Lex Ad Astra

Studies in Space Law

VOLUME 26

The titles published in this series are listed at *brill.com/slaw*

Lex Ad Astra

Non-State Actor Accountability for Space Pollution

By

Matthew Gillett, Katja Grünfeld and Iva Ramuš Cvetkovič

BRILL | NIJHOFF

LEIDEN | BOSTON

This publication was supported by the University of Essex's open access fund.

Library of Congress Cataloging-in-Publication Data

Names: Gillett, Matthew, 1979- editor. | Grünfeld, Katja, editor. | Cvetkovič, Iva Ramuš, editor.
Title: *Lex ad astra*: non-state actor accountability for space pollution / edited by Matthew Gillett, Katja Grünfeld, and Iva Ramuš Cvetkovič.
Description: Leiden ; Boston: Brill/Nijhoff, 2025. | Series: Studies in space law; 26 | Includes bibliographical references and index. | Summary: "Outer space has long been considered the last untouched wilderness.
Identifiers: LCCN 2025000094 | ISBN 9789004724617 (hardback) | ISBN 9789004724624 (ebook)
Subjects: LCSH: Space pollution–Law and legislation. | Space debris–Law and legislation. | Environmental law, International. | Non-state actors (International relations)
Classification: LCC KZD3600 .L49 2025 | DDC 344.04/634–dc23/eng/20250114
LC record available at https://lccn.loc.gov/2025000094

Typeface for the Latin, Greek, and Cyrillic scripts: "Brill". See and download: brill.com/brill-typeface.

ISSN 1871-7659
ISBN 978-90-04-72461-7 (hardback)
ISBN 978-90-04-72462-4 (e-book)
DOI 10.1163/9789004724624

This book is printed on acid-free paper and produced in a sustainable manner.

Abstract

Outer space has long been considered the last untouched wilderness. However, humankind's forays into space have rapidly increased in recent years. Much of this growth comes from the space activities of non-State actors ('NSAs'). While this activity can generate technological advances and access to resources for humans' benefit, it also has created a corresponding accumulation of debris and other forms of pollution in the outer space environment. Traditionally, space conduct was regulated at the State level. As NSAs increase their space activities, the risks of unregulated launches and operations will grow, raising the question of how international law, the naturally applicable regulatory form to address common threats such as space pollution, will respond.

This book explores the novel issue of regulating NSA space pollution under international law. It examines whether the Outer Space Treaty of 1967 and other core space law instruments, as well as principles of international environmental law, international criminal law, international humanitarian law, international human rights law, and associated doctrinal sources, can be feasibly applied to control harm caused to the space environment by NSAs. In doing so, it identifies legal obstacles that will undermine the efficacy of applying these bodies of law. Building on that doctrinal analysis of existing international law, it proposes (and critically evaluates) three prospective approaches to the future application of international law to NSA space pollution. It also provides a detailed survey of States' integration of protections against space pollution under their domestic legal systems. In parallel, the book examines the deeper implications of the seismic increase in NSA activity in the traditionally State-centric domain of space exploration and exploitation.

To my father, Professor Emeritus Grant Gillett, for taking me around the globe from a young age and inspiring me to continue the journey ad astra.
Matthew Gillett

• • •

To my mother, Dr. Monika Grünfeld, and grandfather, Adam Grünfeld, for inspiring and encouraging me to believe anything is possible, to never give up and to always and forever reach for the stars. And to those watching over us: my father Tone, my grandmother Romana, and my darling horses Speedy, Ruella and Amadeus, who all led by example and burned as bright as a supernova.
Katja Grünfeld

• • •

To all the great teachers I have had the chance to meet, who inspired me and shaped me.
Iva Ramuš Cvetkovič

Contents

Preface

The contamination of the outer space environment is epitomized by space debris, which is increasing rapidly at the start of the 21st Century. Space debris ranges from sizeable pieces of satellites, which have been discarded or dislodged from space objects, to tiny paint flakes. All space detritus, however, threatens grave harm, as it orbits the earth at extreme velocities, increasing collision risk and even threatening to create a web of harmful objects orbiting Earth that could entirely obstruct access to outer space, through the so-called 'Kessler Syndrome'. Because of these risks, the United Nations Committee on the Peaceful Uses of Outer Space (UNCOPUOS), experts and space faring nations consider space debris, and space pollution more broadly, to be a high priority issue to address.

One facet of confronting these risks is through better regulation. Ensuring accountability for serious space pollution is a necessary step towards reducing this threat. However, the regulatory responses must keep pace with the rapidly changing operational environment. A major change in recent years has been the growing role of non-State actors (NSA) in space exploration, the so-called New Space industry fueling a growing commercialization of the space domain. NSA are more active than ever in this domain, yet it is the law that traditionally governed State's activities, namely international law, which remains the primary framework governing conduct in space.

In this important work, authors Matthew Gillett, Katja Grünfeld, and Iva Ramuš Cvetkovič confront the difficult question of NSA accountability for space pollution. They explain the novel risks that NSAs present in this environment, examine the traditional approach of regulating NSAs via the construct of the State, and survey in detail the national legal frameworks of space faring nations. They highlight the shortcomings in that well-trodden State-centric route, and in light of these, move on to explore alternative pathways of regulating NSA space pollution directly under international law. Using an innovative approach, they look to other bodies of law, including environmental law, criminal law, humanitarian law, and human rights law, all of which have already seen a tectonic turn towards directly addressing NSAs. That precedent provides impetus for space law to do the same, but also reveals challenges, which might arise in the endeavour.

Through this book, the authors have thus made a significant contribution to the literature on space law, coming at a key moment, as NSAs increase their outer space footprint. The book presents options to develop the doctrine governing NSA space activity. It stands as a major precedent for academic and practitioner consultation over the coming years, potentially decades, as the modern space race heats up and NSAs rapidly expand their activities in this extra-terrestrial domain. All in all, this is a very good book – well worthwhile to read and study.

Prof. Dr. Dr. h.c. Dr. h.c. Stephan Hobe, LL.M.

Acknowledgements

Warm thanks to my energizing co-authors, who have tirelessly joined me on this journey. Thanks also go out to my colleagues at the University of Essex Law School, who have been supportive of my research activities throughout my time there. Equally, I thank my family for keeping me well and truly grounded and able to enjoy the passing seasons while writing this monograph. A particularly heartfelt thanks goes to a person who fits into both the last two categories, my wife Dr. Marina Lostal, whose intellect has always been my guiding North Star.

Matthew Gillett

Foremost thank you to my co-authors, who have shared this exciting journey with me, for their tireless work and belief in us. Warmest thank you to my mentor and supervisor Prof. Stephan Hobe for his support of my research into diverse and enthralling areas of space law, to my colleagues at the Cologne Institute for a wonderful working atmosphere that has helped and entertained during the entirety of this monograph evolution and my European Centre of Space Law Summer Course 2022 co-tutors for many engaging discussions on space law as well as life. A further warm embrace of gratitude to my former mentor Prof. Vasilka Sancin for introducing me to space law by embarking on the 2019 Space Law Moot Court journey with me, my Teammate Iva Ramuš Cvetkovič and our coach Rok Kljajič. A special acknowledgement furthermore to Prof. Em. Christian Brünner and Prof. Em. Sergio Marchisio for their support throughout the Moot Court, and Prof. Wian Erlank for his kind and excellent advice on academic writing and research. A kiss to all my horses, past and present, who have been my joy and teachers, to Tjaša for our many interesting discussions on horseback and off, and finally, the greatest and warmest of thanks to my mother Monika and my grandfather Adam for their unwavering and endless support and love throughout that have made this journey, as well as many others, possible.

Katja Grünfeld

I want to express my gratitude to my distinguished co-authors – to Katja for connecting us and creating an initiative that inspired this work, and to Matthew for his vision of what our initial work could become, as well as then for all his efforts into making that vision possible. It was a privilege and an honor writing this book with you. In addition to that, final edits to the text would be much more difficult and exhausting without Mark Jeršič, who patiently assisted us with citations and bibliography, and Anka Grmek, who helped us with the Index and formatting.

I further want to thank my mentor and PhD supervisor Prof. Aleš Završnik, who recognized the importance of examining the issues of space technology from both legal and criminological perspective, for his ongoing support for my research ideas and plans, valuable advice and numerous opportunities to participate in the multidisciplinary academic sphere, which sharpened my thoughts and expanded my horizons. At the same time, I want to thank all of my colleagues at the Institute of Criminology in Ljubljana, for expressing interest in my research, encouraging my projects and creating a working environment that sparks productivity and creativity on every day basis. As a significant part of this book was written during my research stay at the University of Cologne, I want to also thank everyone who made it possible for me to have a productive time there, but especially the director of the Cologne Criminological Institute, Prof. Frank Neubacher, for a warm welcome and continuous exchange of opinions and ideas, and Ms. Sabine Hackspiel for her generous sponsorship of my DAAD-Stiftung scholarship.

A special acknowledgement goes to my former mentor Prof. Vasilka Sancin, who is, in fact, the primary and the sole reason for the beginning of my journey into the endless challenges of space law. It was also thanks to her, and to Prof. Em. Christian Brünner and Prof. Em. Sergio Marchisio, that I decided to continue that journey.

Lastly, I want to give warmest thanks to those closest to me. To my family, for all their love that surrounds me and guides me in everything I do, and for their endless support and understanding during my studies, including the writing process of this book. Especially to my parents, who both in their own way, have raised me to understand the unparalleled power and importance of thinking and writing. Finally, to all my dear friends and to Kai, for ensuring that my work is (more or less) in balance with life.

Iva Ramuš Cvetkovič

Notes on Authors

Matthew Gillett
is a Senior Lecturer (Associate Professor) of Law at Essex Law School and the United Nations Chair-Rapporteur of the Working Group on Arbitrary Detention. He has published extensively on international law, human rights, and environmental protection.

Katja Grünfeld
is a Research Assistant and PhD Candidate at the Institute of Air Law, Space Law and Cyber Law at the University of Cologne, Group Leader of Working Group Space for the Institute/DLR Project Cologne Manual on the International Law of Space Traffic Management, Member of the Space Law Committee of the International Law Association, and Prospective Member of the International Institute of Space Law with multiple publications in the field of space law.

Iva Ramuš Cvetkovič
is a Researcher and Assistant at the Institute of Criminology at the Faculty of Law Ljubljana, and a PhD Scholar at the Faculty of Law, University of Ljubljana.

CHAPTER 1

Introduction: Regulating Space Pollution by Non-State Actors (NSAs) under International Law

> The effects of human activities on the global commons of outer space have all the potential to be severe, irreversible and wide in scope.[1]

1 Setting the Parameters for the Study of NSA Accountability

Outer space is the staging platform for activities which enhance the lives of billions of people around the world. From satellite navigation systems, to telecommunications, to remote sensing, the range and quantity of space-based activities have escalated rapidly since humankind's first forays into outer space in the 1950s.[2] But as humans have extended their operations into outer space, the risk of anthropocentric pollution[3] has also expanded beyond Earth's atmosphere.

1 Lotta Viikari, *The Environmental Element in Space Law* (Martinus Nijhoff Publishers, 2008), p. 5. See also Lotta Viikari, 'Environmental aspects of space activities, in *Handbook of Space Law* (F.G. von der Dunk & F. Tronchetti, eds.) (2015), pp. 717–768.

2 The rise of non-traditional space activities, fueled by technological advances and predominantly driven by private actors has been termed 'NewSpace'. See Paul Stephen Dempsey and Maria Manoli, *Suborbital Flights and the Delimitation of Air Space Vis-À-Vis Outer Space: Functionalism, Spatialism and State Sovereignty* (International Association for the Advancement of Space Safety, 2017), p. 43 ('[s]uch activities include primarily human space flight, extraterrestrial settlement, exploitation of celestial bodies' natural resources, and any other futuristic space activities that the current space industry plans to achieve in the future. The main characteristics of such activities include the effort to minimize space exploration costs, efficient investment return, incremental development, and broad consumer market targets.').

3 See, e.g. Inter-Governmental Panel on Climate Change (2021), *Sixth Assessment Report of the Intergovernmental Panel on Climate Change*, IPCC AR6 WGI; Frédéric Mégret, 'The Problem of an International Criminal Law of the Environment' (2011) 36 *Columbia Journal of Environmental Law*, p. 195; Kenneth McCallion and Rajan Sharma, 'Environmental Justice without Borders: The Need for an International Court of the Environment to

 DOI:10.1163/9789004724624_002

In recent years, NSAs are increasingly leading the charge into space. With this growing involvement, greater risks emerge. Already in 1996, debris from a misfired Ariane 5 rocket reportedly hit a French satellite. In 2009, a satellite of the American NSA Iridium Satellite LLC collided with the non-functional Russian Kosmos-2251 causing extensive space debris. In April 2019, the landing vehicle of an Israeli NSA called Beresheet crashed into the moon, potentially releasing human DNA and tardigrades onto its surface. In December 2021, there was a near-miss between China's space station and a SpaceX Starlink satellite, and SpaceX has reportedly lost several other satellites since then.[4] Given these threats, it is essential to explore the existing and potential legal bases to regulate NSA space pollution.

Space pollution itself can take many forms.[5] It includes rocket gas and fuel emissions, radioactive belts or other harmful consequences caused by dangerous nuclear or other experiments in outer space, terrestrial organisms (exobiological contamination) brought into outer space, as well as space debris,[6] which constitutes a growing hazard for human access to outer space.

Materially, space debris ranges from sizeable chunks of exploded satellites to tiny paint flakes from spacecraft. This detritus is generated by rockets and satellites colliding and malfunctioning, as well as regular mission materials left in space when they no longer serve a useful purpose.[7] Some has been in orbit since the 1950s.[8] The volume of space debris grows in quantity each year,[9] and increasingly constitutes a blight on the largely pristine outer space environment.[10] For example, the 2007 Chinese anti-satellite weapon test is estimated

Protect Fundamental Environmental Rights' (2000) 32 *George Washington Journal of International Law and Economics*, p. 351.

4 See Chapter 1, Section 3.

5 See Chapter 1, Section 2 for the definition of 'space pollution'.

6 Viikari (2008), pp. 29–52; Vladimir Atanasov and Gianluigi Baldesi, 'An Analysis of Two Space Business Opportunities' in Stella Tkatchova (ed.), *Space-Based Technologies and Commercialized Development: Economic Implications and Benefits* (IGI Global, 2011), p. 210.

7 Michał Pietkiewicz, 'Protection of the space environment against space debris pollution' (2019) 45 *Studia Prawnoustrojowe*, pp. 215, 216; Atanasov and Baldesi (2011), p. 210.

8 See Chapter 1, Section 2 for definitions of these terms.

9 The European Space Agency (ESA) notes that there have been more than 640 break-ups, explosions, collisions, or anomalous events resulting in fragmentation of satellites or rocket bodies', leading to an approximate 10500 tonnes of objects on orbit, ESA, *Space Debris by the Numbers* (22 December 2022) (available at https://www.esa.int/Safety_Security/Space_Debris/Space_debris_by_the_numbers).

10 Joel A. Dennerley, 'State Liability for Space Object Collisions: The Proper Interpretation of "Fault" for the Purposes of International Space Law' (2018) 29(1) *European Journal of International Law*, p. 286 ('The increasing creation and prevalence of space debris in

to have created over a million pieces of space debris, including over 2,000 traceable pieces bigger than a golf ball.[11] The peculiar characteristics of the space environment exacerbate the risk of debris. Because of the absence of atmospheric resistance, space debris can permanently orbit the Earth at over 50,000 kilometres per hour.[12] This heightens the risk of further collisions and the exponential generation of more debris. The upshot is a proliferation of harmful objects orbiting Earth, which may cut off access to outer space completely, in a condition termed the 'Kessler Syndrome'.[13]

The threat posed by space pollution to human lives, property, and the environment is serious. The most tangible form – space debris – can endanger astronauts on space missions. For example, the shrapnel-like belt of debris produced by the Russian destruction of one of its satellites in 2021 threatened the International Space Station (ISS), forcing it into evasive maneuvers and its crew to take shelter in protected pods.[14] Space debris can cause severe damage to functioning satellites in outer space. Several collisions have already occurred and further incidents are becoming statistically more likely with the launch of each new batch of space objects.[15] Satellites, including defunct ones, pose risks to each other and to the critical infrastructure that operates on satellite data, as demonstrated by the Iridium-33/Kosmos-2251 collision in 2009.[16] Many of

orbit is contributing to the environmental pollution of outer space.'); Pietkiewicz (2019), pp. 215, 216.

11 Atanasov and Baldesi (2011), p. 210.

12 Matt Williams, 'Eye-Opening Numbers on Space Debris' *Universe Today* (21 March 2017) (available at https://phys.org/news/2017-03-eye-opening-space-debris.html); Paul B. Larsen, 'Solving the Space Debris Crisis' (2018) 83 *Journal of Air Law and Commerce*, p. 477; Stephan Hobe, *Space Law: a Handbook* (Baden-Baden: Nomos/Hart, 2019), pp. 111–112; NASA, *Space Debris and Human Spacecraft* (26 May 2021) (available at https://www.nasa.gov/mission_pages/station/news/orbital_debris.html).

13 See Donald J. Kessler and Burton G. Cour-Palais, 'Collision Frequency of Artificial Satellites: The Creation of a Debris Belt' (1978) 38 *JGR Space Physics* A6, pp. 2637–2646; Francis Lyall and Paul B. Larsen, *Space Law: A Treatise* (Ashgate, 2009), p. 305; Marit Undseth, Claire Jolly and Mattia Olivari, 'The Economics of Space Debris in Perspective' (2021) in: *8th European Conference on Space Debris*, 20 April 2021–23 April 2021, Darmstadt, Germany (ESA Space Debris Office, 2021); Peter T. Limperis, 'Orbital Debris and the Spacefaring Nations: International Law Methods for Prevention and Reduction of Debris, and Liability for Damage Caused by Debris' (1998) 15 *Arizona Journal of International and Comparative Law*, p. 326.

14 Yannick Radi, 'Clearing up the Space Junk: On the Flaws and Potential of International Space Law to Tackle the Space Debris Problem' (2023) 12(2) *ESIL Reflections*, 9 March 2023, p. 2.

15 Atanasov and Baldesi (2011), pp. 210–212.

16 Atanasov and Baldesi (2011), p. 212.

the satellites at risk provide vital services for Earth.[17] The increasingly crowded space-scape presents a far riskier environment than it did in the early days of space exploration.

On the terrestrial front, space pollution risks harming Earth's environments and inhabitants. It can do so both directly (for example by an uncontrolled de-orbiting of a piece of debris) and indirectly (by causing long-term negative effects on the environment).[18] Up in space, such pollution can persist permanently, as the space environment is in some respects less able to regenerate after disturbances (as can be seen by marks of human presence still visible on the surface of the Moon).[19] For all these reasons, space pollution presents a serious threat to our ability to safely access, explore, and utilize outer space.[20]

The earliest space activities were organized and conducted by a small number of nation-States.[21] However, the range of States involved in space exploration is growing,[22] with up to 80 States now having at least one satellite in space.[23] Moreover, from the 1980s onwards, NSAs[24] have emerged as significant players in the space industry.[25] They are increasingly active across all the

---

17 See generally Lesley Jane Smith, Ingo Baumann and Susan-Gale Wintermuth, *Routledge Handbook of Commercial Space Law* (Taylor and Francis, 2023); Alexander Soucek and Christian Brünner, *Outer Space in Society, Politics and* Law (Springer Vienna, 2012); For Planet Earth and Beyond, European Space Agency (https://connectivity.esa.int/news/satellite-services-and-applications-vital-cornerstone-modern-society); Joseph F. Pelton, Space 2.0 (Springer International Publishing, 2019).

18 See, e.g. Atanasov and Baldesi (2011), p. 210–212; Dennerley (2018), p. 281.

19 Mark Williamson, 'Space Ethics and Protection of the Space Environment' (2003) 19 *Space Policy*, pp. 47–52.

20 Dennerley (2018), p. 281; David S.F. Portree and Joseph P. Loftus, Jr, 'Orbital Debris: A Chronology' *NASA/TP-1999-208856* (1999) (available at Orbital Debris: A Chronology – nasa Technical Reports Server (NTRS)); Joshua Tallis, 'Remediating Space Debris: Legal and Technical Barriers' (2015) 9 *Strategic Studies Quarterly* 86–99, pp. 80–81. See also Sergio Marchisio, 'Article IX' (2009) in: *The Cologne Commentary on Space Law*: Vol. I (Stephan Hobe, Bernhard Schmidt-Tedd, Kai-Uwe Schrogl, Gérardine Meishan Goh (eds.)) (Cologne: Carl Heymanns, 2009), pp. 169–182; Hobe (2019), p. 111.

21 Heather Fogo, 'A Legal Mirage: State Responsibility for Non-State Actor Interference with Space Systems' (2017) 55 *Canadian Yearbook of International Law/Annuaire Canadien De Droit International*, p. 183; Giancarlo Genta, 'Private space exploration: A new way for starting a spacefaring society?' (2014) 104 *Acta Astronautica*, p. 480.

22 Anél Ferreira-Snyman, 'Outer Space Exploration and the Sustainability of the Space Environment – An Uneasy Relationship' (2023) 26 *Potchefstroom Electronic Law Journal*, p. 2.

23 See Chapter 5.

24 This analysis uses the term NSA narrowly, in the sense of entities which are not States and are not constituted by States, and thereby excludes international organizations (IOs).

25 See Peter Stubbe, *State accountability for space debris: a legal study of responsibility for polluting the space environment and liability for damage caused by space debris* (Brill/

major fields of space activities, including satellite technology, space transportation, and space tourism.[26] More prospectively, NSAs are involved in developing technologies for outer space human settlements, as evidenced by SpaceX's stated interest in promoting human inhabitation of Mars.[27]

Financially, the global space economy, which is estimated to be worth over 400 billion US dollars, is now predominantly comprised by private enterprise funding.[28] It is estimated that around three-quarters come from private sources and only one-quarter from government budgets.[29] In many instances, NSAs are able to access space with minimal to no assistance or funding from States.[30] They will do so more frequently as the value of the global communications and data sharing market increases. However, this increase in NSA space exploration widens the circle of actors able to harm the extraterrestrial environment, thereby increasing the overall risk of space pollution.[31] As Ferreira-Snyman notes, 'because of the significant increase in the number of space actors, outer space is becoming a congested and competitive environment'.[32]

Martinus Nijhoff Publishers, 2018), p. 96; Fogo (2017), p. 183; Stefania Paladini and Ignazio Castellucci, 'Sovereign states, private actors, and (national) space laws. A rapidly evolving landscape', in Charles S. Cockell (ed.), *The Institutions of Extraterrestrial Liberty* (Oxford, 2022; online edn, Oxford Academic, 19 January 2023), pp. 366–383.

26 Hobe (2010), pp. 870–874; Ferreira-Snyman (2023), p. 2; Michael Byers and Aaron Boley, *Who Owns Outer Space?* (Cambridge, 2024: Cambridge University Press), pp. 11–13.

27 Ferreira-Snyman (2023), p. 2 (noting that Elon Musk's SpaceX and Jeff Bezos' Blue Origin are currently the most active private enterprises involved in this endeavour). Kenneth Cheng, 'Elon Musk Says SpaceX Could Land on Mars in 3 to 4 Years', *New York Times* (5 October 2023) (available at https://www.nytimes.com/2023/10/05/science/elon-musk-spacex-starship-mars.html).

28 See Chiara Macchi, 'Business, Human Rights And International Space Law: Filling The Gaps Of Corporate Accountability In The 'New Space', in Claudia Cinelli (ed.), *Regulation of Outer Space International Space Law and the State* (Routledge, advance edition (full book forthcoming 2025)), pp. 49–50.

29 Steven Freeland and Danielle Ireland-Piper, 'Space Law, Human Rights and Corporate Accountability', (2022) 26(1) *UCLA Journal of International Law and Foreign Affairs*, p. 2. See also Alexander P. Reinert, 'Updating the Liability Regime in Outer Space: Why Spacefaring Companies Should Be Internationally Liable For Their Space Objects', (2020) 62 *Willian and Mary Law Review*, p. 325 (noting that private corporations have brought down the costs of space exploration).

30 Gregory D. Miller, 'Space Pirates, Geosynchronous Guerrillas, and Non-terrestrial Terrorists: Non-state Threats in Space' (2019) 33(3) *Air and Space Power Journal*, p. 35 ('The ability of western companies (Rocket Lab, Virgin Galactic, and so forth) to develop space capabilities of some type shows that NSAs can access space with minimal assistance or funding from states.').

31 See Chapter 1, Section 3.

32 Ferreira-Snyman (2023), pp. 2–3.

The risk of space pollution arises not just in terms of accidental collisions, but also in terms of the intentional destruction of space objects by NSAs, whether through ill thought-out decommissioning procedures or attempts to harm other entities. This has led to the observation that, although States have a proven capacity for destruction in space, '[t]he more likely threat [in this domain] comes from non-state actors.'[33] Despite this expansion in the cast of space actors, relatively little attention has been paid to the legal means of redress for the danger of NSA space pollution in international legal instruments and the subject is under-developed in scholarly literature.[34] The lacuna is striking given the potential profits deriving from satellite services, the growing interest in space tourism,[35] the enticing lure of mineral resources on celestial bodies, the expanding power and availability of spatial knowledge and technology, and the demonstrated interest and investments of NSAs in space activities.[36] This book seeks to redress that gap in the literature.

Whereas NSAs pose an ever-greater threat to the outer space environment, it is the law that traditionally governed State's activities – namely international law, which provides the core source of regulation for space activities. Given that space lies beyond the sovereign territory of any country,[37] multilateral approaches involving most of the major space-faring nations will be required to create lasting solutions to NSA space pollution.[38] Unilateral strategies or efforts by small groups of States are unlikely to be effective,[39] as they will open the gate for companies and other potential space polluters to move to other

33 Miller (2019), p. 44.

34 See Chapter 1, Section 5.

35 See Hobe (2010), p. 874 citing Clara Moskowitz, 'Private Spaceship Could Start Carrying Tourists Within a Year', *SPACE.com* (30 November 2010); Susan Montoya Bryan, 'CEO Interview: Richard Branson on Space Travel', *The Associated Press* (23 November 2010).

36 Fogo (2017), pp. 183–188; Stubbe (2018), p. 262; Melissa de Zwart, 'GOOGLE in Space? How will space governance accommodate non-State actors?' (2016) *RUMLAE Research Paper* 16–21, pp. 2–3; Kelly Kizer Whitt, 'Who owns all the satellites?' *EarthSky* (8 February 2022) (available at https://earthsky.org/space/who-owns-satellites-company-country/).

37 See Miller (2019), p. 45 ('The fact that space is not sovereign territory for any one country would further complicate things because it would necessarily involve international law.').

38 See Viikari (2008), p. 5 ('although unilateral action is a step forward, it does not alone suffice to remedy the proliferation of debris.').

39 Armel Kerrest, 'International Organizations as Active Subjects of International Law of Outer Space' *Proceedings of Third ECSL Colloquium on International Organizations and Space Law*, Perugia, 6–7 May 1999, pp. 258–259; Viikari (2008), p. 5–6. In this respect, it is notable that a multinational Norwegian, Russian, Ukrainian and US spacecraft launch company operated from 1999 to 2014 providing orbital launch services from a sea platform in international equatorial waters.

States in order to avoid the restrictions on their conduct.[40] This avoidance of regulation through de-camping to another jurisdiction is already known in other domains and is termed 'forum shopping' (also termed 'flags of convenience' from maritime shipping practice).[41] For this and other reasons developed in this monograph, international space law (*corpus iuris spatialis*) is insufficient in its current form to regulate the conduct of private actors.[42]

The United Nations (UN)'s primary body designed to address space activities – the Committee on the Peaceful Uses of Outer Space (UNCOPUOS) – considers space debris to be a central topic of concern.[43] It has a standing issue on the activities of inter-governmental and non-governmental organizations concerning space law.[44] However, its work has not resulted in any new international space law treaty (or adjustment to existing treaties) concerning harmful NSA conduct in space, let alone space pollution.[45] As a result, there is a continuing hole in international law's coverage of harmful human conduct in space, and the gap is particularly acute in relation to NSAs.

To address these growing threats, this monograph explores the facets of international law which can be used to regulate the conduct of NSAs in space, particularly in relation to space pollution. It adopts a largely ecocentric approach, looking to international law for means to protect the space environment from harmful human impacts. To this end, it assesses potential protections of the environment contained in the core international space law conventions, particularly the 1967 Outer Space Treaty,[46] the 1968 Rescue Agreement,[47] the 1972

40 See Chapter 2, Section 3.

41 See Chapter 3, Section 2 citing *inter alia* Larsen (2018), pp. 491–492, 515; Viikari (2008), p. 6; Frans von der Dunk, 'Towards 'Flags of Convenience'in Space?'(2012) 3 *Space and Telecommunications Law Program Faculty Publications Pap*er 76.

42 Christina Isnardi, 'Problems with Enforcing International Space Law on Private Actors' (2020) 58 *Columbia Journal of Transnational Law*, p. 491 (opining that space law is 'not equipped with adequate methods' of enforcement vis-à-vis private actors). See Chapter 3, Section 2.

43 Viikari (2008), p. 6.

44 The Legal Subcommittee of the UNCOPUOS has a regular agenda item concerning information on the activities of international intergovernmental and non-governmental organizations relating to space law.

45 Dempsey and Manoli, (2017), p. 37. See also UNOOSA, *International Space Law: United Nations Instruments*, (United Nations, 2017).

46 By 2022, the Outer Space Treaty had 112 State Parties, including all space-faring States (see UN Doc. A/AC.105/C.2/2021/CRP.10) and its content is largely based on the Declaration of Legal Principles Governing the Activities of States in the Exploration and Use of Outer Space, adopted by the United Nations General Assembly in its resolution 1962 (XVIII).

47 The Rescue Agreement builds on Article V of the Outer Space Treaty, addressing the assistance to be given to astronauts in the event of an accident, distress, or emergency landing,

Liability Convention,[48] the 1975 Registration Convention, and the 1979 Moon Agreement,[49] as well as other branches of international law including criminal, humanitarian, human rights, and environmental. It also looks to State practice, with particular emphasis on the leading space-faring nations, to examine the ways in which NSA conduct has been regulated by States and whether that provides a basis to address space pollution.[50]

Because the inquiry in this book is ecocentrically oriented, the assessment focuses on provisions and principles that protect the environment. Of course, NSA space activities can also harm anthropocentric interests, such as the functioning of global positioning systems and services that rely on them, and telecommunications.[51] Frequently, ecocentric and anthropocentric harms overlap, as in the case of space debris limiting human access to outer space. The intersection between the ecocentric and anthropocentric is most evident in relation to the rights of future generations, which are encompassed by the environmental law principles of intergenerational equity and sustainable development, both of which are analysed below.[52] Nonetheless, the vantage point for the present book remains ecocentric, which provides a contrasting point of entry to works that have taken an anthropocentric approach to the impact of human activities in outer space.[53]

Building on that doctrinal analysis of the current state of the law, it presents a normative assessment, proposing (and critically evaluating) three possible approaches to the future application of international law to NSA space pollution – namely the 'retrenchment', 'reinterpretation', and 'reform' models.[54] In parallel, the analysis examines the deeper implications of the seismic increase in NSA activity in the traditionally state-centric domain of space exploration

---

and Article VIII of the Outer Space Treaty, concerning the return of space objects discovered beyond the territory of the member state (Agreement on the Rescue of Astronauts, the Return of Astronauts and the Return of Objects Launched into Outer Space, 19 December 1967, 672 UNTS 119 (entered into force on 3 December 1968)).

48 Convention on International Liability for Damage Caused by Space Objects, 29 March 1972, 961 UNTS 187 (entered into force on 1 September 1972).

49 Agreement governing the Activities of States on the Moon and Other Celestial Bodies, 5 December 1979, 1363 UNTS 3 (entered into force on 11 July 1984).

50 See Chapter 5.

51 See for example P.J. Blount and Mahulena Hofmann (eds.), *Space Law in a Networked World* (Koninklijke Brill NV, 2023).

52 See Chapter 2, Sections 1, 1.2.

53 See, e.g., Danielle Ireland-Piper and Steven Freeland, 'Human Rights and Space: Reflections on the Implications of Human Activity in Outer Space on Human Rights Law' (2021) 9:1 *Groningen Journal of International Law*.

54 See Chapter 6.

and exploitation.[55] The book includes a novel proposed draft protocol to the Outer Space Treaty (declaration), designed by the authors with the aim of ensuring NSA and State accountability for space pollution under international law. It is formulated flexibly, so that it could be adopted as a declaration, consistent with the approach to developing space law in recent decades. In this way, it would serve as a stepping stone towards the eventual adoption of the full protocol to the Outer Space Treaty.

This book constitutes a significant addition to the literature on space law, as it constitutes a full monograph dedicated specifically to the increasingly important question of NSA accountability for space pollution.[56] It comes at a threshold moment, wherein NSAs are paralleling, and in some respects surpassing, the role of States in the use and exploitation of outer space. Because it addresses NSA accountability for space pollution under a range of potentially relevant sub-domains of international law (including humanitarian, criminal, human rights and environmental),[57] and because it doctrinally assesses the law as it stands while also normatively examining how law on this issue may develop, it constitutes a comprehensive and detailed treatise on the legal issues arising from the growing threat of NSA space pollution. The monograph also provides an original contribution. It reviews legal options through the traditional State-centric positivist international law prism, while also expanding the assessment to explore in detail the unorthodox possibility of directly applying international law to regulate NSA conduct in space. Whereas assessments of the direct application of international law to NSAs have been made in fields such as international humanitarian law,[58] there is no major work focused on NSA accountability for harming the space environment under international law. With its essentially ecocentric central orientation, the book primarily focuses on how international law can be used to protect the environment.

---

55 Gabriela Kütting, *Environment, Society and International Relations: towards more effective international environmental agreements* (Routledge, 2000), p. 3.

56 See Chapter 1, Section 5 below.

57 The book does not focus on *jus ad bellum*, as that is largely an area revolving around the rights of States to use force. For more on the concept of 'force' under international law and its application in space, see Erin Pobjie, *Prohibited Force: the meaning of the 'use of force' in international law*, (Cambridge University Press, 2024), pp. 217–218. See also Jack Beard and Dale Stephens (eds), *The Woomera Manual on the International Law of Military Space Operations*, (Oxford University Press, 2024), p. 111 (noting the attribution of NSA conduct to States under Article VI should not be automatic for the purposes of *jus ad bellum*).

58 See, e.g. Ezequiel Heffes, Marcos D. Kotlik, and Manuel J. Ventura, *International Humanitarian Law and Non-State Actors: Debates, Law and Practice* (Springer, 2020).

Although anthropocentric concerns, such as the impact of space debris on human's access to outer space, are a reoccurring topic, the book addresses these insofar as they are linked to harm to the outer space environment.

The addition of the proposed draft protocol (or declaration) to the Outer Space Treaty is a practical means to seek remedies for the legal lacuna identified throughout this monograph, particularly in relation to NSA space pollution. Consequently, this monograph provides a unique perspective, aimed at highlighting legal incongruities while also presenting avenues for reform of international law to redress the increasing risks presented by NSA space pollution.

The primary research question underlying this analysis is whether international law can be used to effectively regulate NSA space pollution. Underlying questions include whether domains other than space law, such as international humanitarian law, international criminal law, international environmental law, and international human rights law, can be applied directly to NSA conduct in space; what the application of international law to NSA harms in space tells us about the general capacity of international law to regulate NSA conduct; and the extent to which NSAs have sufficient legal personality to influence the formation of international law in the space context. In identifying risks of space pollution emanating from NSAs, this book looks at the launching and operation of satellites in space, human space travel, including space tourism, the extraction of minerals and other resources from celestial bodies, military operations in space, and other forms of exploiting the outer space environment.

To address its core research question, this book surveys relevant sources of international law, from conventional to customary to soft law, and identifies doctrinal bases and challenges for the legal redress of NSA space pollution. It addresses at length the critical gateway issue of whether there is an established prohibition of space pollution under international law. In reviewing the legal bases to operationalize that prohibition, it seeks to adhere to the principle of *effet utile*, as reflected in Article 31(1) of the Vienna Convention on the Law of Treaties[59] and as endorsed by the International Court of Justice, whereby treaty provisions are interpreted to give them, and the treaty as a whole, meaningful effect and to avoid either rendering the provisions superfluous or depriving them of significance in governing the parties' relationship.[60] At the same

59 Vienna Convention on the Law of Treaties, Vienna, done 23 May 1969, entered into force 27 January 1980; 1155 UNTS 331; UKTS 1980 No. 58; Cmnd. 4818; ATS 1974 No. 2; 8 ILM 679 (1969).

60 *Case Concerning Application of the International Convention on the Elimination of All Forms of Racial Discrimination* (*Georgia v Russia*), Preliminary Objections, 2011 *ICJ Reports*

time, it takes a progressive approach to interpreting the terms of international law instruments, looking to their underlying principles and motivating policies rather than looking only at the facial text of the instruments assessed.[61] In this way, the analysis adheres to core precepts of international law, and maintains its coherence as a framework, while ensuring that specific provisions and instruments are interpreted and applied in light of contemporary technological, economic, and societal conditions.

The analysis traverses multiple normative levels, and addresses the connections between those levels. It begins at the purely international level, with the examination of the gateway question of the existence of a prohibition of space pollution under international level.[62] It then turns to the interaction between the international level and the domestic level in relation to the regulation of NSA space conduct, assessing whether this relationship can effectively be mediated through the State construct or whether the two levels can be directly enmeshed through the vertical imposition of international duties on domestic actors.[63] Following that, it examines the enactment of domestic laws and their horizontal application to domestic actors.[64] Those inter-normative level analyzes assist in generating the insights regarding the nature and formation of international law.

The normative focus is also central to the exploration of three major avenues for the legal development of international space law in the face of NSA space pollution.[65] That prospective discussion provides constructive and critical comment on the approaches of retrenching back to a strict traditional application of international law, re-interpreting the existing provisions of international law with a teleological lens aimed at protecting the space environment, and reforming international law to directly redress NSA space pollution. Drawing insights from each of those approaches, the study takes an approach which could be called 'progressive positivism', whereby established instruments and principles of international law are interpreted and applied with due regard to the current technological, societal, and political circumstances that prevail in order to maximize the protection of the space environment.[66]

70, para 134. See also Steven Ratner, 'International Law Rules on Treaty Interpretation' in *The Law and Practice of the Northern Ireland Protocol* (Christopher McCrudden ed.) (Cambridge University Press, 2022), pp. 80–91.

61 See Chapter 6, Section 5.

62 See Chapter 2.

63 See Chapters 3 and 4.

64 See Chapter 5.

65 See Chapter 6.

66 See Chapter 6, Section 4 and 5.

Whereas this book revolves around legal issues, it should not be taken as asserting that the law is the exclusive source of redress for space pollution. Law is just one vehicle to address communal problems, and must be accompanied by political, financial, and diplomatic commitments, among others, to result in effective mitigation of the risk of anthropogenic threats to the space environment. Similarly, whereas the following survey uses international space law as the central anchoring framework, the normative framework of other sub-fields of international law are examined throughout the book for their potential applicability to space pollution by NSAs – including international environmental law as well as international criminal law, international humanitarian law, and international human rights law. Although those legal sub-fields were designed to protect interests other than the space environment, such as human suffering in the case of international humanitarian law and human rights law[67] or the terrestrial environment in the case of international environmental law, they have adapted to increasingly confront threats from NSAs as well as States.

This book is written at a time of rapid technological change, as the internet age now transitions to the age of artificial intelligence. It is likely that space travel, NSA activity, and societal organization more broadly, will grow and adapt in the coming years and decades.[68] For this reason, the current study does not pretend to present a definitive prescriptive framework to resolve all threats to the space environment. Instead, it identifies the strengths and weaknesses of the major approaches to international space law which may be adopted to address the challenge of NSA activity in space. In doing so, the book places considerable weight on the flexibility and adaptability of the potential legal approaches examined. At the same time, it also seeks to highlight foundational principles from space law and other applicable international law regimes which should persist irrespective of the prescriptive framework adopted.

In this introductory Chapter, a foundation for the study is laid by mapping out the escalating threat of space pollution from NSAs and juxtaposing that threat with the traditionally State-centric nature of international space law. Chapter 2 addresses key terminology, explaining the definitions of key terms used throughout the book, and then examines the critical gateway question of whether there is a prohibition on space pollution in general. In Chapter 3, the

67 However, it should be noted that international humanitarian law does contain a small number of explicit protections of the environment and international human rights law has been interpreted by some institutions to include the right to a clean, healthy and sustainable environment. See Chapter 4, Section 2, 2.3 and 2.4 below.

68 See Chapter 1, Section 3.

book explores State responsibility as a vehicle to regulate NSA space pollution. It identifies limitations to this approach, which necessitate the search for alternative and complementary approaches. In Chapter 4, those other pathways to regulating NSA space pollution under international law are assessed. As a platform for that assessment, Chapter 4 contains case studies of two types of NSA threats to the space environment, namely profit-driven NSAs and ideologically motivated NSAs. Against that backdrop, Chapter 4 sets out a topography of legal regimes which could potentially be applied directly to NSAs. It covers space law, international environmental law, international criminal law, international humanitarian law, international human rights law, and private international law. It also reviews fora in which these claims could be brought, including international courts and domestic courts acting under universal jurisdiction. Moving to the domestic level, Chapter 5 provides an important survey of State practice under national law regarding the accountability of NSAs for space pollution. It covers all major space-faring nations and an expansive number of other States and regional organizations with activity relevant to space. Building on the outcomes of the first five chapters, Chapter 6 turns to a more normative assessment, setting out, evaluating, and critiquing three possible paths for future redress of NSA space pollution, namely *retrenchment* back to traditional State-centric approaches, *reinterpretation* of existing legal provisions, and *reform* of space law to provide for direct NSA accountability for space pollution. It discusses the implications for space law, and the construction of international law itself, particularly regarding the role of NSAs, which emerge from the assessment of these three normative approaches. Finally, Chapter 7 contains the conclusions that have been drawn from the study and provides the authors' views regarding the most critical challenges, both legally and practically, which will eventuate when seeking to use international law to redress NSA space pollution.

2 Defining the Key Terms

As a basis for the analysis, several key terms require clarification. These are: 'outer space' (including linked terms such as 'geostationary orbit'; 'lower Earth orbit'; 'medium earth orbit'; 'highly elliptical orbits; and 'celestial body/bodies') 'space object'; 'space debris'; 'space pollution'; 'launching State'; 'State of registration'; 'responsibility'; 'liability'; and 'accountability'. Whilst international law does not provide exhaustive definitions for all of these concepts, it can provide an indication of the meaning and import of each of them.

The initial term requiring definition is 'outer space'. Outer space itself is difficult to scientifically delineate.[69] The atmosphere surrounding the earth gradually changes as it stretches outwards. However, outer space can generally be described as 'the space upwards from the airspace (atmosphere) surrounding the Earth.'[70]

In establishing a more precise definition of outer space, approaches to the altitudinal division between the airspace and outer space diverge. Over 50 years of efforts by the Legal Sub-Committee of UNCOPUOS have not yet resulted in a settled definition.[71] Parts of the international community place the limit at 100 km (62 miles) above mean sea level,[72] on what is called the Kármán line.[73] Named, after scientist Theodore von Kármán, this line is located at the point at which the atmosphere becomes too thin for aeronautical purposes.[74] Although this line has not been legally accepted as the delineation of outer

---

69 For a more detailed analysis see Hobe (2019), pp. 1–3; Frans von der Dunk, 'International space law', in *Handbook of Space Law* (Frans von der Dunk & Fabio Tronchetti, eds.) (2015a), pp. 60–72. See also discussions of the UN COPUOS Legal Subcommittee Working Group on the Definition and Delimitation of Outer Space of the Legal Subcommittee ('Working. Group on the Definition and Delimitation of Outer Space of the Legal Subcommittee' *UNOOSA* (available at https://www.unoosa.org/oosa/en/ourwork/copuos/lsc/ddos/index.html)).

70 Viikari (2008), p. 1. See also Bin Cheng, *Studies in International Space Law* (Oxford University Press, 2004), pp. 227–228; Bartosz Ziemblicki and Yevgeniya Oralova, 'Private Entities in Outer Space Activities: Liability Regime Reconsidered' (2021) 56(2) Space Policy, p. 3.

71 See UNCOPUOS, 'Historical summary on the consideration of the question on the definition and delimitation of outer space', UN Doc. A/AC.105/769/Add.1, 3 February 2020, p. 4 (noting that, according to some delegations, '[c]urrent and foreseeable civil aviation operations would not exceed altitudes of 100–130 km, where there was a potential danger of collision with numerous spacecraft … [i]n this connection, the boundary between airspace and outer space could be established in that range.'). See also Viikari (2008), pp. 2–3.

72 See, e.g. the Australian Space Activities Act of 1998 (as amended in 2002), which refers to the limit of 100 kilometers as the altitude at which outer space begins. See also UNCOPUOS, *Definition and delimitation of outer space*, UN Doc. A/AC.105/C.2/2022/CRP.24 6 April 2022; ESPI, *Executive Brief* No.11 updated: Delimitation of Outer Space 1 March 2017.

73 However, it should be noted that the van Kármán is, as Gangale notes, a theoretical construct with no inherently remarkable practical significance from an engineering point of view, but rather is relevant only from a theoretical legal point of view, see Thomas Gangale, 'The Non Kármán Line: An Urban Legend of the Space Age', 41 *Journal of Space Law* (2017), 151–177.

74 Jean-Francois Mayence, 'Granting Access to Outer Space: Rights and Responsibilities for States and their Citizens, An Alternative Approach to Article VI of the Outer Space Treaty, Notably Trough the Belgian Space Legislation', in Frans von der Dunk (ed.), *National Space Legislation in Europe* (Martinus Nijhoff, 2011a), pp. 96–97.

space, it presents a reasonable demarcation between the domain of aeronautical activities and outer space satellite activities.[75] Nonetheless, the perigee of some satellites does dip below 100 km, and so either this definite figure would have to be adopted with some exceptions or a more descriptive definition, such as the lowest point at which space objects are able to continuously and effectively orbit Earth, would have to be preferred.[76]

Because of this indeterminacy, the upper boundary of the complete and exclusive jurisdiction over airspace, granted under treaties such as the Chicago Convention on Civil Aviation,[77] remains subject to dispute.[78] The dispute over this delineation has significant ramifications. Whereas in air law, the sovereignty of the subjacent State over its airspace is the foundational principle,[79] space law precludes States from asserting sovereignty over the outer space, including its celestial bodies.[80] Moreover, whereas under international aviation law liability is primarily imposed on the airline, under international space law liability is essentially placed on the State.[81] The transition between the legal domains of air and space law results in a shift from greater NSA liability to greater State liability, accentuating the importance of a clear delineation between these regimes.[82] However, such delineation is unlikely to occur anytime soon, as indicated by UNCOPUOS's unsuccessful past attempts.

Within the outer space sphere, there are various sub-domains. Those with particular significance for space debris are the following. The orbit which is key for satellites is the geostationary orbit (GEO).[83] It is located around 35,000

75 Von der Dunk (2015a), p. 67.

76 See von der Dunk (2015a), pp. 67–69. See also, p. 87 (noting that these discussions reflect a deeper divide between 'spatialism' and 'functionalism', with the former favouring determining measurable boundaries to the application of space law (outer space vs within the Earth's atmosphere) and the latter favouring definitions based on the functions assumed by the object or operation).

77 The Convention on International Civil Aviation, 7 December 1944, 15 UNTS 295 (entered into force on 4 April 1947), Article 1.

78 See Dempsey and Manoli (2017), pp. 20, 23, 25.

79 Chicago Convention, Article 1.

80 Outer Space Treaty, Article 2.

81 See Dempsey and Manoli (2017), p. 10.

82 Even the delineation of aircraft vs spacecraft is becoming difficult; such as in the case of reusable spacecraft with systems designed to navigate through the air to come back to ground upon re-entry to Earth's atmosphere. The determination of which legal regime applies carries significant ramifications, as space launches often involve arced trajectories which could potentially cross multiple countries' airspace, and thereby require the consent of the subjacent State(s) under the basic precepts of international aviation law, if the upper limit of airspace were set too high. See Dempsey and Manoli (2017), pp. 20, 23, 25.

83 IADC SDMG, Rev. 3, 2021, para. 3.3.3.

km from Earth. The GEO has a special importance for telecommunications because 'a satellite placed in this orbit has the same period of rotation around the Earth as the Earth has around its own axis, whereby the satellite will appear stationary to an observer on the surface of the Earth – that is, geostationary – 24 hours a day.'[84] The GEO is a 'unique resource' as it 'offers significant benefits to operators from the standpoint of station-keeping requirements, ground visibility and coverage, the absence of the need for tracking facilities in small earth station antennas and a relatively benign orbital environment.'[85] Telecommunications are a major economic commodity. Areas of the GEO above countries with stronger demand for satellite services are highly sought after by countries and entities looking to provide those services to the populations of those areas on Earth. As more space objects occupy GEO trajectories, it will become increasingly crowded and difficult to obtain slots to safely place satellites in.[86] This emphasizes the necessity to ensure the viability of space objects operating at this orbit, which relies on preventing increasing deposits of space debris and clearing that which already exists.

The closest sub-domain of outer space to Earth is the Lower Earth Orbit (LEO).[87] The LEO occurs in altitudes from the start of outer space up to 1-2,000 km.[88] Because objects in the LEO are located closer to Earth than those in the GEO, and because they typically follow relatively unstable paths, there is a greater risk of collisions and space debris in the LEO than the GEO.[89] Due to its proximity to Earth, this orbital domain accommodates telecommunications and imagery – Earth observation satellites – as well as military reconnaissance objects.[90] Most recently, the LEO has become host to large

---

84 Viikari (2008), p. 41.

85 Radiocommunication Sector of the International Telecommunication Union (ITU). Environmental Protection of the Geostationary-Satellite Orbit, Recommendation ITU-R S.1003–2, December 2010, point (a). See also UNCOPUOS SDMG, Commentary, para. 194.

86 Gérardine Goh, *Dispute Settlement in International Space Law: A Multi-Door Courthouse for Outer Space* (Martinus Nijhoff Publishers, 2007), p. 19.

87 IADC SDMG, Rev. 3, 2021, para. 3.3.2.

88 Stubbe (2018), p. 25.

89 Tremayne-Smith (2011), pp. 180–181, 187; Viikari (2008), p. 44.

90 Dragonfly Aerospace, 'Applications of a LEO Satellite', *Dragonfly Aerospace* (19 April 2022) (available at https://dragonflyaerospace.com/what-are-some-applications-of-a-leo-satellite/); Base Camp, 'The Basics of Leo Satellite Systems' (23 February 2022) (available at https://www.basecampconnect.com/leo-satellite-systems/).

satellite-constellations providing internet connectivity services, especially to remote Earth areas, such as Starlink, OneWeb and AmazonKuiper.[91]

A further orbital sub-domain is known as the Medium Earth Orbit (MEO). This covers altitudes of around 2,000–35,000 km above the Earth (though some set the upper limit at 10,000 km).[92] The MEO is suitable for navigation systems such as the GPS and Galileo.[93]

In addition to these domains, there are also Highly Elliptical Orbits (HEO).[94] With high eccentricity (deviation from a circular orbit) and variation between a perigee (closest point on the orbit to Earth) of around 1,000 km to an apogee with an altitude of over 35,000 km, the elongated orbits result in long periods dwelling close to the apogee, which makes them suitable for communications satellites.[95]

Another relevant term is 'celestial body/bodies'. Whereas UNGA Resolutions passed in the lead-up to the adoption of the Outer Space Treaty differentiated between outer space itself and celestial bodies, the Outer Space Treaty itself treats these two facets of the space environment collectively, and also appears to include the Moon as a celestial body.[96] However, some commentators argue that celestial bodies are limited to planetary bodies similar to those in our Solar System.[97]

The term 'space objects' is not exhaustively defined in space treaties, including the Outer Space Treaty.[98] The Liability Convention, which is discussed below, and the Registration Convention provide that the term 'space object' includes 'component parts of a space object as well as its launch vehicle and parts thereof', but add no further explanation.[99] Von der Dunk surmises that 'the only widespread agreement – at least amongst authors – would be that

91 Butash Tom, 'Low-Earth orbit megaconstellations reach record capacity', *Aerospace America* (December 2021) (available at https://aerospaceamerica.aiaa.org/year-in-review/low-earth-orbit-megaconstellations-reach-record-capacity/).

92 Stubbe (2018), p. 27; Tremayne-Smith (2011), pp. 180–181; Viikari (2008), p. 44. Note some of these authors diverge on the precise delineation between the LEO and MEO.

93 Tremayne-Smith (2011), pp. 180–181, 352; Viikari (2008), p. 45.

94 Viikari (2008), p. 45.

95 See Stojce Dimov Ilcev, 'Highly elliptical orbits (HEO) for high latitudes and polar coverage,' (2010) *20th International Crimean Conference 'Microwave and Telecommunication Technology'*, Sevastopol, Ukraine, 2010, pp. 396–399.

96 Cheng (1997), p. 227 referring to Outer Space Treaty Articles I(2) in fine; IV(1), and IV(2) 2nd sentence; V(2); VIII.

97 Hobe (2019).

98 Larsen (2018), p. 483.

99 See Liability Convention, Article 1(d); Registration Convention, Article I(b), which both contain an identical non-substantive circular definition.

a space object concerns any man-made object which is at least attempted to be physically brought into outer space'.[100] Space law expert Dennerly explains that 'space object includes man-made objects used across a broad range of space-related activities for a variety of uses, which are subsequently launched into outer space, such as satellites and rockets, and "all parts used in a launch, even those ... not intended to reach outer space", such as boosters'.[101] There is debate over whether 'space object' is a broad term including all such man-made objects intended for launch into space, or whether it is narrower, excluding space debris.[102] However, distinguishing between these categories in a mutually exclusive way is unnecessary, as space objects can be used in the wide sense, with space debris being a subset thereof. Given that the Liability Convention prefaces its definition of 'space objects' with 'includes' (as does the Registration Convention), a wider interpretation is available and consistent with its framing. Accordingly, space objects for present purposes can be taken to encompass all manner of anthropogenic objects launched into space, irrespective of their specific use or nature.

The term 'space debris' does not have one authoritative overarching legal definition and is not defined in any treaty.[103] However, there are several operational definitions, usually used by space agencies or international organizations. The most commonly cited is the definition in the 2002 Inter-Agency Space Debris Coordination Committee (IADC) Space Debris Mitigation Guidelines (SDMG).[104] It provides that 'space debris are all man-made objects including fragments and elements thereof, in Earth orbit or re-entering

---

100 Von der Dunk (2015a), p. 87.

101 Dennerley (2018), p. 285.

102 Yannick Radi, 'Clearing up the Space Junk: On the Flaws and Potential of International Space Law to Tackle the Space Debris Problem' (2023) 12(2) *ESIL Reflections*, 9 March 2023, p. 8 referring to Nicolas M Matte, 'Environmental Implications and Responsibilities in the Use of Outer Space' (1989) 14 *Annals of Air and Space Law*, p. 435, and Stubbe (2018), p. 388.

103 Radi (2023), p. 8.

104 The IADC was formed in 1993 in response to the issue of space debris; Atanasov and Baldesi (2011), p. 220. The 2002 IADC SDMG were most recently updated in 2021: Inter-Agency Space Debris Coordination Committee (IADC), *IADC Space Debris Mitigation Guidelines*, IADC-02-01, Revision 3, June 2021, available at https://www.iadc-home.org/documents_public/view/id/82#u. The 2002 IADC SDMG formed the key basis for the 2007 UNCOPUOS Space Debris Mitigation Guidelines (UNCOPUOS SDMG), as discussed below at Chapter 1, Section 4. Since 2007, the IADC Guidelines have been updated; see, e.g. IADC-02-01 Rev. 3, June 2021 (available at https://www.iadc-home.org/documents_public/file_down/id/5249).

the atmosphere, that are non-functional.'[105] Similarly, the International Organization for Standardization (ISO) issuance 'Space systems – Space debris mitigation requirements' defines 'space debris' as 'all objects of human origin in Earth orbit or re-entering the atmosphere, including fragments and elements thereof, that no longer serve a useful purpose.'

Among scholarly definitions, Stubbe describes it broadly as 'the remnants of human activities in outer space'.[106] Other experts explain that the term 'space debris' covers objects produced by fragmentation events such as collisions, accidental or deliberate explosions, caused by on-board sources or by for example anti-satellite (ASAT)[107] experiments.[108] The main difference between the IADC definition and that of Stubbe, for example, is the restriction to objects in Earth orbit. Whereas objects that remain in Earth's orbit (or re-enter the atmosphere) pose the greatest risks to satellites and other space objects, this monograph does not adhere to that limitation. Instead, it takes a broader ecocentric approach seeking to protect the outer space environment in general. Consequently, for present purposes, space debris will refer to any man-made object in outer space, the original and/or intended function of which has ceased, as well as any fragments that have broken away from such an object.[109]

105 See Inter-Agency Space Debris Coordination Committee (IADC), *Space Debris Mitigation Guidelines* (2007); which were adopted by the full COPUOS and approved by United Nations General Assembly (UNGA) Resolution 62/217. The International Academy of Astronautics defined it as 'any man-made Earth-orbiting object which is non-functional with no reasonable expectation of assuming or resuming its intended function, or any other function for which it is or can be expected to be authorized, including fragments and parts thereof', see Ad Hoc Expert Group, IAA, 'Orbital Debris – Status and Possibilities for Control' (1993) 9(3) *Space Policy*, pp. 185 et seq; International Law Association defined it as any 'man-made object in outer space, other than active or otherwise useful satellites', see Buenos Aires International Instrument on Damage caused by Space Debris, August 1994, reprinted in 23 *Journal of Space Law* 113 (1995), p. 113 (Article 1 (c)).

106 Stubbe (2018), p. 3.

107 During ASAT tests States deliberately target their own non-functional space objects to test the effectiveness of their anti-satellite weapon systems; see Mark Smith, 'Anti-satellite weapons: History, types and purpose' *Space.com* (10 August 2022) (available at https://www.space.com/anti-satellite-weapons-asats); Ritu S. Lauer, 'When States Test Their Anti-Satellite Weapons' (2022) 20 *Astropolitics*, pp. 1–2.

108 John S. Goehring, 'Can We Address Orbital Debris with the International Law We Already Have? An Examination of Treaty Interpretation and the Due Regard Principle' (2020) 85(2) *Journal of Air Law and Commerce*, pp. 310, 319; Dennerley (2018), p. 285; Stubbe (2018), p.17.

109 Dennerley (2018), p. 286; Alexander Soucek, *Space Law Essentials: Volume 1: Textbook* (NWV, 2020), p. 37 (notwithstanding the 'non-functionality or fragmentary nature of debris, the "object's use or usefulness" is not relevant to the definition of space object').

The term 'space pollution' is a broad expression, which is not subject to any authoritative legal definition at present.[110] As used herein, it connotes the remnants and impact of human activities in outer space.[111] It includes not only 'space debris', which is generally considered to refer to tangible items,[112] but also the impact on the space environment, which may be created by the extraction of resources (such as minerals) from celestial bodies or by the introduction of terrestrial matter to outer space,[113] as well as intangible matter such as radiation.

Beyond space debris itself, various forms of space pollution include nuclear contamination (many satellites utilize nuclear-power sources)[114] and exobiological contamination (both in its forward – contamination from Earth to outer space, and backwards – from outer space to Earth[115] – forms).[116] Regarding nuclear risks, radioactive materials must be properly contained and protected so they will not be leaked into the Earth's environment due to the intense atmospheric forces on re-entry.[117] Moreover, nuclear explosions could result in serious hazards to astronauts in manned space flights because there is no atmosphere to cushion them, and radiation can 'freely spread out over a radius of thousands of kilometers, extending even to the Earth'.[118] Aside from the risk of radioactive space debris returning to Earth and bringing that contamination with it, there is also the risk of space-based weapons or other objects hitting nuclear-power sources in outer space. Therefore, passivation efforts at the end

---

110 There are references to the term 'space pollution' in scholarly literature, but it is not a term explicitly included in legal instruments; see, e.g. Sraavya Poonuganti, 'It's Raining Rockets: Heightening State Liability for Space Pollution' (2023) 23(2) *Chicago Journal of International Law*, pp. 23–24.

111 See Peter Stubbe, 'Legal Consequences of the Pollution of Outer Space with Space Debris' (2020) in: *Oxford Research Encyclopedia of Planetary Science* (Peter Read *et al.* (eds.)) (Oxford University Press), p. 3.

112 See, e.g., Hobe (2019), p. 111.

113 Ouarda Layachi, 'International Liability for Pollution Damage in Outer Space Environment' (2020) 16 *WSEAS Transactions on Environment and Development*, pp. 149–157; Pietkiewicz (2019), pp. 215–219.

114 Nuclear power source-equipped spacecraft can be moved for extended periods of time to disposal orbits, where they can obtain space debris. However, this increased the probability of collisions involving radiation; Viikari (2008), p. 47.

115 In addition to international space law, which is discussed herein, international aviation law (sometimes termed air law) could be used to regulate backwards pollution to Earth by NSAs, as a returning NSA vessel that potentially could qualify as an aircraft is using the Earth's atmosphere to control its movement; see Dempsey and Manoli (2017), pp. 9, 37–43.

116 Viikari (2008), p. 50.

117 Stubbe (2018), p. 246.

118 Viikari (2008), p. 47–48.

of an object's lifespan (such as emptying residual fuel) are considered particularly important as discussed herein.[119]

Human exploration of the moon and eventually other planets could result in space pollution, through the introduction of terrestrial substances onto celestial bodies which may harm any existing indigenous life forms.[120] There is precedent for the careless pollution of celestial bodies. In 1999, the Lunar Prospector, which had not been sterilized or decontaminated and had human remains aboard (cremated remains of lunar geologist Eugene Shoemaker), was 'targeted at the pristine lunar south pole, with the hope that the impact would liberate water molecules from suspected ice deposits.'[121] That contamination of the moon could have unforeseen consequences for the pristine lunar environment.

Turning to the term 'launching State', this is defined in Article VII of the Outer Space Treaty, Article I of the Liability Convention and Article I of the Registration Convention[122] as the State 'which launches or procures the launching of a space object, or the State from whose territory or facility a space object is launched'.[123] Consequently, there are four categories of States in issue:

1) the State which launches [the space object];
2) the State which procures the launching;
3) the State from whose territory a space object is launched, and;
4) the State from whose facility a space object is launched.[124]

---

119 See e.g. Viikari (2008), p. 114; Martha Mejia-Kaiser, *The Geostationary Ring: Practice and Law* (Martinus Nijhoff Publishers, 2020), p. 210; Neta Palkowitz, *Regulating a Revolution* (Wolters International Law BV, 2019).

120 Stubbe refers to 'contamination' as including biological contamination; Stubbe (2018), p. 155.

121 Mark Williamson, Protecting the Space Environment, (2000) 9(4) *Earth Space Review*, pp. 4–5; Viikari (2008), p. 53.

122 For more detail on these conventions, see Chapters 2, Section 1, (a) and 3, Section 1 below.

123 Article I (c) of the Liability Convention defines the launching State as '(i) A State which launches or procures the launching of a space object; (ii) A State from whose territory or facility a space object is launched'. However, the guidance as to potentially liable States stretches wider: 'Article I (c) of the [Liability] Convention: cf. also Article VII of the Outer Space Treaty; in the elaboration of the Convention in the Sub-Committee seven criteria were listed as essential for liability: (a) providing territory for the launching of a space object; (b) providing facilities for the launching of a space object; (c) exercising control over the orbit or trajectory of a space object; (d) owning or possessing a space object; (e) procuring the launching of a space object; (f) participation in the launching of a space object; and (g) registration (international or national) of a space object'; Manfred Lachs, *The Law of Outer Space* (Martinus-Nijhoff Publishers, 2011), p.113 citing Committee on the Peaceful Uses of Outer Space (1965), *Report of the Legal Sub-Committee on the Work of its Fourth Session*, A/AC.105/29, p. 4.

124 See von der Dunk (2015a), pp. 82–84.

Consequently, there can be more than one launching State, as confirmed in Article V of the Liability Convention. If more than one State fulfils these criteria, they will be jointly and severally liable.[125] However, there could also be no territorial State from which a space object was launched; for example, if it took off from an area in the global commons.[126] Accordingly, this definition leaves it uncertain whether a space object launched from global commons by a national of a particular State would be considered a launch by that State, which potentially links to nefarious uses of space that may be sought in the future.[127] In this respect, Radi argues that if private companies are involved in the launch, whether by doing so themselves or procuring such a launch or providing a launch facility, State responsibility should be engaged in line with Article VI of the Outer Space Treaty.[128] However, Radi does not specify which State would incur responsibility in such circumstances and does not address the situation of launches from global commons and areas outside any State's jurisdiction. Some States advocate for a narrow interpretation of the definition of a launching State, which would exclude the liability of launching State(s) in some cases of private activities.[129] However, Kerrest considers this

---

125 See Armel Kerrest, 'The concept of the 'launching State' in commercial launch ventures' (2017) in: *Commercial Uses of Space and Space Tourism* (Jan Wouters, Philip De Man, Rik Hansen (eds.)) (Cheltenham: Edward Elgar), pp. 5–6. An example are INTELSAT satellites launched by France and USA, and later bought on orbit by a Dutch NSA, see Note verbale dated 29 July 2003 from the Permanent Mission of the Netherlands to the United Nations (Vienna) addressed to the Secretary-General, A/AC.105/806; Note verbale dated 18 February 2004 from the Permanent Mission of the Netherlands to the United Nations (Vienna) addressed to the Secretary-General, A/AC.105/824.

126 See Draft Articles on Prevention of Transboundary Harm from Hazardous Activities with Commentaries (DAPTHAA), Yearbook of the International Law Commission, Volume II, Part II (2001) (adopted 53rd Session), Article 1 Commentary, paragraph 10 ('Sometimes, because of the location of the activity, there is no territorial link between a State and the activity such as, for example, activities taking place in outer space or on the high seas.'). Note that the USA has previously indicated that it does not consider outer space to constitute a part of the 'global commons'; Melissa de Zwart; Stacey Henderson; Rachel Neef, 'The Principle of 'Harmful Contamination' Applied to Human Missions to Mars' *Journal of Space Law* 45, no. 2 (2021), pp. 302–303.

127 See Chapter 3, Section 2.

128 Radi (2023), p. 9 (Article VI 'provides that States Parties shall bear international responsibility for national activities in outer space carried on by non-governmental entities').

129 As also noted by von der Dunk (2015a), p. 83, there is generally no fear of escaping liability in instances where an object has been launched from a State's territory or platform, but in cases of private actors launching from global commons or procuring the launch, the situation may not be completely straightforward. This is because the definition of launching State does not elaborate as to whether purely private launches and procurements count under a State launches or a State procures. By virtue of discussions on the

would violate 'the spirit of the Liability Convention, and even of the letter in the context of Article VI Outer Space Treaty' and that it could lead to no State being liable in the case of private activity launched from areas outside of State jurisdiction such as the high seas.[130] While such narrow interpretations remain outside the mainstream of international space law for the moment, they signal the need to explore means to hold NSAs responsible in the absence of State responsibility, as discussed below.[131]

The 'State of registration' is generally regarded as the State that registers an object launched into outer space in its national registry, thereby gaining jurisdiction over it and any personnel thereof pursuant to Article VIII of the Outer Space Treaty. It was later defined in Article I(c) of the Registration Convention as a 'launching State on whose registry a space object is carried in accordance

Outer Space Treaty (Articles II and VI) it could be argued that private launches and procurements are counted under State launches and procurements by virture of the space treaties being State-oriented. However, in cases of on-orbit transfers of ownership, the Netherlands, for example, refused to be seen as the launching State of NSS-6 and NSS-7 bought in-orbit by a private Dutch company (see Note verbale dated 29 July 2003 from the Permanent Mission of the Netherlands to the United Nations (Vienna) addressed to the Secretary-General, A/AC.105/806; Note verbale dated 18 February 2004 from the Permanent Mission of the Netherlands to the United Nations (Vienna) addressed to the Secretary-General, A/AC.105/824; Note verbale dated 29 July 2003 from the Permanent Mission of the Netherlands to the United Nations (Vienna) addressed to the Secretary-General, A/AC.105/806; Note verbale dated 18 February 2004 from the Permanent Mission of the Netherlands to the United Nations (Vienna) addressed to the Secretary-General, A/AC.105/824.). It could of course be argued that in-orbit transfers of ownership are a somewhat separate issue since the object is already in orbit and not at the launching stage. Nonetheless, Dasgupta has argued that the Netherlands should be recognised as the procuring State and thus a launching State, because the satellites were procured by a Dutch NSA, see Upasana Dasgupta, 'On-Orbit Transfer of Satellites Between States: Legal Issues – with Special Emphasis on Liability and Registration' (2016) in: *59th International Institute for Space Law Colloquium on the Law of Outer Space* (Tanja Masson – Zwaan et al. (eds.)) (The Hague: Eleven International Publishing), p. 646. On the problematic of on-orbit transfers of ownership see Hobe (2019), p. 91, Sancin, Grünfeld, Ramuš Cvetkovič (2021), pp. 25–28; Dasgupta (2016), pp. 641–666.

130 See Kerrest (2017), p. 5–6. See also Chapter 3, Section 2. An additional consideration would be whether the vessel from which the launch took off was registered to a country and whether the actions of the persons conducting the launch could be attributed to a State in line with the usual rules on State responsibility; see International Law Commission's Draft Articles on Responsibility of States for Internationally Wrongful Acts, in Report of the International Law Commission on the Work of Its Fifty-third Session, UN GAOR, 56th Sess., Supp. No. 10, at 43, UN Doc. A/56/10 (2001).

131 See Chapter 3, Section 2.

with Article II of the Registration Convention'.[132] Aside from the fact that registration is the basis for jurisdiction, meaning the legal authority of States to control space objects,[133] it furthermore assists in identifying responsible States.[134]

The term 'responsibility' is used herein to denote legal responsibility in accordance with international law and domestic law, to the extent the latter is not displaced by international law. It is used broadly, to encapsulate the sense outlined in the International Law Commission's (ILC) Articles on State Responsibility for Wrongful Acts,[135] which focuses on the attributability of prohibited conduct and the consequences for the responsible party.[136] It is also used herein to refer to the responsibility of NSAs for wrongful acts, whether in their own capacity or when attributed to States.

The term 'liability' is used here to mean 'the legal obligation 'to compensate another ... for injury' after an event which results in damage.[137] It is used herein primarily with reference to the framework of the Liability Convention and does not necessarily require the commission of a wrongful act, only the existence of damage and the obligation to provide compensation for the damage.[138]

---

132 Article II of the Registration Convention demands that an object is registered in a national register and that such registration is communicated to the Secretary General of the UN. It, however, prescribes no specific deadline in which such registration must be carried out, making it difficult in practice to enforce registration.

133 Lachs (2010), p. 66.

134 Larsen (2018), pp. 487–488; Ram S. Jakhu, Bhupendra Jasani, Jonathan C. McDowell, 'Critical issues related to registration of space objects and transparency of space activities' (2018) 143 *Acta Astronautica*, p. 407; see also Bernhard Schmidt-Tedd, Alexander Soucek, 'Registration of Space Objects' in: *Oxford Research Encyclopedia of Planetary Science* (Peter Read *et al.* (eds.)) (Oxford University Press, 2020).

135 Responsibility of States for Internationally Wrongful Acts (ARSIWA), *Yearbook of the International Law Commission, Volume II* (2001), A/CN.4/SER.A/2001/Add.1. See also Sompong Sucharitkul, 'State Responsibility and International Liability Under International Law' (1996) 18 *Loyola of Los Angeles International and Comparative Law Journal*.

136 Rosalyn Higgins, *Problems and Process: International Law and How We Use It* (Clarendon Press, 1994), p. 146.

137 Dennerley (2018), citing 'No-fault liability'. See also Fogo (2017), p. 196 ("international liability' refers to a State's 'obligation to compensate another state for any injury that is caused to the people or property of the latter nation.').

138 See Sucharitkul (1996), pp. 828–832. In space law, no wrongful act is inherently necessary in order to establish liability (with an exception being the notion of fault in Article III of the Liability Convention). The International Law Commission, on the other hand, has commented on liability in both contexts – liability for wrongful acts and liability resulting from acts not prohibited by international law; see, for example, Report of the Working Group on international liability for injurious consequences arising out of acts not prohibited by international law, A/CN.4/L.284 and Corr.1, New York, 1978; Seventh report of the Special Rapporteur Barboza on international liability for injurious consequences

The term 'accountability' is a broader term than 'responsibility' and 'liability'. It denotes 'that there is a liability for internationally wrongful behaviour and that that liability must be discharged'.[139] Accountability is used in a broad sense herein, to encompass criminal accountability, civil accountability, and other forms of enforcing regulatory frameworks.

3 The Escalating Threat of NSA Space Pollution

The threat posed by space pollution increases in magnitude each year. Every object launched into outer space contributes to a form of pollution both during the launching phase, by producing emissions, and at the end of its operation, either by becoming (un)trackable space debris in GEO or by re-entering the orbit, hitting the Earth (damaging the Earth's environment or even becoming a threat to human health and lives), or burning up in the atmosphere (resulting in harmful emissions). Looking at the example of space debris specifically, in 2021, ESA noted that of the approximately 26,000 tracked objects in space, only 2,800 objects are functional spacecraft, with the remaining objects constituting space debris.[140] Many more objects are too small to be tracked with current technology, leading to the estimation that '1 million objects smaller than 10 cm and larger than 1 cm and 130 million objects smaller than 1 cm and larger than 1mm are expected to reside in earth orbits'.[141]

Despite this, the commercial side of space activity is rapidly expanding.[142] Launches are expected to increase tenfold in the short term, largely driven by the launch of small satellites.[143] The global space economy in 2019

arising out of acts not prohibited by international law, UN Doc. A/CN.4/437 and Corr.1, New York, 1991; Tenth report of the Special Rapporteur Barboza on international liability for injurious consequences arising out of acts not prohibited by international law, UN Doc. A/CN.4/459, New York, 1994. Against this background, the application and consequences of liability and responsibility sometimes overlap, which creates an issue with regard to the appropriate legal basis for compensation for damages; see Frans G. von der Dunk, 'Liability versus Responsibility in Space Law: Misconception or Misconstruction?' (1992) 21 *Space, Cyber, and Telecommunications Law Program Faculty Publications*, pp. 364, 367–368.

139 Higgins (1994), p. 146.

140 Williams (2017); ESA, *Space debris: assessing the risk* (16 March 2005) (available at https://www.esa.int/About_Us/ESOC/Space_debris_assessing_the_risk); NASA (26 May 2021).

141 European Space Agency (22 December 2022); UNCOPUOS Technical Report on Space Debris, A/AC.105/720 (1999), p. 14.

142 Stubbe (2018), p. 96 ('[i]t is estimated that out of the currently approximately 1,419 operational satellites, about 557 are associated with commercial purposes.').

143 Larsen (2018), p. 481.

was reportedly valued at 423.8 billion US dollars.[144] Out of this, commercial applications make up the largest share.[145] The majority is being conducted by NSAs,[146] particularly satellite companies.[147]

The trend towards NSAs becoming an essential part of the space sector looks set to continue.[148] Some of the oldest space-active States rely heavily on services provided by NSAs. Prominent among these are the use of commercial satellites operated by NSAs.[149] Launch capabilities for crewed missions, which were, for a long time, primarily the domain of the Russian space agency 'Roskosmos',[150] are now being offered by private providers.[151] The conflict in Ukraine is accelerating this privatization, with many cooperation agreements with Roskosmos having ended, as State agencies are pushed towards a greater

---

144 For more information see: Erick Burgueño Salas, 'Space industry worldwide – statistics and facts' *Statista* (20 November 2022) (available at https://www.statista.com/topics/5049/space-exploration/). See also Yousaf Butt, 'Avoiding Collisions in Outer Space' *New York Times* (19 March 2018) (available at https://www.nytimes.com/2018/03/19/opinion/space-race-regulation.html).

145 Andrea Sommariva, 'The Evolution of Space Economy: The Role of the Private Sector and the Challenges for Europe' *Italian Institute for International Political Studies* (7 December 2020) (available at https://www.ispionline.it/en/pubblicazione/evolution-space-economy-role-private-sector-and-challenges-europe-28604); Matthew Weinzierl and Mehak Sarang, 'The Commercial Space Age Is Here' *Harvard Business Review* (12 February 2021) (available at https://hbr.org/2021/02/the-commercial-space-age-is-here).

146 Due to the complexity of space activities, non-governmental space conduct is usually undertaken by corporations, see Stubbe (2018), p. 262; de Zwart (2016), pp. 2–3; Kizer Whitt (2022).

147 Tereza Pultarova, 'The 10 Hottest Companies in Satellite 2018' *ViaSatellite* (January 2019) (available at http://interactive.satellitetoday.com/via/january-2019/the-10-hottest-companies-in-satellite-2018/); Chris Kolmar, 'The 15 Largest Satellite Companies In The World' *ZIPPIA* (26 July 2022) (available at https://www.zippia.com/advice/largest-satellite-companies/).

148 Stubbe (2018), p. 96; Rachel A. Gabriel and Barnett S. Koven, 'Malicious Non-state Actors and Contested Space Operations' *Report to DHS SandT Office of University Programs and DoD Strategic Multilayer Assessment Branch* (February 2018) (available at https://nsiteam.com/social/wp-content/uploads/2018/07/START_Malicious-Non-state-Actors-and-Contested-Space-Operations-Final.pdf).

149 Fogo (2017), pp. 185, 187; SpaceX Commercial Crew Transportation Capability Contract (CCtCap) NNK14MA74C, signed between NASA and SpaceX (available at https://www.nasa.gov/sites/default/files/files/CCtCap_SpaceX_508.pdf).

150 For more on the influences of Russia, see Katja Grünfeld, *Influences of the Russian Federation on International Law in the 21st Century* (Master Thesis, University of Ljubljana, 2020).

151 See, e.g., Stuart Fox, '6 Private Companies That Could Launch Humans Into Space' *Space.com* (4 June 2010) (available at https://www.space.com/8541-6-private-companies-launch-humans-space.html).

dependency on private launch providers.[152] Moreover, with companies such as SpaceX and Virgin Galactic planning space tourism and various other extraterrestrial exploits, commercial launches are set to become the norm rather than the exception.[153] Futuristic ventures, such as proposed human settlements on Mars, have seen private actors like Elon Musk and his SpaceX corporation taking the lead.[154]

The commercial space sector has already caused an exponential growth of objects, especially in the LEO.po[155] With the development of small satellites, space activity has become cheaper than at any point in history. The launch of a large satellite, such as a weather satellite, typically necessitates over 50 million US dollars. However, small satellites can be launched at a greatly reduced cost of only a few 100,000 US dollars.[156] Many NSAs are using the new technologies to develop satellite swarms or mega constellations of satellites, which can consist of thousands of satellites.[157] These can be potentially harmful to the space environment for many reasons ranging from obstructing astronomical observations to heightening the dangers of space debris due to the higher volume of satellites in orbit.[158] OneWeb, for example, applied for the launch of

---

152 Tzvi Joffre, 'Russia stops space cooperation with US: 'Let them fly on brooms'' *The Jerusalem Post* (3 March 2022) (available at https://www.jpost.com/breaking-news/article-699203); German Aerospace Center (Deutsches Zentrum für Luft- und Raumfahrt; DLR), *DLR ceases bilateral cooperation with Russia* (3 March 2022) (available at https://www.dlr.de/content/en/articles/news/2022/01/20220303_dlr-ceases-bilateral-cooperation-with-russia.html); Florin Zubașcu, 'Ukraine war disrupting East-West cooperation in space' *ScienceBusiness* (8 March 2022) (available at https://sciencebusiness.net/news/ukraine-war-disrupting-east-west-cooperation-space).

153 See David Hsu and Nicolaj Siggelkow, 'Why Big Business Is Making a Giant Leap into Space' *Knowledge at Wharton* (4 June 2019) (available at https://knowledge.wharton.upenn.edu/article/commercial-space-economy/).

154 de Zwart (2016), p. 2.

155 European Space Agency, *ESA's Annual Space Environment Report* (22 April 2022) (available at https://www.sdo.esoc.esa.int/environment_report/Space_Environment_Report_latest.pdf), p. 26.

156 John Nixon and Joseph Michaels, *Modern English for Aeronautics and Space Technology* (2021) Munich: Carl Hanser Verlag, pp. 137–144; Denise Chow, 'To cheaply go: How falling launch costs fueled a thriving economy in orbit', NBC News, 8 April 2022 (https://www.nbcnews.com/science/space/space-launch-costs-growing-business-industry-rcna23488).

157 European Space Agency, 'Managing mega-constellations' (30 May 2017) (available at https://www.esa.int/Enabling_Support/Preparing_for_the_Future/Discovery_and_Preparation/Managing_mega-constellations).

158 See also Miraslava Kazlouskaya, 'Large Satellite Constellations: Legal Challenges in Addressing Space Sustainability and Astronomical Observations' (2021) 70(4) *Zeitschrift für Luft- und Weltraumrecht*, pp. 571–585.

7,000[159] satellites, Amazon Kuiper for 3,000[160] satellites, SpaceX's Starlink constellation has had first approximately 4,000[161] then 12,000[162] satellites approved and filed for another 30,000.[163] To put this in perspective – in 2021 around 4,000 active satellites were noted as orbiting Earth, indicating that exponential increases can be expected.[164] This rapid increase in the number of satellites in orbit constitutes a threat to the outer space environment because of the congestion of space objects (which in turn leads to a higher risk of space debris) and also because of the significant volume of CO_2 released with each satellite launch.[165]

Worryingly, NSA space activity has already been linked to collisions resulting in space debris, as noted above.[166] The 1996 failed launch of the Ariane 5 rocket and its payload, led to debris that reportedly struck and damaged a French micro-satellite.[167] In 2009, the non-functional Russian Kosmos-2251 satellite collided with the functional Iridium-33 satellite operated by an American

---

159 Rachel Jewett, 'OneWeb Adjusts Target Constellation Size Down to 7,000 Satellites' *Via Satellite* (14 January 2021) (available at https://www.satellitetoday.com/broadband/2021/01/14/oneweb-adjusts-target-constellation-size-down-to-7000-satellites).

160 Federal Communications Commission, FCC File No. SAT-LOA-20190704-00057 (30 July 2020) (available at https://fcc.report/IBFS/SAT-LOA-20190704-00057).

161 Federal Communications Commission, FCC File No. SAT-LOA-20161115-00118 (29 March 2018), available at https://www.fcc.gov/document/fcc-authorizes-spacex-provide-broadband-satellite-services.

162 Tamanna Farooque Arzo, 'Starlink satellites increased nearly 50% in space in 2021' *techgenyz* (8 March 2022) (available at https://www.techgenyz.com/2022/03/08/starlink-satellites-increased-nearly-space/).

163 Caleb Henry, 'SpaceX submits paperwork for 30,000 more Starlink satellites' *SpaceNews* (15 October 2019) (available at https://spacenews.com/spacex-submits-paperwork-for-30000-more-starlink-satellites/).

164 Stephen Young, 'The Number of Active Satellites in Space Skyrockets … Literally' *The Equation* (27 July 2021) (available at https://blog.ucsusa.org/syoung/number-of-satellites-skyrockets/#:~:text=In%20the%20four%20months%20between%20January%201%20and,that%20has%20been%20building%20since%202014.%20Given%20the); Statista Research Department, 'Number of satellites in orbit by major country as of January 1, 2022' *Statista* (3 February 2023) (available at https://www.statista.com/statistics/264472/number-of-satellites-in-orbit-by-operating-country/).

165 Ferreira-Snyman (2023), p. 5.

166 Certain examples in the following discussion involve mixed public-private activities, which is increasingly common in space exploration. Some private actors are aware of their contribution to space pollution and are taking steps towards mitigating their space debris. See, for example, the experimental system Remove DEBRIS which was already used by SpaceX, Eli Meixler, 'SpaceX Has Launched an Experimental Space Junk Sweeper Into Orbit' (2 April 2018) (available at https://time.com/5225670/spacex-space-junk-cleaner-launch/).

167 Radi (2023), pp. 1–2.

NSA – Iridium Communications, which is a publicly traded US company that operates the Iridium constellation of 66 communications satellites.[168] The collision was in part blamed on the NSA not taking evasive action.[169] Moreover, in April 2019, a landing vehicle called Beresheet, delivered by a SpaceX Falcon 9 rocket, produced by the Israeli company SpaceIL crashed into the surface of the moon.[170] This privately developed Moon lander was carrying on board cargo containing human DNA as well as tardigrades, micro-animals capable of surviving in extreme environments.[171] Even though it is very unlikely that tardigrades survived the crash (according to commentators), the decision to include them in the cargo of Beresheet was allegedly a private decision.[172] This example demonstrates a growing threat, whereby NSAs disregard preventive

168 This event generated over 1800 new pieces of space debris larger than 10cm, see Nicholas Johnson 'The Collision of Iridium 33 and Cosmos 2251: The Shape of Things to Come', Conference paper 20100002023 at 60th International Astronautical Congress (2009) (available at https://ntrs.nasa.gov/citations/20100002023); A. Tan, T.X. Zhang and M. Dokhanian, 'Analysis of the Iridium 33 and Cosmos 2251 Collision using Velocity Perturbations of the Fragments' (2013) 3(1) *Advances in Aerospace Science and Applications*, pp. 13–25.

169 Michael J. Listner, 'Iridium 33 and Cosmos 2251, Three Years Later' *Space Safety Magazine* (10 February 2012) (available at https://www.spacesafetymagazine.com/space-debris/kessler-syndrome/iridium-33-cosmos-2251-years-later-learned-then/); Michael A. Earl, 'The CASTOR Satellite Survey, 2007 January 1 to 2009 December 31' (2010) 104(4) *Journal of the Royal Astronomical Society of Canada*, pp. 152, 153.

170 Chang Kenneth, 'Moon Landing by Israel's Beresheet Spacecraft Ends in Crash' *New York Times* (11 April 2019) (available at https://www.nytimes.com/2019/04/11/science/israel-moon-landing-beresheet.html); Eric Mack and Jackson Ryan, 'SpaceX sends Israel's historic moon mission on its way' CNET (21 February 2019) (available at https://www.cnet.com/science/spacex-space-x-beresheet-moon-mission-israel/); David Szondy, 'First private moon mission lifts off aboard SpaceX Falcon 9 rocket' *NewAtlas* (22 February 2019) (available at https://newatlas.com/beresheet-lunar-mission-launch/58587/); Loren Grush, 'Israel's attempted Moon landing fails moments before touchdown' *The Verge* (11 April 2019) (available at https://www.theverge.com/2019/4/11/18306294/spaceil-beresheet-lunar-lander-failure-crash-engine-shut-down).

171 Daniel Oberhaus, 'A Crashed Israeli Lunar Lander Spilled Tardigrades on the Moon' *Wired* (5 August 2019) (available at https://www.wired.com/story/a-crashed-israeli-lunar-lander-spilled-tardigrades-on-the-moon/); Mindy Weisberger, 'There Are Thousands of Tardigrades on the Moon. Now What?' *LIVE SCIENCE* (15 August 2019) (available at https://www.livescience.com/moon-tardigrades-future.html); Jonathan O'Callaghan, 'Hardy water bears survive bullet impacts-up to a point' *Science* (18 May 2021) (available at https://www.science.org/content/article/hardy-water-bears-survive-bullet-impacts-point).

172 Oberhaus (2019); Christopher D. Johnson, Daniel Porras, Christopher M. Hearsey, and Sinead O'Sullivan, 'The curious case of the transgressing tardigrades (part 1)' *The Space Review* (26 August 2019) (available at https://thespacereview.com/article/3783/1).

measures and endeavor in activities that endanger the environment of outer space.[173]

Regarding collisions, in December 2021, China complained to the United Nations regarding a near-miss between its space station and a Starlink satellite (operated by the private company SpaceX), citing an unpredictable avoidance maneuver strategy of the novel artificial intelligence system on-board the satellite.[174] Over the years, SpaceX has reportedly lost several of its Starlink satellites.[175] These risks compound on those created by State launched space objects colliding with other space objects. In 2013, Ecuador launched its first satellite called Pegasus, from a Chinese spaceport, however, during orbit insertion the satellite collided with particles of a Soviet rocket, which remained in orbit, and was lost.[176] In 2022, the International Space Station (ISS) was forced to maneuver in order to avoid debris from the Russian satellite Kosmos-1408.[177] The Kosmos-1408 space debris had resulted from an anti-satellite weapon test which Russia undertook in 2021.[178] Other States, including Russia (and previously the Soviet Union), the United States, China, and India have conducted similar tests previously.[179]

---

173 Cirkovic points out another case where a private entity sent potentially dangerous cargo in space without a State's explicit permission – a US aerospace start-up Swarm launched in 2018 four tiny satellites into space on an Indian rocket that lofted a total 31 payloads, despite being denied a license by the Federal Communications Commission expressing concern that the satellites were too small to be tracked in outer space. See Elena Cirkovic, 'International Law beyond the Earth system: Orbital debris and interplanetary pollution' (2022) 13(2) *Journal of Human Rights and the Environment*, p. 337.

174 Note verbale dated 3 December 2021 from the Permanent Mission of China to the United Nations (Vienna) addressed to the Secretary-General, UN Doc. A/AC.105/1262 (10 December 2021).

175 BBC 'SpaceX loses 40 satellites to geomagnetic storm a day after launch' *BBC News* (9 February 2022) (available at https://www.bbc.com/news/world-60317806); Ian Randall, 'SpaceX loses control of three of its Starlink internet satellites just WEEKS after launch amid fears the surge in space junk could one day trap humanity on Earth' *Mail Online* (1 July 2019) (available at https://www.dailymail.co.uk/sciencetech/article-7200885/SpaceX-loses-control-three-Starlink-internet-satellites-just-WEEKS-launch.html).

176 Ronnie Nader, T.S. Kelso, *The Pegasus Incident: The Loss of the First Ecuadorian Satellite and its Recovery*, (2014) Conference Paper at the International Astronautical Congress, October 2014; BBC News, 'Ecuador Pegasus satellite fears over space debris crash', *BBC News* (24 May 2013) (available at https://www.bbc.com/news/world-latin-america-22635671).

177 Radi (2023), p. 2.

178 Radi (2023), p. 2; Mark Smith, 'Anti-Satellite Weapons: History, Types and Purpose', *Space.com* (10 August 2022) (available at https://www.space.com/anti-satellite-weapons-asats).

179 Viikari (2008), pp. 61–62. Laura Grego, 'A History of Anti-Satellite Programs, Union of Concerned Scientists' (January 2012) (available at https://www.ucsusa.org/sites/default/files/2019-09/a-history-of-ASAT-programs_lo-res.pdf); Heather Foye and Gabriela

Threats facing the outer space environment are not limited to the unintentional generation of space debris. Commentators have warned of the threat of 'nefarious' intentional conduct by NSAs,[180] such as terrorist groups.[181] Gregory Miller argues that 'the most likely threat of attacks against the space capabilities of any country will come from non-state actors engaging in new forms of asymmetric warfare.'[182] In 2016, David Livingstone and Patricia Lewis argued that 'cyberthreats against space-based systems include ... well-resourced organized criminal elements seeking financial gain; [and] terrorist groups wishing to promote their causes, even up to the catastrophic level of cascading satellite collisions.'[183] Because it is difficult and expensive to add defensive capacities to space objects, attacks are in some respects 'relatively easy' to conduct against space objects.[184] This makes space a soft underbelly for threat actors seeking to cause maximum shock to governments and the international community.

The risks to the outer space environment from military activities have been recognised from the earliest formation of international space law.[185] However, those risks are now emanating not only from States but also from NSAs. This may include the indirect use of outer space for their military purposes. Already, armed non-State groups have extended their operations to encompass outer space either directly or indirectly. In the 1980s and 1990s, INMARSAT[186] terminals were removed from ships and reportedly used by armed factions in the mountains behind Beirut for military communications.[187] In 2007, the

Rosa Hernandez, 'UN First Committee Cals for ASAT Test Ban, Arms Control Association' (December 2022) (available at https://www.armscontrol.org/act/2022-12/news/un-first-committee-calls-asat-test-ban).

180 Linda Dawson, *War in Space: The Science and Technology Behind Our Next Theater of Conflict* (Springer, 2018), p. 56; Thomas Harding, 'Why space debris is a threat to the world' *The National News* (16 July 2021) (available at https://www.thenationalnews.com/world/2021/07/16/why-space-debris-is-a-threat-to-the-world/).

181 Fogo (2017), pp. 183, 190.

182 Miller (2019), p. 35.

183 David Livingstone and Patricia Lewis, 'Space, the Final Frontier for Cybersecurity?' (2016) Research paper, Chatham House The Royal Institute of International Affairs, International Security Department, London (available at https://www.chathamhouse.org/sites/default/files/publications/research/2016-09-22-space-final-frontier-cybersecurity-livingstone-lewis.pdf).

184 Miller (2019), p. 44.

185 See Viikari (2008), p. 24 ('military applications have contributed significantly to environmental degradation worldwide (and even in outer space): the military is one of the largest polluters in terms of the amount of waste produced and energy consumed.')

186 Inmarsat is a British satellite telecommunications company, which offers telephone and data services via portable or mobile terminals to users around the world, utilising fourteen geostationary telecommunication satellites.

187 Lyall and Larsen (2009), pp. 524–525.

Liberation Tigers of Tamil Eelam (LTTE), in Sri Lanka, were recorded as pirating an InterSat satellite transponder signal and used it to broadcast propaganda transmissions for a period of two years.[188] Less notorious, but potentially just as harmful, threats emanate from hacker groups, which can operate from nondescript locations with minimal equipment and nonetheless still seize control of space assets. Miller notes that, in 1999, 'hackers seized control of a British military communications satellite with a home computer'.[189] Even the 2022 cyber-attack on the KA-SAT satellite, which caused telecommunications disruptions in Ukraine during the Ukraine conflict, was allegedly conducted by two NSA hacking groups.[190]

Despite these risks, the enormous potential profits to be made are prompting States to actively encourage private space ventures. The United States, for example, has passed legislation seeking to remove governmental barriers for the most viable and safe industries as well as to attempt to enable US citizens, including legal entities incorporated in the United States,[191] to commercially explore, recover and even take ownership[192] of space

188 Fogo (2017), p. 182 citing Nina-Louisa Remuss, 'The Need to Counter Space Terrorism: A European Perspective,' *European Space Policy Institute* (6 January 2009), p. 3; Miller (2019), p. 39 citing John Daly, 'LTTE: Technologically Innovative Rebels,' *Asian Tribune* (14 June 2007) (John Daly 'LTTE: Technologically innovative rebels,' (2007) ISN, Centre for Security Studies (CSS)); Peter B. de Selding, 'Intelsat Vows to Stop Piracy by Sri Lanka Separatist Group' *Space News* (18 April 2007) (available at https://spacenews.com/intelsat-vows-stop-piracy-sri-lanka-separatist-group/).

189 Miller (2019), p. 39 citing 'Satellite Hack Raises Security Questions' *CNET* (2 January 2002) (available at https://www.cnet.com/tech/mobile/satellite-hack-raises-security-questions/).

190 Cyberlaw, *Viasat KA-SAT attack* (29 May 2022) (available at https://cyberlaw.ccdcoe.org/wiki/Viasat_KA-SAT_attack_(2022)).

191 United States of America, 51 U.S. Code § 50902 (available at https://www.law.cornell.edu/uscode/text/51/50902).

192 The concept of space resource appropriation presents an open question of space law. It must be clarified that there is a separate question of appropriation of orbital positions or surface area of celestial bodies that is not contested and is considered prohibited (to States as well as NSA and/or natural persons), and a separate question of appropriation of natural space resources, which remains contested. Concerning appropriation of orbital positions or surface area of celestial bodies: Pursuant to Articles I and II of the Outer Space Treaty (*Treaty on Principles Governing the Activities of States in the Exploration and Use of Outer Space, Including the Moon and Other Celestial Bodies*, 27 January 1967, 610 UNTS 205 (entered into force on 10 October 1967)), outer space is the province of all mankind not subject to national appropriation. This means States cannot assert sovereignty or property rights over outer space, including celestial bodies, see Lachs, (2010), pp. 41–44. However, the explicit reference to only 'national' appropriation and the subsequent silence on private appropriation gave rise to arguments that individuals and NSAs are permitted to appropriate portions of outer space, see example of USA citizen Dennis Hope (Lunar Embassy). Since then, two domestic Court cases have refuted this, see *Nemitz v US*, 2004 WL 316704, D. Nevada, 2004 (26. 4. 2004); *Nemitz v N.A.S.A*, 126 Fed Appx. 343, 9th Cir. Nev. (10 February 2004). *Lunar Embassy to China v. Beijing Administration of Industry and Commerce*, Haidian District People's Court, November 2005. Another, more doctrinal view,

agrees with these decisions of domestic court on the basis that, since private property cannot exist in absence of a State to guarantee it and a State cannot guarantee more rights that it itself has (*Nemo plus iuris transferre potest quam ipse habet*), Article II of the Outer Space Treaty encompasses private appropriation within the prohibition on national appropriation (see Hobe (2019), p. 165; Lyall and Larsen (2009), pp. 184–185; Fabio Tronchetti (2013) 'The Legal Framework Regulating International Outer Space Activities' in *Fundamentals of Space Law and Policy* (SpringerBriefs in Space Development, 2013), pp. 13–14; Frans von der Dunk, 'Property Rights Over the Moon or On the Moon? The Legality of Space Resource Exploitation on Celestial Bodies' (2023) 6 *Journal of Law & Innovation*, p. 100, which is confirmed by Outer Space Treaty drafting history (see Steven Freeland, Ram Jakhu, 'Article II' (2009) in: *The Cologne Commentary on Space Law: Vol. 1* (Stephan Hobe, Bernhard Schmidt-Tedd, Kai-Uwe Schrogl, Gérardine Meishan Goh (Eds.)) (Cologne: Carl Heymanns), 2009, pp. 51–53)). Consequently, the Manual on International Law Applicable to Military Uses of Outer Space (MILAMOS) clarified that a prohibition on private appropriation is encompassed under the prohibition on national appropriation. Despite this discussion, the potential legal void remains and can therefore be seen as another shortcoming of a State-centric system. Accordingly, States may still be incentivised to use (or acquiesce in) NSAs appropriation of facets of outer space thereby achieving what international law prohibits them to do, but it is unlikely as the two mentioned cases and the stark response to the Bogota Declaration have shown (and as furthermore this type of action would give NSAs more power than States and leave States vulnerable to NSA influence, for example see the two mentioned Nemitz cases). Concerning appropriation of space (natural) resources, the situation is, however, entirely different. Whereas ownership over celestial bodies *per se* is prohibited, that does not seem to preclude ownership of materials extracted from outer space (such as minerals), whether by States or NSAs, see John G. Wrench, 'Non-Appropriation, No Problem: The Outer Space Treaty Is Ready for Asteroid Mining' (2019) 51 *Case Western Reserve Journal of International Law*, p. 447; Vasilka Sancin, Katja Grünfeld and Iva Ramuš Cvetkovič, 'Contemporary Challenges of International Law-Making for Outer Space' (2021) 76 *Pravnik* 138, pp. 45–84. Here, States may be incentivised to use NSAs to extract and exploit space resources, such as minerals. The Outer Space Treaty does not explicitly address space resources. The Moon Agreement in Article 11 attempts to preclude any entity, State, NSA or natural person, from taking ownership of material extracted from the Moon or its subsurface until an international regime is in place governing the mining and exploitation of natural resources, see United Nations General Assembly, Agreement Governing the Activities of States on the Moon and Other Celestial Bodies, UN Doc. A/RES/34/68 (Dec. 5, 1979); Agreement Governing the Activities of States on the Moon and Other Celestial Bodies (Dec. 5, 1979) [hereinafter Moon Agreement], 1363 UNTS 3, Article 11. However, this treaty has not received support from any major space-faring nation, which heavily impacts its relevance in practice, see Andrew Tingkang, 'These Aren't the Asteroids You Are Looking For: Classifying Asteroids in Space as Chattels, Not Land' (2012) 35 *Seattle University Law Review*, p. 572; Tronchetti (2013), pp. 13–14. The non-legally binding Artemis Accords made a further attempt to clarify the question and give green light to space resource mining, but as of yet, the legal situation regarding space resource appropriation remains unregulated, see The Artemis Accords (2020); Hobe (2019), pp. 162–165. The USA Commercial Space Act has therefore been, by some, criticized as a 'sleight of hand', aimed at circumventing the current prohibition on States exercising property rights over space resources, see de Zwart (2016), p. 5 citing Arindrajit Basu and Arthad Kurlekar, 'Highway to the Danger Zone: United States Legislative Framework Regulating the Commercial Space Sector' (2016) 14(1) *Astropolitics*, p. 60; Cirkovic (2022), pp. 6–8. The same critiques could be levied against the other national acts attempting to ultimately permit space resource activities in line with the USA Commercial Space Act, as the question of the legality of space resource activities remains unclear on an international level and is currently being reviewed by the UNCOPUOS Working Group on the Legal Aspects of Space Resource Activities.

resources.[193] Similar national acts have been adopted by Luxembourg, the United Arab Emirates, and Japan.[194] Internationally, around 40 States are currently Signatories to the Artemis Accords, which form a legally non-binding, instrument that was designed to guide partner States in the execution of the Artemis mission, aiming to return humans to the moon and stay there, including enabling commercial and scientific activities on the surface of the Moon.[195]

The reference in the Artemis Accords to enabling commercial activities, complements domestic legislation in several States which authorizes the extraction and utilization of space resources for commercial purposes.[196] Specifically, Section 10(2) of the Artemis Accords provides that 'the extraction of space resources does not inherently constitute national appropriation under Article II of the Outer Space Treaty'. Although this provision is vague, it may be intended as a basis to argue that NSAs extracting space resources for commercial purposes would not violate the Outer Space Treaty's prohibition of national appropriation.[197] If so, this could potentially open the path to space mining and the commercial exploitation of space resources. However, an extreme interpretation of Section 10(2) of the Artemis Accords that would allow for exploitation of space resources without any limitation, on a first come first serve basis, would conflict with Article II of the Outer Space Treaty.[198] For example, by commencing mining operations without an agreement in place governing cooperation and access to mining areas, actors could

---

193 de Zwart (2016), pp. 3–5, referring to the US *Spurring Private Aerospace Competitiveness and Entrepreneurship Act* of 2015, Pub L No 114–90, 129 Stat 704 (2015) ('*US Commercial Space Launch Competitiveness Act*').

194 See Chapter 5 below.

195 Laura Delgado López, 'What Are the Implications of Peru Joining the Artemis Accords?', (6 June 2024), Center for Strategic and International Studies (available at https://www.csis.org/analysis/what-are-implications-peru-joining-artemis-accords); Stacey Henderson, 'To the Moon and Beyond: Australia's Space Activities and Obligations Under International Law', *Australian Institute of International Affairs: Australian Outlook*, (3 April 2023); Rami Mandow, 'NASA and Australia Continue Strategic Partnership with Artemis' (21 March 2023) (available at https://spaceaustralia.com/news/nasa-and-australia-continue-strategic-partnership-artemis).

196 See Laura Yvonne Zielinski, 'Disputes over space mining on the horizon?', *International Bar Association* (18 January 2023) (available at https://www.ibanet.org/disputes-over-space-mining-on-the-horizon); Rossana Deplano, 'The Artemis Accords: Evolution or Revolution in International Space Law?', (2021) 70 *International and Comparative Law Quarterly*.

197 See Macchi (2025), pp. 65–66.

198 See Chapter 2 1, 1.1. See also Macchi (2025), pp. 65–66.

de facto appropriate certain areas on the surface of the moon or other celestial bodies.[199] This would also contradict the thrust of the Moon Agreement, which provides inter alia for

> An equitable sharing by all States Parties in the benefits derived from [natural resources of the Moon], whereby the interests and needs of the developing countries, as well as the efforts of those countries which have contributed either directly or indirectly to the exploration of the Moon, shall be given special consideration.

However, States are already engaged in bringing back samples from celestial bodies, and the United States contracted private companies to collect lunar regolith as a means of obtaining samples.[200] This initiative was reportedly also designed to create subsequent practice whereby the Outer Space Treaty is interpreted as permitting space mining.[201] A shift to greater exploitation of the minerals on the Moon and other celestial bodies could trigger a race for space resource mining.[202] This would almost certainly pollute or at least endanger the pristine environment of celestial bodies and also risk producing space debris that would make future comparable activities far more difficult or impossible to conduct for others.[203]

Risks of collisions and space pollution are exacerbated by the free rider phenomenon, which refers to those who 'benefit by the actions of others without sharing any of the responsibility or cost'.[204] Because the costs of ensuring

199 Article I of the Outer Space Treaty permits free exploration and use while simultaneously mandating that free access to all areas of celestial bodies be guaranteed, but does not specify parameters for either, which could result in a conflict of the two mandates, see Sancin, Grünfeld, Ramuš Cvetkovič (2021), pp. 22–25.

200 Byers and Boley (2023), pp. 130–132.

201 Byers and Boley (2023), pp. 131–132.

202 Space mining of asteroids alone has been estimated to have a value of 6 trillion USD; Freeland and Ireland-Piper (2022), p. 29. See also Bloomberg News, 'China, US are racing to make billions from mining the moon's minerals' *Mining.com* (17 May 2022) (available at https://www.mining.com/web/china-us-are-racing-to-make-billions-from-mining-the-moons-minerals/); Orbital Today, 'The Lunar 'Gold Rush' Is On: How Could Mining Moon Minerals Change Life On Earth?' *Orbital Today* (9 October 2023) (available at https://orbitaltoday.com/2023/10/09/the-lunar-gold-rush-is-on-how-could-mining-moon-minerals-change-life-on-earth/).

203 Cirkovic (2022), pp. 6–8.

204 Lawrence E. Susskind, *Environmental Diplomacy: negotiating more effective global agreements* (Oxford University Press, 1994), p. 23; Viikari (2008), p. 5.

environmental protection during space missions are relatively high, and the benefits of space exploration and exploitation are obtained by space-faring actors irrespective of their specific conduct, opportunist entities can profit disproportionately while eschewing the full extent of the costs required to ensure safe and sustainable space activities.[205]

A second phenomenon known as the tragedy of the commons compounds these risks.[206] Despoliation of the space environment will often not affect the immediate mission which causes it, thereby removing an immediate incentive to take environmental precautions.[207] Over time, the collective impact on the space environment escalates, eventually spoiling this common area for other potential space explorers. The free rider and 'tragedy of the commons' phenomenon are particularly aggravated in the context of NSAs, as they are typically profit-maximizing entities, and may only exist for short periods of time before being wound up, thereby reducing the incentive for incorporating the costs of longer-term space preservation into their operating budgets.

While this manuscript focuses on pollution to the space environment, it should be noted that NSA conduct also heightens the risk of environmental harm on Earth.[208] Space-originating terrestrial harm may occur directly, as in the case of Kosmos-0954, a defunct Soviet satellite which crash-landed over northern Canada, causing radioactive pollution of the territory.[209] Alternatively, it may arise indirectly, as for example the long-term negative impacts of damaging the ozone layer by rocket engine emissions.[210] Risks of damage are elevated in a small number of countries around the equator, because space objects often re-enter the atmosphere in that area.[211] The indirect effects include the

205 See Chapter 3, Section 2.

206 Viikari (2015), pp. 217–220.

207 Viikari (2008), pp. 5–6.

208 Jasper Schellekens, 'The Legality of Anti-satellite ASAT Weapons', University of Leiden, (2008), p. 32 (noting the 'COSMOS 954 incident, where a Soviet satellite disintegrated over Northern Canada, demonstrates that should the debris of certain satellites return to Earth it could have drastic environmental consequences.135 As a result of the satellite disintegrating debris was scattered over 600 kilometres of Canadian territory and most of the debris was found to be radioactive.').

209 See Chapter 3, Section 1.

210 Settlement of Claim between Canada and the Union of Soviet Socialist Republics for Damage Caused by 'Cosmos 954' (Released on April 2, 1981) (available at https://www.jaxa.jp/library/space_law/chapter_3/3-2-2-1_e.html); Pietkiewicz (2019), pp. 217–218; Kazlouskaya (2021), pp. 573–574.

211 Radi (2023), p. 10; Michael Byers, Ewan Wright, Aaron Boley and Cameron Byers, 'Unnecessary Risks Created by Uncontrolled Rocket Reentries' (2022) 6 *Nature Astronomy*, pp. 1093–1097.

resources consumed in producing rockets and utilizing them. Jeff Bezos' few-minutes-long trip to outer space on Blue Origin's rocket allegedly produced gas emissions greater than an average person's lifetime carbon footprint.[212]

These varied threats of serious environmental harm in the terrestrial and extra-terrestrial zones highlight the need to determine the legal avenues to hold NSAs accountable for space pollution. However, before doing so, it is necessary to review the genesis of space law and the extent to which it was formed on the presumption of the State as the exclusive type of space actor.

4 Space Law Has Been Designed State-Centrically

Whereas there is an increasing presence of NSAs in space, the core legal framework of space law was designed with States in mind. In the era when space law was formed, States were essentially the only entities conducting space exploration.[213] Indeed, in the early years following the Soviet Union's launch of Sputnik 1 in 1957, it was only the United States and the Soviet Union which were active in space.[214] Hobe terms this period the first period of space law-making, marked by the evolution and adoption of space law treaties in the United Nations.[215] Goldman describes it as the 'classical period' of the development of space law from 1957 to 1979, during which the prevailing ethic was 'pro-state, anti-free enterprise'.[216] The major legal architecture of international space law was put in place with the passing of the Outer Space Treaty of 1967

212 Isaac Schultz, 'Jeff Bezos' Space Joyride Emitted a Lifetime's Worth of Carbon Pollution' *GIZMODO* (10 December 2021) (available at https://gizmodo.com/jeff-bezos-space-joyride-emitted-a-lifetime-s-worth-of-1848196182); Angelo Fichera, 'Posts misinterpret space travel carbon emissions finding' *AP NEWS* (14 December 2021) (available at https://apnews.com/article/fact-checking-558398031858).

213 Viikari (2008), p. 21 ('For decades, only states – and very few of them – were capable of carrying out activities in outer space.'); Kütting (2000), p. 3.

214 Stephan Hobe, 'The Impact of New Developments on International Space Law (New Actors, Commercialisation, Privatisation, Increase in the Number of Space-Faring Nations),' (2010) 15(3) and (4) *Uniform Law Review*, p. 869 ('[a]t the beginning of the space age there were only two space powers: the United States of America and what was then the Soviet Union.'); Freeland and Ireland-Piper (2022), p. 25; Bartosz Ziemblicki and Yevgeniya Oralova, 'Private Entities in Outer Space Activities: Liability Regime Reconsidered' (2021) 56 *Space Policy*, p. 1.

215 Hobe (2019).

216 Nathan C. Goldman, 'Space Law. Space Politics and Policy: an evolutionary perspective', in Eligar Sadeh (ed.) *Space Regulations Library*, Vol. 2 (Kluwer Academic Publishers, 2002), pp. 163–180.

among other instruments. Although private companies were involved in a collateral manner, such as for manufacturing hardware, this was typically only on the American side in the initial years of space activity.[217]

Following that classical period, space law entered a second phase, the so-called 'transitional period', during the 1980s, in which the number of States involved in space activities grew significantly and the commercial applications of space activities became increasingly evident.[218] States enacted domestic legislation addressing space activities, as discussed in Chapter 5, and formed contracts with private entities to undertake those activities. The negotiation of new international treaties was hampered due to the entry of new States with a broader range of sometimes differing interests and, in lieu of treaty additions or amendments, UNCOPUOS focused on producing soft law instruments such as guiding norms on specific space applications such as nuclear-power sources in outer space or direct broadcasting.[219]

After that 'transitional period', and with the end of the Cold War signalled by the fall of the Berlin Wall, space law entered into its third and ongoing phase or 'modern period'.[220] In this period, space commerce has rapidly expanded and NSAs have become significant actors in space.[221] States have continued to hold military interests up as key contributors to their positions on the legal frontier, and there have been no major new treaty-based developments in international space law.[222] Despite the growing role of NSAs, no new treaty or protocol has been adopted concerning their conduct in space.[223] Instead this period has featured the adoption of further soft-law documents, such as UNGA Resolutions concerning existing space law treaty terms (such as the launching State), increasing registration practice, expanding national space legislation, and addressing topics like space debris mitigation and the long-term sustainability of outer space activities.

The modern period has coincided with a growing awareness of the importance of the protection of the environment, including that of outer space. The risks of contamination of the outer space environment have become acute and public consciousness is increasing in this respect. Guidelines have been issued

217 Hobe (2010), p. 870.

218 Goldman (2002), pp. 163–180; Ferreira-Snyman (2023), p. 2.

219 Goldman (2002), pp. 163–180.

220 Goldman (2002), pp. 170–185.

221 Ziemblicki and Oralova (2021), p. 1.

222 Dempsey and Manoli (2017), p. 37.

223 See Chapter 6, Section 3 for a discussion of possible reforms to space law treaties to address NSAs.

seeking to mitigate space debris, such as those by the Inter-Agency Space Debris Coordination Committee (IADC),[224] and UNCOPUOS.[225] Furthermore, the International Law Association (ILA) has produced a Model Law on National Space Legislation which has inter alia recommended the adoption of provisions on space debris mitigation and environmental protection of space environment in national legislation.[226] However, these instruments are voluntary in nature and often[227] lack enforcement procedures.[228] Because of this, international space law *per se* remains minimalist in relation to specific protections of the environment.[229]

Since the classic period, the range of States involved in space activities has changed dramatically. By August 2023, there were over 70 States and international organizations which had provided the United Nations with notification of objects launched into outer space, in accordance with the Registration Convention and/or General Assembly Resolution 1721 B (XVI).[230] However, NSAs (other than international organizations, which are not considered NSAs for present purposes), are conspicuously absent from the register of notifications. Other than States, only two other entities have registered space objects – specifically the European Space Agency (ESA) and the European Organization for the Exploitation of Meteorological Satellites (EUMETSAT).[231] In this way, there is a mismatch between the international legal recognition of a growing range of States' space activities and the unrecognized conduct of a growing number of NSAs operating in space.

224 Larsen (2018), p. 479.

225 Viikari (2008), p. 57 (also noting that 'A subcommittee of the International Organization for Standardization (ISO) has started working on standards based on space debris mitigation guidelines developed by the IADC' and 'the Committee on Space Research (COSPAR) has long been working on issues related to planetary protection7 and has also discussed other environmental aspects of space activities to some extent.').

226 See Chapter 5 below.

227 Exceptions occur where these international instruments are adopted into national space legislation and thereby made binding law upon NSAs acting from those jurisdiction, as set out in Chapter 5 below.

228 Larsen (2018), p. 492.

229 Viikari (2008), p. 57.

230 See United Nations Office for Outer Space Affairs, 'United Nations Register of Objects Launched into Outer Space' (United Nations Register of Objects Launched into Outer Space (unoosa.org)). See further below at Chapter 3 for a description of the register process.

231 See United Nations Office for Outer Space Affairs, 'United Nations Register of Objects Launched into Outer Space' (United Nations Register of Objects Launched into Outer Space (unoosa.org)).

4.1 *Conventional Instruments*

Despite their antagonistic relationship, the United States and the Soviet Union used the auspices of the United Nations to entrench a legal framework in the early years of their space activities. They reached an agreement that the legal form of this approach would be public international law.[232] Accordingly, the UN General Assembly recognised in 1961 that '[i]nternational law, including the Charter of the United Nations, applies to outer space and celestial bodies' and that '[o]uter space and celestial bodies are free for exploration and use by all States in conformity with international law and are not subject to national appropriation'.[233] The reference to exploration and use by 'States' in this seminal UNGA Resolution 1721 demonstrates a presumption (and favoured position on the part of the Soviet Union) that States would be the entities conducting space activities. It is consistent with the traditional view of international law as 'a system of rules created by states for states'.[234]

The State-centric approach was enshrined in the five major conventions that make up space law, which were negotiated in UNCOPUOS, and were then adopted as UN General Assembly resolutions.[235] Other pertinent agreements include the 1963 Treaty Banning Nuclear Tests in the Atmosphere, in Outer Space and Under Water (known as the Partial Test Ban Treaty or Moscow Test Ban Treaty),[236] which prohibits nuclear tests in outer space.

Where NSAs are referred to in these treaties, it is to explicitly confirm State control over them.[237] For example, Article VI of the Outer Space Treaty ensures that States Parties bear responsibility for national activities in outer space, 'whether such activities are carried on by governmental agencies or by non-governmental entities.' It specifically provides that all activities of NSAs 'shall require authorization and continuing supervision by the appropriate State Party'.[238] In the same vein, Article VIII provides that the State that registers a launched object in its national registry retains jurisdiction and control over it and any personnel thereof.[239] That rigid system of funneling all NSA space

---

232 Hobe (2010), p. 874.

233 General Assembly resolution 1721 (XVI) of 20 December 1961.

234 See Viikari (2008), p. 21.

235 Hobe (2010), p. 875 citing United Nations Office for Outer Space Affairs, *United Nations Treaties and Principles on Outer Space and related General Assembly Resolutions*, (United Nations publication, October 2009), pp. 3–35.

236 Cheng (1997), p. 218.

237 See also Macchi (2025), pp. 60–61.

238 See Chapter 3, Section 1.

239 Gabriel Lafferanderei, 'Jurisdiction and control of Space objects and the Case of an International Intergovernmental Organization (ESA)' (2005) 54(2) *Zeitschrift für Luft- und Weltraumrecht*, p. 231.

conduct through the sieve of State control reflects the mentality of the Cold War era, when clashes in space were seen as realistic prospects by the US-led Western block and the Soviet-led Eastern block.[240] Indeed, fear of space being used as a launching pad for military strikes was a strong motivation for both sides of the conflict to agree to the 1967 Outer Space Treaty, which recognizes the common interest of humanity in the peaceful exploration and use of outer space and prohibits the placement of weapons of mass destruction in orbit or on celestial bodies as well as the use of celestial bodies for anything other than peaceful purposes.[241]

In the years preceding the agreement of the Outer Space Treaty, efforts had been made to restrain the use of outer space for military purposes. The United Nations had set up a committee (UNCOPUOS) in 1959 to examine the peaceful uses of outer space and set a legal framework in place.[242] US President Eisenhower had proclaimed his country's outer space policy, which included that 'nations of the world shall not engage in warlike activities on [celestial] bodies' and that 'no nation will put into orbit or station in outer space weapons of mass destruction.'[243] However, in 1966, just a year before the enactment of the Outer Space Treaty, the Chairman of the Legal Sub-Committee of UNCOPUOS, lamented that in the preceding years 'little progress had been made towards ensuring that outer space was used for man's advancement and not for his destruction.'[244] At the time, the race to explore and potentially exploit outer space was in full swing. The first man-made satellite had orbited the Earth in 1957. Then after a series of orbits of the moon, the first-ever 'soft' (unmanned) landing on the moon was conducted in 1966 and it was clear that 'no further technological barrier stood between man and the moon.'[245] Aware of the dangerous direction this could take, the superpowers agreed to the peaceful use of outer space as a central premise underlying the 1967 Outer Space Treaty.[246]

---

240 Hobe (2010), p. 870.

241 Outer Space Treaty, Preamble and Article IV.

242 See United Nations Office for Outer Space Affairs, 'Committee on the Peaceful Uses of Outer Space and its Subcommittees', (available at https://www.unoosa.org/oosa/en/ourwork/copuos/comm-subcomms.html#:~:text=The%20Committee%20on%20the%20Peaceful,membership%20has%20continued%20to%20expand).

243 A/PV.868 (22.9.1960), p. 48 cited in Cheng (1997), p. 217.

244 A/AC.105/C.2/SR.57, pp. 2–3 cited in Cheng (1997), p. 215.

245 Cheng (1997), p. 215.

246 See Kai Uwe Schrogl and Julia Neumann, 'Article IV' (2009) in *The Cologne Commentary on Space Law*: Vol. I (Stephan Hobe, Bernhard Schmidt-Tedd, Kai-Uwe Schrogl, Gérardine Meishan Goh (eds.)) (Carl Heymanns, 2009).

Beyond military purposes, States were concerned about other States claiming ownership of celestial bodies.[247] General Assembly Resolution 1721 (XVI) of 1961 had provided that outer space and celestial bodies should be free from national appropriation. This reflected a growing concern that conflict over territory and resources would stretch to outer space.[248] In a similar vein, Article I of the Outer Space Treaty contains references to the exploration and use of space constituting the 'province of all mankind'. However, operationally its focus is on States as the recipients of powers and obligations when conducting activities in space.[249] In this respect, Article II provides that outer space, including the Moon and other celestial bodies, is not subject to 'national appropriation by claim of sovereignty, by means of use or occupation, or by any other means.' However, the reference to 'national' appropriation begs the question of whether NSAs are covered. The lack of explicit reference to NSAs could potentially open the possibility of space and the Moon and other celestial bodies being considered property, even though no specific country can take ownership thereof, however, this remains unlikely given the current examples of State practice.[250] As explained, practice and doctrine confirm that legal appropriation of orbital positions or of surface area on celestial bodies by States or NSAs alike should not be put in question (which is reinforced because Article VI of the Outer Space Treaty, due to the State-oriented nature of the treaty, requires that States guarantee compliance of non-governmental actors with the provisions of the Outer Space Treaty, meaning that they also guarantee the prohibition on national appropriation from Article II); however, the question of appropriation of space (natural) resources is another matter as some claim that the appropriation of space resources by any type of actor is an open issue in space law.[251,252,253]

In relation to the role of NSAs, the Soviet Union's view was thoroughly State-centric and anti-private enterprise during the negotiating of the Outer Space Treaty, to the extent that it sought to explicitly prohibit NSAs from exploring or using outer space at all. It proposed the inclusion of wording that 'all activities of any kind pertaining to the exploration and use of outer space shall be

247 Bing Cheng (1997), pp. 219–220.

248 Freeland and Jakhu (2009), pp. 51–53.

249 See Viikari (2008), p. 22 ('the language of the space treaties promises much more for the humankind as a whole than what space utilization actually provides it with.').

250 See further Chapter 3, Section 2 below.

251 see footnote 192 on page 32.

252 Hobe (2019), p. 165. For more information on space resource activities, see Tronchetti. (2013); Lee (2012).

253 Magdalena Petrova, 'The first crop of space mining companies didn't work out, but a new generation is trying again' *CNBC* (9 October 2022) (available at https://www.cnbc.com/2022/10/09/space-mining-business-still-highly-speculative.html).

carried out solely and exclusively by States.'[254] Although the United States was more flexible than the Soviet Union, as it was in theory open to NSA activity in space, the United States nonetheless agreed to condition any such activity on a comprehensive web of State responsibility for those NSA activities.[255] The negotiating history of the Outer Space Treaty demonstrates this State-centric conception.[256]

Aside from States, international organizations, such as the International Telecommunication Union (ITU), have been involved in space activities for decades.[257] While the issue of international organizations exploring space was contemplated during the classical period of the development of space law,[258] that was relatively embryonic. The Soviet Union was reluctant to include reference to international organizations in the Outer Space Treaty, in line with its position that international organizations should not be considered subjects of international law.[259] Nonetheless, Article VI of the Outer Space Treaty ultimately provides that where space activities are conducted by an international organization, 'responsibility for compliance with this Treaty shall be borne both by the international organization and by the States Parties to the Treaty participating in such organization'. However, in including reference to international organizations, it was nonetheless made clear this 'did not mean that international organizations were being placed, from a legal point of view, on the same footing as States Parties to the Treaty' and instead, it was designed to ensure that no State could evade its responsibilities simply by acting as a member of an international organization.[260] Moreover, it would only cover inter-State organizations, namely, entities 'a) established by a treaty or other instruments governed by international law, and b) capable of generating through its organs an autonomous will distinct from the will of c) its members.'[261] It did not cover the types of NSAs which are focused on in this monograph, such as profit-seeking and politically motivated NSAs.[262]

254 See UN Doc. A/AC.105/C.2/L.1, Proposal of the Union of Socialist Soviet Republics: Declaration of the Basic Principles governing the Activities of States pertaining to the Exploration and Use of Outer Space, 1962, para. 7. See also Stubbe (2018), p. 81.

255 Stubbe (2018), p. 82.

256 Cheng (1997), p. 221.

257 Viikari (2008), p. 25. See also Hobe (2010), p. 870 ('The International Telecommunication Satellite Organization INTELSAT was composed of a group of governmental telecommunications services around the world. It was a public enterprise and provided services both for high technology and developing countries.').

258 Cheng (1997), p. 223.

259 Cheng (1997), p. 240.

260 UN Doc. A/AC.105/C.2/SR.58 (13.7.66), p. 8 cited in Cheng (1997), p. 240.

261 Schmalenbach, K., 'International Organizations or Institutions, General Aspects' (Status: 2014), in Wolfrum, R. (ed.), *The Max Planck Encyclopedia of Public International Law: Online Edition*, (Oxford University Press) (available at <opil.ouplaw.com/home/EPIL>); Stubbe (2018), p. 289.

262 See Chapter 4, Section 1.

This State-centric approach is unsurprising considering the broader context of international law. Even following the end of the Cold War, the primary conception of international law, including environmental obligations, has revolved around the State.[263] Von der Dunk argues that this State centricity is reflected in the use of the expression 'international responsibility' in Article VI of the Outer Space Treaty, which he suggests is an expansion of 'State responsibility' to encompass also activities by NSAs and international organizations.[264] The upshot is a set of core space law treaties which are formulated in terms envisaging the State as the primary actor and bearer of obligations in space exploration. However, an exclusively State-centric approach to international law is not inevitable. For example, core instruments of international aviation law are effectively agreements between national and private airline carriers.[265] Havel and Gabriel Sanchez see these aviation instruments are 'as remarkable examples of a private trade group having a discernible impact on the development of international law'.[266] Whether similar accommodations for space active NSAs constitutes a critical question underlying the current analysis.

4.2 *Soft Law Instruments*

After the initial batch of international law treaties agreed relatively quickly in the 1960s and 1970s, there was a shift towards using non-binding UNGA resolutions to develop standards for space activities.[267] Soft law instruments have considerable potential as a means to address emerging issues of concern to the international community, as they are flexible and can be adopted quickly with immediate effect.[268] Although not legally binding,[269] they can influence the interpretation of terms of treaties and other primary sources of international law.[270] They can also contribute to determining customary international law. The International Court of Justice (ICJ) has explained that UNGA resolutions

263 Viikari (2008), p. 21.

264 Von der Dunk (2015a), p. 46.

265 Havel and Gabriel Sanchez (2014), pp. 271–272.

266 Havel and Gabriel Sanchez (2014), p. 272.

267 Hobe (2010), p. 876.

268 Kenneth Abbott and Duncan Snidal, 'Hard and Soft Law in International Governance' (2000), 54(3) *Legalization and World Politics*, pp. 421–456.

269 Viikari (2008), pp. 56–57.

270 See Sumudu Atapattu, 'International environmental law and soft law: a new direction or a contradiction?', in Cecilia Bailliet (ed.) *Non-state actors, soft law and protective regimes: from the margins*, (Cambridge University Press, 2012).

can be a source from which to 'deduce' the *opinio juris* of States regarding the rules set out in the substance of those resolutions.[271]

Atapattu notes that soft law instruments have a variety of functions at the international level, including to codify existing customary international law; serve as a catalyst or chrysalis for a trend to develop into a norm; highlight new problems; suggest means of addressing gaps in existing conventions; provide interpretative guidance for treaties; generate fresh State practice; and influence the contours of domestic law.[272] Nonetheless, because they are not strictly legally binding, their role is to impact on State conduct and the interpretations of legally binding law rather than constituting the applicable law *per se*.

In the area of international space law, soft law instruments have served an important function,[273] but have largely been State-centric. For example, the 1963 Declaration of Legal Principles Governing the Activities of States in the Exploration and Use of Outer Space exhibits a State-centric orientation, stating in paragraph 2 that 'Outer space and celestial bodies are free for exploration and use by all States on a basis of equality and in accordance with international law'. This State-centric vantage point is also evident in paragraph 5 which provides that

> States bear international responsibility for national activities in outer space, whether carried on by governmental agencies or by non-governmental entities, and for assuring that national activities are carried on in conformity with the principles set forth in the present Declaration [...] The activities of non-governmental entities in outer space shall require authorization and continuing supervision by the State concerned. When activities are carried on in outer space by an international organization, responsibility for compliance with the principles set forth in this Declaration shall be borne by the international organization and by the States participating in it.

---

271 ICJ, Nicaragua, paras. 188, 191 (concerning Resolution 2625 (XXV), '[a]s already observed, the adoption by States of this text affords an indication of their opinio juris as to customary international law on the question'); ICJ, Legality of the Use or Threat of Nuclear Weapons, para. 70; Marko Öberg, 'The Legal Effects of Resolutions of the UN Security Council and General Assembly in the Jurisprudence of the ICJ', (2005) 16(5) *European Journal of International Law*, p. 897.

272 Atapattu (2012), p. 207.

273 See Marboe, I. (ed.), *Soft Law in Outer Space: The Function of Non-Binding Norms in International Space Law* (Böhlau, Wien, 2012), pp. 119–144.

Importantly, for accountability, paragraph 5 of the 1963 Declaration provides that 'each State launching or procuring a launch will be internationally liable for damage to a foreign State or to its natural or juridical persons by the launched object or its component parts on the earth, in air space, or in outer space.'

Similarly, UNGA Resolution 37/92, named the Principles Governing the Use by States of Artificial Earth Satellites for International Direct Television Broadcasting, which was adopted in 1982, stipulates that a State intending to establish such broadcasting services should notify receiving States and should only establish such services in agreements with those States. In addition to the fact that the title of this resolution explicitly signals its State-centric focus, its paragraphs adhere to the traditional approach of funneling the application of international law through State-level apparatuses.[274] Aside from States, UNGA Resolution 37/92 does refer to international organizations, but makes it clear that they are subjects of it because they are constituted by States.

Some antecedents of the recognition of NSA interests appear in the details of the text of Resolution 37/92. For example, paragraph 3, titled 'Purposes and Objectives', provides that activities under its purview should be carried out consistently with 'the development of mutual understanding and the strengthening of friendly relations and cooperation among all States *and peoples* in the interest of maintaining international peace and security'.[275] Those references could accommodate groups other than majority state populations, such as indigenous groups and other ethnic collectivities. Moreover, there are also references to commercial NSAs. For instance, paragraph 11, on copyright and neighbouring rights, requires that States should cooperate on a 'bilateral and multilateral basis' to ensure the protection of copyright and neighbouring rights by means of appropriate agreements between the 'interested States or the competent legal entities acting under their jurisdiction.' However, that reference to legal entities is conditioned on them falling within the relevant State's jurisdiction, again indicating a State-funneling approach to the regulation of these types of broadcasts.

The preeminence of State interests is reiterated in UNGA Resolution 41/65 of 1986, which is titled 'Principles Relating to Remote Sensing of the Earth from Outer Space'. It features a similar largely State-centric framing, while also referring to 'peoples'.[276] Consistent with the approach of emphasizing State

274 See, e.g. paragraphs 5 and 8.

275 Emphasis added. See also paragraph 5.

276 Principle IV provides that such activities shall be conducted with 'respect for the principle of full and permanent sovereignty of all States and peoples over their own wealth and

interests, Principles V to VII refer to States participating in remote sensing activities without addressing NSA involvement in such operations.

Moving into the 1990s, another soft law instrument is UNGA 47/68 of 14 December 1992, which annexes the United Nations Principles Relevant to the Use of Nuclear Power Sources in Outer Space.[277] In Principle 8, it adheres to the traditional State-centric approach, as set out in the Outer Space Treaty, funneling responsibility through the State exercising jurisdiction and control in the circumstances, stating:

> In accordance with article VI of the Treaty on Principles Governing the Activities of States in the Exploration and Use of Outer Space, including the Moon and Other Celestial Bodies, States shall bear international responsibility for national activities involving the use of nuclear power sources in outer space, whether such activities are carried on by governmental agencies or by non-governmental entities, and for assuring that such national activities are carried out in conformity with that Treaty and the recommendations contained in these Principles.

Similar to the incongruency between Articles VI and VII of the Outer Space Treaty, there is a difference in the terms of this Resolution, as Principle 9 on liability refers to 'each State which launches or procures the launching of a space object and each State from whose territory or facility a space object is launched shall be internationally liable for damage caused by such space objects or their component parts.' It is unclear if the italicized phrase is exactly equivalent with the reference to 'national activities' in Principle 8. For example, if an NSA directed by nationals of a State launched a space object from global commons without that State being involved in the launch, the State would not *per se* have launched or procured[278] the launch or provided the launching facility, and so it would not be liable under Principle 9. That would

---

natural resources, with due regard to the rights and interests, in accordance with international law, of other States and entities under their jurisdiction.'

277 United Nations General Assembly, Principles Relevant to the Use of Nuclear Power Sources in Outer Space, UN Doc. A/RES/47/68 (14 December 1992).

278 It is currently unclear what actions would amount to procuring a launch, whether it requires financial action or whether authorisation of space activity would suffice. However, considering the possibility of nefarious action by NSAs, it cannot be discounted that an NSA with the requisite technological capability would attempt a launch without authorisation. Whether at this point the nationality of the NSA would suffice to draw in the liability of a State remains speculative, see Gerhard (2009), pp. 103–125; Kerrest, Smith (2009), pp. 126–146; Kerrest, Smith (2013), pp. 104–116.

result in a liability gap. The likelihood of such launches may be slight, but the consequences could be severe, as it is precisely this type of NSA which may circumvent safety precautions in conducting a launch, raising the risks of a serious incident in space. Cheng observes in the context of the Outer Space Treaty that 'national activities':

> may mean, therefore, in addition to activities of the State, activities of all persons within its territorial, quasi-territorial and personal jurisdiction. But, inasmuch as the system of "authorization and continuing supervision" envisaged by Article VI can be effectively administered only by the State exercising territorial and quasi- territorial jurisdiction, rather than by the State exercising merely personal jurisdiction, it would appear that Article VI is not intended to include within the notion of "national activities" those conducted by the nationals of a State when they are not within either its territorial or quasi-territorial jurisdiction.[279]

Moreover, the principles in Resolution 47/68 do not resolve in any comprehensive manner the issue of the accountability of the launching State for harms produced by an incident involving a nuclear power source.[280] To address such incidents, the Liability Convention would have to be utilized. However, that imports its own set of ambiguities and gaps, as discussed herein.[281]

Since Resolution 47/68 of 1992, there have been several resolutions adopted, including the United Nations Declaration on International Cooperation in the Exploitation and Use of Outer Space for the Benefit and in the Interest of All States, Taking into Particular Account the Needs of Developing Countries, adopted by the United Nations General Assembly in its Resolution 51/122;[282] the 2004/2005 UNGA Resolution 59/115 'Application of the concept of the 'launching State';[283] and the 2007/2008 UNGA Resolution 62/101 'Recommendations

279 Cheng (1997), pp. 238–239. He also notes that 'Art. IX of the treaty where the responsibility of the State extends also to activities and experiments 'planned by … its nationals'.' Cf. Frans von der Dunk, *Advanced Introduction to Space Law* (Edward Elgar 2020), pp. 122–123.

280 Viikari (2008), p. 84.

281 See infra Chapter 2, Section 1.

282 G.A. Res. 51/122, Declaration on International Cooperation in the Exploration and Use of Outer Space for the Benefit and in the Interest of All States, Taking into Particular Account the Needs of Developing Countries (Dec. 13, 1996). See also Stephan Hobe, 'International Space Law in its First Half Century', *Proceedings of the 49th Colloquium on the Law of Outer Space* (2006), p. 373 et seq.

283 This resolution '*Recommends* that States conducting space activities, in fulfilling their international obligations under the United Nations treaties on outer space, in particular the Treaty on Principles Governing the Activities of States in the Exploration and

on enhancing the practice of States and international intergovernmental organizations in registering space objects'. This last resolution contains no explicit reference to NSAs, but recognizes the difficulty with international intergovernmental organizations ensuring a complete web of responsibility for all space activities.[284] That indicates that even within international organizations, which are not the key focus of this study, potential gaps in jurisdiction, and therefore responsibility, are a concern.

On the issue of space debris, the 2002 IADC SDMG, which have since been updated, provided an early example of regulations. The latest version of the IADC SDMG outlines the fundamental principles, which 'should be considered for mission planning, design, manufacture and operational (launch, mission and disposal) phases of spacecraft and launch vehicle orbital stages.' The SDMG clarify that States and international organisations should take voluntary measures 'through national mechanisms or through their own applicable mechanisms, to ensure that these guidelines are implemented, to the greatest extent feasible, through space debris mitigation practices and procedures. These guidelines are applicable to mission planning and the operation or newly designed spacecraft and orbital stages and, if possible, to existing ones.' Content-wise they require States to limit the release of space debris during normal operations, minimize the potential for on-orbit break-ups, ensure post mission disposal (removing spacecraft and orbital stages that have reached the end of their mission operations from the useful densely populated orbit regions), and to prevent on-orbit collisions.[285] However, as guidelines which organizations and operators of space launches and objects are 'encouraged' to apply,[286] these are not internationally legally binding obligations.

However, there have been calls for a greater involvement of NSAs in these types of negotiations. The 2007 Report of UNCOPUOS, states, in relation to designating some areas of the Moon and other celestial bodies as international

---

Use of Outer Space, including the Moon and Other Celestial Bodies, the Convention on International Liability for Damage Caused by Space Objects1 and the Convention on Registration of Objects Launched into Outer Space, as well as other relevant international agreements, consider enacting and implementing national laws authorizing and providing for continuing supervision of the activities in outer space of non-governmental entities under their jurisdiction' and that States 'consider the conclusion of agreements in accordance with the Liability Convention with respect to joint launches or cooperation programmes' and share information in an effort to harmonize approaches.

284 Paragraph 3(a).

285 Inter-Agency Space Debris Coordination Committee (IADC). *IADC Space Debris Mitigation Guidelines*, IADC-02-01, Revision 3, June 2021.

286 IADC SDMG, Rev.3, 2021, p. 7.

scientific preserves and passenger space transport, that the Legal Subcommittee should 'consider this issue and for nongovernmental organizations working in the legal field to be invited to contribute to that work.'[287] The 2007 UNCOPUOS Report also notes that States and also 'entities of the United Nations system' contributed to the 'list of space-related initiatives and programs that corresponded to recommendations contained in the Plan of Implementation of the World Summit on Sustainable Development'.[288] Given that these are entities of the United Nations system, they may be seen as synonymous with an international organization. However, the phrasing is not entirely clear, and it is questionable whether these 'entities' refer to UN Secretariat staff, which would be representatives of an international organizations, or whether they were some other type of entity associated with the United Nations, such as an NGO with official UN observer status. In the latter case, it could provide a precedent for the involvement of NSAs in the formation of international regulatory-related materials.

Clearer reference to NSAs proper is contained later in the 2007 UNCOPUOS report, where it notes that the 'presence of non-governmental entities and the willingness of experts to make special presentations had enriched the Committee and its subcommittees, and that ultimate success in implementing the recommendations of UNISPACE III would depend on their continued involvement.'[289] These potential moves to increase the role of NSAs in space regulation formation could substantively concern sustainable development, which is an area closely linked with protection of the environment including that of outer space. In this way, the approach of the Committee could broadly support the contention that NSAs can serve as participants in the formation of international law, and thereby enjoy a level of subject-hood, including in relation to environmental protection.[290]

Another facet of space law which emerged during the Cold War is the limited explicit protection afforded to the space environment. During the technological race between East and West which characterized space activities during

287 UN Doc. A/62/20, Report of the Committee on the Peaceful Uses of Outer Space, General Assembly Official Records Sixty-Second Session Supplement No. 20 (A/62/20), 2007.

288 UN Doc. A/62/20, Report of the Committee on the Peaceful Uses of Outer Space, General Assembly Official Records Sixty-Second Session Supplement No. 20 (A/62/20), 2007, para. 26.

289 Report of the Committee on the Peaceful Uses of Outer Space (2007), para. 58.

290 On the involvement of NSAs in the formation of IHL, and the controversies that have arisen in this respect, see Anthea Roberts and Sandesh Sivakumaran, 'Lawmaking by Nonstate Actors: Engaging Armed Groups in the Creation of International Humanitarian Law', *The Yale Journal of International Law* (2012), 37:1.

the Cold War, space itself was commonly seen as a 'mere laboratory for scientific activity and a resource for human utilization.'[291] With existential conflict seen as potentially imminent, the idea of restricting the advance of technology in any way to protect the environment was, at most, a minority viewpoint.

This lack of attention given to the threat to the space environment manifests in soft law instruments. Notably, UNGA Resolution 41/65 on Remote Sensing of the Earth from Outer Space provides in Article X that '[r]emote sensing shall promote the protection of the Earth's natural environment.' It notes that 'States participating in remote sensing activities that have identified information in their possession that is capable of averting any phenomenon harmful to the Earth's natural environment shall disclose such information to States concerned.' The reference to using modern technological advances to protect the environment is notable and indicates a willingness to harness the tools at the international community's behest to combat terrestrial environmental harm. However, it does not contain protections for the outer space environment.

As noted, an important guiding instrument to protect the space environment is the set of SDMG established by UNCOPUOS. Although voluntary, the UNCOPUOS SDMG contain benchmark standards for the avoidance and containment of space debris. They were created after the Scientific and Technical Subcommittee of UNCOPUOS set up a Working Group on Space Debris to study the matter. The Working Group based its formulation on the 'technical content and the basic definitions' SDMG designed by the IADC.[292]

The UNCOPUOS SDMG note the 'common understanding' that 'the current space debris environment poses a risk to spacecraft in Earth orbit'. These guidelines are divided into two broad temporal categories. First, they seek to avoid the creation of new debris. Second, they encourage States to ensure efforts to remediate existing space debris will be undertaken. States are directed to limit the creation of space debris and avoid break-ups, while also dismantling and decommissioning existing spacecraft and launch vehicles from orbits populated by operational spacecraft.[293]

Whilst salutary in their aims, the SDMG maintain an exclusive focus on States (and international organizations). They provide that States which are members thereof, as well as international organizations, should take measures to ensure that the guidelines are implemented, as far as possible. The UNCOPUOS SDMG then set out measures to be taken to mitigate space debris

291 Viikari (2008), p. 112.

292 Report of United Nations sixty-second session of the Committee on the Peaceful Uses of Outer Space, A/62/20, Annex, pp. 47–48.

293 UNCOPUOS SDMG, Commentary, p. 47.

generated during 'mission planning, design, manufacture and operational (launch, mission and disposal) phases of spacecraft and launch vehicle orbital stages', including (Guideline 1) limiting debris released during normal operations, (Guideline 2) minimizing the potential for break-ups during operational phases, (Guideline 3) limiting the probability of accidental collision in orbit, (Guideline 4) avoiding intentional destruction and other harmful activities, (Guideline 5) minimizing potential for post-mission break-ups resulting from stored energy, (Guideline 6) limiting the long-term presence of spacecraft and launch vehicle orbital stages in the low-Earth orbit (LEO) region after the end of their mission, and (Guideline 7) limiting the long-term interference of spacecraft and launch vehicle orbital stages with the geosynchronous Earth orbit (GEO) region after the end of their mission.

In 2007, the United Nations General Assembly endorsed the UNCOPUOS SDMG.[294] It invited its Member States to ensure that relevant national mechanisms were available to implement the UNCOPUOS SDMG.[295] However, many States have not yet designated national mechanisms for this purpose.[296]

For the current inquiry, it is apposite that no specific reference is made to NSAs in the UNCOPUOS SDMG. This constitutes an example of adherence to the traditional State-centric model of regulating space pollution. Given the various limitations on the State-centric approach, as set out below,[297] consideration should be given to incorporating an expanded set of regulations, potentially in the form of an annex to the Outer Space Treaty containing an adapted form of the SDMG, to directly govern the conduct of NSAs and provide means to pursue legal avenues against NSAs in case they violate the guidelines without being beholden to whichever State they decide to host themselves in.

Moreover, the legally non-binding nature of the SDMG has been criticized, with some delegations expressing the view that 'a legally non-binding set of guidelines was not sufficient and would disadvantage developing countries.'[298] Reportedly, those delegations were of the view that the 'issue of space debris should also be considered by the Legal Subcommittee, with a view to developing a binding legal framework.'[299] Enshrining a binding legal framework would be a powerful way of providing the regulatory basis to prevent pollution

294 United Nations General Assembly Resolution 62/217 of 22 December 2007, para. 26.

295 United Nations General Assembly Resolution 62/217 of 22 December 2007, para. 27.

296 See Compendium and linked materials concerning Algeria, Argentina, Azerbaijan, Chile, Czech Republic, Indonesia. See also Chapter 5 below.

297 See Chapter 3, Section 2.

298 UN Report of the Committee on the Peaceful Uses of Outer Space, 2007, para. 123.

299 UN Report of the Committee on the Peaceful Uses of Outer Space, 2007, para. 123.

of the space environment. However, extending the prohibitions to NSAs will require political will and continuing efforts, as has already been signalled by the sparse, sporadic, and sometimes inconsistent approaches taken in UN instruments to NSAs.

In 2010, the International Telecommunication Union (ITU) issued a recommendation on 'Environmental Protection of the Geostationary-Satellite Orbit'.[300] In it, the ITU recommends that 'as little debris as possible should be released into the GSO region during the placement of a satellite in orbit'; that 'every reasonable effort should be made to shorten the lifetime of debris in elliptical transfer orbits with the apogees at or near GSO altitude'; that 'before complete exhaustion of its propellant, a geostationary satellite at the end of its life should be removed from the GSO region such that under the influence of perturbing forces on its trajectory, it would subsequently remain in an orbit with a perigee no less than 200 km above the geostationary altitude'; and that 'the transfer to the graveyard orbit removal should be carried out with particular caution in order to avoid RF interference with active satellites.' While this evinces an ecocentric concern for the space environment, it places no explicit obligations on NSAs to contribute to that purpose.

More recently, the European Union's 2014 Draft International Code of Conduct on Outer Space Activities provides an example of an instrument which is explicitly not legally binding,[301] and is largely State-centric, even though it acknowledges the increasing involvement of NSAs in space activities.[302] Notably, the Draft International Code of Conduct has two divergent underlying rationales when it comes to space debris. First, there is the goal of ensuring free exploration and use of outer space by States.[303] Second, there is

300 Radiocommunication Sector of the International Telecommunication Union (ITU). Environmental Protection of the Geostationary-Satellite Orbit, Recommendation ITU-R S.1003–2, December 2010, available at https://www.itu.int/rec/R-REC-S.1003-2-201012-I/en.

301 Provision 1.4: 'this Code is not legally binding, and is without prejudice to applicable international and national law'.

302 Preamble: 'Recalling the increasing importance of outer space transparency and confidence- 2 building measures in light of the growing use of outer space by governmental and non-governmental entities'; Provision 1.2 'This Code addresses outer space activities involving all space objects launched into Earth orbit or beyond, conducted by a Subscribing State, or jointly with other States, or by non-governmental entities under the jurisdiction of a Subscribing State, including those activities conducted within the framework of international intergovernmental organizations'.

303 Provision 4.1 ('The Subscribing States resolve to establish and implement policies and procedures to minimize the risk of accidents in space, collisions between space objects, or any form of harmful interference with another State's peaceful exploration, and use, of outer space').

the goal of limiting the impact of space debris on outer space in general.[304] While both aim to prevent or restrict the creation of space debris, the former does so based on a utilitarian ethic of ensuring the ongoing use of outer space, whereas the latter has a potentially more ecocentric motive seeking to protect the outer space environment. Neither rationale is reinforced by legal accountability, however. This renders their impact subject to the will of States' voluntary observance.

Of a similar character is the 2013 report of the Group of Governmental Experts on Transparency and Confidence-Building Measures in Outer Space Activities, appointed by the United Nations Secretary-General. While this is focused on States' conduct, it also encourages relevant international intergovernmental and non-governmental organizations to consider and implement the proposed transparency and confidence-building measures as appropriate and to the greatest extent practicable.[305]

4.3 *Conclusion on the State-Centric Formation of International Space Law*

The State-centric framing of international space law is a natural corollary of the epoch in which it was formed. In the post World-War Two era, States were the only entities engaging in serious space exploration and States were essentially the exclusive contributors to the formation of international law. However, over the ensuing decades, NSAs have played an increasingly prominent role in space activities. At the same time, the role of NSAs as subjects and objects of international law has expanded. With roots going back to the 1949 Advisory Opinion of the International Court of Justice (ICJ) in the *Reparation for Injuries Suffered in the Service of the United Nations* case, there have been legal moves to increase the range of actors with international legal personality beyond States, beginning with international organizations and then eventually expanding to NSAs.[306] In 1980, the ICJ recognised that international organizations, as subjects of international law, are bound by the treaties to which they

304 Provision 4.3 ('In order to minimize the creation of space debris and to mitigate its impact in outer space, the Subscribing States resolve to limit, to the greatest extent practicable, any activities in the conduct of routine space operations, including during the launch and the entire orbital lifetime of a space object, which may generate long-lived space debris.').

305 Group of Governmental Experts on Transparency and Confidence-Building Measures in Outer Space Activities UN Doc A/68/189 (2013), para.74.

306 See ICJ, *Reparation for Injuries Suffered in the Service of the United Nations,* Advisory Opinion, 11 April 1949, *ICJ Reports* (1949) 174 (holding that the United Nations was intended to exercise functions and rights which could be explained only on the basis of it possessing international legal personality and the capacity to operate on the international level).

are parties, by their internal rules, and by the 'general rules of international law'.[307] However, it was with the emergence of the *ad hoc* international criminal tribunals in the 1990s that the possibility of NSAs other than international organizations, such as armed groups, having a measure of international legal personality emerged.[308] The law of armed conflict has also seen increasing debates over the role of NSAs in the formation of the law.[309]

In parallel, NSAs, particularly businesses, have increasingly become key players in space exploration.[310] This prompts questions as to the role of such NSAs in the formation and application of international law. As Viikari states

> Private companies are no longer mere national-level lobbyists but partners of governments globally. Sometimes governments even seem to have turned into spokespersons for business. Such contradictions between the formal and the actual status of the different stakeholders in the space sector are proving increasingly problematic – not least from the point of view of international norm-making.[311]

The incongruity between the significant role of NSAs, particularly private companies, in conducting and enabling space activities versus their lack of status under traditional conceptions of international space law is glaring.[312] Moreover, it is growing more pronounced, as NSAs are increasingly operating autonomously in outer space, as in the case of SpaceX, for example.[313] As set out above, the increase in NSA activities in space brings with it greater risks of the pollution of the space environment, whether by intentional overexploitation or by accidental discharge of space debris or collisions.[314] The State-centric formation of the core instruments of international space law clashes sharply with the prevalence of NSAs in modern day space activities, resulting in legal dissonance. To illustrate, SpaceX, an American NSA, owns the majority of satellites currently in orbit.[315] Against this backdrop, the current

307 See ICJ, *Interpretation of the Agreement of 25 March 1951 between the WHO and Egypt*, Advisory Opinion, 20 December 1980, *ICJ Reports* (1980) 73, para. 37.

308 See Chapter 4, Section 2.2.

309 See Anthea Roberts and Sandesh Sivakumaran (2012).

310 Viikari (2008), p. 22.

311 Viikari (2008), p. 27.

312 Goh, (2007), pp. 161–162.

313 See Chapter 4, Section 1.

314 Chapter 1, Section 3.

315 Bruno Venditti and Miranda Smith, 'Space: Which Companies Own the Most Satellites?' *Visual Capitalist* (23 September 2023) (available at https://www.visualcapitalist.com/who-owns-the-most-satellites/).

study seeks to examine how law and scholarship has responded to the growing role of NSAs in space and the threat this presents to the previously pristine space environment.

5 The Limited Scholarly Attention Given to Regulating NSA Space Pollution

Space law has come under increasing attention in recent years, including in relation to the protection of the space environment. Studies have mainly been dedicated to State responsibility and liability under international space law.[316] In particular, space debris has been the subject of multiple publications during the last decade,[317] including an entire monograph on State accountability for space debris.[318]

However, very little of that scholarship has addressed NSA responsibility for misconduct in space,[319] and even less so for space pollution. Where attention has been paid to NSAs, it has sought to filter their accountability under international law through State structures.[320] The incongruity between traditionally State-centric space law and the growing recognition of NSA rights and

316 Stubbe (2018), p. 8 citing inter alia Wins, E., *Weltraumhaftung im Völkerrecht* (Duncker and Humblot, 2000); Bin Cheng, 'Article VI of the 1967 Space Treaty Revisited: "International Responsibility", "National Activities", and "the Appropriate State"', in (1998) 26(1) *Journal of Space Law*, pp. 7–32.

317 Dennerley (2018); Benjamin Jacobs, 'Debris Mitigation Certification and the Commercial Space Industry: A New Weapon in the Fight against Space Pollution' (2011) 20(1) *Media Law and Policy* pp. 117–141; Sophie Kaineg, 'The Growing Problem of Space Debris' (2020) 26(2) *Hastings Environmental Law Journal*, p. 277; David Tan, 'Towards a New Regime for the Protection of Outer Space as the "Province of All Mankind"' (2000) 25(145) *The Yale Journal of International Law*, pp. 145–194; Joseph N. Pelton, *Space Debris and Other Threats from Outer Space* (Springer, 2013); Viikari (2008).

318 See Stubbe (2018).

319 See Macchi, (forthcoming 2025), pp. 49–50 ('Both policy-makers and scholars have thus far paid limited attention to the human rights and environmental implications of the private sector's growing involvement in outer space').

320 See Ziemblicki and Oralova (2021), pp. 6–8 ('on an international level, only states are liable for damages caused by companies, and the liability of private companies is, therefore, subject to national law.'). See further Jennifer Friedberg, 'Bracing for the Impending Rocket Revolution: How to Regulate International Environmental Harm Caused by Commercial Space Flight' (2013) 24(1) *Colorado Natural Resources, Energy & Environmental Law Review*, p. 223 (focusing on State-to-State dispute resolution rather than the direct application of international law to NSAs).

obligations under international law has resulted in a confused legal picture.[321] As Freeland and Ireland-Piper observe:

> The reality is that there are gaps in space law when it comes to regulating private actors and legal uncertainty relating to corporate and personal nationality.[322]

It is unsurprising that commentators have focused on State responsibility. Traditionally, States were seen as the subjects of international law, with concomitant rights and duties, as detailed above.[323] Conversely, NSAs were seen as mere objects of international law which States must control.[324] This approach emanates throughout the writings of legal positivists such as Austin,[325] Kelsen,[326] as well as Fitzmaurice and Spender,[327] and others. Thirlway explains the conceptual basis for this approach:

321 See Goh (2007), p. 162 ('Sovereign states and inter-governmental organizations have been the exclusive subjects of international space law. Individuals and private enterprises remain under the jurisdiction of their respective governments and national laws. They have no independent legal status in international space law, and their rights and interests are represented by their government at the international level. With burgeoning commercialization of space activities however, private enterprises have also become entities with rights and obligations under international law. This is so even if they have not been formally recognized as such.').

322 Freeland and Ireland-Piper (2022), p. 3.

323 See Chapter 1, Section 4.

324 Robert Jennings and Arthur Watts (Eds.), *Oppenheim's International Law (9th Edition): Volume 1 Peace* (Oxford University Press, 2008), p. 120; Daragh Murray, *Human Rights Obligations of Non-State Armed Groups* (Hart Publishing Limited, 2016), pp. 23–24. See also Fergus Green, "Fragmentation in Two Dimensions': The International Court of Justice's Flawed Approach to Non-State Actors and International Legal Personality' (2008) 9 *Melbourne Journal of International Law*, p. 50.

325 John Austin, *Lectures on Jurisprudence or the Philosophy of Positive Law* (5th Edition) (John Murray, 1885) ('Every positive law, or every law simply and strictly so-called, is set by a sovereign individual or a sovereign body of individuals, to a person or persons in a state of subjection to its authority').

326 Hans Kelsen, *General Theory of Law and State* (Harvard University Press, 1949), p. 113 (referring to the existence of a grundnorm – the highest fundamental norm from which all others derived their binding force).

327 ICJ, *South West Africa Cases* (Ethiopia v. South Africa; Liberia v. South Africa), Preliminary Objections, Judgment of 21 December 1962, *ICJ Reports* (1962), p. 319 [hereinafter: South West Africa cases]; *South West Africa Cases*, Joint Dissenting Opinion of Sir Percy Spender and Sir Gerald Fitzmaurice, 465–563, p. 466, (referring to their 'duty of reaching a conclusion strictly on the basis of what we believe to be the correct legal view').

> The reason why international law is built round States is not because they have selfishly created such a system, or fought off any strivings for equality on the part of other entities: it is because they represent the interests of their human citizens in general terms, in the area where it matters, literally 'on the ground'.[328]

Although authoritative bodies, such as the International Court of Justice, have recognised that international law does not exclusively concern States,[329] the dominant approach still remains State-centric.[330]

However, the role of NSAs under international law has been transformed in practice, leading to a reconceptualization of the actors under this legal framework.[331] Notwithstanding the dominance of the State-centric approach,[332] NSAs are increasingly treated as participants[333] in the formation and application of international law.[334] International humanitarian law, international

---

328 See H.W.A. Thirlway, *International Customary Law and Codification* (Sijthoff, 1972), p. 147.

329 In its *Reparations* Advisory Opinion, the International Court of Justice ascribed legal personality to the United Nations, a non-state actor, because of 'its functions, the capacity to possess rights and duties and the possession of organs with separate will from that of its member states.', see *Reparation for injuries in the service of the United Nations*, Advisory Opinion: *ICJ Reports* (1949), p. 174; Nicolas Tsagarious, 'Non-State Actors, Ungoverned Spaces and International Responsibility for Cyber Acts' (2016) 21(3) *Journal of Conflict and Security Law*, pp. 455–474.

330 Fogo (2017), p. 188.

331 See James Crawford, 'The System of International Responsibility' (2010) in: *The Law of International Responsibility* (James Crawford, Alain Pellet, Simon Olleson and Kate Parlett (Eds.)) (Oxford University Press, 2010), p. 20. See further Andrew Clapham, 'Human Rights Obligations of Non-State Actors in Conflict Situations' (2006) 88(863) *International Review of the Red Cross*, pp. 491–523; Commission on Human Rights, Report of the Special Rapporteur, Philip Alston, Addendum, Mission to Sri Lanka, UN Doc. E/CN.4/2006/53/Add.5 (27 March 2006), pp. 25–27.

332 See, e.g., Jennings and Watts (Eds.) (2008), pp. 16, 120; Colin Warbrick, 'States and Recognition in International Law' (2006) in Malcolm Evans (Ed.) *International Law* (2nd ed.) (Oxford University Press, 2006), p. 22; Green (2008), p. 50. See also Austin (1885), p. 34; Kelsen (1949), p. 113; South West Africa Cases, p. 319; South West Africa Cases, Joint Dissenting Opinion of Sir Percy Spender and Sir Gerald Fitzmaurice, p. 466.

333 See Higgins (1994), p. 50; Murray (2016), p. 27. See also Clapham (2006), p. 29; Fogo (2017), p. 188.

334 See Cedric Ryngaert, 'Non-State Actors: Carving out a Space in a State-Centred International Legal System' (2016) 63 *Netherlands International Law Review*, pp. 188–190 (highlighting the role of certain NSAs in international law-making and policy-making, arguing that 'International law or, more accurately, the community of states has [conferred] certain rights and obligations on categories of NSAs' and stating 'an NSA enjoys international legal personality because it enjoys certain obligations.').

criminal law, and even international human rights law, have, to varying degrees, seen NSA treated not only as objects, but also entities with both rights and obligations.[335] Even the *jus ad bellum*, which is a traditional preserve of State-to-State conduct, has seen initiatives seeking to attribute NSAs with responsibility for armed attacks sufficient to activate the right to self-defence.[336] On this basis, Shaw notes that 'the gradual sophistication of positivist doctrine, combined with the advent of new approaches to the whole system of international relations, has broken down this exclusive emphasis and extended the roles played by non-state entities, such as individuals, multinational firms and international institutions.'[337] He refers to these moves as being 'indicative of the trend away from the exclusivity of the state [as the sole type of actor under international law]'.[338]

In the realm of international humanitarian law, for example, Common Article 3 of the Geneva Conventions binds parties to non-international conflicts, including non-State armed groups, and affords protections to members of NSAs who are not taking an active part in hostilities.[339] Specifically, it sets out legal guarantees covering members of NSAs (both in the sense of protecting their members against these harms and in prohibiting their members from inflicting these harms). These include prohibitions against violence to life and person, cruel treatment and torture, hostage-taking, outrages upon personal dignity, violations of basic due process, and lack of care for the sick and wounded.[340] Several other provisions of international humanitarian law

335 Clapham (2006), pp. 522, 523.

336 Shaw (2008), pp. 1137–1138 (noting that the Chatham House Principles on International Law on the Use of Force in Self-Defence, 55 ICLQ, 2006, pp. 963, 969, 'provide that the right to self-defence may apply to attacks by non-state actors where the attack is large-scale; if the right to self-defence is exercised in the territory of another state, then that state is unable or unwilling to deal itself with the non-state actors and that it is necessary to use force from outside to deal with the threat in circumstances where the consent of the territorial state cannot be obtained; and the force used in self-defence may only be directed against the government of the state where the attacker is found in so far as is necessary to avert or end the attack.').

337 Shaw (2008), pp. 46–47.

338 Shaw (2008), p. 47.

339 See, e.g., Convention (III) relative to the Treatment of Prisoners of War, Geneva, 12 August 1949; ICRC, Commentary Convention (III) relative to the Treatment of Prisoners of War, 2020, paras. 427–428. See also Protocol to the Geneva Conventions of 12 August 1949, and relating to the protection of victims of international armed conflict (Protocol I) (Jun. 8, 1977) [hereinafter Protocol I to the Geneva Convention (1949)], 1125 UNTS 3, Article 3.

340 Convention (III) relative to the Treatment of Prisoners of War, Geneva, 12 August 1949, Article 3. Note that common Article 3 also provides that it shall not affect the legal status of the Parties to the conflict.

refer explicitly to organized armed groups (which are NSAs).[341] The content of these provisions, including their application to NSAs, has been confirmed to reflect customary international law.[342] Instruments outside international humanitarian law also impose obligations on NSAs, for example the Terrorism Suppression Conventions and the Genocide Convention.[343]

International law not only explicitly places obligations on NSAs as a matter of black letter law, but also increasingly applies those obligations directly to NSA conduct. For example, international criminal tribunals and similar institutions have recognised the responsibility of NSAs for atrocity crimes, often based on violations of the laws and customs of war, based *inter alia* on Common Article 3 of the Geneva Conventions.[344] In turn, leaders and commanders of

341 These documents include Protocol II Additional to the Geneva Conventions of 12 August 1949 and Relating to the Protection of Victims of Non-International Armed Conflicts (Additional Protocol II) 1977, 1125 UNTS 609, Article 1(1), referring to 'dissident armed forces or other organized armed groups', Convention IV Respecting the Laws and Customs of War on Land and Its Annex: Regulation Concerning the Laws and Customs of War on Land (Hague Regulations) 1899, 187 CTS 227, Annex, Article 1, stating that 'The laws, rights, and duties of war apply not only to armies, but also to militia and volunteer corps [fulfilling specified conditions]', and the Convention for Protection of Cultural Property in the Event of Armed Conflict 1954, 249 UNTS 240, Article 19(1), stating that '[i]n the event of an armed conflict not of an international character occurring within the territory of one of the High Contracting Parties, each party to the conflict shall be bound to apply, as, a minimum, the provisions of the present Convention which relate to respect for cultural property'. See generally Thibaud de La Bourdonnaye, 'Greener insurgencies? Engaging non-State armed groups for the protection of the natural environment during non-international armed conflicts' (2020) 102 *International Review of the Red Cross* 914, pp. 579–605. See also Vladyslav Lanovoy, 'The Use of Force by Non-State Actors and the Limits of Attribution of Conduct' (2017) 28(2) *European Journal of International Law*, p. 564.

342 See Jean-Marie Henckaerts and Louise Doswald-Beck, *Customary International Humanitarian Law* (Cambridge University Press, 2005). When it comes to the formation of customary international law, the ILC has stated that the '[c]onduct of other actors [sc., other than States and international organizations] is not practice that contributes to the formation, or expression, of rules of customary international law, but may be relevant when assessing the practice', see International Law Commission, Identification of customary international law, UN Doc. A/CN.4/L.872 (May 30, 2016). See also Anthea Roberts and Sandesh Sivakumaran (2012).

343 Lanovoy (2017), p. 564 citing, e.g., International Convention for the Suppression of the Financing of Terrorism, 9 December 1999, 2178 UNTS 197 (entered into force on 10 April 2002), Article 2; Convention on the Prevention and Punishment of the Crime of Genocide, 9 December 1948, 78 UNTS 277 (entered into force on 12 January 1951), Article 4: 'Persons committing genocide or any of the other acts enumerated in article III shall be punished, whether they are constitutionally responsible rulers, public officials or private individuals.'

344 See ICC, *Prosecutor v. Katanga*, Case No. ICC-01/04-01/07, Decision pursuant to Article 74 of the Statute (7. 3. 2014), paras. 679–681, 785, 849, 879 (finding that members of the

NSAs have been held criminally accountable for violations of international law before the International Criminal Tribunal for the former Yugoslavia (ICTY), the International Criminal Tribunal for Rwanda (ICTR), the International Criminal Court (ICC) and other international and quasi-international tribunals.[345] Domestic courts have also recognised the possibility of members of NSAs being responsible for crimes which would constitute human rights violations, such as when they exercise quasi-official powers.[346]

This view can be found in UN emanations from the highest levels; UNSC Resolutions 2170 and 2379 refer to unlawful acts carried out by ISIS/ISIL, the Al-Nusrah Front, and other individuals or entities associated with Al-Qaeda as

---

Ngiti militia committed crimes included violations of common article 3 against civilian population and civilians not taking direct part in hostilities in Bogoro on 24 February 2003); United Nations Security Council, Resolution 2235 (2015), UN Doc. S/RES/2235 (7 August 2015), para. 4 and 5 (expressing the Security Council's determination to identify those responsible for these acts and reiterates that those individuals, entities, groups, or governments responsible for any use of chemicals as weapons, including chlorine or any other toxic chemical, must be held accountable, and calls on all parties in the Syrian Arab Republic to extend their full cooperation in this regard, and requiring the OPCW-United Nations Joint Investigative Mechanism to identify to the greatest extent feasible individuals, entities, groups, or governments who were perpetrators, organisers, sponsors or otherwise involved in the use of chemicals as weapons); United Nations Security Council, Third Report of the Organization for the Prohibition of Chemical Weapons – United Nations Joint Investigative Mechanism, UN Doc. S/2016/738/Rev.1 (Aug. 2016, 24), paras.58–60 and Annex X (concluding that the Islamic State in Iraq and the Levant was responsible for the use of a chemical weapon (sulphur mustard) in Marea in 2015). See also ICTY, *Prosecutor v. Tadić*, Case No. IT-94-1-AR72, Decision on the Defence Motion for Interlocutory Appeal on Jurisdiction (2. 10. 1995), para. 130 (noting that 'during the Nigerian Civil War, both members of the Federal Army and rebels were brought before Nigerian courts and tried for violations of principles of international humanitarian law.').

345 See, e.g. ICTY, *Prosecutor v. Lahi Brahimaj*, Case No. IT-04-84-T, Public Judgment with Confidential Annex (29.11.2012) (finding Lahi Brahimaj guilty of cruel treatment and torture as war crimes committed in his capacity as Member of the Kosovo Liberation Army General Staff); ICC, *Prosecutor v. Thomas Lubanga Dyilo*, Case No. ICC-01/04-01/06-2842, Judgment pursuant to Article 74 of the Statute (14 March 2012); ICC, *Prosecutor v. Thomas Lubanga Dyilo*, Case No. ICC-01/04-01/06 A5, Judgment on the appeal of Mr Thomas Lubanga Dyilo against his conviction (1 December 2014); ICC, *Prosecutor v. Katanga*, paras. 1691.

346 *R v Reeves Taylor* [2019] UKSC 51, para 76–79; *R v TRA* [2018] EWCA Crim 2843, para 69 (concerning Agnes Reeve Taylor, a member of the NPFL, which was Charles Taylor's rebel group in Liberia. Reeve Taylor was accused of committing torture during the 1990s. Whereas the Court of Appeal and Supreme Court ruled that an NSA figure could theoretically be responsible for such acts, a trial judge eventually determined that a jury could not properly conclude that the rebel forces exercised functions of a governmental or quasi-governmental nature, and the case was dismissed); Clapham (2022), p. 590.

crimes against humanity, war crimes, or genocide, and insist that the perpetrators be held accountable.[347] Moving to the human rights domain, UN bodies have held NSAs accountable for human rights abuses,[348] notwithstanding the ongoing debates regarding the applicability of human rights obligations to NSAs.[349]

While international law has served as a vehicle to impose obligations on NSAs, it has also been a source of rights for them. For example, corporations and other entities have relied on bilateral investment treaties to assert their rights against foreign governments encroaching on their commercial practices.[350]

---

347 Vincent-Joël Proulx, 'A Postmortem for International Criminal Law? Terrorism, Law and Politics, and the Reaffirmation of State Sovereignty' (2020) 11(1) *Harvard National Security Journal*, pp. 151–213, p. 187.

348 See, e.g. Annual Report of United Nations Assistance Mission in Afghanistan, 2020, p. 99 citing United Nations Secretary-General, Report of the Secretary-General's Panel of Experts on Accountability in Sri Lanka, 31 March 2011, para. 188. See also Human Rights Council, Report of the International Commission of Inquiry to investigate all Alleged Violations of International Human Rights Law in the Libyan Arab Jamahiriya, UN Doc. A/HRC/17/44 (1 June 2011); Human Rights Council, Report of the International Commission of Inquiry on the Syrian Arab Republic, UN Doc. A/HRC/19/69 (22 February 2012), para. 106; United Nations Mission in the Republic of South Sudan (UNMISS), Conflict in South Sudan: A Human Rights Report (8 May 2014), para. 18.

349 In contrast to the UN documents recognizing the responsibility of NSAs for human rights abuses, several authors argue contrary to the existence of the international obligation of NSAs to respect human rights and advise caution in establishing such obligation, as human rights norms presuppose the existence of an entity exercising governmental functions. See Thirlway (1972), p. 148; Els Debuf, *Captured in War: Lawful Internment in Armed Conflict* (Hart Publishing, 2013), p. 481; Liesbeth Zegveld, *Accountability of Armed Opposition Groups in International Law* (Cambridge University Press, 2002), pp. 9, 38; Duncan B. Hollis, 'Private Actors in Public International Law: Amicus Curiae and the Case for the Retention of State Sovereignty' (2002) 25 *Boston College International and Comparative Law Review*, pp. 235–255.

350 The most obvious examples of such a trend are International Investment Treaties, among which are Bilateral Investment Treaties (BITs), international treaties between two States, conferring and guaranteeing direct rights to private investors of one State regarding their investments in the other. Yadira Castillo, 'The Appeal to Human Rights in Arbitration and International Investment Agreements' (2012) XII *Anuario Mexicano Derecho Internacional*, p. 63; Catharine Titi, Public Actors in International Investment Law (Springer Nature: Open Access, 2021), pp. 50, 99, 122, 159. Investment tribunals often refer to judgments of the European Court of Human Rights, which was the case, for example in ICSID, *Mondev Internationall Ltd. v. United States*, Case No. ARB(AF)/99/2, Award (11 October 2022), para. 144 and ICSID, *Total S.A. v. Argentine Republic*, Case No. ARB/04/1, Decision on Liability (27 December 2010), paras. 128–34 – see Anthea Roberts, 'Clash of Paradigms: Actors and Analogies Shaping the Investment Treaty System' (2013) 107(1) *American Journal of International Law*, pp. 51–52.

Individual leaders of NSAs before international criminal tribunals are able to directly rely on international law to assert rights, such as fair trial rights and rights to compensation.[351] In relation to international humanitarian law, agreements between warring parties including NSAs,[352] and other practices of NSAs, have been taken into account in discerning the rules of customary international humanitarian law.[353] More broadly, NSAs have reportedly been accepted as parties before international courts, such as the Seabed Disputes Chamber of the International Tribunal for the Law of the Sea.[354] Some even argue that multinational corporations are effectively able to directly create international law.[355]

The domain of international aviation law epitomizes the direct applicability of international law to NSAs. Although not applicable to outer space,[356] international aviation law provides a model whereby the primary rules governing NSA rights and obligations are set out in international treaties and related instruments.[357] For example, the Convention for the Unification of Certain Rules for International Carriage by Air of 1999 (Montreal Convention 1999),[358] and the 1929 Warsaw Convention it replaced, 'established a private legal regime that

351 ICTR, *Jean-Bosco Barayagwiza vs. Prosecutor*, Case No. ICTR-97-19-AR72, Decision of the Appeals Chamber (03 November 1999).

352 See, e.g. Henckaerts and Doswald-Beck (2005), p. 4; paragraph 2.5 of the 1992 Agreement on the Application of IHL between the Parties to the Conflict in Bosnia and Herzegovina requires that hostilities be conducted in accordance with Article 48 AP I.

353 See, e.g. Henckaerts and Doswald-Beck (2005), p. XXV (referring to the category of VI. Other Practice – 'This category includes statements by armed opposition groups, reports by non-governmental organizations and other types of publications from nongovernmental sources.' And making frequent references to such practice in its assessments).

354 United Nations Convention on the Law of the Sea (UNCLOS), 10 December 1982, 1833/1834/1835 UNTS 3 (entered into force on 16 November 1994), Article 187(c) (recognising the tribunal's jurisdiction over *inter alia* 'disputes between parties to a contract, being States Parties, the Authority or the Enterprise, state enterprises and natural or juridical persons'). See further Ziemblicki and Oralova (2021), p. 4.

355 See Julian Arato, 'Corporations as Lawmakers', (2015) 56(2) *Harvard International Law Review*, pp. 229–296.

356 See Dempsey and Manoli (2017), p. 9 ('[t]he legal regimes that govern air space and outer space are distinct, and create a distinct conflict: while air space is an area to which State sovereignty can be attributed, outer space falls beyond sovereignty claims').

357 Brian Havel and Gabriel Sanchez, *The Principles and Practice of International Aviation Law* (Cambridge University Press, 2014), pp. 251, 257–258.

358 Convention for the Unification of Certain Rules for International Carriage by Air, 1999, UNTS 2004, p. 309. This consolidates and updates developments originally enshrined in the 1929 Convention for the Unification of Certain Rules Relating to International Carriage by Air ('Warsaw Convention'); Havel and Gabriel Sanchez, p. 252.

directly affects human and corporate persons'.[359] The Montreal Convention explicitly covers the liability of carriers for death and injury to passengers, damage to cargo, and delays, while also assigning rights to carriers.[360] Whereas the Montreal Convention sets out specific NSA obligations at the international level, it directs that claims for damages must be in the courts of one of the relevant States Parties (either the domicile of the carrier, its principal place of business, where it has a place of business through which the contract has been made, or the State of destination).[361] Claims based on the Warsaw Convention of 1929 (the predecessor to the 1999 Montreal Convention which replaced it) have been litigated in domestic courts many times.[362] Concerning environmental protection, Annex 16 to the Chicago Convention on Civil Aviation contains environmentally oriented obligations which are directly applicable to aircraft operators, covering topics including CO_2 emissions and carbon offsetting and reduction.[363]

Despite these established strands of law and practice, the question of NSA status under international law continues to divide scholarly opinion. This has led one observer to conclude that the position of NSAs under international law remains an area 'shrouded in remarkable uncertainty'.[364] That uncertainty is acknowledged herein and constitutes a driving motivation for the current scholarly investigation of the potential responsibility of NSAs for space pollution.

5.1 *Conceptual Underpinnings of the Increasing Recognition of NSAs as Subjects and Objects of International Law*

Unlocking the potential application of international law to NSAs requires latching onto a shift in international law which already has theoretical antecedents. As noted, international law was historically conceived as a State-centric system.[365] In the late 18th century, Jeremy Bentham referred to it as the 'law betwixt states'.[366] Noting this ontology, Noortmann observed that

359 Havel and Sanchez (2014), pp. 257–259 ('Its effectiveness lay in the fact that contracting States were undertaking to treat the Convention's provisions as the applicable domestic law in all airline liability cases in all of their national courts').

360 See Chapter 6, Section 3.

361 Convention for the Unification of Certain Rules for International Carriage by Air, 1999, Article 33(1).

362 Havel and Gabriel Sanchez, p. 252 referring to inter alia Eastern Airlines, Inc. v. Floyd, 499 U.S. 530 (1991) (holding that Article 17 of the Warsaw Convention does provide for recovery for mental or emotional injuries unaccompanied by physical injury).

363 See Chapter 6, Section 3.

364 Murray (2016), p. 23 (commenting on the legal personhood of non-State armed groups).

365 Stubbe (2018), p. 8.

366 Noortman, p. 180 citing Bentham 1781.

> In the prevailing and pervasive legal positivist approach to international law, NGOs [broadly referring to NSAs] are not considered to be international legal persons or subjects of international law.[367]

Anthony Clark Arend encapsulates this view of international law in the following passage:

> [S]tates are still the main actors in the international system and the primary creators of international law. Even though nonstate actors exist, and, in some cases, these nonstate actors have entered into international agreements, these actors do not enter the process of creating general international law in an unmediated fashion. In other words, the interactions of nonstate actors with each other and with states do not produce customary international law. Only state interactions can produce custom.[368]

But this perception is increasingly being questioned at the theoretical level, and commentators are re-evaluating the nature and parameters of international law. Some have begun to recognize that the traditional conception of international law as an exclusively State-oriented framework has been displaced by a more nuanced (and potentially more chaotic) understanding.[369]

For example, Andrew Clapham states:

> There is an assumption that human rights treaties only address state actors. This is not really the case.[370]

According to former President of the International Court of Justice Rosalyn Higgins[371] the traditional subject-object dichotomy of legal positivists, founded

367 Math Noortmann, 'NGOs in international law', *Routledge Handbook of NGOs and International Relations* (Routledge, 2019), p. 180.

368 Arend (1999), p.176.

369 See, e.g., Murray (2016), p. 27 ('the traditional view that states are the sole entities endowed with international legal personality is no longer valid, and today it is accepted that non-state entities may, under certain circumstances, possess international legal personality.').

370 Clapham (2022), p. 590 (noting that arguments have been made for years that human rights obligations can bind NSAs and citing Meron, *Human Rights in Internal Strife: Their International Protection* (Grotius, 1987), pp. 33–40).

371 Higgins (1994), p. 8. See also Roland Portmann, *Legal Personality in International Law* (Cambridge University Press, 2010), p. 213.

on the idea of States essentially being the exclusive subjects forming international law, has been supplanted by a 'process' based approach whereby:

> [in international law] there are no 'subjects' and 'objects', but only participants. Individuals are participants, along with States, international organizations, ... multinational corporations, and indeed private non-governmental groups.[372]

Similarly, Ezequiel Heffes, Marcos Kotlik and Manuel Ventura challenge the traditional understanding of international law and argue that:

> it is necessary to shift the focus beyond States, in order to encompass the various types of functions and interactions in which every entity participates, and that constitute international decision-making processes.[373]

Andrew Clapham explains, in the context of human rights, that

> the most promising theoretical basis for human rights obligations for non-state actors is to remind ourselves that the foundational basis of human rights obligations is best explained by recalling that these rights belong to the individual in recognition of each person's inherent dignity. The implication is that these natural rights should be respected by everyone and every entity.[374]

In this light, a wide conceptual schism persists between Higgins, Clapham and others who treat NSAs as subjects of international law as opposed to those strict positivists who hold adhere to the traditional view.

Because of this, the position of NSAs under international law remains subject to uncertainty, which in the view of some commentators 'inhibit[s] an accurate understanding of the contemporary legal reality'.[375] With NSAs expanding their activities in space, the implications of this legal uncertainty are growing more acute. The stakes are high. As Daragh Murray notes, 'entities devoid of personality simply do not exist (directly at least) in the eyes of the

372 Higgins (1994), p. 50.

373 Ezequiel Heffes, Marcos D. Kotlik, and Manuel J. Ventura, *International Humanitarian Law and Non-State Actors: Debates, Law and Practice*, (Springer, 2020), p. 1.

374 Clapham (2022), p. 586.

375 Murray (2016), p. 23 (commenting on the legal personhood of non-State armed groups).

law, and are excluded from the international legal system.'[376] If NSAs have no legal personality under international law, then all processes and applications of international law must be funneled through States. However, if NSAs do possess international legal personality, at least to an extent, then the question arises as to which international legal processes they can play a role in, how international law applies to them and before which fora.

Given that international law contains 'no written provisions that unambiguously determine who has legal personality',[377] detailed scholarly attention is essential to avoid exacerbating the lack of attention to areas in which NSAs play critical roles in international events. For this purpose, the present study postulates the following:(i) NSAs can play a role in international law, not only as entities subject to the law (passive international legal personality) but also as entities recognised as being capable of affecting the formation of international law (active international legal personality);[378] (ii) the recognition of NSA international legal personality must accord with the broader framework and secondary rules of international law (such as customary law formation; responsibility and liability);[379] (iii) the extent to which NSAs have international legal

376 Murray (2016), p. 25 citing Jan Klabbers, "The Concept of Legal Personality" (2005) 11 *Ius Gentium* pp. 35–66; Portmann (2010), p. 5.

377 Noortmann, (2019), p. 180.

378 See, e.g. Noortmann (2019), pp. 186–187 referring to the 'formal recognition' of NSAs in inter alia Article 71 of the Charter of the United Nations, which provides that: 'The Economic and Social Council may make suitable arrangements for consultation with nongovernmental organizations which are concerned with matters within its competence. Such arrangements may be made with international organizations and, where appropriate, with national organizations after consultation with the Member of the United Nations concerned.' In addition, he refers to 'art. 4.2 (consultation and cooperation) of the Agreement establishing the World Trade Organization; art. 6.3 (assistance) and art. 6.7.f (implementation) of the landmine treaty; art. 15.2 (information) and 44.4 (expertise of the Statute of the International Criminal Court), and the preamble (raising awareness and implementation) and art. 16 (assistance) of the arms trade treaty.' By contrast, agreements between sub-State entities will not per se constitute international law; Hari Osofsky, 'The creation of the international law of climate change: complexities of sub-state actors', in Bailliet (2012), p. 187 (referring to actions of sub-State entities related to the UNFCC and observing that '[t]hese actions have no formal international legal significance under traditional notions of international law. They are formed among subnational actors who, as a matter of international law, are not subjects and objects of international law and could rescind their commitments at any time. The commitments themselves involve subnational, not international, legal action.').

379 This approach proceeds on what could be called a liberal-positivist basis, whereby recognition of NSAs' active legal personality must be based on recognised sources of international law, such as international conventions, whether general or particular, establishing rules expressly recognized by the contesting states; international custom, as evidence

personality varies between different domains (for example, it is more extensive in international humanitarian law than in the law of the sea); (iv) in the field of space law NSAs have nascent international legal personality, which must be closely examined to determine its parameters, as is done herein. These postulations are tested throughout this work and used to generate meta-insights into the conceptualization of the nature of international law.[380]

As space activities increase, the range of actors engaging in space exploration has accordingly increased. This has revealed several deficiencies in the space law regime. The gaps are particularly acute when it comes to liability for space activities that cause harm.[381] As Stubbe notes in relation to liability, 'the possibility of being penalized for damage clearly increases the incentive for avoiding the occurrence of that damage in the first place.'[382] By implication, if there is no serious prospect of being penalized, it will undermine the incentive to limit and avoid damage to the outer space environment particularly for profit-seeking entities such as corporations. Identifying and synthesizing the provisions and principles of international law that apply to NSA conduct in space is important to establish a precise diagnosis of the current situation and thereby provide a foundation to assess the feasibility and coherence of available future approaches to the regulation of NSA space pollution.[383]

---

of a general practice accepted as law; the general principles of law recognized by civilized nations; and, as subsidiary means for the determination of rules of law, judicial decisions and the teachings of the most highly qualified publicists of the various nations. See ICJ Statute, Article 38. Examples of such formal recognition being ascribed to NSAs are provided in Noortman's recitation of relevant treaties in the preceding footnote. This approach has analogies with the new governance theory; whereby traditional foundational precepts regarding the formation of international law are respected, but the implementation of those precepts is broadened to a less traditional array of actors and expanded to include voluntary targets; see Kenneth W. Abbott and Duncan Snidal, 'Strengthening International Regulation Through Transnational New Governance', (2009) 42 *Vanderbilt Journal of Transnational Law*, p. 501. An alternative approach would be the global legal pluralist school of thought, whereby international law is understood from a socio-legal perspective which conceptualises the creation of law as occurring through a variety of simultaneous formal and informal processes among stakeholders; see, e.g., Ofosky (2012), p. 193. However, that approach carries little utility in delineating what counts as international law, as discussed below in Chapter 6.

380 See infra Chapter 6 (insights from the avenues for redress regarding NSA space pollution).

381 See Viikari (2008), p. 66 ('all space activities are ultra-hazardous and it has been deemed appropriate that those engaged in such activities (and gaining profit from them) should also bear the risk of any ensuing damage, whereas possible victims on Earth deserve full compensation.').

382 Stubbe (2018), p. 6.

383 See Miller (2019), p. 35 ('As states become more reliant on space and as the cost of participating in space declines, it would be overly optimistic to believe that nonstate actors will

5.2 *The Need for Scholarly Analysis of NSA Responsibility for Space Pollution*

Despite the increasing recognition of NSAs as subjects of international law, and despite their accelerating activity in the space environment, very little scholarly attention has been paid to the issue of regulating of NSA responsibility for space pollution under international law.[384] This accords with the broader trend of analyses on space law, which overwhelmingly focus on States rather than NSAs.[385] Typifying this State-centric approach is Peter Stubbe's monograph on space debris, which explicitly refrains from addressing NSAs accountability, stating 'the accountability of non-state entities will not be considered, because they are normally subject to national rather than international law.'[386] Similarly, James Gutzman focuses on how NSA responsibility can be imposed via the route of State responsibility,[387] without looking at the direct application of international law to NSAs.

The lack of attention given to legal responses to the threat posed by NSAs in space, leads Gregory Miller, who focuses on the military aspects of this threat, to concludes that 'states and the international community need to expand discussions dealing with non-state threats to space because such responses will necessarily rely on a mix of individual state laws, international law, and international norms.'[388] Notwithstanding this explicit recognition of the gap in the legal literature, there continues to be an ongoing disregard of NSA

---

not become increasingly greater threats, not to mention that nonstate actors can already carry out attacks on the ground that would have negative consequences for a state's interests in space, such as targeting launch facilities or personnel. To prepare for some of these potential challenges, it is important to understand the nature of the actors that may present a threat.').

384 See Fogo (2017), pp. 185, 187 (discussing responsibility for NSA interference with space systems and mentioning space debris but focusing on interference with 'space assets' rather than the space environment per se); Larsen (2018) (discussing the IADC Guidelines on Space Debris, and noting the relevance of non-governmental space operations, but assessing the accountability of non-governmental entities through the lens of State accountability). Other works on international space law which touch on NSA accountability but do not address it in detail are referred to throughout this book.

385 Freeland and Ireland-Piper (2022), p. 3.

386 Stubbe (2018), p. 8. In footnote 36, Stubbe acknowledges that 'individuals may also possess subjectivity in international law', but he does not explore the direct application of international law to NSAs.

387 James Gutzman,'State Responsibility for Non-State Actors in Times of War: Article VI of the Outer Space Treaty and the Law of Neutrality' (2017), *Institute of Air and Space Law McGill University*, p. 1.

388 Miller (2019), p. 46.

accountability under international space law, which is ever more difficult to sustain in light of the growing risk of NSA space pollution.

Even if States must shoulder most of the burden of protecting the outer space environment, assessing the extent to which international law can regulate NSA space pollution is necessary. It will help determine key issues, including: the limitations on NSA conduct (which are not necessarily equal to those on States); what form of accountability should be imposed on NSAs; which State should impose that accountability; and, fundamentally, what type of space pollution, if any, violates international law. The legal vagaries regarding NSA legal accountability contrast with the growing certainty that NSAs are contributing to space pollution.

In light of the need for assessment of NSA accountability under international law for space pollution, and given the conceptual schism regarding the applicability of international law to NSAs, this manuscript serves three interlinked purposes. First, it examines whether and how international law, in its current state, can be used to regulate the conduct of NSAs in space, particularly in relation to space pollution. Second, based on the analysis of the first issue, it gleans insights into the nature of international law and the feasibility of applying it directly to NSAs. Third, these assessments provide the foundation for a prospective normative analysis of the options for redressing international space law in the future to better confront the pressing threat of NSA space pollution.

CHAPTER 2

Gateway Considerations for the Application of International Law to Space Pollution

Given the rapid rise in space activities in recent years, it is striking that there has been no corresponding change or addition to the core space law treaties since they were adopted in the 1960s and 1970s. There have also been very few cases before courts, whether international, regional, or domestic, in which the provisions and principles of space law have been authoritatively interpreted or applied.[1] As a result, the legal approach to establishing State accountability for space pollution is not particularly settled.[2] When it comes to NSAs, the legal framework is even more embryonic.[3] Because of this, it is particularly important to examine the legal regimes potentially relevant to NSA accountability for space pollution.[4] In order to do so, it is necessary to address the fundamental prefatory question of whether there is a prohibition of space pollution under international law.

1 The Quest to Discern a Prohibition of Space Pollution

1.1 *Does International Space Law Prohibit Space Pollution?*

> The presence of debris in outer space should be considered a form of environmental degradation on a global scale.[5]

1 Most of the cases are related to torts and contracts, very few cases relate to the environment. See, e.g., Rick Adams, 'The New York Times Co. v. National Aeronautics and Space Administration' (available at https://rickadams.org/chall/legal.html). For a more detailed overview of cases, see the list of cases sorted according to the subject matter of the case on: ESA, *Space law cases* (17 March 2022) (available at https://www.esa.int/About_Us/ECSL_-_European_Centre_for_Space_Law/Space_law_cases). See further Chapter 5.

2 See Viikari (2008), p. 6.

3 Clapham identifies national courts (civil and criminal liability) and the International Criminal Court (individual criminal liability) for NSA liability and relevant international human rights treaty monitoring bodies and courts for State liability (accountability for treaty violations), see Clapham (2006), p. 32.

4 See, e.g. Fogo, pp. 182–190.

5 Stubbe (2018), p. 3. See also Viikari (2008), p. 31.

© MATTHEW GILLETT ET AL., 2025 | DOI:10.1163/9789004724624_003

To assess whether NSAs can be held accountable for space pollution, it first must be determined whether space pollution is prohibited under international law. This question remains subject to debate,[6] notwithstanding the existence of entire volumes assessing responsibility for causing space debris (bearing in mind that space debris is the major, though not only, sub-component of space pollution).[7] It is a critical question, both in determining the current state of international, and informing the nature of reforms that are required to establish a legal architecture capable of redressing space pollution.

As noted above, the nucleus of international space law[8] is made up of several conventions, namely the 1967 Outer Space Treaty, the 1968 Rescue Agreement, the 1972 Liability Convention, the 1975 Registration Convention, and the 1979 Moon Agreement, along with the 1963 Partial Test Ban Treaty. Soft law instruments provide additional interpretive aides and sources of guidance. These instruments constitute the core body of legal provisions to explore in the effort to determine whether a prohibition of space pollution exists.

Widely recognized as the 'constitution' of international space law,[9] the Outer Space Treaty of 1967 is the most authoritative instrument from which a prohibition of space pollution could be derived. The Outer Space Treaty is a fundamental instrument regulating human activities in outer space, which has attracted broad acceptance in the international community.[10]

In line with the tenor of space law, the Outer Space Treaty makes very little express provision for the protection of the environment.[11] In fact, one of its core underlying principles could be seen as providing a green light for the exploitation of space, rather than its preservation. Specifically, Article I(2) of the Outer Space Treaty refers to the principle of freedom of use and exploration of space.

---

6 Contrast Hobe (2019), pp. 88–90 with Stubbe (2018), p. 163.

7 See Chapter 1 (definition of 'space pollution'). See further, Stubbe (2018).

8 Yun Zhao, 'Space Commercialization and the Development of Space Law' (2018) *Oxford Research Encyclopedia of Planetary Science*, p. 1.

9 Viikari (2008), p. 58.

10 The Outer Space Treaty has 114 State Parties at the time of writing, including all space-faring States (see UN Doc. A/AC.105/C.2/2024/CRP.3; UNOOSA, Status of International Agreements relating to Activities in Outer Space, UNOOSA (available at: https://www.unoosa.org/oosa/en/ourwork/spacelaw/treaties/status/index.html)) and its content is largely based on the Declaration of Legal Principles Governing the Activities of States in the Exploration and Use of Outer Space, adopted by the United Nations General Assembly in its Resolution 1962 (XVIII).

11 Isabella Diederiks-Verschoor, 'Environmental Protection in Outer Space' (1987) 30 *German Yearbook of International Law* 144, cited in Zhao (2018), p. 10.

> Outer space, including the moon and other celestial bodies, shall be free for exploration and use by all States without discrimination of any kind, on a basis of equality and in accordance with international law, and there shall be free access to all areas of celestial bodies.

The Preamble to the Outer Space Treaty contains similar language. However, Article I(2) could also be read in a more environmentally protective way, namely, to mean that all space activities must be carried out with a view to ensuring that space remains free to access for future expeditions and activities. In this manner, it would require actors engaged in space activities to pay due heed to the environmental impact of their endeavours. That would be consistent with the context of the Outer Space Treaty, including Article IX. It would prioritize an *effet utile* interpretation in light of the object and purpose of the Outer Space Treaty, which is also evolving[12] in light of the modern situation of increasing numbers of satellites and space objects clogging up access to space and risking collisions and the exponential increase of space debris.[13] The core purpose of the Outer Space Treaty focuses on ensuring that the exploration and use of outer space remains the 'province of all mankind'. This could be significantly undermined if space becomes overcrowded with non-operational pieces of junk hurtling around at astronomic speeds, as access to space will become increasingly difficult and expensive, putting it out of reach of the vast majority of States, people, and organisations throughout the world.

Among the Outer Space Treaty's provisions, the most important potential basis for environmental protection is contained in Article IX.[14] This provision

12 On the evolving interpretation of provisions of international law, see ICJ, *Award in the Arbitration regarding the Iron Rhine ('Ijzeren Rijn') Railway (Belgium v. Netherlands)* ICJ Reports 2005, para. 80 (in addition to conceptual or generic terms, 'new technological developments' are subject to 'an evolutive interpretation, which would ensure an application of the treaty that would be effective in terms of its object and purpose'). See also ICJ, *In the Case concerning the Gabčikovo-Nagymaros Project (Hungary v. Slovakia)* ICJ Reports 1997, para. 112 ("By inserting these evolving provisions in the Treaty, the parties recognized the potential necessity to adapt the Project. Consequently, the Treaty is not static, and is open to adapt to emerging norms of international law. By means of Articles 15 and 19, new environmental norms can be incorporated in the Joint Contractual Plan.").

13 See Report of the Scientific and Technical Subcommittee on its 42nd session 2005, para. 97 (containing the proposal made in the deliberations of the UNCOPUOS that 'in order for States to continue having unrestricted access to outer space, all spacefaring nations should be implementing space debris mitigation measures as expeditiously as possible'); Viikari (2008), p. 59.

14 Viikari (2008), p. 59 ('Limitations on conducting space activities in environmental terms in particular are dealt with more directly in Article IX, which is the basic provision for all environmental protection of outer space.').

is designed to protect outer space and celestial bodies from harmful contamination and pollution while also protecting State's space exploration programs from undue interference.[15] Its full terms provide that:

> In the exploration and use of outer space, including the moon and other celestial bodies, States Parties to the Treaty shall be guided by the principle of co-operation and mutual assistance and shall conduct all their activities in outer space, including the moon and other celestial bodies, with due regard to the corresponding interests of all other States Parties to the Treaty. States Parties to the Treaty shall pursue studies of outer space, including the moon and other celestial bodies, and conduct exploration of them so *as to avoid their harmful contamination and also adverse changes in the environment of the Earth* resulting from the introduction of extraterrestrial matter and, where necessary, shall adopt appropriate measures for this purpose. If a State Party to the Treaty has reason to believe that an activity or experiment planned by it or its nationals in outer space, including the moon and other celestial bodies, would cause potentially harmful interference with activities of other States Parties in the peaceful exploration and use of outer space, including the moon and other celestial bodies, it shall undertake appropriate international consultations before proceeding with any such activity or experiment. A State Party to the Treaty which has reason to believe that an activity or experiment planned by another State Party in outer space, including the moon and other celestial bodies, would cause potentially harmful interference with activities in the peaceful exploration and use of outer space, including the moon and other celestial bodies, may request consultation concerning the activity or experiment.[16]

Article IX does not explicitly refer to space pollution or debris. Indeed, the Outer Space Treaty was 'negotiated and established before debris was recognized as a problem'.[17] Nonetheless, Article IX does prohibit '*harmful contamination*', which are the key words on which a prohibition of space pollution can be based.[18]

---

15 Paul G. Dembling and Daniel M. Arons, 'The Evolution of the Outer Space Treaty', *Journal of Air Law and Commerce* 33 (1967), p. 440.

16 Emphasis added.

17 Larsen (2018), p. 482.

18 Stubbe (2018), p. 163 (referring to 'the central question [of] whether space debris pollution of outer space can be characterized as a harmful contamination.'); Hobe (2019), p. 88; Howard A. Baker, 'Protection of the Outer Space Environment: History and Analysis of

The precise meaning of 'harmful contamination' remains unsettled. Some authors set out an abstract evaluation, noting simply that the threshold to be considered harmful must be set relatively high.[19] Others set out more concrete examples. Kramer, for example, argues that attempts of certain NSAs to build facilities on the Moon are likely to be perceived as 'harmful contamination' for the purposes of Article IX.[20] Baker does not define 'harmful contamination' but refers to four types of space debris in connection with his discussion of harmful contamination:

> inactive payloads (former payloads which can no longer be controlled by their operators), operational debris (objects associated with space activities, remaining in outer space), fragmentation debris (products of explosions and collisions) and microparticulate matter (a catch-all category including micro-sized objects, such as solid-propellant rocket motor effluent, paint flakes and thermal coatings, and spacecraft-induced phenomena such as outgassing of heavy molecules and space glow).[21]

Negotiators of the Outer Space Treaty considered that the treaty's prime objective was the effective utilization of outer space. Given that view, it could be argued that any environmental protection provided by the Outer Space Treaty would merely be a 'fortuitous by-product'.[22] Reportedly, the US 'West Ford Experiment' (a military experiment in the 1960s in which millions of copper dipoles were placed in orbit in an attempt to allow long distance communications by bouncing radio waves off them) prompted the 'harmful contamination' formulation of Article IX.[23] Because of fears of cutting off access to space, the wording of Article IX stresses the obligation to pay due regard to

---

Article IX of the Outer Space Treaty' (1987) 12 *Annals of Air and Space Law*, p. 158; Viikari (2008), p. 50; Stephen Gorove, 'Pollution and Outer Space: A Legal Analysis and Appraisal' (1972) 5 *NYU Journal of International Law and Politics*, pp. 55–56.

19 Gordon Chung, 'The Emergence of Environmental Protection Clauses in Outer Space Treaty: A Lesson from the Rio Principles' (2018) in Annette Froehlich (ed.), *A Fresh View on the Outer Space Treaty* (Springer, 2018), pp. 3–5. See also Zwart et. al., pp. 301–302 ('concerns of harmful contamination that were raised during the drafting process [of the Outer Space Treaty] were largely theoretical. States persistently chose not to engage with the question of what contamination would be considered harmful').

20 William R. Kramer, 'In dreams begin responsibilities – environmental impact assessment and outer space development' (2017) 19 *Environmental Practice*, p. 132.

21 Howard A. Baker, *Space Debris: Legal and Policy Implications* (Nijhoff, 1989) pp. 3–9.

22 Baker (1987), pp. 163, 166, 167.

23 Marchisio (2009), pp. 169–183.

the interests of other States and avoid 'interference' with their interests, rather than protection of the outer space environment *per se*.[24]

Nonetheless, the fact that Article IX uses the word 'contamination' signals a bifurcated scope of protection. It encompasses both the prohibition of harm to the outer space environment (and backwards contamination of Earth) and the obligation for States to avoid restricting others' access to outer space, which they enact through measures such as consultation when their activities or experiments could interfere with other State Parties' space operations. Encompassed within the obligation to pay 'due regard' is the responsibility to 'avoid creating hazards that could adversely affect the safe conduct of space activities by other states', such as space pollution.[25] Moreover, access to space and space pollution are inherently interconnected. As set out above, if the current production of space debris continues unchecked, then the freedom to use and explore outer space (the main objective of the Outer Space Treaty)[26] will be rendered extremely dangerous and difficult, if not impossible.[27] By guaranteeing free exploration and use, the Outer Space Treaty places the same obligation on States to keep outer space in a condition that permits free exploration and use, in line with the object and purpose of this treaty.[28]

Bearing in mind the range of opinions on the interpretation of Article IX of the Outer Space Treaty, it is nonetheless clear that pollution in space would constitute 'harmful contamination', so long as more than merely *de minimis* or negligible.[29]

---

24 Marchisio (2014), pp. 172–173.

25 See Hobe, 'Handbook' (2019), pp. 729–730; Giulia Pavesi, 'Legal Consequences of Environmental Pollution in Outer Space' (2018) in Froehlich (2018), pp. 21–22.

26 Baker (1987), pp. 163, 166, 167; Larsen (2018), p. 484 (Article I of the Outer Space Treaty, which provides that outer space is the province of all mankind where free utilization without discrimination of any kind must be guaranteed and therefore indicates that 'continued deposits of space debris that may preclude access to outer space would be contrary to [its terms]').

27 See Cirkovic (2022), p. 1080.

28 Marietta Benkö, Kai-Uwe Schrogl, Denise Digrell, Esther Jolley, *Space Law: Current Problems and Perspectives for Future Regulation* (Eleven International Publishing, 2005), p. 226; Philip De Mann, Ward Munters, 'Reciprocal Limits to the Freedom to Use Outer Space by All States: Common but Differentiated Responsibilities?' (2018) 43 *Air and Space Law*, p. 1; Timiebi Aganaba-Jeanty, 'Space Sustainability and the Freedom of Outer Space' (2018) 14 *Astropolitics: The International Journal of Space Politics and Policy*, p. 5.

29 See, e.g. Stubbe (2018), p. 163; Layachi (2020); Annette Froehlich and Vincent Seffinga, *National Space Legislation* (Springer, 2018), p. 90; Ram S. Jakhu, Joseph N. Pelton, *Global Space Governance: An International Study* (Springer, 2017), p. 436; George T. Hacket, *Space Debris and the Corpus Iuris Spatialis* (Gif-sur-Yvette: Editions Frontières, 1994), p. 115; Anja Nakarada Peculjic, Matteo Tugnoli, *Promoting Productive Cooperation Between*

However, other interpretive issues also arise from this provision in relation to harm to Earth's environment. First, Article IX refers explicitly to adverse changes resulting from the introduction of extraterrestrial matter. This is termed backward pollution, as it involves bringing back harmful elements from space into Earth's environment.[30] That differs from forward pollution, which is harmful material brought by humans from Earth into space.[31]

Another textual feature of this provision is that Article IX refers explicitly to avoiding harmful contamination in 'studies' and 'the exploration' of outer space, but does not explicitly extend this prohibition to its 'use'.[32] Space pollution often arises from activities such as launching satellites and sending testing equipment to the moon or Mars, which do not necessarily constitute 'exploration' in the sense of searching for new unexplored areas. For commercial activities by NSAs in particular, the label of exploration will often not be the most fitting. Profit-seeking companies will instead look to exploit outer space and celestial bodies to generate income. Given that those activities will raise risks of accidental or purposeful creation of space debris, this interpretive issue is of potential future consequence for any legal proceedings based thereon. It places a significant doubt over the utility of Article IX to found a prohibition against space pollution.

In light of the context, object and purpose of the Outer Space Treaty, the term 'exploration' in Article IX can be interpreted in a broad manner, to encompass activities in general.[33] That interpretation is available on the basis of the text alone. Activities in space have traditionally been referred to with the language of exploration, as immortalized in the phrase 'space, the final frontier'.

Lawyers and Engineers (IGI Global 2019), p. 188. By contrast, see Joanne Wheeler, 'Space Debris: Legal Framework, Issues Arising and New ISO Guidelines in 2010/2011' (2013) *Yearbook on Space Policy 2010/2011*; Peter Hulsroj, Spyros Pagkratis, Blandina Baranes (eds.), *The Forward Look* (Springer), p. 256; Fawaz Haroun, Shalom Ajibade, Philip Oladimeji, and John Kennedy Igbozurike, 'Toward the Sustainability of Outer Space: Addressing the Issue of Space Debris' (2021) 9 *New Space* 1, p. 69. See also Chapter 5 containing national legislation supporting this interpretation, e.g. Austria, Outer Space Act, para. 4(1)(4) and (5) – authorization procedures require operators to ensure precautions for the avoidance of harmful contamination of outer space by space debris (summarized in Martha Mejia-Kaiser, *The Geostationary Ring: Practice and Law* (Martinus Nijhoff Publishers, 2020), p. 217).

30 Zwart et. al. (2021), p. 277.

31 Viviana Iavicoli, 'The legal regime of outer space in light of the Law of the Sea' (2015) in Salvatore Aricò (ed.) *Ocean Sustainability in the 21st Century* (Cambridge University Press, 2015), p. 258; Viikari (2008), p. 50; Zwart et. al (2021), p. 277.

32 Radi (2023), pp. 6–7.

33 See Stubbe (2018), p. 154.

The term 'astronaut' harks back to the Greek tale of Jason and the argonauts, which is a story of exploration. Second, a broad reading of 'exploration' aligns with the purpose of the Outer Space Treaty (because avoiding harming outer space in all activities ensures that it remains pristine and accessible for all other States Parties), which is a requisite consideration under Article 31(1) of the Vienna Convention on the Law of Treaties.[34]

However, an argument could be made that this broad reading of 'exploration' would clash with the other terms of the Outer Space Treaty, as provisions such as Article VI refer to 'activities' in space. If the drafters had wanted 'exploration' to cover all space activities they could have used that wider term. Nonetheless, the context signals that a broad reading of the terms 'studies' and 'exploration' should be preferred; the second sentence of Article IX adds to the due regard principle in the first sentence, which covers all activities in space, and the context does not provide a strong indication that it was meant to be restricted to the mapping out of space for its discovery, and instead was meant to encompass a range of human activities in space.[35]

There is a further question regarding the requirement that State Parties 'shall adopt appropriate measures for this purpose [avoiding harmful contamination]'.[36] The term 'appropriate' is a wide and malleable one, which could invite self-serving interpretations by States looking to minimize their responsibility and maximize their range of maneuver. However, an interpretation in line with the *effet utile* approach would see the term 'appropriate' given an objective meaning – namely the proportionate measures objectively required to address the harm, rather than what a State claims it subjectively considered appropriate in the circumstances.

Additionally, Article IX imposes an obligation on State Parties to adhere to the principle of cooperation and mutual assistance when conducting exploration and use of outer space. This expands on the direct obligation to avoid harmful contamination and provides a strong basis to read Article IX as requiring States to communicate and coordinate when a risk of harmful contamination arises.[37] Additionally, the 1968 Rescue Agreement, the 1972 Liability Convention, and the 1975 Registration Convention provide useful tools for regulating international cooperation during space activities, which will be useful

34 Vienna Convention on the Law of Treaties, 23 May 1969, 1155 UNTS 331 (entered into force on 27 January 1980).

35 Stubbe (2018), pp. 154–155.

36 Radi (2023), p. 7.

37 Viikari (2008), pp. 59–60.

for space environment remediation efforts, but do not contain protections for the space environment *per se*.

Complimentary to Article IX are Articles I and II of the Outer Space Treaty, which specify that exploration and use of outer space shall be free to all States and shall be the province of all mankind. Importantly, Article II provides that '[o]uter space, including the moon and other celestial bodies, is not subject to national appropriation by claim of sovereignty, by means of use or occupation, or by any other means.' These two provisions together designate outer space as *res communis*.[38] In this way, the outer space environment, including on celestial bodies, can be seen as protected by existing space law insofar as its protection is necessary to ensure humankind's access to as well as the use and exploration of outer space.[39] Although causing space pollution, such as through space debris, would not naturally constitute appropriation, the broader message of protecting the accessibility of space and avoiding its cluttering with anthropogenic matter is consistent with the approaches taken above.[40]

Separately, Article IV, forbids the stationing of 'any objects carrying nuclear weapons or any other kinds of weapons of mass destruction' in outer space and provides that the Moon and other celestial bodies are reserved for 'exclusively peaceful purposes', thereby banning all military activity on celestial bodies at least. By prohibiting a major potential source of pollution, Article IV provides a measure of indirect protection for the space environment. However, the prohibition centres on the weapons per se, and any benefits for the space environment are only incidental to that aim.

In addition to the Outer Space Treaty, the Moon Agreement has potentially relevant provisions concerning a prohibition of space pollution, including

38 Hobe (2019); Shaw (2008); von der Dunk (2015a), pp. 55–60. See also, Chapter 2, Section 1.2 below.

39 Viikari (2008), p. 59 ('preservation of the space environment can be regarded as a basic condition for guaranteeing equal opportunities in exploration and use by all countries.').

40 In other words, should debris rise to the level where it is obstructing free access, exploration and use of outer space it could be considered as violating not only the freedoms from Article I of the Outer Space Treaty, but also the prohibition on national appropriation from Article II of the Outer Space Treaty. For example, due to Article VIII of the Outer Space Treaty granting States that nationally register launched objects, jurisdiction over these and any personnel thereof and as furthermore this jurisdiction does not depend on functionality of an object (See Chapter 3, Section 1 below) an abandoned registered object could not lawfully be removed without the respective State's consent. If the State would be unwilling to grant consent or remove the object itself, this would mean that the object was permanently possessing a part of outer space (such as for example surface area of celestial bodies or an orbital position) thus resulting in de-facto appropriation of outer space, see Sancin, Grünfeld, Ramuš Cvetkovič (2021), pp. 22–25.

explicit references to preserving the Moon's environment. It provides in Article 4(1) that' due regard shall be paid to the interests of present and future generations' and in Article 7(1) that '[i]n exploring and using the Moon, States Parties shall take measures to prevent the disruption of the existing balance of its environment, whether by introducing adverse changes in that environment, by its harmful contamination through the introduction of extra-environmental matter or other-wise.' Moreover, it reiterates the Outer Space Treaty requirement that the Moon be used for peaceful, non-military purposes only.[41]

These provisions are consistent with an interpretation of space law which precludes space pollution. In this light, the Moon Agreement has been described as 'the most advanced of the space treaties in an environmental sense.'[42] Indeed, its protections are formulated in a broader and more concrete way in comparison to the Outer Space Treaty. However, the Moon Agreement (likewise) does not have any sanctions provisions.[43] Moreover, due to its low ratification status, the Moon Agreement is currently of limited legal weight.[44] It had only 17 ratifications as of January 2024, with leading space-faring countries not among them. Nonetheless, it entered into force in July 1984 when Austria became the fifth State to ratify the Agreement.

Beyond the Outer Space Treaty and the Moon Agreement, there is the Liability Convention. Article XXI of the Liability Convention refers to damage caused by space objects constituting 'a large-scale danger to human life' or threatening to seriously interfere with 'the living conditions of the population or the functioning of vital centres'. These terms could cover environmental destruction, whether anthropocentric or due to natural disasters.[45] However, the interpretation is not beyond debate, and its reference to 'damage' could also be seen as related primarily to matters of harm to anthropogenic objects or possessions. Indeed, Articles III and IV of the Liability Convention indicate that the damage has to be inflicted on the space object of a launching State, or persons or objects aboard, (unless it occurs on the surface of the Earth).[46]

41 Article 3.1.

42 Viikari (2008), p. 62.

43 Viikari (2008), p. 63.

44 Antonella Bini, 'The Moon Agreement: Its effectiveness in the 21st century' (2008) 14 *European Space Policy Institute Perspectives* 14, pp. 1–7. See also von der Dunk (2015a), pp. 99–100, where the author assessed that the provisions of the Moon Agreement in this particular context are not particularly controversial.

45 Viikari (2008), p. 69.

46 This also raises the question of whether objects that are not 'launched' from Earth but are created in space are covered by the Liability Convention, which primarily places liability on the 'launching State'; see Ziemblicki and Oralova, pp. 2–3.

Under Article I, the extent of damage covered does not refer to the environmental harm, but could potentially encompass facets of the environment as 'property' of States. Where such property is covered by these provisions, this could provide indirect protection to the environment. Indeed, collisions in space, for example, will result in space debris and thereby impact the outer space environment.[47]

Amongst the other international space law treaties, there is little that could be construed as a direct prohibition of space pollution. The 1963 Partial (Nuclear) Test Ban Treaty is the most relevant, as it removes a major source of potential space pollution by banning nuclear tests in the atmosphere. However, it is focused on the nuclear explosion rather than environmental pollution per se, and only provides incidental protection for the space environment.

When interpreting the Outer Space Treaty and other international treaties, it is useful to look at subsequent agreements, soft law, and domestic laws, which provide context for the interpretation of the articles of the Outer Space Treaty.[48] As detailed in Chapter 5, Germany, United States, Canada and the Russian Federation, for example, have explicit national policies focused on mitigation of space debris.[49] Similarly, the European Space Agency (ESA) 'Space Debris Mitigation Policy for Agency Projects' generally requires all ESA projects to limit space pollution.[50] Another example is provided by international standards, like the ISO Standards,[51] and Radiocommunication Sector of the International Telecommunication Union (ITU), Recommendation on the 'Environmental Protection of the Geostationary-Satellite Orbit' of 2004, and the IADC and UNCOPUOS SDMG.[52] These instruments essentially aim

47 Chapter 1, Section 3.

48 For more see P.J. Blount, 'Renovating Space: The Future of International Space Law' (2011) 40(1) *Denver Journal of International Law and Policy*.

49 See Compendium on Space Debris Mitigation Standards Adopted by States and International Organizations, 8 April 2021.

50 European Space Agency Director General's Office (2014), *Space Debris Mitigation Policy for Agency* Projects, ESA/ADMIN/IPOL(2014).

51 See International Organization for Standardization (ISO) issuance ISO 24113:2023 'Space systems – Space debris mitigation requirements'. See also Compendium (2021).

52 However, SDMG explicitly address States, urging them to formulate national mechanisms to control NSAs (space activity operators), see Committee on the Peaceful Uses of Outer Space, *Space Debris Mitigation Guidelines of the Committee on the Peaceful Uses of Outer Space*, UN Doc. ST/SPACE/49 (2010), Point 3, p. 2, declares: 'Member States and international organizations should voluntarily take measures, through national mechanisms or through their own applicable mechanisms, to ensure that these guidelines are implemented, to the greatest extent feasible, through space debris mitigation practices and procedures'. However, the content and rationale of the SDMG is the minimization and mitigation of space debris emission during normal space operations and therefore seem

to mitigate the proliferation of space debris by providing technical standards to minimize its generation during normal operations and removing inactive spacecraft from usable orbits.[53] In 2021, a reported 35 States explicitly expressed that they adhere or would adhere to the SDMG and other international standards relating to space debris mitigation.[54] In 2021, approximately 18 States had national laws which included space debris or environmental provisions.[55] This relatively widespread practice among the most active space-faring nations supports the interpretation of Article IX's 'harmful contamination' as entailing a prohibition on space pollution (or at least excessive space pollution), as further detailed in Chapter 5.

UN General Assembly (UNGA) declarations or recommendations[56] concerning national legislation relevant to the peaceful exploration and use of outer space can be indicative of the subsequent interpretation of hard law obligations. Importantly, States' contributions to these instruments can also provide evidence of *opinio juris*[57] and potentially State practice,[58] which are the building blocks of customary international law. Adopted without a negative vote, in 2013 the UN General Assembly noted in Resolution 68/74 the 'need to maintain

---

to be addressed to the space activity operator, often a private actor, see SDMG, Point 4, p. 2: 'The following guidelines should be considered for the mission planning, design, manufacture and operational (launch, mission and disposal) phases of spacecraft and launch vehicle orbital stages'. This is supported by national legislation incorporating SDMG. On this basis, the SDMG in part address space activity operators, whether States or NSAs, and Point 3 of the SDMG simply obliges States and international organizations to ensure SDMG application. Up to date, several States have incorporated SDMG into national legislation, See, e.g., Finland Space Act; Austrian Space Act; French Space Act (all detailed in Chapter 5).

53 See IADC (2007). However, experts warn that even with full observance of SDMG, mitigation efforts will not be sufficient to resolve the issue if we keep to the *status quo* (see European Space Agency, *Space debris mitigation: the case for a code of conduct* (*available at* https://www.esa.int/Enabling_Support/Operations/Space_debris_mitigation_the_case_for_a_code_of_conduct) *and* space debris remediation, or the active removal of debris, would be required, which however faces legal obstacles (for more see: Annette Froehlich, *Space Security And Legal Aspects of Active Debris Removal* (Springer, 2019)).

54 See Compendium (2021).

55 See Compendium (2021). See also Zhao (2018), p. 4. However, not all of the space faring States require private entities conducting space exploration from their territories to take on environmental protection obligations in order to be licensed; Marboe and Hafner in von der Dunk (1992), p. 63 (Table 1).

56 ICJ, *Legality of the Threat or Use of Nuclear Weapons,* Advisory Opinion of 8 July 1996 (I.C.J Reports 1996, p. 226), paras. 68–70.

57 ICJ, Nicaragua, paras. 188, 191.

58 Hilary Charlesworth, 'Customary International Law and the Nicaragua Case', (1984–87) 11 *Australian Year Book of International Law*, p. 24. But see Öberg (2005), pp. 899–900.

the sustainable use of outer space, in particular by mitigating space debris, and to ensure the safety of space activities and minimize the potential harm to the environment'.[59] Similarly, UNGA Resolution 73/91 from 2018 in its preamble notes that space debris plays a significant role in the fragility of the outer space environment.[60] Other instruments, such as the UNCOPUOS Guidelines for the Long-term Sustainability of Outer Space Activities provide strong hortatory support for a prohibition (and make explicit reference to NSAs), but are not binding in a strictly legal sense.[61]

From these materials, it can be concluded that space law prohibits the pollution of the outer space environment. However, that claim is not beyond dispute, as the relevant provisions and instruments are not as explicit and definitive as well-established interdicts under international law.[62] The leading provision of international space law remains Article IX of the Outer Space Treaty. Its reference to 'harmful contamination' can encompass anthropogenic pollution in space which meets the threshold of 'harm'. UN issuances, such as Resolution 68/74 support the conclusion that space pollution is prohibited. Nonetheless, the genesis of Article IX of the Outer Space Treaty and the lack of consistent State practice condemning space pollution means that the extent of the conventional basis for a prohibition of space pollution will continue to be contested as long as it is not explicitly spelt out in an international convention.

In this light, it is apposite to look beyond international space law and survey international environmental law to discern whether and how it further supports a prohibition against space pollution under international law.

1.2 *Does International Environmental Law Prohibit Space Pollution?*

Having examined whether a prohibition of causing space pollution can be found in space law, the survey now expands to address whether causing harmful pollution in space would violate existing principles of international environmental law. Although the Outer Space Treaty was negotiated before a majority of the environmental law instruments were adopted, Article III of the Outer Space Treaty provides that State Parties involved in the exploration and

59 See: UN General Assembly Resolution A/RES/68/74, adopted on 11 December 2013 (available at https://www.unoosa.org/oosa/oosadoc/data/resolutions/2013/general_assembly_68th_session/ares6874.html).

60 UN General Assembly Resolution A/RES/73/91, adopted on 18 December 2018; Cirkovic (2022), p. 6.

61 UNCOPUOS, Guidelines for the Long-term Sustainability of Outer Space Activities, UN Doc. A/AC.105/2018/CRP.20 (28th June 2018), para.15.

62 For example, the prohibition of genocide is emphatic and detailed. See Genocide Convention, Article 1.

use of outer space shall do so in accordance with 'international law, including the Charter of the United Nations, in the interest of maintaining international peace and security and promoting international cooperation and understanding'.[63] Consequently, Article III provides a basis for the integration of the broader framework of international law as a relevant set of regulatory conditions which are applicable to space activities.[64]

Because Article III ensures that the Outer Space Treaty framework is not a hermetically-sealed 'self-contained regime',[65] it should be interpreted in line with, and as complemented by, international law. Accordingly, rules of general international law, including customary international law particularly customary international environmental law,[66] can be used to interpret the meaning of

---

63 Experts, however, diverge on the question whether Article III imports all relevant provisions and principles of international law and generally divide into two potential interpretations. A natural reading is that Outer Space Treaty Article III neither expands nor restricts existing international law, but simply holds that States must carry out activities under Outer Space Treaty without violating international law. That means that, for example, if an existing international obligation is limited to Earth, or a specific area thereof, then that obligation is not transposed to outer space by the Outer Space Treaty. An alternative reading is that Article III of the Outer Space Treaty automatically transposes obligations under international law to the outer space environment. Thus, the Basel Convention on movement of toxic goods would automatically apply to activities in space, irrespective of definitions in the Basel Convention as to its ambit of application. Dennerley (2018) writes in favour of this alternative reading: 'Article III provides for the inclusion of customary rules of international law relating to state liability and state responsibility as elements of the regime of space law.' Several other authors support such a view; Sergio Marchisio, 'The ITU Regulatory System: a Self-Contained Regime or a Part of International Law?' (2014) in Guilhem Penent (ed.) *Governing the Geostationary Orbit Orbital Slots and Spectrum Use in an Era of Interference* (Space Policy Programme, 2014), pp. 75, 78; Stephan Hobe and Erik Pellander, 'Space Law: A 'Self-Contained Regime?' (2012) in Stephan Hobe, Steven Freeland (eds.) *In Heaven as on Earth? The Interaction of Public International Law on the Legal Regulation of Outer Space* (Bonn: Institute of Air and Space Law of the University of Cologne, 2012), p. 7.

64 Olivier Ribbelink, 'Article III' (2009) in Stephan Hobe, Bernhard Schmidt-Tedd, Kai-Uwe Schrogl, Gérardine Meishan Goh (eds.) *The Cologne Commentary on Space Law*: Vol. I (Carl Heymanns, 2009), pp. 64–70.

65 Marchisio (2014), pp. 75, 78; Hobe, Pellander (2012), p. 7; Hobe (2019), pp. 53–55.

66 See Fawaz Haroun, Shalom Ajibade, Philip Oladimeji, John Kennedy Igbozurike, 'Toward the Sustainability of Outer Space: Addressing the Issue of Space Debris', (2012) 9:1 *New Space*, 63–71 ('In recognition of the importance of space being a common heritage of mankind, a proper legal regime should extend the environmental law principles applicable on Earth to space. This should include the precautionary principle, the polluter-pays principle, the transboundary harm principle, environmental impact assessment, among others.'); Brunner and Soucek, Outer Space in Society (2011), p. 382; Viikari (2008), pp. 119–206.

space law provisions and to fill lacunae in the coverage of space law.[67] In the words of Pierfrancesco Breccia

> it is without any doubt that a substantial part of international law and the UN Charter apply to human activities in outer space. Furthermore, [through] [A]rticle III, developments in international law, such as new international agreements, rules of customary law or new interpretations of the provisions of the UN Charter, which are compatible with the peculiarity of the space activities, can be extended to the use of outer space.[68]

The phrase 'in accordance with' in Article III provides a basis to interpret the Outer Space Treaty's consistently with international law more broadly.[69] Further, it also potentially permits other principles and facets of international law to be read into the treaty, to complement the provisions of the Outer Space Treaty.[70] This later reading of Article III would build on the interpretive approach of systemic integration of international space law with other branches of international law.[71] However, that reading, which would effectively incorporate by reference general international law into the Treaty's framework,

---

67 Ribbelink (2009), pp. 64–65; Hobe (2019), pp. 53–56; Lachs (2010), pp. 11–17; Fogo (2017), p. 197; Lyall and Larsen, pp. 39–43.

68 Pierfrancesco Breccia, 'Article III of the Outer Space Treaty and Its Relevance in the International Space Legal Framework' (2016) in 67th International Astronautical Congress (IAC), pp. 1, 3.

69 For a discussion of systemic integration, whereby treaty provisions are interpreted consistently with the broader framework of international law; see Campbell McLachlan KC, *The Principle of Systemic Integration in International Law* (2024; online edn, Oxford Academic); Campbell McLachlan, 'The Principle of Systemic Integration and Article 31(3) (C) of the Vienna Convention', *International and Comparative Law Quarterly*, 54 (2005), p. 318.

70 Note that there is a difference between the phrase 'in accordance with' in Article III of the Outer Space Treaty and 'apply' in Article 21 of the Rome Statute of the ICC. Whereas the latter explicitly empowers the ICC to rely on external legal sources beyond the Rome Statute (and Elements of Crimes and Rules of Procedure), the former is more ambiguous and is arguably oriented towards interpreting in light of international law rather than importing external legal sources to substantively rely on *per se*.

71 Concerning systemic integration, see McLachlan (2024); Lauren Nishimura, *Adaptation and Anticipatory Action: Integrating Human Rights Duties into the Climate Change Regime* (Brill, 2022) (which seeks to systemically integrate IHRL obligations into a key area of IEL); Karen Hulme, 'Using International Environmental Law to Enhance Biodiversity and Nature Conservation During Armed Conflict', (2022) 20 *Journal of International Criminal Justice*, pp. 1155–1190 (which conducts a rule-by-rule and treaty-by-treaty assessment of the complementary aspects of these two branches for the protection of the environment during armed conflict).

relies on an expansive reading of Article III's terms. That interpretation is contestable, as the terms do not go as far as explicitly saying that broader international law may be applied via Article III of the Treaty.[72] Irrespective of which approach is taken, Article III facilitates a harmonious approach, which has the benefit of bringing different sub-branches of international law closer together and mitigating the fragmentation of international law.[73]

The most dynamic source of international law that may apply to activities in outer space is that of customary international law.[74] Customary international law imports a broad array of principles and rules to complement the provisions of the Outer Space Treaty framework.[75] Breccia argues that several key principles of international environmental law are relevant to space activities, namely 'prevention and precaution', 'environmental impact assessments', 'access to information', 'participation in the decision-making process', and 'common but differentiated responsibilities'.[76] He acknowledges that one cannot begin with the assumption that all environmental principles are 'indiscriminately' applicable to space activities and instead asserts that that it is necessary to assess the environmental principles' applicability from both a technical-scientific standpoint and from a strictly legal perspective, and to discern whether any of the principles need adaption to apply in the space environment.[77] Accordingly,

72 This contrasts with Article 21 of the Rome Statute of the International Criminal Court, for example, which explicitly allows the Court to apply exogenous facets of international law, such as customary and conventional international humanitarian law.

73 International Law Commission (2006), *Report of the ILC to the fifty-eight session of the General Assembly*, A/61/10 [Fragmentation Report], paras. 36, 488; Anne Peters, 'The refinement of international law: From fragmentation to regime interaction and politicization' (2017) 15(3) *International Journal of Constitutional Law*, pp. 690, 692, 702. For more on the role of *lex specialis* in combating fragmentation of international law regarding the regulation of space activities see Iva Ramuš Cvetkovič, *Space law as lex specialis to international law* (Master Thesis) (2021) (University of Ljubljana, Faculty of Law) (available at https://repozitorij.uni-lj.si/IzpisGradiva.php?id=130477&lang=eng).

74 Breccia (2016), p. 8.

75 Breccia, (2016) 'Article III of the Outer Space Treaty and Its Relevance in the International Space Legal Framework', 67th International Astronautical Congress (IAC), 2016, p. 3 ('In this sense, although every field of international relations would be regulated most directly by its *lex specialis*, it does not mean that a significant part of international law, such as rules of customary international law and general principles of international law, are not applicable generally.'). See also Lachs (2010), p. 11–17.

76 Breccia (2016), p. 8. See also Viikari (2008), pp. 22–23.

77 Breccia (2016), p. 8. An example of a principle potentially requiring adaptation is that of common-but-differentiated responsibilities, given that some States have simply no space program whatsoever; see below Chapter 5.

this analysis will survey those international environmental law principles to discern their application to the space environment.

To assess the applicability of customary international environmental law, it is necessary to know whether outer space qualifies as part of the 'natural environment'. However, there are multiple definitions of the term 'natural environment', some of which do not cover outer space. Whereas the International Law Commission (ILC) appears to limit its enumerated definition to the earth, seas and the atmosphere (and elements therein), it does allow for the natural environment to extend to 'where the human race develops'.[78] The Partial or Limited Nuclear Test Ban Treaty lists outer space as 'man's environment'.[79] The United Nations body UNCOPUOS reports routinely refer to the 'space environment',[80] and several other organizations refer routinely to the 'space environment'.[81] The Council of Europe included outer space in its definition of the 'human environment'.[82] Moreover, in 2021, an Independent Expert Panel released a definition of ecocide for consideration by the States Parties to the ICC in which it defined the environment to mean 'the earth, its biosphere,

---

78 Draft Code of Crimes Against the Peace and Security of Mankind, *Yearbook of the International Law Commission* (1991), p. 107, para. 4 reads 'the words 'natural environment' should be taken broadly to cover the environment of the human race and where the human race develops, as well as areas the preservation of which is of fundamental importance in protecting the environment. These words therefore cover the seas, the atmosphere, climate, forests, and other plant cover, fauna, flora and other biological elements.'.

79 Treaty Banning Nuclear Weapon Tests in the Atmosphere, 5 August 1963, 480 UNTS 43 (entered into force on 10 October 1963), see Article I: 'in Outer Space and Under Water'.

80 See, e.g., United Nations General Assembly (2006), *Report of the Committee on the Peaceful Uses of Outer Space*, A/61/20, p. 19, where it is stated that 'Efforts should continue to be made to devise the technical ability to begin removing existing space debris from their orbits in order to halt the decline in the space environment.'; Guidelines for the Long-term Sustainability of Outer Space Activities, UN COPUOS, UN Doc. A/AC.105/2018/CRP.20 (27th June 2018); UNGA Resolution, UN Doc. A/RES/77/120 (15th December 2022); UNGA Resolution, UN Doc. A/RES/77/121 (15th December 2022); UNGA Resolution, UN Doc. A/RES/73/6 (31st October 2018); UNCOPUOS Report, UN Doc. A/77/20 (30th June 2022).

81 For example, the European Space Policy Institute, see Space Environment Capacity, ESPI Report 82 (April 2022); European Space Agency, see ESA's Annual Space Environment Report, ESA Space Debris Office Report (22nd April 2022); Thomas Colvin, John Karcz, and Grace Wusk, 'Cost and Benefit Analysis of Orbital Debris Remediation' NASA Office of Technology, Policy, and Strategy Report (10 March 2023) (available at https://www.nasa.gov/wp-content/uploads/2023/03/otps_-_cost_and_benefit_analysis_of_orbital_debris_remediation_-_final.pdf).

82 See Council of Europe, Model Act on the Protection of the Environment 1994, Dela/Model Act (94)1, Article 1(b)(i).

cryosphere, lithosphere, hydrosphere and atmosphere, as well as outer space.'[83] As for scholarly works, notable authors on space law, such as Hobe and Stubbe, refer to outer space as part of the environment, using such phrases as 'space environment'.[84] A broader approach is suggested by Marie-Louise Larsson who addresses the environment in a far-reaching way, including 'all those elements which in their complex interrelationships form the framework, setting and living conditions for mankind, by their very existence or by virtue of their impact'.[85]

In light of the multiple ways in which outer space can be included in the definition of the 'natural environment', this article proceeds on the basis that outer space can be encompassed by that term and that international environmental law principles are potentially applicable to outer space pursuant to Article III of the Outer Space Treaty. At the same time, these international environmental law principles must be applied subject to any necessary adjustments in light of the differing considerations arising from the terrestrial and spatial settings.

With those preliminary issues addressed, there are several established principles of international environmental law which could impact on the prohibition of space pollution. The following environmental principles are those considered to have the greatest potential application to human activities in outer space.

1.2.1 No-Harm Principle

Of primary importance to space pollution is the 'no harm' principle.[86] This was famously set down in the *Trail Smelter*

83 Independent Expert Panel, *Definition of Ecocide*, June 2021 (https://www.stopecocide.earth/legal-definition).

84 See, e.g., Hobe (2019); Stubbe (2018); Viikari (2008); Dennerley (2018); Tateo Goka, 'The Space Environment: Natural and Induced' (2009) in Gary Eugene Musgrave, Axel (Skip) M. Larsen, Tommaso Sgobba (Eds.) *Safety Design for Space System* (Butterworth-Heinemann, 2009); Annette Froehlich (ed.), *Space Resource Utilization A View from an Emerging Space Faring Nation*, (ESPI/Springer, 2018); Isabella Diederiks-Verschoor and Vladimir Kopal, *An Introduction to Space Law* (3rd Revised Version) (Wolters Kluwer International, 2008); Philip De Man, The Commercial Exploitation of Outer Space and Celestial Bodies – A Functional Solution to the Natural Resource Challenge, in Mark J Sundahl and V Gopalakrishnan (eds) *New Perspectives on Space Law* (International Institute of Space Law, 2011).

85 Marie-Louise Larsson, 'Legal Definitions of the Environment and of Environmental Damage' (1999) *Scandinavian Studies in Law* (available at https://www.scandinavianlaw.se/pdf/38-7.pdf), p. 156.

86 Stubbe (2018), p. 168.

arbitration.[87] Thereafter, it has been repeated by international courts, including the International Court of Justice.[88] This can be seen as closely related to the prevention principle.[89] It is also reflected in the Stockholm declaration and the Rio Declaration,[90] such as Rio Principle 2, which provides that 'States have, [...] the responsibility to ensure that activities within their jurisdiction or control do not cause damage to the environment of other States or of areas beyond the limits of national jurisdictions.'

Under the 'no harm' principle, States must ensure that activities within their jurisdiction do not cause significant environmental damage outside their jurisdiction.[91] The International Court of Justice has confirmed that, under this international obligation, States must ensure that activities within their jurisdiction and control respect the environment of other States or of areas beyond national control.[92] The 'no harm' principle is violated when the damage reaches the threshold of *significant harm*, as determined by the International Law Commission in its Draft Articles on the Prevention of Transboundary Harm from Hazardous Activities.[93] In this regard, *harm* encompasses 'harm caused to persons, property or the environment'.[94] The term

---

87 *Trail Smelter Arbitration* (*USA v. Canada*), Decision of 16 April 1938, published in: 33 *American Journal of International Law* 1, 1938 ('*Trail Smelter Arbitration*'), p. 182; and *Trail Smelter Arbitration* (*USA v. Canada*), Decision of 11 March 1941 ('*Trail Smelter Arbitration2*'), Published in 35 *American Journal of International Law* 4, 1941, p. 716.

88 See ICJ, *Corfu Channel Case* (U.K. v. Albania), Judgment of 15 December 1948 (ICJ Reports 1948, p. 15).

89 See ICJ, *Pulp Mills on the River Uruguay* (Argentina v. Uruguay), Judgment of 20 April 2010 (ICJ Reports 2010, p. 14), para. 101 ('The Court points out that the principle of prevention, as a customary rule, has its origins in the due diligence that is required of a State in its territory. It is "every State's obligation not to allow knowingly its territory to be used for acts contrary to the rights of other States" (Corfu. Channel (United Kingdom v. Albania), Merits, Judgment, I.C.J. Reports 1949, p. 22). A State is thus obliged to use all the means at its disposal in order to avoid activities which take place in its territory, or in any area under its jurisdiction, causing significant damage to the environment of another State. This Court has established that this obligation "is now part of the corpus of international law relating to the environment" (Legality of the Threat or Use of Nuclear Weapons, Advisory Opinion, I.C.J. Reports 1996 (I), p. 242, para. 29).').

90 Radi (2023), p. 7.

91 *Trail Smelter Arbitration 2.*

92 ICJ, *Legality of the Threat or Use of Nuclear Weapons*, Advisory Opinion of 8 July 1996 (ICJ Reports 1996), para. 29; ICJ, *Case Concerning the Gabčikovo-Nagymaros Project* (Hungary v. Slovakia), Judgment of 25 September 1997 (ICJ Reports 1997, p. 7), para. 53.

93 Draft articles on Prevention of Transboundary Harm from Hazardous Activities with Commentaries (DAPTHAA), *Yearbook of the International Law Commission, Volume II, Part II* (2001), Article 2(b).

94 DAPTHAA, Article 2(b).

significant,[95] according to the International Law Commission, which based this claim upon an extensive research of case law, international conventions and domestic legal instruments, is to be understood as something more than 'detectable' but need not reach the level of 'serious' or 'substantial'.[96] Consequently, significant harm is required for the 'no harm' principle to be engaged.

There is a relatively direct line of argument to show that the causation of space pollution would constitute a violation of the international environmental law 'no-harm' principle. Schellekens argues that causing space debris constitutes a violation of the no-harm principle.[97] According to Dennerly, the no-harm threshold would appear to be met, as he argues that 'space activities, such as the operation of space objects, that encompass the potential to create space debris in orbit is considered ultra-hazardous for the purposes of the Articles on Transboundary Harm.'[98] Similarly, Stubbe concludes that 'there can be no doubt that debris pollution in outer space is of a transboundary nature because it occurs in a *res communis* area beyond national jurisdiction' and that space debris can qualify as 'any detrimental change to the environment [including outer space]'.[99] Given the risk of exponential harm deriving from ever fragmenting items of space debris, and the looming Kessler effect, the risk engendered by even a small amount of space debris is greater than the immediate harm it can cause to another space object, and should be considered significant in most, if not all, instances.[100]

Regarding the obligations that arise from the no-harm principle, in the case concerning Pulp Mills on the River Uruguay (*Argentina v. Uruguay*) the

95 In the Trail Smelter case, the term 'serious consequence' is used. The term 'seriously' is further highlighted in the *Lake Lanoux Arbitration* (France v. Spain), Decision of 16 November 1957, 12 R.I.A.A. 281, 24 I.L.R. 101.

96 DAPTHAA, p. 152, para. 4.

97 Jasper Schellenkens, *The Legality of Anti-satellite Weapons* (University of Malta Thesis, 2008). p. 32 ('any activity that causes damage to the environment in space can be considered a violation of Principle 2 of the Rio Declaration').

98 Dennerley (2018), p. 296.

99 Stubbe (2018), pp. 187, 197–198 citing inter alia Andrea Bianchi, 'Environmental Harm Resulting from the Use of Nuclear Power Sources in Outer Space: Some Remarks on State Responsibility and Liability' (1991) in Francesco Francioni (ed.) *International Responsibility for Environmental Harm*, (Graham and Trotman, 1991), p. 237; Nicolas Matte, 'Environmental Implications and Responsibilities in the Use of Outer Space' (1989) 14 *Annals of Air and Space Law*, pp. 419–421;Wolfgang Graf Vitzthum, *Volkerrecht, 5th edition* (De Gruyter Recht, 2010), p. 451; Lyall and Larsen (2009), p. 303. See also Breccia (2016), p. 8.

100 See above, Chapter 1 (The growing threat of NSA space pollution).

International Court of Justice referred to the 'no harm' rule in the context of the 'principle of prevention' and noted that it entails a level of due diligence.[101] In turn, due diligence in environmental matters includes the obligation to conduct a conclusive environmental impact assessment,[102] as the ICJ recognised.[103] Therefore, States have an obligation to conduct such an assessment when engaging in potentially harmful activities in outer space. Causing space pollution without conducting proper precautionary measures or without conducting an environmental impact assessment and harm mitigation plan, whether done deliberately or negligently, could be considered a violation of the 'no harm' principle.

However, in practice, the requirement to exercise due diligence, typically in the form of an environmental impact assessment, is not exhaustively complied with. Several states require an environmental impact assessment within their national space authorization procedures and national space laws.[104] But the assessments are mainly directed at impact on the terrestrial environment, and it is unclear whether they are consistently adhered to even in States where they are required.[105]

Consequently, there is a strong basis to assert that the no-harm principle should apply to outer space, as it constitutes an area beyond national jurisdiction and the environment is generally interpreted to encompass outer space. Significant harm must be shown at minimum to trigger the application of this principle to a specific case. While a violation of due diligence obligations may demonstrate a violation of this principle, the support for the enforceability of such obligations is somewhat undermined by the lack of universal adherence to this duty in State practice.[106]

1.2.2 Precautionary Principle

The precautionary principle, which is recognised in Principle 15 of the 1992 Rio Declaration, provides that 'where there are threats of serious or irreversible environmental damage, a lack of full scientific certainty shall not be used

101 See ICJ, *Pulp Mills on the River Uruguay* (Argentina v. Uruguay), Judgment, para. 101.

102 Mara Tignino, Christian Bréthaut, 'The role of international case law in implementing the obligation not to cause significant harm' (2020) 20 *International Environmental Agreements: Politics, Law, and Economics*, pp. 639, 640; Adrian Di Giovanni, 'A Pebble in the Shoe: Assessing the Uses of Do No Harm in International Assistance' (2014) 47(2) *Law and Politics in Africa, Asia and Latin America*, p. 218.

103 ICJ, *Pulp Mills on the River Uruguay* (Argentina v. Uruguay), Judgment, para. 101.

104 See Chapter 5.

105 See Chapter 5. See also Hobe (2019); Viikari (2008), pp. 104–111.

106 See Chapter 5 for the mixed practice in this respect.

as a reason for postponing cost-effective measures to prevent environmental degradation'. Whereas there is some dispute as to its customary status,[107] it is reflected in various instruments of international law.[108] For example, the principle has been applied to carbon emissions and climate change where scientific uncertainties surround humankind's impact on the outer space environment. To address these uncertainties, and prevent them from becoming obstacles to progress in protecting the environment, Article 3 of the United Nations Framework Convention on Climate Change (UNFCCC) provides that '[t]he Parties should take precautionary measures to anticipate, prevent, or minimize the causes of climate change and mitigate its adverse effects. Where there are threats of serious or irreversible damage, lack of full scientific certainty should not be used as a reason for postponing such measures.' Ultimately, notwithstanding debates the precautionary principle has a strong legal standing at its core.[109]

In relation to space activities, Larsen argues that the precautionary principle could be used to impose accountability for space debris. He states that it could be 'read into' Article IX of the Outer Space Treaty, and that:

> the Precautionary Principle would require a launching state as well as a non-governmental operator to take extra precaution in launching a space object that may result in space debris. Such a precaution would,

107 See Meinhard Schröder, 'Precautionary Approach/Principle' (2014) in Rüdiger Wolfrum (ed) *Max Planck Encyclopedia of Public International Law* (online edition), paras. 16–21 (disputing that the precautionary principle is customary international law). But see Michael Bothe, 'Protection of the Environment in Relation to Armed Conflicts' (2021) in Dieter Fleck (ed.) *The Handbook of International Humanitarian Law, 4th ed.* (Oxford University Press, 2021), p. 343 (arguing that the principle of precaution is a 'fundamental rule of modern customary environmental law'); Haroun et al. (2021), 67 (arguing that the precautionary principle is established in customary international law and citing the 'MOX Plant Case, Ireland v United Kingdom, Order, Request for Provisional Measures, ITLOS Case No 10, ICGJ 343 (ITLOS 2001), 3rd December 2001, International Tribunal for the Law of the Sea [ITLOS]). See generally Matthew Gillett, *Prosecuting Environmental Harm before the International Criminal Court* (Cambridge University Press, 2022), pp. 170–173.

108 Jose Felix Pinto-Bazurco, 'Deep Dive: The Precautionary Principle' *International Institute for Sustainable Development* (23 October 2020) (available at https://www.iisd.org/articles/deep-dive/precautionary-principle) (referring to the 1985 Vienna Convention for the Protection of the Ozone Layer and the 1987 Montreal Protocol on Substances that Deplete the Ozone Layer); Convention for the Protection of the Marine Environment of the Baltic Sea Area, (9 April 9, 1992), Art. 3 (2); see Viikari (2008), fn. 189. See further the Climate Convention 1992, the UNECE Water Convention, Treaty Establishing the European Community.

109 Viikari (2008), p. 134.

> at a minimum, require a state and an operator to observe the Space Debris Mitigation Guidelines, which are founded on normal operating procedures.[110]

This approach would require reading Article IX's prohibition of harmful contamination as incorporating a *precautionary facet*. While it is important that States do not use the absence of scientific certainty to avoid taking precautionary measures, the question arises how this principle would be applied in the space sector as a legal doctrine.

One manifestation of environmental law related to the precautionary principle is the requirement to conduct environmental impact assessments. This reflects the reasonable regard due to the rights of other States.[111] Environmental assessments have been incorporated into some national space legislation in multiple countries including Belgium and the United Arab Emirates.[112] However, to date these have largely focused on the impact of space activities on the earthly environment.[113] Beyond this, the precautionary principle can be read into several other principles of space law, including for establishing liability for harm caused in space,[114] as well associated with soft law instruments such the space debris mitigation guidelines.[115] In this way, the failure to take precautions would not itself constitute a violation of the prohibition of space pollution but would constitute an ancillary and complementary protection of the outer space environment.

Despite this grounding in customary international law, there is currently no legal instrument that would explicitly decree the observance of the

---

110 Larsen (2018), p. 491. See also Freeland and Ireland-Piper (2022), p. 21 ('The precautionary principle might possibly be relevant, although not necessarily directly applicable, to both human rights and human activities in outer space, particular given that so much is unknown about the environmental consequences for Earth of destabilizing the Moon through mining activities.').

111 Viikari (2008), p. 157.

112 Chapter 5.

113 See Chapter 5.

114 For example the responsibility and liability regimes included in the space treaties exemplify elements of precautionary approach, for a more in depth analysis see: Claudia Cinelli and Katarzyna Pogorzelska, 'The Current International Legal Setting for the Protection of the Outer Space Environment: The Precautionary Principle Avant La Lettre' (2013), 22 *RECIEL* 2, pp. 186–201; Paul B. Larsen, 'Application of the Precautionary Principle to the Moon' (2006), 71(2) *Journal of Air Law and Commerce*, pp. 295–306.

115 See Cinelli and Pogorzelska (2013), p. 191. See further Larsen (2006), pp. 295–306; Olavo Bittencourt Neto, 'Preserving the outer space environment: The 'precautionary principle' approach to space debris' (2013) *International Institute of Space Law*, p. 341.

precautionary principle in the space sector. The generally formulated space law principles mentioned briefly in this section leave room for State discretion to be exercised, given that there are substantial differences in various States' understanding and application of the precautionary principle.[116] Hence, space law will require further bolstering to secure the implementation of precautionary measures for the space environment.

1.2.3 Principle of Sustainable Development

The principle of sustainable development is a core environmental tenet, which features in several principles of the 1972 Stockholm Declaration,[117] in at least 12 of the Rio Principles of 1992,[118] along with several international treaties,[119] soft law instruments[120] and national acts.[121] It was first authoritatively described in the epoch defining Brundtland report as 'development that meets the needs of the present without compromising the ability of future generations to meet their own needs'.[122]

In 1997, the International Court of Justice poignantly described this principle, stating:

> Throughout the ages, mankind has, for economic and other reasons, constantly interfered with nature. In the past, this was often done without consideration of the effects upon the environment. Owing to new scientific insights and to a growing awareness of the risks for mankind – for present and future generations – of pursuit of such interventions at an unconsidered and unabated pace, new norms and standards have

---

116 For example, See Chapter 5 for examples of a wide application of the precautionary principle.

117 1972 Stockholm Declaration, Principles 2, 3, 4, 7 and Preamble.

118 1992 Rio Declaration, Principles 1, 4, 5, 7, 8, 9, 12, 20, 21, 22, 24, 27; Virginie Barral, 'Sustainable Development in International Law: Nature and Operation of an Evolutive Legal Norm' (2012) 23(2) *European Journal of International Law*, pp. 377, 379.

119 This principle has also been incorporated into numerous and various international and national instruments such as the 2002 World Summit on Sustainable Development; the 1991 Protocol on Environmental Protection to the Antarctic Treaty; the 1992 Convention on Biological Diversity; the 1992 UN Framework Convention on Climate Change (Article 3.4); the 1992 Convention on Biological Diversity (Article 6(b)).

120 United Nations Agenda 21 (UNCED Report, A/CONF.151/26/Rev.1 (vol. I)) (1993).

121 See Patricia Birnie and Alan Boyle, *International Law and the Environment* (2nd ed. Oxford University Press, 2002), p. 87 (referring to numerous national acts of developed countries); Viikari (2008), p. 134.

122 Report of the World Commission on Environment and Development: 'Our Common Future', UN Doc. A/42/427, Annex I, 4 August 1987, 54.

> been developed, set forth in a great number of instruments during the last two decades. Such new norms have to be taken into consideration, and such new standards given proper weight, not only when States contemplate new activities but also when continuing which activities begun in the past. This need to reconcile economic development with protection of the environment is aptly expressed in the concept of sustainable development.[123]

Sustainable development has three facets – environmental, economic and social. The goal is consequently 'to balance environmental protection and economic development in a way that is sustainable for both present generations and the future of humankind.'[124] In this respect, it is closely linked to the principle of intergenerational equity, which is addressed below.[125]

The basic goal of the principle is to balance environmental protection and economic growth in a sustainable manner. In practice this has been explained as ensuring environmental concerns are considered when developing developmental policy, whereby the environment is treated as a resource and sustainable is taken to mean 'non-exhaustive'.[126] In other words, development and growth should be achieved in a manner that does not exhaust the natural resources available.[127] As such, for the principle of sustainable development, the environment itself is not the primary core protected value, but its protection is the by-product of promoting human welfare,[128] as humans inherently live within nature and thus depend on it.[129]

In the field of space law, sustainable development therefore has *particular resonance*. Modern life has become heavily dependent on satellite services.[130] Space-based satellites form an integral part of the proposed means to ensure

---

123 ICJ, *Case Concerning the Gabčikovo-Nagymaros Project* (Hungary v. Slovakia), Judgment, para. 140.

124 Viikari (2008), p. 129 and Ferreira-Snyman (2023), p. 3.

125 See Birnie-Boyle (2002), p. 4; Viikari 2008, p. 130.

126 Viikari 2008 p. 130; see also Birnie-Boyle (2002), p. 84.

127 See also Principle 12 of the Rio Declaration, which declares that the sovereign right of states 'to exploit their own resources pursuant to their own environmental and developmental policies', tempered by the responsibility for transboundary environmental protection.

128 Viikari (2008), pp. 131–132.

129 See also Verschuuren (2003), pp. 46–49, 144; Viikari (2008), pp. 133–134.

130 See also Larsen (2018), p. 481.

sustainable development on Earth.[131] But sustainable development relies on continued access to space, which is necessary to utilize the space environment for human development. However, space pollution jeopardizes sustainable development by cutting off access to space, which would in turn undermine intergenerational equity.

Considering that copious amounts of space debris already orbit the Earth, ensuring the continued sustainability of utilizing outer space will be a key challenge confronting humanity. For this reason, Breccia notes that 'the principle of sustainable development is acquiring relevance even in the space sector'.[132] This is demonstrated aptly by yearly UNCOPUOS Subcommittee meetings, which include space sustainability as a regular item on the agenda. It is also shown by the Long-Term Sustainability Guidelines, and the UNCOPUOS Space Sustainability Working Group,[133] as well as by various initiatives levied to achieve space sustainability.

However, the justiciability of the concept of sustainable development is disputed.[134] Specifically, because it is so broad-ranging, it would pose challenges to courts to enforce. Institutions in which environmental damage could be prosecuted are unlikely to have provisions imposing criminal sanctions for

131 See Vladimir Atanasov and Gianluigi Baldesi, 'An Analysis of Two Space Business Opportunities' in Stella Tkatchova, *Space-Based Technologies and Commercialized Development: Economic Implications and Benefits* (IGI Global, 2011), p. 210.

132 Declaration of the United Nations Conference on the Human Environment (Stockholm Declaration), 15 December 1972. Stockholm Principle 21 points to international acceptance of the proposition that states are also required to protect global common areas, including Antarctica and those areas beyond the limits of national jurisdiction, such as the high seas, deep sea-bed, and outer space. Principle 21 (which was reproduced in Principle 2 of the Rio Declaration) provides that 'States have, in accordance with the Charter of the United Nations and the principle of international law, the sovereign right to exploit their own resources pursuant to their own environmental policies, and the responsibility that activities within their jurisdiction or control do not cause damage to the environment of other states or of areas beyond the limits of national jurisdiction.'

133 UNCOPUOS, UN Doc. A/AC.105/2018/CRP.20 (28 June 2018).

134 It is disputed whether the principle of sustainable development constitutes a principle or rather a goal with broad buy-in. Given the lack of consensus on its specific content, there is considerable divergence in its interpretation and application; see Birnie-Boyle (2002), p. 45; Viikari (2008), p. 134. Moreover, the anthropocentrism and utilitarianism at the core of this formulation limits its eco-centric value (the Rio Declaration states that 'human beings are at the centre of concerns for sustainable development', and the Stockholm Declaration preamble states that 'of all things in the world, people are the most precious' – but does mention in Principle 4 humankind's special responsibility to wildlife and its habitat), See, e.g., Verschuuren (2003), pp. 20–25; Viikari (2008), pp. 129, 131.

violating the concept of sustainable development.[135] Therefore, while playing an important role in developing policies and regulation,[136] it does not constitute an established and tested basis for concrete obligations.

1.2.4 Principle of Intergenerational Equity

The principle of intergenerational equity holds that resources should not be used by current generations in such a way that it will prejudice future generations' access to those resources.[137] It is intertwined with the principle of sustainable development outlined above. Non-renewable resources are particularly important concerns for this principle, as equity demands that they are not exhausted or overly dissipated by current generations to the prejudice of succeeding ones.

In relation to space activities, this principle has a clear basis of applicability.[138] In addition to non-renewal resources such as minerals on celestial bodies, Goh observes that

> some space resources, while undepletable, are limited. The radio spectrum on which all space communication depends and the geostationary orbit on which most communication satellites are deployed are examples of these limited resources. These have to be equitably shared.[139]

As noted above, this has been more clearly formulated in the fifth space treaty, the Moon Agreement. Article 4 provides that the exploration and use

---

135 However, the Independent Expert Panel which has proposed a definition of ecocide has placed an analogous concept to the idea of sustainable development (namely balancing environmental harm against social and economic benefits) at the heart of its definition of Ecocide. For a critique, see Matthew Gillett, 'A Tale of Two Definitions: Fortifying Four Key Elements of the Proposed Crime of Ecocide', *Opinio Juris*, 20 June 2023 (https://opiniojuris.org/2023/06/20/a-tale-of-two-definitions-fortifying-four-key-elements-of-the-proposed-crime-of-ecocide-part-i/).

136 Integrating environmental considerations in developmental considerations is more likely to guarantee environmental values are taken into account in decision-making processes than separating the two. This has been demonstrated by Principle 4 of the Rio Declaration, which highlights the fundamental role of sustainable development principle in environmental management and protection, which 'cannot be considered in isolation from it.' Therefore, the principle of sustainable development is nonetheless relevant and valuable to space activities, in particular during the planning and design phases. For more see Viikari (2008), p. 134.

137 Edith Brown Weiss, 'Climate Change, Intergenerational Equity, and International Law' (2008) *Vermont Journal of Environmental Law*, pp. 622–623.

138 Freeland and Ireland-Piper (2022), pp. 21–22.

139 Goh (2007), p. 19.

shall be the province of all mankind, carried out for the benefit of all countries and decrees that '[d]ue regard shall be paid to the interests of present and future generations as well as to the need to promote higher standards of living and conditions of economic and social progress and development in accordance with the Charter of the United Nations.' However, due to the Moon Agreement's low ratification numbers,[140] this provision does not have extensive reach. Beyond the Moon Agreement, the UNCOPUOS SDMG refer to intergenerational equity in providing that '[t]he prompt implementation of appropriate debris mitigation measures is therefore considered a prudent and necessary step towards preserving the outer space environment for future generations'.[141] Furthermore, the principle of intergenerational equity is also referenced, at least indirectly, in the UNCOPUOS Guidelines for the Long-term Sustainability of Outer Space Activities.[142] However, these guidelines are not strictly legally binding. Consequently, while there are bases on which to find violations of intergenerational equity resulting from space activities, these are not found in the major space law instruments, such as the Outer Space Treaty, and so have limited direct applicability.

Space has been described as an environment shared by all States, populations and generations.[143] It has been observed that the current exponential increase of space launches and space objects risks depriving future generations of fair opportunities to explore and utilize space. Radi states that '[t]his would create a fundamental intergenerational inequity by depriving – partly or fully – future generations of the enjoyment of the most fundamental space right: the right to explore and use space freely.'[144]

Breccia argues that the principle of intergenerational equity applies to outer space activities as it can be found in Article I of the Outer Space Treaty implicitly.[145] By decreeing that outer space shall be free to be explored and used by all

---

140 As of January 2024, the number will stand at 17, following Saudi Arabia's withdrawal in January of 2023.

141 Report of United Nations sixty-second session of the Committee on the Peaceful Uses of Outer Space, A/62/20, Annex, p. 47.

142 UNCOPUOS Guidelines for the Long-term Sustainability of Outer Space Activities, para. 4.

143 Viikari (2008), p. 65 ('[o]uter space is an environment that in principle is shared by all states, populations and generations, and its contamination could jeopardize their rights of exploration and use.').

144 Radi (2023), p. 2 (referring for support for the principle to Article I of the Treaty on Principles Governing the Activities of States in the Exploration and Use of Outer Space, including the Moon and Other Celestial Bodies (adopted 27 January 1967, entered into force 10 October 1967) 610 UNTS 205).

145 Breccia (2016), p. 8.

countries without any discrimination, for the benefit of all, and as a province of mankind, Article I demands guaranteeing access to outer space for present and future generations.[146] However, this does not necessarily require engage the principle of intergenerational equity *per se*.

A practical facet of the equitable principle is that the limited resources of outer space, such as geostationary orbital positions, should be shared equitably among countries. This is set out in the 2007 UNCOPUOS report.[147] Although it is focused on the division of benefits at the present time, it will also have an impact on future generations as they will be impacted by the level of equity achieved in sharing out these orbital positions. If they are deprived of such opportunities at present, then the situation will only become more entrenched and inequitable as time marches on and future generations arrive.

In essence, the principle of intergenerational equity suffers from the same strengths and weaknesses as the principle of sustainable development. In the space domain it is strongly heralded by developing States, who are currently unable to partake in space activities and therefore wish to ensure that they will have this opportunity in the future. However, its practical application is less commonly discussed and so it remains unclear how it could impact on the use of international law to redress space pollution.

1.2.5 Principle of Common-but-Differentiated Responsibilities

According to the principle of common-but-differentiated responsibilities those States which have historically created more pollution bear a higher responsibility to mitigate the damage to the environment.[148] This has emerged as a key principle supported by many in the Global South, particularly in the context of combating climate change. In accordance with this approach, international law instruments often differentiate, at least in some manner, between industrialized and developing States.[149] Whilst the Outer Space Treaty does not explicitly contain this principle, it does provide that space exploration and use should be carried out for the benefit of all countries irrespective of their economic development. The rationale for this is two-fold; first, is that

146 See also Stephen Gorove, 'The Concept of "Common Heritage of Mankind": A Political, Moral or Legal Innovation?' (1972) 9 *San Diego Law Review*, p. 394.

147 UNCOPUOS Report (2007), para. 44.

148 Viikari (2008), pp. 138, 178–179.

149 See, for example, United Nations Framework Convention on Climate Change, 9 May 1992, 1771 UNTS 107 (entered into force on 21 March 1994); Vienna Convention for the Protection of the Ozone Layer, 22 March 1985, 1513 UNTS 323 (entered into force on 22 September 1988); Convention on Biological Diversity, 22 May 1992, 1760 UNTS 79, (entered into force on 29 December 1993).

the environmental degradation seen today originates from the past actions of industrialized states, resulting in these states today possessing the greater capacities for responding to the degradation, and second, that developing countries still require the use of polluting technologies and resources to achieve a level of development equal to the already industrialized states.[150] However, developed states have been reluctant to agree to anything other than ambiguous or relatively irrelevant commitments.[151]

There is a basis in space law to incorporate the principle of common-but-differentiated responsibilities. The Principles Governing The Use By States Of Artificial Earth Satellites For International Direct Television Broadcasting contained in the Annex to UNGA Resolution 37/92 of 1982, provide in Paragraph 2 that '[s]uch activities should promote the free dissemination and mutual exchange of information and knowledge in cultural and scientific fields, assist in educational, social and economic development, particularly in the developing countries, enhance the qualities of life of all peoples and provide recreation with due respect to the political and cultural integrity of States.'[152] Similarly, Paragraph 11 provides that, in cooperating on the protection of copyright and related rights, States 'should give special consideration to the interests of developing countries in the use of direct television broadcasting for the purpose of accelerating their national development'.

Against this background, it should be noted that the impact of the recognition of the common-but-differentiated responsibilities in space law on a putative prohibition of space pollution is distributive rather than prohibitive. It does not constitute a basis for banning space pollution per se. Nonetheless, it would potentially affect the levels of chemical emissions and other pollutants in space which would be justifiable depending on the launching State in question (more developed States would be expected to have the highest environmental protections and therefore the lowest emissions).

Relatedly, common-but-differentiated responsibilities imply a responsibility on the part of developed States to assist developing States. This would be relevant to space remediation efforts to clear space debris for example. A basis for this can be seen by analogy in the 1986 UNGA Resolution 41/65 on the 'Principles Relating to Remote Sensing of the Earth from Outer Space' which provides in Principle II that '[r]emote sensing activities shall be carried out for the benefit and in the interests of all countries, irrespective of their degree of economic, social or scientific and technological development, and taking

---

150 Viikari (2008), pp. 289–290.

151 Viikari (2008), p. 181.

152 Emphasis added.

into particular consideration the needs of the developing countries.' Principle XII is specific in its guidance, requiring that as soon as primary data and processed data concerning a territory under its jurisdiction are produced, 'the sensed State shall have access to them on a non-discriminatory basis and on reasonable cost terms.' It augments these 'non-discrimination' and 'reasonable costs' requirements with a most-favoured nation type requirement, holding that '[t]he sensed State shall also have access to the available analyzed information concerning the territory under its jurisdiction in the possession of any State participating in remote sensing activities on the same basis and terms, taking particularly into account the needs and interests of the developing countries.'[153]

Similarly, the United Nations Declaration on International Cooperation in the Exploitation and Use of Outer Space for the Benefit and in the Interest of All States, Taking into Particular Account the Needs of Developing Countries was adopted by the United Nations General Assembly in its Resolution 51/22 of 13 December 1996. Although Resolution 51/22 is 'soft law', it can be used as a significant source to impact the interpretation of provisions of 'hard' space law, particularly as it is directly relevant to Article I(1) of the Outer Space Treaty.[154] Again, these principles would be primarily relevant to space environment remediation efforts rather than the prohibition of space pollution per se.

The principle of common-but-differentiated responsibilities has been adopted in multiple environmental law instruments in order to better achieve environmental policies across all States, particularly in the global South.[155] However, this principle is not without dangers, as many industries or NSAs could effect a transfer to developing states in order to undertake environmentally degrading activities for higher gain, thus actually increasing environmental degradation.[156] To counter this it is necessary to stress that common-but-differentiated responsibilities measures must be temporary in nature and only designed to apply as long as the developing State is at significant disadvantage in its ability to engage in relevant activity.[157]

Two differentiating views can be found in doctrine regarding the applicability of the common-but-differentiated responsibilities principle to outer space

153 UNGA Resolution 41/65.

154 Hobe (2010), p. 876. See Chapter 1.

155 See, e.g. United Nations Framework Convention on Climate Change, 9 May 1992, 1771 UNTS 107 (entered into force on 21 March 1994).

156 Viikari (2008), p. 182.

157 Viikari (2008), p. 182.

activities.[158] The first one claims that this principle is not suited for space activities and therefore cannot be translated into outer space.[159] This is connected to the ultra-hazardous nature of space activities; and is essentially premised on the notion that space activities are so dangerous that there cannot be any lowering of standards of safety in order to avoid harmful consequences. As with nuclear safety, pollution of the seas by ships, dumping at sea, deep sea activities, trade in endangered species, and Antarctic activities, for example, it has been regarded essential that observance of protective standards with regard to space activities is maintained.[160]

The second view, relying on Article III of the Outer Space Treaty, claims that it is through that Article that the common-but-differentiated responsibilities principle applies to outer space, and that such interpretation is in line with Article I of the Outer Space Treaty.[161] It could be operationalized by assigning different obligations to States at different levels of economic development, while also encouraging the sharing of knowledge to advance all States' knowledge and advancement.[162]

Generally, industrialized States, which have the desire and existing capacity to engage in space activities, will be more likely to pollute the environment and are therefore pushing back against any blanket prohibition of space pollution.[163] This is not to say these are opposed to action being taken to protect the space environment. To the contrary, space faring nations are highly concerned about the space environment and the connected access to space.[164] These protections are, however, in essence directed at all parties already partaking in space activities, thus not in line particularly with common-but-differentiated

158 See Svitlana Kravchenko, Tareq M.R. Chowdhury, Jahid Hossain Bhuiyan, 'Principles of International Environmental Law' (2013) in Shawkat Alam, Jahid Hossain Bhuiyan, Tareq M.R. Chowdhury and Erika J. Techera (eds.) *Routledge Handbook of International Environmental Law* (Routledge, 2013), p. 54.

159 See generally Birnie–Boyle (2002), pp. 568–588. See also Peter Stubbe, 'Common but Differentiated Responsibilities for Space Debris – New Impetus for a Legal Appraisal of Outer Space Pollution' (2010), *European Space Policy Institute Perspectives*, p. 11 ('the principle must not be construed in a way that tempts states to refrain from mitigation measures. … Only collective action can reverse the trend of ongoing degradation of the outer space environment which is in the interest of all states – be it developing or developed').

160 Viikari (2008), p. 183.

161 Ferreira-Snyman (2013), pp. 35–36; Philip De Man, Ward Munters, 'Reciprocal Limits to the Freedom to Use Outer Space by All States: Common but Differentiated Responsibilities?' (2018) 41 *Air and Space Law*, p. 21.

162 See Viikari (2008), 183, Uchitomi (2000), at 77.

163 Uchitomi (2000), pp. 77, 80; Viikari (2008), p. 182.

164 Viikari (2008), 182.

responsibilities. On the other hand, developing states, which currently do not possess the technology and resources necessary, but hope to do so in future, are demanding regulation for the preservation of the space environment so that they might have the opportunity to partake in space activities in future.[165] In this connection, non-spacefaring nations are demanding that space-faring nations that have the capabilities take the lead in environmental remediation.[166]

As noted, according to the common-but-differentiated responsibilities principle, a greater responsibility for the maintenance of the environment should be assigned to the space powers that have carried out majority launches in the past.[167] However nowadays, more and more launches are conducted by NSAs. By extending the ratio of the principle of common-but-differentiated responsibilities to apply to NSAs, one could argue that NSAs that cause the most space pollution carry more responsibility to mitigate it. It is not evident that any such trend is materializing in practice. Nevertheless, common-but-differentiated responsibilities could be used in this manner to require NSAs to engage in remediation efforts, particularly NSAs from developed States. Another proposal has been that of a fund for space activities, to provide a ready means of facilitating common-but-differentiated responsibilities, as well as other principles such as the polluter-pays or inter-generational equity ones.[168] But this is a prospective financial measure rather than a legal adjustment to impose accountability for space pollution.

1.2.6 Polluter-Pays Principle

Another important customary international environmental rule is the polluter-pays principle ascribing liability for damages to the polluter.[169] The principle was first introduced by the Organization for Economic Co-operation and Development in 1972 and can furthermore be found, for example, in Article 16 of the Rio Declaration.[170] According to this principle, where harm arises to any facet of the environment, it is the person or entity which caused the harm which should pay for the full remediation of that environmental harm. It

165 Uchitomi (2000), pp. 77, 80; Viikari (2008), p. 182.

166 See, e.g., Committee on the Peaceful Uses of Outer Space, Report of the Scientific and Technical Subcommittee on its 42nd session, held in Vienna from 21 February to 4 March 2005, UN Doc. A/AC.105/848 (21 February – 4 March 2005), para. 99.

167 Ferreira-Snyman (2013) 47.

168 Viikari (2008), p. 182.

169 Viikari (2008), p. 184.

170 OECD, Recommendation of the Council on Guiding Principles concerning International Economic Aspects of Environmental Policies, 2020; Rio Declaration Art. 16.

has been argued that that applying the polluter-pays principle to outer space would protect the space environment in two ways: '[f]irst, it shall create a form of deterrence structure, making space farers more conscious of the debris being created' and, second, 'it shall create a veritable avenue to create funds to address whatever space debris are created in an equitable manner.'[171]

The applicability of this principle to outer space activities, however, remains disputed. The principle was initially designed for terrestrial activities, and the closest rule in space law to it is the concept of liability for damages caused by space objects, even though the damage defined in Liability Convention does not explicitly cover environmental damage. In the terrestrial context, proportionality between pollution and demanded compensation are easier to define and lower than in the space sector, where the expenses of activities are extremely high even without compensation for the pollution, and establishing proportionality is a more novel field.[172] There is likely little doubt that application of the polluter-pays principle would help deter the proliferation of space debris, however, at present the principle is not being applied in practice to space activities. Moreover, it would not contribute to showing a violation of the prohibition of space pollution but instead assist the determination of where responsibility and liability should fall in cases of harm to the outer space environment.

1.2.7 The Principle of Permanent Sovereignty over Natural Resources

The principle of permanent sovereignty over natural resources seeks to establish a right of 'governments to exploit the State's natural resources on behalf of the State and its people on condition that it does so for national development and the well-being of the people of the State.'[173] Its foundational document is the 1962 General Assembly Resolution 1803 on Permanent Sovereignty over Natural Resources, which recognizes that 'respect [for this principle] must be based on the recognition of the inalienable right of all States freely to dispose of their natural wealth and resources in accordance with their national interests, and on respect for the economic independence of States'.[174] In relation to space law, the 1986 Resolution 41/65 of the United National General Assembly ('Principles Relating to Remote Sensing of the Earth from Outer Space'), makes

171 Haroun et. al. (2021), p. 68.

172 Viikari (2008), pp. 202, 203.

173 UNGA Resolution 1803 (XVII), 14 December 1962, 'Permanent sovereignty over natural resources', preamble.

174 UNGA Resolution 1803 (XVII), 14 December 1962, 'Permanent sovereignty over natural resources'.

reference to the principle of permanent sovereignty over natural resources in Principle IV, which calls for 'respect for the principle of full and permanent sovereignty of all States and peoples over their own wealth and natural resources, with due regard to the rights and interests, in accordance with international law, of other States and entities under their jurisdiction.'

Given that outer space, including the Moon and other celestial bodies, is not subject to national appropriation whether by claim of sovereignty of otherwise,[175] the principle of permanent sovereignty over natural resources should not have application in this environment. However, space exploration can involve the exploitation of natural resources on earth, such as rare metals and compounds. To the extent these natural resources are exploited for the construction of space objects or for their launch, those natural resources should be utilized with respect for the principle of disposing of wealth in the interests of the peoples of the relevant State in question.

1.2.8 Other Bases under International Environmental Law to Prohibit Space Pollution

Among key international environmental law instruments, several accord the environment intrinsic value. Of greatest general import is the 1992 Convention on Biological Diversity, which is motivated by the 'the intrinsic value of biological diversity' and 'the importance of biological diversity for evolution and for maintaining life sustaining systems of the biosphere', while also noting 'the ecological, genetic, social, economic, scientific, educational, cultural, recreational and aesthetic values of biological diversity and its components'.[176] Moreover, the 1972 World Heritage Convention defines natural heritage as natural features, geological and physiographical formations, and natural sites of 'outstanding universal view' from the 'point of view of science' and 'conservation', as well as due to aesthetic value.[177] To date, the application of these instruments has been limited to terrestrial environments, and it remains unclear whether and how they could be applied to the context of outer space. Von der Dunk argues that outer space constitutes a 'global commons', and he specifies that this has different legal implications from a 'common heritage of mankind' designation. Whereas the former protects the fundamental freedom to act except to the extent that specific obligations have been agreed to the contrary, the latter establishes a presumption against any exploitation of

175 Chapter 1.

176 Convention on Biological Diversity 1992, 1760 UNTS 30619, Preamble.

177 Convention concerning the Protection of the World Cultural and Natural Heritage, 23 November 1972 ('World Heritage Convention'), 1037 UNTS 151, article 2.

the area unless the applicable international regime permits it.[178] Conversely, the Moon Agreement designates the Moon (and other celestial bodies as per Article 1(1)) as the 'common heritage of mankind'.[179] However, although the provisions of the Moon Agreement substantively overlap with the Outer Space Treaty's contents, the Moon Agreement has not received sufficient acceptance to be considered a connected instrument accepted by the parties to the Outer Space Treaty (under the Vienna Convention on the Law of Treaties) which could directly impact its interpretation in this respect.[180]

Another potential source of a prohibition of space pollution is the Convention on the Prohibition of Military and Other Hostile Use of Environmental Modifications (ENMOD). Adopted in 1977, this treaty was essentially a reaction to events during the Vietnam War, including the use of high quantities of chemical defoliants against large tracts of forest, by the United States Army, which resulted in significant destruction of forests and wildlife as well as high levels of human ill-health and death.[181] In its Article II, it provides that 'the term 'environmental modification techniques' refers to any technique for changing – through the deliberate manipulation of natural processes – the dynamics, composition or structure of the earth, including its biota, lithosphere, hydrosphere and atmosphere, or of outer space.'[182] It prohibits State Parties from engaging in 'military or any other hostile use of environmental modification techniques having widespread, long-lasting or severe effects as the means of destruction, damage or injury to any other State Party.'

Military uses of outer space are increasingly being researched by States and other entities. Because of the nature of outer space, and the lack of gravity or atmospheric friction, the spreading of space debris through military activities, collisions or other activities is likely to be long-lasting unless specifically

---

178 See von der Dunk (2015a), p. 58.

179 See in Article 11(1). Article 11 goes on to provide that 'Neither the surface nor the subsurface of the Moon, nor any part thereof or natural resources in place, shall become property of any State, international intergovernmental or non-governmental organization, national organization or non-governmental entity or of any natural person.'

180 See Vienna Convention on the Law of Treaties 1969, Article 31.

181 Eliana Cusato, 'From Ecocide to Voluntary Remediation Projects: Legal Responses to Environmental Warfare in Vietnam and the Spectre of Colonialism' (2018) 19 *Melbourne Journal of International Law* ('Cusato (2018)'), pp. 499–500; Elizabeth Maruma Mrema, Carl Bruch, and Jordan Diamond, *Protecting the Environment during Armed Conflict: An Inventory and Analysis of International Law* (United Nations Environment Programme, 2009) (UNEP, 2009), p. 12.

182 Convention on the Prohibition of Military and Other Hostile Use of Environmental Modification Techniques (ENMOD), 10 December 1976, 1108 UNTS 151 (entered into force on 5 October 1978), p. 151, see Article II.

cleaned up. Moreover, the constant movement of space debris covers long distances, and so could be considered widespread. Finally, because even a small object can cause significant damage to space vessels, the effects of even a small release of space debris could potentially be considered severe. The ENMOD Convention has significant global coverage, as it has over 70 State Parties, covering many of the key space-faring nations, including the United States, the United Kingdom, China, Germany, India, and the Russian Federation. However, it is not definitively settled that the terms of ENMOD constitute customary international law.[183] Moreover, it would have to be determined whether space pollution constitutes environmental modification. This would be unlikely in cases of accidental (but potentially culpable) collisions, which are often the cause of space debris.

1.2.9 Conclusion on International Environmental Law

There is considerable overlap between several of the environmental law principles discussed above, particularly when it comes to space law. However, for present purposes it is striking they all have the common element of not having been applied in legal cases on the space environment. While the principles such as no-harm, prevention, precaution, polluter-pays, intergenerational equity, common-but-differentiated responsibilities, conducting environmental impact assessments and access to information are 'cornerstones of international environmental law',[184] they cannot be 'indiscriminately' transposed to the context of outer space, but instead must be assessed from technical-scientific and legal points of view.[185] Moreover, the status and content of the majority of international environmental law principles mentioned in this chapter remain open to debate, particularly when applied to outer space. They permit various interpretations and therefore make it difficult to establish specific obligations for application in legal settings such as courts. This is because they are principles, formulated vaguely and thus suffering from the same issue plaguing the Outer Space Treaty in this regard. On the other hand, as Lyall and Larsen point out, '[i]t would be wrong to consider the law of space environment as something separate, distinct and different from the concepts

183 See Roman Reyhani, Protection of the Environment During Armed Conflict, 14 Missouri Environmental Law and Policy Review 323 (2006); Yoram Dinstein, *The Conduct of Hostilities Under the Law of International Armed Conflict* 178 (Cambridge University Press, 2004), p. 1801.

184 Breccia (2016), p. 8.

185 Breccia (2016), p. 8.

of terrestrial environmental law … [e]nvironmental space law is simply a specialized area of environmental law.'[186]

The ambiguity and vagueness of international environmental law limits the legal applicability of its specific principles. This, coupled with the fact that international environmental law treaties and principles were designed with terrestrial environment in mind, lead to it providing few clear instructions for States' activities in space. As such, environmental law principles may help guide the development and interpretation of space law from an ecocentric perspective, but at present remain insufficient on their own to indisputably demonstrate a prohibition of space pollution.

In relation to the contrast of anthropocentric and ecocentric views, much of space law was developed at a time when the anthropocentric view was in the ascendency and the ecocentric view was in its infancy.[187] As a result, space law is largely focused on benefits that humans may draw from space exploration. The reference to harmful contamination in Article IX of the Outer Space Treaty is one of the few acknowledgements of the potential harm that humans may cause to the outer space environment. This human-centred ontology means that space law could result in largely untrammeled damage to the space environment, so long as done with a profit motive or other human-oriented benefit in mind. This is an escalating risk, particularly with the rising number and breadth of NSAs interested in space exploration. In line with the views of Viikari,

> [a]s space exploration expands further into outer space and takes more extensive forms, such as construction of permanent facilities and the utilization of natural resources for the support of missions, anthropogenic alterations of this environment and the related hazards will be of an order of magnitude far greater than those seen today.[188]

This augurs in favour of a re-orientation in space law towards more ecocentric inclusivity. Such a shift would not mean removing the opportunity for space exploration or utilization by humans, but rather adopting a viewpoint prioritizing the protection of outer space as a fundamental starting point among the values to weigh when adopting or amending the international legal framework governing space activities.

---

186 Lyall and Larsen (2009), p. 275.

187 Viikari (2008), p. 55.

188 Viikari (2008), p. 54.

At the operational level, international environmental customary international law (particularly the no-harm principle) can reinforce Article IX's prohibition of harmful contamination of the outer space environment and can support its interpretation to cover space pollution. In this way, Articles III and IX of the Outer Space Treaty serve to combine conventional and customary international law to result in a robust basis for the prohibition of space pollution.

1.3 *The Relevance of the Human Right to a Clean, Healthy and Sustainable Environment*

An alternative legal regime that has recently been growing in relevance to environmental harm is that of international human rights law. Although there are several human rights which may be affected by events in space, the present analysis focuses on those human rights intertwined with harm to the environment. In this respect, the most notable potential human right is that to a clean, healthy and sustainable environment, recognised in 2022 by the United Nations General Assembly.[189] Notably, Resolution 76/300 had 161 votes in favour, eight abstentions, and no votes against. This followed similar recognition by the Human Rights Council in 2021 and within the inter-American system of human rights.[190]

Concerning the potential application of this right to the outer space environment, there is little guidance provided in the implementing resolution. The United Nations General Assembly notes 'that the right to a clean, healthy and sustainable environment is related to other rights and existing international law' and affirms 'that the promotion of the human right to a clean, healthy and sustainable environment requires the full implementation of the multilateral environmental agreements under the principles of international environmental law'.[191] At the same time, this language leaves open the question of whether the environment would include outer space. In recognizing the same right, the Inter-American Court of Human Rights has held that it 'protects the components of the environment, such as forests, seas, rivers, and other [environmental features] as legal interests in themselves, even in the absence of certainty or evidence of a risk to individuals' and that '[t]his means that nature must be protected, not only because of its benefits or effects for humanity, 'but because of its importance for the other living organisms with which we share

189 See UNGA Resolution A/RES/76/300 The human right to a clean, healthy and sustainable environment, A/RES/76/300 (28 July 2022).

190 UNGA, HRC, A/HRC/RES/48/13 (18 October 2021).

191 UNGA Resolution A/RES/76/300, paras. 2–3.

the planet'.[192] The Inter-American Court's language would imply that the right is linked to the health of Earth itself. Nonetheless, given the various definitions of the natural environment in international law instruments referred to above,[193] the presumptive position is that outer space is encompassed by the term 'environment'.[194] Consequently, there is a strong argument albeit untested that space pollution could violate this right, as it would impinge on the clean, healthy and sustainable nature of the outer space environment.

International human rights law is increasingly being used to litigate environmental concerns, including before the European Court of Human Rights and the Inter-American Court on Human Rights.[195] In addition to the right to a clean, healthy and sustainable environment, there are several pre-existing human rights that have been found to undergird the right to a healthy environment, which was recently recognised by the HRC among other notable bodies.[196] Chief among these rights are the right to life and the right to private and family life.[197] These rights have been found to have been violated by environmental harm on Earth, but remain untested in this respect in the context

---

192 IACtHR, *Comunidades Indígenas Miembros de la Asociación Lhaka Honhat (Nuestra Tierra) v. Argentina* (6 February 2020) ('Lhaka Honhat'), para. 203.

193 See above Chapters 1 and 2, Section (2).

194 See Chapter 2, Section 1.

195 EctHR, *Giacomelli v. Italy,* Judgment of 2 November 2006 (Application no. 59909/00), where the EctHR recognized that the applicant's right to respect for her home and her private and family life was impaired by the negative environmental impacts of an industrial plant nearby; the currently pending EctHR case *Verein KlimaSeniorinnen Schweiz v. Switzerland,* application lodged on 26 November 2020 (Application no. 53600/20); and Inter-American Court of Human Rights, Advisory Opinion OC-23/17 from 2018 (referring to the Inter-American cases recognizing an autonomous right to a healthy environment).

196 Human Rights Council (2012), *Report of the Independent Expert on the issue of human rights obligations relating to the enjoyment of a safe, clean, healthy and sustainable environment (Preliminary Report),* UN Doc. A/HRC/22/43, para. 10; see also: Inter-American Court of Human Rights, *State Obligations in Relation to the Environment in the Context of the Protection and Guarantee of the Rights to Life and to Personal Integrity,* Advisory Opinion of 15 November 2017 (OC-23/17), pp. 22–23 (In the Advisory Opinion OC-23/17 from 2018, the Inter-American Court of Human Rights stated that there is an undeniable interrelationship between realization of human rights and the protection of the environment; as the human rights, including the right to a healthy environment, are affected by degradation to the environment, see paras. 47, 48).

197 See, e.g. Human Rights Committee, *Portillo Cáceres et al. v. Paraguay,* Communication No. 2751/2016, Views of 25 July 2019, UN Doc. CCPR/C/126/D/2751/2016; EctHR, *Öneryıldız v. Turkey,* Grand Chamber Judgment of 30 November 2004 (Application no. 48939/99), pp. 6, 59 (disposition); ECtHR, *Verein KlimaSeniorinnen Schweiz and Others v. Switzerland,* no. 53600/20, judgment (Grand Chamber), 9 April 2024, para. 435. See also Freeland and Ireland-Piper (2022), p. 16.

of outer space. There are several other rights, such as the right to the benefits of scientific progress, which may be affected by space exploration, but do not directly relate to the outer space environment.[198] To demonstrate a violation of human rights on these bases, it must be shown that the environmental harm has caused, or risks causing, harm to the human victims. This anthropocentric linkage is inherent in the notion of these rights being human rights.

Applying human rights in the outer space context can draw lessons from climate change litigation before human rights bodies. For example, in the recent case of *KlimaSeniorinnen*, the ECtHR addressed the risks to elder Swiss citizens produced by climate change. It noted that it is not sufficient it for an applicant to complain of general damage to the environment.[199] Instead it looked at criteria such as the 'minimum level of severity of the harm in question, its duration and the existence of a sufficient link with the applicant or applicants, including, in some instances, the geographical proximity between the applicant and the impugned environmental harm.'[200]

When it came to assessing responsibility for related human rights violations, it held that, although 'climate change is undoubtedly a global phenomenon which should be addressed at the global level by the community of States', it remains the case that 'each State has its own share of responsibilities' and that 'a respondent State should not evade its responsibility by pointing to the responsibility of other States'.[201] On a related point concerning the 'drop-in-the-ocean' argument, the Court recalled that 'sufficient to engage the responsibility

198 See Freeland and Ireland-Piper (2022), pp. 16–17.

199 ECtHR, *KlimaSeniorinnen*, para. 472.

200 ECtHR, *KlimaSeniorinnen*, para. 487, 502. Specifically, it held that, in cases of climate change, for individuals '(a) the applicant must be subject to a high intensity of exposure to the adverse effects of climate change, that is, the level and severity of (the risk of) adverse consequences of governmental action or inaction affecting the applicant must be significant; and (b) there must be a pressing need to ensure the applicant's individual protection, owing to the absence or inadequacy of any reasonable measures to reduce harm'. For associations, it must be shown that they are '(a) lawfully established in the jurisdiction concerned or have standing to act there; (b) able to demonstrate that it pursues a dedicated purpose in accordance with its statutory objectives in the defence of the human rights of its members or other affected individuals within the jurisdiction concerned, whether limited to or including collective action for the protection of those rights against the threats arising from climate change; and (c) able to demonstrate that it can be regarded as genuinely qualified and representative to act on behalf of members or other affected individuals within the jurisdiction who are subject to specific threats or adverse effects of climate change on their lives, health or well-being as protected under the Convention.' Notably, the association does not need to show that the victims it represents would have specifically met the criteria for individuals.

201 ECtHR, *KlimaSeniorinnen*, para. 442.

of the State, is that reasonable measures which the domestic authorities failed to take could have had a real prospect of altering the outcome or mitigating the harm.'[202] Notably, the Court highlighted that 'intergenerational burden-sharing assumes particular importance' in relation to climate change,[203] which is an observation with parallels to space debris given that it risks cutting off access to outer space for future generations.

Ultimately, the Court found Switzerland to have violated its obligations under Article 8 concerning private and family life (which it saw as 'encompassing a right for individuals to effective protection by the State authorities from serious adverse effects of climate change on their life, health, well-being and quality of life'), as well as access to justice, but only in relation to the association and not in relation to the individual victims.[204] Specifically, it pointed to 'critical lacunae in the Swiss authorities' process of putting in place the relevant domestic regulatory framework, including a failure by them to quantify, through a carbon budget or otherwise, national green-house gas emissions limitations.'[205]

When applied to the space context, these findings suggest two potential points of applicability. First, in relation to State responsibility (and potentially corporate responsibility), the multifarious nature of harm to the environment will not preclude findings against specific States of violating human rights for failing to carry out their obligations, even if the State is relatively small and has little overall impact on the environmental threat in question. Second, in relation to the status of complainants, the test is more stringent for individual humans than for associations. Groups interested in protecting and preserving the space environment should pay due heed to this jurisprudential development if they want to lay the platform for potential future claims of human rights violations due to spoliation of the outer space environment.

In terms of implementing accountability for human rights, violations of these rights in outer space would typically occur outside of a State's territorial jurisdiction.[206] In this respect, courts, including the International Court of Justice, have confirmed that human rights have an extraterritorial

202 ECtHR, *KlimaSeniorinnen*, para. 444.
203 ECtHR, *KlimaSeniorinnen*, para. 420.
204 ECtHR, *KlimaSeniorinnen*, paras. 526 535.
205 ECtHR, *KlimaSeniorinnen*, para. 573.
206 In *KlimaSeniorinnen* extra-territoriality of effects was raised by the respondent State but dismissed by the Court, as there was sufficient conduct by the State within its territory, and the victims were located within its jurisdiction, which enabled the Court to proceed.

application.[207] Human rights obligations also extend to persons living beyond a State's own territory where a State takes control over areas outside its borders or where persons otherwise come under the effective control of the State(s) in question.[208] In the latter respect, Lubell explains that the 'recurring proposition is that the action taken by the state agent brings the person at the receiving end of the action into the jurisdiction of the state'.[209] Expansive applications of extra-territorial obligations of human rights treaties have also been taken by United Nations treaty bodies and the Inter-American Court of Human Rights, extended States duties to the regulation of NSAs under their jurisdiction to prevent them from violating human rights abroad, including corporations.[210] The extraterritorial application of human rights is also enshrined in the Principle 3 of Maastricht Principles on the Extraterritorial Obligations of States,[211] which further supports the contention that States must not only avoid directly undermining fundamental rights, but must also take measures to ensure that persons and entities within their jurisdiction do not violate these rights. Noting the extra-territorial application of human rights law, Freeland and Ireland-Piper conclude that 'at the very least, human rights obligations may extend into the use of space and outer space where effective control is present.'[212] Several other authors support this view.[213]

However, at the conceptual level, harm to the space environment is not as directly linked to human beings as terrestrial environmental harm is.[214] This

207 See, e.g. *Legal Consequences of the Construction of a Wall in the Occupied Palestinian Territory,* Advisory Opinion, I.C.J. Rep. 136 (July 2004), para. 109. See also Noam Lubell, *Extraterritorial Use of Force Against Non-State Actors*, (Oxford University Press, 2010) p. 193.

208 Joseph Sinchak, 'The Extraterritorial Application of Human Rights Treaties: Al-Skeini et al. v. United Kingdom (2011)' (2013) 3 *Pace International Law Review*, pp. 419–425; Samantha Besson, 'Due Diligence and Extraterritorial Human Rights Obligations – Mind the Gap!' (2020) 9(1) *ESIL Reflections*, p. 3; Theodor Meron, 'Extraterritoriality of Human Rights Treaties' (1995) 89(1) *American Journal of International Law*, pp. 78–80.

209 Lubell (2010), p. 212.

210 Macchi (2025), pp. 54, 76 referring to CESCR, *General comment 24 on State obligations under the International Covenant on Economic, Social and Cultural Rights in the context of business activities* (2017) E/C.12/GC/24; Inter-American Court of Human Rights, Advisory Opinion OC-23/17, 'The environment and human rights' (2017), paras. 101–103.

211 See Olivier De Schutter et al., 'Commentary to the Maastricht principles on extraterritorial obligations of states in the area of economic, social and cultural rights' (2012) 34(4) *Human Rights Quarterly*, pp. 5–8.

212 Freeland and Ireland-Piper (2022), pp. 8–9.

213 Ribbelink (2009); Hobe (2019); Annette Froehlich and Claudiu Mihai Taiatu, *Space in Support of Human Rights* (ESPI/Springer, 2022), pp. 21–29; Macchi (2025), pp. 53–54.

214 Baker (1987), p. 169 ('Different characteristics of outer space and terrestrial environments demand different approaches; although the principles may be identical, the details vary considerably.'). See also Lachs (2010), p. 106.

is not only because humans are currently unable to live in outer space for any length of time, let alone permanently, and thus are reliant on the environment on Earth for the basics of life, but also because of our societal organization. Earth is largely divided up into States and the officials of those States responsible for respecting the human rights of human beings under their jurisdiction.[215] Conversely, in outer space there are no settled populations and no permanent representatives of States to ensure that their rights are upheld. Because of this, it should not be presumed that human rights applicable on Earth will automatically be applicable outside of Earth's atmosphere. Regarding extraterritorial human rights obligations, Lubell notes that States must refrain from taking direct action that violate human rights, even if taken extraterritorially, and that additionally, where State agents exercise authority or control extraterritorially which brings individuals under the State's jurisdiction, it can create human rights obligations for that State but only in relation to those rights for which the individual(s) in question is 'directly dependent' on the State agents.[216]

Applying this to the outer space environment, it must be noted that different forms of harm to the space environment affect human rights in different ways. Space debris, which risks cutting off human access to space, has a clear and demonstrable link to human suffering as set out above. Where State agents taken actions within their jurisdiction, including in a flagged space shuttle, which result in space debris, or otherwise maneuver a space object to as to directly cause debris that could undermine human rights, they will potentially have violated human rights obligations. For other forms of space pollution – such as the introduction of radio waves into outer space – a case-by-case assessment will be required to determine if there is a sufficient link between the environmental harm and human rights deprivation, but the jurisdictional assessment would remain the same as for debris.

When it comes to space active NSAs, such as corporations, the question of applying human rights obligations arises both in relation to States and to the corporations themselves. Corporations can impact on human rights through their activities in space, as 'corporations are usually part of complex supply chains through which, not unlike other business enterprises, they might contribute or be linked to human rights, labour rights and environmental impacts.'[217] For State-focused obligations, a corporation may be considered to

215 Thirlway (1972), p. 147 ('The reason why international law is built round States is not because they have selfishly created such a system, or fought off any strivings for equality on the part of other entities: it is because they represent the interests of their human citizens in general terms, in the area where it matters, literally 'on the ground'').

216 Lubell (2010), pp. 230–231.

217 Macchi (2025), pp. 50–51.

be acting as a State agent, for example due to the requirements in Article VI of the Outer Space Treaty whereby NSA space activities 'shall require authorization and continuing supervision by the appropriate State Party to the Treaty'.[218] On this basis NSA activities could be read as 'national activities',[219] and the relevant States' obligations would inure in them.[220] But to the extent NSAs in space are not considered State agents, the basis to require States' to control their conduct extraterritorially (extra-terrestrially) is untested. For corporations, according to the Ruggie principles, NSAs should adhere to human rights obligations. However, the bindingness of these obligations remains a developing position in this respect, as discussed below.[221]

Nonetheless, the recognition of the human right to a clean, healthy and sustainable environment marks a significant step towards the broader recognition of a prohibition on serious environmental pollution, which can be extended to the outer space environment in line with several principles of international space law discussed above, most notably the prohibition on causing harmful contamination under Article IX of the Outer Space Treaty. Because space pollution threatens humankind's very access to space and because of the potential importance of space for human survival in the long-term, it could arguably constitute a significant incursion on the human right to a clean, healthy and sustainable environment.[222]

2 Conclusion regarding a Prohibition of Space Pollution

As a result of these countervailing strands of interpretive factors, eminent experts have widely divergent views regarding the prohibition of space pollution. Some, such as Professor Hobe, contend that causing space debris is not a violation of international law, at least during normal operations.[223] Others, such as Professor Stubbe, argue that causing space debris is definitively prohibited[224] on the basis of Article IX of the Outer Space Treaty.[225] For present

218 Outer Space Treaty, Article VI. See also Chapter 3, Section 1.

219 Macchi (2025), pp. 61–62.

220 However, determining which State is the 'appropriate State' can be subject to interpretation, as discussed above.

221 See Chapter 4, Section 2.4. See also Macchi (2025), p. 70.

222 Freeland and Ireland-Piper (2022), pp. 17–18.

223 Hobe (2019), pp. 114–115.

224 Stubbe (2018), p. 163.

225 Stubbe (2018), p. 154 ('article IX sentence 2 of the Outer Space Treaty further obliges states not to contaminate outer space in a harmful manner and to refrain from adversely

purposes, while it is acknowledged that considerable ambiguity surrounds the existence, extent, and enforceability of any such prohibition, it is concluded that Article IX provides a robust basis capable of encompassing harm to the space environment. That prohibition is essential to uphold the object and purpose of the Outer Space Treaty, as enshrined in Article I, as space pollution impairs namely the freedom of exploration and use of outer space, by denying or significantly reducing access to the outer space environment and by posing risks to the safety of the launched space objects and their crew. It is further reinforced when interpreted in accordance with international environmental law in its modern form. The analysis in Chapter 5 below further indicates that many States have integrated aspects of the requirement to avoid space pollution into their domestic laws, at least insofar as requiring operators to provide plans for the avoidance of space debris in order to obtain licenses to conduct space launches and activities.[226]

In addition, several established principles of international environmental law, imported into space law by virtue of Article III of the Outer Space Treaty could theoretically *per se* be violated by space pollution. Nonetheless, this application of terrestrially-conceived notions to the extra-terrestrial domain is novel and untested. Whereas it is clear that international environmental law principles can assist the interpretation of the provisions of the Outer Space Treaty, it is more contestable whether those principles can be directly read into this leading convention. Several authors warn that the application of principles of international law by means of Article III of the Outer Space Treaty cannot be automatic, but must rather be a result of a considerate deliberation whether such application is appropriate and reasonable, and to what extent.[227] In this regard, questions arise, for example, whether the no-harm (and also the preventive) principle can be applied to harmful effects emitted from a space object to outer space in general or whether those effects need to specifically

changing the environment of the Earth.'). Although the second sentence of Article IX reads superficially as though the obligations are limited to when conducting studies and exploration, Stubbe and others have argued that this appears to be poor drafting rather than reflecting any intent to limit the ambit of these responsibilities; Stubbe (2018), p. 154 citing Frantzen, 'Umweltbelastungen durch Weltraumaktivitaten' (1991) in *Handbuch des Weltraumrechts* (Carl Heymanns Verlag, 1991), pp. 611–612; Peter Malanczuk, 'Review of the Regulatory Regime Governing the Space Environment' (1996) 45(1) *Zeitschrift fur Luft und Weltraumrecht*, p. 47.

226 See Chapter 5.

227 Ribbelink (2009), pp. 64–69 (noting nonetheless that a considerable portion of conventional and customary international law is applicable to outer space). See also Breccia (2016), p. 8.

impact on one or more other State's space objects, and what level of harmful impact would be required in each instance.[228] In relation to the principle of sustainable development, there are key resources, such as GEO spots, that are not finite in the same way as terrestrial resources, but can be used in an unsustainable manner which may more broadly cut off human access to outer space.[229] As regards the polluter-pays principle, determining the level of costs is difficult and raises the issue of whether and how to factor in the costs and probability of a potential collision with another space object.

In sum, the robust basis for a prohibition of space pollution under international law is discernible and provides an important foundational platform for the remaining examination of NSA accountability for space pollution. Moreover, given the trend towards regulating anthropocentric harm to the natural environment, and the tendency for definitions of the environment to extend to outer space, the basis for the prohibition of space pollution will most likely grow increasingly robust in the coming years.

---

228 Stubbe (2018) considers this not to preclude the application of the 'no harm' principle; notwithstanding the wording of the original arbitral decision referring to damage to another State or its nationals or property.

229 See Chapter 1, Section 2.

CHAPTER 3

The Classical Approach: Regulating NSA Space Pollution via State Responsibility

> [i]n international space law, however, all private actions are attributed to the State.[1]

∴

The analysis above has shown that the existence of a prohibition against States causing space pollution has a demonstrable basis in international space law, particularly when interpreted in line with leading principles of international environmental law. However, whereas there has been scholarly work on the responsibility of States for space debris, the legal bases to hold NSAs accountable for such harm is essentially unexplored.[2] The discussion in this Chapter seeks to redress that gap.[3] To do so, it looks at provisions and instruments of international law to determine how they can apply to regulate NSA conduct (whereas domestic laws applicable to space activities are assessed in Chapter 5). That multi-level analysis of the interplay between international law, State law, and the conduct of NSAs provides an important and novel means of producing a holistic view appraisal of legal protections of the outer space environment.

As detailed above, space law originated in a highly State-centric legal context.[4] Consistent with this, and in light of its genesis in the 1960s, the obligations in the Outer Space Treaty and other leading space treaties are largely

---

1 Gutzman (2017), p. 1.

2 See Chapter 1, Section 5.

3 See Zhao (2018), p. 6 citing Juan Davalos, 'International standards in regulating space travel: Clarifying ambiguities in the commercial era of outer space' (2016) 30 *Emory International Law Review* p. 4, ('with more and more countries joining the space club, space legislation at the international level proves to be difficult.').

4 Fogo (2017), p. 182. See also James Crawford, *Brownlie's Principles of Public International Law* (9th ed.) (Oxford University Press, 2019) ('international law remains highly state-centric, a position reinforced from the early nineteenth century by the development and subsequent dominance of positivism as an account of law and legal obligation.').

directed towards States.[5] Accordingly, this section on accountability first looks at State responsibility and State liability as a means of imposing accountability for space pollution caused by NSAs.

1 The Outer Space Treaty and NSAs: Key Provisions

Any assessment of space law must begin with the Outer Space Treaty. Accordingly, the most relevant provisions of the Outer Space Treaty for State accountability for harmful activities in space are assessed in the following sections, most notably Articles VI, VII, VIII and IX.

1.1 *Article IX*

Beginning with Article IX, which has been discussed above as the core basis for a prohibition of space pollution,[6] the terms of this provision contain obligations relevant to space pollution, but convey them in elliptical terms which require considerable interpretation. Of central importance, it does not explicitly provide that States must take any particular action if NSAs under their control and/or jurisdiction cause harmful contamination to the space environment. On its own, Article IX does not provide an enforcement mechanism for States to take measures against NSAs which cause such harm (albeit it is the basis for the substantive prohibition of space pollution).

Of ancillary relevance to responsibility, Article IX enshrines principles of co-operation and mutual assistance and dictates that States shall conduct all their activities in outer space, including the moon and other celestial bodies, with due regard to the corresponding interests of all other states. Furthermore, it includes an obligation of consultation. However, the consultation obligation is hampered by the lack of concrete requirements as to the extent or form of any such consultation. as well as an undetermined time component of when such a consultation needs to be undertaken as Article IX declares that if a State Party has 'reason to believe that an activity or experiment planned by it

5 Dan St. John, 'The Trouble with Westphalia in Space: The State-Centric Liability Regime' (2012) 40(4) *Denver Journal of International Law and Policy*, p. 687; Elena Cirkovic, 'The Next Generation of International Law: Space, Ice, and the Cosmolegal Proposal' (2021) 22 *German Law Journal*, p. 151; Frans von der Dunk, 'The Origins of Authorization: Article VI of the Outer Space Treaty and International Space Law' (2011b) 69 *Space, Cyber, and Telecommunications Law Program Faculty Publications*, pp. 1–3; S.G. Sreejith, 'Whither International Law, Thither Space Law: A Discipline in Transition' (2008) 38 *California Western International Law Journal*, p. 392.

6 Chapter 2, Section 1, 1.1.

or its nationals (...) would cause potentially harmful interference'. This leaves States with a wide discretion to determine the obligation for themselves.[7] Such discretion undermines the consistent and firm adherence to the consultation obligation.

Further, interpretive issues surround Article IX. These include the fact that it only refers explicitly to 'the exploration' of outer space, but not its 'use', as noted above.[8] Given that serious space pollution can occur when launching satellites and sending testing equipment to the moon or Mars, in addition to when exploring in the traditional sense, this interpretive issue bears consequence for the legal obligations and proceedings deriving from Article IX. However, an interpretation of 'exploration' to cover all uses of space is potentially available, as discussed above.[9] Nonetheless, that will render space law dependent on the interpretation of law by scholars and judges in the future, which may itself alter and vacillate.

1.2 *Article VI*

The key provision in the Outer Space Treaty emphasizing the State-centric approach to accountability for NSA conduct is Article VI. Uniquely, it decrees in its first part that:

> States Parties to the Treaty shall bear international responsibility for national activities in outer space, including the moon and other celestial bodies, whether such activities are carried on by governmental agencies or by non-governmental entities, and for assuring that national activities are carried out in conformity with the provisions set forth in the present Treaty. The activities of non-governmental entities in outer space, including the moon and other celestial bodies, shall require authorization and continuing supervision by the appropriate State Party to the Treaty.[10]

---

7 Michael C. Mineiro, 'FY-1C and USA-193 ASAT Intercepts: An Assessment of Legal Obligations under Article IX of the Outer Space Treaty' (2008) 34 *Journal of Space Law* p. 355; Biswanath Gupta, Tamoghna Agasti, 'The Curious Case of Article IX and Outer Space Environment' (2022) 2 *Journal of Environmental Impact and Management Policy*, pp. 2, 11.

8 See Chapter 2, Section 1.1.

9 Chapter 2, Section 1.1.

10 In doctrine, two distinct views on the effects of Article VI can be discerned. The first is based on a premise that Article VI concerns merely primary obligations of States, namely to authorize and supervise acts of private persons (see Gaetano Arangio-Ruiz, 'State Responsibility Revisited: The Factual Nature of the Attribution of Conduct to the State' (2017) 6 *Rivisita di diritto internazionale*, pp. 126, 127; Sergio Marchisio, 'Il Trattato sullo spazio: passato, presente e future' (2018) 1 *Rivisita di diritto internazionale*, p. 201), whereas the second view claims that Article VI concerns secondary rules on attribution

In broad terms, Article VI makes States responsible for all national activities in outer space that are carried out by their authorities, their nationals or by NSAs operating from their territory or otherwise connected to the State. Under Article VI, States must ensure that these entities comply with the Outer Space Treaty.[11] Furthermore, Article VI suggests that NSAs are only allowed to conduct space activities with State authorization and continuous supervision. That raises the issue of how to address an NSA which lies beyond the power of a State to control, such as a rebel movement in control of part of a country. If the territorial State is unable to control such an NSA, then it is unclear how it can be attributed responsibility for the NSA's actions.[12]

Two distinct views emerged as to the effect of Article VI. The first one considers that Article VI concerns merely primary obligations of States, namely to authorize and supervise acts of private 'persons', which would include corporations and other NSAs.[13] This would result in only a type of due diligence obligation incumbent on States during the authorization and supervision process.[14]

The second view claims that Article VI concerns secondary rules on attribution and that it acts as *lex specialis* to less strict customary rules of State

---

(as a form of *lex specialis* to the customary rules of State responsibility on attribution from Articles on State Responsibility) (see Hobe, Pellander (2012); BinCheng, 'Article VI of the 1967 Space Treaty Revisited: 'International Responsibility', 'National Activities' and 'The Appropriate State'' (1998) 26 *Journal of Space Law* 1, p. 14; von der Dunk (2011b), pp. 3, 5; Stubbe (2018), p. 95; Horst Bittlinger, 'Private Space Activities: Questions of International Responsibility, in Proceedings of the 30th Colloquium on the Law of Outer Space (Brighton, United Kingdom)).

11 Stubbe notes that, because the first sentence of Article VI does not differentiate between governmental and non-governmental entities, '[t]his can only be understood to mean that a state is responsible for all national space activities, included those carried out by non-governmental entities.' See Stubbe (2018), p.95. Consequently, he asserts that '[a]rticle vi sentence 1 of the Outer Space Treaty establishes a specific attribution rule for all outer space activities, in addition to those of ILC Articles on State Responsibility and in derogation from the non-attributability of private conduct under customary law (also citing Horst Bittlinger, 'Private Space Activities: Questions of International Responsibility' (1987) *Proceedings of the 30th Colloquium on the Law of Outer Space* (American Institute of Aeronautics and Astronautics, 1987), pp. 191–196). See also Gutzman (2017), p. 8.

12 See Chapter 3, Section 2. See also Beard and Stephens (2024), pp. 111–112 (arguing that automatic attribution of NSA conduct to a State in the context of *jus ad bellum*, 'it could give rise to manifestly absurd results').

13 Arangio-Ruiz (2017), pp. 126, 127; Marchisio (2018), p. 201.

14 Dennerley calls it a 'duty of conduct, not of result, meaning that the obligation incumbent on states is to use their best efforts to try to prevent damage or harm occurring to other states.', see Dennerley (2018), p.294.

responsibility on attribution based on the Articles on State Responsibility.[15] If the second view is taken, the State automatically inherits the acts of the NSA without the need to establish the link of attribution. In this way, it would be held to have essentially carried out the acts itself, rather than merely being responsible for a failure to adequately supervise the conduct of space-faring entities under its jurisdiction as per the first view. On either view of Article VI, it is the State Party that is ultimately ascribed with international responsibility under the treaty, in case it fails to take required action, rather than the NSA being directly bound by the Outer Space Treaty.

Under general international rules on attribution, State responsibility does not arise automatically. In broad terms, there are the following major categories whereby attribution can be established: acts by *de jure* organs of State, acts by *de facto* organs of a State or entities that carry out "governmental authority", acts carried out by entities under a State's control, acts of insurrectional movements which become governments, and acts that are subsequently adopted by a State as its own.[16] However, if the second view of Article VI is accepted, then Article VI exceeds these grounds; as it makes States responsible for acts of non-State entities when they emanate from its territory whether by organs of government or by NSAs,[17] as well as for actions by their nationals falling under the national authorisation and supervision regime.[18] In this respect, it can be seen as a hyper State-centric approach.

The responsibility of States for NSA conduct under Article VI imports obligations. In general, willful blindness and inaction in the face of private space activities will not fulfill the State's obligations and will not absolve the appropriate State of responsibility.[19] Dennerly calls it a 'duty of conduct, not of result, meaning that the obligation incumbent on states is to use their best efforts to try to prevent damage or harm occurring to other states.'[20] However, Stubbe goes so far as to call it a 'responsibility to ensure' – meaning the 'obligation of a state to assure that the conduct of a state's private individuals complies with

15 Hobe, Pellander (2012), p. 9; Cheng (1998), p. 14; von der Dunk (2011b), pp. 3, 5; Stubbe (2018), p. 95; Bittlinger (1987), pp. 191–196.

16 See Chapter 3, Section 2 on Articles on State Responsibility.

17 Article VI provides that 'States Parties to the Treaty shall bear international responsibility for national activities in outer space, [...] by non-governmental entities, and for assuring that national activities are carried out in conformity with the provisions set forth in the present Treaty.'

18 Beard and Stephens (2024), pp. 114–115.

19 Stubbe (2018), p. 89, fn. 139; von der Dunk (2011b), pp. 7–8.

20 Dennerley (2018), p. 294.

that state's duties under international law.'[21] Von der Dunk takes a similar line, calling it 'private activity public responsibility'. He argues that Article VI clearly establishes that a State must always be responsible for private activities and that this is shown by the change in language, as previous declarations employed a due diligence language for responsibility for private actors whereby Article VI of the Outer Space Treaty equates governmental and non-governmental activities.[22] Equally, Cheng argues that all activities, whether carried out by states or NSAs 'are deemed to be governmental activities involving direct state responsibility',[23] imposing a form of strict responsibility on States for NSA conduct.[24]

Strict State responsibility for NSA conduct follows from the etymology of the provision. The terms of Article VI emerged in this format as a compromise between the view of the Soviet Union, whereby NSA activities would be excluded from space altogether, and that of the United States, which opposed that approach.[25] As a result, the wording of Article VI allowed for the possibility of non-governmental space activities, but established a strict state responsibility regime for private space activities.[26]

Article VI also refers to the governmental authorization process. The specific way in which that authorization process is converted to domestic law is set out in detail in Chapter 5. Nonetheless, for present purposes the implementation of international law duties, the authorization process 'is the major tool for states to ensure that their authorized operators are able and willing to comply with existing regulations'.[27] However, the provisions of the Outer Space Treaty do not specify *how* States have to implement this obligation. Similarly, while authors refer to a due diligence obligation to ensure the 'effective regulation

---

21 Stubbe (2018), p. 90 referring to Article 139 para. 1 UNCLOS; and Article 4 para. 4 Annex iii UNCLOS; ITLOS, *Responsibilities and Obligations of States Sponsoring Persons and Entities with Respect to Activities in the Area*, Advisory Opinion of 1 February 2011 (ITLOS Reports 2011, p. 10), para. 108.

22 See von der Dunk (2011b), p. 4.

23 Cheng (1997), p. 237. But see Stubbe, arguing that Article VI should be read to open the gate to responsibility on the part of States, but not to displace the requirement of showing the usual objective and subjective requirements of State responsibility ('[t]he criterion that needs to be fulfilled for entailing international responsibility of a state – the internationally wrongful act with its objective and subjective elements – is not at all modified by Article VI sentence 1 of the Outer Space Treaty.'); Stubbe (2018), p. 87.

24 Stubbe (2018), p. 87.

25 Ribbelink (2009), pp. 64–69.

26 See von der Dunk (2011b), p. 4.

27 Larsen further notes that 'unauthorized operators cannot launch legally' and that 'delinquent operators should be required by the authorizing country to deorbit', see Larsen (2018), p. 483.

of national activities that have the potential to cause environmental harm',[28] the parameters governing this obligation are not set out in binding space law instruments. Broad duties based on general international law can be gleaned from the jurisprudence of the International Court of Justice. But this provides little guidance specifically tailored towards the outer space environment.[29] Larsen notes that 'unauthorized operators cannot launch legally' and that 'delinquent operators should be required by the authorizing country to deorbit'.[30] However, aside from the legislative moves by States which are mapped out in detail in Chapter 5, there are few examples of States taking enforcement actions in court against NSAs. There are examples of State authorities stepping in to halt NSAs space launches. SpaceX's launch of a batch of Starlink satellites was delayed due to the Federal Aviation Administration requiring changes to be made to the satellites following a complaint from the space community.[31] Nonetheless, these are sporadic examples, which do not evince clear State practice establishing how States must regulate the conduct of NSAs under their control.

Having reviewed the basis for States to be held responsible for NSAs under the Outer Space Treaty, a key question remains as to how to determine national activity, especially in cases of large multinational NSAs. In this respect, it is necessary to determine which State is the 'appropriate State' under Article VI.[32] While the Outer Space Treaty does not further define the 'appropriate

---

28 Stubbe (2018), p. 200.

29 ICJ, *Corfu Channel Case* (U.K. v. Albania), Judgment; Dennerley (2018), p. 293; ICJ, *Case Concerning Application of the Convention on the Prevention and Punishment of the Crime of Genocide* (Bosnia and Herzegovina v. Serbia and Montenegro), Judgment of 11 July 1996 (ICJ Reports 1996, p. 595), para. 430; ICJ, *Pulp Mills on the River Uruguay* (Argentina v. Uruguay), Judgment, para. 101; ICJ, *Construction of a Road in Costa Rica along the San Juan River* (Nicaragua v. Costa Rica), Judgment of 16 December 2015 (ICJ Reports 2015, p. 665), para. 104. See also Dennerley (2018), p. 294.

30 Larsen (2018), p. 483.

31 Jeff Foust, 'FAA again delays completion of Starship environmental review' *Space News* (26 March 2022) (available at https://spacenews.com/faa-again-delays-completion-of-starship-environmental-review/); Ry Crist, 'Starlink Explained: What to Know About Elon Musk's Sattelite Internet Service' *CNET* (15 April 2023) (available at https://www.cnet.com/home/internet/starlink-satellite-internet-explained/https://www.faa.gov/newsroom/faa-requires-spacex-take-over-75-actions-mitigate-environmental-impact-planned); Jeff Foust, 'FAA proposes fining SpaceX for missing launch data' *Space News* (17 February 2023) (available at https://spacenews.com/faa-proposes-fining-spacex-for-missing-launch-data/).

32 See Karl-Heinz Bockstiegel, 'Term Appropriate State in International Space Law, The Definitional Issues in Space Law' (1994) 37 *Proc Law Outer Space*, p. 77. See also Ziemblicki and Oralova (2021), p. 4.

State', a plain meaning interpretation would refer to the State of nationality of space actors, due to the use of the phrase 'States Parties to the Treaty shall bear international responsibility for *national* activities in outer space.'[33] The most relevant entity under Article VI under this approach would be the national State. This necessitates determining the nationality of the person(s) or entities conducting the space activities.

For natural persons, determining nationality is usually a routine matter. However, for legal entities there are various routes to determining nationality. Three criteria are normally accepted to determine the nationality of corporate entities: 'either from the fact of incorporation, that is creation as a legal person, within a given system of domestic law, or from links to a particular state such as the center of administration (siège social) or the nationality of the natural or legal persons that own or control the company.'[34] The Permanent Court of International Justice in the *Barcelona Traction* case focused on the State in which the company is incorporated, on whose territory it holds its seat.[35]

However, there is a lack of clarity regarding distinction or overlapping of the terms appropriate State, launching State, and State of registry. The relation between Articles VI, VII and VIII of the Outer Space Treaty is complex in this respect. Zannoni notes that the opacity contributes to inconsistency, but is also something that States are not particularly eager to resolve, as it serves "as a convenient buffer against responsibility and liability".[36] A second option is the launching State(s), which may be held liable for any damage caused by space objects. In the case of multiple States, the launching States are jointly and severally liable for any damage caused, as determined by Article V of the Liability Convention. Finally, one view with a basis in both State practice and doctrine, though disputed, is that a launching State cannot rid itself of liability even in cases of a transfer of ownership or loss of control over the space objects.[37] This then means the launching State will remain indefinitely liable for any damage caused by its space objects/space debris, even if such objects are actually owned (and launched) by private entities.

33 Pavesi (2018), p. 19.

34 Stubbe (2018), p. 262.

35 ICJ, *Case Concerning the Barcelona Traction, Light and Power Company, Limited* (Belgium v. Spain), Judgment of 5 February 1970 (ICJ Reports 1970, p. 3), para. 70.

36 Diego Zannoni, 'The Liability Regime for Private Activities in Outer Space: Is There a Normative Gap?' (2021) 59(1) *Archiv des Völkerrechts*, p. 2.

37 See Stubbe (2018), pp. 278–279. See also Viikari, p. 78 (noting that the Registration Convention does not address the situation of registering space objects in case of transfer of ownership to an entity in a different State).

A third option is the State of Registry, which according to Article VIII of the Outer Space Treaty holds jurisdiction and control over the objects registered in its national registry and any personnel thereof, as discussed below. According to the Registration Convention it is the duty of a launching State to register.[38] The Registration Convention furthermore envisions the conveyance of certain information regarding space objects to the United Nations.[39] However, NSAs are not subject to the Registration Convention, and therefore it is up to States to enact appropriate national legislation to require from NSAs the necessary information and register it.[40]

Commentators opine that multiple States may be the 'appropriate State' notwithstanding the grammatical awkwardness of this interpretation.[41] This accords with the overarching aim of Article VI, namely to ensure that at least one State is responsible and accountable for all human actions and activities that occur in outer space.[42] Significantly, the survey of State practice set out in Chapter 5 below indicates that States with space legislation have frequently framed it as applying to any NSAs operating from their territory as well as to their nationals whichsoever territory they are operating from, or even to activities under their jurisdiction elsewhere.[43] That nationality and/or territoriality and/or jurisdiction linkage would provide a clear and robust test for ascertaining whether any particular State is sufficiently connected to any particular NSA under Article VI. However, it would also mean that multiple States would frequently be implicated, potentially leading to disputes over which should bear primary responsibility for the NSAs conduct.

Judicial practice relevant to Article VI includes examples of States regulating the conduct of NSAs. This can be seen in attempted applications of Article II of the Outer Space Treaty, which forbids national appropriation of outer

38 Registration Convention, Article II.

39 Registration Convention, Article IV.

40 Mick Schmidt-Tedd, 'Article VIII' (2009) in Stephan Hobe, Bernhard Schmidt-Tedd, Kai-Uwe Schrogl, Gérardine Meishan Goh (eds.) *The Cologne Commentary on Space Law* (Vol. 1) (Carl Heymanns, 2009), p. 153.

41 Stephan Hobe *et al.*, *'Cologne Commentary on Space Law: In Three Volumes'* (2009) Köln: Carl Heymanns, at p. 110 In a case of cooperation between two States' entities, 'a national activity (of the governmental agency or non-governmental entity) in cooperation with another national activity (of another governmental agency or non-governmental entity). Consequently, two or more States might be internationally responsible.' Gutzman (2017), p. 8.

42 Hobe et al. (2009), p. 9.

43 See Chapter 5. Interestingly, this territoriality and/or nationality approach approximates the key jurisdictional bases of the International Criminal Court, as established under Article 12 of the Rome Statute.

space, including the Moon and other celestial bodies.[44] In the 1980s, a citizen of the United States called Dennis Hope started selling property on the Moon, stating that the prohibition entailed in Article II of the Outer Space Treaty forbids only national, but not private appropriation.[45] This was rebuffed in two national legal cases before national courts, where the courts interpreted Article II of the Outer Space Treaty to find that private property is not permitted, as it is encompassed under the prohibition on national appropriation in that Article.[46] This is explained in doctrine *inter alia* by the belief that private property cannot exist without State authority to guarantee it, and since a State cannot grant more rights than it itself has, it cannot grant private property rights in outer space (this is analogous to the widely recognised principle of *nemo dat quod non habet*).[47] Furthermore, the rationale of including private property under national appropriation was reportedly the intention the Outer Space Treaty's drafters, in accordance with States being responsible for all space activity.[48] In 2022, the Manual on International Law Applicable to Military Uses of Outer Space (MILAMOS) reiterated the provisions of the Outer Space Treaty, but added that the prohibition on national appropriation entails a prohibition on national appropriation by non-governmental entities.[49]

However, some authors argue that the Outer Space Treaty only prohibits the appropriation of orbital spots or areas in space and not resources extracted from celestial bodies.[50] That view could be used to argue that Section 10 of the Artemis Accords confirms that there is no prohibition on extracting space resources under Article II of the Outer Space Treaty.[51] However, an alternative view maintains that all resources are part of outer space including the Moon and other celestial bodies and therefore their appropriation is prohibited

---

44 This is developed further in Chapter 5.

45 Virgiliu Pop, 'The men who sold the Moon: science fiction or legal nonsense?' (2001) 17(3) *Space Policy*, p. 196; Alan Wasser, Douglas Jobes, 'Space Settlements, Property Rights, and International Law: Could a Lunar Settlement Claim the Lunar Real Estate It Needs to Survive' (2008) 73(1) *Journal of Air Law and Commerce*, p. 50.

46 United States District Court for the District of Nevada, *Nemitz v. US*, 2004 WL 316704 (26 April 2004).

47 S. Hobe (2019), p. 165; Lyall, Larsen (2009), pp. 184–185; F. Tronchetti (2013), pp. 13–14. This opinion is further confirmed by Outer Space Treaty drafting history (see Steven Freeland, Ram Jakhu, 'Article II' in Hobe et. al. (2009), pp. 51–53).

48 Freeland, Jakhu (2009), pp. 51–53.

49 Ram Jakhu and Steven Freeland, *McGill Manual on International Law Applicable to Military Uses of Outer Space: Volume 1 – Rules* (McGill University, 2022), Rule 113.

50 Hobe (2019), pp. 165; Freeland and Jakhu (2009), pp. 51–53.

51 See Chapter 1, Section 3.

by Article II.[52] Given that the Moon Agreement indicates that it is generally not permitted to extract resources unless an international regime on space resource exploitation is established beforehand,[53] there is contextual support for reading Article II of the Outer Space Treaty broadly to also prohibit State Parties appropriating space resources, including those extracted from celestial bodies. Extraction would only be permitted following the creation of an international regime. In this way, it would prevent unilateral exploitation and support the fair distribution of benefits globally, in accordance with Article I of the Outer Space Treaty. However, the fact that the Moon Agreement is so poorly subscribed weakens this interpretive reading.

While the governmental authorization process is primarily a tool designed to make States ensure that their authorized operators comply with international law,[54] the provisions of the Outer Space Treaty do not specify how States have to implement this obligation. Similarly, while authors refer to a due diligence obligation to ensure the 'effective regulation of national activities that have the potential to cause environmental harm',[55] the parameters governing this obligation are not set out in binding space law instruments. Broad duties to avoid harm emanating from a State's territory can be gleaned from the jurisprudence of the International Court of Justice,[56] but this provides little guidance specifically tailored towards the outer space environment. The consequences of disobedience are also unclear. Larsen, for example, notes that 'unauthorized operators cannot launch legally' and that 'delinquent operators should be required by the authorizing country to deorbit'.[57] However, the actual practice

---

52 See Chapter 1, Section 3.

53 Moon Agreement Article 11. See also Gaja Čeferin, *Mednarodnopravna Ureditev Rudarjenja na nebesnih telesih* (Master Thesis, University of Ljubljana, 2018); Ricky Lee, *Law and Regulation of Commercial Mining in Outer Space* (Springer, 2012).

54 Larsen further notes that 'unauthorized operators cannot launch legally' and that 'delinquent operators should be required by the authorizing country to deorbit', see Larsen (2018), p. 483.

55 Stubbe (2018), p. 200.

56 ICJ, *Corfu Channel Case* (U.K. v. Albania), Judgment; Dennerley (2018), p. 293; ICJ, *Case Concerning Application of the Convention on the Prevention and Punishment of the Crime of Genocide* (Bosnia and Herzegovina v. Serbia and Montenegro), Judgment, para. 430; ICJ, *Pulp Mills on the River Uruguay* (Argentina v. Uruguay), Judgment, para. 101; ICJ, *Construction of a Road in Costa Rica along the San Juan River* (Nicaragua v. Costa Rica), Judgment, para. 104. See also Dennerley (2018), p. 294.

57 Larsen (2018), p. 483.

with regard to enforcing these bans, which are reflected in legislation in many States as set out in Chapter 5, remains opaque.[58]

Based on the foregoing, Article VI of the Outer Space Treaty imposes an ostensibly strict mesh of State responsibility for national acts under their jurisdiction. However, such responsibility is merely an indirect responsibility, as States are the subjects directly responsible under Article VI. Consequently, under this provision, NSAs can be held directly responsible only under national legislation of the appropriate State, which must authorize and supervise their activities, as determined by Article VI.[59]

1.3 *Article VII*

Article VII of the Outer Space Treaty defines the launching state as the entity liable for any damage caused by launched objects. It provides that;

> Each State Party to the Treaty that launches or procures the launching of an object into outer space, including the moon and other celestial bodies, and each State Party from whose territory or facility an object is launched, is internationally liable for damage to another State Party to the Treaty or to its natural or juridical persons by such object or its component parts on the Earth, in air or in outer space, including the moon and other celestial bodies.[60]

This focus on the launching State diverges from Article VI's concentration on 'national activities'. However, Dennerly notes that the launching State is best placed to prevent acts that would cause damage such as space collisions, suggesting a 'best efforts obligation of due diligence to prevent acts, such as space object collisions, that would cause damage to another state is a duty incumbent on launching states.'[61]

Because Article VII encompasses States that launch or procure the launches of space objects, or from whose territory or facility such object is launched, and allow their territory to be used for launches, as well as State launches, it covers a wide array of conduct. However, two distinct questions appear in connection to Article VII: firstly, whether this provision can cover any environmental

58 SpaceX's launch of a batch of Starlink satellites was delayed due to the FAA requiring changes to be made to the satellites following a complaint from the astronomical community.

59 See Chapter 4, Section 2.1.

60 Outer Space Treaty, Article VII.

61 Dennerley (2018), p. 294.

damage in outer space; and, secondly, whether this liability is purely State-oriented as the initial reading of the terms of Article VII would suggest or whether it covers NSA activity as well.

Turning first to whether Article VII is capable of addressing environmental damage in outer space, the terms of Article VII of the Outer Space Treaty are unclear as to whether they would cover any environmental damage, or be restricted to damage that manifests against another State or natural or juridical person.[62] Article VII does not define damage, simply declaring 'damage to another State Party to the Treaty or to its natural or juridical persons'.[63] Whether this could include the environment of outer space as an area beyond national jurisdiction and a *res communis* remains unclear.

Article VII can be interpreted in light of subsequent practice, agreements, and relevant rules of international law, in accordance with Article 31(3)(a)-(c) of the Vienna Convention on the Law of Treaties. In the *Nicaragua* judgment, the International Court of Justice held that *lex specialis* has precedent over *lex generalis*.[64] In this respect, a subsequent treaty, the 1972 Liability Convention, complements Article VII of the Outer Space Treaty, defining damage in Article I(a) as follows:

> For the purposes of this Convention: (a) The term 'damage' means loss of life, personal injury or other impairment of health; or loss of or damage to property of States or of persons, natural or juridical, or property of international intergovernmental organizations.

Under the Liability Convention, Articles I to VII reiterate the obligation in Article VI of the Outer Space Treaty to compensate for damage caused by space objects,[65] but divide the obligation into absolute liability for damages occurring on Earth or to an aircraft in flight and fault-based liability for damages in

62 See Chapter 2, Section 1.1.

63 For more on the definition of damage see Kerrest and Smith (2009), pp. 126–146.

64 ICJ, *Case Concerning Military and Paramilitary Activities in and against Nicaragua* (Nicaragua v. United States of America), Judgment of 27 December 1986 (ICJ Reports 1986, p. 14), p. 137.

65 As discussed in Chapter 1, there is no authoritative definition of space object and whether it encompasses space debris. However, this article works on the premise that the term space object from article I of the Liability Convention encompasses space debris, and both space object and space debris are encompassed under 'object launched into outer space' from article VII of the Outer Space Treaty. For a discussion on the matter see Hobe (2019), p. 111; Smith and Kerrest (2013), pp. 109–110; Kerrest and Smith (2009), pp. 50–56; Schmidt-Tedd and Mick (2009), pp. 153–155.

outer space. The Liability Convention sets out two separate regimes of liability: first on absolute liability for cases of damage caused by a space object 'on the surface of the Earth or to aircraft flight'.[66] Second, a fault-based liability which applies when the damage occurs in outer space.[67] Importantly, it refers to liability for 'damage' in space, where it is the launching State's fault that resulted in the 'damage' or where it is the 'fault' of persons for whom the State is responsible.

However, the Liability Convention provisions face challenges. Environmental damage and damage to outer space or celestial bodies by space debris is not explicitly covered by the Liability Convention. It could be argued that indirect damage to the environment is encompassed. This could occur, for example, if the damage to the space environment caused impairment of health to persons or resulted in loss of or damage to property of States, persons or international organizations. This would be in line with the victim-oriented nature of the Liability Convention, which has been set with the objective of affecting swift and just compensation to victims.[68] However, the justification for liability would only be indirectly related to environmental harm.

Historic precedent provides a measure of support for this reading of 'damage' to encompass harm caused by space pollution such as debris. Under the Liability Convention, the sole claim presented is Canada's in the Kosmos-954 case in 1978, which involved a former Soviet Union nuclear powered satellite disintegrating over remote areas of northern Canada.[69] Canada claimed six million dollars (Canadian currency) of damages based on the Liability Convention, the Outer Space Treaty and general principles of international law. The damages covered 'the costs of restoring the territory rendered partly unfit for use by radioactive debris scattered over large areas, hence constituting damage to property within the meaning of the Liability Convention' as well as potentially the costs to establish a Compensation Commission.[70] However, the dispute was resolved by a settlement, which was founded on a 1981 protocol

66 Liability Convention, Article II.

67 Liability Convention, Article III. See also Viikari (2008), p. 66.

68 See Liability Convention, Preamble; Lyall and Larsen (2009), p. 107; Lesley Jane Smith and Armel Kerrest, 'The 1972 Convention on International Liability for Damage Caused by Space Objects' (2013) in Stephan Hobe, Bernhard Schmidt-Tedd, Kai-Uwe Schrogl (eds.), Peter Stubbe (assist. Ed.) *The Cologne Commentary on Space Law: Vol. II* (Carl Heymanns, 2013), pp. 83–227.

69 Viikari (2008), p. 72.

70 Viikari (2008), p. 72.

between the two States and not the Liability Convention.[71] Ultimately, the Soviet Union paid three million dollars (Canadian) which was termed 'full and final compensation'.[72] Nonetheless, this resolution between Canada and Soviet Union regarding the Kosmos-954 case demonstrates a notable precedent in that 'space debris was evidently considered a 'space object' as it sufficed, in the light of the initial Canadian claim, to establish liability under the Liability Convention.'[73]

On the other hand support for the Liability Convention indirectly covering space pollution could be gleaned from Article XXI, which decrees that in the event that 'the damage caused by a space object presents a large-scale danger to human life or seriously interferes with the living conditions of the population or the functioning of vital centres, the States Parties, and in particular the launching State, shall examine the possibility of rendering appropriate and rapid assistance to the State which has suffered the damage, when it so requests'. This recognition of affecting living conditions of all the population or the functioning of 'vital centres' would accord with including damage to the human environment that seriously affects the health or living conditions of persons. However, causation and fault on the part of the launching State Party to the Convention (or on the part of an entity for which the State Party was responsible) would have to be established in accordance with Article III. Establishing causation and fault would be difficult in the outer space environment given the uncertainties of space travel, the presence of unregistered space debris, and the lack of space traffic rules.[74]

Regarding the status of Article VII of the Outer Space Treaty and provisions of the Liability Convention, the Outer Space Treaty currently has 114 State Parties including all space faring nations, and the Liability Convention has 98 State Parties with equally all space faring nations included. Overall, the Liability Convention should be consulted when addressing any liability for damage by space objects, particularly when read in light of the obligation under Article VI of the Outer Space Treaty concerning the supervision of NSA activities.[75] The construction of the Liability Convention indicates an underlying presumption of States bringing legal suits thereunder for damage in outer

71 See Bilateral and Multilateral Agreements Governing Space Activities: Disintegration of Cosmos 954 Over Canadian Territory in 1978, Protocol Between The Government of Canada and The Government of the Union Of Soviet Socialist Republics, 2 April 1981.

72 Viikari (2008), p. 72.

73 Viikari (2008), pp. 72–73.

74 See further Chapter 3, Section 2.

75 See, e.g., Smith and Kerrest (2013), pp 108–110.

space. In this respect, the construction is similar to the Outer Space Treaty. Such a State-centric view further reflects the era in which these conventions were drafted and adopted, whereby States were seen as the sole actors in the system of international law.[76]

Turning to the second question of whether NSAs could be held liable for damages caused by such harm, in line with the State-oriented nature of the Outer Space Treaty, Article VII focuses on the State for liability, and its terms do not provide for any direct application to NSAs. However, it covers damages resulting from private space activities also, as it makes no distinction between damage caused by governmental and non-governmental entities. It simply makes the launching State(s) liable for any damage caused by their launched object, objects which launch they procured, or objects launched from its territory or platform. This approach is arguably in line with Article VI of the Outer Space Treaty,[77] which seeks to render all space activity national/State activity.[78]

Moreover, the procedure specified in Articles VIII to XXI of the Liability Convention provides further valuable insight. These specify that only a State, either the State 'whose natural or juridical persons suffer damage',[79] the State on whose territory the damage occurred or the State whose permanent residents were harmed, can present a claim for damages to the launching State via diplomatic channels.[80] Should these attempts fail, the States may establish a Claims Commission,[81] similar in character to arbitration.[82] This then corroborates the State-centric character of the Liability Convention, whereby States are made accountable for all damages and all conduct, including that of natural or juridical persons.

76 See Chapter 1, Section 3.

77 Armel Kerrest, '*Remarks on the Notion of Launching State*' (1999) 42 *Proceedings of the International Institute of Space Law*, p. 314; Armel Kerrest and Lesley Schmidt, '*Article VII*' (2009) and Bernhard Schmidt-Tedd and Stephan Mick, '*Article VIII*' both in Hobe et. al (2009), at pp. 128–30 and p. 147, respectively.

78 Michael Gerhard, '*Article VI*' (2009) in Hobe et. al. (2009), pp. 109–116. But see Ziemblicki and Oralova (2021), p. 4 (noting that the USA and India became engaged in a dispute regarding responsibility for NSA activites and that '[i]t became apparent that Articles VI and VII of the Outer Space Treaty were interpreted differently by the states involved and that the current space law regime is unable to resolve this type of transnational disagreement.').

79 Liability Convention, Article VIII.

80 Liability Convention, Articles VIII, IX, X.

81 Liability Convention, Article XIV.

82 See Lesley Jane Smith and Armel Kerrest and Fabio Tronchetti, 'The 1972 Convention on International Liability for Damage Caused by Space Objects' (2013) in Hobe et. al. (2013), pp. 244–372.

The only potential exception to the State-centric approach in both the Outer Space Treaty and Liability Convention is Article XI(2) of the Liability Convention, which provides that '[n]othing in this Convention shall prevent a State, or natural or juridical persons it might represent, from pursuing a claim in the courts or administrative tribunals or agencies of a launching State.' Under the domestic national jurisdiction of the launching State then claims can be presented directly to the NSA that caused the damage.[83] Kerrest analyzes that while these claims may be based on the Liability Convention, national court proceedings will be subject to various national laws in this respect,[84] which might cap the compensation awarded. This can be seen, for example under the legislative framework of Belgium, and might furthermore be plagued by problems of execution.[85] However, it does present an alternative to the otherwise State-focused liability regime of the Outer Space Treaty and Liability Convention.

1.4 *Article VIII*

A further provision relevant to ensuring accountability for NSA space pollution via the prism of States is Article VIII of the Outer Space Treaty. Article VIII decrees that the State that registers a launched object in its national registry retains jurisdiction and control over it and any personnel thereof.[86] Control is the factual element enabling actual supervision of the object's activity and jurisdiction is the legal right to determine the activity of a space object and to require other States to refrain from interfering with it.[87] In this way, jurisdiction constitutes an aspect of State sovereignty, including 'the rights and powers to exercise legislative, judicial and administrative authority over persons and objects in outer space'.[88] Article VIII of the Outer Space Treaty therefore effectively creates State sovereignty in space objects by granting launched objects a quasi-territorial character, similar to ships and aircraft.[89]

In international law, jurisdiction is typically understood as the legal right of a State to exercise legislative, judicial and administrative authority over personnel and objects. Former International Court of Justice President Judge

83 Kerrest (2017), pp. 9–14.
84 See Chapter 5.
85 Kerrest (2017), pp. 13–18.
86 Lafferanderei (2005), pp. 230–231.
87 Lachs (2010), pp. 65–75; Schmidt-Tedd and Mick (2009), pp. 156–160.
88 V.S. Vereshchetin, 'International Space Law and Domestic Law: Problems of Interrelations' (1981) 9 *Journal of Space Law*, pp. 31–32.
89 Cheng (1997), p. 467; Lachs (2010), pp. 65–75; Gbenga Oduntan, *Sovereingty and Jurisdiction in the Airspace and Outer Space* (Routledge, 2012).

Manfred Lachs posits that Article VIII, by granting jurisdiction in space objects and over any personnel thereof, grants to States the exclusive right to supervise the activities of its space object.[90] This in effect creates quasi-territorial sovereignty in space objects, bringing them akin to vessels and aircraft.[91] Arguably jurisdiction, like liability, does not end and cannot be abandoned once an object has been classified as debris or has been sold. The continuity of jurisdiction is important, as Article VI of the Outer Space Treaty presupposes situations of State jurisdiction and control for supervision of national activities.[92]

Article VIII does not depend on the functionality of an object. This means even space debris – man-made, non-functional objects[93] – remains under the jurisdiction of the State of registry.[94] That feature of Article VIII can be problematic for space debris remediation efforts.[95] According to the jurisprudence of the International Court of Justice, the customary international law requirement to respect the sovereignty of other States includes a prohibition of unauthorized interferences in the jurisdiction of another State.[96] Taken together, this would mean that other States may not interfere with an object and its space activity.[97] Consequently, active debris removal efforts by third parties would require the consent of the State of registry before a piece of space debris can be removed.[98]

Article VIII also establishes that national laws apply to and regulate human activities within a space object.[99] This is for example the case at the International Space Station, where the astronauts/cosmonauts are subject to the jurisdiction of the State that has registered the module they are located

90 Lachs (2010), p. 166.

91 Cheng (1997), p. 480.

92 Mark Sundahl, 'Legal Status of Spacecraft' in: *Routeledge Handbook of Space Law* (Ram Jakhu, Paul Stephen Dempsey (eds.)) (Routledge) p. 44; Setsuko Aoki, 'In Search of the Current Legal Status of the Registration of Space Objects' (2010) in *61st International Astronautical Congress 2019* (IAC 2010), Prague, Czech Republic.

93 Hobe (2019), pp. 111–112.

94 Schmidt-Tedd and Mick (2009), p. 154.

95 For more on the topic see Annette Froehlich (ed.), *Space Security and Legal Aspects of Active Debris Removal* (Springer, 2019).

96 ICJ, *Case Concerning Military and Paramilitary Activities in and against Nicaragua* (Nicaragua v. United States of America), Judgment, para. 202.

97 See Gordon Chung, '*Jurisdiction and Control Aspects of Space Debris Removal*' (2019), in Froehlich (2019), p. 38; Lachs 2010, p. 69; Cheng (1997), pp. 72, 86.

98 Chung (2019), pp. 38–40.

99 Stephan Hobe, '*The Legal Framework for a Lunar Base Lex Data and Lex Ferenda*' (1997), in Gabriel Lafferranderie und Daphné Crowther (eds) *Outlook on Space Law over the Next 30 Years* (Kluwer Law International, 1997) pp. 135–143.

in.[100] There have already been a few cases of States exercising their national legislation for offenses committed on the ISS, namely the case of Annie McClain, a NASA astronaut, accused of illegally accessing her partner's bank account while onboard the ISS.[101]

The International Space Station is governed by public entities, and is based on an Intergovernmental Agreement between the United States, Russia, Japan, Canada and 10 of the ESA member States.[102] Given this international agreement, the ISS constitutes a public project par excellence, made for States to control. The involvement of multiple States makes the legal position complex. If persons on the ISS visit another module, they arguably cross from one jurisdiction to another.[103] This quasi-territorial jurisdiction within space objects arguably prevails over all other legal bases, such as, for example, their personal jurisdiction with respect to the nationality of astronauts.[104] The picture is complicated further, as private entities are increasingly involved in trips to the ISS. For example, Space Adventures, a private company, reports that it has arranged all nine of the space flights undertaken by private citizens to date.[105] Clients of Space Adventures flying to the International Space Station have stayed on the Russian Soyuz spacecraft, where they live and work alongside professional astronauts for 10 days or more.[106] With multiple States potentially involved, and with private enterprise also conducting space tourism activities on it, the ISS presents one of the most multi-faceted contexts for space activities, in the sense of implicating multiple regulatory frameworks, and calls for academic

100 Agreement Between the United States of America and Other Governments Concerning Cooperation on the Civil International Space Station (29 January 1998) (available at https://www.state.gov/wp-content/uploads/2019/02/12927-Multilateral-Space-Space-Station-1.29.1998.pdf), Article 5(2); ESA, *International Space Station Legal Framework* (available at https://www.esa.int/Science_Exploration/Human_and_Robotic_Exploration/International_Space_Station/International_Space_Station_legal_framework).

101 See Loren Grush, 'The first alleged crime committed in space raises questions about jurisdiction in orbit' *The Verge* (27 August 2019) (available at https://www.theverge.com/2019/8/27/20833761/nasa-iss-international-space-station-alleged-crime-anne-mcclain-jurisdicition-framework).

102 Hobe (2010), p. 872.

103 ISS IGA Article 5; 'The International Space Station', Frans von der Dunk and Marcel M.T.A. Brus, (Eds.) (Brill, 2006); Percy J. Blount, 'Jurisdiction in Outer Space: Challenges of Private Individuals in Space' (2007) *Journal of Space Law*, pp. 312–313.

104 Vereshchetin (1981), p. 32.

105 Space Adventures, Live Onboard The International Space Station' (available at https://spaceadventures.com/experiences/space-station/#:~:text=When%20you%20reach%20Earth%20orbit,by%20private%20citizens%20to%20date.).

106 See Hobe (2010), p. 873.

scrutiny to assess whether and how NSAs could be held responsible for wrongdoing in this context.

In relation to space pollution, Article VIII provides a basis to hold States responsible for NSA acts. Stubbe argues that Article VIII acts as a type of fail-safe and extends the responsibility of States from Article VI of the Outer Space Treaty by transposing 'the obligations of the state with respect to preventing harm (...) to any actor under its jurisdiction carrying out a space activity; actors that would not normally be bound by the international obligation of a state.'[107] He explains that this is because States are under international law obligated to regulate certain environmental protection in national laws, which through Article VIII then become binding on national space actors as well. He argues that States have, for example, a 'due diligence duty' which requires them to regulate any national activities which could result in harm to the space environment. In effect, the provision transposes State obligations to any actor under its jurisdiction engaging in space activities.[108] According to Stubbe, one such due diligence duty is the environmental impact assessment.[109] However, it is not firmly established that States are required to force NSAs to undertake environmental impact assessments if the State fails to do so itself.[110] Nonetheless, Belgium and France, for example, require an environmental impact assessments for authorization of NSA space activity, considering effects beyond Earth's atmosphere within their national space legislation adopted in accordance with Article VI of the Outer Space Treaty.[111]

---

107 Stubbe (2018), p. 200.

108 Stubbe (2018), p. 200.

109 Stubbe (2018), p. 200 (arguing that conducting an EIA accords with Article 7 of the Articles on Transboundary Harm and that this would apply to space debris causing damage to other space objects under control or jurisdiction of another state. For the Articles on Transboundary Harm see Article 1 'The present articles apply to activities not prohibited by international law which involve a risk of causing significant transboundary harm through their physical consequences.'; Article 2(a) "risk of causing significant transboundary harm" includes risks taking the form of a high probability of causing significant transboundary harm and a low probability of causing disastrous transboundary harm;' Article 2(c): '"transboundary harm"' means harm caused in the territory of or in other places under the jurisdiction or control of a State other than the State of origin, whether or not the States concerned share a common border; ... ').

110 See generally Stephen Eric Mustow, 'Environmental impact assessment (EIA) screening and scoping of extraterrestrial exploration and development projects' (2018) 36(6) *Impact Assessment and Project Appraisal*, pp. 467–478.

111 Mustow (2018), pp. 467–469. See also William R. Kramer, 'In dreams begin responsibilities – environmental impact assessment and outer space development' (2017) 19(3) *Environmental Practice*, p. 130. See also Chapter 5.

In light of the above, Article VIII of the Outer Space Treaty certainly helps to regulate and even hold accountable private space actors, including NSAs. However, it does so indirectly – by ascribing the State's jurisdiction and control over the space objects listed in its national register belonging to NSAs and any personnel thereof. The way in which States regulate NSA conduct within their jurisdiction under domestic law is addressed in Chapter 5.

2 Problems Arising from the Exclusive Focus on States to Ensure NSA Accountability

Given that space law was conceived of in a State-centric manner, it is unsurprising that the first recourse for NSA space pollution is channeling accountability via States. However, several factors restrict the utility of seeking accountability for space pollution caused by NSAs exclusively via State accountability.

First, States may not be able to sufficiently monitor the wide range of NSA activities in outer space.[112] As space activities generally increase and space market becomes more segmented and globally integrated,[113] the amplitude and volume of private space activities may increase to the point that States cannot comprehensively supervise the totality of NSA conduct. For example, certain companies are already developing technology that may rival or even surpass that of States making it very difficult for States to supervise or even detect private space activity.[114] This trend could foreshadow an age of increased space activity, producing a potentially unregulated production of space debris.

---

112 For the growing range of space activities by private actors, see Alessandra Vernile, *The Rise of Private Actors in the Space Sector* (Springer, 2018), Introduction, p. xxii.

113 Guglielmo S. Aglietti, 'Current Challenges and Opportunities for Space Technologies' (2020) 1 *Frontiers in Space Technologies*, p. 1; Bhavya Lal, 'Reshaping Space Policies to Meet Global Trends' (2016) 32 *Issues in Science and Technology*, p. 4.

114 Aerospace startup Swarm Technologies already launched a few satellites that were deemed too small to be trackable, which is why they were at first denied a license. See: Loren Grush, 'Company that launched satellites without permission gets new license to launch more probes' *The Verge* (4 October 2017) (available at https://www.theverge.com/2018/10/4/17928452/swarm-technologies-spacebees-satellites-spacex-falcon-9-fcc-license). Similarly, New Zealand start-up Rocket Lab created a launch vehicle offering launch to a great number of miniature satellites. See Morgan Bailey, 'Frequent and Reliable Launch for Small Satellites: Rocket Lab's Electron Launch Vehicle and Photon Spacecraft' (2020) in Joseph N. Pelton, Scott Madry (Eds.) *Handbook of Small Satellites* (Springer, 2020); Adam Mann, 'Rocket Lab poised to provide dedicated launcher for CubeSat science' *Science* (6 December 2017) (available at https://www.science.org/content/article/rocket-lab-poised-provide-dedicated-launcher-cubesat-science); Victor L. Shammas, Thomas B. Holen,

Second, some States may not be willing or able to regulate activities emanating from their territories. This may occur due to a lack of organization, resources, authority, or even a lack of will to ensure that all activities originating from their territory are monitored and controlled. These limitations can be exacerbated by the presence of increasingly sophisticated NSAs in outer space, which often outpace States in terms of adapting and utilizing new technology.

There are demonstrated cases of States that are unwilling or unable to repress acts risking serious harm to the environment committed by entities operating from or on their territory even on earth let alone in space. For example, Houthi rebels reportedly fired a missile from Yemen's territory towards Israel in November 2023, which was intercepted by Israeli air defence.[115] Given the hostilities in Yemen and its lack of control over areas from which the Houthi's operate, it is questionable whether it could have interceded to prevent the rebels launching this strike even if it had wanted to. Moreover, States may engage in hiding behind NSAs in order to keep or reach the strategic advancement – letting NSAs achieve what these States are not allowed to do under international law. Even though States usually regulate their space activities, the commercial space market remains far less regulated.[116] Some States, due to conflict, famine, or other disasters of human and non-human origins, are unable or unwilling to take measures even in the face of earthly environmental pollution.[117]

Moreover, certain powerful multinational corporations with a growing interest in space exploration have financial resources outstripping many States.[118] Some large transnational corporations 'may wield more power and influence in international environmental fora than smaller states.'[119] Although Thirlway

---

'One giant leap for capitalist kind: private enterprise in outer space' (2019) 5 *Palgrave Communications*, p. 3.

115 Harriet Barber, 'How Israel shot down a ballistic missile in space for the first time', *Telegraph*, 5 November 2023 (available at https://www.telegraph.co.uk/world-news/2023/11/04/how-israel-shot-down-ballistic-missile-in-space-houthis/).

116 Stephen M. McCall (2020) *Challenges to the United States in Space*, Congressional Research Service Report IF10337.

117 Whilst such States would typically not have the financial means to launch space objects, they may nonetheless attempt to do so, just as the Ugandan dictator Idi Amin attempted to do so. Moreover, the prospect of private entities using such States as launching locations is a potential risk.

118 Amazon's market cap, for example, is larger than the GDPs of 92 percent of the world's countries. See Omri Wallach, 'The World's Tech Giants, Compared to the Size of Economics' *Visual Capitalist* (7 July 2021) (available at https://www.visualcapitalist.com/the-tech-giants-worth-compared-economies-countries/).

119 Philippe Sands and Jacqueline Peel, *Principles of International Environmental Law* (4th ed.) (Cambridge University Press, 2018), p. 53.

argues that 'even the most powerful international corporation is – in theory, at least – [...] under State sovereignty: it has its existence, is incorporated, under the law of some sovereign State, and that State could in theory and principle dissolve it at any time',[120] corporations can shift their headquarters rapidly and are able to force countries to compete for their business.

Additionally, the inability to regulate matters within their borders may also occur where parts of States' territories lie outside their control, typically in circumstances of armed conflict. Euphemistically termed 'ungoverned spaces' ('encompassing under-governed, misgoverned, contested, and exploitable areas as well as ungoverned areas'),[121] international law literature is increasingly recognizing that threats to international peace and security may emerge from such areas.[122] According to Nicholas Tsagourias '[s]uch places are viewed as breeding grounds for non-state actors to pursue nefarious activities'.[123] Interference with space activities is a growing threat; such incidents perpetrated by NSAs are reportedly on the rise.[124]

---

120 Hugh Thirlway, 'The Role of Non-State Actors: A Response to Professor Ryngaert' (2017) 64, *Netherlands International Law Review*, p. 145.

121 Nicholas Tsagourias notes that an ungoverned space is defined in a RAND report as '[a]n area in which a state faces significant challenges in establishing control. Ungoverned territories can be failed or failing states, poorly controlled land or maritime borders, or areas within otherwise viable states where the central government's authority does not extend.' See Nicholas Tsagourias, 'Non-State Actors, Ungoverned Spaces and International Responsibility for Cyber Acts' (2016) 21 *Journal of Conflict and Security Law* 3, pp. 458 citing Angel Rabasa, Steven Boraz, Peter Chalk, Kim Craigin, Theodore W. Karasik, *Ungoverned Territories: Understanding and Reducing Terrorism Risks* (2007) (Rand: Project Air Force). See also Anne L. Clunan and Harold A. Trinkunas, *Ungoverned Spaces: Alternatives to State Authority in an Era of Softened Sovereignty* (Stanford University Press, 2010), pp. 28–29.

122 Tsagourias (2016), p. 455 citing Robert D. Lamb, *Ungoverned Areas and Threats from Safe Havens: Final Report of the Ungoverned Areas Project*, Office of the Deputy Assistant Secretary of Defense for Policy Planning (2008) (available athttps://dgi.umd.edu/sites/default/files/2019-07/ugash_report_final.pdf); US Department of Defense, *Quadrennial Defense Review* (2014) (available at https://www.acq.osd.mil/ncbdp/docs/2014_Quadrennial_Defense_Review.pdf).

123 Tsagourias (2016), p. 455. He notes that, under Article 9 of the Articles on State Responsibility, the conduct of a person or group exercising elements of governmental authority due to the absence or default of the official authorities (for example where there is total or partial collapse of governmental authority) can constitute an act of the State where they are located. Under Article 10, the conduct of an insurrectional movement that replaces governmental authority or establishes a new state are considered an act of the State where it occurs.

124 Fogo (2017), p. 190 citing Deborah Housen-Couriel, 'Disruption of Satellite Transmissions Ad Bellum and In Bello: Launching a New Paradigm of Convergence' (2012) 45(3) *Israel Law Review*, pp. 431, 440.

Examples of State unwillingness to address NSA risks (partly due to a divergent understanding of the international legal framework) have already emerged in which environmental consequences could have been grave. For instance, in 1992, an Indonesian company called Pasifik Satellite Nusantara (PSN) company launched a satellite into a GEO orbital slot which had been assigned to Tonga but had remained unfilled.[125] Tonga then leased the GEO slot out in 1993 to a company from the United States and the company launched its own satellite into this position. In 1996, Tonga leased the same spot to a Chinese company. A direct collision was avoided as PSN jammed the satellite.[126] Eventually, the crisis was resolved, as PSN had a financial collapse. However, the incident demonstrates that a company operating within a State which refuses to abide by international frameworks cannot be directly proceeded against under the current framework of international law. Indonesia declined to recognize the ITU's competence to allocate GEO slots and the ITU did not have an enforcement mechanism capable of overriding this refusal.[127]

Third, enterprising corporations, and other individuals or groups, may seek to exploit weaker regulatory regimes to engage in potentially more profitable space exploration. Certain States may adopt a less stringent regulatory approach in order to attract the investment associated with space ventures. Even if the variation in regulation arises merely as a matter of different interpretations of instruments such as the IADC guidelines, these variations may still introduce incentives for private entities to seek out the lowest common regulatory denominator.[128]

This raises the risk of non-State entities engaging in a form of forum shopping by utilizing 'flag of convenience countries'.[129] By registering in countries with less rigorously enforced standards, they may obtain a competitive

125 Space Security 2004, p. 14; Viikari (2008), p. 90.

126 Space Security 2004 (available at https://www.belfercenter.org/sites/default/files/pantheon_files/files/publication/ssi2004.pdf); Viikari (2008), p. 90.

127 Space Security 2004, p. 14; Viikari (2008), p. 90.

128 Larsen notes that the implementation of the IADC Guidelines is not uniform as they must be 'implemented in accordance with their interpretation by each nation-state'; see Larsen (2018), p. 480.

129 Larsen (2018), pp. 491–492, 515 ('Because the regime would not be universal, it would suffer from the competitive freedom of countries which remain unregulated and become flag of convenience countries. Experience indicates that some non-government operators find it to be in their commercial interest to establish themselves in such flag-of-convenience countries in order to enjoy a competitive advantage. If major operators chose to move to flag-of-convenience countries, then the effort of more stringent space debris regulation could be defeated.').

advantage.[130] In the shipping domain, this practice and the consequent lowered safety standards led to an increase in accidents and environmental disasters.[131] The legal response was the adoption of the Geneva Convention on the High Seas of 1958, which required that the ship have a 'genuine link' with the State in which it was registered, a requirement that was further entrenched in the 1982 UN Convention on the Law of the Sea.[132] However those treaties only directly apply to States Parties, and the flag of convenience problem continues to plague the high seas.[133]

When translated to the outer space domain, flag of convenience practices also pose a risk. While the Liability Convention provides a financial incentive for launching States to ensure that NSAs adhere to rigorous safety procedures,[134] the growing number of States involved in space activities increases the risk of opportunistic practices. Neither the Liability nor the Registration Convention, for example include references to a genuine link, therefore leaving open how the definitions of the launching State, that is 'the State that launches' or 'the State that procures' are to be interpreted, thus leaving it unclear whether procurement or launch by NSA from a global commons would fall under State that launches or procures. This risks NSAs registering their activities under jurisdictions with lower controls. A correspondingly heightened possibility of incidents resulting in space pollution will follow. With private actors increasingly involved in space activities, the likelihood of seeking out locations with more permissive regulatory approaches is heightened, elevating the risk of NSAs gravitating to States that are unable or unwilling to enforce strict responsibility for causing space pollution rises.[135] Already examples of this forum shopping have emerged, such as in the case of Swarm Technologies, which effectively circumvented a license denial by the US Federal Communications Commission, which had safety concerns, by launching experimental satellites

130 Larsen (2018), p. 515.

131 Frans von der Dunk, 'Towards "Flags of Convenience" in Space?' (2012) *Space, Cyber, and Telecommunications Law Program Faculty Publications*, pp. 76–78.

132 Convention on the High Seas, Geneva (1958), Article 5.

133 Von der Dunk (2012), pp. 78–79.

134 Von der Dunk (2012), pp. 86–90.

135 On the meaning of 'likelihood', guidance can be taken from Principle 2(3) of United Nations General Assembly Resolution 47/68, 'Principles Relevant to the Use of Nuclear Power Sources In Outer Space', which provides that 'the terms "foreseeable" and "all possible" describe a class of events or circumstances whose overall probability of occurrence is such that it is considered to encompass only credible possibilities for purposes of safety analysis'.

from the territory of India after it had purchased a spot on an Indian-owned and operated launch vehicle.[136]

In the area of ITU allocation of GEO slots for satellites, there is a discernable risk of enterprising companies exploiting the system. The structure of the Constitution of the International Telecommunication Union and the Convention of the International Telecommunication Union indicate that only States can be members.[137] Protections against harmful interference also refer to those of 'countries'.[138] States have been accused of gaming the allotment system, such as Tonga's request for six slots for the reported purpose of 'parking spaces' which it could sell to private entities.[139] However, the system also lends itself to private entities, which will effectively pay the fees required by the ITU to administer the designation of slots,[140] misusing the system and potentially clogging up the relatively limited number of orbits, particularly in the geo-stationary band.[141] The over-subscription of satellite spots can result in the congestion of these bands and potentially heighten the risk of harmful collisions and the generation of space pollution.

Fourth, the indeterminacy of the attributes of statehood constitutes a further issue with exclusively focusing on States for accountability for space pollution. A fixation on entities formally recognised as States (or officially recognized governments) will run into the problematic reality of entities with debated or contested status, such as Afghanistan, Myanmar, Libya, Syria, Kosovo, and other areas where either the government or the entity itself are not recognised by all other established States.[142] In the gray area of States or territories under

136 Macchi (2025), p. 63–64.

137 See, e.g. Constitution of the International Telecommunication Union, Article 1(a) ('to maintain and extend international cooperation among all its Member States for the improvement and rational use of telecommunications of all kinds.'). See also the Radio Regulations which operate in conjunction with the International Telecommunication Union framework, Section 1, 1.2: defining '*administration*' as '[a]ny governmental department or service responsible for discharging the obligations undertaken in the Constitution of the International Telecommunication Union, in the Convention of the International Telecommunication Union and in the Administrative Regulations (CS 1002).'

138 Constitution of the International Telecommunication Union, Article 2(b).

139 Jannat C. Thompson, 'Space for Rent: The International Telecommunications Union, Space Law, and Orbit/Spectrum Leasing', (1996) 62 *Journal of Air Law and Commerce*, pp. 280–283.

140 Viikari (2008), pp. 89, 92–93.

141 Thompson, p. 284. See also Jan Smits, Legal Aspects of Implementing International Telecommunications (Martinus Nijhoff, 1991).

142 Tsagourias (2016), pp. 455–460.

the control of unrecognized governments, the potential for NSAs to exploit the unregulated opportunity is a potential risk.

Fifth, the State sovereignty approach is premised on NSAs only being able to act under the jurisdiction of States. However, NSA activities may emanate from areas outside any State's control, such as the high seas or the poles, and without State authorization.[143] In such circumstances, it is unclear which State, if any, would be obliged to take action and under which legal notion they could do so, particularly if the NSA disclaimed or hid any nationality (such as in the case of an irredentist movement).

Finally, addressing NSA space pollution through the indirect route of State accountability inherently requires extra layers of linkage to connect the conduct to a State. The issues of causation and attribution are complex and dynamic. Causation of space pollution, for example by significant amounts of space debris, will be very hard to establish due to the unclear legal standard and the typically unclear factual circumstances.[144] As Viikari notes, '[i]n most cases it is almost impossible to prove in a given case that the damage was even caused by space debris, that a particular piece of debris is part of a registered space object of a certain state and, furthermore, that there exists such fault (when the incident takes place in outer space) on the part of the launching state that it can be held liable for the damage.'[145]

For these linkages, legal ambiguities cause difficulties. Legally, to characterize conduct as negligent requires a sufficiently common understanding and acceptance of the applicable yardstick to assess negligence. As noted by Radi, 'the characterization of conduct as negligent begs the question of the applicable yardstick to appraise negligence'.[146] Given that the Liability Convention provides no explicit definition of negligence, another source which may be

143 Chapter 4, Section 1; Diego Zannoni, 'The Liability Regime for Private Activities in Outer Space: Is There a Normative Gap?' (2021) 59(1) *Archiv des Völkerrechts*, pp. 1–2.

144 Viikari (2008), p. 71 (Viikari notes that '[r]egardless of the interpretation of 'space object', mere activity involving a risk of damage, no matter how hazardous, can never result in liability under the provisions of the UN space treaties. Moreover, even in cases of indisputable material damage, proving the fault and the causality required is often an insurmountable obstacle. For instance, even if debris particles of all sizes were included in the legal definition of a 'space object', great practical difficulties would remain in establishing liability of the launching state.').

145 Viikari (2008), p. 71.

146 Radi (2023), p. 11.

looked to is that soft law (and thereby non-binding) space debris technical guidelines.[147]

The issue becomes particularly complex when multiple States are involved. To provide an example, a US company called IntelSat, LLC, which was wholly owned by IntelSat Global, SA, a Luxembourg company, launched IntelSat-22 in 2012. This was a geosynchronous telecommunications satellite. Whereas the satellite itself was licensed by the United States, it had a payload licensed by Australia (the Australian Defense Forces had placed an ultra-high frequency (UHF) communications payload on the satellite for military communications purposes).[148] In the event of an explosion or other incident causing space debris, a detailed investigation would likely be required to identify the cause and source of the damage in order to address questions of accountability, as well as for the purposes of indemnification between joint launching States under Article 5 of the Liability Convention.

A further legal restriction that arises from placing all NSA acts in space under the rubric of State control is the prospect of non-justiciability being argued on the basis of foreign act of State doctrine. If all NSA conduct were attributable to States, then any efforts to redress harmful conduct through courts may be rendered inadmissible pursuant to the act of State doctrine.[149] This would significantly restrict the prospects of exercising universal jurisdiction to address serious space pollution in domestic courts, as discussed below.[150]

Individually, these problems have varying degrees of risk of harm to the outer space environment. The probabilistic risk of a terrorist organization, acting beyond the control of any State, managing to launch an object to space designed to detonate and cause large emissions of space pollution is low, but the impact would be extremely high. Contrastingly, the likelihood of corporate NSAs using flags of convenience to lower regulatory constraints is relatively

147 Radi (2023), p. 11; Joel A Dennerley, 'State Liability for Space Object Collisions: The Proper Interpretation of 'Fault' for the Purposes of International Space Law' (2018) 29 *European Journal of International Law* 281–301.

148 Gutzman (2017), p. 2 citing United States Federal Communications Commission, *Intelsat-22 Grant of Application for Satellite Space Systems Authorization with Attachment to Grant (IBFS File No. SAT-LOA-20110929-00193)* (2012) and Jeff Foust, 'An opening door for hosted payloads' *SpaceNews* (30 October 2012) (available at http://spacenews.com/an-opening-door-for-hosted-payloads/).

149 See generally Philippa Webb, 'International Law and Restraints on the Exercise of Jurisdiction by National Courts of States', in Malcolm Evans (ed.) *International Law* (5th ed.) (Oxford University Press, 2018), pp. 316–348.

150 Chapter 4, Section 3.

high, and might even increase over time. Although corporate NSAs would not be intentionally looking to detonate their space objects, the increasingly unregulated activity in space would heighten the risks of accidental collisions and explosions occurring. Collectively, these risks emphasize the need to regulate NSA activity through means other than State enforcement.

CHAPTER 4

The New Horizon: Direct NSA Accountability under International Law for Space Pollution

Given the significant limitations of the State-centric model and consequent risk of NSAs escaping accountability for space pollution, it is apposite to examine other means of recourse exist outside of that traditional paradigm. An alternative to exclusive State accountability under international space law, is to examine the direct application of international law to NSAs. Other branches of international law have been applied directly to NSAs, as detailed above. In this light, it is important to examine whether international space law itself can be used to directly redress NSA space pollution, and whether other branches, such as international criminal law, international humanitarian law, international human rights law, international environmental law, and private international law could serve that function. However, before engaging in the substantive analysis, two case studies of contrasting sources of NSA potential space pollution are set out. These are presented in order to provide a substrate for the ensuing discussion of the applicability of international legal regimes to NSA conduct.

1 Two Case Studies Exemplifying the New Threat Emanating from NSAs

The rise of NSA space activity has brought with it increased risks of space pollution.[1] There are two primary types of NSAs which present the most concrete threats in this respect. First, there is the paradigm of the profit-driven NSA, such as Jeff Bezos's space tourism with Blue Origin, Richard Branson's orbital flight with Virgin Galactic, or Elon Musk's increased launching of satellites into space. Second, there is the paradigm of the politically-motivated NSA.[2] The specific risks of space pollution that arise from these two types of NSAs differ. Examining these threats provides an important factual context, onto which

1 Chapter 1, Section 3.

2 See Miller (2019), p. 34; Tsagourias (2016), p. 455.

the legal analysis can be superimposed, in order to highlight regulatory challenges that arise when seeking to redress NSA space pollution.

1.1 *Profit-Driven* NSA*s*

With the United States and the Soviet Union being the early explorers of space, military interests were at the forefront of their considerations when crafting space law, along with scientific advances for the States to harness. Civilian and commercial uses of space were a 'by-product' of those uses of outer space.[3] However, as the Cold War ended, the interest in the commercial use of outer space escalated rapidly,[4] and this is now among the most significant development areas of outer space activities.

By the 1980s, private entities were increasingly involved in space activities. For example, in 1980, a semi-private entity called Arianespace was established in Europe.[5] It became heavily involved in commercial launches. Moreover, some public telecommunications enterprises which were active in space were privatized, such as INTELSAT which became Intelsat Inc.[6] Private satellite companies also sprang up, such as Iridium in the United States. This trend has manifested with remote sensing satellites, which are increasingly operated by semi-private and purely private entities.[7] Navigation satellites are largely run by public infrastructures such as the Global Positioning System (GPS), but services based on those systems are offered by private corporations.[8]

Launching services are likewise increasingly often offered by semi-private or wholly private corporations. An example of a semi-private profit-seeking entity which has sent objects to space is that of Sea Launch. This limited partnership was reportedly a joint venture between Boeing and companies in Russia, Ukraine, and Norway, which intended to launch satellites from a converted North Sea oil rig called 'Ocean Odyssey' that had been moved to the Pacific.[9] Sea Launch eventually conducted over 30 launches. Most were successful but three failed, with one 5.9 tonne rocket exploding on the launch pad

---

3 Zhao (2018), p. 1–2.

4 Stella Tkatchova, *Space-Based Technologies and Commercialized Development: Economic Implications and Benefits* (2011) IGI Global, p. 90.

5 European Space Agency, 'The origins of Ariane', 18 December 2009, (available at https://www.esa.int/About_Us/ESA_history/The_origins_of_Ariane). Hobe (2010), p. 871.

6 Hobe (2010), p. 872.

7 Zhao (2018), p. 4; Hobe (2010), p. 872.

8 Hobe (2010), p. 872.

9 Colin Woodard, 'High-seas launch worries islanders', *The Christian Science Monitor* (22 September 1999) (available at https://www.csmonitor.com/1999/0922/p5s1.html).

in a huge fireball.[10] Conducting launches from a sea-based platform near the equator drew several significant potential advantages, particularly in reducing the amount of fuel required to successfully propel the rockets to outer space. The Earth's rotational speed at the equator provides an extra launch boost, as sites at that point are already moving at over 1650 km per hour relative to Earth's center.[11] Launching from the sea can also limit risks for human populations in comparison with ground-based launches.

From an early stage, observers noted that the structure of the enterprise could be used in an effort to evade regulatory restrictions and potential liability in case of an explosion or crash.[12] Challenges were mounted against Sea Launch's plans, including from the International Transport Workers Federation, which objected to its use of flags of convenience, in this case Liberia.[13] In response to the litigation, the US State Department fined the US company Boeing 10 million US dollars for allegedly sharing sensitive technology with their foreign partner companies, and it suspended Sea Launch's operations for two months.[14] Those penalties had no direct link with environmental harm, but demonstrated the risk of NSAs attempting to evade regulatory scrutiny, as well as the need for enforcement to send a deterrent message to other NSAs looking to maximize their profits.

In relation to the environment, the small Island State of Kiribati objected to Sea Launch's planned operations occurring around 500 miles from its easternmost islands in the Pacific. It appealed to the South Pacific Regional Environmental Program, which carried out an independent environmental study and considered that in addition to problematic aspects concerning Sea Launch's safety and accident planning, it anticipated that each launch would

10 Woodard (1999).

11 NASA, 'Basics of Space Flight: Section 3: Operations, Chapter 14: Launch' (available at https://solarsystem.nasa.gov/basics/chapter14-1/#:~:text=If%20a%20spacecraft%20is%20launched,hour%20relative%20to%20Earth's%20center).

12 Woodard (1999) ('By launching from the middle of nowhere – far outside national borders – the venture reduces infrastructure and labor costs, ducks regulatory bodies, and minimizes the risk of liability in the event one of the Sea Launch rockets crashes back to earth.').

13 As noted herein, the practice of using flags of convenience is often used by ship operators to avoid regulatory oversight and tax burdens.

14 Woodard (1999); Walter Pincus, 'Boeing Fined $10 Million For Data Transfer To Ukraine, Russia', *Washington Post* (3 October 1998) (https://www.washingtonpost.com/archive/politics/1998/10/03/boeing-fined-10-million-for-data-transfer-to-ukraine-russia/307b7709-655a-4572-84f9-0202ce5e5352/).

entail 4.5 tons of unused fuel from discarded stages creating a kerosene oil slick 'several square kilometers wide.'[15]

Despite its completion of many launches, Sea Launch became embroiled in financial disputes. It filed for bankruptcy because of weaker demand for its sea-based launches and a failed launch which led to growing debt, including a large arbitration award against the company.[16] The arbitral award reportedly arose due to Sea Launch's launch pad failure in January 2007 forcing its customers to seek alternatives or suffer delays for their booked launches.[17] One customer, Hughes Network Systems (HNS) canceled its contract and asked for a panel of the American Arbitration Association to order Sea Launch to 'refund $44.4 million in advance payments made to Sea Launch to prepare to place HNS's Spaceway 3 Ka-band broadband satellite into orbit.'[18] The arbitration panel ordered Sea Launch Co. to pay HNS 53.2 million US dollars. Upon Sea Launch filing for bankruptcy in 2009, one partner – Boeing Co BA.N – sued its Russian and Ukrainian partners (RSC Energia, a company partially owned by the government of Russian, and two state-owned Ukrainian companies, PO Yuzhnoye Mashinostroitelny Zavod and KB Yuzhnoye), alleging that they failed to provide it with 350 million US dollars which it had been promised from them if the joint venture failed.[19] These legal moves demonstrate the precarious nature of NSAs and the risk they will dissolve when confronted with fines, which reinforces the need for *ex ante* protections against causing communal harms in preference to *ex post facto* dispute resolution after the harm has already been incurred.[20]

The trend towards profit-seeking companies exploring means of exploiting the space environment looks set to continue, as outer space has considerable commercial potential. Zhao notes that the 'zero-gravity environment in outer space provides an excellent condition for scientific experiments, with the scientific results readily available for commercialization'.[21] Moreover, valuable

15 Woodard (1999).

16 Nate Raymond, 'Boeing sues Sea Launch partners for $350 million', Reuters (4 February 2013) (https://www.reuters.com/article/us-boeing-sealaunch-idUSBRE9130RU20130204).

17 Peter B. de Selding, 'Sea Launch Ordered to Pay HNS $52 Million', Space News (23 April 2009) (https://spacenews.com/sea-launch-ordered-pay-hns-52-million/).

18 Peter B. de Selding (2009).

19 Nate Raymond (2013) citing *The Boeing Company v. KB Yuzhnoye et al.*, U.S. District Court, Central District of California, 13-00730.

20 Contra see Goh (2007), pp. 168–181.

21 Zhao (2018), p. 4 citing NASA, '15 Ways the International Space Station is Benefiting Earth' *nasa.gov* (30 October 2015) (available athttps://www.nasa.gov/missions/station/15-ways-the-international-space-station-benefits-humanity-back-on-earth/).

mineral resources present an attractive prospect for entrepreneurs seeking astronomical profit margins.[22] The most profitable space activity for private entities have thus far been telecommunications.[23] Space mining presents a potentially even more profitable venture for private companies in the future.[24] Commercial activities therefore include space launches, satellite direct broadcasting, remote sensing, telecommunications, space tourism, space mining, the operation of small satellites, and the exploitation of digitization potential in space.[25]

The potential profitability of these activities is increasingly captured international attention. Major international personalities have promoted the virtues of space tourism. In 2017, Richard Branson celebrated as Virgin Galactic's SpaceShipTwo completed its first test flight, utilizing an updated re-entry system.[26] SpaceX has conducted rocket recycling experiments in 2015, 2018, and 2021, with some success.[27] It has offered launches with reusable Falcon 9 and Falcon Heavy rockets ever since.[28] Satellites exemplify the rapid recent development of space commercialization. Since the first commercial global satellite communications system was launched in 1965 by INTELSAT (an

22 See John G. Wrench, 'Non-Appropriation, No Problem: The Outer Space Treaty Is Ready for Asteroid Mining' (2019) 51 *Case Western Reserve Journal of International Law*, p. 447; Zhao (2018), p. 4 citing Yu Hui, 'Joint development of mineral resources: An Asian solution' (1994) in Seokwoo Lee, Hee Eun Lee (eds.) *Asian Yearbook of International Law* (Brill Nijhoff, 1994).

23 Hobe (2010), p. 872.

24 Petrova (2022).

25 Zhao (2018), p. 4 citing Steven Freeland, 'Impact of space tourism on the International Law of Outer Space' (2005) in 48th Colloquium on the Law of Outer Space, 17 October 2005 – 21 October 2005, Fukuoka, Japan, published by the American Institute of Aeronautics and Astronautics Inc.; Anita Rinner, 'Small Satellites – Smart Laws – Small Satellite Projects in the Face of National Space Legislation – Austria' (2013) *Proceedings of the International Institute of Space Law*.

26 Irene Klotz, 'Virgin Galactic's SpaceShipTwo Makes 1st Test Flight of Revamped Re-Entry System' (2 May 2017), Space.com (https://www.space.com/36679-virgin-galactic-space shiptwo-unity-feather-system-test-flight.html); see also Fox News. (3 May 2017) 'Virgin Galactic's Space Ship Two makes 1st test flight of revamped re-entry system'; Space.com (https://www.space.com/36679-virgin-galactic-spaceshiptwo-unity-feather-system-test -flight.html).

27 Cara McGoogan, 'What is SpaceX and is it the future of space exploration?' *Telegraph* (26 July 2017) (available at https://www.telegraph.co.uk/technology/0/spacex-future-space -exploration/); Marcia Dunn, 'SpaceX successfully uses recycled parts to launch third crew into orbit', PBS (23 April 2021) (available at https://www.pbs.org/newshour/scie nce/spacex-successfully-uses-recycled-parts-to-launch-third-crew-into-orbit).

28 'SpaceX – Reusable Rockets' *The Index Project* (https://theindexproject.org/award/nomin ees/1692).

intergovernmental organization which became a private enterprise),[29] telecommunications services have expanded significantly. Remote image capture and sensing is growing business and commercial providers like the US company Quick Bird and the German company Rapid Eye offer products and services to States and private entities lacking their own means of offering remote sensing capabilities.[30] Navigation services also provide a burgeoning service around the world.[31]

SpaceX alone has deployed thousands of broadband satellites called Starlink and has developed many more earth-based ground transmitters.[32] As satellite technology improves yearly, the costs of launching satellites are being reduced.[33] These trends render it likely that major areas of new commercial exploitation will emerge rapidly, including human space flight, the generation of space energy, the use of space stations, and space mining.[34] With the growth of these activities, the risk of NSA space pollution will increase commensurately.

Space activities conducted by private companies can result in both terrestrial and extra-terrestrial harm to the environment. Elon Musk's SpaceX's has set up a 'spaceport' known as 'Starbase', which is a production and launch site, in the Texan town of Boca Chica. Because its employees number over 1,600 people, it provides an attractive opportunity for local regions seeking to spur economic growth and opportunities.[35] However, reports have emerged of harm to the environment. The US Fish and Wildlife Service has recorded 'a decline of endangered piping plovers in habitat surrounding [Starbase],' and noted that Space X's activities may also potentially harm sea turtles and other shorebirds.[36] Ecological groups such as the Centre for Biological Diversity have

29 Chapter 3, Section 2.

30 Zhao (2018), p. 5 citing Steven Livingston, 'Commercial Remote Sensing Satellites and the Regulation of Violence in Areas of Limited Statehood' (2015) 5 *CGCS Occasional Paper Series on ICTs, Statebuilding, and Peacebuilding in Africa*.

31 Paul B. Larsen, 'International Regulation of Global Navigation Satellite Systems' (2017) 80(2) *Journal of Air Law and Commerce*, p. 365.

32 Miller (2019), p. 35 citing Arthur Villasanta, 'SpaceX to Build 1 Million Earth Stations to Track 12,000 Satellites, FCC License Details,' *International Business Times*, (10 February 2019) (available at https://www.ibtimes.com/spacex-build-1-million-earth-stations-track-12000-satellites-fcc-license-details-2761987).

33 Zhao (2018), p. 5 citing Ram S. Jakhu, Joseph N. Pelton, *Small satellites and their regulation* (Springer, 2014).

34 Zhao (2018), p. 4.

35 Alex Brown, 'New space race holds promise, but possible environmental risks, too', *Washington Post* (31 July 2022) (https://www.washingtonpost.com/science/2022/07/31/spaceports-environmental-harm/).

36 Brown (2022).

argued that the environmental harm caused by launches has exceeded that which was initially reported by Space X, demonstrating that, even in highly regulated States, the conduct of NSAs may create risks to the environment that are difficult to manage via the sole route of State responsibility.[37] In 2023, the Centre for Biological Diversity, along with four other organizations, filed a lawsuit in the District of Columbia Federal District Court challenging 'the Federal Aviation Administration's authorization of the SpaceX Starship/Super Heavy Launch Vehicle Program at Boca Chica, Texas', and asserting that the FAA failed to properly assess Space X's launch program's contribution to climate change.[38] This proceeding appears to be ongoing.[39]

Efforts to explore outer space stretch to other celestial bodies. Soft law instruments have been signed by States indicating their interest in lunar exploration, for example the Artemis Accords,[40] and the Chinese-Russian Memorandum of Understanding.[41] In 2021, several developments occurred concerning the exploration of Mars. The 'perseverance' rover program commenced, along with the United Arab Emirates' Mars mission, and China's Zhurong rover taking steps forward.[42] This signals the opening of a new market, which may be highly lucrative for those corporations able to obtain access to the mineral resources and other commercial opportunities presented by Mars exploration

37 *Centre for Biological Diversity et. al. vs Federal Aviation Administration and Billy Nolen*, US District Court for the District of Columbia, Case No. 1:23-cv-01204 (1 May 2023) (available at https://climatecasechart.com/wp-content/uploads/case-documents/2023/20230501_docket-123-cv-01204_complaint.pdf).

38 *Centre for Biological Diversity et. al. vs Federal Aviation Administration and Billy Nolen*, District Court in the District of Colombia, Docket No.1:23-cv-01204.

39 See https://climatecasechart.com/case/center-for-biological-diversity-v-federal-aviation-administration/.

40 NASA, Artemis Accords, available at: https://www.nasa.gov/artemis-accords/.

41 Andrew Jones, 'China, Russia enter MoU on international lunar research station' (9 March 2021) (available at https://spacenews.com/china-russia-enter-mou-on-international-lunar-research-station/); For more on the influences of Russia on international law, see Grünfeld (2020).

42 See Liping Liu, Puqi Jia, Yalin Huang, Jie Han, Eric Liechtfouse, 'Space industrialization' (2023) 21 *Environmental Chemistry Letters* 1, pp. 1–7 citing NASA, 'NASA's Perseverance Rover Begins its First Science Campaign on Mars' *nasa.gov* (9 June 2021) (available at https://www.nasa.gov/solar-system/nasas-perseverance-rover-begins-its-first-science-campaign-on-mars/); United Arab Emirates Space Agency, 'About UAE Space Agency' *space.gov.ae* (available at https://space.gov.ae/Page/20120/20230/About-UAE-Space-Agency); China National Space Administration (CNSA), 'Probe makes historic landing on Mars' *China National Space Administration* (17 May 2021) (available at https://www.cnsa.gov.cn/english/n6465652/n6465653/c6812005/content.html).

and potential settlement. Already the Artemis Accords signal a growing interest in the profits presented by space mining.[43]

Many legal issues have arisen as this commercialization of space has intensified. These include the legality of space resource appropriation, issues of licensing of privately owned small satellites (including nano-satellites), the regulation of radio frequencies and orbits, the registration of satellites, and the allocation of responsibility and liability between government and private entities for the environmental pollution and other negative impacts.[44]

Alongside these legal concerns regarding NSA conduct, the overarching issue of protecting outer space looms large. For the outer space environment, the biggest risk is inadvertent collisions. Additional risks are space debris being cast off in order to save costs and insufficient planning for disposal or destruction on re-entry. The risk of damage caused on re-entry is likely to affect the natural environment, particularly the marine environment on Earth.[45] This has been shown in the locality of Point Nemo in the Pacific Ocean, where space agencies have sunk over 260 space objects. These objects include the Russian space station MIR, and have led to the zone being called the 'spacecraft cemetery'.[46]

Examples of anthropocentric damage deriving from space activities have already occurred. In 2021, debris created by a Chinese Long March 5B rocket reportedly fell and struck two villages in Cote d'Ivoire, causing damage to several buildings.[47] In 2022, SpaceX debris was listed as found in the Snowy Mountain region of Australia.[48] Such destruction would, in theory, be covered by the Article VII of the Outer space Treaty, which provides that the launching State is the entity liable for any damage caused by the launched object.[49]

---

43 See Chapter 1, Section 3. See also Macchi (2025), p. 65.

44 Zhao (2018), pp. 5–6 citing Paul Steven Dempsey, 'National laws governing commercial space activities: Legislation, regulation, and enforcement.' (2016) 36 *Northwestern Journal of International Law and Business*.

45 Radi (2023), p. 3.

46 Radi (2023), p. 3; Vito De Lucia, 'Splashing Down the International Space Station in the Pacific Ocean: Safe Disposal or Trashing the Ocean Commons' *EJIL:Talk!* (23 February 2022) available at https://www.ejiltalk.org/splashing-down-the-international-space-station-in-the-pacific-ocean-safe-disposal-or-trashing-the-ocean-commons/.

47 Radi (2023), p. 2; Edward Helmore, 'Chinese Rocket's Chaotic Fall to Earth Highlights Problem of Space Junk' The Guardian (8 May 2021) (available at https://www.theguardian.com/science/2021/may/08/chinese-rocket-space-junk-long-march-5gb).

48 Elsa Maishman, 'Space Debris Australia: Piece of SpaceX capsule crashes to Earth in field' *BBC News* (3 August 2022) (available at https://www.bbc.com/news/world-australia-62414438).

49 Outer Space Treaty, Article VII ("Each State Party to the Treaty that launches or procures the launching of an object into outer space, including the moon and other celestial

However, obtaining such compensation can sometimes be challenging, particularly where there are major power discrepancies between the States involved.[50]

A separate threat is that of space tourism. In 2021, the space tourism race heated up. US-based Virgin Galactic conducted its first suborbital test flight in a rocket-powered space plane called VSS Unity.[51] On 11 July 2021, VSS Unity took a group of space tourists up to the edge of space.[52] The next week, Amazon founder Jeffrey Bezos and three others were aboard Blue Origin's New Shepard rocket. During their trip, they passed the Kármán Line.[53] On 18 September 2021, SpaceX's Dragon and the Inspiration4 were successfully launched via a Falcon 9 rocket and managed to complete the first commercial crewed space mission. They sent four civilians into space for three-days, which ended with them safely returning to land off the Floridian coast.[54] Space tourism is potentially highly lucrative, and has been predicted to be worth over three billion dollars by 2030.[55] This pending surge will inevitably increase the number of objects and actors in space, including NSAs, and thereby raise the risk of variable safety and environmental standards being adhered to.

From this brief overview of profit-driven NSA conduct, it can be seen that the race to commercialize and profit from space tourism will create pressure to send increasing numbers of launches into outer space, at increasing regularity,

---

bodies, and each State Party from whose territory or facility an object is launched, is internationally liable for damage to another State Party to the Treaty or to its natural or juridical persons by such object or its component parts on the Earth, in air or in outer space, including the moon and other celestial bodies.').

50 See Chapter 3, Section 1.

51 See Liping Liu, 'Puqi Jia, Yalin Huang, Jie Han, Eric Liechtfouse, Space industrialization' (2023) 21 *Environmental Chemistry Letters*, pp. 1–7 citing Tariq Malik, 'Virgin Galactic's SpaceShipTwo Unity 22 launch with Richard Branson' *space.com* (11 July 2021) (available at https://www.space.com/virgin-galactic-richard-branson-unity-22-launch-explained).

52 Nola Taylor Tillman, 'Virgin Galactic launches researchers to suborbital space on 5th commercial flight', Space.com (2 November 2023) (https://www.space.com/virgin-galactic-05-mission-success-stern-gerardi); Liu *et. al.* (2023) citing Virgin Galactic, 'Virgin Galactic successfully completes first fully crewed spaceflight' *Virgin Galactic* (available at https://www.virgingalactic.com/news/virgin-galactic-successfully-completes-first-fully-crewed-spaceflight).

53 Liu et. al. (2023) citing Blue Origin, 'Blue Origin safely launches four commercial astronauts to space and back' *Blue Origin* (available at https://www.blueorigin.com/news/first-human-flight-updates).

54 Scott Dutfield and Vicky Stein 'Inspiration4: the first all-civilian spaceflight on SpaceX Dragon' *space.com* (5 January 2022) (available at https://www.space.com/inspiration4-spacex.html).

55 Liu et. al. (2023), pp. 1–7.

which will lead to increased risks of collisions, further space debris being created and proliferating and other forms of space pollution degrading the space environment. In light of the heightened risks, these commercial risks necessitate the incorporation of environmental protection into the re-shaping of space law and practice.[56]

1.2 *Politically-Motivated Violent NSAs*

Politically-motivated NSAs prepared to use violence to achieve their goals can vary from rebel movements using guerilla tactics to protect people under their control, to separatist movements seeking international recognition, to terrorist organizations targeting civilians to spread fear and intimidate States. The risks from these entities are varied. They include attacks in space, or through the use of space, using 'computer viruses, jamming, lasers, and anti-satellite missiles', as well as NSAs which seek to disrupt and overturn the international stability and/or the power structures in their own countries.[57] NSAs such as terrorist groups may carry out attacks in non-space domains, in order to disrupt and destroy terrestrially based equipment, or else in the outer space domain, in order to destroy or otherwise incapacitate deployed space objects.[58]

Challengingly, such NSAs may be less susceptible to deterrence than other actors, such as corporations or States, as they do not fear reprisals, escalation to war, or the targeting of space assets (and in fact may well welcome the extra attention generated by such reactions).[59]

Moreover, because they will not necessarily seek conventional military advantages such as control over territory, they can achieve their goals of maximizing disruption through multiple means, including targeting communications satellites.[60] The potentially escalatory costs to the global economy created by attacks in space will serve as an attraction rather than a deterrent for maliciously motivated NSAs.[61] The risk is growing more realistic. As noted,

56 Haroun et. al. (2021), pp. 68–72.

57 Miller (2019), p. 34.

58 Rachel A. Gabriel and S. Koven Barnett, 'Malicious Non-state Actors and Contested Space Operations,' Report to DHS SandT Office of University Programs and DoD Strategic Multilayer Assessment Branch. College Park, MD: START, (2018), p. 5.

59 Miller (2019), p. 34.

60 Rachel A. Gabriel and S. Koven Barnett, 'Malicious Non-state Actors and Contested Space Operations,' Report to dhs SandT Office of University Programs and DoD Strategic Multilayer Assessment Branch. College Park, md: start, (2018), pp. 5–6.

61 Miller (2019), p. 34.

in November 2023, Houthi rebels reportedly fired a missile from Yemen's territory into space, in an unsuccessful attempt to strike Israel.[62]

Among this category of NSAs, Miller highlights the differences between guerrillas and terrorists. Whereas guerrillas perceive the population as an essential source of support and seek to convince them of the worthiness of their cause, terrorist groups tend to target civilians to further their political ends,[63] and this can impact satellites, as shown by Hamas reportedly disrupting Israeli satellite broadcasts during Operation Cast Lead.[64] Both types of groups will also sometimes deviate from these tactics, with guerillas erring into criminal conduct and terrorist groups sometimes carrying out lawful acts, such as erecting hospitals and allowing humanitarian access to wounded and ill persons under their control.[65] However, whereas 'guerrillas are more likely to use conventional military tactics and are organized in a hierarchical way, much like a conventional military organization', terrorists are more liable to make use of unconventional methods of attacks, and are typically organized in cells or other forms of non-traditional hierarchical formations, with small units operating largely autonomously with only limited concrete connections across or between cells and with the overall leadership.[66]

Terrorist groups, which are less concerned by negative international opinion (and in some cases, such as ISIS, seem to seek pariah status), would be more likely to engage in highly destructive kinetic attacks.[67] Terrestrially, their attacks often involve significant violence and destruction, through bombings, armed strikes and assassinations.[68] This suggests that similarly destructive tactics would be likely in the space environment. Additionally, more sophisticated tactics, such as 'satellite systems being used for microwave-like attacks',

62 Harriet Barber, 'How Israel shot down a ballistic missile in space for the first time', *Telegraph* (5 November 2023) (https://www.telegraph.co.uk/world-news/2023/11/04/how-israel-shot-down-ballistic-missile-in-space-houthis/).

63 Miller (2019), p. 36.

64 Deborah Housen-Couriel, (2012) 'Disruption of Satellite Transmissions ad Bellum and in Bello: Launching a New Paradigm of Convergence' *Israel Law Review*, 45(3), p. 440.

65 Miller (2019), p. 36.

66 Ekaterina Stepanova, *Terrorism in Asymmetrical Conflict Ideological and Structural Aspects* (*SIPRI Research Report No. 23*) (Oxford University Press, 2008); Miller (2019), pp. 36–37.

67 Miller (2019), pp. 39–40.

68 Miller (2019), p. 40 citing Global Terrorism Database, 'National Consortium for the Study of Terrorism and Responses to Terrorism' *Global Terrorism Database* (2018) (available at https://www.start.umd.edu/gtd), ('bombings account for 49 percent of all terrorist activity between 1970–2017 … the next most common tactics are armed assaults and assassinations, accounting for 25 percent and 11 percent, respectively, though there is some temporal and regional variation.').

are conceivable threats.[69] There is a whole taxonomy of disruptions to satellite systems, including 'satellite collision, harm caused by space debris, and damage to ground stations; as well as jamming, laser blinding, morphing and piggybacking of signals, and interference with the satellite's computer systems housed in ground stations', which terrorists seek to emulate.[70]

Terrorist groups typically lack access to the resources required to access space and will frequently be reliant on State sponsors.[71] However, the increasing number of actors in space means that 'attribution will become more difficult', which could in turn incentivize States to utilize proxies to carry out attacks to weaken adversaries.[72] Terrorist groups have shown an interest in targeting space programs for decades; the Black September Palestinian group, which notoriously killed Israeli athletes at the 1972 Munich Olympics, reportedly were planning an attack against members of the Apollo 17 mission, which necessitated heightened security measures around the Cape in Florida.[73] In August 1984, a French left-wing group called Action Directe exploded a bomb at the European Space Agency's (ESA) Paris headquarters, injuring six people.[74]

In addition to terrorist and guerrilla groups, another possible type of threat actor is space pirates. Although driven by a profit motive, this type of group would be prepared to use violent means to achieve it.[75] Space pirates straddle the categories of the profit-driven and politically motivated, being subjectively closer to the former in attitude but objectively linked to the latter in behaviour. This could coincide with State and corporate interests to form State-sponsored piracy, and corporate-backed piracy, particularly to gain a geo-political or market-based advantage.[76]

Legally, if treated like maritime pirates, space pirates would be considered *hostis humani generi* and therefore fall under the jurisdiction of any State.[77]

---

69 Miller (2019), p. 40.

70 Housen-Couriel (2012), pp. 432–435. Cyber attacks against a satellite could disrupt a country's energy systems, as shown by the attack on Ka-sat on the eve of the invasion on Ukraine on 24 February 2022.

71 Cottam (2022).

72 Miller (2019), p. 40.

73 David Schlom, 'When Terrorists Threatened Apollo', *Ad Astra*, November 2001; Miller (2019), p. 41.

74 Associated Press, 'Bomb Shatters Office of Europe Space Unit,' *New York Times* (3 August 1984) (available at https://www.nytimes.com/1984/08/03/world/bomb-shatters-office-of-europe-space-unit.html); Miller (2019), p. 41.

75 Miller (2019), p. 34.

76 Miller (2019), p. 42.

77 Lawrence Azubuike (2009), 'International Law Regime Against Piracy', *Annual Survey of International and Comparative Law*: Vol. 15(1), Article 4.

However, whereas the 1982 Convention on the Law of the Sea has specific provisions defining piracy and requiring international cooperation to combat it, there is no analogous instrument governing space piracy.[78] This results in a lacuna, which exploitative groups may fill,[79] and thereby creates greater risk of attacks or accidents in the space environment.

Another group which could be engaged in space activities, is that of private military security contractors and security companies. If human settlements are created in space, these groups may be engaged to provide protection against other threat actors. To the extent this occurs, they will be bound by international humanitarian law, international criminal law, and potentially aspects of international human rights law, as discussed herein. These obligations are collated in a soft law instrument, the International Code of Conduct for Private Security Service Providers.[80] However, contractors will typically prefer to avoid destruction, as that may reduce the political aims sought or the value of any goods taken or bring unwanted attention.

Consequently, for all groups – guerillas, terrorists, space pirates, and private military security contractors, there is a discernible risk of attacks being intentionally conducted against space objects or assets. These threats are becoming less remote, due to the decreasing costs of space equipment and the growing availability of advanced space capabilities on the commercial market.[81] Because satellite systems combine physical apparatus and virtual data transfers, disruptions may be conducted kinetically against satellites or ground stations or through interference with the electromagnetic communications systems between satellite receivers on Earth and satellites in space.[82] That creates a long chain of vulnerability for threat actors to exploit.

Although the risk of destructive tactics is less with guerillas, pirates, and private military contractors, it is not negligible, particularly as their access to space becomes more feasible. With terrorists, major destruction is often an intentional tactic. Given the major international interest in space, it would be an attractive target for ambitious terrorists seeking to intimidate populations

---

78 See United Nations Convention on the Law of the Sea (UNCLOS), 10 December 1982, 1833/1834/1835 UNTS 3 (entered into force on 16 November 1994), Articles 100 to 107 and 110.

79 See Michael Viets, 'Piracy in an Ocean of Stars: Proposing a Term to Identify the Practice of Unauthorized Control of Nations' Space Objects' (2018) 54 *Stanford Journal of International Law*, p. 2; Miller (2019), p. 44.

80 See Responsible Security Association (available at https://icoca.ch/the-code/); Scott Jerbi, 'The International Code of Conduct for Private Security Service Providers', (2013) Geneva Academy of International Humanitarian Law and Human Rights.

81 Cottam (2022).

82 Housen-Couriel (2012), p. 436.

and force authorities to do their bidding. That threat of kinetic destruction raises the corresponding risk of an exponential proliferation of space debris, which highlights the need to examine accountability mechanisms capable of applying international law to NSA conduct.

2 The Direct Application of International Law to NSAs regarding Space Pollution

Having set out two examples illustrating the emerging risk of NSA space pollution, the following survey examines whether and how international law could be directly applied to NSAs. It does so in accordance with the postulates set out in Chapter 1 of this Book,[83] namely by paying particular heed to the precept that recognition of NSA responsibility must accord with the broader framework and secondary rules of international law. In this way, it seeks to identify well-founded bases in international law for the attribution of responsibility to NSAs for space pollution.

2.1 *Space Law*

The discussion in Chapters 1, Section (4) and 3 has highlighted that space law is largely State-centric and funnels accountability through the medium of States. This reflects its etymology during the State-dominated geo-strategic era of the Cold War. During that period, the United Nations was keenly aware of, and reactive to, the growing spectre of the space race escalating into conflict in the outer space environment. After the first manmade satellite (Sputnik) was launched in 1957, the United Nations rapidly reacted with the establishment of an *ad hoc* committee to examine the peaceful uses of outer space as well as a UN General Assembly Resolution the same year.[84] As a result of this vintage, current international space treaties only expressly impose obligations on States (at least according to their explicit terms) and NSAs are currently not parties to such treaties.[85] Moreover, even where the Outer Space Treaty references NSAs[86] or

83 See Chapter 1 (the lack of scholarly attention to NSA responsibility for space pollution).

84 Zhao (2018), p. 2 referring to UN General Assembly Resolution (UN Res. 1348, 1958).

85 Ziemblicki and Oralova (2021), p. 2 ('the existing regime does not recognize the status that private companies have achieved.').

86 Outer Space Treaty, Article VI ('activities are carried on by governmental agencies or by non-governmental entities, and for assuring that national activities are carried out in conformity with the provisions set forth in the present Treaty.').

nationals,[87] it imposes an obligation for their conduct on States rather than on NSAs/nationals themselves.

Building on the broader analysis set out above in Chapter 3, the following section focuses on provisions relevant to the direct application of international law to NSAs for space pollution. This is an experimental and novel analysis. There is limited scholarly attention paid to the application of international law to NSA space pollution. Whereas Chapter 5 provides a detailed description of how States are implementing their obligations at the international level, the present analysis focuses on the direct application of international space law to NSA conduct.

It is difficult to envisage any reading of this provision which permits for NSAs to bear direct obligations under the Outer Space Treaty,[88] particularly when bearing in mind the usual interpretive principle in Article 31 of the Vienna Convention on the Law of Treaties whereby '[a] treaty shall be interpreted in good faith in accordance with the ordinary meaning to be given to the terms of the treaty in their context and in the light of its object and purpose.' Article IX of the Outer Space Treaty is indicative in this respect. This provision, which crucially contains the most explicit basis on which to base a prohibition of space pollution,[89] requires that 'States Parties to the Treaty shall pursue studies of outer space, including the moon and other celestial bodies, and conduct exploration of them so as to avoid their harmful contamination'. This suggests that States are the exclusive repository of obligations under the Treaty. Similarly, Article VI of the Outer Space Treaty provides that 'States Parties to the Treaty shall bear international responsibility for national activities in outer space [...], whether such activities are carried on by governmental agencies or by non-governmental entities, and for assuring that national activities are carried out in conformity with the provisions set forth in the present Treaty', the Outer Space Treaty places the obligations to ensure adherence to its terms squarely on States.[90]

As noted, the context for the purpose of the interpretation of a treaty must take into account its text. Here the additional text further reinforces the central and essentially exclusive role of States as the recipients of obligations

87 Outer Space Treaty, Article IX ('activity or experiment planned by it or its nationals in outer space, including the Moon and other celestial bodies, would cause potentially harmful interference with activities of other States Parties in the peaceful exploration and use of outer space, including the Moon and other celestial bodies, it shall undertake appropriate international consultations before proceeding with any such activity or experiment.').

88 See Isnardi (2020), pp. 591–593.

89 See Chapter 2.

90 See above Chapter 3, Section 1.

under space law. For example, the rest of Article VI holds that '[t]he activities of non-governmental entities in outer space, including the moon and other celestial bodies, shall require authorization and continuing supervision by the appropriate State Party to the Treaty.' Moreover, Article VII makes State Parties 'internationally liable for damage to another State Party to the Treaty or to its natural or juridical persons by such object or its component parts on the Earth, in air or in outer space, including the moon and other celestial bodies'.[91] In light of this context, there is little space for creative or even evolving interpretations whereby NSAs attract obligations under the Outer Space Treaty.

By referencing general international law via Article III, the Outer Space Treaty does provide a basis for consistency with the wider body of international law, including customary international environmental law, as discussed above in Chapter 2. However, even in this respect, the basis to assert that NSAs have direct obligations, which are enforceable against them as a matter of law, is currently thin.[92] While there is a trend towards NSAs being full actors in international environmental law,[93] this trend has not manifested in specific legal obligations being placed on NSAs at the international level in a consistent manner. Moreover, international environmental law is largely aspirational, in the sense of setting goals to be achieved and processes for cooperation, without containing many absolute prohibitions.[94] Accordingly, even if international environmental law can be imported into the reading of the Outer Space Treaty,[95] it still requires further interpretation of environmental principles, such as the no-harm principle to envisage their application to space pollution by NSAs.

Beyond the Outer Space Treaty, space law also encompasses the Liability Convention. The Liability Convention has an ostensible reference to NSAs and also has sufficient reference in its terms to cover environmental harm. However, that environmental harm is more directly linked to Earth and would be highly attenuated in relation to outer space. On the former issue, the instrument does refer to 'natural or juridical persons [which] suffer damage'.[96] However, it specifies that only States be held liable and can claim damages from the launching

---

91 Chapter 5 sets out the ways in which some States require NSA space operators to compensate them for any such expenses and to have insurance covering such claims.

92 See above Chapter 2 (the discussion of Article III).

93 Sands and Peel (2018), pp. 52–53.

94 Darryl Robinson, 'Ecocide – Puzzles and Possibilities' (2022) 20 *Journal of International Criminal Justice* 2, pp. 315, 326.

95 Chapter 2, Section 1.

96 Liability Convention, Article VIII.

State for damage caused by its space object in diplomatic processes.[97] Article II refers to launching States being liable rather than NSAs. There is further provision for States to establish a Claims Commission should their diplomatic efforts to obtain relief fail,[98] but that is also State-centric on its face. It could be interpreted broadly by States, and eventually see them establish commissions to look into the potentially wrongful conduct of NSAs to establish liability therefore. However, as a matter of conventional law, it would still constitute a procedural funnel through State structures and entities.

Article XI(2) of the Liability Convention provides that '[n]othing in this Convention shall prevent a State, or natural or juridical persons it might represent, from pursuing a claim in the courts or administrative tribunals or agencies of a launching State'. Again, this terminology (particularly the term 'represent') indicates that only States can make claims for damage in the outer space environment, and that any claims of other legal entities, including natural or juridical persons (which would likely encompass NSAs) would potentially have to be routed through State representation. That would cause an incongruity, with States seeking claims in the domestic courts of other States. A better reading of Article XI(2), in line with the *effet utile* principle, would be that it allows an opportunity for natural and juridical persons to take direct legal action in the national jurisdiction of the launching State.[99] This is however still plagued by several difficulties as laid out in Chapter 3, including questions as to whether environmental damage in outer space could be claimed at all and under what basis. Consequently, there is no facet of the Liability Convention which lends support to the notion of proceeding directly against NSAs for environmental harm in outer space.

Finally, Article 7 of the Moon Agreement contains an ostensible prohibition of harming the celestial environment, but lacks reference to NSAs in this respect, and has few States Parties, as discussed above.[100] Its context indicates that States are seen as the key repositories of obligations under this instrument. On these bases, it can be concluded that space law currently provides negligible opportunity to directly apply its provisions to NSAs. Christina Isnardi concludes that the leading instruments (the Outer Space Treaty and the Moon Agreement)

---

97 Liability Convention, Article VIII, IX, X.

98 Liability Convention, Article XIV.

99 Kerrest (2017), pp. 3–18.

100 See Chapter 3.

> do not offer detailed provisions on the involvement of private entities in space activities,' [and] 'the treaties may cover private entities only to the extent that such an interpretation can be implicated, and such implications are ambiguous at best.[101]

In addition to the lack of prescriptive foundation for directly imposing obligations on NSAs under international space law, there are no established enforcement mechanisms under the core treaties of space law which could apply their provisions to NSAs.[102] In the absence of the direct application of the most relevant field of law to outer space activities, only a few options are open to hold NSA directly accountable, as analyzed below, namely the domestic courts under universal or extra-territorial jurisdiction, the International Criminal Court or similar tribunals dealing in international criminal law, and potentially under international humanitarian law, human rights law (insofar as applicable to NSAs), or under a private law mechanisms.[103] Given the paucity of provisional hooks on which to hang NSA responsibility, it is apposite to survey other branches of international law to discern their potential means of holding NSAs accountable when they cause space pollution.

2.2 *International Criminal Law*

An alternative means of addressing NSA misconduct to conventional space law is that of international criminal law. This domain has rapidly developed in the last three decades and can now be considered a well-established feature of international legal practice, with several cases ongoing before international courts (or domestic courts enforcing international prohibitions such as war crimes, crimes against humanity and genocide under universal jurisdiction) at any one time.[104] Convictions for a wide range of international law violations have been entered against leaders and commanders of NSAs. These include in the ICC cases of Thomas Lubanga from the *Union des patriotes congolais*,[105]

---

101 Isnardi (2020), p. 511.

102 Isnardi, p. 512; Freeland and Ireland-Piper (2022), p. 30; Macchi (2025), p. 57.

103 Chapter 4, Section 3.

104 See, e.g., Hague Institute for the Internationalisation of Law (2011), *General Rules and Principles of International Criminal Procedure and Recommendations of the International Expert Framework*, (available at https://www.legal-tools.org/doc/ee4de3/pdf/), p. 4; Gillett (2022), p. 25.

105 See ICC, *Prosecutor v. Thomas Lubanga Dyilo*, Case No. ICC-01/04-01/06-2842, Judgment pursuant to Article 74 of the Statute, Trial Chamber I (14 March 2012); See ICC, *Prosecutor v. Katanga*, Case No. ICC-01/04-01/06 A5, Judgment on the appeal of Mr Thomas Lubanga Dyilo against his conviction (1 December 2014).

Germaine Katanga from the *Force de résistance patriotique en Ituri*,[106] and Ahmad Al Faqi Al Mahdi and al Hassan from the *Ansar Dine* and *Al-Qaeda in the Islamic Maghreb* groups,[107] along with the ICTY cases against Radovan Karadžić[108] and Ratko Mladić,[109] the President of the Bosnian Serbs and Commander of the Bosnian Serb Army, respectively. Until the emergence of international criminal law, individuals, such as these leaders and high State officials, could expect few legal repercussions for their deeds and misdeeds while in office, at least at the international level. Yet, in recent years dozens of heads of States or self-proclaimed States (such as the Republika Srpska) have been charged before courts applying international law. The move to ensure accountability builds on the observation of the International Tribunal at Nuremberg that 'crimes are committed by men, not by abstract entities, and only by punishing individuals who commit such crimes can the provisions of international law be enforced.'[110] Establishing individual responsibility has been at the core of the modern flourishing of international criminal law.

Looking at the possibility of prosecuting NSAs for space pollution, a gateway consideration is the ICC's personal jurisdiction, which is limited to natural persons.[111] Accordingly, an organizational NSA could not be convicted *per se* under international criminal law in its current state.[112] However, the lack of direct enforcement powers against NSAs does not exhaust the potential utility of international criminal law. In line with the insight of the Judges at Nuremberg set out above, prosecuting natural human beings, such as leaders or executives of an NSA, could result in even greater deterrent value than proceedings against an NSA as an entity. Consequently, pursuing individual criminal responsibility for international crimes is a viable means of identifying NSAs responsible for serious harms to communal values.

106 ICC, *Prosecutor v. Germain Katanga*, Case No. ICC-01/04-01/07, Judgment pursuant to article 74 of the Statute, Trial Chamber II (7 March 2014).

107 ICC, *Prosecutor v. Ahmad Al Faqi Al Mahdi*, Case. No. ICC-01/12-01/15, Judgment and Sentence, Trial Chamber VIII (27 September 2016).

108 ICTY, *Prosecutor v. Radovan Karadžić*, Case No. IT-95-5/18-T, Judgment (24 March 2016).

109 ICTY, *Prosecutor v. Ratko Mladić*, Case No. IT-09-92-T, Judgment (22 November 2017).

110 Nuremberg Judgement, 1 'Trial of the Major War Criminals Before the International Military Tribunal', Nuremberg 14 November 1945 – 1 October 1946, at 186 (1947); reprinted in 172 *American Journal of International Law* (1947) 186 ('Nuremberg Judgement'), pp. 220–221.

111 Rome Statute, Article 25(1).

112 Under the laws put in place by the victorious allies in response to the Axis powers actions during World War Two, organizations such as Nazi groups were able to be banned. However, those were essentially State affiliated entities at the time they were operating, which is distinct from NSAs being targeted by criminal laws.

Separate from the prosecution of NSAs for substantive crimes, there have been completed cases under international law in which corporations have been held guilty for offences against the administration of justice. In particular, the Special Tribunal for Lebanon held in its second contempt trial (the *Al Amin* case) that convictions should be entered against a corporate entity, the Akhbar Beirut Corporation, as well as a natural person, namely, Ibrahim Mohamed Al Amin. These convictions were not appealed and became final.[113] Accordingly, there is a limited basis for considering corporate entities criminally responsible before international courts.

Beyond this, substantive charges were successfully laid against the Lundin corporation in Sweden, for aiding and abetting war crimes in Sudan[114] and the LaFarge corporation in France, which pleaded guilty to conspiring to provide material support to foreign terrorist organizations in the United States and agreed to pay fines and forfeitures amounting to 778 million US dollars.[115] This demonstrates the incipient but strengthening movement among civil society to have corporations held responsible under international criminal law and related bodies of law for their actions, including for environmental harm.

Nonetheless, prosecuting space pollution under international criminal law will be difficult, particularly due to the strict substantive jurisdictional parameters governing this branch of international law. The Court's geographic jurisdiction (*ratione loci*), in the case of a State Party referral or a *proprio motu* initiation of an investigation by the Prosecution, is limited to acts on the territory of a State Party or on a vessel or aircraft registered to a State Party (though the Court would also have jurisdiction if the crime were committed by a national of a State Party). If the reference to vessels and aircraft is interpreted to encompass spacecraft for jurisdictional purposes, this will cover space activities occurring on board or in connection with spacecraft. Alternatively, if space activities emanate from, or are controlled by persons acting in, the territory of States Parties, then those activities could be equated with acts occurring within the respective jurisdictions, also giving the Court a basis to act in the situation.

113 Public Redacted Version of the Judgment, *Akhbar Beirut S.A.L. and Al Amin* (STL-14-06/I/CJ), Contempt Judge, 15 July 2016 (hereinafter 'Al Amin Trial Judgment').

114 Taylor and Francis Online, (2023) *The proliferation of corporate war-crimes cases*, Strategic Comments, 29:8.

115 US Department of Justice, 'Lafarge Pleads Guilty to Conspiring to Provide Material Support to Foreign Terrorist Organizations', 18 October 2022 (https://www.justice.gov/opa/pr/lafarge-pleads-guilty-conspiring-provide-material-support-foreign-terrorist-organizations).

The Rome Statute does not indicate that it is terrestrially bound, and there are strong bases to apply international humanitarian law in outer space, as set out in the following section of this discussion. However, that extra-terrestrial application remains untested and will likely be contested in any case that concerns harm in outer space.[116] Even presuming the Rome Statute can apply to acts in outer space, launches conducted from non-State parties' territory or global commons, as discussed herein, would only be covered if the launching individuals were nationals of a State Party to the Rome Statute. Alternatively, even if they were not committed on the territory (or vessel) or by a national of a State Party, the Court can exercise its powers regarding acts occurring anywhere when the case is referred to the Court by the Security Council.[117] Beyond the jurisdictional challenges, the problematic nature of obtaining admissible evidence of space pollution capable of fulfilling the elements of an international crime will also present difficulties.

In terms of which substantive crime to charge, currently there is no international crime explicitly addressing space pollution. Indeed, even the gateway question of whether space pollution constitutes a violation of international law is still subject to debate.[118] When determining whether space pollution can be envisioned as an international crime per se, the parameters have been authoritatively set down by the ICTY Appeals Chamber in the *Tadić* case.[119] Importantly, this includes 'state practice indicating an intention to criminalize the prohibition, including statements by government officials and international organizations, as well as punishment of violations by national courts

116 Chapter 4, Section 2.3.

117 Rome Statute, Articles 12 and 13(b). See also Gillett (2022), p. 58.

118 See Chapter 2, Section 1.

119 ICTY, *Prosecutor v. Tadić*, Case No. IT-94-1-AR72, Decision on the Defence Motion for Interlocutory Appeal on Jurisdiction (2 October 1995) ('Tadić Jurisdictional Decision'), para. 94 (The conditions that must be fulfilled for a violation of international humanitarian law to be subject to Article 3 of the Statute are ('Tadić conditions'): i) the violation must constitute an infringement of a rule of international humanitarian law; ii) the rule must be customary in nature or, if it belongs to treaty law, the required conditions must be met [...]; iii) the violation must be 'serious', that is to say, it must constitute a breach of a rule protecting important values, and the breach must involve grave consequences for the victim. Thus, for instance, the fact of a combatant simply appropriating a loaf of bread in an occupied village would not amount to a 'serious violation of international humanitarian law' although it may be regarded as falling foul of the basic principle laid down in Article 46, paragraph 1, of the Hague Regulations (and the corresponding rule of customary international law) whereby 'private property must be respected' by any army occupying an enemy territory; iv) the violation of the rule must entail, under customary or conventional law, the individual criminal responsibility of the person breaching the rule.').

and military tribunals.'[120] The Special Tribunal for Lebanon added to this '[t]o turn into an international crime, a domestic offence needs to be regarded by the world community as an attack on universal values (such as peace or human rights) or on values held to be of paramount importance in that community; in addition, it is necessary that States and intergovernmental organizations, through their acts and pronouncements, sanction this attitude by clearly expressing the view that the world community considers the offence at issue as amounting to an international crime.'[121]

Based on this jurisprudence, it is far from clear that space pollution, even if it could be considered a substantive violation of international law (which has a robust basis, as set out above),[122] would also be considered sufficiently well-established as a criminal matter to be a basis for criminal prosecution *per se*. Given that the exploration and use of outer space are the 'province of all mankind'[123] and of increasing importance for humanity, it could satisfy the requirement of being 'of paramount importance' in the global community. Moreover, in some countries there are criminal penalties available for violating the licensing requirements for space operators, which include space debris mitigation or other general environmental provisions.[124] However, this is not a particularly explicit basis for a criminal prohibition, and is only reflective of several States rather than the vast majority of space-active States. Aside from this, there is insufficient practice to evince an intention to criminalize the prohibition of space pollution as a matter of international law, even if such an outcome may emerge in the future. Currently, it is difficult to envisage a prosecution of space pollution as a crime *per se* under international law.

Having addressed the prefatory question about whether causing space pollution is a crime *per se*, the inquiry turns to whether causing such pollution could violate an *existing* provision under the Rome Statute. Taking the example of an individual leader of an NSA that deliberately caused disproportionate proliferation of space debris, for example by deliberating destroying a satellite, there are several provisions that serve as analytical frameworks to test the feasibility of proceeding before the ICC.

---

120 ICTY, *Prosecutor vs. Stanislav Galić*, Case No. IT-98-29/A, Appeals Chamber Judgment. Para. 92 citing Tadić Jurisdiction Decision, para. 128.

121 STL, Interlocutory Decision on the Applicable Law: Terrorism, Conspiracy, Homicide, Perpetration, Cumulative Charging (STL-11-01/I), Appeals Chamber, 16 February 2011, para. 91.

122 Chapter 2, Section 1.

123 Outer Space Treaty, Article I.

124 Chapter 5.

In the context of an international armed conflict,[125] creating space pollution through the intentional destruction of a satellite may be argued to amount to the war crime of launching an attack in the knowledge that it will cause excessive environmental harm, set out in Article 8(2)(b)(iv) of the Rome Statute. This would depend on whether the 'natural environment' were interpreted to include outer space.[126] As noted above, the Independent Expert Group's proposed definition of ecocide potentially covers space pollution, as the 'environment' is defined to include outer space,[127] and several other definitions of the environment support this broad interpretation.[128] By way of analogous support, it can be noted that Higgins *et alia* report that the International Law Commission reportedly endorsed a proposal whereby harming the natural environment could constitute an international crime with similarity to Article 8(2)(b)(iv), and in doing so they invoked in this regard several international documents demonstrating international precedence, including the Outer Space Treaty.[129] On this basis, if NSAs were to undertake acts involving such a risk to the outer space environment, they could potentially harm the natural environment as referred to in Article 8(2)(b)(iv).

However, Article 8(2)(b)(iv) typically applies to acts by State armed forces. For an NSA to be covered by the provisions of Article 8(2)(b) would require it to be operating in the context of an international armed conflict. That could occur in particular if the NSA were contracted by a State to conduct security or offensive operations, but this is not a well-tested scenario. The elements of Article 8(2)(b)(iv) also require that the perpetrator launch an attack (in the context of an international armed conflict), knowing that the attack would result in widespread, long-term and severe harm to the environment, and that the harm would be clearly excessive to the anticipated military advantage arising from the attack. These are exacting elements to establish.[130] While it is not

125 The provisions of the Rome Statute applicable to IACs could encompass harm by NSAs if, for example, the NSA were acting within the overall control of a State actor; as established by the ICTY in the *Tadić* case and followed by the ICC; see, e.g., ICC, *Prosecutor v. Bosco Ntaganda*, Case No. ICC-01/04-02/06, Trial Chamber, Judgment, 8 July 2019, para. 717.

126 See Chapter 1, Section 1.

127 Independent Expert Panel, Definition of Ecocide, 2021 (available at https://static1.squarespace.com/static/5ca2608ab914493c64ef1f6d/t/60d1e6e604fae2201d03407f/1624368879048/SE+Foundation+Commentary+and+core+text+rev+6.pdf). However, the expert panel's opinion is not a legal source under Article 21 of the Rome Statute and so would be of incidental guidance only.

128 See Chapter 2.

129 Polly Higgins, Damien Short, Nigel South, 'Protecting the planet: a proposal for a law of ecocide' (2013) 59(3) *Crime, Law and Social Change*, pp. 259–260.

130 See Gillett (2022), Chapter 2.

inconceivable that an NSA could launch such an attack in outer space while operating in conjunction with a State, the circumstances would be highly specific and would not encompass most of the situations in which space pollution arises. Consequently, Article 8(2)(b)(iv) remains a theoretical but highly constrained possibility for prosecuting this form of NSA harm.[131]

Broadening the contextual scope, if space pollution were linked to an international armed conflict, it could fall under the crime of deliberately targeting civilian objects, enshrined in Article 8(2)(b)(ii),[132] which prohibits intentionally directing attacks against civilian objects. The corresponding international humanitarian law grave breach that is most directly applicable is Article 85(3)(b) of Additional Protocol I, which concerns launching indiscriminate attacks on civilian objects with knowledge that they would result in excessive damage to civilian objects.

However, it is hard to envisage space pollution being used to target civilian objects (rather than the targeting of civilian objects in space resulting in pollution to the outer space environment). Simply put, space pollution typically arises from accidental deterioration or impacts, rather than any kind of deliberate means of seeking to harm civilian property or items. It is possible that a nefarious NSA could seek to damage or destroy a space object seeking to impart a political message or terrorize human populations.[133] While more detail is set out in the section below on international humanitarian law, it is sufficient to note for present purposes that the high burden of proof in the context of international criminal law means that theoretical or highly indirect forms of harm are unlikely to lead to successful prosecutions.

In a similar line, the destruction of a satellite or other space object could amount to a violation of the war crime set out under Article 8(2)(a)(iv) and 8(2)(b)(xiii) (also 8(2)(e)(xii) for non-international armed conflicts as discussed below), which in broad terms prohibit the destruction and appropriation of enemy (or an adversary's) property. Key elements to prove in such a case are that the destruction or appropriation was not justified by military necessity; the destruction or appropriation was extensive and carried out wantonly; and that the property was protected under one or more of the Geneva Conventions of 1949.[134]

---

131 Few, if any, of the instances of space pollution noted above could be considered to constitute an attack in the context of armed conflict.

132 The provision underlying this is Article 52(1) of Additional Protocol I. There is no equivalent provision for non-international armed conflicts under the Rome Statute.

133 See Chapters 3, Section 2, 4, Section 1.

134 ICC Elements of Crimes, p. 15.

On the element of military necessity, there are potential circumstances in which a satellite or other space object could be used to advance military activities. The use of Starlink satellites in the current Ukrainian conflict against Russia has demonstrated the important value that satellite communications can make to integrated military attacks.[135] Starlink, which was launched by SpaceX in 2019, is a 'private sector-run, low earth orbit satellite constellation that provides high-speed, low-latency broadband internet across the globe.'[136] Starlink has important civilian and military uses. Mykhailo Fedorov, Ukraine's Minister of Digital Transformation has said that Starlink 'is crucial support for Ukraine's infrastructure and restoring the destroyed territories' and reportedly, the Ukrainian military forces applied it in a creative manner, such as using it to 'control unmanned surveillance and reconnaissance aerial vehicles and unmanned combat aerial vehicles (aka drones).'[137] SpaceX itself has acknowledged the potential for Starlink's use in military operations.[138] On this basis, it could arguably be militarily necessary to attempt to destroy its satellites. If that argument were accepted, it would undermine the criminal prosecution of such destructive acts.

In determining whether an object is a military object at a certain time and whether a strike against such an object would be justified by military necessity, the provisions of Additional Protocol I provide guidance, particularly Article 52(2):

> In so far as objects are concerned, military objectives are limited to those objects which by their nature, location, purpose or use make an effective contribution to military action and whose total or partial destruction, capture or neutralization, in the circumstances ruling at the time, offers a definite military advantage.

Even if a military aim is present, the attacker must not cause excessive incidental harm to civilians and civilian objects. Article 51(5)(b) provides that:

---

135 For more information see for example ESPI, Briefs No. 57 (2022).

136 Belfer Center for Science and International Affairs, Harvard Kennedy School, 'Starlink and the Russia-Ukraine War: A Case of Commercial Technology and Public Purpose?' (9 March 2023) (available at https://www.belfercenter.org/publication/starlink-and-russia-ukraine-war-case-commercial-technology-and-public-purpose), citing Starlink Homepage (https://www.starlink.com/)/.

137 Belfer Center (2023) citing Ukrainian Cities Are Suffering Internet Blackouts.' *The Economist*. The Economist Newspaper, (26 February 2023) (available at https://www.economist.com/graphic-detail/2022/02/26/ukrainian-cities-ar).

138 Belfer Center (2023).

> an attack which may be expected to cause incidental loss of civilian life, injury to civilians, damage to civilian objects, or a combination thereof, which would be excessive in relation to the concrete and direct military advantage anticipated.

In assessing the excessiveness of any such anticipated damage, the ongoing threat of environmental harm in space would be a key consideration. Unlike most terrestrial pollution,[139] pollution in space continues to present a significant danger for an essentially unlimited time. Flying around at missile-like velocities, the harm from even a small piece of space debris can be catastrophic for satellites, spacecraft and astronauts.[140] Consequently, the potential for excessive harm caused by the targeting of a space object is high.

The most direct provision of the Rome Statute under which to prosecute the destruction of a satellite or space object during a non-international armed conflict is Article 8(2)(e)(xii). That would require an NSA to be in conflict with a State or two NSAs to be engaged in armed conflict in space, which is conceivable but unprecedented (conversely, on Earth, such non-international armed conflicts frequently occur). This provision prohibits: '[d]estroying or seizing the property of an adversary unless such destruction or seizure be imperatively demanded by the necessities of the conflict.' The elements of this crime are that (1) 'the perpetrator destroyed […] certain property; (2) 'such property was property of an adversary'; (3) 'such property was protected from that destruction […] under the international law of armed conflict'; (4) 'the perpetrator was aware of the factual circumstances that established the status of the property'; and (5) 'the destruction […] was not required by military necessity'. This crime concerns destruction, which the Trial Chamber in *Katanga* has explained as follows: 'destruction entails acts such as setting ablaze, demolishing, or otherwise damaging property.'[141] In the present scenario of a satellite being deliberately attacked, the targeted space object itself would be considered 'property'.[142]

139 Radioactive pollution on earth could be considered an exception in this respect, due to its ongoing dangerous effects for nature and humans.

140 Chapter 1, Section 3.

141 Katanga TJ, para. 891.

142 This would fit with the broad interpretation taken by the *Katanga* Trial Chamber, which held that the property in question 'whether moveable or immoveable, private or public – must belong to individuals or entities aligned with or with allegiance to a party to the conflict adverse or hostile to the perpetrator, which can be established in the light of the ethnicity or place of residence of such individuals or entities'; Katanga TJ, para. 892

However, the impact on the environment would only be indirectly addressed, by virtue of the impact on the space environment caused by the destruction of the space object. To qualify under Article 8(2)(e)(xii), the partially or totally destroyed property must be protected by the international law of armed conflict, that is, it must not constitute 'military objectives'. As set out above, civilian objects are usually defined negatively by reference to the definition of military objects under Article 52(2) of Additional Protocol I.[143] Whether space objects would be considered protected objects for these purposes remains to be assessed on the facts in a specific case, taking into account factors such as its effective contribution to the military activities of the opposing force.

Additionally, Article 8(2)(e)(xii) refers to the property of an 'adversary', which has been interpreted as 'any person, who is considered to belong to another party to the conflict, such as the government, insurgents or, as Article 8(2)(f) of the Statute demonstrates, belongs to an opposing organized armed group'.[144] If an armed conflict extended to outer space, then efforts to destroy enemy property may also occur in that domain.

Consequently, depending on the nature of the conflict, the most directly potentially relevant provisions of the Rome Statute in relation to an attack on a space object resulting in harm to the space environment are Article 8(2)(a)(ii), 8(2)(b)(ii), 8(2)(b)(iv), and Article 8(2)(e)(xii). However, there is no precedent for prosecutions of this type of conduct at the international level, and so even the question of the applicability of the Rome Statute to activities in space would likely be subject to significant and contested litigation.

Beyond the property destruction, if an NSA representative caused space debris or other form of space pollution that would kill astronauts or other persons in outer space, this could potentially constitute murder as a war crime (in the context of armed conflict) or a crime against humanity (in the context of a widespread or systematic attack on a civilian population) within the jurisdiction of the ICC.[145] The key issue here would be intent; establishing the intent to kill the astronauts or other persons in outer space would be a difficult burden to meet. It is not a particularly likely scenario but could arise if such harm were caused intentionally or through a criminal level of recklessness, or if an NSA

(interpreting the elements of the war crime under Article 8(2)I(xii)). In NIACs, the concept of property has largely been regulated by national law; Gillett (2022), p.120–121.

143 Katanga TJ, para. 893 citing Additional Protocol I, Article 52(2).

144 Andreas Zimmerman and Robin Geiß, 'Article 8 – para. 2 (e)' in Otto Triffterer and Kai Ambos (eds.), *The Rome Statute of the International Criminal Court: A Commentary 2.3*, Substantive Crimes (C.H. Beck/Hart/Nomos, 2016), p. 568, para. 969; Gillett (2022), p. 115.

145 ICC Rome Statute, Articles 8(2)(a)(i)/(c)(i) and 7(1)(a).

intentionally caused the death of an individual in space. Other crimes, such as persecution, torture, and inhumane acts, are not impossible to envision. While these are currently remote possibilities, they will grow in likelihood as terrestrial activities are increasingly extended to outer space.

In sum, these scenarios are unprecedented and difficult to foresee. The ICC has not yet adopted the crime of ecocide,[146] and there is no other international criminal forum capable of prosecuting such harm. As with other areas of international law examined above, there is potential for the future application of ecocide, war crime or crime against humanity to intentional pollution of outer space by NSAs, but no current operational means to do so in a direct manner.

2.3 *International Humanitarian Law*

The domain of international humanitarian law offers a fertile potential basis to impose accountability on NSAs for environmental harm that occurs during armed conflict.[147] However, its application in the outer space environment is less well-tested. Although scholars have examined its relevance in the context of anti-satellite missile testing and related areas,[148] international and domestic courts have not yet applied international humanitarian law to the outer space environment sufficiently to develop any consistent jurisprudence. In the absence of judicial guidance, the following assessment relies on extrapolating from the established international humanitarian law doctrine and case-law to assess its application in outer space.

Armed conflicts have the potential to disrupt all facets of space activity. The threat of hostilities can prevent State launches of rockets and satellites and interfere with communications networks, undermining exploration of space and development of infrastructure for space operations. Similar impacts can be felt by NSAs, particularly due to disruptions to commercial activities such as launches of satellites, satellite broadcasting, remote sensing, telecommunications, space tourism, and even the mining of resources in space.[149] Additionally,

146 Proposed definitions of ecocide, include those of the Independent Expert Panel for the Legal Definition of Ecocide, *Commentary and Core Text*, June 2021, available at https://www.stopecocide.earth/legal-definition; and Matthew Gillett, *Prosecuting Environmental Harm before the International Criminal Court* (Cambridge University Press, 2022), pp. 326, 353.

147 See, e.g. Bourdonnaye (2020), p. 599 ('all NSA[s] have environmental obligations under IHL'). For a more traditional State-centred approach, see Gutzman (2017).

148 Cassandra Steer and Dale Stephens, 'International Humanitarian Law and Its Application in Outer Space' (2020), in Cassandra Steer, and Matthew Hersch (eds), *War and Peace in Outer Space: Law, Policy, and Ethics* (Oxford Academic Press, 2020).

149 Zhao (2018), p. 4 citing Steven Freeland, 'Impact of space tourism on the International Law of Outer Space' (2005) in 48th Colloquium on the Law of Outer Space, 17 October 2005–21

some space activities may even give rise to disputes that escalate to armed conflicts, particularly with the growing spectre of space resource mining.[150]

Already, it is well established that NSAs have obligations under humanitarian law insofar as they are parties to a conflict.[151] These include the core prohibitions set out under Common Article 3 of the Geneva Conventions, which bans violence to life and person, including murder, cruel treatment and torture, hostage-taking, outrages upon personal dignity, violations of basic due process, and lack of care for the sick and wounded.[152] Moreover, Additional Protocol II to the Geneva Conventions applies specifically to non-international armed conflicts, which inherently involves armed NSAs,[153] thereby placing obligations on actors operating within the territory of State Parties.

However, novel questions arise in relation to the application of international humanitarian law to pollution in outer space. Two key questions are: first, whether this body of law applies beyond the Earth's terrestrial limits, and second, which specific provisions could address environmental harm in space.

Regarding the first question, it is clear that the possibility of armed conflict in outer space (or the extension of terrestrial conflict to the outer space theatre) is increasing. The importance of satellite communications for real-time information regarding enemy positions and coordination of multi-faceted military operations has been demonstrated repeatedly. As noted above, Elon Musk's provision of Starlink satellites were essential for the early successes of Ukraine's military forces after the escalation of the Russo-Ukrainian conflict in 2022.[154] Integrated military operations, involving drones, tanks, and artillery, are likely to become the dominant form of conducting large-scale combat, which will accentuate the importance of reliable satellite communications. Correspondingly, disabling (or at least disrupting) those networks will be an increasingly central aim of opposing parties in modern warfare. Given the increasing likelihood of conflict extending to outer space, it would be incongruous to prevent international humanitarian law from applying beyond the Earth's atmosphere.

October 2005, Fukuoka, Japan, published by the American Institute of Aeronautics and Astronautics Inc.; Anita Rinner, 'Small Satellites – Smart Laws – Small Satellite Projects in the Face of National Space Legislation – Austria' (2013) *Proceedings of the International Institute of Space Law*.

150 See Chapter 1, Section 3.

151 Sandesh Sivakumaran, *The Law of Non-International Armed Conflict* (Oxford University Press 2012), pp. 236–242.

152 Geneva Conventions of 12 August 1949, 1125 UNTS 3, Common Article 3.

153 Additional Protocol II to the Geneva Conventions.

154 Chapter 4, Section 2, 2.2.

The extension of international humanitarian law to outer space finds support from a range of sources. In its 1986 *Nuclear Weapons Advisory Opinion*, the International Court of Justice noted that international humanitarian law applies to 'all forms of warfare and to all kinds of weapons, those of the past, those of the present and those of the future.'[155] The ICRC has also concluded that international humanitarian law applies to armed conflicts occurring in space or extending out to it'[international humanitarian law] applies to any military operations conducted as part of an armed conflict, including those occurring in (or extending to) outer space.'[156] Several commentators have reiterated this approach.[157] Addressing the question of which body (or bodies) of law apply to armed conflicts in outer space, Frans von der Dunk has developed a matrix of applicable laws in descending order. At the top, he places the United Nations Charter as an overarching normative framework, which follows from Article 103 of the Charter. Alongside the Charter, he places the non-domain specific international humanitarian law principles that apply generally.[158] His matrix then descends through other branches of international law including space law and then further treaties which may be applicable.[159]

155 ICJ, *Legality of the Threat or Use of Nuclear Weapons*, Advisory Opinion of 8 July 1996, para. 86.

156 ICRC (2021), *The Potential Human Cost of the Use of Weapons in Outer Space and the Protection Afforded by International Humanitarian Law: Position paper submitted by the International Committee of the Red Cross to the Secretary-General of the United Nations on the issues outlined in General Assembly Resolution 75/36* (available at https://www.icrc.org/en/document/potential-human-cost-outer-space-weaponization-ihl-protection), ('The applicability of IHL in outer space is confirmed by Article III of the Outer Space Treaty, which requires States to "carry on activities in the exploration and use of outer space ... in accordance with international law". International law includes IHL'); ICRC (2022), *Constraints under International Law on Military Operations in Outer Space during Armed Conflicts* (Working paper submitted by the International Committee of the Red Cross to the open-ended working group on reducing space threats through norms, rules and principles of responsible behaviours, as convened under United Nations General Assembly Resolution 76/231, and to the Secretary-General of the United Nations in reply to General Assembly Resolution 76/230 on Further practical measures for the prevention of an arms race in outer space').

157 See, e.g., Steer and Stephens (2020); Wen Zhou, 'War, law and outer space: pathways to reduce the human cost of military space operations', *Humanitarian Law and Policy* (15 August 2023) (https://blogs.icrc.org/law-and-policy/2023/08/15/war-law-outer-space-reduce-human-cost-of-military-space-operations/).

158 See Frans von der Dunk, 'Armed Conflicts in Outer Space: Which Law Applies?' 97 *International Law Studies* (2021), pp. 188–231.

159 See von der Dunk (2021), pp. 188–231.

Looking to the treaties, various international humanitarian law provisions provide a basis for its application to outer space. For international armed conflicts (which may be the context in which an NSA conducts operations by or on behalf of a State), Common Article 2 of the Geneva Conventions,[160] which constitute core instruments of humanitarian law, refer to their applicability to 'any … armed conflict'. Additional Protocol I[161] arguably also applies to conflicts in outer space, as it refers to that same Article of the Geneva Conventions to define the scope of its application.[162] However, although Article 49 of Additional Protocol I (which concerns 'attacks' and the scope of application), provides that the provisions on attacks apply 'to all attacks in whatever territory conducted', it continues that Articles 48–67 'apply to any land, air or sea warfare which may affect the civilian population, individual civilians or civilian objects on land'. On a narrow reading, this could exclude 'attacks' purely conducted in space. But, given that space-based attacks would risk impacting essential services on which civilians depend,[163] these international humanitarian law provisions for international armed conflicts would also likely apply to attacks in space in most circumstances.[164]

For non-international armed conflicts, the jurisdictional question is more complex. Factually, the increased presence of NSAs in space raises the clear possibility of clashes between States and armed non-State organisations amounting to non-international armed conflicts. Legally, the situation is less clear. In its working paper on "Constraints under International Law on Military Operations in, or in Relation to, Outer Space during Armed Conflicts", the ICRC refers to prohibitions applicable in non-international armed conflicts, including provisions of Additional Protocol II.[165] However, Article 1(1) of Additional Protocol II provides that it:

160 Geneva Conventions of 1949, Article II.

161 Additional Protocol I, Article 1(3).

162 Additional Protocol I, Article 1(3); ICRC (2022), p. 3.

163 Zhou (2023) ('Today, space systems, particularly navigation, communications and remote-sensing satellites, play an indispensable role in the functioning of critical civilian infrastructure, especially in the energy and communications sectors. These sectors enable the provision of the essential services on which civilians depend, such as food production and supply, water, electricity, health care, sanitation, and waste management.').

164 ICRC (2022) ('Article 49(3) of Additional Protocol I demonstrates that the protocol's rules on the conduct of hostilities were meant to apply to all types of warfare that may affect civilians on land. This would include hostilities in outer space, or the effects of which extend to outer space').

165 Additional Protocol II; ICRC (2021), p. 5.

> shall apply to all armed conflicts which are not covered by Article 1 of the Protocol Additional to the Geneva Conventions of 12 August 1949, and relating to the Protection of Victims of International Armed Conflicts (Protocol I) and which take place *in the territory of a High Contracting Party* between its armed forces and dissident armed forces or other organized armed groups which, under responsible command, exercise such control over a part of its territory as to enable them to carry out sustained and concerted military operations and to implement this Protocol.[166]

Similarly, Common Article 3, which provides a set of basic protections applicable to armed conflicts not of an international character, refers to armed conflicts 'in the territory of one of the High Contracting Parties'. These references to conflicts in the 'territory' of a Contracting Party are difficult to reconcile with space warfare, particularly given that outer space, including the Moon and celestial bodies, is precluded from being subject to national appropriation and so, under current understandings of international space law, it cannot become the territory of a State.[167]

Nonetheless, beyond the terms of the conventions themselves, there is customary international law. Nils Melzer has argued that a non-international armed conflict occurring outside the territory of any contracting Party would still be covered by the humanitarian provisions of Common Article III, as they reflect customary international law.[168] He concludes that 'in situations of non-international armed conflict, not only does international humanitarian law apply in areas exposed to active hostilities, it governs essentially any act or operation carried out for reasons related to the conflict (nexus to the conflict), regardless of territorial location.'[169] This supports the ICRC's statement that 'most rules governing the conduct of hostilities today are part of customary international humanitarian law and apply wherever hostilities take place during armed conflicts, including in, or in relation to, outer space.'[170] Schmitt notes

166 Emphasis added. This provision also sets out a minimum threshold, which must be surpassed before lighter clashes will be considered to amount to armed conflict: 'This Protocol shall not apply to situations of internal disturbances and tensions, such as riots, isolated and sporadic acts of violence and other acts of a similar nature, as not being armed conflicts.' See also Rome Statute, Article 8(2)(d) and (f), reiterating these lower-level thresholds.

167 Outer Space Treaty, Article II.

168 Nils Melzer, *International Humanitarian Law: A Comprehensive Introduction* (International Committee of the Red Cross, 2016), pp. 71–72.

169 Nils Melzer, *International Humanitarian Law: A Comprehensive Introduction* (International Committee of the Red Cross, 2016), pp. 71–72.

170 ICRC (2022), p. 3.

that space-based attacks against land targets and attacks against space-based resources, whether from land of space, that affect civilians, would be covered by international humanitatrian law and that customary law fills the conventional gaps in this respect, without specifically addressing non-international armed conflicts.[171] However, given the extremely limited State practice regarding the applicability of international humanitarian law to non-international armed conflicts in space, the application of customary humanitarian law to this type of conflict in space requires further development.

In light of the foregoing, there is a basis to apply international humanitarian law to outer space, even if it remains largely untested in judicial fora. However, the source of this legal position depends on the nature of the conflict. For international armed conflicts, both conventional and customary law can apply in principle to the outer space theatre, whereas for non-international armed conflicts the primary basis on which to apply international humanitarian law would be custom. This means that the customary basis of any specific prohibition may become a significant factor depending on the nature of the conflict being examined, which is particularly relevant given the focus on this book on NSAs.

Turning to the second question, given that international humanitarian law can apply to NSA conduct in space at least in some circumstances,[172] several prohibitions are relevant to environmental harm. Under the Outer Space Treaty itself, there is the prohibition against the placement into orbit of objects carrying nuclear weapons or other weapons of mass destruction, or the installation of such weapons on celestial bodies. Such conduct carries an obvious risk to the space environment.[173] The Outer Space Treaty also prohibits establishing military bases, installations, or fortifications, and testing weapons or conducting military maneuvers on celestial bodies could harm the environments on those bodies.[174]

Beyond the Outer Space Treaty, there is the environmentally linked prohibition on the use of 'methods or means of warfare that are intended, or may be expected, to cause widespread, long-term and severe damage to the natural environment'.[175] A closely related prohibition covers military or any other

171 Michael N Schmitt, 'International Law and Military Operations in Space', *Max Planck Yearbook of United Nations Law*, (2006) 10, p. 114-124.

172 See Zhou (2023).

173 Outer Space Treaty, Article IV(1). See also ICRC (2022), p. 4; Zhou (2023).

174 Outer Space Treaty, Article IV(2). See also ICRC (2022), p. 4; Zhou (2023).

175 Michael N Schmitt, 'International Law and Military Operations in Space', *Max Planck Yearbook of United Nations Law*, (2006) 10, p. 121 (listing Article 35(3) of AP1 as applicable to outer space conflict); Zhou (2023) (listing this as an applicable prohibition when

hostile use of environmental modification techniques, which could apply in the outer space context.[176] Additionally, reprisals against the natural environment could also theoretically extend to outer space and are prohibited to States during international armed conflict.[177] However, it remains contested whether this prohibition also extends to non-international armed conflict.[178] Each of these environmentally-oriented provisions would require interpreting the term 'natural environment' to encompass outer space. That notion receives support from Article II of the Convention on the Prohibition of Military or Any Other Hostile Use of Environmental Modification Techniques of 1976[179] which explicitly refers to outer space.

The prohibitions against attacking civilians and against acts or threats of violence the primary purpose of which is to spread terror among the civilian population, would be relevant if NSAs intentionally targeted civilians in outer space or sought to terrorize the civilian population through such attacks.[180] A gateway consideration would be whether the personnel targeted were civilian in nature. This is not always a clear-cut distinction.[181] In space, the blurring between civilian and military personnel is frequent. In the United States, for example, astronauts from the armed forces usually continue to be on active duty while seconded to the National Aeronautics and Space Administration

discussing the outer space context). See further ICRC Customary International Law Study, Rule 45 (finding this rule is applicable during the international form of conflict but is contested as being applicable during non-international conflicts); Matthew Gillett, 'Eco-Struggles: Using International Criminal Law to Protect the Environment During and After Non-International Armed Conflict' (2017) in Carsten Stahn, Jens Iverson, Jennifer S. Easterday (eds.) *Environmental Protection and Transitions from Conflict to Peace: Clarifying Norms, Principles and Practices* (Oxford University Press), p. 238.

176 See *Convention on the Prohibition of Military or Any Other Hostile Use of Environmental Modification Techniques*, 1976, Article II (which explicitly refers to environmental modification techniques in outer space). See also ICRC (2022), p. 4; Zhou (2023).

177 Additional Protocol I to the Geneva Conventions, Article 55(2).

178 Matthew Gillett, 'Criminalizing reprisals against the natural environment' *International Review of the Red Cross* (2023) 105. Compare David Turns, 'Implementation and Compliance' (2007) in Elizabeth Wilmshurst and Susan Breau (eds.) *Perspectives on the ICRC Study on Customary International Humanitarian Law* (Cambridge University Press, 2007), pp. 354, 372 (arguing that it does not extend to NIACs) with Rule 148 of the ICRC rules on customary IHL (which applies the prohibition to NIACs).

179 ENMOD, 1976.

180 See Jean-Marie Henckaerts, Louise Doswald-Beck, *Customary International Humanitarian Law Vol. 1: Rules* (Cambridge University Press, 2005), [hereinafter ICRC Customary Law Study], Rules 2, and 7 to 10.

181 Schmitt (2006), pp. 123–124. See also e.g. ICTY, *Prosecutor v Mrkšić (Mile) and Šljivančanin (Veselin)*, Judgment, Case No. IT-95-13/1-A, ICL 758 (ICTY 2009), 5 May 2009.

(NASA),[182] but serve alongside civilian scientists, engineers, and medical professionals.[183] Moreover, even if an attack were directed against civilians, the harm to the environment would be an incidental factor, rather than the protected object behind the prohibition and so the condemnation of the space pollution would only be collateral in nature.

A directly relevant prohibition is the targeting of the outer space environment as a civilian object.[184] Many commentators consider the natural environment to be civilian in nature.[185] The ICRC has also argued that the natural environment is by default considered to be of civilian character unless it becomes a military objective through its nature, use, purpose or location.[186] The civilian qualification of the natural environment would likely extend to outer space, particularly given the definitions of the natural environment which include outer space.[187] Consequently, an intentional attack on the outer space environment could qualify as an attack against a civilian object, subject to those interpretations being favoured. Conversely, attacks on space objects that are dual-use would be more difficult to assess. Many space objects are designated as dual-use, as they could serve both military and civilian purposes.[188]

In relation to attacks on space satellites and similar objects, a relevant prohibition is Rule 42 of the ICRC Study on customary international law, which covers attacks against works or installations containing dangerous forces (such

182 Miller also notes that these military officers would not qualify as combatants while engaged in a space flight 'since they are not armed, nor are they in a combat zone', see Miller (2019), p. 38.

183 Miller (2019), pp. 37–38.

184 ICRC Study, Rule 7 ('Attacks may only be directed against military objectives. Attacks must not be directed against civilian objects', and asserting that 'State practice establishes this rule as a norm of customary international law applicable in both international and non-international armed conflicts.'). Note that the Rome Statute, Article 8(2)(b)(ii) contrast with Article 8(2)(c) and (e) which do not include a corresponding war crime to Article 8(2)(b)(ii), as discussed in the ICRC customary law study, p. 27.

185 Michael N. Schmitt, *Tallinn Manual on the International Law Applicable to Cyber Warfare* (Cambridge University Press, 2013), pp. 231–233, Rule 83 (Protection of the Natural Environment): (a) '[t]he natural environment is a civilian object.'

186 See ICRC Customary Law Study, commentary on Rule 43(A), p. 143. But see Wolff Heintschel von Heinegg and Michael Donner, 'New Developments in the Protection of the Natural Environment in Naval Armed Conflicts' (1994) 37 *German Yearbook of International Law*, p. 289.

187 See Chapter 1, Section 1.

188 Clark McFadden and Dewey Ballantine, 'Dual-Use Technologies and National security' (1997) in National Research Council, *International Friction and Cooperation in High-Technology Development and Trade: Papers and Proceedings* (The National Academies Press, 1997), p. 130.

as dams and nuclear power stations) if such attacks 'may cause the release of dangerous forces and consequent severe losses among the civilian population'.[189] Another provision of international humanitarian law applicable to NSAs is the prohibition of attacks on 'objects indispensable to the survival of the civilian population'.[190] Although facially relevant, this provision concerns starvation of the civilian population and thus is hard to equate with space pollution *per se*.[191] Whilst indirect impacts of space debris could theoretically impact terrestrial economic and security conditions to the extent that food shortages became problematic, this would be an extremely indirect chain of causation and difficult to attribute to an entity for legal responsibility.

Turning to indiscriminate attacks, which can apply in the space context,[192] this prohibition is said by the ICRC to have attained customary status in international and non-international armed conflicts.[193] Notably, this prohibition is not disputed by India, Israel, and the United States, at least in relation to the context of international armed conflicts.[194] The prohibition against indiscriminate attacks covers

> (a) those which are not directed at a specific military objective;
> (b) those which employ a method or means of combat which cannot be directed at a specific military objective; or
> (c) those which employ a method or means of combat the effects of which cannot be limited as required by this Protocol; and consequently, in each such case, are of a nature to strike military objectives and civilians or civilian objects without distinction.

Kinetic strikes in space potentially raise the issue of space debris proliferating in an uncontrollable way, with inherent dangers to civilians and civilian objects (such as non-military space objects) and thereby being inherently

189 ICRC Customary Law Study, Rule 42; Zhou (2023). See also Protocol II to the Geneva Conventions, Article 15.

190 ICRC Customary Law Study, Rule 54; Zhou (2023). See also Article 14 of Additional Protocol II.

191 See generally, Federica D'Alessandra and Matthew Gillett, 'The War Crime of Starvation in Non-International Armed Conflicts' (2019) 17 *Journal of International Criminal Justice*, pp. 815–819.

192 See ICRC (2022), p. 4; Zhou (2023), both citing ICRC Customary Law Study, Rules 70–84.

193 ICRC Customary Law Study, Rule 12.

194 See Michael Schmitt, Kieran Tinkler, 'War in Space: How International Humanitarian Law Might Apply' (2020) *Just Security* (available at https://www.justsecurity.org/68906/war-in-space-how-international-humanitarian-law-might apply/#:~:text=Accordingly%2C%20the%20ICRC%20rightly%20concludes,those%20occurring%20in%20outer%20space.%E2%80%9D).

indiscriminate.[195] Some commentators conclude that such attacks automatically violate the prohibition on indiscriminate attacks.[196] Presuming that the prohibition applied to the conflict in question, indiscriminate attacks resulting in the destruction of satellites and the creation of space debris may qualify as this grave violation.

The core principles of international humanitarian law, particularly distinction, necessity, and proportionality, could all potentially apply to the conduct of NSAs and their potential harm to the environment.[197] However, these are general principles, which would be difficult for courts to apply in any direct manner. At most, they would assist in the interpretation of applicable provisions and laws relevant to environmental harm in outer space.

On this basis, international humanitarian law provides a fertile body of law that could apply to the conduct of NSAs in space. In the context of international armed conflicts, this would require showing that the NSA was acting under the overall control of a State, or a similar qualifying circumstance. For a non-international armed conflict to occur in space would require at least one belligerent to be an NSA acting beyond the control of a State. In such circumstances, there is a basis in customary international law for international humanitarian law to apply to non-international armed conflicts, but it is largely untested, as set out above.

Regarding specific prohibitions, many questions would arise regarding the nature of the conduct that would be prohibited and how that would apply to particular factual scenarios. The primary issue in most foreseeable scenarios would be whether or not the space object in question were considered to be a military object, such as if it were making an effective contribution to military action and whose total or partial destruction, capture or neutralization would offer a definite military advantage.[198] Additional issues would include whether the harm was foreseeable and foreseen by the perpetrator, as well as whether the actions were argued to be lawful reprisals. These issues would have to be addressed by competent adjudicative bodies. Identifying such bodies presents a challenge in and of itself, particularly in relation to international

195 Schmitt and Tinkler (2020); Zhou (2023).

196 David A. Koplow, 'ASAT-isfaction: Customary International Law and the Regulation of Anti-Satellite Weapons' (2009) 30 *Michigan Journal of International Law*, pp. 1244–1245, 1262; Percy Blount, 'Targeting in Outer Space: Legal Aspects of Operational Military Actions in Space' *Harvard Law School: National Security Journal* (25 November 2012) (available at https://harvardnsj.org/2012/11/25/targeting-in-outer-space-legal-aspects-of-operational-military-actions-in-space/).

197 Bourdonnaye (2020), pp. 587–590; Zhou (2023).

198 Additional Protocol I, Article 52(2).

humanitarian law.[199] In recent decades, it has been international criminal bodies that have been the primary institutions applying international humanitarian law. However, those bodies have additional restrictions including the requirement to apply their own statutes rather than an unmediated version of the law of armed conflict. In this light, the application of international humanitarian law to space pollution remains a theoretical but untested possibility, which would nonetheless likely pivot on critical questions that arise in terrestrial settings, particularly the civilian nature of the targeted object or persons and the foreseeability of collateral harm to other persons and objects, including the environment.

2.4 *International Human Rights Law*

International human rights law has increasingly been interpreted as containing protections of the environment, notwithstanding its inherently anthropocentric orientation and genesis. The most obvious manifestation of this trend is the July 2022 UNGA Resolution recognizing the human right to a clean, healthy and sustainable environment.[200] While this has ecocentric utility, exercising this right (and other human rights that may be violated by environmental harm) requires a showing of harm, or potential harm, to anthropocentric interests. In this light, international human rights law provides a form of indirect protection for the environment, mediated through the prism of human interests.

However, human rights law has traditionally been formulated along State-centric lines.[201] International human rights obligations are primarily owed by States, and questions remain about the extent to which NSAs can owe human rights.[202] Institutions, such as the Human Rights Committee, typically supervise and monitor the implementation of Covenant obligations by States parties,

---

199 See Chapter 4, Section 3 below.

200 This culmination builds on various strands of recognition from regional contexts, including the 2017 IACtHR Advisory Opinion of the Inter-American Commission on Human Rights, which recognised the right to a healthy environment as an autonomous human right, found that States have an obligation to take measures to prevent environmental harms both within their borders, and in transboundary scenarios and thus extraterritorially, and held that 'as an autonomous right, the right to a healthy environment, unlike other rights, protects the components of the environment, such as forests, rivers and seas, as legal interests in themselves, even in the absence of the certainty or evidence of a risk to individuals'. See Chapter 2, Section 1.3.

201 Andrew Clapham, Chapter 28 'Non-State Actors' in Moeckli et. al. (eds), *International Human Rights Law* (4th ed.), (Oxford University Press, 2022), p. 584.

202 Bourdonnaye (2020), pp. 592–593.

rather than NSAs. Some commentators categorically refute the application of international human rights law to NSAs.[203] Accordingly, even if there were a link between space pollution and a human right within the Committee's remit, its determinations would primarily concern a relevant State rather than the specific NSA in question.

Nonetheless, experts such as Andrew Clapham note that the legal picture is more complex than a simple binary between States which bear human rights obligations and NSAs which do not.[204] In this vein, tribunals ruling on investor-State disputes under international law (in the context of ICSID) provide corporations with standing to bring claims against States and have attributed corporations with potential responsibility for human rights obligations.[205] For example, in *Urbaser v. Argentina* (which in part concerned the right of access to water), the Tribunal held that it was 'reluctant to share Claimants' principled position that guaranteeing the human right to water is a duty that may be born solely by the State, and never borne also by private companies like the Claimants', and that 'it can no longer be admitted that companies operating internationally are immune from becoming subjects of international law.'[206] The Tribunal also noted that peremptory norms (*jus cogens*) of international law would also be relevant to its assessments as they would prevail over any contrary treaty law.[207] Ultimately, the Tribunal ruled that the investing corporation's obligation to provide access to water to the population in that case was based on the specific concession under which it was operating, rather than by the direct application of the human right to water under international law.[208] However, it held this because of the nature of the claim in question, which was an obligation to perform. In doing so, it expressly acknowledged that the legal position would be different in the case of a prohibition against conduct on the

203 Lindsay Moir, *The Law of Internal Armed Conflict* (Cambridge University Press 2002), pp. 194–195.

204 Clapham (2022), p. 590 (noting that arguments have been made for years that human rights obligations can bind NSAs and citing Meron, *Human Rights in Internal Strife: Their International Protection* (Grotius, 1987) pp. 33–40).

205 See Arato (2015), pp. 232–233.

206 *Urbaser v The Argentine Republic*, ICSID Case No. ARB/07/26, Award, 8 December 2016, paras. 1193–1195.

207 *Urbaser v The Argentine Republic*, para. 1203 citing *Phoenix Action, Ltd. v. The Czech Republic*, ICSID/ARB/06/5, para. 78 (LARA-68) ('nobody would suggest that ICSID protection should be granted to investments made in violation of the most fundamental rules of protection of human rights, like investments made in pursuance of torture or genocide or in support of slavery or trafficking of human organs.').

208 ICSID, *Urbaser v. The Argentine Republic*, Case No. ARB/07/26, Award (8 December 2016), para. 1210.

part of the corporation, stating that '[t]he situation would be different in case an obligation to abstain, like a prohibition to commit acts violating human rights would be at stake. Such an obligation can be of immediate application, not only upon States, but equally to individuals and other private parties.'[209]

Depending on the obligation in question and the State of the law, there are areas where obligations incumbent on NSAs have attained legal status through direct or indirect application, and there are areas where such obligations are developing and may well crystallize in the near future.[210] In this light, there are several emerging tracks of human rights law which could extend the right to a clean, healthy and sustainable environment to provide a basis for the responsibility of NSAs for space pollution.

First, if the offending NSA is a corporation, then it would bear responsibilities[211] under the 2011 UN Guiding Principles on Business and Human Rights (known as the 'Ruggie Principles' after former UN Special Representative for Business and Human Rights, Professor John Ruggie).[212] The 31 directives, are part of a soft law instrument, which collates the binding obligations of States to ensure that businesses adhere to human rights protections, as well as the responsibilities of businesses to regulate their own adherence to human rights standards. Under Principle 12 of this instrument:

> The responsibility of business enterprises to respect human rights refers to internationally recognized human rights understood, at a minimum, as those expressed in the International Bill of Human Rights and the principles concerning fundamental rights set out in the International Labour Organization's Declaration on Fundamental Principles and Rights at Work.

Under the Ruggie principles, business must not cause or contribute to human rights abuses.[213] Also among the responsibilities of businesses is one of due

209 ICSID, *Urbaser v. The Argentine Republic*, Case No. ARB/07/26, Award (8 December 2016), para. 1210.

210 Clapham notes the draft Convention on the Right to Development, Article 7 of which provides that States Parties 'agree that all human and legal persons, peoples, groups and States have the general duty under international law to refrain from participating in the violation of the right to development'.

211 The term 'responsibilities' is not used in a strict legal sense in this specific paragraph; compare Chapter 1, Section 2 containing the definitions.

212 See Carlos López, 'The 'Ruggie process': From legal obligations to corporate social responsibility?', in Surya Deva, David Bilchitz (eds), *Human Rights Obligations of Business: Beyond the Corporate Responsibility to Respect?*, (Cambridge University Press, 2013), pp. 58, 68.

213 UN Guiding Principles on Business and Human Rights (2011) A/HRC/17/31, Principle 13.

diligence, which includes environmental and social impact assessments.[214] These assessments should be anchored to all internationally recognized human rights, which would include the right to a clean, healthy and sustainable environment.[215] Moreover, corporations have a responsibility to adopt policy statements approved at the highest level of their governance structure signaling their acceptance of human rights obligations.[216]

Although the Ruggie Principles were not conceived of as being *per se* binding on businesses,[217] the Office of the High Commissioner for Human Rights has explained that they reflect binding legal obligations of States, and that vis-à-vis businesses 'responsibility to respect human rights may also be incorporated in binding contractual requirements between companies and their corporate and private clients and suppliers' which can be 'enforced through judicial means.'[218] This potential basis for legal responsibility via businesses accepting obligations is developing and in recent years United Nations Special Procedures have written communications to corporations reminding them of the responsibility to adhere to human rights obligations, including in relation to environmental concerns.[219]

Under the Ruggie principles, the due diligence requirements for businesses to conduct environmental and social assessments can be linked to space pollution. If failures to perform those assessments properly and in accordance with standards such as the IADC SDMG leading to crashes or excessive emissions of space pollution, it could potentially violate the right to a clean, healthy and sustainable environment, as well as the right to family and private life. Cases such as *KlimaSeniorinnen* provide a model for litigation to enforce those rights

---

214 UN Guiding Principles on Business and Human Rights (2011) A/HRC/17/31, Principles 17 and 18. Several European States have adopted domestic due diligence laws; Macchi (2025), p. 73.

215 OHCHR, *Guiding Principles on Business and Human Rights: Implementing the United Nations 'Protect, Respect and Remedy' Framework* (2011), Principle 18, p. 20.

216 OHCHR, *Guiding Principles on Business and Human Rights: Implementing the United Nations 'Protect, Respect and Remedy' Framework* (2011).

217 Clapham, p. 596. In June 2014, an open-ended intergovernmental working group (OEIGWG) on transnational corporations and other business enterprises with respect to human rights was established by HRC Resolution 26/9, with a mandate 'to elaborate an international legally binding instrument to regulate, in international human rights law, the activities of transnational corporations and other business enterprises'.

218 OHCHR, *Frequently Asked Questions about the Guiding Principles on Business and Human Rights* (2014), pp. 8–9.

219 See Letter from United Nations Special Procedures to Saudi Arabia and to companies operating on behalf of Saudi Arabia in relation to the NEOM project, April 2023. See also Clapham, p. 597.

when threatened by harm to the environment, as discussed above.[220] A key challenge would be establishing a jurisdictional link to the relevant judicial body and demonstrating actionable harm to human beings sufficient to render the case admissible, particularly where the harm in question occurs in outer space, well beyond the normal territorial jurisdiction of any State. Nonetheless, if space pollution were to interfere with important satellite services used for transport, health, and other critical services, then harm to specific humans or groups of humans may be possible to demonstrate with sufficient specificity. Moreover, in circumstances where the harm originated from a space object (under the jurisdiction of the registering State pursuant to Article VIII of the Outer Space Treaty)[221] in outer space or in an area under the control of a State or by a State agent exercising powers in such a way as to undermine others human rights protections on Earth, that may be sufficient to establish the State's human rights responsibilities therefore, as discussed above.[222]

Second, there is the route of domesticated human rights obligations, which provide a basis for the human rights responsibilities of NSAs. Whereas this typically requires a national law, such as the Alien Tort Claims Act in the United States,[223] those pieces of legislation often incorporate international law by reference, without explicitly codifying its contents into domestic law in a detailed manner. In this sense, it can be seen as an indirect application of international law, rather than purely an application of domestic law.[224] In this way, domestic courts have recognised that NSAs can violate international law, namely the law of nations.[225] However, the link between domesticated human rights and space pollution is attenuated and lacking in established lines of jurisprudence from authoritative courts.

Third, the responsibility of legal persons for human rights violations amounting to international crimes is increasingly recognised, as discussed above.[226] Cases such as those against the Lundin corporation in Sweden and the Lafarge corporation in France stand as lead examples in this respect.[227]

---

220 Chapter 2, Section 1.3.

221 See Chapter 3, Section 1.

222 See Chapter 2, Section 1.3 citing Lubell (2010), p. 212.

223 Alien Tort Statute (codified in 1948 as 28 U.S.C. para. 1350).

224 Clapham (2022), pp. 594–595.

225 See, e.g. *USA: Kadic v Karadzic* 70 F 3d 232, 243–4 (1995); Canada: Nevsun Resources Ltd v Araya (2020) SCC 5, para. 113.

226 Clapham (2022), pp. 598–599. This sits at the intersection of international human rights law and international criminal law.

227 Taylor and Francis Online, (2023) *The proliferation of corporate war-crimes cases*, Strategic Comments, 29:8.

Fourth, armed NSAs, which are clearly bound by obligations under bodies of law such as international humanitarian law,[228] are increasingly recognised as being bound by international human rights law in situations in which they control areas of territory.[229] For example, in 2019 the Group of Eminent International and Regional Experts on Yemen noted that:

> It is now widely recognized, including by various United Nations organs and bodies, as well as scholars, that non-State armed entities have human rights obligations, in particular when they exercise territorial control over certain areas.[230]

Clapham notes that the practice of a wide range of experts and expert bodies involves considering NSA responsibility for human rights violations:

> commissions relating to places such as Gaza, Libya, Sri Lanka, the Central African Republic, and South Sudan, we might conclude that the more recent practice of the UN Secretary-General, the UN Human Rights Council, relevant UN experts, panels, and commissions, as well as the Office of the High Commissioner is to investigate and condemn violations of human rights by de facto regimes and armed groups in more or less the same terms as those used for states.[231]

The increasingly blurred line between governmental roles and those of private entities (or governmental-private partnerships), creates a fertile context in which NSAs may attract human rights obligations.

In sum, there are a variety of circumstances and legal avenues in which NSAs are recognised as being able to violate international law and as having responsibilities and in some cases obligations. The clearest scenarios are where such entities are conducting quasi-governmental functions and/or are in control of an area or territory. To the extent space launches were carried

228 See Clapham (2022), p. 599 ('it is 'undisputed' that the core international humanitarian law (IHL) rules, such as those found in Common Article 3 of the 1949 Geneva Conventions, apply to the non-state party to a non-international armed conflict').

229 See Liesbeth Zegveld, *Accountability of Armed Opposition Groups in International Law* (Cambridge University Press, 2002), pp. 38–55. See also Katharine Fortin, *The Accountability of Armed Groups under Human Rights Law* (Oxford University Press, 2017), pp. 3–5.

230 A/HRC/42/CRP.1 (3 September 2019) paras 82–84 (internal citations omitted); Clapham (2022), pp. 599–600.

231 Clapham (2022), p. 600.

out under the control of, or in the controlled territory of, NSAs in such circumstances, or to the extent that NSAs controlled space objects in orbit, those NSAs could be attributed human rights obligations, including that of ensuring a clean, healthy and sustainable environment.[232] In this manner, the causation of space pollution, particularly significant or excessive amounts of space debris, could amount to a violation of that recognised human rights obligation, and raise the possibility of the various human rights institutions and actors intervening to address such violations at the international level. However, that would require the relevant human right to be applicable to conduct in space. For the right to a healthy environment to be applicable, it would require the environment extending to outer space and a finding that an NSA were bound by human rights obligations. Even if these hurdles could be met, human rights courts are encumbered by several admissibility restrictions, such as showing significant harm to the claimants at the European Court of Human Rights. Moreover, even if a violation were found it would reflect the suffering of natural humans rather than the environmental harm *per se*, demonstrating the anthropocentric orientation of international human rights law.

Turning to the specific instances in which harm to the outer space environment may implicate NSA responsibility under human rights law, the discussion above in Chapter 2 demonstrated that key rights include the right to life, the right to privacy and family life, and potentially the right to benefit from scientific progress.[233] Cutting off human access to outer space, or severely limiting its ability to benefit from space-based activities, would impact on human life in several ways. Telecommunications networks, transport systems, weather prediction and disaster relief are all heavily dependent on satellite-based communications and data relaying. Cutting human society off from those systems would have severe consequences for the well-being of many members of society and potentially indirectly contribute to accidents and avoidable deaths through its impact on critical infrastructural systems. Space activities can also impact the terrestrial environment, though the re-entry of space junk and potentially contaminating substances. Although the re-entry risks are relatively limited at present, they are growing in magnitude with the ever-increasing number of space launches being conducted. The risks to the terrestrial environment can also be linked to harms to humans in some instances, such as through the contamination of water or food sources, along with more intangible harms such as to human privacy.[234]

232 Chapter 2, Section 1.3.
233 Chapter 2, Section 1.3.
234 See Macchi (2025), pp. 51–54.

2.5 *International Environmental Law*

Several key principles of international environmental law were discussed above in examining whether there is a prohibition of space pollution under general international law.[235] These include the no-harm principle, the precautionary principle, the preventive principle, the principle of sustainable development, intergenerational equity, and the polluter pays principle.[236] However, to apply environmental law for present purposes it is necessary to examine how these principles could apply to NSA conduct.

Given the focus on NSA responsibility in the present inquiry, a gateway issue is whether international environmental law can apply directly to NSAs, or whether its principles are entirely State-directed. It is notable in this respect that NSAs have a well-established history of participating in international environmental law processes, which is widely accepted.[237] Sands observes that NSAs 'have played a central role in developing international environmental law'.[238] However, participation is a broad term and what is critical for the current inquiry is the extent to which international environmental law is directly applicable to NSAs so as to bind them to its prohibitions. At its core, this issue remains largely 'unexplored' (or at least under-explored).[239] Consequently, the following section of the analysis seeks to disentangle the provisions of international environmental law that may apply to NSAs.

Based on the precepts of established international law, NSAs have a highly circumscribed role as actors under international environmental law. For example, in the context of climate change, the most significant multilateral regime consists of the United Nations Framework Convention on Climate Change (UNFCCC)[240] and the agreements negotiated pursuant thereto, most notably the Kyoto Protocol.[241] These instruments treat States as singular decision-making entities, which take on obligations and implement international

---

235 See Chapter 2, Section 1 (discussion of prohibition of space pollution).

236 See above Chapter 2.

237 Philippe Sands, *Principles of International Environmental Law* (2nd Edition) (2012), p. 51.

238 Sands (2012), p. 86 citing inter alia Mario Bettati, Pierre-Marie Dupuy and Yves Beigbeder (eds.), *Les ONG et le Droit International* (1986); Maria Garner, 'Transnational Alignment of Non-Governmental Organizations for Global Environmental Action' (1991) 24 *Vanderbilt Journal of Transnational Law*, p. 653; Steve Charnovitz, 'Two Centuries of Participation: NGOs and International Governance' (1997) 18 *Journal of International Law* p.183; Philippe Sands, 'International Law, the Practitioner and Non-State Actors', in Chanaka Wickremasinghe (ed.), *The International Lawyer as Practitioner* (2000).

239 See La Bourdonnaye (2020), pp. 596–597.

240 United Nations Framework Convention on Climate Change, 1992.

241 Kyoto Protocol to the United Nations Framework Convention on Climate Change, 11 December 1997, 2303 UNTS 148 (entered into force on 16 February 2005).

law in dialogue with other States.[242] The obligations under major environmental treaties are primarily directed towards States, such as in the Basel Convention on the Control of Transboundary Movements of Hazardous Wastes and Their Disposal;[243] the Convention on Biological Diversity;[244] the Convention on International Trade in Endangered Species of Wild Fauna and Flora;[245] the International Convention for the Prevention of Pollution from Ships;[246] the Vienna Convention for the Protection of the Ozone Layer;[247] and the Convention for the Prevention of Marine Pollution from Land-Based Sources.[248]

Moreover, the very nature of environmental law regulation at the international level is not easily transferable to NSAs. Most international environmental instruments do not have specific prohibitions but instead set up voluntary targets and oblige States to cooperate and share technical means and knowledge.[249] These types of collaborative goals differ significantly from the largely proscriptive provisions of international humanitarian law and international criminal law. Whereas concrete prohibitions are content-focused and can be transferred to different entities, obligations under this branch of international law are largely consultative and distributive in character. That process-based orientation is difficult to envisage as a means of ensuring accountability for NSAs.

Nonetheless, there are environmental instruments which potentially provide a basis for the direct application of international environmental law to NSAs. First, at the level of principle, some of the most prominent declaratory environmental instruments note that NSAs are required to implement international law for the protection of nature.[250] The World Charter for Nature

242 Osofsky (2012), pp. 180–181.

243 Basel Convention on the Control of Transboundary Movements of Hazardous Wastes and Their Disposal, 22 March 1989, 1673 UNTS 125 (entered into force 5 May 1992).

244 Convention on Biological Diversity, 5 June 1992, 1760 UNTS 79, 143 (entered into force on 29 December 1993).

245 Convention on International Trade in Endangered Species of Wild Fauna and Flora, 3 March 1973, 993 UNTS 243 (entered into force on 1 July 1975).

246 International Convention for the Prevention of Pollution from Ships, 2 November 1973, 1340 UNTS 61 (entered into force on 2 October 1983).

247 Vienna Convention for the Protection of the Ozone Layer, 22 March 1985, 1513 UNTS 323 (entered into force on 22 September 1988).

248 Convention for the Prevention of Marine Pollution from Land-Based Sources, 4 June 1974, 1546 UNTS 119 (entered into force on 6 May 1978).

249 Darryl Robinson, 'Ecocide – Puzzles and Possibilities' (2022) 20(2) *Journal of International Criminal Justice*, p. 315 ('IEL simply does not have concrete and absolute 'prohibitions' on conduct in the same manner as IHL or IHRL').

250 See La Bourdonnaye (2020), pp. 596–597.

provides that 'States and, to the extent they are able, other public authorities, international organizations, individuals, groups and corporations shall: [...] implement the applicable international legal provisions for the conservation of nature and the protection of the environment.'[251] Similarly, the 1992 Rio Declaration and Agenda 21, place international organizations and NSAs in a central role, including in relation to the international legal process.[252] Although those instruments are soft law, they provide a persuasive guide for the interpretation of binding international law and a source from which to determine *opinio juris*.[253]

In relation to binding international law, there are several instruments which directly apply to NSAs, whether by ascribing them with rights or responsibilities. For example, Sands notes the

> 1998 Aarhus Convention which, no doubt because of its subject matter, entitles non-governmental organizations to participate in the Meeting of the Parties and – uniquely – to nominate candidates for election to the Convention's implementation committee.[254]

Similarly, Viikari notes that

> the ITLOS permits non-state entities (including state enterprises, natural or juridical persons, and the International Seabed Authority which is an international organization) to take part in proceedings in limited, well-specified instances concerning disputes relating to activities in the international deep seabed (see Art. 187).[255]

Under the Montreal Protocol on Substances that Deplete the Ozone Layer,[256] NSAs are ascribed standing to file reports on their State's efforts to adhere to the obligations imposed by the Protocol. In this light, Sands observes that 'it is clear that international law has moved away from an approach which treats

---

251 United Nations General Assembly, World Charter for Nature, UN Doc. A/RES/37/7 (28 October 1982), paI 21(c).

252 Sands and Peel, (2018), p. 53 referring to United Nations Agenda 21 (UNCED Report, A/CONF.151/26/Rev.1 (vol. I) (1993)) and Rio Declaration on Environment and Development, (United Nations Conference on Environment and Development, U.N. Doc. 31 ILM 874 (1992)).

253 See Chapter 2.

254 Sands (2012), p. 87.

255 Viikari (2008), pp. 308–309.

256 1987 Montreal Protocol on Substances that Deplete the Ozone Layer 1522 UNTS 3.

international society as comprising a community of states, and increasingly encompasses the persons (both legal and natural) within and among those states.'[257] Against that backdrop, the notion of NSAs being given a measure of legal personality under international environmental law is feasible.

Narrowing in on discrete bases for NSAs to be held liable for space pollution, the provisions of international environmental law bear broad potential but lack in specific applicability. In this respect, a critical question is whether the environmental law principles identified above can apply directly to NSAs, namely the no-harm principle, the precautionary principle, the preventive principle, the principle of sustainable development, intergenerational equity, and the polluter-pays principle.

There is some support for the direct applicability of principles of international environmental law to NSAs. For example, Article 32 of the 1997 UN Watercourses Convention allows 'victims of transboundary pollution or damage to have direct recourse to local remedies in the State where the source of the harm is located.'[258] Article 32 is notable in that it requires a State Party to grant 'persons, natural or juridical' from other States, 'who have suffered or are under a serious threat of suffering significant transboundary harm as a result of activities related to an international watercourse', access to their legal systems to pursue claims for compensation or other legal relief for significant harm caused by such activities.[259] This recognizes that NSAs can suffer from transboundary pollution and have rights protected under international law (albeit a procedural right to access domestic courts, rather than a substantive right under international environmental law *per se*). It could also be read *implicitly* recognizing that the prohibition of transboundary harm applies generally irrespective of whether the wrongdoer is a State or an NSA, thereby implying that the transboundary harm principle can directly bind NSAs.[260]

Regarding quasi-international fora, investor-State disputes heard by International Centre for Settlement of Investment Disputes (ICSID) panels have also increasingly seen environmental obligations raised. These are

257 Sands and Peel (2018), p. 13.

258 Alan Boyle and Catherine Redgwell, *Birnie, Boyle, and Redgwell's International Law and the Environment* (4th edn.) (Oxford University Press, 2021), p. 325.

259 The provision permits States to agree to alternative arrangements to this general approach.

260 Boyle and Redgewell (2021), p. 326. Article 15 of the ILC's 2001 Articles on Prevention of Transboundary Harm, which is based on Article 32 of the Watercourses Convention, contains substantially the same obligation. Similarly, the 1992 Convention on the Transboundary Effects of Industrial Accidents, 'underlines' the principle of non-discrimination and 'affords reciprocal access to justice.'

typically cited as a basis for States restricting the operations of the investor's enterprise. ICSID panels have visited these issues on a number of occasions over the past decade.[261] Regarding the source of these environmental obligations, the usual basis has been domestic environmental law. In *Burlington v Ecuador*, for example, 'the ICSID tribunal awarded US$39.2 million to Ecuador for environmental harm caused by the investor in breach of the Ecuadorian statutory environmental regulation regime'.[262]

Nonetheless, in some cases, investor liability is based on the direct application of international law rules governing the environment.[263] For example, in the *Urbaser v Argentina* dispute, discussed above, the Tribunal recognised that the relevant agreement was not an isolated self-contained set of rules but rather extended the legal framework to applicable domestic law and general international law.[264] It expressly recognised that international law could be directly applicable to private entities such as corporations, particularly if international law imposed an obligation to abstain, in which case it would be 'of immediate application, not only upon States, but equally to individuals and other private parties.'[265]

That approach is consistent with the construction of the European Union Energy Charter Treaty.[266] This instrument, which is a multilateral investment and trade treaty for fifty countries plus the European Union, explicitly recognizes environmental protections. Article 19 enjoins State Parties to 'strive to take precautionary measures to prevent or minimize environmental degradation', and to 'take account of environmental considerations throughout the formulation and implementation of their policies.' Importantly, these

---

261 See Arato (2015), pp. 233–234.

262 Kate Parlett and Sara Ewad, 'Protection of the Environment in Investment Arbitration – A Double-Edged Sword', Kluwer Arbitration Blog (22 August 2017) (https://arbitrationblog.kluwerarbitration.com/2017/08/22/protection-environment-investment-arbitration-double-edged-sword/) citing *Burlington Resources Inc v Republic of Ecuador*, ICSID Case No. ARB/08/5, Decision on Ecuador's Counterclaims, 7 February 2016, para 1075.

263 Parlett and Ewad (2017), citing ICSID, *Urbaser v. The Argentine Republic,* Case No. ARB/07/26, Award (8 December 2016), paras. 1182–1192.

264 See paras. 1190–1192 (referring to the sources of law being the Agreement and alternatively, another treaty in force between the Parties, the host State's domestic law, or the 'general principles of international law.').

265 See para. 1210.

266 Energy Charter Treaty (opened for signature 17 December 1994, entered into force 16 April 1998) (ECT).

environmental obligations may be relied upon by 'international tribunals' for the interpretation of other provisions of the treaty.[267]

However, aside from the theoretical novelty of this approach, there are practical problems with its implementation. Relying on domestic institutions in foreign countries can be restricted by principles such as *forum non conveniens*,[268] and the denial of jurisdiction in actions affecting foreign land, or the refusal to allow transboundary access to administrative proceedings on the basis that national legislation does not have extraterritorial application.[269]

Consequently, there are discrete but established areas in which international environmental law can potentially be directly applicable to NSAs on its own terms and in accordance with the formal precepts of international law.[270] However, the directly applicable provisions and principles of international environmental law do not include a specific prohibition of space pollution which could be imposed on NSAs. Although there is an implicit basis for the no-harm principle to be applied directly to NSAs and although environmental principles of international law have been accepted in specific instances as potentially binding on NSAs, these remain theoretical bases at best, lacking an established body of international jurisprudence behind them. As a result, there is a nascent possibility of directly applying international environmental law to prohibit NSA space pollution, but this is far from an established legal paradigm.

2.6 *Private International Law*

The preceding discussion of international environmental law referred to arbitral-type awards. In this respect, a legal regime that could potentially lend itself to remedying space pollution by corporations is private international law.[271] Private international law consists of the 'rules governing cross-border

267 Thomas Waelde and Abba Kolo, 'Environmental Regulation, Investment Protection and 'Regulatory Taking' in International Law' (2001) 50(4) *The International and Comparative Law Quarterly*, p. 817.

268 See Macchi (2025), p. 71. However, see Boyle and Redgwell (2021), pp. 326–327 ('[a] good example is the litigation resulting from the Sandoz chemical spillage in the Rhine, which was successfully handled without any resort to interstate claims or international proceedings').

269 Boyle and Redgwell (2021), pp. 326–330.

270 Sands (2012), p. 93 ('Many international organizations already rely heavily on the efforts and activities of nonstate actors, either informally or formally.'); Viikari (2008), p. 27 ('Despite the traditional focus on states as stakeholders at the international level, domestic politics and non-state actors increasingly affect international developments.').

271 There are instruments which straddle private and public international law, such as the Cape Town Convention which regulates ownership interests in aircraft assets (Convention on International Interests in Mobile Equipment and Protocol on Matters Specific to

legal disputes between private citizens or other private entities'. It encompasses jurisdictional and forum questions, the applicable body of law (whether from one State or a neutral source such as the UNIDROIT principles in international commercial transactions),[272] and the enforcement of judgments made in a foreign court. Private international law addresses the prefatory jurisdictional and *forum conveniens* questions but it often relies on domestic private law and other sources of law, including international law, for its substance.

Private international law is typically applied in the context of arbitration. Arbitration relies on the polluting party being willing to participate in the proceedings (or bound by a legal agreement). Given this context, private international law will be relevant for the first category of NSAs presenting a risk of space pollution that were highlighted above, namely corporations, rather than the second category of armed NSAs using violence to achieve political or similar goals, as the latter are unlikely to accept the strictures of an arbitral awards.[273]

With respect to the prospects of arbitration being used in the context of outer space, there is a procedure referred to in the Liability Convention, which sets out that States may establish a Claims Commission[274] for damage suffered from space objects and collisions, including to 'natural or juridical persons [which] suffer damage'.[275] However, the Liability Convention is consistently State-oriented, noting that only States can claim damages from the launching State for that damage.[276]

Aircraft Equipment, both concluded in 2001); Brian Havel and Gabriel Sanchez, *The Principles and Practice of International Aviation Law* (Cambridge University Press, 2014), pp. 251–252. Although aviation law does not apply to outer space by definition, it can provide useful guidance for the application of international law to NSAs, as discussed above; Chapter 6, Section 2.

272 UNIDROIT Principles of International Commercial Law, pmbl. (International Institute for the Unification of Private Law, 1994).

273 See Chapter 4, Section 1.

274 Liability Convention, Article XIV.

275 Liability Convention, Article VIII.

276 Liability Convention, Article VIII, IX, X. There is also a significant exclusion in Article VII of the Liability Convention, which provides that the Convention – including Articles II and III on liability – does not apply when the damage is caused by a space object of a launching State to nationals of that same launching State. This is not a minute risk; often NSAs which own satellites will have the nationality of the State which is active in launching activities, and so accidents may well occur involving only one nationality. That would essentially deprive the damaged nationals of a right to compensation; Radi (2023), p. 10. Although this relates to damage to the question of nationals' compensation rather than the environment per se, it further demonstrates the growing shortcomings of the State-centric model which has been prevalent in international space law. The risk of harm to nationals will only grow as NSAs become increasingly active in space.

On the issue of arbitration for harms caused in space, the Permanent Court of Arbitration adopted a set of Optional Rules for Arbitration of Disputes Relating to Outer Space Activities in 2011.[277] The modification of the 2010 United Nations Commission on International Trade Law Arbitration (UNCITRAL) Rules was done 'to better serve and reflect the particular characteristics of disputes having an outer space component involving the use of outer space by States, international organizations and private entities'.[278] Consequently, there is an established forum in which claims for damages arising from space pollution could potentially be heard, albeit this is of an optional nature. Nonetheless, this remains procedural in nature, and does not explicitly provide support for holding NSAs responsible for space pollution.

In terms of specific substance of the outcomes of arbitrations concerning outer space conduct will depend on the substantive law applied. In this respect, the contract between the parties to the dispute will be essential. Article 35(3) of the Optional Rules for Arbitration of Disputes Relating to Outer Space Activities provides that '[i]n all cases, the arbitral tribunal shall decide in accordance with the terms of the contract, if any, and shall take into account any usage of trade applicable to the transaction.' That provision brings the assessment back to the substantive provisions, such as those of international environmental law, which may have either been incorporated in contracts between the parties or imposed on them by customary international law, as discussed above.[279]

When it comes to protecting ecocentric interests, whilst commercial arbitration can be a suitable dispute settlement method,[280] and can assist space-related industries to resolve commercial disputes,[281] arbitration engenders the risk of accountability being avoided in the interests of reaching a commercially advantageous arrangement. Companies are unlikely to have an interest in ensuring environmental protection on behalf of the broader public. Moreover, even if States or other parties willing to take proceedings to protect the environment are involved in arbitration,[282] dispute resolution is not an

277 These rules note in their introduction that they 'reflect the particular characteristics of disputes having an outer space component involving the use of outer space by States, international organizations and private entities'. See also Fausto Pocar, 'An Introduction to the PCA's Optional Rules for Arbitration of Disputes Relating to Outer Space Activities' (2012) 38 *Journal of Space Law* p. 171 cited in Zhao (2018), pp. 6–7.

278 Pocar (2012) as cited in Zhao (2018), pp. 6–7.

279 Chapter 4, Section 2.

280 Mykola Selivon, 'Cooperation Between Judiciary and International Commercial Arbitration' (2011) *Law of Ukraine: Legal Journal*, p. 139.

281 See Goh (2007), pp. 166–181.

282 See Friedberg (2013), p. 223.

ideal vehicle to prevent environmental harm, as it is inherently *ex post facto* rather than *ex ante* in nature.[283]

In connection with these characteristics, arbitration relies on a harm or legal wrong being suffered by a particular State, person, or other legal entity. Harm to the environment *per se*, such as that caused by space debris being intentionally left in orbit to save costs, will not necessarily manifest and in any direct damage to another space vessel, person or entity. Examples from practice in cases involving NSAs indicate that the damages awarded will focus on contractual liabilities and monetary damages suffered rather than environmental harm itself. For instance, an arbitral award against Sea Launch in 2007, following its launch-pad explosion, resulted in an award of $53.2 million to be repaid to HNS.[284] However, there was no aspect of the award, or other regulatory sanction or fine, explicitly directed to the harm to the environment which was caused by the explosion. In the absence of direct damage to property or life or limb, it is unclear what award an arbitral panel could make directly referring to environmental harm.

Nonetheless, there is the potential for ancillary recognition of harm to the space environment. Arbitration between States has made reference to principles of international environmental law, including the duty of prevention.[285]

While novel in relation to NSA accountability for space pollution, substantively, there are several private law instruments, methods, and principles, aimed at combating pollution that could be relevant by analogy. The first one that could be used in this regard is a contract clause demanding disclosure of environmental and sustainability information of the party performing a certain activity.[286] Such disclosure improves transparency and enables other actors (such as civil society) to oversee certain potentially harmful activities

283 Havel and Sanchez (2014), pp. 255–256.. Contra: Goh (2007), p. 88.

284 See Chapter 4, Section 1.

285 *Award in the Arbitration regarding the Iron Rhine ('Ijzeren Rijn') Railway between the Kingdom of Belgium and the Kingdom of the Netherlands*, decision of 24 May 2005 24 May 2005 VOLUME XXVII pp.35–125.

286 Abdulaziz Mohammed Alsahlawi, Kaouther Chebbi, Mohammed Abdullah Ammer, 'The Impact of Environmental Sustainability Disclosure on Stock Return of Saudi Listed Firms: The Moderating Role of Financial Constraints' (2021) 9(4) *International Journal of Financial Studies*, pp. 1, 2; Susan A. Maslow, 'Non-Financial Reporting and the Model Contract Clauses, Version 2.0' *Business Law Today* (26 May 2021) (available at https://businesslawtoday.org/2021/05/non-financial-reporting-and-the-model-contract-clauses-version-2-0/). See examples of such clauses at (11 March 2022) (available at https://www.lawinsider.com/clause/environmental-disclosure).

of NSAs.[287] In the context of space activities, this would mean that the Launch Services Agreement would include a clause demanding that the transporter provides conclusive environmental and sustainability information. Failure to provide such information would be a breach of contract obligation and could represent grounds for termination of the contract. Other private law solutions could include clauses on contamination and environmental insurance, for example.[288] In this manner, the UNCOPUOS SDMG (or similar guidelines) could be introduced into contract clauses. However, in all cases, the plaintiff would need to prove the causation of the pollution of the space environment caused actual damage to his health, person or property. On this basis, private international law demonstrates the nascent potential to provide redress for NSA space pollution, but remains untested in legal proceedings.

2.7 *Conclusion on Alternative International Law Domains*

Having reviewed those alternative legal domains to international space law, there are several regimes of international law which could potentially adjudicate a claim of harm caused by NSAs in terms of space pollution. International humanitarian law has several relevant provisions but no courts for the direct enforcement thereof. International environmental law has broader provisions, which are typically not framed as prohibitions, and which also lack a specific international court for enforcement. International criminal law presents an alternative option which has been applied to NSAs and has established courts to ensure enforcement. However, it is purely a potentiality at this time, in light of its highly restrictive substantive criminal parameters and jurisdictional limits governing its application. Should the crime of ecocide be enshrined in law, that will significantly increase the potential application of international criminal law to NSAs but that remains a possibility rather than a probability. Some private law solutions may have potential merit such as through environmentally protective contractual clauses, but will lack the teeth of enforcement via binding criminal law, as they are essentially optional and subject to agreement by the parties.

In this light, and given the continuing increase of total NSA activity in space and the rising risks of NSA space pollution, it is apposite to look at means to

287 See, e.g., the EU legislation on environment and sustainability reporting at: https://ec.europa.eu/info/business-economy-euro/company-reporting-and-auditing/company-reporting/corporate-sustainability-reporting_en (11 March 2022).

288 Jeff Slivka, 'Managing Environmental Liabilities through Contracts' *IRMI* (1 January 2003) (available at https://www.irmi.com/articles/expert-commentary/managing-environmental-liabilities-through-contracts).

adjust the approach under space law regarding pollution caused by NSAs, as is done in Chapter 6. However, before moving to that prospective inquiry, the review first examines where these relatively limited substantive legal bases could be operationalized under the current framework of international law and how States have enacted their space law obligations under domestic law.

3 Operationalizing NSA Accountability for Space Pollution: Fora in Which to Proceed against NSAs under International Law

Space law has negligible formal provisions for the enforcement of its substantive provisions.[289] Sanctions for violating the terms of the Outer Space Treaty are not set down, and the Liability Convention largely focuses on compensatory relief without any punitive facet, let alone any penalties. In this vacuum, the substantive protections in other legal regimes under international law must be examined, as has been set out above. However, for the provisions of those other regimes to be enforceable there must be venues in which the provisions can be asserted and used as a basis to impose credible sanctions.

3.1 *International Courts and Institutions*

To the extent that international criminal law, international humanitarian law, international environmental law, and potentially international human rights law are applicable to the conduct of NSAs in outer space, along with international space law is adapted to provide for NSA responsibility,[290] the potential fora in which to seek remedies would include international courts.

An institution that does have jurisdiction over acts by the leaders of NSAs is the International Criminal Court, as discussed above.[291] With its established jurisdiction over the conduct of all nationals of State Parties as well as acts in their territory from 2002 onwards, and its prospective jurisdiction over any acts pursuant to a UN Security Council referral, the ICC has a large potential ambit of operation. However, in relation to conduct in outer space, several difficulties present themselves when considering the ICC's ability to provide judicial relief. First, the Court does not have experts on the outer space environment on staff. Second, it is unclear to what extent outer space law instruments would apply.

289 Chapters 2, Section 1.1 and Chapter 3, Section 1.

290 See Chapter 6.

291 See Chapter 4, Section 2.2, referencing the ICC's bases concerning the ICC cases of Katanga and Lubanga.

Article 21 of the Rome Statute permits reference to 'applicable' treaties,[292] as well as principles and rules of international law, but only when 'appropriate' and only when there is a lacuna in the Statute and Rules.[293] It also refers to principles deriving from national law, but again only when there is a lacuna in the Statute and Rules. Without detailed prescriptive enforcement provisions in space law to provide guidance, the judiciary could easily stray into fragmenting the approach of international criminal law and outer space law, which would undermine the message sent to States and entities operating in space. Third, the ICC lacks jurisdiction over corporate entities.[294] Given that these are likely to be the main drivers of private space exploration and exploitation, they are also the most likely NSAs to cause space pollution. Simply prosecuting individuals in their personal capacity who are members of NSAs will provide some deterrence but not necessarily compensate for the full scope of the harmful acts, as dispersed responsibility in corporate structures may mean that no one natural person has the requisite *mens rea* to qualify for criminal prosecution even though the composite acts of the corporation amount the criminal damage.

Beyond the International Criminal Court, there are few if any institutional options for judicial relief at the international level. The International Court of Justice has addressed environmental harm cases, such as the *Pulp Mills* case, in which it recognized environmental impact assessment as a practice that has become an obligation of general international law.[295] The International Court of Justice arguably has a broad jurisdiction over the destruction of nature, including in the outer space environment.[296] Moreover, it has commented on

---

292 Rome Statute, Article 21.

293 See ICC, *Prosecutor v. Thomas Lubanga Dyilo*, Case No. ICC-01/04-01/06-772, Judgment on the Appeal of Mr. Lubanga Dylo against the Decision on the Defence Challenge to the Jurisdiction of the Court pursuant to article 19(2)(a) of the Statute, Appeals Chamber (13 December 2006), para. 34 (holding that, if 'a matter is exhaustively dealt with by [the Statute] or [...] the Rules of Procedure and Evidence, [...] no room is left for recourse to the second or third source of law [in article 21(1) of the Statute] to determine the presence or absence of a rule governing a given subject'); ICC, Case No. ICC-01/18-143, Decision on the 'Prosecution request pursuant to article 19(3) for a ruling on the Court's territorial jurisdiction in Palestine, Pre-Trial Chamber I (5 February 2021), para. 111.

294 Rome Statute, Article 25; Andrew Clapham, 'The Complexity of International Criminal Law: Looking Beyond Individual Responsibility to the Responsibility of Organizations, Corporations and States' (2004) in Ramesh Thakur and Peter Malcontent (eds.) *From Sovereign Impunity to International Accountability: The Search for Justice in a World of States*, (United Nations University Press, 2004), pp. 233, 245–246.

295 Chapter 2, Section 1.2.

296 See the ENMOD Convention, discussed above, the text of which refers to consultation and cooperation being handled 'within the framework of the United Nations and in

international humanitarian law and environmental law principles in its advisory opinion on the threat or use of nuclear weapons.[297] However, it is a jurisdiction limited to State disputes (with the consent of the States) and advisory opinions concerning the responsibility of States under international law, and accordingly will not provide a forum for directly adjudicating the responsibility of NSAs for their conduct in space.

In terms of other fora, the International Tribunal for the Law of the Sea is operational but is maritime bound and so has no direct applicability to the outer space environment.[298] The rulings of the WTO's dispute settlement bodies do sometimes touch on environmental protection, but only in an incidental manner. The Dispute Settlement Body of the World Trade Organization addresses trade disputes rather than accountability for environmental harm *per se*.[299] Arbitral panels do not have the kind of enforcement powers and mandatory jurisdiction that are required to promote effective compliance for common threats such as that to the environment, as they are based on consent as discussed above.[300]

Under international human rights law, there are quasi-judicial bodies such as the Human Rights Committee established under the International Covenant on Civil and Political Rights (ICCPR). Notwithstanding the reference to a State Party's obligations arising with respect to individuals 'within its territory and subject to its jurisdiction' in Article 2(1) of the ICCPR, these terms have been interpreted broadly and thereby could potentially stretch on conduct in outer space.[301] There are also regional human rights bodies, such as the European

---

accordance with its Charter' and that the 'international procedures may include the services of appropriate international organizations.'

297 ICJ, *Legality of the Threat or Use of Nuclear Weapons*, Advisory Opinion of 8 July 1996 (I.C.J Reports 1996, p. 226), para. 29.

298 But see Goh (2007), pp. 236–237 ('it is submitted that the UNCLOS provides a legally workable and politically acceptable framework for the peaceful settlement of disputes in an area of extreme international, economic and scientific interest.').

299 See generally, Sean D. Murphy, 'Does the World Need a New International Environmental Court?' (2000) 32(3) *George Washington Journal of International Law and Economics*, p. 333.

300 Chapter 4, Section 2.6.

301 Danielle Ireland-Piper, 'Space Laws: Criminal Jurisdiction in Outer Space' *ILA Reporter* (17 October 2019) (available at https://ilareporter.org.au/2019/10/space-laws-criminal-jurisdiction-in-outer-space-danielle-ireland-piper/) ('If the legal authority of the State can stretch extraterritoriality into space, it follows that human rights obligations do as well. The United Nations Human Rights Committee, which hears complaints of violations of the International Covenant on Civil and Political Rights, might have jurisdiction to hear complaints relating to space.').

Court of Human Rights and the Inter-American Court of Human Rights, which have adjudicated terrestrial claims of human rights violations perpetrated via environmental harm.[302] However, the applicability of human rights frameworks to NSAs remains largely untested before these fora, and may potentially be rejected as inadmissible. Moreover, the linking of harm to the space environment and human rights is already an indirect one which is relatively novel. Together, these factors demonstrate the highly speculative basis of relying on human rights for enforcement of a prohibition of space pollution by NSAs.

As an alternate to the use of existing international courts, the proposal has been made to establish a purpose-built international court focused on serious environmental harm – an 'International Court for the Environment' (ICE).[303] As formulated, the ICE would be able to address criminal matters as well as disputes and compensatory matters. In this way, it would cover the hard enforcement of serious crimes, alongside the adjudication of competing interests as is typically done in arbitral panels and international trade and investment mechanisms. The institution would have jurisdiction over situations of armed conflict and peacetime. The latter is important as considerable environmental harm occurs outside of armed conflict.[304] Importantly for present purposes, the ICE could have jurisdiction over corporate entities.

Penalties at the proposed ICE would range from custodial sentences to fines, as well as orders to engage in remedial action, injunctions to cease the harmful conduct and declarations of non-compliance with international law. Reparations and compensation could encompass the harm to the environment as well as economic loss and symbolic reparative measures such as scientific centres and research programs to avoid future repetition of such harms. Procedures before the ICE could integrate the precautionary principle from international environmental law by placing the burden on the party which failed to take measures to protect the environment despite scientific uncertainty as to the potential consequences of their acts. Additionally, the ICE adjudicators could comprise experts on environmental and space degradation, alongside legally trained judges.[305] To the extent that any such institution

---

302 See, e.g. ECtHR, *Öneryıldız v. Turkey* (48939/99) ECHR Grand Chamber [30 November 2004]; IACtHR, *State Obligations in Relation to the Environment in the Context of the Protection and Guarantee of the Rights to Life and to Personal Integrity*, Case No. OC-23/17, Advisory Opinion (15 November 2017); IACtHR, *Case of the Indigenous Communities of the Lhaka Honhat (Our Land) Association v. Argentina*, Inter-American Court of Human Rights, Judgment of 6 February 2020 (Merits, Reparations and Costs), para. 208.

303 Gillett (2022), pp. 337–346.

304 Gillett (2022), p. 341.

305 Gillett (2022), pp. 337–346.

is created and seeks to address the conduct of NSAs, it will be important to have jurisdiction over corporations and enforcement options, such as financial penalties and injunctive relief, capable of encompassing the extensive harm that may eventuate to the outer space environment from relatively contained initial collisions and incidents. Additionally, the support of the leading space-faring nations will be essential to ensuring the institution's relevance and reach regarding conduct in outer space.

It must be borne in mind that previous efforts to create international environmental courts have not been fruitful. Most notably, the International Court of Justice's environmental chamber was abandoned in 2006, as no case had been submitted to it in the entire thirteen years of its existence.[306] Consequently, the idea of an international court for the environment being established and having effective jurisdiction to address cases of NSA harm to the environment remains a putative prospect at best.

3.2 *Domestic Courts Acting under Universal Jurisdiction*

An additional manner in which NSAs may potentially be held accountable under international law is through actions before national courts, including via universal jurisdiction. Domestic courts import several advantages over international bodies. These include that domestic courts de-escalate disputes 'to their ordinary neighbourhood level', they avoid turning disputes into interstate controversies, they allow 'direct recourse against the enterprise causing the damage' in accordance with the 'polluter pays' principle of allocating environmental costs, and they 'empower[] individuals by enabling the private plaintiff to act without the intervention of a government, and to that extent facilitate[] further development of a rights-based approach to environmental issues.'[307] It is also significant that domestic courts will typically be able to enforce their jurisdiction over NSAs.

As discussed above,[308] the most applicable jurisdictions will be those of the domestic courts of the national State (whether the national State of the NSA or the territorial State where the space activity was authorized), the launching State or the State of registry, whichever holds jurisdiction.[309] Some experts

---

306 Basile Chartier, 'Chamber for Environmental Matters: International Court of Justice (ICJ)', *Max Planck Encyclopedias of International Law* (2018) (available at https://opil.ouplaw.com/display/10.1093/law-mpeipro/e3339.013.3339/law-mpeipro-e3339).

307 Boyle and Redgewell (2021), p.323.

308 Chapter 3, Section 1.

309 There have been a few examples of domestic courts resolving space disputes, but these have mainly addressed standard civil matters, for more See Chapter 5.

have advocated for direct accountability before the courts of the launching State.[310] These approaches would approximate the approach taken in international aviation law, which does not have any independent or supranational judicial body established to adjudicate liability actions against NSAs (typically air carriers).[311] However, in light of the potential difficulties that may arise due to forum shopping and other limits of accountability in some national States,[312] a further option would therefore be relying on universal jurisdiction or extra-territorial jurisdiction to invoke the domestic jurisdiction of a wider range of states as possible fora.

For States to proceed to prosecute NSAs for space pollution on the basis of customary international law, presuming there is no other jurisdictional link, one basis would be to rely on the doctrine of universal jurisdiction. Universal jurisdiction 'refers to jurisdiction established over a crime without reference to the place of perpetration, the nationality of the suspect or the victim or any other recognized linking point between the crime and the prosecuting State.'[313] For crimes falling under universal jurisdiction, any State is authorized 'to search for and bring to trial – or, alternatively, extradite to a requesting state – any person suspected or accused of [having committed that crime] (whatever his or her nationality and the territory where the grave breach has allegedly been perpetrated) who happens to be on its territory.'[314]

If States are Parties to treaties with positive obligations to repress grave offences, such as the Geneva Conventions of 1949 and the Additional Protocols thereto of 1977, then they are not only authorized, but required to carry out such activities and can use universal jurisdiction (subject to their own

310 Kerrest (2017), pp. 5–13.

311 Havel and Gabriel Sanchez (2014), p. 258. The International Civil Aviation Organisation (ICAO) often acts as a quasi-judicial (dispute resolution) body for civil aviation matters, but is not as such an official judicial body. For more see Matthew H. Ormsbee, 'Fair Enough?: Procedural Fairness When the ICAO Council Excercises Its Judicial Function' (2023) 48 Air and Space Law 4/5, pp. 457–476; see also generally Michael Milde, *International Air law and ICAO* (Essential Air and Space Law Series) (2008) (The Hague: Eleven International Publishing).

312 Chapter 3, Section 2.

313 Robert Cryer et al., An Introduction to International Criminal Law and Procedure (2nd ed.) (Cambridge University Press, 2010), pp. 50–51. See also 'universal jurisdiction is criminal jurisdiction based solely on the nature of the crime, without regard to where the crime was committed, the nationality of the alleged or convicted perpetrator, the nationality of the victim, or any other connection to the state exercising such jurisdiction' (Princeton Principles on Universal Jurisdiction).

314 Antonio Cassese and Paola Gaeta, *International Criminal Law* (2nd ed.) (Oxford University Press, 2008), p. 89.

constitutional limits).[315] Similarly, if the duties to repress such crimes have reached the status of customary international law, then non-State Parties are also obliged to undertake these measures. However, in many States there is a requirement to enact domestic legislation to enforce prohibitions against any crimes, even if they are subject to universal jurisdiction.[316]

The fundamental question which serves as a gateway to applying universal jurisdiction is whether the offence in question is recognised as attracting universal jurisdiction. This means not only that the conduct is regulated in a sufficient number of States, but that it is considered to constitute such a grave violation of communal standards, that universal jurisdiction is merited.[317] Crimes that are widely accepted as attracting universal jurisdiction are genocide, torture, war crimes, and crimes against humanity.[318] These categories of crimes have all been recognised as reflecting customary international law, and all (apart from crimes against humanity) are subject to extensively subscribed treaties. Conversely, space pollution has not been criminalized in a near-universal manner.[319]

Another offence seen as subject to universal jurisdiction is piracy.[320] It does not fall under the same category as the aforementioned crimes and some argue it is subject only to extra-territorial jurisdiction and not universal jurisdiction as set out in the following section, but it is nevertheless prosecuted universally, as any and every state may prosecute it.[321] Two most important reasons for such universal criminalization of piracy are, firstly, its international reach and, secondly, the negative effects on international trade, commercial activities and consequently the general well-being of nations.[322] In the first respect, an analogy could be drawn with space pollution, as it is also a problem on

---

315 First Geneva Convention, Article 49; Second Geneva Convention, Article 50; Third Geneva Convention, Article 129; Fourth Geneva Convention, Article 146; Additional Protocol I, Article 85(1).

316 Casesse and Gaeta (2008), pp. 12, 436.

317 See Cryer (2010), p. 51 ('The purpose of universal jurisdiction … is linked to the idea that international crimes affect the international legal order as a whole.).

318 Cryer (2010), p. 51.

319 See Chapters 2, Section 1 and Section 5.

320 Malcolm Shaw, *International Law* (6th edition) (Cambridge University Press, 2008), p. 458.

321 Shaw (2008), p. 458.

322 John Anderson, 'Piracy and World History: An Economic Perspective on Maritime Predation' (1995) 6(2) *Journal of World History*, pp. 179, 182; La'Nita M. Johnson, 'The Consequences of Somali Piracy on International Trade' (2014) 8 *Global Tides* pp. 2, 5; Giacomo Morabito, Bruno S. Sergi, 'How Did Maritime Piracy Affect Trade in Southeast Asia?' (2018) 18 *Journal of East Asian Studies*, p. 257.

international rather than on a national level (space pollution does not cause damage locally, but in most cases causes damage to the environment of the whole Earth – for example: emissions harm atmosphere and space debris is present in geostationary orbit around the Earth). In the second respect, space pollution in the form of space debris negatively affects (and will continue to do so on a much greater scale in the future) space exploration, as it is becoming more and more difficult and risky to launch a space object into outer space without hitting debris.[323] Even the objects already present in outer space are endangered by space debris, for example, in 2013 pieces of debris caused the loss of Ecuadorian Pegasus satellite,[324] and in 2021 pieces of debris reportedly hit an International Space Station module and endangered the lives of astronauts on board.[325] Therefore, at least space pollution in the form of significant or excessive amounts of space debris could be considered as an offence with similar rationales to piracy for being subject to universal jurisdiction. However, this scenario is not likely to occur in the near future. As set out above, even the existence of a substantive prohibition against causing reckless space pollution is contested, let alone one that would reach the threshold of invoking universal jurisdiction.[326]

Potentially, a case could be made for universal jurisdiction due to the very specific and special nature of space activity and the outer space environment. The Outer Space Treaty dictates that the exploration and use of outer space, including the Moon and other celestial bodies, are the 'province of all mankind'.[327] The Moon Agreement, in Article 11(1), goes even further, calling it the 'common heritage of mankind'. However, other provisions of these conventions do not clearly support a principle of universal jurisdiction. Articles VI and VIII of the Outer Space Treaty imply that only the specifically designated State of nationality has jurisdiction. Article VII binds it to several possible States, which must still be somehow linked to the space object causing damage

323 Gershon Hasin, 'Confronting Space Debris Through the Regime Evolution Approach' (2021) 97 *International Law Studies*, p. 1080.

324 Nader and Kelso (2014).

325 Mark Rigby, Brad Carter, 'A chunk of Chinese satellite almost hit the International Space Station. They dodged it – but the space junk problem is getting worse' *The Conversation* (12 November 2021) (available at https://theconversation.com/a-chunk-of-chinese-satellite-almost-hit-the-international-space-station-they-dodged-it-but-the-space-junk-problem-is-getting-worse-171735); Rebecca Heilweil, 'The space debris problem is getting dangerous' *Vox* (16 November 2021) (available at https://www.vox.com/recode/2021/11/16/22785425/international-space-station-russia-missle-test-debris).

326 See Chapter 2, Section 1.

327 Outer Space Treaty, Article I.

(launching States). Article XIII sets out collective responsibility for collective acts, but that still does not equate to universal jurisdiction. Given this lack of precision, the argument for any State being able to enforce a prohibition of space pollution is speculative.

Ultimately, domestic cases under the principle of universal jurisdiction have occurred in other areas[328] but are unlikely to occur for space pollution. This is partly due to the lack of an established crime of causing space pollution at the international level and partly because of the limited number of cases conducted under universal jurisdiction in general. However, if the cause of the space pollution also involved acts amounting to crimes against humanity, war crimes or genocide, universal jurisdiction could form the basis for domestic proceedings and incidentally address the space pollution.

3.3 *Domestic Courts Acting under Extra-Territorial Jurisdiction*

Separate from universal jurisdiction, an alternative way of proceeding against NSAs would be domestic States exercising extra-territorial jurisdiction. This would be based on the concept of common areas, akin to the regulation of piracy.[329] Under the International Convention on the Law of the Sea, any State can seize a ship or aircraft on the high seas or any other location outside of the jurisdiction of any State (as well as inside the seizing State's own jurisdiction) and arrest persons on board and confiscate their property if they are perpetrating piracy.[330] In theory, this conceptual approach could see States assert their enforcement powers over NSAs which caused disproportionate and reckless or intentional space pollution while acting outside of the territorial jurisdiction of any other State (albeit without a prescribed basis equal to the Convention on the Law of the Sea).

However, multiple issues arise. First, there is the practical question of when, if ever, an NSA could launch or operate a space object from outside of any State's territory. While NSAs may face difficulties launching space objects from the high seas or other areas outside of the control of any State, it is conceivable that NSAs could operate space objects from such areas (for example from super platforms), as demonstrated by the establishment of Sea Launch to conduct water-based launches outside of any particular territorial jurisdiction.[331] These NSAs may try and avoid association to a State by evading authorization

328 Michael P. Scharf, Milena Sterio, Paul R. Williams, *The Syrian Conflicts Impact on International Law* (Cambridge University Press, 2020).

329 See Casesse (2008), p. 12.

330 See UNCLOS, Article 105.

331 See Chapter 3, Section 2.

and otherwise shunning legal links to States. In operating space objects, NSAs could negligently or intentionally cause space debris, whether by colliding with other space objects or by causing the space object itself to disintegrate. Accordingly, the possibility of harmful space debris being caused from areas outside of any State's control is not completely hypothetical.

Second, the possibility of NSAs launching or operating space objects from outside of any State's jurisdiction clashes with the requirement in Article VI of the Outer Space Treaty that all space activities should be under the authorization and continuing supervision of States. In this respect, even if the activities were undertaken outside of any State's territory, the participants would typically have the nationality of one or more States, which could potentially qualify as the 'appropriate' State under Article VI of the Outer Space Treaty.

Third, whereas piracy involves acts that are widely considered criminal, such as theft, space pollution does not have the same level of criminalization. In a scenario where an NSA coming from one State were to participate in a joint launch with another State or an NSA coming from another State, multiple States would be involved. That case would see domestic courts of one State decide upon liability for damages caused by a jointly launched space object, meaning that the prosecuting State would *de facto* sit as a judge over the actions of another State. Such an act would potentially conflict with the International Court of Justice State Immunities case, where the Court prohibited such endeavours as they violate immunity of a State.[332] By allowing the direct application of international law to the NSA, without the intermediary of a State, this would open up an avenue to circumvent the application of State immunities.

A further possibility for domestic adjudication are courts of the State of registry, as that is the State with quasi-territorial jurisdiction in space objects.[333] A few cases have occurred where the courts of the State of registry were involved, such as the case of the American astronaut aboard the ISS[334] or as attempted by the Russian space agency Roskosmos to bring a charge in national courts

332 *Monetary Gold Removed from Rome in 1943* (It. v. Fr., UK and U.S.), Judgment, 1954 ICJ Rep. 19 (15 June 1954).

333 Article VIII, Outer Space Treaty and Article II, Registration Convention, dictate that the State that registers a space object in its national registry retains jurisdiction over it and any personnel thereof, for more See Chapter 3, Section 1.

334 Mike Baker, 'NASA Astronaut Anne McClain Accused by Spouse of Crime in Space' *The New York Times* (23 August 2019) (available at https://www.nytimes.com/2019/08/23/us/astronaut-space-investigation.html); Mike Baker, 'Space Crime Allegation Leads to Charges Against Astronaut's Ex-Wife' *The New York Times* (6 April 2020) (available at https://www.nytimes.com/2020/04/06/us/space-crime-allegation-indictment.html).

against an American astronaut (after a hole had been discovered in the side of the Soyuz spacecraft).[335] An additional option is that of the national State as the State responsible for all national space activities, as discussed above.[336] NSAs could be judged before courts in a national State for space pollution if such provision were available in the national system. However, some NSAs may potentially operate without a nationality (or at least without an easily discernible one).[337]

The assertion of extra-territorial jurisdiction would depend on the existence of domestic legislation covering the prohibition of space pollution, for example through the negligent causation of space debris. As noted in Chapter 5's extensive survey below, there are several States which have legislation regulating space activities including space debris and environmental protection, and some of those States impose criminal sanctions on such activity.[338] However, domestic laws in States implementing their international obligations are far from uniform or comprehensive as set out in the following section of this chapter. Consequently, using the doctrine of extra-terrestrial jurisdiction would result in sporadic coverage at best.

In sum, the fora for operationalizing the prohibition of space pollution are relatively limited and each type of institution faces considerable restraints. Both at the international and domestic levels, the options are multiple but all have significant jurisdiction or operational features which make it unlikely that they would provide effective enforcement options in their current form. The proposed International Court for the Environment remains putative, but would be the preferable venue to adjudicate space pollution if established.

This lack of effective options for hearing cases and enforcing protections of the space environment constitutes a major impediment to the efficacy of combating space pollution by NSAs. It is incongruous with the prohibition of

335 Though no charges seem to have been brought by Russia, the Russian space agency Roscosmos alleged an American astronaut had caused the damage and was demanding charges be brought against the astronaut, see: Eric Berger, 'Russia threatens criminal charges against a NASA astronaut' *arstechnica* (30 November 2021) (available at https://arstechnica.com/science/2021/11/russia-threatens-criminal-charges-against-a-nasa-astronaut/).

336 As discussed in Section 3, Outer Space Treaty, Article VI dictates that the appropriate State shall authorize and continuously supervise the activities of NSAs. As the Outer Space Treaty does not elaborate on the concept of appropriate State, several options are possible, among them the national State as Outer Space Treaty, Article VI decrees that the State shall be internationally responsible for all national activities in outer space.

337 Freeland and Ireland-Piper (2022).

338 See Chapter 5.

harmful contamination, particularly when the serious shortcomings in relying on enforcement exclusively via the State route are considered, as set out above in Chapter 3, Section 2. It could even call into question whether NSAs are capable of possessing international legal personality, due to their inability to bring legal claims based on international law. However, that argument has been rejected as a misreading of the UN Reparations case,[339] which instead saw the United Nations recognised as having legal personality and therefore the ability to bring legal claims, rather than that ability being necessary for its legal personality.[340] Nonetheless, this highlights two important issues. First, the extent to which domestic systems ensure accountability for NSA space pollution, which is addressed in the following Chapter 5, is an important factor in providing some measure of protections for the environment. Second, this gap in the enforcement armory highlights the need for reform of the architecture of international space law, which is addressed in Chapter 6 below.

339 *Reparation for injuries in the service of the United Nations*, Advisory Opinion: *ICJ Reports* (1949).

340 Murray (2016), p. 45.

CHAPTER 5

Domestic and Regional Practice: Legislation, Enforcement Frameworks, and Jurisprudence

The preceding chapters have demonstrated means to hold NSAs accountable for space pollution under existing international law. But the analysis has also highlighted significant restrictions which make those approaches likely inadequate in light of the rising threat emanating from NSAs in space. In line with the generally State-oriented nature of international law,[1] outer space law primarily places the burden on States to regulate NSA space activities.[2] Thus, to assess the effectiveness of relying on the existing approach of funneling NSA regulation through States, it is important to survey national and regional legislation relevant to the accountability of NSAs for space pollution.[3]

The assessment of States' regulatory frameworks provides an important contribution to the analysis in this book in two respects. First, it shows the manner and extent to which States regulate NSAs under domestic law. Pursuant to Article VI of the Outer Space Treaty, States are mandated to both authorize and supervise NSA space activity.[4] However, Article VI does not prescribe how these two elements are to be satisfied, instead leaving that to States' discretion.[5] States must navigate between the need to respect their international obligations through the regulation of NSA activities on one hand, and the pressure to ensure their economic growth through the development of private space activities and attracting foreign investments on the other. Mapping out commonalities and divergences in how States formulate their domestic regulations in

1 For an analysis of individual States power in the space arena see Marco Aliberti, Ottorino Cappelli, and Rodrigo Praino, *Power, State and Space*, (Springer, 2023).

2 See Chapter 3 (on Article VI of the Outer Space Treaty).

3 See also Annette Froehlich, Vincent Seffinga, National Space Legislation: A Comparative and Evaluative Analysis (Springer, 2018); Ram S. Jakhu, National Regulation of Space Activities (Springer, 2010); Joanne Wheeler, *The Space Law Review* (4th ed.) (Lexology, 2023).

4 See Chapter 3, Section 1.

5 For further discussions on this topic See Chapter 3, Section 1; Gerhard (2009), pp. 103–126; Hobe (2019), pp. 127–133; Stephan Hobe, 'The ILA Model Law for National Space Legislation' (2013) *62 ZLW 81*, pp. 81–95; Irmgard Marboe, 'National space law' in von der Dunk and Tronchetti (2015), pp. 127–39; Frans von der Dunk, *Advanced Introduction to Space Law* (2020), pp. 115–21.

DOI:10.1163/9789004724624_006

this respect helps to demonstrate the level of consistency across States, which illustrates the efficacy of relying on the State sovereignty approach.

Secondly, examining the domestic implementation of international space law obligations provides an important platform for the normative assessment of options to develop space law set out in Chapter 6. It provides examples of State practice relevant to whether a prohibition on space pollution exists under conventional or customary space law. As the primary subjects of international law, State practice is a key indicator of the development and crystallization of customary international law. Domestic law is also a key vehicle for the implementation of international law obligations. States and international organizations are becoming increasingly oriented towards using soft-law instruments for space activities.[6] It nonetheless remains possible for binding rules of customary international law to emerge through 'consistent state practice'.[7] Accordingly, this Chapter provides a detailed guide to State practice regarding the regulation and prohibition of space pollution, particularly by NSAs, under domestic law.

In terms of customary international law formation, these binding principles and/or rules of international law are formed by the combination of an objective and subjective element. According to Article 38(1)(b) of the Statute of the International Court of Justice,[8] international custom is evidenced by 'a general practice accepted as law' amongst the actors in public international law. The International Court of Justice has required that there must be a settled practice of State practice as well as the *opinio juris* that this conduct is legally obligatory.[9] National legislation can be an important source from which to discern

6 See also Steven Freeland, 'Overview of Current International Space Law in the Context of Planetary Defense' (2021) in Irmgard Marboe (ed.) *Legal Aspects of Planetary Defense* (Martinus Nijhoff, 2021), pp. 109–119.

7 ICJ, *Case concerning Military and Paramilitary Activities in and against Nicaragua*, Merits, Judgment; ICJ Rep. 1986, para. 186.

8 Statute of the International Court of Justice, 26 June 1945, 33 UNTS 993 (entered into force on 24 October 1945) ('ICJ Statute').

9 See ICJ, *The North Sea Continental Shelf Cases* (Federal Republic of Germany v. Denmark; Federal Republic of Germany v. Netherlands), Judgment of 20 February 1969 (ICJ Reports 1969, p. 4), para. 77: ('[n]ot only must the acts concerned amount to a settled practice, but they must also be such, or to be carried out in such a way, as to be evidence of a belief that this practice is rendered obligatory by the existence of a rule requiring it. The need for such a belief, i.e., the existence of a subjective element, is implicit in the very notion of the opinio juris sive necessitatis') and para. 74 referring to extensive and uniform state practice. In the Nicaragua case, the ICJ provided a more flexible guide to the level of State practice: ICJ, *Case concerning Military and Paramilitary Activities in and against Nicaragua*, Merits, Judgment (ICJ Reports 1986), para. 186 ('[i]n order to deduce the existence of customary rules, the Court deems it sufficient that the conduct of States should, in general, be

customary international law.[10] Judicial decisions of national courts can also be evidence of State practice or acceptance as law (*opinio juris*) for the purpose of determining the existence and the content of customary international law under Article 38(1)(b) of the ICJ Statute. Additionally, they can be a subsidiary means of identifying international law.[11]

With those considerations in mind, the following survey of relevant State legislation, regulatory instruments and, where existent, judicial decisions is designed to assist with the determination of customary law regarding NSA obligations to avoid space pollution. In this manner it complements other instruments, including soft international law provisions, set out in preceding chapters.[12] In accordance with the research question at the core of this monograph, the survey highlights domestic rules concerning space pollution and the responsibility of regulation of NSAs.

As an overview, from an estimated 70 to 80 States with at least one satellite in orbit, around 50 States have been evaluated to have national legislation of some type in place specifically governing space activity.[13] This chapter provides a brief analysis of the national acts available in the UNOOSA archive,[14] as well as additional examples of national and regional legislative documents and policies, with a particular emphasis on NSAs and the space environment. However, the analysis is not designed to be a comprehensive examination of every aspect of their regulatory framework. Instead, it covers the major legislative features, particularly in relation to space pollution and NSA accountability. In this way, it provides an important guide to the current practice of States, as

---

consistent with such rules, and that instances of State conduct inconsistent with a given rule should generally have been treated as breaches of that rule, not as indications of the recognition of a new rule. If a State acts in a way prima facie incompatible with a recognized rule, but defends its conduct by appealing to exceptions or justifications contained within the rule itself, then whether or not the State's conduct is in fact justifiable on that basis, the significance of that attitude is to confirm rather than to weaken the Rule').

10 ICJ, *Case concerning the Arrest Warrant of 11 April 2000* (Democratic Republic of the Congo v. Belgium), Jurisdiction of the Court and Admissibility, Judgment (ICJ Reports 2002, p. 3), at pp. 23–24, paras. 56–58; International Law Commission, 'Identification of customary international law', A/CN.4/691, 9 February 2016, para. 21.

11 See International Law Commission, 'Identification of customary international law', A/CN.4/691, 9 February 2016, pp. 5–6.

12 See Chapter 1, Section 4.

13 See, e.g., UNOOSA, *National Space Law* (20 December 2023) (available at https://www.unoosa.org/oosa/en/ourwork/spacelaw/nationalspacelaw/index.html).

14 See UNCOPUOS, Schematic Overview of National Regulatory Frameworks for Space Activities, UN Doc. A/AC.105/C.2/2023/CRP.28 (20 March 2023).

well as an indication to how State practice may develop in the coming years and decades.

In measuring State activity in space, one indicator is the number of satellites attributable to a State. As of 2023, it is evaluated that between 6,000 and 10,000 satellites are in orbit around the earth.[15] While the numbers of satellites vary, reports indicate that the United States is the frontrunner with over 5,000 satellites, followed by China, the Russian Federation (the Russian Federation possesses more than 1,000 satellites including the former Soviet satellites) and the United Kingdom with several hundred.[16] Japan has 141 according to the UN Online Index of objects launched into outer space (as of November 2023),[17] and others with less than 100 include France, Germany, India, Canada, Luxembourg,

---

15 All evaluations, including evaluations about how many satellites different States have in orbit, have been taken from the UNOOSA, *Online Index of Objects Launched into Outer Space* (20 December 2023) (available at https://www.unoosa.org/oosa/osoindex/index.jspx?lf_id), cross referenced with UNOOSA, *Notifications to the UN (20 December 2023)* (available at https://www.unoosa.org/oosa/sk/spaceobjectregister/submissions/states-organisations.html) as well as various independent websites such as Union of Concerned Scientists, *UCS Satellite Database* (1 January 2023) (available at https://www.ucsusa.org/resources/satellite-database; https://nanoavionics.com/blog/how-many-satellites-are-in-space/); Statista, *Number of satellites in orbit as of February 2023, by leading nations and organizations* (21 February 2023) (available at https://www.statista.com/statistics/1367699/number-of-satellites-in-orbit-by-country/); Primoz Rome, 'Every Satellite Orbiting Earth and Who Owns Them' *DEWESoft* (18 January 2022) (available at https://dewesoft.com/blog/every-satellite-orbiting-earth-and-who-owns-them).

16 UNOOSA, *Online Index of Objects Launched into Outer Space* (20 December 2023) (available at https://www.unoosa.org/oosa/osoindex/index.jspx?lf_id), cross referenced with UNOOSA, *Notifications to the UN (20 December 2023)* (available at https://www.unoosa.org/oosa/sk/spaceobjectregister/submissions/states-organisations.html); UNOOSA, United Nations Register of Objects Launched into Outer Space (20 December 2023) (available at https://www.unoosa.org/oosa/sk/spaceobjectregister/index.html); Kongsberg Nano Avionics, How Many Satellites are in Space? (4 May 2023) (available at nanoavionics.com/blog/how-many-satellites-are-in-space/); Union of Concerned Scientists, *UCS Satellite Database* (1 January 2023) (available at https://www.ucsusa.org/resources/satellite-database; https://nanoavionics.com/blog/how-many-satellites-are-in-space/); Statista, *Number of satellites in orbit as of February 2023, by leading nations and organizations* (21 February 2023) (available at https://www.statista.com/statistics/1367699/number-of-satellites-in-orbit-by-country/); Primoz Rome, 'Every Satellite Orbiting Earth and Who Owns Them' *DEWESoft* (18 January 2022) (available at https://dewesoft.com/blog/every-satellite-orbiting-earth-and-who-owns-them).

17 UNOOSA, 'United Nations Register of Objects Launched into Outer Space: Notifications from States and Organizations' (available at https://www.unoosa.org/oosa/sk/spaceobjectregister/submissions/states-organisations.html).

Italy, Republic of Korea, Israel, Uruguay, Australia, Finland, Norway, Spain, and Singapore.[18] Switzerland, Argentina, Belgium, Brazil, Denmark, Saudi Arabia, United Arab Emirates, Sweden, The Netherlands, and Turkey are estimated to possess between 10 and 20 satellites. States with satellites in single digits include Slovenia, Slovakia, Ukraine, Algeria, Armenia, Austria, Azerbaijan, Belarus, Bulgaria, Chile, Colombia, Czech Republic, Ecuador, Egypt, Estonia, Ethiopia, Portugal, Rwanda, South Africa, Thailand, Tunisia, Venezuela, Vietnam, Zimbabwe, Mexico, Kazakhstan, Indonesia, Ecuador, Peru, Greece, Malaysia, Morocco, Nigeria, Pakistan, Lithuania, Bangladesh, Bolivia, Hungary, Iran, Iraq, Qatar, Peru, Jordan, Kuwait, Laos, Mauritius, Monaco, Nepal, New Zealand, Paraguay, Sri Lanka, Sudan and Turkmenistan. State expenditure generally matches this distribution, with the United States the frontrunner, for example, spending an estimated 19.65 billion US dollars in 2017, China in second, and Russia in third place.[19]

Some of these States are part of regional organizations, including Arabsat, EUTELSAT, EUMETSAT, ESA or the European Union. However, as for regional organizations only ESA and the European Union are examined herein. This is because they are the international organizations with most satellites in orbit and they exert influence over European States, such as the United Kingdom, France, and Germany, which together account for almost 1,000 satellites in orbit.

With regard to NSAs, the United States, European countries and Japan are linked to the most NSA space activity.[20] Under the Registration Convention, only States have the obligation and ability to nationally register satellites and forward this information to the United Nations. Commercial actors may therefore own and operate satellites, but it falls to their respective States to register the satellite for inclusion in the UNOOSA Online Index of Objects Launched into Outer Space. The number of NSA satellites is large. Although the private operation of satellites is highly dynamic, there are some major private players with a significant presence in space far outstripping many States. For example, at the time of writing SpaceX (United States) owns as much as a third

18 See Online Index of Objects Launched into Outer Space; Notifications to the UN, available at https://www.unoosa.org/oosa/osoindex/index.jspx?lf_id and https://www.unoosa.org/oosa/sk/spaceobjectregister/submissions/states-organisations.html.

19 Marc Carns, *Orbital Debris Prevention and Mitigation Efforts Among Major Space Actors*, (Martinus Nijhoff, 2023), p. 162.

20 Primoz Rome, 'Every Satellite Orbiting Earth and Who Owns Them' *DEWESoft* (18 January 2022) (available at https://dewesoft.com/blog/every-satellite-orbiting-earth-and-who-owns-them).

of all satellites in orbit. OneWeb (United Kingdom) is a distant second with almost three hundred satellites. The remaining companies with considerable satellite numbers are Planet Labs Inc. (United States) over a hundred, Spire Global Inc. (United States), Swarm Technologies Inc. (United States), Iridium Communications Inc. (United States), ORBCOMM Inc. (United States), Global Star (United States) and ICEYE Ltd. (Finland).[21] In this respect, a particularly important aspect of State practice in their interactions with NSAs is their licensing systems, which have been recognised as critical to the preservation of the outer space environment.[22]

With regard to the preservation of the space environment, the main (international) efforts presently seem to be space debris mitigation efforts such as international standards and guidelines the likes of the UNCOPUOS SDMG, the IADC SDMG, the ESA Space Debris Mitigation Policy for Agency Projects, International Telecommunications Union (ITU) Recommendation ITU-R S.1003, the International Organization for Standardisation (ISO) standards and technical reports such as ISO 24113: Space Systems, along with the Italian Space Agency (ASI), British National Space Centre (BNSC), French Space Agency (CNES), German Aerospace Agency (DLR), and the European Space Agency (ESA)'s European Code of Conduct for Space Debris Mitigation,[23] complimented by studies on long-term sustainability of outer space.[24]

Importantly, out of the 43 States that submitted statements to the UNCOPUOS for the production of the Compendium of space debris mitigation standards adopted by States and international organizations, 17 States (Australia, Austria, Belgium, Canada, Denmark, Finland, France, Germany, Greece, Italy, Japan, Netherlands, Russian Federation, Ukraine, United Kingdom, United States, Nigeria) have national mechanisms on space debris mitigation in place.[25] A further 22 (Algeria, Argentina, Azerbaijan, Chile, Czech Republic, Slovakia, Spain, Switzerland, Kingdom of Thailand, Brazil, Cuba, Hungary,

21 Kizer Whitt (2022); Rome (2022).

22 Tremayne-Smith, 'Environmental Protection and Space Debris Issues in the Context of Authorization' in von der Dunk (2011a), pp. 187–188.

23 European Code of Conduct for Space Debris Mitigation (Issue 1.0) (28 June 2004). See also Viikari (2008), Hobe (2019); UNCOPUOS, Compendium of space debris mitigation standards adopted by States and international organizations, UN Doc. A/AC.105/C.2/2021/CRP.19 (4 June 2021).

24 UNCOPUOS, Guidelines for the Long-term Sustainability of Outer Space Activities, UN Doc. A/AC.105/2018/CRP.20 (28 June 2018).

25 See UNCOPUOS, Compendium of space debris mitigation standards adopted by States and international organizations, UN Doc. A/AC.105/C.2/2021/CRP.19 (4 June 2021).

Jordan, Nicaragua, Pakistan, Peru, Indonesia, Lao PDR, Mexico, Myanmar, Tunisia, Philippines) do not have a national mechanism in place, despite the fact that 18 out of these 22 support adherence to international standards on debris mitigation (Slovakia, Switzerland, Philippines, Myanmar, Mexico, Lao PDR, Indonesia, Peru, Hungary, Jordan, Pakistan, Kingdom of Thailand, Spain, Chile, Czech Republic, Argentina, Algeria, Azerbaijan). A further 3 States (India, Morocco, Poland) are in the process of developing and adopting national legislation.[26] The final State which made a submission, Colombia, declared only that it is signatory of the Liability Convention and that it promotes space debris mitigation measures and registration practice.[27] National mechanisms are critical for implementation of international obligations, as has been shown with the experience of the implementation of the prohibition of torture through national preventive mechanisms, for example.[28] The fact that over half of the States reporting to UNCOPUOS have not yet put in place national mechanisms is a strong indication that the regulatory frameworks set out below lack the architecture for meaningful implementation, which is required for effective enforcement of these international obligations.

With those overarching considerations in mind, it is apposite to assess how specific States which have space operations have adopted laws and issued judgements governing NSA conduct in their domestic systems. However, the analysis is largely based on laws rather than judicial pronouncements. National jurisprudence regarding licensing and supervision of NSA space activities is currently scarce, with the majority available concentrating on standard civil matters such as lawsuits for noise pollution, unlawful termination of contracts, competition law and related matters which do not directly concern space pollution. Consequently, the major focus of the analysis below, which is conducted State-by-State in regional groupings, is legislative and regulatory in nature.

26 See UNCOPUOS, Compendium of space debris mitigation standards adopted by States and international organizations, UN Doc. A/AC.105/C.2/2021/CRP.19 (4 June 2021).

27 See Statement of Colombia to UNCOPUOS in the UNCOPUOS, Compendium of space debris mitigation standards adopted by States and international organizations, UN Doc. A/AC.105/C.2/2021/CRP.19 (4 June 2021).

28 These are required for signatories to the Optional Protocol to the Convention against Torture (OPCAT) of 2002, under Article 17.

1 Oceanic States[29]

1.1 *Australia*[30]

Australia has set the goal of becoming a major space actor and is an increasingly important player in space exploration, with around three billion Australian dollars invested in the national space industry between 2018 and 2023.[31] It is investing heavily in space start-ups and developing and ever-evolving national space legislation to facilitate NSA space activity by for example streamlining licensing procedures.[32]

Australia's main space legal instruments are the Space Activities Act of 1998,[33] the Space (Launches and Returns) Act 2018 (the 2018 Act)[34] and the Space (Launches and Returns) (General) Rules 2019 (the 2019 Rules).[35] The 1998 Act covers the operation of a launch facility in Australia; the launch of a space object in Australia; the launch of an Australian space object from a facility located outside Australia; and the return of a space object to a place anywhere in Australia.[36] It regulates the issuing of launch permits for space

29 For more on space activities in Australia and New Zealand see Maria A. Pozza, Joel A. Dennerley, *Risk Management in Outer Space Activities: An Australian and New Zealand Perspective* (Springer, 2022).

30 For an analysis see also Thomas Jones, Tom Macken, *Australia*, in Joanane Wheeler (ed.) *The Space Law Review*, (Law Business Research Ltd., 2019), pp. 21–36.

31 Australian Government, *Space* (5 November 2023) (available at https://www.globalaustralia.gov.au/industries/space) See also: ACIL Allen, 'Australian Space Industry Capability' (October 2017) (available at https://acilallen.com.au/uploads/projects/673/ACILAllen_AustralianSpaceIndustryCapability_2017.pdf); Norton Rose Fulbright, *Global Outer Space Guide: Australia* (5. November 2023), available at https://www.nortonrosefulbright.com/de-de/wissen/publications/f0a97b4e/global-outer-space-guide-australia.

32 Urszula McCormack, Kate Creighton-Selvay, 'Developing Australia's Space Industry: How Can the Government Help You?' *KingandWood Mallesons* (7 December 2020) (available at https://www.kwm.com/au/en/insights/latest-thinking/developing-australias-space-industry.html).

33 Space Activities Act 1998 (No. 123, 1998) (as amended, taking into account amendments up to Act No. 8 of 2010).

34 Space Launches and Returns Act 2018 (No. 74, 2023) (as amended and in force on 18 October 2023).

35 Space (Launches and Returns) (General) Rules 2019 made under section 110 of the Space (Launches and Returns) Act 2018.

36 For a more detailed analysis of this Act, see Dylan McGirr, Matthew Bovaird and Thomas Jones, 'In review: space law, regulation and policy in Australia' (5 January 2023) (available at https://www.lexology.com/library/detail.aspx?g=29a0fde0-b441-4d49-858d-f7b5759fd050). Arranging launches from aircraft while in flight and launches of high-power rockets are also now covered under the new legislation.

activities carried out in Australia or by nationals of Australia,[37] launch permits or authorizations for the return of space objects,[38] and space licenses to operate a launch facility.[39] This means that if an NSA wants to conduct any of those space activities connected to Australia, it needs to obtain a permit or a license.

The 1998 Act requires that the operator has obtained the environmental approvals required under Australian law and made an 'adequate environmental plan' for the construction and operation of the launch facility.[40] The license application must provide, for each launch, the appropriate information from the following: '(a) evidence that the environmental impact of the launch and any connected return is addressed by the environmental plan of the licensed launch facility from which the launch is proposed; (b) information about environmental approvals required for the launch under any other law of the Commonwealth or a law of a State or Territory; (c) an assessment of the likely impact of the launch and any connected return on the environment, and information on how any adverse effects on the environment are to be monitored and mitigated.'[41] The inclusion of an environmental impact assessment supports the argument that such assessments are a general obligation under customary international law for space activities.

Whereas the 1998 Act was unclear as to whether it only referred to the environment on Earth, this has since been clarified with the 2018 Act and 2019 Rules. Under the 2018 Act, any 'launch of an Australian space object overseas or a launch to space from Australia [must] include consideration of the space environment, including space debris'.[42] An application from an Australian entity to be licensed to obtain an overseas payload permit or an Australian launch permit must include a strategy to address space debris. The strategy must be founded on a guideline or standard which has international recognition, like the UNCOPUOS SDMG or the IADC SDMG; the guideline or standard used must be identified; planned mitigation measures must be described; and

37 See Articles 11 and 12.

38 See Articles 13 and 14.

39 Article 15.

40 1998 Act, Article 18, point b.

41 See Space Activities Act of 1998. See also Space (Launches and Returns) (General) Rules 2019, Article 55 and Space (Launches and Returns) (High Power Rocket) Rules 2019, Article 28. See further Maximum Probable Loss Methodology, Section 6.4.

42 See Statement of Australia to UNCOPUOS, Compendium of space debris mitigation standards adopted by States and international organizations, UN Doc. A/AC.105/C.2/2021/CRP.19 (4 June 2021).

an orbital debris assessment must be provided.[43] Notably, the object of the Act includes the implementation of Australia's obligations under the UN space treaties.[44]

Australia cooperates with the United States in space activities, primarily through NASA. Current activities include operation of the Canberra Deep Space Communication Complex and, most recently, joining the Artemis Accords, with which Australia aims to increase commercial uses of space, as discussed above.[45] Separately, an agreement between the Government of Australia and the Government of the Russian Federation on Cooperation in the Field of the Exploration and Use of Outer Space for Peaceful Purposes, defines areas of cooperation, including 'research on matters relating to the protection of the outer space environment', though no new initiatives appear to be have been adopted under this agreement since Russia's invasion of Ukraine in February 2022. Separately, Australia has signalled its interest in space mining.[46]

At the judicial level, there have no cases directly addressing space pollution. However, one prominent lawsuit for nearly 5 million US dollars was filed against Equatorial Launch Australia, a start-up that facilitated NASA's first launch from Australian territory. The lawsuit, filed by company director Michael Jones, alleged unlawful dismissal and discrimination, and so is not directly linked to space pollution.[47] However, it signals that NSA companies engaged in space activities under Australia's jurisdiction can be proceeded

43 See Statement of Australia to UNCOPUOS, Compendium of space debris mitigation standards adopted by States and international organizations, UN Doc. A/AC.105/C.2/2021/CRP.19 (4 June 2021).

44 See Statement of Australia to UNCOPUOS, Compendium of space debris mitigation standards adopted by States and international organizations, UN Doc. A/AC.105/C.2/2021/CRP.19 (4 June 2021).

45 For more on Australian endeavours in that field, see Stacey Henderson, 'To the Moon and Beyond: Australia's Space Activities and Obligations Under International Law', *Australian Institute of International Affairs: Australian Outlook*, (3 April 2023) (available at https://www.internationalaffairs.org.au/australianoutlook/to-the-moon-and-beyond-australias-space-activities-and-obligations-under-international-law/); Rami Mandow, 'NASA and Australia Continue Strategic Partnership with Artemis' (21 March 2023) (available at https://spaceaustralia.com/news/nasa-and-australia-continue-strategic-partnership-artemis).

46 Rami Mandow, 'NASA and Australia Continue Strategic Partnership with Artemis' (21 March 2023) (available at https://spaceaustralia.com/news/nasa-and-australia-continue-strategic-partnership-artemis).

47 Matt Garrick, 'Equatorial Launch Australia hit with lawsuit, including allegations of bullying against director Michael Jones' (13 October 2022) (available at https://www.abc.net.au/news/2022-10-13/michael-jones-equatorial-launch-australia-ceo-bullying-lawsuit/101526340).

against in the same manner as other corporations. Although there have been no high-profile cases of lawsuits for space pollution (or terrestrial pollution caused by space activities), the possibility is not far-fetched; in 2022, 'space junk' reportedly from SpaceX's Crewed Dragon Resilience – fell on fields in the Snowy Mountains region of Australia.[48]

In sum, Australia's space sector is growing. Its regulatory framework echoes the desire to increase such growth, and seeks to streamline license granting as a way to authorize and supervise activities of the NSAs. Nonetheless, even though Australia's space legislation references the environment, calling for compliance with the provisions of Australian environmental regulations and requires an environmental impact assessment, it does not include specific reference to NSAs bearing criminal liability for space pollution.

1.2 *New Zealand*

New Zealand has a rapidly developing and internationally connected space sector that features a mix of start-up and well-established companies, servicing both governmental and non-governmental customers.[49] Its core space legislation consists of the Space Activities Act[50] and the Regulations issued pursuant thereto.[51]

The Space Activities Act covers procedures for the authorization and supervision of space activities. It regulates licenses and permits.[52] Article 7 declares that every launch from a launch facility in New Zealand, or from a vehicle in the air that was launched from New Zealand, must have a license. According to Article 9, such license can be granted only if the Minister for Space is satisfied *inter alia* that: 'the applicant has an orbital debris mitigation plan that meets any prescribed requirements' and 'the proposed launch or launches under the license are consistent with New Zealand's international obligations.' Article 10 refers to environmental safety as a condition for issuing a license. The Act also

48 Luke Dale, Nikki Macor Heath, 'Space Law Update: One Person's Space Junk is Another's Treasure – Who is Legally Responsible for Damage Caused by Space Debris?' HWL Ebsworth Lawyers (6 February 2023) (available at https://hwlebsworth.com.au/space-law-update-one-persons-space-junk-is-anothers-treasure-who-is-legally-responsible-for-damage-caused-by-space-debris/).

49 Deloitte, 'New Zealand Space Sector: Its value, scope and structure' (November 2019) (available at https://www.mbie.govt.nz/assets/new-zealand-space-sector-its-value-scope-and-structure.pdf).

50 Outer Space and High-altitude Activities Act 2017.

51 Outer Space and High-altitude Activities (Licenses and Permits) Regulations 2017.

52 Articles 7–56.

regulates other types of licenses, including payload permits,[53] and licenses for launch of launch vehicles overseas.[54]

Regarding sanctions in relation to space debris mitigation, a person can be 'liable on conviction to imprisonment for a term not exceeding 3 months or to a fine not exceeding $2,000, or both'. For other offences, imprisonment can be set up to 5 years (see, for example, Article 72 – interfering with launch vehicle and payload), indicating that safety matters are treated more seriously than environmental harm per se.

New Zealand's 2017 Regulations provide more detail governing orbital debris mitigation plans, including that (i) the release of debris during normal operations of the vehicle or payload be limited; (ii) the potential for break-up of the vehicle or payload while in orbit is minimized; (iii) the potential for the vehicle or payload to collide with debris other than debris released in the course of the activity to which the license or permit relates is minimized; and (iv) at the end of the activity to which the license or permit relates, the vehicle or payload is disposed of in a way that 'minimizes risks to, or in, Earth's environment and in the space environment (including the risk of collisions)'. These obligations essentially reflect the various space debris mitigation guidelines issued by international bodies, as referred to above.

The space legislation of New Zealand is robust and directly addresses the issue of debris. It is somewhat unique in establishing several different sorts of licenses, as sets out a number of offences and sanctions for breaches of this framework. By referring to space debris mitigation, this legislation adds to State practice broadly supporting a prohibition on space pollution (other than minimal emissions essential to the regular completion of a mission) along with ancillary obligations such as an environmental impact assessment preceding the launch.

2 European States

Among the European space-faring States, the large majority are members of the European Space Agency (ESA) and the European Union (EU). Both actors influence the space operations of NSAs in European States. However, their

53 Articles 15–22.

54 Articles 23–30.

approaches and procedures vary.[55] Accordingly, the following section examines their position regarding environmental harm and NSAs separately, as they provide valuable guidance as to the State practice among these countries, but in different ways.

2.1 *The European Space Agency*[56]

Initially founded by Belgium, Germany, Denmark, France, the United Kingdom, Italy, the Netherlands, Sweden, Switzerland and Spain, ESA was created in 1975 with the conclusion of the ESA Convention.[57] ESA is an international organization with international legal personality,[58] authorized by its Member States to act on their behalf when engaging with third parties.[59] As ESA views are often seen as reflecting those of 'values of Europe as a whole', it wields considerable influence in directing the development of international space law.[60] With a budget of over 7 billion Euros and estimated to be the international organization with most satellites in orbit, ESA is an influential space actor in and of itself.[61]

As of late 2023, ESA has 22 Member States, four Associated States and four States with Cooperation Agreements in place which enable these four to partake in some of ESA's programs.[62] Canada, in addition, has a specific Cooperation Agreement with ESA and sits on its council.[63] NSAs from those States may bid for and receive ESA contracts.[64] An example is the French NSA

55 For the main differences between the EU and ESA regulatory frameworks see Jane Lesley Smith, 'EU Competition Law and Issues of National Authorization of Private Space Activities,' in von der Dunk (2011a), p. 358.

56 See also Jenni Tapio, Alexander Soucek, *The European Space Agency's Contribution to National Space Law* (Springer, 2022).

57 ESA Convention and Council Rules of Procedure (SP-1337/EN, November 2019 – consolidated ESA-C-M/CXXII?Res. 1 8Final) Chapter 4, adopted on 20 October 1995; ESA/C-m/CLIV/Res. 2 (Fina), Chapter 3, adopted on 15 November 2001; ESA/C/CLXXIX/Res, 6 (Final), adopted on 22 June 2005; ESA/C(2009)73, adopted on 10 June 2009.

58 ESA Convention, Article 15.

59 See Carns (2023), p. 222; Smith (2011), pp. 346–352.

60 Carns (2023), p. 222.

61 ESA, 'ESA Facts' (2023) (available at https://www.esa.int/About_Us/Corporate_news/ESA_facts); Primoz Rome, 'Every Satellite Orbiting Earth and Who Owns Them' *DEWESoft* (18 January 2022) (available at https://dewesoft.com/blog/every-satellite-orbiting-earth-and-who-owns-them).

62 ESA, 'Member States and Cooperating States' (2 November 2023) (available at https://www.esa.int/About_Us/Corporate_news/Member_States_Cooperating_States).

63 ESA, 'Member States and Cooperating States' (2 November 2023) (available at https://www.esa.int/About_Us/Corporate_news/Member_States_Cooperating_States).

64 European Space Agency and Programs Handbook: Strategic Information and Contacts (BOOK); For an overview of all ESA Basic Documents see: ESA, 'Highlights of ESA rules

Arianespace, which has been providing launch services to ESA. The activity of authorizing and supervising NSAs is, due to its nature, divided between ESA, which oversees the implementation of its contracts, and the relevant Member State(s) as the sovereign authority overseeing the NSAs general activities.[65] ESA does this primarily through procurement procedures, dictated by ESA Procurement Regulations and annexes, in accordance with ESA industrial policy spelled out in Article VII of the ESA Convention and its Annex V.[66] One of the prescribed requirements is the fair-return or geographical-return principle, meaning it seeks to award contracts in accordance with the member State's contribution.[67] As an intergovernmental organization, ESA is generally immune from jurisdiction, and therefore its decisions are not subject to judicial review.[68] Consequently, any dispute between ESA and industry entities is resolved through administrative channels, namely by the Head of procurement, or via voluntary arbitration.[69]

ESA has been environmentally conscious since its inception. It adopted its first series of measures in the 1980s, *inter alia* forming a Space Debris Working Group, which in 1988 issued a report leading to the first ESA Resolution on the Agency Policy vis-a-vis the Space Debris issue.[70] In 1999, it issued a Space Debris Mitigation Handbook in 1999 (updated in 2002),[71] and then in 2000, it adopted a resolution on space debris,[72] and that same year a European Code of Conduct for Space Debris Mitigation.[73] These instruments require the

and regulations' (2 November 2023), available at https://www.esa.int/About_Us/Law_at_ESA/Highlights_of_ESA_rules_and_regulations.

65 See Carns (2023), pp. 211–249; Smith (2011), pp. 346–352.

66 ESA, *European Space Agency Procurement Regulation* (*ESA/REG/001, Rev.5*) (2019); ESA, *ESA Convention and Council Rules of Procedure* (*SP-1337*) (2019), Art. VII, Annex V.

67 See, e.g., ESA, *ESA Convention and Council Rules of Procedure* (*SP-1337*) (2019), Annex 5, Article IV. See also overall references in ESA, *European Space Agency Procurement Regulation* (*ESA/REG/001, Rev.5*) (2019). For a further analysis see: Smith (2011), pp. 346–352.

68 See, e.g., ESA, *ESA Convention and Council Rules of Procedure* (*SP-1337*) (2019), Article XV, Annex I. For a further analysis see: Smith (2011), p. 351.

69 See, e.g., ESA, ESA Procurement Regulations (ESA/REG/001), Part VI; ESA, Clause 35; General Clauses and Conditions for ESA Contracts (ESA/REG/002, rev.3) (2019); For a further analysis see Smith (2011), p. 351.

70 Carns (2023), pp. 223–22; see also Howard Baker, 'The ESA and USS reports on Space Debris' (1990) 6 *Space Policy*, p. 332.

71 ESA Contract 14471/00/D/HK: Update of the ESA Space Debris Mitigation Handbook, Ref: QINETIQ/KI/SPACE/CR021539.

72 ESA Res. E/SA/C/(2000)93 (resolution for a European Policy on the Protection of the Space Environment from Debris).

73 ASI, BNSC, CNES, DLR, ESA, European Code of Conduct for Space Debris Mitigation (2004).

prevention of on-orbit breakups and collisions, the removal of inactive spacecraft (end-of-life missions), and it prescribes limiting the release of debris during normal operations to be executed through a mitigation plan led by a space debris manager.[74] Notably, the Code of Conduct is directly applicable to NSAs, along with States.[75]

More recently, the Code of Conduct has been updated by International Organization for Standardization's (ISO) space debris mitigation guidance,[76] called Space Systems – Space Debris Mitigation requirements, endorsed by the European Cooperation on Space Standardisation (ECSS) in 2012, and adopted by ESA in 2014 as standards to be applied to all ESA space operations.[77] To ensure compliance, ESA simultaneously adopted two annexes, the first requiring that a Space Debris Mitigation Plan should be established for each project to ensure compliance, and that a Space Debris Mitigation Report must be issued for purposes of verifying and documenting the plan, while the second annex clarified terms and definitions.[78]

According to ESA's own statement to UNCOPUOS, its main document for debris limitation is its Space Debris Mitigation Policy for Agency Projects, which is an administrative instruction of the ESA executive organ – headed by the ESA Director General. Within ESA, this instruction is binding for all ESA staff, who in turn have to ensure its correct implementation in relation to third parties.[79] The document applies to procurement of ESA space systems and operations under the responsibility of ESA (including end-of-life missions). It defines a set of requirements for debris and risk reduction, in line with

74 See Carns (2023), pp. 226–227.

75 See paragraph 1.2 'The present Code is applicable to all outer space activities conducted by a Subscribing State or jointly with other State(s) or by non-governmental entities under the jurisdiction of a Subscribing State, including those activities within the framework of international intergovernmental organizations.'

76 Under the number ISO 24113:2010 (first updated to ISO 24113:2011, then ISO 24113:2019, and most recently ISO 24113:2023).

77 ESA Space Debris Mitigation Policy for Agency Projects, EUR SPACE AGENCY, ESA/ADMIN/IPOL (2014)2 (28 March 2014); Space Sustainability Adoption Notice of ISO 24113: Space Systems Space Debris Mitigation Requirements, Eur. Cooperation for Space Standardization, ECSS-U-AS-10C (10 February 2012). See also Carns 2023, at 232–247.

78 ESA Space Debris Mitigation Policy for Agency Projects, European Space Agency, ESA/ADMIN/IPOL (2014)2 (28 March 2014).

79 ESA Space Debris Mitigation Policy for Agency Projects, European Space Agency, ESA/ADMIN/IPOL (2014)2 (28 March 2014), replacing ESA instruction from 2008. See also Statement of ESA to UNCOPUOS in: UNCOPUOS, Compendium of space debris mitigation standards adopted by States and international organizations, UN Doc. A/AC.105/C.2/2021/CRP.19 (4 June 2021).

international standards such as IADC SDMG, UNCOPUOS SDMG, ISO international standard ISO 24113:2011.[80]

Various ESA announcements continue to signal its environmental commitment.[81] Under its 2012 Clean Space Initiative,[82] ESA is pursuing a 'Zero Debris Approach' to achieve space sustainability and safety of critical space services, which encompasses space debris mitigation, remediation (including on-orbit servicing and active debris removal), upgrading spacecraft platforms and space traffic management.[83] To monitor the situation, ESA issues an annual Space Environment Report in cooperation with many governmental and NSA partners.[84] ESA has acknowledged that the space sector and the space environment are not exempt from the fast evolving European environmental legislation. It proposed a common eco-design framework for the European space sector through the recognition of the application of environmental legislation in outer space, such as the (in force) Montreal Protocol on Substances that Deplete the Ozone Layer, the European Commission's Restriction of Hazardous Substances (RoHS) directive and the Registration, Evaluation, Authorization and Restriction of Chemicals (REACH) regulation, as well as the requirement for environmental impact assessments for each project.[85]

In summary, ESA regulations and policies influence all Member States (including Associated States and Cooperating States taking part in ESA projects) and all NSAs working under ESA contracts, resulting in considerable influence over a vast number of space actors. In its projects ESA pays close

---

80 Statement of ESA to UNCOPUOS in: UNCOPUOS, Compendium of space debris mitigation standards adopted by States and international organizations, UN Doc. A/AC.105/C.2/2021/CRP.19 (4 June 2021). See also ESA, ESA Space Debris Mitigation Requirements, Reference: ESSB-ST-U-007 Issue 1 (30 October 2023).

81 See, e.g., ESA, 'ESA Green Agenda' (2 November 2023) (available at https://www.esa.int/About_Us/Responsibility_Sustainability/ESA_Green_Agenda), where it indicates its intention to reduce the Agency's environmental footprint and informs on the environment and sustainability projects of ESA.

82 For more information on Clean Space see: ESA, 'Clean Space' (2. November 2023) (available at https://www.esa.int/Space_Safety/Clean_Space/Clean_Space2); ESA, *Clean Space – Latest* (2 November 2023) (available at https://www.esa.int/Space_Safety/Clean_Space).

83 ESA, Zero Debris Charter (2022). See also ESA, 'The Zero Debris Charter' (available at: https://www.esa.int/Space_Safety/Clean_Space/The_Zero_Debris_Charter); ESA, 'Towards a Clean Space: ESA's Zero Debris Approach' (2 November 2023) (available at hhttps://blogs.esa.int/cleanspace/2023/06/16/a-clear-path-to-a-sustainable-space-esas-zero-debris-approach/).

84 See generally: ESA, 'ESA's Space Environment Report 2023' (2 November 2023) (available at https://www.esa.int/Space_Safety/ESA_s_Space_Environment_Report_2023).

85 ESA, 'ecodesign' (2 November 2023) (available at https://www.esa.int/Space_Safety/Clean_Space/ecodesign).

attention to the space environment, in particular the space debris threat, by, for example, implementing ISO standards on space debris mitigation, and pursuing newer endeavours such as in-orbit servicing, active debris removal and space traffic management initiatives. However, as an international organization, its supervision is subject to an administrative procedure under the procurement process and Head of Procurement, rather than subject to judicial mechanisms. Therefore, apart from enforcing its contracts through arbitration, ESA does not have any independent legal mechanism to ensure NSA accountability for space pollution. However, given its status, it could play an important role in the formation of rules and procedures under international law applicable to NSA space pollution, as is discussed below.[86] Considering its high number of space-faring Member States, the fact that it is officially the international organization with the most satellites in orbit (evaluated at 48),[87] and that it is responsible for the operational development of the major EU space program components (including Galileo, Copernicus, and Iris2),[88] ESA can exert considerable influence and has the potential to be a strong driver for environmentally sound regulation of NSA space activity.

2.1.1 The European Union

The European Union has 27 Member States, of which 19 are simultaneously members of ESA, while the remaining States comprise four Associated States and four with Cooperation Agreements. Of the full ESA members, only Norway, Switzerland and the United Kingdom are not Member States of the European Union. In the Treaty on the Functioning of the European Union, Articles 4, 179 and 189, space activities have been designated as a shared competence between the European Union and its Member States, with the European Union given the prerogative to establish a European space program, which it has done.[89]

The Union operates its own space activities, such as the European global navigation services Galileo, EGNOS, Earth observation constellation Copernicus, Govsatcom, Space situational awareness (SSA) and the recently established

86 See Chapter 6 on Lex Ferenda.

87 ESA, 'ariane' (5 November 2023) (available at https://www.esa.int/Enabling_Support/Space_Transportation/Ariane); Arianespace, 'Who does what?' (5 November 2023) (available at https://www.arianespace.com/spaceport-facility/who-does-what/).

88 Regulation (EU) 2021/696; Regulation (EU) 2023/588.

89 Consolidated Version of the Treaty on the Functioning of the European Union, OJ C 326, 26 October 2012. See, e.g. Regulation (EU) 2021/696 of 28 April 2021 establishing the Union Space Programme and the European Union Agency for the Space Programme, supplemented by the Commission implementing decision (EU) 2022/1245 of 15 July 2022. For more see Stephan Hobe 'Article 189 AEUV'.

secure connectivity network Iris2.[90] For the operation of these activities, the European Union adopted various regulations determining the Union's space program and capacities and establishing the EU Agency for the EU Space Programme (EUSPA).[91] In EU regulation (EU) 2021/696, the European Union made the European Commission responsible for the implementation of the Program, the EUSPA for market development, and ESA for technical and operational development and expertise.[92] An EU space law is expected to be drafted and proposed for adoption in 2024.[93] Until then, however, the EU Regulations and EU competition law will continue to be the primary sources of the European Union's space activity regulatory framework.[94] This distinguishes it from ESA,[95] which functions on the basis of its Convention and the Industrial Policy's Procurement procedure.[96]

The European Union, in the domains granted to it by the Treaty of Lisbon, assigns contracts subject to EU competition law, as supplemented by the World

90 Regulation 2023/588 Of The European Parliament And Of The Council of 15 March 2023, establishing the Union Secure Connectivity Programme for the period 2023–2027; EUSPA, *The EU Space Programme* (2 November 2023) (available at https://www.euspa.europa.eu/european-space/eu-space-programme).

91 Initially the European Global Navigation Satellite Systems Supervisory Authority (GSA) established through Regulation (EU) No 1321/2004, reorganized into the European Global Navigation Satellite Systems Agency (also GSA) by means of Regulation (EU) No. 912/2010, and finally into EUSPA by Regulation (EU) 2021/696.

92 Regulation (EU) 2021/696, Articles 28–31.

93 European Commission, 'Targeted consultation on EU space law' (2. November 2023) (available at https://defence-industry-space.ec.europa.eu/public-consultations/targeted-consultation-eu-space-law_en).

94 See Smith (2011), pp. 323–358.

95 For an analysis of the differences between ESA and EU space competences and legal procedures see Smith (2011), pp. 323–358.

96 Von der Dunk (2015a), p. 206, highlights that within the European framework ESA acts as the 'operational' integration, while the European Union designated the 'legislative' integration of European space capabilities and actors. This approach furthermore seems included in the EU Regulation REGULATION (EU) 2021/696 OF THE EUROPEAN PARLIAMENT AND OF THE COUNCIL of 28 April 2021 establishing the Union Space Programme and the European Union Agency for the Space Programme, which in Article 28 has tasked the EU Commission with overall responsibility for the implementation of the EU Programme, in Article 29 the EU Agency for the Space Programme with security accreditation, communication, market development and promotion, and in Article 30 ESA with space system evolution (design and development of the space components). For more see Stephan Hobe, 'Artikel 189 AEUV' (2015) in: H von der Groeben, J Schwarze, A Hatje (eds.) (7th ed) *Europäisches Unionsrecht, Vertrag über die Europäische Union – Vetrag über die Arbeitsweise der Grundrechte der Europäischen Union, Band 4*, (Nomos Baden-Baden: Verlag).

Trade Organization's GATT[97] (except in matters of national security, such as for example the Galileo Program) and the principles of the internal market.[98] The European Court of Justice has adjudicated space cases but these mainly concerned the transmission of television signals and the European free market, rather than environmental protection *per se*.[99] In a recent decision from 2022, for example, the European Court of Justice decided that EU law precludes the general and indiscriminate retention of traffic and location data except in cases of serious threat to national security.[100]

Like ESA, the European Union has signaled an environmentally conscious approach. In its regulations on space activity, the European Union has made repeated references to the space environment and to the private sector. For example, Regulation (EU) 2021/696 references the UN Sustainable

---

97 GATT 1994: *General Agreement on Tariffs and Trade 1994, 15 April 1994, Marrakesh Agreement Establishing the World Trade Organization*, Annex 1A, 1867 U.N.T.S. 187, 33 I.L.M. 1153 (1994).

98 Smith (2011), pp. 340–352.

99 See, e.g., Court of Justice of the European Union, 'Press Release No. 156/22' (20 September 2022) (available at https://curia.europa.eu/jcms/upload/docs/application/pdf/2022-09/cp220156en.pdf); European Communities, Court of Justice, Judgement of April 30, 1974 (C-155/73). Guiseppe Sacchi; European Communities, Court of Justice, Judgement of March 18, 1980 (C-52/79). Procureur du Roi v. Marc LV.C. Debauve and Others; European Communities, Court of Justice, Judgement of March 18, 1980 (C-62/79). S.A. Compagnie Gènérale pour la Diffusion de la Télévision, Coditel, and Others; European Communities, Court of Justice, Judgement of April 26, 1988 (C-352/85). Bond van Adverteerders and Others v. The Netherlands State; European Communities, Court of Justice, Judgement of September 10, 1996 (C-222/94). Commission of the European Communities v. United Kingdom of Great Britain and Northern Ireland; European Communities, Court of Justice, Judgement of September 10, 1996 (C-11-11/95). Commission of the European Communities v. Kingdom of Belgium; European Communities, Court of Justice, Judgement of December 12, 1996. Reti Televisive Italiane SpA (RTI) (C-320/94), Radio Torre (C-338/94), Rete A Srl (C-329/94), Vallau Italiana Promomarket Srl (C-337/94), Radio Italia Solo Musica Srl and Others (C-338/94) and GETE Srl (339/94) v. Ministerio delle Poste e Telecommunicazioni; European Communities, Court of Justice, Judgement of July 9, 1997 (Joined Cases C-34/95 and C-36-95); see also Stephan Gorove and Michael A. Gorove, *Cases on Space Law* (Journal of Space Law, University of Mississippi, 1996); Karl-Heinz Böckstiegel, Marietta Benkö, Stephan Hobe, *Space Law: Basic Legal Documents* (Eleven Publishing, 2005).

100 European Court of Justice, Joined Cases C-793/19, SpaceNet and C-794/19 | Telekom Deutschland. See also European Communities, Court of Justice, Judgement of September 20, 2022 (C-793/19 and C-794/19). SpaceNet and Telekom Deutschland, available at https://curia.europa.eu/jcms/upload/docs/application/pdf/2022-09/cp220156en.pdf. See also: European Communities, Court of Justice, Judgement of 5 April 2022, *Commissioner of An Garda Síochána and Others*, C-140/20 (see also Press Release No 58/22), and of 6 October 2020, La Quadrature du Net and Others, C-511/18, C-512/18 and C-520/18 (see also Press Release No 123/20).

Development Goals and decrees that one of its objectives is to 'enhance the safety, security and sustainability of all outer space activities pertaining to space objects and debris proliferation, as well as space environment, by implementing appropriate measures, including development and deployment of technologies for spacecraft disposal at the end of operational lifetime and for space debris disposal.'[101]

Regulation (EU) 2023/588 of 15 March 2023, which establishes the Union Secure Connectivity Programme for the period 2023–2027, makes extensive reference to the private sector (procurement and contracts),[102] as well as the environment, both of earth and outer space, and sustainability of space activities. In its introduction the Regulation mentions the necessity for 'good practices in space traffic management and in space surveillance and tracking (SST), in order to reduce the amount of space debris produced, prevent on-orbit break-ups and on-orbit collision, and provide appropriate end-of-life spacecraft measures.'[103]

Significantly, Article 8 of Regulation (EU) 2021/695 specifically addresses environmental and space sustainability by requiring that contracts and procedures to implement the program shall include provisions on minimization greenhouse gas emissions, the establishment of a scheme to offset the remaining greenhouse gas emissions, appropriate measures to reduce visible and invisible radiation pollution caused by spacecraft (and those that can hamper astronomical observations or any other type of research and observation), the use of appropriate collision-avoidance technologies for spacecraft and the submission, implementation of a comprehensive mitigation plan regarding space debris before the deployment phase, including orbital positioning data, in order to ensure the avoidance of space debris by the satellites of the constellation, and sharing data, in particular ephemeris data and planned maneuvers, to the entities in charge of producing SST.[104] It provides that the European Commission will maintain a database of the program's space assets, containing, in particular, data relating to environmental and space sustainability aspects, and shall adopt further Acts to supplement the Regulation, limited to space assets owned by the European Union and contractors.[105] Lastly, the Regulation decrees that for public procurement procedures the contracting authority shall act in accordance with the principle 'to enhance the safety and

101 Regulation (EU) 2021/696, Article 4(e).
102 Regulation (EU) 2021/695, Chapter 4, Articles 19–23.
103 Regulation (EU) 2023/588, Introduction (26).
104 Regulation (EU) 2023/588, Articles 8(1), 8(2).
105 Regulation (EU) 2023/588, Articles 8(3), 8(4), 8(5).

sustainability of outer space activities',[106] and that the European Commission would evaluate implementation of the program in light of objectives for which it will assess, *inter alia*, the environmental impact of the program, taking account of the criteria specified in the preceding provision.[107]

The European Union's non-space specific legislative frameworks refer extensively to the environment as well. Given the environmentally conscious views of ESA and the European Union more generally,[108] the 'environment' as mentioned in these instruments may encompass outer space.[109] These instruments include its policies on Green Public Procurement,[110] and European environment and climate change commitments,[111] including the European Green Deal.[112] EU environmental policy and law, resting on principles of precaution, prevention and rectifying pollution,[113] influences all NSA space activity based in, or under the jurisdiction of, the European Union.

---

106 Regulation (EU) 2023/588, Article 20(2)(h).

107 Regulation (EU) 2023/588, Article 42(3)(g).

108 EUSPA, 'How EU Space Supports Europe's environmental policies' (1 June 2023) (available at https://www.euspa.europa.eu/newsroom/news/how-eu-space-supports-europe-environmental-policies); ESA 'European space sector commits: Earth is ours, we must cherish it' (21 November 2022) (available at https://www.esa.int/Space_Safety/European_space_sector_commits_Earth_is_ours_we_must_cherish_it); Niklas Nienass, 'Europe leads on environmental concerns on earth, it must do the same in space' *Euractiv* (3 July 2023) (available at https://www.euractiv.com/section/global-europe/opinion/europe-leads-on-environmental-concerns-on-earth-it-must-do-the-same-in-space/); European Commission, 'The future of the European Space Sector' *European Investment Bank* (2019) (available at https://www.eib.org/attachments/thematic/future_of_european_space_sector_en.pdf).

109 See Chapter 2.

110 Vanessa Schmidt, Anna Brüning-Pfeiffer, 'Environmental Aspects in Public Procurement in Europe: Conference Report' (2021) Berlin: German Environmental Agency (available at https://www.umweltbundesamt.de/sites/default/files/medien/5750/publikationen/2021-04-22_dokumentationen_02-2021_public_procurement_0.pdf); André Sapir, Tom Schraepen, Simone Tagliapietra, 'Green Public Procurement: A Neglected Tool in the European Green Deal Toolbox' (2022) Intereconomics: review of European Economic Policy Volume 57, Number 3 (available at https://www.intereconomics.eu/contents/year/2022/number/3/article/green-public-procurement-a-neglected-tool-in-the-european-green-deal-toolbox.html).

111 EUR-Lex, 'Environment and climate change' (available at https://eur-lex.europa.eu/summary/chapter/20.html).

112 See European Commission, 'The European Green Deal' (available at https://commission.europa.eu/strategy-and-policy/priorities-2019-2024/european-green-deal_en).

113 European Parliament, 'Environment policy: general principles and basic framework' (available at https://www.europarl.europa.eu/factsheets/en/sheet/71/environment-policy-general-principles-and-basic-framework); Institute for European Environmental Policy ('IEEP') (Andrew Farmer (ed.)), *Sourcebook on EU Environmental Law* (IEEP,

In summary, the European Union's regulatory framework states its commitment to protecting the space environment and sets in place obligations to impose environmental due diligence when approving contracts and procurement. The European Union's environmental approach includes space debris mitigation, space debris remediation and the management of space traffic. Recently, the European Union proposed development and implementation of an EU space traffic management approach,[114] which focuses heavily on the utilization of EU space situational awareness database and EU SST capabilities.[115] However, the EU framework governing space activities contains no other enforcement mechanism to ensure compliance by NSAs with its environmental aims and does not indicate explicitly whether NSAs are bound by these environmental aims. It leaves enforcement to EU procurement (competition and environmental laws) and Member States procurement processes, and the consequent judicial mechanisms of domestic or EU courts.

2.1.2 France

France is one of the oldest European space powers and a founding member of ESA. It is one of the fastest growing and most active European space States, with numerous start-ups,[116] a considerable space sector,[117] the seat to the largest private launcher Arianespace providing launch services to both ESA and the European Union, and is in control of the main European spaceport in French Guiana.

2010) (available at https://www.eib.org/attachments/strategies/sourcebook_on_eu_environmental_law_en.pdf); WECOOP, 'EU Environment Policy' (available at https://wecoop.eu/regional-knowledge-centre/eu-policies-regulations/). Problems often encountered in EU environmental law are however inconsistent application of existing laws, See, e.g., European Environmental Bureau, 'Environmental Law and Justice' (available at https://eeb.org/work-areas/environmental-law-and-justice/EU-environmental-law/).

114 EUSTM, 'European space traffic management for the 21st century' (available at https://eustm.eu/); European Commission – Defense Industry and Space, 'Space Traffic Management' (available at https://defence-industry-space.ec.europa.eu/eu-space-policy/space-traffic-management_en).

115 EU SST, 'EU SST is the key operational capability for the EU approach to Space Traffic Management' (available at https://www.eusst.eu/newsroom/eu-sst-key-operational-capability-eu-approach-stm/).

116 See, e.g.,: Tracxn, *NewSpace Startups in France* (available at https://tracxn.com/d/explore/newspace-startups-in-france/__cRjAOQ4LjYjRQRTbpe8ZNxuwovS2FRTMkXyNx4zC4Aw/companies).

117 CNES, *French Space Industry Capabilities Catalogue* (available at https://cnes.fr/en/entreprises/catalogue-industrie-spatiale).

The two main acts regulating NSA space activity in France are the French Space Operations Act of 2008,[118] relating to space operations, and the Decree on Technical Regulation issued pursuant to Act number 2008-518 of 3 June 2008, updated 31 March 2011.[119] Both are mandatory acts, applicable to NSA activity.[120] Regarding NSA space activity, the French law defines 'Space operator' or 'operator' as any natural or legal person who conducts, under their own responsibility and independently, a space operation.[121] The French Space Operations Act of 2008 is applicable to launch and return operations carried out from French territory, by a French operator acting from French territory or from abroad, as well as to procurement of a launch by a French entity and control of space objects by French entities irrespective of where they are acting.[122]

Operators wishing to launch or return an object to or from territory or a facility under French jurisdiction, or any French operator, must first obtain an authorization to be issued by the relevant administrative authority,[123] which is the Minister in charge of space activities, who decides taking into account 'a technical assessment carried out by the French Space Agency CNES [Centre National D'Études Spatiales]'.[124] Consequently, any NSA operating from French territory, along with any French NSA, will require a license before engaging in

118 French Space Operations Act No. 2008-518 (2008) (Law No. 2008-518 of June 3, 2008 relating to space operations (1)).

119 Decree No. 2009-643 of June 9, 2009 relating to authorizations issued pursuant to Law No. 2008-518 of June 3, 2008 relating to space operations. To a lesser extent see also Decree No. 2009-1657 of December 24, 2009 relating to the National Defense and Security Council and the General Secretariat for Defense and National Security; Decree No. 62–153 of February 10, 1962 NATIONAL CENTER FOR SPACE STUDIES. See also B. Lazare, 'The French Space Operations Act: Technical Regulations (2013) 92 Acta Astronautica 2, pp. 209–212.

120 Statement of France to UNCOPUOS, Compendium of space debris mitigation standards adopted by States and international organizations, UN Doc. A/AC.105/C.2/2021/CRP.19 (4 June 2021).

121 French Space Operations Act also referred to as Law No. 2008–518 of 3 June 2008, Article 1(2).

122 Statement of France to UNCOPUOS, Compendium of space debris mitigation standards adopted by States and international organizations, UN Doc. A/AC.105/C.2/2021/CRP.19 (4 June 2021).

123 Article 2.

124 Statement of France to UNCOPUOS, Compendium of space debris mitigation standards adopted by States and international organizations, UN Doc. A/AC.105/C.2/2021/CRP.19 (4 June 2021). For more on French legislative framework and CNES see Philippe Clerc, *Space Law in the European Context: National Architecture, Legislation and Policy in France* (Eleven International Publishing, 2018).

space activity. The subsequent transfer of control over a space object is likewise subject to authorization (or licensing) by the French authorities.[125]

The licensing conditions refer to the protection of public health and the environment,[126] and indicate that a key goal is to limit risks of space debris.[127] Specific requirements and instructions are set down in the 2008 Decree, including that '[t]he launcher must be designed, produced and implemented in such a way as to minimize the production of debris during nominal operations, including after the end-of-life of the launcher and its component parts.'[128] The Decree contains provisions related to space debris mitigation, applicable to launch systems[129] and orbital systems.[130] These are consistent with international standards (for example, the IADC SDMG, the UNCOPUOS SDMG, the European Code of Conduct for Space Debris Mitigation, and ISO 24113).[131]

French agents are empowered to search operators' facilities and report any infringements to the public prosecutor within five days.[132] Violations of the Act may be investigated by officers and agents of the judicial police, acting in accordance with the provisions of the Code of Criminal Procedure (including violations noted by the agents carrying out inspections). The Act provides for fines of up to 200,000 euros for undertaking space activity (control, operation, launch, return) without authorization, for transferring to a third party control of an object or group of coordinated space objects without authorization, for taking control via transfer of a space object (or objects) that have not been authorized under this Act, for continuing space operations in contravention of an administrative measure or a judicial decision of arrest or suspension, or failing to comply with a formal notice from the administrative authority, or obstructing inspections carried out in accordance with the law.[133] In instances

125 Article 3.

126 Article 4.

127 Article 5. See also Statement of France to UNCOPUOS, Compendium of space debris mitigation standards adopted by States and international organizations, UN Doc. A/AC.105/C.2/2021/CRP.19 (4 June 2021).

128 French Decree on Technical Regulation issued pursuant to Act no. 2008-518 of 3rd June 2008, 31 March 2011, Article 21.

129 Article 21.

130 Article 40, 55.

131 Statement of France to UNCOPUOS, Compendium of space debris mitigation standards adopted by States and international organizations, UN Doc. A/AC.105/C.2/2021/CRP.19 (4 June 2021).

132 Article 10.

133 Article 11.

of the mentioned actions harming national defense, penalties are increased to three years' imprisonment and a fine of 300,000 euros.[134]

The French Act contains extensive references to damage[135] caused by space objects or activity,[136] including determining sole responsibility of operators for damages caused (which is essentially automatic on Earth and in airspace, but fault-based in outer space, in accordance with the Liability Convention). Responsibility can potentially be mitigated through the victims' proven fault.[137] In instances of services carried out on behalf of the State in the interest of national defense, an exception may be made through conclusion of an agreement between the State and the operator, conditioning and limiting the exemption.[138] In all instances when the State is required, as the launching State, to pay under Liability Convention, it can take recourse action against the operator (there is an exception when the space object has been targeted in the course of acts targeting State interests).

French space legislation regulating the conduct of the NSAs makes a reference to environmental protection, as well as to space debris mitigation. With this it makes an important contribution towards mitigation of further space pollution. Furthermore, it regulates liability for damage, in line with the Liability Convention, making sure that NSAs can be held liable for certain damages.

2.1.3 Germany

Germany is one of Europe's most active space states, with the German Aerospace Center (DLR) being its primary space organ. It is highly active on the global space scene, including through its participation in the Artemis mission and ensuing research.[139] Germany's private sector is likewise thriving, with numerous new companies, such as Isar Aerospace Technologies and Rocket

134 Article 11(v).

135 Regarding the space environment, the law defines damage as any harm to people, property, and in particular public health or the environment directly caused by a space object in the context of a space operation, excluding the consequences of using the signal emitted by this object for users (Article 1(1)). However, the act does not clarify whether the mention of the environment pertains to the Earthly or the space environment.

136 Articles 13–20.

137 Article 13.

138 Article 13-1.

139 Norton Rose Fulbright, *Global Outer Space Guide: Germany* (available at https://www.nortonrosefulbright.com/de-de/knowledge/publications/582a6d62/global-outer-space-guide-germany).

Factory Augsburg, in addition to the existing older NSAs, such as Airbus.[140] Germany is furthermore examining the possibilities of a national spaceport in the North Sea.[141]

The key German instruments include the Delegation of Space Activities Act[142] and the Telecommunications Act.[143] German legislation on space activities is, however, not extensive. Detailed licensing procedures are specified in the Act to give Protection against the Security Risk to the Federal Republic of Germany by the Dissemination of High-Grade Earth Remote Sensing Data (known as the Satellite Data Security Act – SatDSiG).[144] In other words, these procedures are set out in an act specific to Earth Remote Sensing activities, and not space activities in general, despite Germany and German NSAs participating a wider range of space activities.

The Satellite Data Security Act applies to high-grade earth remote sensing systems and data dissemination by German nationals, or by legal persons or associations of persons under German law, or by foreign legal persons, or foreign associations of persons with their head office within the territory of the Federal Republic of Germany, or if unalterable sequences of instructions to command an orbital system are transmitted from the territory of the Federal Republic of Germany. The Act therefore includes NSA space activity. Under the Satellite Data Security Act, licenses are required for NSAs to participate in these activities. In relation to the outer space environment, the conditions for a permit are mainly concerned with security risks related to third parties gaining access to ground stations or space-based assets. The conditions for a permit do not explicitly address the environment, leaving a considerable gap in the domestic coverage of space activities.

The DLR, which implements the German space program, operates a policy under which each contractor must provide product assurance and ensure that

---

140 Deutschland.de, *Strong start-ups* (available at https://www.deutschland.de/en/topic/business/germany-aerospace-start-ups-innovative-technology-in-space); Airbus, Space technology made in Germany (available at https://www.airbus.com/en/products-services/space/space-technology-made-in-germany).

141 German Offshore Spaceport Alliance (OHB), First launches in the North Sea planned for 2024 (available at https://www.ohb.de/en/news/first-launches-in-the-north-sea-planned-for-2024-gosa-starts-its-first-demo-mission).

142 Raumfahrtaufgabenübertragungsgesetz, 22 August 1998, BGBl. I, 2510.

143 Telekommunikationsgesetz, 23 June 2021, BGBl. I, 1858, as amended 10 September 2021, BGBl. I, 414.

144 2590 Bundesgesetzblatt Jahrgang 2007 Teil I Nr. 58, ausgegeben zu Bonn am 28. November 2007 – Gesetzzum Schutz vor Gefährdung der Sicherheit der Bundesrepublik Deutschland durch das Verbreiten von hochwertigen Erdfernerkundungsdaten (Satellitendatensicherheitsgesetz – SatDSiG).

safety requirements, including debris measures, are met throughout all phases of a project.[145] Mitigation requirements are mandatory as part of the Product Assurance and Safety Requirements for DLR Space Projects, and include requirements for space debris mitigation assessments and reports. Measures pertaining to design, passivation, disposal maneuvres, re-entry safety, consistent with the IADC SDMG, the UNCOPUOS SDMG, and the European Code of Conduct, are included, along with reference to ISO standard 24113, with NASA STD 8719.14 (Process for Limiting Orbital debris) and NASA-NPR-8715.6A (Procedural Requirements for Limiting Orbital Debris) as informative references.[146] While this applies specifically to DLR projects, Germany has asserted that the ITU recommendation ITU-R S.1003.2 is a condition which all users of German orbit and frequency rights must fulfill in light of Article 56 of the Telecommunications Act.[147]

In light of the above, it can be seen that Germany has national mechanisms in place for NSA licensing as well as for ensuring environmental protection in accordance with European standards, however, a general comprehensive law is yet to be developed and punitive sanctions are not as specific as in some other States.

2.1.4 Austria

Austria is one of the smaller, but long-standing, space States. It invests approximately 60 million euro annually in ESA and EUMETSAT, and around 30 million euro in EU space activities.[148] It operates a relatively large industry with around 120 organizations.[149] As a European State, Austria's regulatory approach is closely aligned with other European States and the ESA.

---

145 Statement of Germany to the UNCOPUOS in the UNCOPUOS, Compendium of space debris mitigation standards adopted by States and international organizations, UN Doc. A/AC.105/C.2/2021/CRP.19 (4 June 2021).

146 Statement of Germany to the UNCOPUOS in the UNCOPUOS, Compendium of space debris mitigation standards adopted by States and international organizations, UN Doc. A/AC.105/C.2/2021/CRP.19 (4 June 2021).

147 Statement of Germany to the UNCOPUOS in the UNCOPUOS, Compendium of space debris mitigation standards adopted by States and international organizations, UN Doc. A/AC.105/C.2/2021/CRP.19 (4 June 2021).

148 See, e.g., Federal Ministry for Transport, Innovation and Technology, Austrian Space Applications Programme; FFG, 'Austria in Space' (available at https://www.ffg.at/en/space/austria-in-space); Austria in Space, 'Space Activities' (available at https://austria-in-space.at/en/european-space-activities/).

149 Austria in Space, 'Austrian Space Industry and Research' (available at https://austria-in-space.at/en/austria-in-space/austrian-space-industry-and-research.php).

Austrian national legislation consists of the Outer Space Act of 2011,[150] and a supplementary Outer Space Regulation of 2015.[151] Space activities under its jurisdiction require the authorization by the Minister for Transport, Innovation and Technology.[152] Amongst the conditions for such authorization, some are relevant for preventing space pollution, namely 'the space activity does not run counter Austria's obligations under international law', that 'appropriate provision has been made for the mitigation of space debris', and that 'the space activity does not cause harmful contamination of outer space or celestial bodies or adverse changes in the environment'.[153] The Act provides also for the possibility of modification or termination of an authorizing license.[154]

The Austrian Outer Space Act requires operators to 'take out an insurance covering a minimum amount of € 60,000,000 per insurance claim'.[155] In this way, Austria will be secured and can demand recourse from a private operator if damage is caused by a space object launched by that private operator which results in Austria having to pay liability under rules of international law (for example under Article VII of the Outer Space Treaty or under the Liability Convention).[156] In this way, NSAs are not directly liable under international law, but indirectly pay to cover the risk through insurance premiums. However, this appears to only cover damage to other space objects, rather than harm to the outer space environment *per se*. In this way, the regulatory framework arguably invisibilizes the costs of environmental harm in space.

Nonetheless, the Outer Space Act transposes the UNCOPUOS Space Debris Mitigation Guidelines into the national legislation.[157] It demands that 'the

---

150 Federal Law on the Authorization of Space Activities and the Establishment of a National Registry (Outer Space Act), BGBl. I No. 132/2011 of 27 December 2011.

151 Regulation of the Federal Minister for Transport, Innovation and Technology in Implementation of the Federal Law on the Authorization of Space Activities and the Establishment of a National Space Registry (Outer Space Regulation; Bundesgesetzblatt II Nr. 36/2015 of 26 February 2015) issued on the basis of § 12 of Outer Space Act (Bundesgesetzblatt. I No. 132/2011).

152 Outer Space Act, Articles 2 and 3.

153 Article 4.

154 Article 7.

155 However, if the space activity is in the public interest, meaning, that it serves science, research or education, 'the Minister for Transport, Innovation and Technology may determine a lower sum or release the operator from the insurance requirement by administrative decision, taking into account the risks connected to the activity and the operator's financial capacity'.

156 Article 11.

157 In its Statement to the UNCOPUOS, Austria specifically stated that in the Explanatory Report to the Austrian Outer Space Act that the IADC SDMG, UNCOPUOS SDMG and ESA requirements on Space Debris Mitigation were referred to by the phrase 'internationally

operator has to make provision for the mitigation of space debris in accordance with the state of the art and in due consideration of the internationally recognised guidelines for the mitigation of space debris', highlighting further that 'measures limiting debris released during normal operations have to be taken'.[158] Concretization of this obligation is done through the Outer Space Regulation, prescribing that 'the operator has to submit: 1. a report [on the measures adopted] according to the state of the art and in consideration of the internationally accepted guidelines, in particular a) for the avoidance of space debris and mission residue released during normal operations, b) for the prevention of on-orbit break-ups of the space object, c) for the removal of the space object from Earth orbit at the end of the space activity, either by controlled re-entry or by moving the space object to a sufficiently high Earth orbit ('graveyard orbit'), while for non-maneuverable space objects the Earth orbit is to be chosen such that they do not remain in Earth orbit for more than 25 years after the end of their operation, 2. a demonstration of measures adopted for the prevention of on-orbit collisions with other space objects.'[159]

Operators of space activities are subject to supervision by the Minister for Transport, Innovation and Technology. This means that 'the operator is obliged to grant the organs of the supervisory authority access to all business premises [and plants], [and] allow them to inspect relevant documents and provide them with information'.[160] The Outer Space Act also provides sanctions for operators infringing upon its provisions. However, the fines prescribed are relatively low in comparison to the costs of space activity and insurance requested, as they rise to 100,000 euros.

Austrian space legislation comprehensively regulates the authorization and supervision of NSA space activities, including detailed provisions on the process and conditions for granting a license, obligations of the operator, and

recognised guidelines for the mitigation of space debris' in Article 5, and are paid particular attention during the authorization process and non-compliance risks the license. While the ITU Recommendations are only mentioned when referring to frequency allocation and the European Code of Conduct for Space Debris Mitigation Requirements and ISO Standards are not explicitly referenced, they may nonetheless be taken into account during the authorization process 'in the application of' Article 5. See Statement of Austria to UNCOPUOS, Compendium of space debris mitigation standards adopted by States and international organizations, UN Doc. A/AC.105/C.2/2021/CRP.19 (4 June 2021).

158 Article 5.

159 Article 2 of the Regulation. See also Statement of Austria to the UNCOPUOS in the UNCOPUOS, Compendium of space debris mitigation standards adopted by States and international organizations, UN Doc. A/AC.105/C.2/2021/CRP.19 (4 June 2021).

160 Article 13.

the termination of the authorization. The legislation makes several references to environmental protection, including through space debris mitigation. It is important to note that Austrian Law is one of few examples of national legislations that transpose the UN SMDG onto the domestic level, making it legally binding, which is an important contribution towards lowering space pollution.

2.1.5 Slovenia

Slovenia launched its first two satellites in 2020,[161] with a third joining in 2022.[162] Its space sector is composed primarily of mixed public-private initiatives.[163]

Slovenia adopted space legislation in 2022, which is very similar to the Austrian model. It consists of the 2022 Space Activities Act[164] and a subsequent Decree[165] governing the Act's implementation. Notably, Article 3 of the Space Activities Act refers to space debris, when defining space activity as 'the launch of a space object into outer space, the operation and operational control of the space object in outer space, and the controlled termination of the space object's operation in outer space and/or its return to Earth, including the procedures for limiting the generation of space debris'.

Articles 4 and 5 of the Act establish that, to perform a space activity, an operator must obtain a license, subject to certain conditions including that the 'space activities do not pose a threat to national defence, public order, the safety of people or their property, national intelligence and security operations, and protection against natural or other disasters and do not negatively affect public health, the environment or aviation'. The environmental condition is examined by the Ministry for the Environment. Additionally, Article 15 regulates the obligation of the operator to notify the ministry on certain emergencies, including the risk for the environment.

The most important condition in the present context is the obligation that 'space activities envisage measures for limiting the generation of space debris in accordance with the applicable UN Space Debris Mitigation Guidelines

---

161 Government of the Republic of Slovenia, *First Slovenian satellites launched into orbit* (5. November 2023) (available at https://www.gov.si/en/news/2020-09-03-first-slovenian-satellites-launched-into-orbit/).

162 STA, *Third Slovenian satellite launched in space* (5. November 2023) (available at https://english.sta.si/3060191/third-slovenian-satellite-launched-in-space).

163 Ministry of the Economy, Tourism and Sport, Catalogue of Slovenian Space Industry (2023), (available at https://www.gov.si/assets/ministrstva/MGTS/Dokumenti/ESA/Slovenia-space-catalogue-2023-SPREAD.pdf).

164 Space Activities Act, Official Gazette of the Republic of Slovenia, 43/22.

165 Decree on the Implementation of the Space Activities Act, Official Gazette of the Republic of Slovenia 122/22.

and for limiting adverse environmental effects on Earth or in outer space or adverse changes in the atmosphere'.[166] With this, Slovenia essentially transposes the UN SMDG into its national legislation.

Despite the fact Slovenia joined the space-faring nations relatively recently, its space legislation is relatively comprehensive and its provisions regarding environmental protection can be described as progressive, transposing the UN SMDG into domestic law and containing certain other safeguards against environmental pollution, similar to the ones contained in the Austrian law.

2.1.6 Luxembourg

Luxembourg has one of the most active commercial space sectors in Europe.[167] Despite being a small State, its ambitions in space are significant. It currently registers approximately 75 space companies and space sector research laboratories, which employ nearly 1,200 people.[168] In comparison with other States, whose space legislation consists of only one or two pieces of legislation, Luxembourg's legislation governing NSA space activities is more complex and fragmented.

Firstly, Article 20 of the Law on Electronic Media sets out that no one may establish and operate a satellite system under Luxembourg's legislation without having previously obtained a concession, granted by the Government.[169] There is no explicit reference to the environment in the conditions for the concessions. Despite the use of the term 'concession' instead of 'license', this provision is comparable to provisions of other states concretizing their obligations under Article VI of the Outer Space Treaty through establishing proceedings for authorizing and supervising space activities of their NSAs. However, this provision only concerns operating a satellite system, not other space activities.

Second, a general regulation of space activities in Luxembourg is laid down by the Law on Space Activities.[170] This law applies to space activities carried out by NSAs, which operate under the control and jurisdiction of Luxembourg, either due to their national or territorial link with the State. An explicit reference to the environment is made in Article 9, where the withdrawal of

166 Space Activities Act, Article 5.

167 Deloitte, *Space Galaxy* (5. November 2023) (available at https://www2.deloitte.com/lu/en/pages/technology/articles/luxembourg-space-initiatives.html).

168 Luxembourg Space Agency, 'Space Campus: The Future Centre of Gravity of the Luxembourg Space Ecosystem' (3 August 2022) (available at https://space-agency.public.lu/en/news-media/news/2022/spacecampus.html).

169 Law of 27 July 1991 on Electronic Media.

170 Law of December 15, 2020 relating to space activities.

authorization is regulated. It requires that all necessary measures be taken to prevent space activities from harming the safety of people or property or the environment or causing an increased risk of international liability for the Luxembourg State. This law therefore enables the State to take action (including taking control of the space object) instead of the NSA in order to protect people, property or the environment. The law also provides for sanctions in form of a monetary fee or imprisonment up to 5 years.[171] This national regulation is comparable with the majority of domestic laws analyzed in this chapter.

However, an innovative feature of the domestic space legislation is the Luxembourgish Law on the Exploration and Use of Space Resources.[172] This law allows for certain entities – public companies limited by shares (*société anonyme*) or corporate partnerships limited by shares (*société en commandite par actions*) or private limited liability companies (*société à responsabilité limitée*) of Luxembourg law or a European Company (*société européenne*) having its registered office in Luxembourg – to be authorized to explore and use space resources for commercial purposes.[173] The authorization of exploration and use of space resources is, just like other space activities under the Luxembourgish law, subject to an annual fee, ranging from 5,000 to 500,000 euros depending on the complexity of the application and the amount of work involved in its processing.[174] The authorization may be withdrawn under similar conditions to other activities.[175] Sanctions to the breaches of this law are comparable with sanctions for other space activities.[176]

Luxembourg's space legislation contains an important novelty, which allows private entities to extract and appropriate space resources. However, this Law does not contain any provisions that would prevent space pollution by the NSAs. Given that this is one of the first laws on this matter, which may serve as a precedent for others, it is important that the environmental aspect is sufficiently addressed. On the other hand, the Law on Space Activities makes a reference to the environment, which will have to be expanded on in the future for the purpose of effectively preventing space pollution.

171 Article 14.
172 Law of 20 July 2017 on the exploration and use of space resources.
173 See Articles 2, 3 and 4.
174 Article 13.
175 Article 14.
176 Article 18.

2.1.7 Belgium

Belgium's space industry plays an important role within the European space sector, with its companies (both private and mixed public-private) having received ESA contracts in value of 746 million euro between 2015 and 2020.[177]

Belgium regulated its space activities in its national law on the Activities of Launching, Flight Operation or Guidance of Space Objects of 2005 (revised in 2013).[178] The law is applicable to the activities of NSAs when they are carrying out launches, flight operations, and the guidance of space objects or installations or property under Belgian ownership, jurisdiction or control. Article 2 further extends the applicability of the law to 'the activities [...] carried out by natural or legal persons of Belgian nationality, irrespective of the location where such activities are carried out'. Thus, the law can apply to both foreign and domestic NSAs, insofar as the former carry out activities linked to Belgium.

The law declares that '[t]he activities must be carried out in accordance with international law and, in particular, with the principles laid down in the Outer Space Treaty and the other treaties and agreements to which Belgium is a party', reaffirming the principle stated in Article III of the Outer Space Treaty. The Law also concretizes Belgium's obligation under Article VI of the Outer Space Treaty, dictating that any person wanting to carry out the activities referred to in the Law must obtain the prior authorization of the Belgian Minister.[179] Authorization is granted on a personal basis to the particular operator and is non-transferable.

Under Article 5 of the Belgian law, the Belgian king may determine further conditions for granting authorization, observing various important factors, such as 'ensuring the safety of people and property, protecting the environment, ensuring the optimal use of air space and outer space, protecting the strategic, economic and financial interests of the Belgian State, as well as in order to satisfy the Belgian State's obligations under international law'. Against this background, a Royal Decree[180] has been issued, applying further conditions to certain types of space activities. Article 7 of the Royal Decree lists all

177 BELSPO, 'The Belgian Space Industry' (available at https://www.belspo.be/belspo/space/beindu_en.stm).

178 Law of 17 September 2005 on the Activities of Launching, Flight Operation or Guidance of Space Objects (*consolidated text as revised by the Law of 1 December 2013 (B.O.J. of 15 January 2014)*).

179 Article 4.

180 Royal Decree implementing certain provisions of the Law of 17 September 2005 on the activities of launching, flight operations and guidance of space objects form the legal basis for the regulation of space activities.

the necessary information that an application of the operator must contain, including 'the study of the impact on the environment'.

According to Article 8 of the Royal Decree, the environmental impact study must include four parts. The first part consists of a description of the activity and its objectives, including a demonstration of its compatibility with the recommendations adopted by UNCOPUOS, and where applicable, any other models or technical standards identified by the Minister prior to the application for authorization. The second part concerns the potential impact of the activity on the terrestrial environment, including the atmosphere and, in particular, on the natural and human environment of the place of launching, and includes a description of the measures taken or planned to reduce or limit this impact (where these locations are not under the jurisdiction of Belgium, the applicant must attach to this part all available information or documentation relating to the environmental protection measures applicable to these locations). The third part deals with the potential impact of the activity on the outer space environment, and includes a description of the measures taken or planned to reduce or limit such impact and, where appropriate, the measures taken or planned to ensure the sustainable and rational use of the natural resources of the outer space environment. The fourth part includes a non-technical summary of the activity, a description of the expertise available to the applicant in carrying out the activities, and a descriptive summary of activities similar to that for which the application was made and in which the operator has participated in the three years preceding the application for authorization.

For the second and third parts, the activity and its environmental impacts are considered in the short, medium and long term. This activity shall be assessed from the point of view of the risks of the space object falling back to Earth and with regard to the compliance of the activities with the applicable international standards intended to limit space debris and designated as applicable by the Minister.[181] Amongst these requirements, the compatibility with the UNCOPUOS recommendations and the standards intended to limit space debris are relevant. In its Statement to UNCOPUOS, Belgium stated that neither the Law nor Decree refer specifically to standards, which leave the Minister with the possibility of imposing compliance with international technical standards, such as the IADC SDMG, UNCOPUOS SDMG, ESA and ISO norms, and may be supervised by a technical expert designated by the Minister, for

181 For details, see Article 8 of the Decree.

which purpose a specific agreement between the national authority BELSPO and ESA has been concluded.[182]

When the description of the environmental impact of the space activity reveals a substantial risk to the safety of persons, property or the environment, the applicant must attach to the impact study a description of the designed alternatives to the activity that can reasonably be considered, particularly with regard to the location, parameters or manner of carrying out the activity, and the protection of the environment.[183] The costs of these impact studies are to be borne by the operator, meaning that the NSAs must take on financial risks in order to prove that their activities will not result in uncontrollable pollution of outer space.

If the space launch or operations include the use of sources of nuclear energy, the operator shall mention this explicitly in his application for authorization, and the Minister shall only grant the authorization in that case after taking into consideration, in particular, the danger that the use of such sources of energy may represent, precautions to be taken with regard to public health and safety, protection of the environment and standards of national and international law applicable to the case in question.[184]

According to Article 10 of the Belgian Law, the Minister may also designate experts charged with controlling the activities carried out by the operator, and require that they be granted extensive access to the documents, data and premises related to the activity. The minister has far-reaching powers to take measures to ensure the environment, including by taking control of a space object and destroying it. In case the space activities are transferred to another operator, the authorization of the Minister is also required.[185] This provision is aimed at ensuring that the Belgian State keeps track of the operators and can effectively exercise its obligations under Outer Space Treaty.

The Belgian Law provides for the rules regarding the compensation for damage caused by space objects. Article 15 of the Belgian Law states: '[w]hen the Belgian State is liable, pursuant to Article VII of the Outer Space Treaty, the provisions of the Convention on International Space Liability or the provisions

182 See also Statement of Belgium to UNCOPUOS, Compendium of space debris mitigation standards adopted by States and international organizations, UN Doc. A/AC.105/C.2/2021/CRP.19 (4 June 2021). In this Statement, however, Belgium declares that it is likely that conditions imposed on an operator will refer more to all the mentioned documents, including ITU-R S.1003 and ISO 24113, with the possibility for the King to impose the same on all operators once implementation and thus revision of the legal framework truly begins.

183 Article 9 of the Decree.

184 Article 8.

185 Article 13.

of this law, for reparation, it shall have the right to institute a counterclaim against the operator(s) involved up to the amount of the compensation.' The damages between the State and the Operator[186] (NSA) are determined in one of the following two ways, depending on the type of victim:

- when the damage is caused to a third-party State or foreign nationals, the damage shall be first assessed between the Belgian State and the State representing the victim, in accordance with the Convention on International Space Liability or any other applicable clause. The operator, or the person designated by the latter for that purpose, may participate in the discussions or be a party to the damage assessment procedures between the representatives of the States involved, so as to defend his own interests; and
- when the damage is caused to Belgian nationals, the damage shall be assessed by a college of three experts, two of whom shall be designated by each of the parties and the third by mutual agreement between the parties. The Minister may make the prior designation of experts one of the conditions for granting the authorization.

The Belgian Law regulates the operator's duty to inform. The duty enshrined in Article 16 demands that the operator immediately informs the Belgian space crisis centre in case of 'any malfunctioning or any anomaly of the space object, likely to result in a danger for persons on the ground, aircraft in flight or other space objects, or to cause any damage.' Non-compliance with this duty results in the operator's obligation to guarantee the Belgian State for the total of the compensation due by it pursuant to its international liability or pursuant to the national law at hand.

The costs of all the services of technical experts, that the Minister calls upon in accordance with his legal duties and powers, are borne by the operator.[187] As penalties for breaches of its provisions. Article 19 dictates that '[a]ny person carrying out the activities referred to in article 2 without authorization, shall be liable to a period of imprisonment of between eight days and one year and a fine of between 25 and 25,000 euros, or to one of these sanctions. [...] The same

186 The Operator is now defined (in the revised text) as the person who exercises the ultimate authority over the activity (that is, the manoeuvring of the space object). In the case of non-manoeuvrable space objects, the Operator is identified by the Law as the person who orders the launch of the object according to specific parameters'; Statement of Belgium to UNCOPUOS in UNCOPUOS, Compendium of space debris mitigation standards adopted by States and international organizations, UN Doc. A/AC.105/C.2/2021/CRP.19 (4 June 2021).

187 Article 18.

sanctions [...] shall apply to anyone who, having submitted an application for authorization, communicates intentionally false or incomplete information concerning the activities in question.' This means that Belgian law in certain cases allows for a prison sentence for exercising space activities contrary to its provisions.

Belgian legislation sets out detailed regulation regarding the authorization and supervision of space activities. Environmental safety is considered as one of the considerations when granting a license. Belgium is one of the few States that explicitly demand that environmental impact assessment must be conducted and that international soft-law standards must be complied with. In terms of enforcement, Belgian law provides for the possibility of prison sentences as well as monetary fines, including for failure to take environmental precautions.

2.1.8 Finland

Finland participated in the space industry in a passive manner from the late 1950s, but has become active in space since the 1980s. It has quickly integrated itself into European space activities, particularly in relation to satellite equipment, structures and software supply chains, focusing mainly on telecommunications and Earth observation.[188] Its NSAs include ICEYE, which in 2022 interceded in the Russo-Ukrainian conflict, providing satellite imagery to Ukraine.[189]

In line with its environmental and sustainability orientation, Finland included both NSA and environmental provisions in its national space regulation. Finnish national law regulating space activities is titled the Act on Space Activities.[190] As with other laws analyzed in this section, the Act defines its scope of application, according to which the Act covers all space activities carried on within the territory of the State of Finland, on board a vessel or aircraft registered in Finland; or carried out by a Finnish citizen or a legal person incorporated in Finland. This means that the Act concerns NSAs conducting space activities on the Finnish territory, vessel or aircraft, as well as NSAs incorporated in Finland which operate anywhere around the globe.

188 Publication of the Ministry of employment and the economy, Finland's space strategy for years 2013 to 2020, p. 6.

189 ICEYE, 'ICEYE Signs Contract to Provide Government of Ukraine with Access to Its SAR Satellite Constellation' (18 August 2022) (available at https://www.iceye.com/press/press-releases/iceye-signs-contract-to-provide-government-of-ukraine-with-access-to-its-sar-satellite-constellation).

190 Act on Space Activities (63/2018).

Section 1 allows for the application of Finnish criminal law, under the conditions laid down in the Criminal Code,[191] including in relation to penalties. This means that NSAs under the jurisdiction of Finland may in certain cases be subject to its criminal law alongside with the legislation governing space activities.

Amongst the conditions for the authorization of a license to conduct space activities is the requirement that 'the operator seeks to prevent the generation of space debris and adverse environmental impacts on the earth, in the atmosphere and in outer space'.[192] This means that environmental concerns are included in the consideration whether a particular NSA shall be enabled to carry on a specific space activity. This condition is further concretized in Section 10, which includes the requirement that the operator 'assess the environmental impacts of the activities on the earth, in the atmosphere and in outer space, and present a plan for measures to counter and reduce adverse environmental impacts'. The operator must ensure that the space activities do not generate space debris, and must do so in accordance with generally accepted international guidelines. In its Statement to UNCOPUOS, Finland clarified this point by stating that recognised international guidelines are listed in a Governmental Proposal as UNCOPUOS SDMG, IADC SDMG, European Code of Conduct for Space Debris Mitigation and the ISO standards for space debris mitigation.[193] Section 10 further sets out that the operator must restrict the generation of space debris during the normal operations of the space object, reduce the risks of in-orbit break-ups and in-orbit collisions and, after the space object has completed its mission, seek to move it into a less used orbit or into the atmosphere.[194]

Section 7 of the Act regulates the issue of liability. As a general rule it sets out that '[c]ompensation for any damage caused by a space object shall be paid from State funds, with the exception of damage caused to the operator'. The State, however, 'has the right to recover the compensation paid to the injured party from the operator' to the extent that the operator would have

191 Criminal Code (39/1889).

192 Section 5.

193 See Statement of Finland to UNCOPUOS, Compendium of space debris mitigation standards adopted by States and international organizations, UN Doc. A/AC.105/C.2/2021/CRP.19 (4 June 2021).

194 Decree of the Ministry of Economic Affairs and Employment on Space Activities (74/2018) (this obligation is further concretized in the following terms: '[t]he operator shall seek to ensure that, within 25 years from the end of the functional operating period of the space object, the space object moves or is moved into the atmosphere or is moved into an orbit where it is considered not to cause any danger or harm to other space objects or other space activities.').

been liable himself for the damage done to the injured party under the Finnish Tort Liability Act.[195] The regulation of liability in the Finnish Act on Space Activities follows the model established in the Liability Convention, as it provides that 'if the damage has been caused on the earth or to aircraft in flight or its passenger or crew member, the State has the right to recover the paid compensation from the operator even if the operator had not caused the damage deliberately or negligently', meaning that in this particular case the liability is essentially absolute, mirroring the Article 2 of the Liability Convention. The State's right to recourse is, however, limited to the amount of 60 million euro, which is the amount of obligatory insurance that the operator must take,[196] unless the operator (the NSA) has violated the Act on Space Activities – in which case, there is no limit on the recourse.

After receiving authorization, operators (the NSAs) are under obligation to provide information about any changes that could affect the conditions for the authorization without delay, as well as any changes of ownership over a space object or discontinuation of space activities.[197] This means that the NSAs need to fulfill the conditions for authorization prior to the process and also after authorization is given. This obligation is further concretized by the Ministerial Decree, which calls for an annual report, provided by the operator, in which the progress of the space activities, the functionality and any failures of the space object, any warnings and risks of collision, any environmental impacts and a plan for continuing, need to be described.[198] Additionally, the respective Ministry must supervise compliance with the law, and has the right to conduct an inspection of the operators' activities and space objects, conducted by an independent expert.[199]

In summary, Finnish national legislation lays down the legal framework for state authorization and supervision of NSA space activity. The process contains an environmental component and as noted by scholars, comprehensively addresses the problem of space debris.[200] Furthermore, the Act on

195 Tort Liability Act (412/1974).

196 The Ministry of Economic Affairs may, however, determine that insurance is not obligatory if the collision-factor and the probability of space objects or parts thereof surviving re-entry are very low, thus seemingly insurance seems to be dependent on the danger of causing damage and on the factor of space debris mitigation (see Section 5 Paragraph 2).

197 Section 12.

198 See Section 8 of the Decree.

199 Section 14.

200 Jenni Tapio, 'The Finnish Space Act: En Route to Promoting Sustainable Private Activities in Outer Space' (2018) 43 *Air and Space Law* 4/5, pp. 387–409.

Space Activities explicitly allows for the application of Finnish criminal law in certain cases related to space activities.

2.1.9 Denmark

Denmark's national space institute, DTU Space, is hailed as one of the world's leading institutes in space science. It has over 50 years' experience and a number of international and national partners, including NASA, ESA and numerous NSAs.[201] While Denmark has no national space agency, its space sector participates in almost all ESA programs and utilizes EU Horizon 2020 funding scheme to advance its sector, which operates in numerous fields including suborbital flights.[202]

The main document regulating space activities in Denmark is the Danish Outer Space Act.[203] As stated in its Part 1, this Act applies to all 'space activities carried out within the Danish State'. Besides its applicability on the State's territory, the Act applies also to space activities carried out on Danish craft or facilities, or by Danish operators. Operator means a 'natural or legal person who performs, or undertakes to perform, space activities'. Regarding NSAs, this Act applies to all NSAs operating space objects and exercising essential activities related to those which are on the territory, craft or facilities of Denmark, as well as Danish NSAs operating in the described way outside of their home country.

As set out in Part 3, such activities may only be performed after obtaining prior approval from the Danish Minister for Higher Education and Science. In the application for such approval, the operator must establish *inter alia* that appropriate measures with regard to space debris management are taken and that the space activity which the application concerns is carried out in an environmentally safe manner.

Consequently, space debris management and environmental safety are explicitly listed as the conditions for granting an approval to carry out space activity. Moreover, these facets are regulated more concretely in the Executive Order[204] regarding space activities. In Part 3, the Executive order lays down

201 GlobalSecurity.org, 'Denmark in Space' (available at https://www.globalsecurity.org/space/world/denmark/index.html).

202 See, e.g., Copenhagen Suborbitals, 'About us' (available at https://copenhagensuborbitals.com/about-us/); Ministry of Higher Education and Science, 'Space and Denmark' (22 August 2023) (available at https://ufm.dk/en/research-and-innovation/space-and-denmark).

203 Outer Space Act (Act no. 409 of 11 May 2016).

204 Executive Order No. 552 (31 May 2016) also known as the Executive Order on requirements in connection with approval of activities in outer space, etc.

a general rule regarding space debris, which dictates that 'within 25 years of the end date of the functional operating period of the space object, the space object must either safely leave its earth orbit again or safely be placed into an orbit where it is deemed not to constitute a danger to other space activities.' The Order explicitly refers to ISO and ECSS, and also leaves it open that other international guidelines, for example ITU Recommendation ITU-R S.1003, may be taken into consideration, even if this is not explicitly referenced.[205] From the requirements listed above, it can be concluded that both the Earth environment as well as the environment of outer space, must be considered when authorizing NSA space activity.

Part 6 of the Danish Outer Space Act regulates liability and insurance. Under the law, the operator is 'obliged to compensate for any damage caused by a space object to persons or property on Earth as well as damage to aircraft in flight'. For other damage caused by a space object, the operator is liable under the general rules of Danish law on compensation. NSAs may, therefore, be held liable for damages caused by the space object they are operating. In cases when the Danish State has paid compensation for damage caused by a space object operated by the NSA, the State may make claims against the operator of the space object to the extent that the operator is liable. The operator's liability can, however, be limited in cases when the claimant of the damage contributed to the damaging event, either by intent or gross negligence. The executive order placed a limitation on the operators' liability at 450 million Danish Kroner (approximately 60 million euros), but has provided also for exceptions in which this limitation does not apply.

Insurance or other security to cover liability for damage caused by a space object is not obligatory under Danish law. Instead, the law provides in Part 6 that the Minister may impose the obligation to take out insurance on the operator as a condition for granting approval to conduct space activity. Insurance by the NSAs is thus a possibility, but not a necessity in all cases.

The transfer of space objects or space activities to another owner or operator may, as regulated in Part 7, only take place after prior approval from the Minister. A transfer to another owner or operator domiciled in another State may demand additional requirements for an advance agreement with said State to take over the liability to pay damages. This means that if an NSA sells a space object to an NSA from another State, the question of liability would need to be addressed between the two States.

205 Statement of Denmark to UNCOPUOS, Compendium of space debris mitigation standards adopted by States and international organizations, UN Doc. A/AC.105/C.2/2021/CRP.19 (4 June 2021).

Part 9 of the Act regulates penalties for violations of legal rules, enshrined in other parts of the law. Several violations of the provisions of the Act, listed explicitly in Part 9, 'carry a fine or a term of imprisonment of up to four months, unless a higher penalty is incurred under other legislation'. Furthermore, for intentional violations under particularly aggravating circumstances, 'the penalty may be increased to imprisonment of up to two years'. Regarding aggravating circumstances, it provides that they 'include, in particular, situations in which persons are exposed to risk of death or injury, or when the violations are of a more systematic nature'. The most important provision regarding acts of NSAs included in the Part 9 of the Act, however, is the last paragraph, stating that the '[c]ompanies, etc. (legal persons) may incur criminal liability according to the regulations in Chapter 5 of the Criminal Code.'

In summary, Denmark's laws regulate NSA activity and explicitly make a reference to environmental protection as a criterion in the authorization and supervision process, and imposes criminal liability on corporations in connection with space misconduct. In this way, they make sure that environmental concerns play a role in decision-making regarding NSA space activities.

2.1.10 Italy

Italy, despite being one of the oldest space-faring nations, has not enacted laws that specifically address the space environment or NSA licensing procedures.[206] Its instruments contain the obligation to register any object launched by natural and legal persons of Italian nationality or commissioned by them, launches from any base located on national territory or under Italian control by natural or legal persons of any nationality, as well as the obligation to inform the Italian Space Agency of any abandonment of such objects in Earth's orbit.[207] All of the preceding, as well as the information which must be notified to the Italian Space Agency to be recorded in the National Register, is in accordance with the Registration Convention, to which Italy has acceded in the relevant national act. This, however, does not amount to comprehensive national mechanisms on space pollution and NSA activity. Instead, those facets

206 Italy has enacted Law Decree No. 128, 4 June 2003, Reorganization of the Italian Space Agency (A.S.I.) and Law No. 7, 11 January 2018 on Measures for the coordination of space and aerospace policy and provisions concerning the organization and operation of the Italian Space Agency (18G00025) (Official Gazette, General Series, No. 34, 10 February 2018).

207 Law of the 12 July 2005, n. 153 Accession of the Italian Republic to the Convention on the registration of objects launched into outer space, made in New York on 14 January 1975 and its execution. (GU General Series n.177 of 01-08-2005).

are currently limited to the mandatory standards provisions of the Italian Space Agency (ASI), which is tasked with defining, operating and managing the Italian space program, international and European (ESA) cooperation, and through which Italy applies the European Code of Conduct for Space Debris Mitigation. In this way, Italy adheres to international standards on debris mitigation, such as the ITU and ISO standards as well as the IADC SDMG.[208]

2.1.11 The Netherlands

The Netherlands is primarily focused on European cooperation with ESA and EUMETSAT.[209] The Dutch space sector, one of the country's top economic sectors, includes approximately 250 entities, such as corporations and knowledge institutions, that engage in designing and building components for rockets and satellites,[210] as well as several businesses that are developing services on the basis of processing satellite data.[211]

National legislation in the Netherlands consists of several documents. First amongst them is the Space Activities Act.[212] Under Section 2, this Act applies to space activities that are performed in or from within the Netherlands or else on or from a Dutch ship or Dutch aircraft, and it can be also declared wholly or partly applicable to designated space activities that are performed by a Dutch natural or juridical person or by any other natural or juridical person acting from within the Netherlands. This means that the Act concerns NSAs performing their activities in the Netherlands, as well as Dutch NSAs performing their activities abroad.

Section 3 prohibits operators performing space activities without a license issued for this purpose by the Minister, and provides for the possibility of

208 See Statement of Italy in UNCOPUOS, Compendium of space debris mitigation standards adopted by States and international organizations, UN Doc. A/AC.105/C.2/2021/CRP.19 (4 June 2021).

209 Statement of the Netherlands in UNCOPUOS, Compendium of space debris mitigation standards adopted by States and international organizations, UN Doc. A/AC.105/C.2/2021/CRP.19 (4 June 2021).

210 Government of the Netherlands, 'Space research generates new technologies' (available at https://www.government.nl/topics/space/space-research-generates-new-technologies#:~:text=The%20Dutch%20space%20sector%20is,services%20based%20on%20satellite%20data).

211 Government of the Netherlands, 'Space Research Generates New Technologies' (available at https://www.government.nl/topics/space/space-research-generates-new-technologies#:~:text=The%20Dutch%20space%20sector%20is,services%20based%20on%20satellite%20data).

212 Rules Concerning Space Activities and the Establishment of a Registry of Space Objects (Space Activities Act), in force since 1 January 2008.

attaching regulations and restrictions to such licenses. Amongst the purposes, the protection of the space environment is explicitly mentioned. The issuance of a license is conditional on the fact that the prospective holder has and maintains what the Minister considers to be the maximum possible cover for the liability arising from the space activities for which a license is requested.

A license may be refused for several reasons, including a situation where in the Minister's view 'facts or circumstances suggest that the safety of persons and goods, environmental protection in outer space, the maintenance of public order or national security might be jeopardized by issuing the license'.[213] In that case, before the license is revoked, the Minister must take all the steps necessary to ensure the safety of persons and goods, environmental protection in outer space, the maintenance of public order or national security, and must provide the necessary instructions to the party whose license will be revoked, which is then obliged to follow the instructions.

Section 10 places an obligation upon the holder of the license when an incident occurs that may jeopardize the safety of persons and goods, or threaten the outer space environment or the maintenance of public order or national security, or otherwise cause damage. The operator must 'without delay, take the steps that can reasonably be expected of it to prevent the consequences of that event or, where those consequences cannot be prevented, to limit and rectify them as far as possible'.

Section 12 regulates the State's right to redress, in case it is obliged to pay compensation for damage under Article VII of the Outer Space Treaty or the Liability Convention, vis-à-vis the NSA whose activity caused such damage. The violations of the Act can result in administrative penalties.[214]

In summary, the Dutch national legislation regulates in a relatively detailed way the process of authorization and supervision of space activities. It makes an important reference to the protection of the environment in outer space. Whilst it does not explicitly mention the environment on Earth, that can be read into other conditions for license, such as public order or safety of property and people, or from other national and international regulation. Most importantly, however, the Unguided Satellites Decree represents an important novelty amongst national space legislation. Namely, it extends the obligation to obtain a license also to the controlling of unguided objects in outer space.[215]

---

213 Sections 6 and 7.

214 Sections 13–23.

215 Decree of 19 January 2015 expanding the scope of the Space Activities Act to include the control of unguided satellites (Unguided Satellites Decree). See also Tanja Masson-Zwaan, 'Registration of Small Satellites and the Case of the Netherlands', in *Small Satellites – Regulatory Challenges and Chances* (Brill, 2016), pp. 187–193.

2.1.12 Norway

Norway is another of the older space-active States, having celebrated 50 years of space activity in 2012, with the first rocket having launched in 1962 from the Andøya launching facility.[216] In 2023, it inaugurated a new spaceport in northern Andøya.[217] The northern islands of Svalbard host Galileo's largest ground segment, relaying commands to Europe's global navigational service. These islands act as a Mars-simulation ground and are overall geographically suitable for space activity.[218] In Norway, the private space industry has flourished, with Ariane rockets relying on Norwegian-made parts, and Norwegian electronics used in telecommunication satellites, and components and experiments for the International Space Station designed and created in Norway.[219]

Norwegian legislation on space activities is enshrined in the Launching Act.[220] As noted by Frans von der Dunk, this Act is the first example of national legislation on space activities and has been in force since before Liability Convention and the Registration Convention were adopted.[221] The text of the Act, however, is short. Article 1 enshrines the obligation to obtain permission before launching an object. In particular, it is stated that it is forbidden to launch any object into outer space without a license, from 'a) Norwegian territory, also including Svalbard, Jan Mayen and the Norwegian external territories; b) Norwegian vessels, aircrafts and suchlike; c) [a]reas that are not subject to the sovereignty of any state, when the launching is undertaken by a Norwegian citizen or person with habitual residence in Norway.'

Article 1 does not explicitly cover legal persons. However, it is significant that it prohibits the launch of space objects from areas outside the jurisdiction of any State, if conducted by Norwegian subjects. Nonetheless, the limited

216 ESA, *50 years of space activity for Norway* (available at https://www.esa.int/About_Us/ESA_history/50_years_of_space_for_Norway); Pål Brekke, *»Norwegian Space Activities – Arctic Access to Space«* (2015) 2(2) Journal of Space Safety Engineering, pp. 91–97.

217 See Andrew Jones, 'Norway opens Andøya spaceport' *Spacenews* (available at https://spacenews.com/norway-opens-andoya-spaceport/).

218 ESA, *50 years of space activity for Norway*, available at https://www.esa.int/About_Us/ESA_history/50_years_of_space_for_Norway.

219 ESA, *50 years of space activity for Norway*, available at https://www.esa.int/About_Us/ESA_history/50_years_of_space_for_Norway.

220 Act on launching objects from Norwegian territory etc. into outer space, 13 June. No. 38. 1969.

221 Frans von der Dunk & Atle Nikolaisen, 'Vikings First in National Space Law: Other Europeans to Follow the Continuing Story of National Implementation of International Responsibility and Liability' (2001) *Proceedings of the Forty-Fourth Colloquium on the Law of Outer Space* 111–122, p. 114.

scope of the Norwegian legislation is notable given its long history of activity in space.

2.1.13 Portugal

The Portuguese space industry consists of several start-ups as well as large space companies, which are connected internationally with other companies abroad.[222] Its core space legislation consists of a Decree-Law[223] and a Regulation,[224] both adopted in 2019.

The Decree-Law defines its scope of application in Article 2, declaring that it applies to 'space activities (space operations or launch centre operations) carried out on national territory, including sea space and airspace under Portuguese sovereignty or jurisdiction, on-board Portuguese vessels and aircraft or from facilities under Portuguese jurisdiction or sovereignty, regardless of the operator's nationality; or carried out outside the national territory by Portuguese operators or operators established on national territory'. This means that it concerns both Portuguese NSAs as well as all other NSAs operating under Portuguese jurisdiction.

Article 4 of the Decree-Law demands that space activities are subject to a license and registration. There are two types of licenses that can be obtained from the Space Authority, namely, a 'Unitary license', that applies to each type of space operation and is granted to the respective operator, and the so-called 'Global license', that applies to a number of space operations of the same type and is granted to the respective operator.[225] The Decree-Law lists the conditions for granting a license in its Article 7. This places considerable emphasis on environmental factors and so are set out in full hereunder:

a) The applicant has technical, economic and financial capacity for space operations intended to be carried out;
b) The space operation provides appropriate safeguards against damage to the Earth's surface, airspace and outer space, according to applicable national and international obligations;

---

222 Portugal Space, 'Space Catalogue: Industry' (available at https://www.newspaceportugal.org/en).

223 Decree-Law no. 16/2019, of 22 January, Legal regime of access to and exercise of space activities.

224 Regulation no. 697/2019, of 5 September, regulation on access to and exercise of space activities.

225 Article 6.

c) The space operation guarantees the minimization of space debris, to the greatest possible extent, according to international principles and obligations;
d) The space operation is compatible with applicable public security standards, including those relating to public health and physical security of citizens;
e) The space operation does not jeopardize internal security and the strategic interests of the Portuguese Republic, nor does it violate international obligations upon it;
f) All other authorizations and certificates required for the purpose of the space operation have been issued by the respective competent bodies;
g) The applicant has the compulsory civil insurance as required under article 19.

Additional conditions other than those already provided in the Decree-Law may be imposed, including in relation to environmental protection. The operator must expressly agree to these conditions, but without them the license shall not be granted.[226] According to Article 9, the license holder has a right to carry out the corresponding space operations, subject to several duties including compliance with space exploitation principles contained in the space treaties that Portugal has ratified. These include the minimization of space debris and predicting and duly safeguarding against any damage to Earth and the outer space, either directly or indirectly, in accordance with applicable national and international obligations. In this way, Portugal has transposed its international space obligations into national legislation.

Liability is regulated under Article 18, which provides that '[w]ithout prejudice to other legally applicable liability regimes, operators shall be liable for damage caused in the exercise of the space activity'. Types of liability are regulated in accordance with the Liability Convention; objective liability is foreseen for damage caused by the space operation on the Earth's surface or to aircraft in flight; whereas fault liability is foreseen for damage occurring anywhere else. The Portuguese State has the right of recourse against the operator responsible for that space object, up to the limits provided by subsequent legislation. However, in case of fault liability, the limit does not apply. Complementing that liability regime, Article 19 demands that operators take compulsory insurance for liability cases.

Reporting requirements are set out in Article 20, whereby operators have a duty to 'report to the Space Authority within 24 hours of becoming aware of

226 Article 7.

an incident involving their launch or space operations, from which a serious incident or accident may arise'. NSAs are thus obliged to share the potential risks with the Space Authority, which is the body tasked with the supervision of space activities. Sanctions for violations of its provisions include monetary fines for administrative offences,[227] or additional penalties in the form of suspension or prohibition to develop space activities.[228]

The Portuguese Regulation places additional obligations on the operator, including in relation to environmental protection, such as providing 'safeguards against damage to the earth's surface, airspace and outer space'.[229] The operator must also submit a plan regarding mitigation of space debris, which may, but does not have to, 'include measures to be implemented to international best practices and principles, especially those provided for in the ISO 24113:2011 standard (Space systems – Space debris mitigation requirements), in the 2007 'IADC Space Debris Mitigation Guidelines', and in the UNCOPUOS SDMG, laid down in UN General Assembly Resolution 62/217, of 22 December 2007.[230]

In summary, the Portuguese legislation requires the State to authorize and supervise NSA space activities. NSA operators are given considerable duties, and must adhere to several safeguards in place to ensure the environmental aspect is taken into account. There is also an explicit reference to several international space debris mitigation instruments, albeit as a voluntary matter.

2.1.14 Sweden

Sweden began development of its space activities in earnest in the 1970s, with the launch of the research satellite Viking and telecom satellite Tele-X.[231] Currently, Sweden is one of the rising space actors, having established its own commercial spaceport,[232] which will likely also be used by the German launcher startup Isar Aerospace Technologies.[233]

227 Article 24.

228 Article 25.

229 Article 15 of the Regulation.

230 Article 14 of the Regulation.

231 ESA (Nina Wormbs and Gustav Källstrand), A Short History of Swedish Space Activities (December 2007) (available at https://www.esa.int/esapub/hsr/HSR_39.pdf).

232 Thomas Erdbrink, Christina Anderson, 'In Sweden's Far North, a Space Complex Takes Shape', *New York Times* (23 May 2021) (available at https://www.nytimes.com/2021/05/23/world/europe/sweden-space-arctic-satellites.html).

233 See Isar Aerospace, 'Isar Aerospace participates in inauguration of new Spaceport Esrange in Sweden' (13 January 2023) (available at https://www.isaraerospace.com/press/isar-aerospace-participates-in-inauguration-of-new-spaceport-esrange-in-sweden).

The Swedish Act on Space Activities[234] is relatively short. Section 1 defines the term 'space activities' broadly, stating that in addition to activities carried out entirely in outer space, the term also encompasses launching of objects into outer space and all measures to maneuver or affect objects launched into outer space.

Section 2 imposes the obligation to obtain a license before carrying out space activities on Swedish territory or by Swedish natural or legal persons. This means that the Act applies to the NSAs operating in, or being incorporated in, Sweden. Section 3 provides that a license to carry on space activities may be granted by the Swedish government, subject to certain conditions.[235] In terms of liability, Section 6 of the Act allows the Swedish State to demand reimbursement for liability paid for damage that has resulted from space activities carried out by subjects other than the State, including NSAs.

On this basis, Swedish space legislation is relatively limited in detail, but does impose requirements for NSAs to obtain licenses to engage in space activities.

2.1.15 United Kingdom

The United Kingdom is one of the most active space States, with an estimated 400 or more active satellites. In recent years, heightened government investment into space research and development has resulted in the development of the United Kingdom's space infrastructure and rise in its global competitiveness.[236] The United Kingdom has also centralized oversight of its space strategy and used the UK Space Agency as a central point to coordinate with other public and private bodies. A number of launch sites (currently evaluated at seven) have been opened or are in the process of opening,[237] with some launch sites composed of various launch locations.[238]

The private space sector has grown exponentially in recent years. Influential NSAs operating in the United Kingdom include Skyrora or Surrey Satellite

234 Act on Space Activities (1982:963).

235 Decree on Space Activities (1982:1069).

236 Skyrora, 'Trends in the UK Space Industry' (available at https://www.skyrora.com/trends-in-the-uk-space-industry/).

237 Launch UK, 'A guide to UK spaceports' (available at https://assets.publishing.service.gov.uk/government/uploads/system/uploads/attachment_data/file/1151003/Spaceport_brochure_17.4.23.pdf); Orbital Today, 'The Magnificent Seven' (5. August 2021) (available at https://orbitaltoday.com/2021/08/05/the-magnificent-seven-the-main-uk-rocket-launch-sites-their-benefits/).

238 See, e.g. Orbex, 'Launch Services' (available at https://orbex.space/launch-services/launch-site).

Technology. Airbus has a large OneWeb constellation consisting of over 500 satellites.[239] Lockheed Martin, a large US NSA, maintains subsidiaries in the United Kingdom.[240] One of the most successful providers of suborbital flight activity, including private suborbital tourism, Virgin Galactic, though headquartered in the United States, is owned by its founder's – British citizen Richard Branson's – Virgin Group, headquartered in London. Moreover, the UK Space Agency is cooperating with NSAs, highlighted by the recent deal with Axiom Space, the leading company in offering orbital space tourism to the International Space Station.[241] These activities in turn have produced a chain of services, including private law firms offering legal advice to space companies.[242]

The United Kingdom regulates space activities in the Outer Space Act of 1968.[243] It applies to launching or procuring a launch of a space object, operating a space object, and any other activity in outer space carried out in the United Kingdom, or elsewhere by British citizens,[244] British Dependent Territories citizens, British Nationals (Overseas), or British Overseas citizens. Citizens include natural and legal persons, thus also covering NSAs.[245]

Environmental concern is not mentioned as a mandatory condition for granting an operator's license.[246] However, the Secretary of may impose conditions, including *inter alia* a condition 'requiring the licensee to conduct his operations in such a way as to – (i) prevent the contamination of outer space or adverse changes in the environment of the earth, (ii) avoid interference with the activities of others in the peaceful exploration and use of outer space'.[247] Consequently, the UK legislation covers NSAs, but the environment

239 Airbus, 'Constellations' (available at https://www.airbus.com/en/space/telecom/constellations).

240 Ria Urban, 'The 20 Most Important UK Space Companies' *Space Impulse* (24 April 2023) (available at https://spaceimpulse.com/2023/04/24/the-20-most-important-uk-space-companies/).

241 Andrew Jones, 'UK Space Agency signs deal with Axiom Space for human spaceflight mission' (27 October 2023) (available at https://www.space.com/uk-space-agency-axiom-human-spaceflight-mission).

242 See, e.g., the services offered by the following law firms: Burges Salmon, Alden Legal, Clyde and Co, London Institute of Space Policy and Law, Bird and Bird, Linklaters, Norton Rose Fullbright, Brodies, Hogan Lovells, Dentons, Harper MacLeod, Taylor Wessing, KandL Gates, Mayer Brown.

243 UK Outer Space Act of 1968 (c. 38).

244 Outer Space Act of 1968, Article 1.

245 Article 2.

246 Outer Space Act of 1968, Article 4.

247 Article 5.

is only a discretionary rather than a mandatory consideration for issuing and upholding a license. According, however, to the UK statement to UNCOPUOS, in performing license application analysis, international standards such as the UNCOPUOS SDMG, the IADC SDMG, ITU Recommendation ITU-R S.1003 and ISO Standards (24113) are regularly evaluated.[248]

Of particular significance to the activities carried out by NSAs is the United Kingdom's 2018 Space Industry Act.[249] This Act aims to regulate space activities, sub-orbital activities, and associated activities, defining space activities as 'launching or procuring the launch or the return to earth of a space object or of an aircraft carrying a space object, [...] operating a space object, [...] or any activity in outer space' (see Article 1).

Article 2 of the Act dictates that the regulator must exercise its functions primarily with a view to securing public safety and secondarily in accordance with several conditions, including 'any environmental objectives set by the Secretary of State', 'any international obligations of the United Kingdom' and 'any space debris mitigation guidelines issued by an international organisation in which the government of the United Kingdom is represented'. The later provision constitutes a transposition of international guidelines for space debris mitigation into United Kingdom's national legislation.

Article 3 of the Act prohibits carrying out spaceflight activities in the United Kingdom, or operating a spaceport in the United Kingdom, without first obtaining a license in accordance with this Act, listing such actions (as well as making any false statements in order to obtain a license) as an offence. The Act provides several conditions for granting a license. Among them, it sets out obligations to carry out a risk assessment (see Article 9) and an assessment of the environmental effects (see Article 11). With this provision, the United Kingdom seeks to ensure that NSAs conduct environmental impact assessments prior to launching a space object or operating a spaceport.

The Space Industry Act includes regulations on the issues of liability, indemnities and insurance. The regulation of liability differs from the one set out in the 1968 Outer Space Act. According to Article 34 of the Space Industry Act, in cases when 'injury or damage is caused to persons or property on land or water in the United Kingdom or in the territorial sea adjacent to the United Kingdom, or to aircraft in flight over any such land, water or sea, or to persons or property on board any such aircraft [...] (a) by any craft or space object being used by a

---

248 Statement of United Kingdom to UNCOPUOS in: UNCOPUOS, Compendium of space debris mitigation standards adopted by States and international organizations, UN Doc. A/AC.105/C.2/2021/CRP.19 (4 June 2021).

249 UK Space Industry Act of 2018 (c. 5).

person ("the operator") for spaceflight activities, (b) by anything falling from such a craft or object, or (c) by any person in such a craft, damages in respect of the injury or damage are recoverable without proof of negligence or intention or other cause of action, as if the injury or damage had been caused by the wilful act, neglect, or default of the operator'. This does not apply to (a) injury or damage sustained by an individual of a prescribed description taking part in, or otherwise engaged in connection with, the spaceflight activities or (b) injury or damage caused or contributed to by the negligence of the person by whom it is sustained. This means that Article 34 contemplates damage to the general public in the United Kingdom and imposes absolute liability. However, damages to the general public outside of the United Kingdom are not covered by this provision. Article 34 of the Act provides some limitations on such liability, for example in cases when injury or damage caused or contributed is caused by the negligence of the person by whom it is sustained.

Both the Outer Space Act and the Space Industry Act take into account provisions of Liability Convention and establish that the operator must indemnify the State for the liability it would be required to pay under this Convention. Similarly, both Acts regulate the obligatory insurance which must be taken by the operator for such cases. In Articles 51 to 59, the 2018 Space Industry Act provides for both criminal and civil sanctions for breaches of its provisions.

The 2018 Space Industry Act is an important addition to UK space legislation, introducing a detailed regulatory framework for licensing procedure. It limits the application of the Outer Space Act, as the latter is now only valid for the space activities carried out by UK entities acting outside the United Kingdom. It highlights environmental concerns, among which the most relevant are the requirements for risk and environmental effects assessments and the adherence to international guidelines on space debris mitigation. It is important to note that the Space Industry Act includes sub-orbital activities, which are most often operated by NSAs, such as those associated with space tourism, which has been criticized for its disproportionate negative environmental effects.[250]

In conclusion, the United Kingdom has enacted one of the earliest pieces of national space legislation, with the view of regulating private, particularly commercial, space activity. The Act leaves wide discretion to the Secretary of State, responsible for authorizing and supervising private space activity, with the authority to revoke or modify the authorization. Environmental provisions, including space debris provisions, are not specifically referenced. However,

250 See, for example, examples of space tourism described in Chapter 4, Section 1.

the language permits their indirect inclusion, particularly by referencing the United Kingdom's international obligations, albeit in a discretionary way, and according to the United Kingdom international standards are regularly evaluated during licensing processes.

2.1.16 Greece

Though it is not a major space nation, Greece's regulatory framework merits a mention. In 2017, Greece adopted its Law on Authorization of space activities, – the Registration in the National Register of Space Objects – Establishment of a Greek Space Organization and other provisions, which was amended in 2020.[251] It established the Greek space agency and national space object registry, and elucidated necessary conditions that must be fulfilled for space activities carried out from Greek territory by natural or legal persons (Greek or other nationality) or abroad, in cases where if Greek infrastructure (facility) is used, and for activities carried out under Greek jurisdiction or performed by Greek nationals or legal entities based in Greece (if provided for in international agreements). The conditions furthermore include proof of adequate provision for mitigation and management of space waste, in line with international practices and technological developments, and of non-contamination (including adverse changes) of the space environment or celestial bodies. Additionally, reports on the impact of space objects on the environment are required before and post launch, and at the end of an object's operational life.[252]

A further technical standard is expected to be adopted at national level (the Joint Ministerial Decision on the definition of the content of environmental impact reporting by space activities). Currently however Greece as a participant in ESA maintains that its law implements existing national, European and international standards and good practices, and moreover enables the Minister of Digital Governance to request technical assistance from third parties (national, European or international) to determine conditions (for example of location or insurance).[253] In sum, the reference to mitigating space waste broadly supports the prohibition of excessive harm to the space environment.

251 Law 4508/2017 (22 December 2017), on 'Authorization of space activities, Registration in the National Register of Space Objects- Establishment of a Greek Space Organization and other provisions' (amended by Law 4712/2020/146/A'/29-07-2020) (29. July 2020).

252 Statement of Greece in UNCOPUOS, Compendium of space debris mitigation standards adopted by States and international organizations, UN Doc. A/AC.105/C.2/2021/CRP.19 (4 June 2021).

253 Statement of Greece in UNCOPUOS, Compendium of space debris mitigation standards adopted by States and international organizations, UN Doc. A/AC.105/C.2/2021/CRP.19 (4 June 2021).

3 North American States

3.1 *United States of America*

The United States is one of two oldest space powers, along with the former Soviet Union. Today, it is the undisputed forerunner in space activity, with over half of the satellites in orbit registered to it, and a majority of the commercial space NSAs incorporated in it. Among them are some of the world's most powerful NSAs, including SpaceX with the largest number of NSA satellites in orbit and many government contracts in place.[254] Correspondingly, its national space legislation is among the most detailed and extensive national regulations worldwide, and its private space sector the most active, with numerous well publicized cases.

The US national framework features numerous acts regulating all aspects of space activity.[255] Title 51 of the United States Code (USC) dictates, *inter alia*, the United States' space goals, which include the promotion of private industry, ensuring US space leadership, and creating a safe, stable, secure, and sustainable environment for space activities, which it explains as including the promotion of responsible behaviour and measures to mitigate orbital debris.[256] The Act goes on to specify several environmental provisions, targeting the space environment protection, and commercial space activity, namely commercial space guidelines, including licensing and monitoring activity.[257]

Regarding environmental protection, Title 51 decrees that the United States 'shall', for the preservation of the space environment, promote, pursue and develop space debris mitigation measures (including mandating compliance with the US Government Orbital Debris Mitigation Standard Practices), space debris remediation (active debris removal), and space traffic management efforts, for which it will share and maintain space situational awareness

---

254 See, e.g., Michael O'Shea, 'The Wild, Wild West of Space Law' *The Walrus* (4 April 2023) (available at https://thewalrus.ca/space-the-wild-wild-west-of-space-law/).

255 The following is not a detailed analysis of the American space regulation, but provides an overview of the licensing regimes that affect the majority commercial actors in the United States and whether these contain provisions on environmental protection. For more information on space debris mitigation practices of the United States see Carns (2023); For a further analysis of US national space law and licensing systems see Milton Smith, 'United States' in Joanne Wheeler (ed.), *The Space Law Review* (Law Business Research Ltd., 2019), pp. 100–115; Statement of the USA to UNCOPUOS, Compendium of space debris mitigation standards adopted by States and international organizations, UN Doc. A/AC.105/C.2/2021/CRP.19 (4 June 2021).

256 United States Code (USC), Title 51, Section 3.

257 USC Title 51, 50905; USC Title 51, 50907.

data.[258] The United States is required to 'continue leading the development and adoption of international and industry standards and policies, such as the Guidelines for the Long-term Sustainability of Outer Space Activities and the Space Debris Mitigation Guidelines of the United Nations Committee on the Peaceful Uses of Outer Space.'[259] The US Government's Orbital Debris Mitigation Standard Practices are said to have served as a primary source for the development of the UNCOPUOS SDMG.[260] These activities are reconfirmed in the U.S. Commercial Space Launch Competitiveness Act 2015,[261] which sets out new requirements for assessments and studies to keep US space assets safe and the United States at the forefront of the international space scene.[262]

Title 51 establishes commercial space guidelines,[263] decreeing that activities by private sector enterprises must be encouraged and developed in harmony with governmental activities, while also being protected from predatory foreign investments, in order to promote innovation and global competitiveness and foster development of space collision warning measures.[264] NSAs are included in the US vision for civil space guidelines, including the push for the Moon and Mars, as private industry is believed to be conducive to US competitiveness and space dominance, and is therefore included in the national security guidelines as well as an integral part of US space security.[265]

NSA space activities are again addressed in the US Commercial Space Launch Competitiveness Act 2015,[266] which grants to US citizens the right to appropriate space resources, including water and minerals, with asteroid resources given special attention.[267] The right of private citizens to exploit space

258 USC Title 51, Section 4(3)(a) decrees: *3. Preserving the Space Environment to Enhance the Long-term Sustainability of Space Activities.*

259 USC Title 51, Section 4(3)(a) decrees: *3. Preserving the Space Environment to Enhance the Long-term Sustainability of Space Activities.*

260 Statement of the USA to UNCOPUOS, Compendium of space debris mitigation standards adopted by States and international organizations, UN Doc. A/AC.105/C.2/2021/CRP.19 (4 June 2021).

261 U.S. Commercial Space Launch Competitiveness Act 2015 (Public Law No. 114–90).

262 U.S. Commercial Space Launch Competitiveness Act 2015 (Public Law No. 114–90), Section 108.

263 USC Title 51, Section 5(1).

264 USC Title 51, Section 5(1).

265 USC Title 51, Section 5(2), 5(3).

266 U.S. Commercial Space Launch Competitiveness Act 2015 (Public Law No. 114–90).

267 U.S. Commercial Space Launch Competitiveness Act 2015 (Public Law No. 114–90), Chapter 513; 51 USC 51301. See also U.S. Commercial Space Launch Competitiveness Act 2015 (Public Law No. 114–90), Section 51303 (Asteroid resource and space resource rights) ('A United States citizen engaged in commercial recovery of an asteroid resource or a space resource under this chapter shall be entitled to any asteroid resource or space

resources accords with the Artemis Accords. However, it appears to clash with the Moon Agreement's obligation not to engage in national appropriation of materials on celestial bodies, as discussed herein.[268] This raises the question of how and to what degree NSA activity in the United States will take into account environmental protection of extraction sites on celestial bodies, as well as contamination protection measures on celestial bodies, aboard spacecraft or upon return to Earth, bearing in mind the current lack of international as well as national legislation on the matter.[269] The inclusion of the reference to an appropriate national framework, as well as international obligations, including supervision and authorization, could act as vehicles to apply environmental protection from other national or international legislation. However, how this particular issue will be tackled in practice remains to be seen.

On the issue of mining space resources, existing NSAs have already proposed asteroid or lunar mining. This attitude is apparent in the United States, as well as in a range of countries from the United Kingdom, to Luxembourg, to Japan.[270] While two of the earliest companies, DeepSpace Industries and Planetary Resources have been acquired by other NSAs and repurposed due to cash-flow issues in 2019 and 2020 respectively, numerous new NSAs have nonetheless drawn life and continue the quest for space mining (for example, AstroForge and TransAstra).[271] This has prompted new movements within the United Nations, namely the establishment of the Working Group on Legal Aspects of Space Resource Activities, to examine and propose an international legal framework for space resource activities.[272]

Returning to the authorization and monitoring of all US NSA space activities involving satellites, two agencies appear to be of central interest; the Federal Aviation Administration (FAA), responsible for licensing launch and re-entry

resource obtained, including to possess, own, transport, use, and sell the asteroid resource or space resource obtained in accordance with applicable law, including the international obligations of the United States.').

268 See Chapter 1, Section 3.

269 See, e.g., Hobe (2019); Fabio Tronchetti, *The Exploitation of Natural Resources of the Moon and Other Celestial Bodies* (Koninklijke Brill, 2009).

270 Mordor Intelligence, 'Space Mining Market Size and Share Analysis – Growth Trends and Forecasts (2023 – 2028)' (available at https://www.mordorintelligence.com/industry-reports/space-mining-market-industry).

271 Magdalena Petrova, 'The first crop of space mining companies didn't work out, but a new generation is trying again' (9 October 2022) (available at https://www.cnbc.com/2022/10/09/space-mining-business-still-highly-speculative.html).

272 UNOOSA, 'Working Group on Legal Aspects of Space Resource Activities' (available at https://www.unoosa.org/oosa/en/ourwork/copuos/lsc/space-resources/index.html).

activities, and the Federal Communications Commission (FCC) responsible for licensing and regulating radio signals (frequencies and attendant orbits).[273]

There is also the National Environmental Satellite Data, and Information Service (NOAA), acting under supervision of the Secretary of Commerce, which is responsible for licensing of exclusively remote sensing systems.[274] These agencies have enacted detailed regulation pertaining to NSAs operating from US territory or otherwise subject to US jurisdiction as will be discussed below, beginning with a general environmental overview. As federal agencies, they are required to act in accordance with the National Environmental Policy Act (NEPA) of 1969,[275] thus private activities under their purview that require federal license must also satisfy the NEPA requirements.[276]

The NEPA has been adopted with a view of encouraging harmony between humans and the natural environment and to promote efforts for the prevention of damage to the environment and biosphere, and to stimulate human health

273 Other agencies and departments could be relevant. For example, any NSA working with NASA is obliged to follow regulations binding NASA (including National Aeronautics and Space Act, Title 51 USC Section 10101, NASA Procedural Requirements for Limiting Orbital Debris (NPR 8715.6A (2007) revised 2009), NASA Process for Limiting Orbital Debris (NS 8719.14A (2007) revised 2011)). NSAs working for the Department of Defense are required to apply Title 10 USC, DoD Directive 3100.10 (Space Policy of 2012), DoD Instruction 3100.12 (Space Support of 2000). Any NSA working for the National Oceanic and Atmospheric Administration Authority is bound by USC Title 51 Section 60122, CFR Title 15 Part 960, and for NOAA Satellites per national Environmental Satellite, Data, and Information Service Policy NQP-0304 as well as NASA policy and best practices. See, e.g., Statement of the USA to UNCOPUOS, Compendium of space debris mitigation standards adopted by States and international organizations, UN Doc. A/AC.105/C.2/2021/CRP.19 (4 June 2021). However, this does not cover every single piece of legislation potentially relevant to commercial NSA space activity in the USA. See also Frans von der Dunk, 'From Space Tourists to Unruly Passengers? The US Struggle with 'On-Orbit' Jurisdiction', in *Proceedings of the International Institute of Space Law 2014* (Institute of International Space Law, 2015b), pp. 391–405; Frans von der Dunk, 'Effective Exercise of "In-Space Jurisdiction": The US Approach and the Problems it is Facing' 40 *Journal of Space Law* (2015–2016), pp. 147–185.

274 NOAA, 'Regulatory Affairs', (available at www.nesdis.noaa.gov/commercial-space/regulatory-affairs); 51 U.S.C. Sections 60101; CFR 15 Part 960.

275 FAA, *Environmental Review* (21 December 2020), available at https://www.faa.gov/space/stakeholder_engagement/spacex_starship/environmental_review; FAA, *Licensing and Permitting Process* (12 November 2020) (available at https://www.faa.gov/space/stakeholder_engagement/spacex_starship/license_review_process).

276 EPA, 'What is the National Environmental Policy Act?' (available at www.epa.gov/nepa/what-national-environmental-policy-act); ESSEL, 'What is NEPA? What Does it Require?' (available at: www.esseltek.com/blog/nepa-what-does-it-require/#:~:text=While%20NEPA%20primarily%20applies%20to%20federal%20"actions%2C"%20private,it%20applies%20to%20public-private%20partnerships%20and%20similar%20arrangements).

and welfare by obligating federal agencies to consider environmental impact in their decisions and work.[277] The Act specifically highlights the human environment and provides that environmental impact assessments shall be undertaken to foresee any potential significant effect of an activity on the quality of the human environment.[278] Though it does not specifically reference outer space, it could be argued that by mentioning the human environment, and making references to US international legal obligations, this term covers the environment of outer space as the space environment has been shown to constitute human environment, inter alia due to the simple fact that human activities are being conducted in it.[279]

Even outside NEPA, the US framework makes frequent reference to the environment, including the space environment, in various regulatory documents. For example, under Title 14, Chapter 5 of the Code of Federal Regulations, the National Aeronautics and Space Administration (NASA) is obligated to respect the space environment as well as the Earthly environment, which could arguably cover all NASA contractors. US legislation provides that 'the United States Government, in coordination with other countries and the private sector, has a responsibility to be a good steward of the space environment.'[280] It additionally recommends tackling the problem of congested orbits by employing space situational awareness data and coordinating space traffic, directing that 'space safety and sustainability tools, voluntary consensus standards, and risk mitigation information and practices,' and ensuring that space situational awareness data be made available to governmental and non-governmental space operators, free of charge.[281] Due to the ever increasing traffic on-orbit, and with it the increased necessity for greater precise space situational awareness services, it furthermore, recommended a transition (including formulating a transition plan) to civil capability, as the increased occurrence and volume of such data requires personnel and resources, not related to the Department of Defense's primary mission.[282]

In relation to the environment, national policies, namely the US National Space Policy (the Presidential Policy Directive 4 (PPD-4) of 2010) and US

277 Section 2 [42 USC, Section 4321].

278 Section 106 [42 USC, Section 4336]. See also NEPA Implementing policy in CFR 40 Part 1500.

279 See Chapter 1, Section 2.

280 Section 202, H.R.5431 – 118th Congress (2023–2024).

281 Section 202, 203, H.R.5431 – 118th Congress (2023–2024).

282 Section 301 H.R.5431 – 118th Congress (2023–2024) (concerning the need to transition to civil space situational awareness capabilities).

Governmental Orbital Debris Mitigation Standard Practices of 2001, are seen as consistent with international mitigation guidelines such as the IADC SDMG, which are regularly applied by agencies.[283] Additionally, the Standard Practices of 2001 serve as 'the overall U.S. Government space debris mitigation technical guidance and as the foundation for specific orbital debris mitigation requirements issued by individual US Government departments and agencies.'[284]

To address the safety and sustainability of the space environment, effective space traffic management is regulated as a form of mitigating the future growth of space debris. The Orbital Sustainability Act of 2023 has been proposed to tackle and provide measures for active remediation of orbital debris, to develop a uniform practice and safeguard the safety and sustainability of the orbital environment.[285] The National Space Council, which is the White House policy council responsible for space activities,[286] has issued several papers on orbital debris population, finding *inter alia* that orbits are dangerously congested and calling for the application of best practices (to be shared between governmental and non-governmental actors inter alia through consultations) to protect critical space services. It furthermore called for the United States to develop programs and update regulation, as well as to lead international efforts, to minimize orbital debris, including debris mitigation (including deorbiting or passivation through moving spent spacecraft to a higher orbit). It adds that the United States should lead 'initiatives to demonstrate active debris remediation of orbital debris generated by the United States or under its jurisdiction, and sharing of data, tying into 'space traffic coordination' taken to mean the planning, coordination, and on-orbit synchronization of activities to enhance the safety and sustainability of operations in the space environment.'[287] The document established a list of orbital debris to be periodically updated by all space actors and stakeholders, and determined that the orbital

283 See Carns (2023); Statement of the United States to UNCOPUOS, Compendium of space debris mitigation standards adopted by States and international organizations, UN Doc. A/AC.105/C.2/2021/CRP.19 (4 June 2021).

284 Statement of the United States to UNCOPUOS, Compendium of space debris mitigation standards adopted by States and international organizations, UN Doc. A/AC.105/C.2/2021/CRP.19 (4 June 2021).

285 Orbital Sustainability Act of 2023 – S.447 – 118th Congress (2023–2024) (The Bill was passed by US Senate on 1. November 2023), see Jeff Foust, 'Senate passes orbital debris bill' (1 November 2023) (available at https://spacenews.com/senate-passes-orbital-debris-bill/).

286 The White House, 'National Space Council' (available at https://www.whitehouse.gov/spacecouncil/).

287 U.S. Government, *Orbital Debris Mitigation Standard Practices* (November 2019 Update).

debris mitigation standard practices should likewise be subject to periodical review every five years.

Turning to licensing of NSA space activity, it is evident that the United States foresees a number of different licenses for different space activities. The FAA, for example, acts on the basis of the Commercial Space Launch Act of 1984, which decrees that the Secretary of Transportation will oversee and license commercial space launch and re-entry activity on US territory or carried out by US citizens, including natural and legal persons.[288] Under the legislation in force, each launch or re-entry shall require licensing, different licenses are foreseen (launch, ren-entry and experimental) all of which require environmental review in accordance with inter alia the NEPA.[289] Additionally, the law details necessary insurance, financial responsibility provisions of the operator and penalties.[290] The FAA is also the agency with which space objects must be registered and which forwards the information to the UN Secretary General in accordance with the Registration Convention.[291]

The FCC on the other hand acts on the basis of, *inter alia*, Communications Act of 1934,[292] tasked with regulating interstate and international communications by radio, television, wire, cable and satellite.[293] Satellite communications are managed by its Space office, subdivided into an Earth station licensing division and a Satellite licensing division.[294] Both rely primarily on what is generally known as Part 25,[295] which provides for a number of different licenses and procedures, includes environmental conditions,[296]

288 The Commercial Space Launch Act, as amended and codified by 51 U.S.C. Sections 50901–50923. FAA, SpaceX Starship Super Heavy Project at the Boca Chica Launch Site (17 November 2023), available at https://www.faa.gov/space/stakeholder_engagement/spacex_starship; Code of Federal Regulations (CFR) Title 14, Chapter III, Parts 413, 415.

289 FAA, *Environmental Review* (21 December 2020), available at https://www.faa.gov/space/stakeholder_engagement/spacex_starship/environmental_review; FAA, *Licensing and Permitting Process* (12 November 2020), available at https://www.faa.gov/space/stakeholder_engagement/spacex_starship/license_review_process.

290 CFR Title 14, Chapter 3, Parts 404, 405, 406, 440.

291 CFR Title 14, Section 450.217.

292 CFR Title 47 Chapter 5, 151 et seq.

293 For more information see Federal Communications Commission, 'About the FCC' (available at: https://www.fcc.gov/about/overview).

294 FCC, 'Satellite Licensing Division' (available at: www.fcc.gov/satellite-licensing-division-page).

295 U.S.C. Title 47 Chapter 1 Subchapter B Part 25.

296 See, e.g., CFR 47, Chapter 1 Subchapter B Part 25, Sections 109, 110; CFR 47, Chapter 1 Subchapter B Part 97.

and coordinates contact with the International Telecommunications Union.[297]

In contrast to the FAA and the FCC, the NOAA (under supervision of the Secretary of Commerce), regulates a narrow(er) field of remote sensing industry (in cooperation with the Department of Defense and Department of State in matters concerning national security), which seems primarily concerned with mitigating national security risks. Regulated in Title 51, Subtitle VI, Chapter 601 (Land Remote Sensing Policy) and detailed in the more recent CFR 15 Part 960 (Licensing of Private Remote Sensing Space Systems), which responded to changes in the remote sensing industry, such as for instance the growing number of remote sensing systems,[298] CFR 15 specifies inter alia definitions, applicability, license conditions and a detailed procedure for granting as well as amending licenses, including appeal instruments available to NSAs and inter-agency (inter-federal government department) coordination where required.[299] It divides licenses into a three-tier system based on risk posed by the sensed data, with the first tier subject to the fewest conditions as it concerns systems and data that have considerable comparable competition both domestically and abroad.[300] The second tier concerns systems that have domestic competition and the third tier addresses systems that have little to no competition, both of which are therefore subject to "modified operators" or what is colloquially known as "shutter control" whereby the US Government can, in times of "increased concerns for national security and where necessary to meet international obligation or foreign policy interests" temporarily (for a maximum of three years) limit operations of certain remote sensing systems.[301] Certainly, this would cover security risks posed by action of nefarious NSAs, such as for example terrorist groups, conducting cyberattacks. This seems confirmed in the licensing provisions which specify that remote sensing systems should have cybersecurity plans in place that are capable of preventing unauthorized access and notifying in event of unauthorized access.[302] US regulation does not specify the details or technical specifics of such action plans,

297 See, e.g., CFR 47, Chapter 1 Subchapter B Part 25, Section 111; See also FCC, 'Part 25 Space Station License and Market Access Checklist' (available at: www.fcc.gov/space/how-prepare-usa-itu-filing; www.fcc.gov/part-25-space-station-license-and-market-access-checklist).

298 See, e.g., Federal Register, Vol. 85, No. 98 (Wednesday May 20th 2020) Rules and Regulations: 15 CFR Part 960.

299 See CFR 15 Part 960.

300 CFR 15 Sections 960.8, 960.9, 960.10.

301 See, e.g., CFR 15 Sections 960.9, 960.10.

302 See, e.g., CFR 15 Sections 960.9, 960.10.

aside from counselling adoption of industry best practices.[303] This could then, at least indirectly, aid in the mitigation of space pollution by NSAs. However, whether the phrase "where necessary to meet international obligation" could be interpreted widely enough to (directly) include safety concerns arising from space pollution, for example debris, remains unclear.

In the United States, substantial media publication shows several instances of demands to modify space activity licenses, as well as sanctions leveraged against NSAs in cases of violations. Many instances show that NSAs apply for modification of licenses, which may be opposed by interested parties and which are ultimately ruled on by the FCC. For example, SpaceX applied for a license amendment to move one of its satellites.[304] Several instances show violations of national space legislation were met with stern response from both the FCC and the FAA. For example, in 2018 the FCC fined a startup company, Swarm Technologies, 900,000 US dollars (as part of a settlement with the FCC) for unauthorized launch of four of its 'SpaceBEE' satellites aboard Indian rocket PSLV-C40.[305] According to public reports, the company had applied for a license in December 2017 and, despite not having received authorization, it launched the satellites in January of 2018. It had been suggested that Swarm Technologies had been 'likely the first time a private organization has launched spacecraft without the explicit approval of any government.'[306] Swarm Technologies CEO Sara Spangelo has since then labeled the event a mistake and expressed regret.[307] However, the satellites remain in orbit,[308] and the

303 See, e.g., CFR 15 Sections 960.9(1)(ii).

304 FCC, FCC Grants SpaceX's Satellite Broadband Modification Application, Document FCC-21–48 (36 FCC Rcd 7995 (11)) (27 April 2021); Michael Sheetz, 'FCC approves SpaceX change to its Starlink network, a win despite objections from Amazon and others' (available at https://www.cnbc.com/2021/04/27/fcc-approves-spacex-starlink-modification-despite-objections.html); Jeff Foust, 'FCC approves Starlink license modification' (27 April 2021) (available at https://spacenews.com/fcc-approves-starlink-license-modification/).

305 FCC, 'FCC Reaches $900,000 Settlement for Unauthorized Satellite Launch' (20 December 2018) (available at https://www.fcc.gov/document/fcc-reaches-900000-settlement-unauthorized-satellite-launch).

306 Tim Fernholz, 'An unauthorized satellite launch in India threatens US regulatory reform in space' (13 March 2018) *Quartz* (available at https://qz.com/1226962/an-unauthorized-satellite-launch-in-india-threatens-us-regulatory-reform-in-space).

307 Marina Koren, 'Launching Rogue Satellites Into Space Was a 'Mistake'' *The Atlantic* (7 September 2018) (available at https://www.theatlantic.com/technology/archive/2018/09/spacebees-swarm-unauthorized-satellite-launch/569395/).

308 Victor Tangermann, 'FCC Fines Startup for Launching Satellites Without Permission' *Futurism* (21. December 2018) (available at https://futurism.com/fcc-fine-settlement-swarm-technologies-unauthorized).

FCC expressed doubt as to whether the fine would be sufficient to deter future rogue behavior.[309]

On 2 October 2023, the FCC's Enforcement Bureau issued a first ever 'space debris' enforcement fine to DISH for 'failure to properly deorbit its EchoStar-7 satellite'.[310] The FCC announced that '[t]he settlement includes an admission of liability from the company and an agreement to adhere to a compliance plan and pay a penalty of $150,000.'[311] This followed its finding that the company violated 'the Communications Act, the FCC rules, and the terms of the company's license by relocating its direct broadcast satellite ('DBS') service EchoStar-7 satellite at the satellite's end-of-mission to a disposal orbit well below the elevation required by the terms of its license.'[312] The fine comes as part of the FCC's wider step-up action in satellite policy efforts, which *inter alia* also include the establishment of the Space Bureau and implementing its Space Innovation Agenda.

The FAA seems to have stepped up its pre-emptive action, proposing a 175,000 US dollar civil penalty fine against SpaceX for not submitting pre-launch data, more specifically launch collision analysis trajectory data, used to assess the probability of the launch vehicle colliding with one of the thousands of tracked objects orbiting the Earth, to the FAA at least seven days prior to the 19 August 2022 launch of Starlink Group 4–27 mission.[313] Furthermore, the FAA has investigated incidents and issued corrective action orders, for example after a SpaceX Starship incident.[314] It also ordered a stay of activity, as for example the recent grounding of a SpaceX Starship.[315]

As for anti-satellite testing, during the Cold War both the Soviet Union and the United States developed anti-satellite weapons and tested them. It has been evaluated that more than ten satellites were destroyed by the two States

309 FCC, 'Statement of Commissioner Michael O'Really', FCC 18–184.

310 FCC, 'FCC Takes First Space Debris Enforcement Action', DOC-397412A1 (2 October 2023) (available at https://docs.fcc.gov/public/attachments/DOC-397412A1.pdf).

311 FCC, 'FCC Takes First Space Debris Enforcement Action', DOC-397412A1 (2 October 2023) (available at https://docs.fcc.gov/public/attachments/DOC-397412A1.pdf).

312 See FCC, 'FCC Takes First Space Debris Enforcement Action', DOC-397412A1 (2 October 2023) (available at https://docs.fcc.gov/public/attachments/DOC-397412A1.pdf).

313 FAA, 'FAA Proposes $175,000 Fine Against SpaceX for Not Submitting Required Pre-Launch Data' (17 February 2023) (available at https://www.faa.gov/newsroom/faa-proposes-175000-fine-against-spacex-not-submitting-required-pre-launch-data).

314 FAA, 'FAA Closes SpaceX Starship Mishap Investigation' (8 September 2023) (available at https://www.faa.gov/newsroom/faa-closes-spacex-starship-mishap-investigation).

315 Lora Kolodny, 'FAA orders Musk's SpaceX to take 63 corrective actions on Starship, keeps rocket grounded' (8 September 2023) (available at https://www.cnbc.com/2023/09/08/faa-starship-grounded-corrective-action.html).

with anti-satellite weapons during the Cold War.[316] Since the fall of the Soviet Union, however, anti-satellite testing and use decreased. Since 2000, only four States destroyed their own decommissioned satellites with anti-satellite missiles; China (2007), United States (2008), India (2019), and the Russian Federation (2021). While the other three performed tests (displays) of anti-satellite weaponry, the United States claimed it engaged in a necessary use of an anti-satellite missile to dispose of one of its old weather satellites, which it deemed dangerous to active objects, but generally criticized the destruction of satellites for testing of anti-satellite weaponry. In 2022, the United States announced that no further ASAT tests[317] should be conducted due to their high negative impact on the space environment.[318] So far, several countries have expressed support,[319] which resulted in the adoption of a United Nations General Assembly resolution on this matter.[320]

In terms of jurisprudence, several space industry related cases have made it to national courts in the United States.[321] In several instances, tort claims have been brought by private persons against NSAs under contract with NASA, alleging, *inter alia*, negative and harmful seismic activity emanating from rocket

316 Daryl G. Kimball, 'U.S. Commits to ASAT Ban' Arms Control Association (May 2022) (available at https://www.armscontrol.org/act/2022-05/news/us-commits-asat-ban).

317 This should be distinguished from the actual use of ASAT weapons.

318 The White House, 'FACT SHEET: Vice President Harris Advances National Security Norms in Space' (18 April 2022) (available at https://www.whitehouse.gov/briefing-room/statements-releases/2022/04/18/fact-sheet-vice-president-harris-advances-national-security-norms-in-space/).

319 See, for example: UK Government, 'Press Release from 3. October 2022' (3 October 2022) (available at https://www.gov.uk/government/news/responsible-space-behaviours-the-uk-commits-not-to-destructively-test-direct-ascent-anti-satellite-missiles). See also: Heather Foye and Gabriela Rosa Hernández, 'UN First Committee Calls for ASAT Test Ban' (December 2022) (available at https://www.armscontrol.org/act/2022-12/news/un-first-committee-calls-asat-test-ban#:~:text=(See%20ACT%2C%20November%202022.,United%20Kingdom%20have%20followed%20suit); Sarwat Nasir, 'UK and South Korea join US-led efforts to ban anti-satellite testing' (6 October 2022) (available at https://www.thenationalnews.com/world/uk-news/2022/10/06/uk-and-south-korea-join-us-led-efforts-to-ban-anti-satellite-testing/); Jeff Foust, 'More countries encouraged to commit to halt destructive ASAT tests' *SpaceNews* (15 June 2023) (available at https://spacenews.com/more-countries-encouraged-to-commit-to-halt-destructive-asat-tests/).

320 K. Cowig, 'United Nations General Assembly Adopts Draft Resolutions Regarding Space Weapons' (9. 12. 2022) *SpaceRef.* (available at https://spaceref.com/newspace-and-tech/united-nations-general-assembly-adopts-draft-resolution-regarding-space-weapons/).

321 In the present Chapter only a brief overview of some chosen cases will be provided. For more information on the cases see: Stephen Gorove and Michael A. Gorove, *Cases on Space Law* (The Space Law Journal, 1996); ESA, 'Space Law Cases' (available at https://www.esa.int/About_Us/ECSL_-_European_Centre_for_Space_Law/Space_law_cases).

engine testing sites, and damages have been issued.[322] However, in the case of *Pigott v. Boeing Co.*,[323] the Court held that the company was acting under direction of NASA and therefore was not responsible for remedying any damages caused.[324]

Several more contractual cases have also been filed relating to space activity.[325] In *Martin Marietta v. Intelsat*,[326] the plaintiff launched two INTELSAT satellites under contract for a fixed price. However, after the launch of the first satellite with a Titan III rocket, the satellite and booster that were supposed to deliver the satellite to its orbital position failed to separate from Titan at the correct time and the satellite was not delivered to its target orbital position. INTELSAT paid 112 million US dollars, with the cost of rescuing the satellite evaluated at around 90 million US dollars, prompting Marietta to bring a pre-emptive action to absolve itself of liability and INTELSAT counterclaimed for negligence. The initial findings absolved Marietta due to the fact that the US Congress affirmed that US public policy requires those using the services of a licensed space launch provider do so at their own risk, and additionally because the contract between the two parties included waivers of gross and normal negligence.

A series of recent cases have seen some of the largest US NSAs pitted against each other. These include an antitrust case,[327] a lawsuit seeking to stop Boeing and SpaceX working on a NASA contract while another bid is on the table,[328] another by Blue Origin against the United States complaining about an award bestowed by NASA to SpaceX,[329] a claim against Amazon's board regarding a

322 *Berg v. Reaction Motors Division*, 37 NJ 396, 181 A.2d 487 (N.J. 1962); *Smith v. Lockheed Propulsion Co.* 246 Cal. App. 2d 774, 56 Cal. Rptr. 128 (Cal.App. 4th Dist. 1967).

323 *Pigott v. Boeing Co.* 240 So. 2d 63 (Miss. 1970).

324 See *Pigott v. Boeing Co.* 240 So. 2d 63 (Miss. 1970).

325 *Martin Marietta v. Intelsat* 763 F. Supp. 1327 (D.Md. 1991); *Martin Marietta v. INTELSAT* 991 F.2d 94 (4th Cir. 1992).

326 *Martin Marietta v. Intelsat* 763 F. Supp. 1327 (D.Md. 1991); *Martin Marietta v. INTELSAT* 991 F.2d 94 (4th Cir. 1992) (Appeal).

327 Brian Berger, 'SpaceX Sues Boeing and Lockheed Martin' *Space.com* (Oct 21 2005) (available at https://www.space.com/1701-spacex-sues-boeing-lockheed-martin.html); Braddock Gaskill, 'SpaceX vs Boeing and Lockheed: Case Closed' *Nasa Spaceflight* (20 May 2006) (available at https://www.nasaspaceflight.com/2006/05/spacex-vs-boeing-and-lockheed-case-closed/).

328 Irene Klotz, 'Lawsuit seeks to stop Boeing, SpaceX work on NASA space taxi' *Reuters* (16 October 2014) (available at https://www.reuters.com/article/idUSKCN0I52O8/).

329 Blue Origin v. United States and Space Exploration Technologies Corp (Federal Court of Public Opinion November 4, 2021). See also Michael Sheetz, 'Bezos' Blue Origin loses NASA lawsuit over SpaceX $2.9 billion lunar lander contract' *CNBC* (4 November 2021) (available at https://www.cnbc.com/2021/11/04/bezos-blue-origin-loses-lawsuit-against-nasa-over-spacex-lunar-lander.html).

Kuiper launch contract with Blue Origin and others,[330] and a case concerning an investor lawsuit against Astra Space.[331] These cases do not directly relate to environmental harm, but do show that US NSAs are becoming embroiled in legal actions against each other and the Government, which may well portend developments in other jurisdictions.

Two cases which concern environmental protection have arisen in the United States.[332] These two cases concerned two NASA missions (joint ventures with ESA) for which the plaintiff, an environmentalist group 'Florida Coalition for Peace and Justice', sought an injunction citing that NASA had not met the requirements of the National Environmental Policy Act (NEPA), which mandates that federal agencies must evaluate and report effects on the quality of the human environment in an Environmental Impact Assessment. The plaintiffs claimed that NASA's Environmental Impact Assessment was defective and sought to stop the launch. However, in both cases the court found insufficient evidence presented by the plaintiff, rejecting an injunction as the missions would benefit humanity and should therefore not be delayed.

In sum, the United States has extensive provisions in place for the regulation of private NSA space activities, dividing activities between different agencies and determining different categories of licenses. The respective entities are active in the area as shown by several documents on license amendments, grounding orders and fines, and space activities have even reached the threshold for admissibility of national courts, mainly for claimed torts and contractual breaches, with a few cases on antitrust and environment. The United States furthermore has several environmental provisions in place, for governmental and non-governmental actors, focusing on the mitigation of space debris and space traffic management, with the newest efforts focusing on establishing rules on remediation of space debris. This survey of the domestic law presents a positive view for the future. However, whether these provisions will be successful, remains dependent on whether they will be effectively enforced through licensing mechanisms.

---

330 Jeff Foust, 'Lawsuit claims Amazon's board erred in awarding Kuiper launch contracts to Blue Origin and others' *Space News* (31 August 2023) (available at https://spacenews.com/lawsuit-claims-amazons-board-erred-in-awarding-kuiper-launch-contracts-to-blue-origin-and-others/).

331 Martina Barash, 'Astra Space Fends Off Investor Lawsuit Over Rocket Launch Claims' *Bloomberg Law News* (3 August 2023) (available at https://news.bloomberglaw.com/securities-law/astra-space-fends-off-investor-lawsuit-over-rocket-launch-claims).

332 *Florida Coalition for Peace and Justice v. George Herbert Walker Bush*, Civil Action No. 89-2682-OG, D.D.C. 10 October 1989; *Florida Coalition for Peace and Justice v. George Herbert Walker Bush*, Civil Action No. 89-2682-OG, D.D:C. 5 October 1990.

3.2 *Canada*

Canada is a highly developed space nation, with high investments in its booming space sector. It has particular expertise in robotics, which it supplies for the ISS and will supply for the Gateway and Artemis projects.[333] In 2022, Canada's leading space companies formed a national industry association called Space Canada, with the aim of providing a united voice for Canada's space sector and fostering its ongoing development.[334] In 2023, the Government expanded its support for commercial space launch activities in Canada.[335] Some of the most successful space companies in Canada are MDA, Telesat, GHGSat and Magellan Aerospace.[336]

There are several pieces of Canadian legislation relevant to NSA space activity. The most important act concerning NSAs is the Remote Sensing Space Systems Act of 2007.[337] The Act provides that 'no person shall operate a remote sensing space system in any manner, directly or indirectly, except under the

---

333 Government of Canada, 'Canadian space industry' (available at https://ised-isde.canada.ca/site/canadian-space-industry/en); Aerospace Review, 'Volume 2: Reaching Higher: Canada's Interests and Future in Space' (November 2012) (available at https://publications.gc.ca/site/eng/432242/publication.html); Government of Canada, 'Programs' (available at https://ised-isde.canada.ca/site/canadian-space-industry/en/programs); Government of Canda, 'Stakeholder directories' (available at https://ised-isde.canada.ca/site/canadian-space-industry/en/stakeholder-directories); Government of Canada, '2020 State of the Canadian Space Sector Report – Facts and Figures 2019' (available at https://www.asc-csa.gc.ca/pdf/eng/publications/2020-state-canadian-space-sector-facts-figures-2019-v2.pdf); Brunswick Shelli, 'How Canada is Shaping the World's Future in Space' *SpaceNews* (23 January 2023) (available at https://spacenews.com/op-ed-how-canada-is-shaping-the-worlds-future-in-space/); For Artemis Mission see: Howell Elizabeth,' Canada assigns astronauts to launch on Boeing's Starliner, back up Artemis 2 moon mission' *Space.com* (22 November 2023) (available at https://www.space.com/canadian-space-agency-astronaut-assignments-spaceflight); Trinh Theresa Do, 'Canada's space agency to take back seat to private sector' *CBC News* (7 February 2014) (available at https://www.cbc.ca/news/politics/canada-s-space-agency-to-take-back-seat-to-private-sector-1.2527149).

334 SatNews, 'Nine Canadian Space Companies Create The Space Canada Association' (20 March 2022) (available at https://news.satnews.com/2022/03/20/nine-canadian-space-companies-create-the-space-canada-organization/).

335 Government of Canada, 'Government of Canada supports commercial space launches in Canada' (20 January 2023) (available at https://www.canada.ca/en/transport-canada/news/2023/01/government-of-canada-supports-commercial-space-launches-in-canada.html).

336 Urban Ria, 'Top 4 Canadian Space Companies and their Contribution' *Space Impulse* (4 July 2023) (available at https://spaceimpulse.com/2023/07/04/canadian-space-companies/).

337 Remote Sensing Space Systems Act (S.C. 2005, c. 45) (amended 5 April 2007).

authority of a license'.[338] This means that a license is a prerequisite for every NSA to carry out space activity in Canada aimed at operating a remote sensing space system. Article 9 provides that applications for a license require showing 'a system disposal plan … that, among other things, provides for the protection of the environment, public health and the safety of persons and property'. Though vague, this provides a legislative entry point for environmental considerations. The Minister may grant exemption from these requirements, but only if satisfied that, amongst certain other conditions, 'adequate provision will be made for the protection of the environment, public health and the safety of persons and property'.[339] According to Article 11 of the Act, the Minister may suspend the license in certain situations, including the situation where the licensed system is likely to be in violation of Canadian international obligations. In this way, Canada's obligations under international treaties are indirectly incorporated by reference into the obligations under the Act. Arguably, this would also cover its obligations under customary international law.

Penalties vary for different offenses and can go up to 5,000 dollars (Canadian), in the case of an individual, and 25,000 dollars, in any other cases, but for certain offenses they can be set much higher, namely, in the case of an individual, to a fine not exceeding 50,000 dollars or to imprisonment for a term not exceeding 18 months, or to both; and in any other case, to a fine not exceeding 250,000 dollars.[340]

Another important instrument for space activities is the Canadian Space Agency Act.[341] While the Canadian Space Agency has principally adopted the IADC SDMG in 2012, which it intends to apply during all phases of the Agency's activities and to all Agency projects,[342] the Canadian Space Agency Act contains no specific references to the environment. Nonetheless, Canada has submitted views on reducing space threats through norms, rules and principles of responsible behaviour, under which it recognised both the rising threat of space debris and the expansion in the number of space actors (including NSAs) as potential man-made threats. To promote the safety, security, and sustainability of outer space activities and the space environment, Canada supports the adoption of international soft-law standards, on cooperation, communication,

338 Article 5.

339 Article 3.

340 Articles 23 and 38.

341 Canadian Space Agency Act (S.C. 1990, c. 13) (10 May 1990).

342 Statement of Canada to UNCOPUOS, Compendium of space debris mitigation standards adopted by States and international organizations, UN Doc. A/AC.105/C.2/2021/CRP.19 (4 June 2021).

transparency, space surveillance and tracking, and has signalled its intent to undertake confidence-building measures with all stakeholders including non-space faring states and private entities.[343] Canada has decried any behaviour that damages the space environment, including any activity that causes wide-spread debris such as development, use and testing of ASATs, non-consensual interference with other space operations, or operations in proximity to space systems.[344]

A further significant instrument is the Procedure for the Submission of Applications for Spectrum Licenses for Space Stations issued by the Innovation, Science and Economic Development Department of Canada.[345] It makes a distinction between satellites in the GEO and those in non-geostationary orbits,[346] with the former required to have a plan for their de-orbiting in line with the ITU Recommendation on Environmental Protection of the Geostationary Satellite Orbit,[347] but the latter required to de-orbit within 25 years of the end of their operational life in accordance with the IADC SDMG.[348]

As expected for its large-scale space activities, Canada has enacted relatively detailed legislation regulating space operations. It sets out the proceedings and the conditions for issuing licenses for space activities, in which environmental concern is addressed as well. Besides its hard-law instruments, Canada endorses several international soft-law mechanisms aimed at ensuring sustainability and environmental protection.

343 Government of Canada, 'Canada's Views on Reducing Space Threats through norms, rules and principles of Responsible Behaviour' (2021) (available at https://documents.unoda.org/wp-content/uploads/2022/05/EN-Canada-working-Paper-on-Norms-75-36.pdf).

344 Government of Canada, 'Canada's Views on Reducing Space Threats through norms, rules and principles of Responsible Behaviour' (2021) (available at https://documents.unoda.org/wp-content/uploads/2022/05/EN-Canada-working-Paper-on-Norms-75-36.pdf).

345 Client Procedures Circular (CPC) 2-6-02 – Procedure for the Submission of Applications for Spectrum Licenses for Space Stations issued by the Innovation, Science and Economic Development Department of Canada.

346 See Chapter 1, Section 2 on the definition of the GEO.

347 ITU, Recommendation ITU–R S.1003-2, Environmental Protection of the Geostationary Satellite Orbit (December 2010).

348 See Statement of Canada to the UNCOPUOS in UNCOPUOS, Compendium of space debris mitigation standards adopted by States and international organizations, UN Doc. A/AC.105/C.2/2021/CRP.19 (4 June 2021).

4 Eastern European (Non-EU) and Central Eurasian States

4.1 *The Russian Federation*

The Russian Federation is, as the legal successor to the Soviet Union, the oldest space faring nation. In 1957, the Soviet Union launched the first artificial satellite, Sputnik-I. It continued a series of firsts, sending the first living being (a dog named Laika), the first man (Yuri Gagarin) and the first woman (Valentina Tereshkova) into orbit, as well as developing and operating the first orbital space station, Mir, and some of the first anti-satellite weaponry. Since the collapse of the Soviet Union and the establishment of the Russian Federation, the State Corporation for Space Activities, called 'Roscosmos', was created and made primarily responsible for space activities. In the 1990s, Roscosmos made a name for itself by providing launch services for actors worldwide, including astronauts from the United States, Canada, European States and Japan traveling to the International Space Station. Historically, the Soviet Union was resistant to private sector activities in space,[349] but more recently the Russian Federation has decreed to promote private industry,[350] and engaged in public-private arrangements in this respect.[351]

Space activities conducted in the Russian Federation, under the jurisdiction of the Russian Federation or by subjects of the Russian Federation worldwide (natural and legal), are regulated in the Law of the Russian Federation on Space Activities of 1993, which has been amended several times over the years, most recently in 2022.[352] This legislation aims to legally regulate space activity for the purpose of developing the economy, science and technology, as well as strengthening State security.[353] It defines 'space activity' to encompass all stages of the space industry from development and manufacturing of necessary technology, to operation of objects to use of results,[354] thus making the act applicable throughout the different stages of any space activity.

Turning to its contents, Article 1 begins with a decree that all space activities must be carried out in accordance with the Constitution, generally recognized

349 Gerhard (2009), pp. 109–116.

350 Act No. Pr-906 (19 April 2013) on 'Main Provisions of the Fundamentals of the Russian Federation State Policy in the Field of Space Activities for the Period up to 2030 and beyond'.

351 For more information on Russian space activities see Marco Aliberti and Ksenia Lisitsyna, *Russia's Posture in Space* (Springer, 2019), p. 18.

352 Law of the Russian Federation No. 5663-I (20 August 1993) 'On Space Activities'.

353 Preamble as amended by Federal Law No. 147-FZ of November 29, 1996.

354 Article 2(2), as amended by federal laws dated November 29, 1996 No. 147-FZ, dated July 13, 2015 No. 216-FZ.

principles and norms of international law and international treaties of the Russian Federation, as well as other laws of the Russian Federation.[355] The Law references international law again as it declares unlawful any space activities prohibited by international treaties. This consequently incorporates obligations from Articles VI and IX of the Outer Space Treaty.

The Law contains direct references to the space environment. In Article 22, paragraph 1 requires that 'space activities are carried out with a view to ensuring the level of permissible anthropogenic burden on the environment and the near-Earth space.' On these bases, it appears that unauthorised NSA space activity and pollution of the space environment are forbidden, in as far as these acts are also prohibited by the Outer Space Treaty, in particular Articles VI, VII, VIII and IX. However, this leaves open the question of how the mentioned Articles of the Outer Space Treaty could be and are being concretized in practice, as discussed herein.

Turning to NSA space activity, NSAs are referenced several times throughout the Law, with provisions primarily directed at strengthening the technical and intellectual potential of the space industry and its infrastructure under goals.[356] However, some of the provisions broader matters, such as Article 17, which decrees that every space object of the Russian Federation is subject to registration and must have markings certifying their belonging to the Russian Federation.[357] Pursuant to the Registration Convention, to which the Russian Federation is a State Party, this provision obliges NSAs to provide the Russian Federation with the requisite information to be recorded by the State in a national space object registry and pass the information to UNOOSA, in accordance with Article IV of the Registration Convention.

If a space object is created by Russian organizations and citizens jointly with foreign states, organizations and citizens or international organizations, then issues of the object's registration, jurisdiction and control over it, and ownership rights are to be resolved on the basis of appropriate international treaties.[358] Rights of jurisdiction and control over a space object, as well as ownership rights pertaining to such an object does not affect the legal status of the zone it occupies in outer space, surface or interior of a celestial body.[359] Moreover, in the immediate vicinity of a space object of the Russian Federation, the Federation may establish rules that are binding on Russian and

355 Article as amended by Federal Law dated November 29, 1996 No. 147-FZ.
356 See, e.g., Article 3, as amended by Federal Law dated November 29, 1996 No. 147-FZ.
357 Article 17(1).
358 Article 17(4).
359 Article 17(4).

foreign organizations and on citizens within zones necessary to ensure the safety of space activities.[360] This regulation pertains then to interpretation of the Registration Convention and Article VIII of the Outer Space Treaty, giving the Federation a relatively wide ambit to affect NSA behaviour.

The Law addresses international responsibility and liability, decreeing that State organizations and their officials, as well as other organizations and their officials, along with citizens, that are guilty of violating acts regulating space activities bear responsibility in accordance with legislation of the Russian Federation.[361] Liability for damage caused by a space object of the Russian Federation, while carrying out space activities on the territory of the Russian Federation or elsewhere on Earth or in its atmosphere, arises regardless of the guilt of the perpetrator of such harm.[362] Conversely, for damage in outer space, caused to a space object of the Russian Federation or property on board such an object by another space object of the Russian Federation when carrying out space activities, compensation from the organization or citizen owning the space object that caused the harm is required under the conditions provided for by the Civil Code of the Russian Federation.[363]

Most importantly, the law makes Roskosmos responsible for authorizing and supervising Russian NSA space activity, except in relation to damage caused by military or dual use components when this is done either by or in cooperation with the federal executive body for defence.[364] The licensing obligation of Roskosmos was augmented and expanded on by the Law on Roskosmos of 2015[365] which added that Roskosmos carries out licensing of space activities,[366] 'in accordance with the legislation of the Russian Federation space activities, maintenance of the registry of issued licenses and the federal Licensing control (supervision) of space activities'.[367]

360 Article 17(5).

361 Article 29.

362 Article 30(1).

363 Article 30(2).

364 Articles 6, 9.

365 Russian Federation Federal Law N 215-FZ (13 July 2015) 'On the State Corporation for Space Activities ROSCOSMOS'; Federal Law of the Russian Federation N 216-FZ (8 July 2015), 'On Amendments to Certain Legislative Acts of the Russian Federation Following the Adoption of the Federal Law on the State Space Corporation 'Roscosmos' of 13 July 2015' as amended by Federal Law N 578-FZ (29 December 2022).

366 Russian Federation Federal Law N 215-FZ (13 July 2015) 'On the State Corporation for Space Activities ROSCOSMOS', Article 6, Paragraph 17, Article 7 Paragraph 11, Article 11, Article 14 (As amended by the Federal Law of 11. 06. 2021 No. 170-FZ).

367 Article 7 Paragraph 11 (As amended by the Federal Law of 11. 06. 2021 No. 170-FZ).

While licensing conditions are not detailed under the same provisions, the remaining duties of Roskosmos provide an insight into the possible requirements. For example, Roskosmos is given responsibility for establishing an inventory and catalogue of space processes, testing, operations, disposal, technology, objects and infrastructure.[368] It must identify, assess and ensure quality of effective methods and safety of space activities, objects, and infrastructure, population and territories, as well as security measures in accordance with international legislation, for which it participates in the definition and coordination of national and international standards for safety of space operations (including organizing work on standardization, including international, of rocket and space technology).[369] It organizes investigations into accidents and catastrophes, and ensuing consequences.[370] Article 12 furthermore clarifies that Roskosmos must protect the population and territories from natural and man-made emergencies, *inter alia,* by a system of prevention and responses. It adds, in Article 14, that Roskosmos will oversee the organization and conduct of expert examinations of projects on the creation of rocket and space technology, of scientific and technical, investment and other programs.[371]

To assure it fulfills its objectives, Roskosmos may invest or participate in projects, conclude contracts,[372] strengthen Russia's capacity to monitor space objects and events in near-Earth space,[373] promote, organise and coordinate work on commercial space projects, assess the feasibility of defence, weapons and space programs and industry, issue permits for the construction or commission of space infrastructure, monitor its development and quality, and conduct inspections of organizations within the rocket and space industry.[374] The Roskosmos corporation furthermore prepares regulatory technical and organizational documents for the standardization and regulation of space activities and their procedures.[375] All of the above, however, indicate matters which Roskosmos may require for licenses, for example standards to be followed to ensure the safety and security of space operations, including the protection of the environment (both of Earth and outer space as indicated by the Law on Space Activities).

368 Articles 11, 14.
369 Article 11.
370 Article 11.
371 Article 14 Paragraph 13.
372 Article 14.
373 Article 7.
374 Article 11.
375 Article 8 paragraph 5.

Roskosmos is given responsibility for participating in the formation of the national State space program, organizing its implementation, and approving (jointly with the federal executive body on defense) an annual launch plan for the realization of international and commercial space programs and projects.[376] The current State program states that space activities are one of the factors determining the influence and level of development of the Russian Federation in the modern world.[377] For this purpose, it demands the strict observance of Russia's obligations under international law,[378] ensuring the safety and long-term sustainable development of space activities, including compliance with environmental protection measures, in near-Earth space and outer space.[379] It is required to actively participate in discussions and studies at the international level of man-made debris, including mitigation and removal methods,[380] and to inform the international community on Russia's capabilities and achievements.[381] The policy explicitly mentions removal methods, which likely refer to active debris removal methods. In Section IX, paragraph 20, the policy declares that implementation of public policy is ensured by the creation of means of removal, service systems for automated spacecraft, new generations of crewed spacecraft, elements of infrastructure for activities in deep space, breakthrough technologies to solve target tasks and production technologies.

For present purposes, it is therefore important to reiterate that Roskosmos is required to prevent possible space threats to the Earth and its biosphere,[382] and ensure the environmental safety of space activities, through *inter alia* the introduction of technologies and designs that reduce the formation of space debris during launch and operation products of rocket and space technology.[383]

Turning to environmental provisions and principle requirements deriving from Article IX of the Outer Space Treaty,[384] Article 4 of the Law on Space

---

376 Article 7 Paragraphs 10, 20, 50.

377 Act No. Pr-906 (19 April 2013) on 'Main Provisions of the Fundamentals of the Russian Federation State Policy in the Field of Space Activities for the Period up to 2030 and beyond', Section I.

378 Section II (7) (d).

379 Sections II and VII.

380 Section VII.

381 Section VII.

382 Section IX.

383 Section VIII (19) (d).

384 This Chapter creates an overview of documents pertaining to licensing and environmental provisions. For a further study of Russian Federation's measures on combating orbital debris see Carns (2023), pp. 188–210.

Activities provides that space activity must be carried out to promote international peace and security, as well as, for example, ensuring the safety of space activities and environmental protection.[385] Space activities must be carried out taking into account the level of acceptable anthropogenic loads on the environment and near-Earth space.[386] If there is a threat to the safety of the population or the environment, the body for space activities and the federal executive body for defence must immediately inform the relevant government authorities, as well as organizations and citizens.[387]

The proceeding provisions are supplemented by the Law on the State Corporation for Space Activities Roskosmos,[388] which makes Roskosmos responsible for managing debris reduction activities in the near-Earth space,[389] and for carrying out measures to ensure the safety of space activity (design, manufacture, testing, operation, utilization of rocketry, space objects and space infrastructure).[390] The Russian Federation introduced national standards (with accompanying goals and principles) and a national system standardizing technical equipment, manufacture, and related matter,[391] in an effort to bring the Russian industry in line with best international practices, standards and agreements.[392]

The majority of the debris mitigation and limiting measures are, however, intended to be carried out through the Federal Space Program of Russia for 2016–2025 (which mandates that State policy regarding pollution shall be approached through required deployment and maintenance of spacecraft and satellite constellations, international cooperation and protection of the population through *inter alia* appropriate groundwork for future oriented space complexes and systems) and the 'Fundamentals of the Russian Federation's State Policy in the Field of Space Activities for the Period up to 2030 and

---

385 As amended by Federal Law No. 309-FZ dated December 30, 2008.

386 Article 22(1) (As amended by Federal Law No. 309-FZ dated December 30, 2008).

387 Article 22(2) (As amended by Federal Law No. 309-FZ dated December 30, 2008, No. 216-FZ dated July 13, 2015; Article as amended by Federal Law No. 147-FZ dated November 29, 1996).

388 Federal Law of the Russian Federation N 215-FZ (13 July 2015) 'On the State Corporation for Space Activities ROSCOSMOS'.

389 Federal Law of the Russian Federation N 215-FZ (13 July 2015) 'On the State Corporation for Space Activities ROSCOSMOS', Article 14, Paragraph 16.

390 Article 11, Paragraph 1.

391 Federal Law of the Russian Federation N 162-FZ (29 June 2015) 'On Standardisation in the Russian Federation'.

392 Statement of the Russian Federation to the UNCOPUOS in the UNCOPUOS, Compendium of space debris mitigation standards adopted by States and international organizations, UN Doc. A/AC.105/C.2/2021/CRP.19 (4 June 2021).

beyond'. This instrument states that the objective of the Russian Federation is to participate in finding international solutions,[393] and determines that the safety of space activities will be guaranteed by ensuring environmental safety through the adoption of new technologies and designs that reduce space debris at launches and during the operation of rockets and space equipment.[394]

In addition, in 2018, the Russian Federation transposed international standards into national standard Outer Space Treaty R 52925-2018,[395] which is not legally binding, but does contain requirements that must be fulfilled by all new space systems. These requirements are consistent with the IADC SDMG provisions (doc A/AC.105/C.2/L.260), UNCOPUOS SDMG (A/RES/62/217 from 10 January 2008) and International standard ISO 24113:2011 'Space Systems – Space Debris Mitigation Requirements'.[396]

The aforementioned instruments apply during all stages of space activity (design, development, operation, passivation and end-of-life missions). They mandate, *inter alia,* that design and development include analysis of possible effects of space object failure, that periodical check-ups are performed during the operational phase and accounted for in design documentation, that measures are taken for prevention of in-orbit break-ups, intentional destruction (through, for example, self-destruct codes), passivation plans (for example removing residual fuel after end-of-mission), preventing in orbit collision with for example risk assessment, as well as end-of-life procedures (for example de-orbiting), and provide legal regulation for the space industry.[397]

---

393 Act N Pr-906 (19 April 2013) on 'Fundamentals of the Russian Federation's State Policy in the Field of Space Activities for the Period up to 2030 and beyond', Section VII(18)(e).

394 Act N Pr-906 (19 April 2013) on 'Fundamentals of the Russian Federation's State Policy in the Field of Space Activities for the Period up to 2030 and beyond', Section VII(19). See also Statement of the Russian Federation to the UNCOPUOS in the UNCOPUOS, Compendium of space debris mitigation standards adopted by States and international organizations, UN Doc. A/AC.105/C.2/2021/CRP.19 (4 June 2021).

395 Outer Space Treaty R 52925-2018 (1 January 2019) on 'Space Technology Items. General Requirements for Space Vehicles for Near-Earth Space Debris Mitigation' (developed by the Federal State Unitary Enterprise Central Research Institute for Machine Building, approved by Order of the Federal Agency for Technical Regulation and Metrology on September 21, 2018 N 632-st).

396 Statement of the Russian Federation to the UNCOPUOS in the UNCOPUOS, Compendium of space debris mitigation standards adopted by States and international organizations, UN Doc. A/AC.105/C.2/2021/CRP.19 (4 June 2021).

397 Statement of the Russian Federation to the UNCOPUOS in the UNCOPUOS, Compendium of space debris mitigation standards adopted by States and international organizations, UN Doc. A/AC.105/C.2/2021/CRP.19 (4 June 2021).

In sum, the Russian Federation has a wide-reaching legislative framework in place to govern NSA space activity and ensure its compliance with and supervision by the Russian State, including provisions on guarding the environment of outer space.

4.2 *Kazakhstan*

In relation to space exploration, the Republic of Kazakhstan is best known for its Baikonur Cosmodrome, which is reputed to be the world's largest operational spaceport.[398] The entities carrying out space activities from Kazakhstan are essentially all operated and overseen by the State, with the exception of one private space company called Eurasian Space Ventures.[399]

Kazakhstan's main regulatory instrument is its Law on Space Activities.[400] However, in Article 2, it provides that when Kazakhstan ratifies an international treaty containing rules that contradict the domestic legislation, the treaty rules prevail. This means that all the rules in international treaties that Kazakhstan is a party to apply to the NSAs under its jurisdiction, including those in the Outer Space Treaty, which Kazakhstan acceded to in 1998.[401]

Under the Law on Space Activities, the Government of Kazakhstan has responsibility for deciding on launches of space objects from Kazakhstan's territory, approving technical regulations in the field of space activities, and defining arrangements regarding the Baikonur cosmodrome. Article 3 of the Law sets out a number of principles to guide Kazakhstan's implementation

398 Guillaume Tiberghien, Raushan Mukhamedjanova, and Philip Feifan Xiw, 'Authenticity and spectrality of space heritage: Baikonur Cosmodrome, Kazakhstan' (14 July 2023) 25 *An International Journal of Tourism Space, Place and Environment* 5 (Taylor and Francis Online) (available at https://www.tandfonline.com/doi/full/10.1080/14616688.2023.2231422), pp. 1445–1464.

399 Mark Holmes, 'Activities in Kazakhstan' *Via Satellite* (24 September 2021) (available at https://www.satellitetoday.com/business/2021/09/24/eurasian-space-ventures-looks-to-boost-space-activities-in-kazakhstan/); Eurasian Bank, 'A Private Space Company from Kazakhstan Together with SpaceChain is Preparing to Launch a Satellite on Elon Musk's SpaceX Falcon 9 Rocket' (available at https://astanatimes.com/2021/07/kazakh-company-launches-cryptocurrency-and-quran-satellite-projects-on-board-of-spacex-falcon-9-rocket/). But see Silk Way, 'Startups in aerospace industry to be developed in Kazakhstan (25. August 2022) (available at https://jibekjoly.tv/en/startups-in-aerospace-industry-to-be-developed-in-kazakhstan); Spacewatch Global, 'Kazakhstan to start its own satellite design and manufacturing industrial base' (available at https://spacewatch.global/2020/02/kazakhstan-to-start-its-own-satellite-design-and-manufacturing-industrial-base/).

400 Law of the Republic of Kazakhstan on Space Activities, No. 528-IV (6 January 2012).

401 United Nations Treaty Series, 'Treaty on principles governing the activities of States in the exploration and use of outer space, including the moon and other celestial bodies', (https://treaties.un.org/pages/showdetails.aspx?objid=0800000280128cbd).

of its space program. These include 'compensation for harm to health of individuals, damage to the environment, property of individuals and legal entities [and] the State arising out of the implementation of space activities' as well as 'compliance with ecological requirements, requirements in the field of technical regulation and provision of sanitary and provision of sanitary and epidemiological wellbeing of [the] population'.[402]

The safety of space activities is regulated in Chapter 5 of the Law, under Article 27, which requires that measures be taken to protect 'people's health and environment protection'. Before the launch of a space object, participants in the space activities must notify the relevant national environmental authority of the coordinates of the designated drop areas for the separated parts of the carrier rocket. If the environment is harmed as a result of the launch, the participants in the space activities should indemnify the damage caused. These rules demonstrate that the Kazakhstan law takes addresses environmental concerns arising from space launches, both *ex ante* (the obligation to inform the authorized body about the coordinates) and *ex post facto* (indemnification for the damage caused).

Article 27 of the Kazakhstan Law also regulates foreign NSAs. It provides that a space object belonging to a foreign individual or legal entity can fly through Kazakhstan's airspace while ascending to outer space or returning to Earth subject to the prior agreement of the Ministry of Defence and authorized bodies in the field of emergency situations of natural and anthropogenic character and environment protection.

Importantly, Article 29 provides that state authorities will monitor the impact on the environment and natural resources arising from space activities. Information regarding the protection of the environment and emergency situations should be distributed to the public through a system of notifications via the media and other forms of communication.

Article 30 lists four prohibitions, namely the creation of immediate threats to people's lives and health, the launching into orbit or deployment in outer space of weapons of mass destruction, the use of space engineering to negatively impact the outer space environment, and the infringement of international norms and standards regarding the pollution of outer space. The pollution of outer space is thus only covered as far as it represents a violation of international standards.

402 Law of the Republic of Kazakhstan on Space Activities, No. 528-IV (6 January 2012), Article 3.

At the international level, Kazakhstan signed an agreement with Russia in 2019 concerning cooperation (in the implementation of launches) of Soyuz-2 carrier rockets. The treaty's coverage of the environment is notable, as it requires environmental impact assessments, and provides that environmental damage linked to the launch (or associated search and rescue operations) must be compensated by the organisation conducting the activities.[403]

The fact that space activities in Kazakhstan are predominantly conducted by the State is clear from its legislation, which consists of mostly general principles and does not prescribe a detailed procedure for licensing or State authorization of private activities. Its laws contain several references to the environment, and are notable for providing that its international obligations override inconsistent domestic obligations.

4.3 *Ukraine*

The 2022 full-scale Russian invasion of Ukraine has severely disrupted its space operations (along with many other facets of Ukraine's societal structures). Consequently, the following discussion focuses on Ukraine's activities prior to 2022. After the end of the Cold War, Ukraine developed its space capacity based on the infrastructure and frameworks it inherited from the Soviet Union.[404] It successfully cooperated with the European Union on matters concerning space exploration, including in relation to the Global Navigation Satellite Systems (EGNOS and Galileo) and the joint use of Ukraine's ground satellite telemetry stations.[405]

In 2019, Ukraine made a significant turn towards the commercialization of space activities, adopting legislation that opened the door for private actors to enter the space sector, including corporations from abroad.[406] Shortly after this legislative change, investments in the Ukrainian space sector increased, as demonstrated by the US-based NSA Firefly Aerospace, which placed an order with Ukrainian-owned entity YuzhMash for a 15 million US dollars value

403 Ziemblicki and Oralova (2021), p. 6 citing Agreement between the government of the Republic of Kazakhstan and the government of the Russian Federation on the procedure for interaction in the event of accident during space launches from the Baikonur Cosmodrome, signed at Astana 18 November 1999.

404 ESPI, 'ESPI Perspectives 51: Space Activities Ukraine Looking for New Developments' (August 2011).

405 ESPI, 'ESPI Perspectives 51: Space Activities Ukraine Looking for New Developments' (August 2011).

406 Kinstellar, 'Ukraine allows private sector involvement in space activities' (November 2019) (available at https://www.kinstellar.com/news-and-insights/detail/971/ukraine-allows-private-sector-involvement-in-space-activities).

mass production of rocket parts.[407] YuzhMash produces engines for the ESA Vega rocket, which delivered numerous satellites into orbit.[408] However, the 2022 Russo-Ukrainian conflict has significantly impacted the Ukrainian and subsequently European space industry, and its long-term effects remain to be seen.[409]

The key Ukrainian space legislation is the 1996 Law on Space Activity.[410] Within this legislation, Section I concerns 'space activity', and covers NSA activity. It requires State authorization and supervision of any NSA activity.[411] This accords with Article VI of the Outer Space Treaty, to which Ukraine is a State party. The scope of application of the Law is defined to apply to space activity, including all phases and all types of activity 'connected with research and use of outer space',[412] conducted within the territory of Ukraine or abroad, when under its jurisdiction.[413]

In Articles 24 and 25, the Law provides that compulsory insurance for certain types of space activity shall be obtained, and that compensation shall be provided if any damage occurs. Article 29 goes on to describe that offences under this legislation shall be punishable by disciplinary, civil-law or criminal penalties in conformity with Ukrainian legislation in force.

Among the prohibited or restricted actions are misuses of space technology. For example, this covers where such technology is used as a means of producing effects upon the environment for military purposes or other purposes posing a threat to humankind, or where such is used to present a direct threat to the life and health of human beings, or to cause damage to the environment. These abuses cover violations of international norms and standards regarding

---

407 Kinstellar (2019); Ilya Timtchenko, 'Firefly looks to bolster aerospace ties with US, investing in Ukraine for the long-haul' (20 August 2018) (available at https://www.kyivpost.com/post/8390); Metallurgprom, 'Firefly Aerospace ordered at the Pivdenmash missile parts to $ 15 million' (31 October 2019) (available at https://metallurgprom.org/en/news/ukraine/1657-firefly-aerospace-zakazala-na-juzhmashe-detali-raket-na-15-millionov-dollarov.html).

408 UkraineInvest, 'Ukrainian Yuzhmash is developing engines for the Vega launch vehicle that injected 53 micro and nanosatellites to orbit' (available at https://ukraineinvest.gov.ua/en/news/ukrainian-yuzhmash-is-developing-engines-for-the-vega-launch-vehicle/).

409 ESPI, 'Executive Brief No. 57' (5 May 2022).

410 Law of Ukraine of 15 November 1996: Ordinance of the Supreme Soviet of Ukraine on Space Activity.

411 Articles 5 and 10.

412 Law of Ukraine (15 November 1996): Ordinance of the Supreme Soviet of Ukraine on Space Activity, Preamble.

413 Preamble.

pollution of outer space or other acts related to space activity which are not permissible under international law.[414]

Furthermore, activities "conducted under a specific project which has led to the loss of human lives, substantial material damage or substantial damage to the environment may be restricted or prohibited in conformity with the legislation of Ukraine currently in force."[415] According to Ukraine's statement to UNCOPUOS, this in effect means that infringing international norms and standards concerning outer space pollution is forbidden when carrying out space activity from Ukraine.[416]

Several other references to the environment are made throughout the Law. It defines an '[i]ncident' as a space activity related event that has led to a threat to the life or health of persons or damage to or destruction of the property of citizens, enterprises, institutions or organizations, or damage to the environment. Similarly, the term '[e]mergency' is explained to mean an event related to a space activity which has led to the death of persons or to serious bodily injury, or to destruction of the property of citizens, enterprises, authorities or organizations, or substantial damage to the environment.

Article 21 of the Ukrainian Law decrees that subjects of space activity shall comply with safety requirements with regard to the life and health of the public, the property of citizens, enterprises, institutions and organizations and protection of the environment. Article 23 specifies that, should there arise in the course of space activity a threat to the population of Ukraine or to its environment or to foreign States, the Ukrainian National Space Agency shall, in conformity with legislation currently in force, immediately inform the competent State authorities of Ukraine. The Law also addresses space facilities (including in Articles 10 and 12–16). For example, Article 15 requires that space facilities must not be operated in violation of Ukrainian legislation. These provisions could open a pathway for establishing further environmental protection, dependent on environmental laws of the State and applicability of international standards such as the debris mitigation guidelines.

According to Ukraine's statement to UNCOPUOS, such standards, consistent with the UNCOPUOS SDMG and IADC SDMG, are transposed into a national mechanism complimentary to the law, namely Industrial Standard URKT-03

414 Article 9.

415 Article 9.

416 Statement of Ukraine to the UNCOPUOS (regarding Article 9 of the Law of Ukraine) (15 November 1996) in the UNCOPUOS, Compendium of space debris mitigation standards adopted by States and international organizations, UN Doc. A/AC.105/C.2/2021/CRP.19 (4 June 2021).

from 2006. The requirements of this standard are compulsory for all entities performing space activities in Ukraine. They apply to launch vehicles as well as spacecraft, whether developed for domestic or foreign contractors, unless other debris mitigation standards are specified in a contract.[417]

Finally, in the Agreement between the Government of the Russian Federation and the Cabinet of Ministers of Ukraine on Technology Safeguards Associated with Cooperation in the Field of the Exploration and Use of Outer Space for Peaceful Purposes and in the Development and Operation of Space Rocket and Rocket Equipment,[418] the environment is mentioned in Article 13(7)(b), which allows the 'imposition of limitations on the movement and use of protected items and technologies within the territory of the State of the importing Party … in case of a threat to security, public order, human life and health and (or) the natural environment.'

In sum, Ukraine has adopted important changes to its legislation in 2019, allowing for the increasing involvement of NSAs in space activities. The analysis of the legislation shows that it pays attention to environmental protection, but it is not clear how this goal is being carried out through the authorization and supervision procedures in specific instances. The 2022 Russian invasion of Ukraine will no doubt significantly impact Ukraine's ability to maintain the proper regulation of its space programme.

4.4 *Armenia*

Armenia's space sector is rapidly developing.[419] The Armenian Law on Space-Related Activities,[420] sets out the goals of strengthening its security and

417 Industrial Standard URKT-11.03 on 'Limitation of the Near-Earth Orbital debris Making at Operation of Space Technical Equipment' (19 July 2006). See also Statement of Ukraine to the UNCOPUOS in the UNCOPUOS, Compendium of space debris mitigation standards adopted by States and international organizations, UN Doc. A/AC.105/C.2/2021/CRP.19 (4 June 2021).

418 Agreement between the Government of the Russian Federation and the Cabinet of Ministers of Ukraine on Technology Safeguards Associated with Cooperation in the Field of the Exploration and Use of Outer Space for Peaceful Purposes and in the Development and Operation of Space Rocket and Rocket Equipment, Signed in Moscow on 11th of June 2009.

419 Manya Israyelyan, 'Fostering a SpaceTech Ecosystem in Armenia' *EVN Report* (3 August 2023) (available at https://evnreport.com/creative-tech/fostering-a-spacetech-ecosystem-in-armenia/); Armenpress, 'Bazoomq becomes first Armenian licensed private space operator' (8 September 2023) (available at https://armenpress.am/eng/news/1119066.html); RFE/RL's Armenian Service, 'Armenian's First Satellite Reaches Orbit After SpaceX 'Rideshare' Launch' (27 May 2022) (available at https://www.rferl.org/a/armenia-first-satellite-spacex/31870989.html).

420 Basic Law No. HO-152-N on Space-related Activities of the Republic of Armenia (Original Source: RAPT 2020.04.01/30(1585) Art. 356), Yerevan: RA National Assembly (Date of Signature by RA President 26.03.2020, Date of entry into force 11.04.2020).

expanding its international cooperation.[421] It clarifies that all relations in the field are regulated both by Armenian law, including the Constitution, and international treaties,[422] including the Outer Space Treaty. This includes all aspects of space activity, from manufacture, to operations, to end-of-life activities.[423]

Under its core principles of space activities, international security and cooperation are listed alongside ensuring Armenia's international responsibility and environmental protection.[424] The Law decrees that NSA activity shall require a license by the properly authorized body, that the registration of space objects shall be required, that launch facilities will be supervised and that safety shall be assured, *inter alia*, through compliance with safety requirements and Armenian legislation on environmental protection, and by an effective and efficient information system whereby operators must immediately inform the authorized bodies of any dangers, in the fields of defence, security, emergency and other threat to population or environment. It ends with clarifying that insurance for space activities shall be required, damages shall be compensated in accordance with the law, and that the State shall supervise activities carried out by inspection bodies authorized by the government.

The Law was accompanied by two annexes, namely Annex 1 on procedures and conditions of licensing space activity and Annex 2 on the space activity license form. Annex 1 specifies that licensing is carried out by the Armenian Ministry for Industry and shall be mandatory for legal entities engaging in any space-related activity.[425] It shall be granted for an indefinite period, but only to the specific entity and for the specific location.[426] Having regard to the provisions and objectives spelled out in the Law, the Annex requires an approved program, detailed description of the company's activities, information about expected investments, technical specifications, and construction documents.[427] Any change in the activity has to be reported within 10 days.[428] If an operator is changed, that must be notified to the authority and a new license application submitted.[429] A license may be suspended, terminated or

421 Article 1.
422 Article 3.
423 Article 4.
424 Article 5.
425 Section I Article 1.
426 Section II Article 5.
427 Article 8.
428 Article 8.
429 Article 17.

amended,[430] and compliance with mandatory requirements and license provisions must be supervised by inspection bodies.[431]

Based on the preceding, the Armenian Law and accompanying documents are broadly formulated, with few mentions of the environment and international responsibility. This leaves it unclear whether the guiding thought behind it is the Earthly or the space environment.

5 South American States

5.1 *Brazil*

Brazil[432] is an emerging space State, with an ideal geolocation for launching.[433] It is currently in a process of establishing its space industry, for which it cooperates with other States, such as India, Russia, China and the United States, as well as various NSAs.[434] In 2021, Brazil's Earth observation satellite, AMAZONIA-1, was successfully launched by the Indian Space Research Organization (ISRO).[435] At the end of 2022, Brazil entered into formal cooperation with UNOOSA and the UN Development Programme.[436] To prepare for the commercialization of space activities, it is inviting NSAs to make use of

---

430 Part III Article 15.

431 Part III Article 16.

432 For an analysis see also Francisco Werneck Maranhao, Guillermo Zuma Hoorn, and Antonio Carlos Almeida Braga, 'Brazil' in Joanne Wheeler (ed.), *The Space Law Review* (Business Law Research Ltd, 2020), pp. 41–53.

433 Andrea Cabello, Lucia Helena Michels Freitas, and Michele Melo, 'Brazilian Space Sector: Historical Analysis of the Public Budget' (2022) 62 *Space Policy*.

434 See, e.g., Michele Melo and Paulo Vasconcellos, 'High hopes for Brazil's space ambitions' (2020) 25 *Room: Space Journal of Asgardia*, p.3 (available at https://room.eu.com/article/high-hopes-for-brazils-space-ambitions); International Trade Administration, 'Brazil Space Sector' (15 March 2021) (available at https://www.trade.gov/market-intelligence/brazil-space-sector).

435 Michele Melo and Paulo Vasconcellos, 'High hopes for Brazil's space ambitions' (2020) 25 *Room: Space Journal of Asgardia*, p.3 (available at https://room.eu.com/article/high-hopes-for-brazils-space-ambitions); International Trade Administration, 'Brazil Space Sector' (15 March 2021) (available at https://www.trade.gov/market-intelligence/brazil-space-sector); Andrea Cabello, Lucia Helena Michels Freitas, and Michele Melo, 'Brazilian Space Sector: Historical Analysis of the Public Budget' (2022) 62 *Space Policy*.

436 UNOOSA, Press Release: New Partnership between UN Office for Outer Space Affairs, UN Development Programme and Brazilian Space Agency, UN Doc. UNIS/OS/575 (15 December 2022) (available at https://www.unoosa.org/oosa/en/informationfor/media/2022-unis-os-575.html).

Brazilian infrastructure, such as the Alcantara Space Center,[437] and has passed national legislation to establish a national space agency, tasking it with coordination, as well as NSA oversight and licensing.

Under law number 8,854 of 10 February 1994, Brazil established the Brazilian Space Agency, which is tasked with the establishment of standards and issuing of licenses and authorizations relating to space activities, as well as applying quality and productivity standards in space activities. There is no explicit requirement to observe environmental protections in order to obtain a license to operate from the Government. Moreover, the definition of damage omits harm to the space environment,[438] which aligns with the non-ecocentric definition of harm in Article I of the Liability Convention.

Whereas Brazil has enacted national regulation of licenses, including avenues to suspend or revoke them when agreed conditions specified in national law are not adhered to, the conditions do not pertain to environmental safety, but rather to the business soundness of the operator. This seems in line with Brazil's continued efforts to build up its space sector but not in line with international standards seeking environmental protection and space debris mitigation.

5.2 *Costa Rica*

In 2021, Costa Rica enacted a Law establishing the Costa Rican Space Agency and another establishing a national registry of space objects pursuant to Article VIII of the Outer Space Treaty.[439] Both hint at NSAs having obligations, but provide no further details.

The Law on the creation of a national registry does not mention the environment and holds no further references to NSA activity, other than indirect obligations to provide information on launched objects. However, the law on the creation of the Costa Rican Space Agency details the functioning and functions of the Agency, reaffirming among the latter the principles of international space law, namely that the exploration and use of outer space shall promote the protection of the Earth's natural environment and that all means

437 See, e.g., Andrea Felippe Cabello, Michele Christina de Melo, Guilherme Viana Ferreira, Lucia Helena Michels Freitas, Fernando Moreira Couto de Lima, 'The Incipient Brazilian Private Space Sector: A Brief Description' (2022) 11 *NewSpace* 3; Alejandro J. Afonso, 'Brazil relaunches its space industry by opening the Alcantara base to the US' *Universidad de Navarra* (available at https://www.unav.edu/web/global-affairs/detalle/-/blogs/brazil-relaunches-its-space-industry-by-opening-the-alcantara-base-to-the-us).

438 Article 3.

439 Law No. 9960 (8 February 2021) on the creation of the Costa Rican Space Agency, Article 3; Law No. 9770 (29 October 2019) on the Creation of the Registry of Spatial Objects.

shall be used to protect humanity against natural disasters. Likewise, the environmental effects in the space of these activities must be taken into account.

The Law specifies that the State will be responsible for national activities carried out in outer space by governmental organizations or non-governmental entities, and must ensure that said activities are carried out in accordance with the international principles applicable to space law.[440] It furthermore decrees that the Agency will be the national institution in charge of authorizing and supervising national activities carried out in outer space by government agencies or non-governmental entities. Likewise, it will be in charge of ensuring that said activities are in accordance with the provisions of international law.[441] It makes no further mention of the environment or specifies any conditions for granting of a license. However, the reference to the goals of solving humanity's problems and pursuing objectives of sustainable development of the United Nations, focusing on well-being in Article 4, could act as a way of introducing space sustainability and associated environmental protection into Costa Rican space activities.

The Act makes several mentions of NSA activities by, for example, noting that the national space policy should promote the development of space systems, technology and infrastructure, facilitating the incorporation of the productive sector into this activity so that they become more competitive in the markets for space goods and services, as well as promoting competitive advantages and innovation capacity of industries for the development of science, technology and innovation in space matters, in collaboration with state universities.[442]

5.3 *Peru*

Peru took a similar approach to Costa Rica, adopting a Law on the establishment and operation of a national Centre for Satellite Imagery Operations, a Decree-Law on the establishment of the Commission National of Investigation and Aerospace development and a Supreme Decree establishing a national register of objects launched into outer space pursuant to Article VIII of the Outer Space Treaty.[443] Peru's space legislation requires the submission of

440 Article 2.

441 Article 2.

442 Article 5.

443 Decree-Law No. 20643 (11 June 1974) on establishing the Comision Nacional de Investigacion y Desarrollo Aeroespacial – CONIDA; Law No. 28799 'Declaring the establishment and operation of a National Centre for Satellite Imagery Operations' (Ley 28799, Que declara de interés nacional la creación, implementación y desarrollo de un Centro Nacional de Operaciones de Imágenes Satelitales); Supreme Decree No. 008-2016-DE

data about the non-contamination of outer space.[444] More broadly, Peru's constitution contains several environmental protections, but nothing that directly addresses outer space. In this light, it is notable that Peru signed on to the Artemis Accords in 2024, despite also being a State Party to the Moon Agreement, which potentially clashes with the more permissive provisions of the Artemis Accords in relation to private entities engaging in space resource exploitation.[445] In its statement to the United Nations, Peru stated that it does not have any space debris mitigation standards, but plans to deorbit the PeruSAT-1 at end of its useful life.[446]

6 Asian States

6.1 *Japan*[447]

Japan is a powerful actor on the space scene, with over one hundred satellites in orbit, and an active space agency – the Japan Aerospace Exploration Agency Act (JAXA).[448] Japan's aerospace market is dominated by Mitsubishi Heavy Industries, IHI Aerospace, Mitsubishi Electric Corporation and NEC Space Technologies, often supported by venture capital-backed startups like Astroscale (a debris removal NSA).[449] JAXA is planning to further increase investments to invest in private businesses.[450] Japan cooperates closely with

establishing the National Register of Objects Launched into Outer Space (Decreto Supremo N° 008-2016/DE que crea el Registro Nacional de Objetos Lanzados al Espacio Ultraterrestre).

444

445 Delgado López (2024) See also above Chapter 1, Section 3.

446 Statement of Peru to UNCOPUOS in UNCOPUOS, Compendium of space debris mitigation standards adopted by States and international organizations, UN Doc. A/AC.105/C.2/2021/CRP.19 (4 June 2021).

447 Daiki Ishikawa, Hiroko Yotsumoto and Tetsuji Odan, 'In review: space law, regulation and policy in Japan' *Lexology* (5 January 2023) *Lexology* (available at https://www.lexology.com/library/detail.aspx?g=f0a661ce-b787-4bb5-95ab-d07fd4159fe6).

448 National Research and Development Agency Japan Aerospace Exploration Agency Act No. 161 (13 December 2002).

449 International Trade Administration, 'Japan Space Industry Commercialization' (26 August 2021) (available at https://www.trade.gov/market-intelligence/japan-space-industry-commercialization); Forbes, 'These Japanese Startups Are Powering Space Development' (18 March 2021) (available at https://www.forbes.com/sites/japan/2021/03/18/these-japanese-startups-are-powering-space-development/); JAXA, 'Japan's Space Industry' (available at https://aerospacebiz.jaxa.jp/en/partner/).

450 Hiroyuki Akiyama, 'Japan's space agency to be freed to invest in private businesses' *NikkeiAsia* (13 June 2023) (available at https://asia.nikkei.com/Business/Aerospace-Defense-Industries/Japan-s-space-agency-to-be-freed-to-invest-in-private-businesses).

the United States, either through various partnerships or trading activities.[451] The Japanese NSA iSpace was further set to become the first NSA to have a presence on the Moon, but was set back as its lander ultimately failed to land successfully.[452]

The most important document of Japanese space legislation is the Basic Space Law,[453] which sets out Japan's priorities and goals, formulating a broad space policy aimed at the improvement of people's lives through space technology.[454] The Act makes specific references to the environment. First, in Article 1, it decrees that space development and use in Japan, based on the pacifist philosophy of the country's constitution, and while giving due consideration to harmony with the environment, shall improve the lives of the people, contribute to the improvement of society and the development of the economy, as well as to contribute to world peace and the improvement of human welfare. Similarly, Article 7 provides that space development and utilization must be carried out with due consideration to the environment. Article 20 demands the State to take necessary measures to promote space development and use in harmony with the environment, including international cooperation to preserve the outer space environment.

The Basic Law furthermore entails several references relevant to NSA space activity. It determines that all space activities shall be carried out in accordance with international treaties,[455] and that the State has the corresponding responsibility to formulate and implement comprehensive policies[456] and take necessary legislative, fiscal, tax, financial, and other measures to implement these.[457] These encompass Japan's obligation to authorize and supervise NSA space activity pursuant to Article VI of the Outer Space Treaty. The Law furthermore determines that space development and utilization will improve the technological strength and international competitiveness of Japan's space industry and other industries,[458] that to promote this development and

451 International Trade Administration, 'Japan Space Industry Commercialization' (26 August 2021) (available at https://www.trade.gov/market-intelligence/japan-space-industry-commercialization).

452 Luke Hurst, 'Japan's ispace is set to become the first private company to land on the Moon' *Euronews* (25 April 2023) (available at https://www.euronews.com/next/2023/04/25/japans-ispace-is-set-to-become-the-first-private-company-to-land-on-the-moon.

453 Basic Space Law, Law No. 43 of 2008 (27 August 2008).

454 See Article 3.

455 Article 2.

456 Article 8.

457 Article 11.

458 Article 4.

utilization the State shall cooperate with local governments, universities, private business operators, and other such entities,[459] and shall promote such business activities, recognizing the importance of the role played by the private sector in space development and utilization.[460]

Following the Basic Space Law, Japan adopted legislation with accompanying Regulations and Enforcement Orders, on handling of remote sensing records and the Act on the launch of artificial satellites and the management of artificial satellites of 2016.[461] Any person intending to launch an artificial satellite, as well as any launch facility aboard a ship or aircraft located in Japan or having Japanese nationality must receive permission from the Prime Minister for each launch, by written application along with documents specified by Cabinet Office Ordinance.[462] Considering that the Act is aimed at promote inclusion of and competitiveness of companies,[463] it is assumed that '*person*' includes natural and legal persons, thus encompassing NSAs, as confirmed by the following provisions.

The Act refers to standards for permission to manage satellites in Article 6. Environmental provisions are included in conditions set out in Article 22, notably that the satellite is designed to prevent the equipment and parts of it from scattering, to prevent other harmful effects on outer space, to prevent harmful pollution of outer space and potentially harmful interference with the space activities of other countries as stipulated in Article IX of the Outer Space Treaty, and to ensure public safety.[464] The product must therefore meet standards specified by the Cabinet Office Ordinance, and the management plan presented must entail collision avoidance measures, harmful pollution prevention measures and termination of space activity measures, such as safely deorbiting or moving the satellite to another orbit.[465] Further detailed procedures are specified in the 'Guidelines on Permission Related to launching of Spacecraft', 'Guidelines on License Related to Control of Spacecraft', and 'Review Standards and Standard Period of Time for Process to Procedures under the Act on Launching of Spacecraft, etc. and Control of Spacecraft', of the National Space Policy Secretariat (Cabinet Office) from 15 November

459 Article 10.

460 Article 16.

461 Act No. 76 (16 November 2016), the Act on the launch of artificial satellites, and the management of artificial satellites.

462 Article 4.

463 Article 3.

464 Article 22.

465 Article 22.

2017.[466] Nonetheless, JAXA maintains its own space debris mitigation standard (currently JAXA Management Requirements 003D (JMR-003D)), applicable to all JAXA projects, governed by domestic law and international standards (e.g. UNCOPUOS SDMG, IADC SDMG, ISO standards).[467]

In addition to the preceding Act, the government issued a Cabinet Office Ordinance titled 'Regulations for Enforcement of the Act on the Launch of Artificial Satellites and Management of Artificial Satellites'.[468] It addresses NSA conduct and mentions the environment specifically once in Article 22, where it decrees that mechanisms must be put in place to prevent deterioration of the environment, which appears to cover both the earthly environment and that of celestial bodies. On this basis, Japan has incorporated an environmental consciousness into its legislation, at least in part.

The 2016 Act continues that operators are entirely responsible for damage caused by their satellites, with courts being authorized to determine the amount, specifically to consider if force majeure contributed to the onset of damage.[469] The Act entails a penalties section,[470] specifying four types of penalties for offenses committed in respect of space activities. The highest penalties are imprisonment with work for not more than three years, a fine of not more than three million yen, or both, for launching without a license or non-compliance with license conditions for such offenses as launching without a license or violation of license. The lowest penalty is a non-penal fine of not more than 100,000 yen for any person who fails or submits a false notification. For corporations, the representative or agent who committed the offence is subject to the above-described penalties, with the corporation itself subject to the fine prescribed in the Act in addition. The preceding is well formulated to enable supervision of NSA activity.

Regarding actual practice, Ishikawa, Yotsumoto and Odan highlight that test launches (namely, launches without payloads) and suborbital flights may be outside the scope of the Space Activities Act. While permission for launch activity is in principle given on a case by case basis, in reality the fact that the

466 Statement of Japan in UNCOPUOS, Compendium of space debris mitigation standards adopted by States and international organizations, UN Doc. A/AC.105/C.2/2021/CRP.19 (4 June 2021).

467 Statement of Japan in UNCOPUOS, Compendium of space debris mitigation standards adopted by States and international organizations, UN Doc. A/AC.105/C.2/2021/CRP.19 (4 June 2021).

468 Cabinet Office Ordinance No. 50 of 2017, 'Regulations for Enforcement of the Act on the Launch of Artificial Satellites and Management of Artificial Satellites'.

469 Articles 53, 54.

470 Articles 60–65.

same rocket design is often used for numerous years has led to applications for launches not being required to provide detailed information every time.[471] The same furthermore applies to launch facilities that have already been licenses, leading to a detailed license evaluation of the facility not being required for each following launch.[472] Ishikawa, Yotsumoto and Odan furthermore analyze that space related acts do not establish any particular dispute resolution system with respect to licenses. Consequently, any dispute will be processed in accordance with the Japanese Administrative Complaint Act.[473] Nonetheless, Japan appears to be one of the most environmentally conscious space-faring States, with active space agencies and a growing debris-removing or debris-mitigating NSA market.

However, on the issue of resources, Japan's record is less environmentally oriented. In 2021, Japan became the fourth country in the world to enact national legislation permitting extraction and appropriation of space resources.[474] In this respect, it fits with the emerging trend of State signatories of the Artemis Accords, which claims that the extraction of space resources is not inconsistent with Article II of the Outer Space Treaty.[475]

In summary, Japan thoroughly regulates NSA space activity in several respects. Japan lists the environment under goals of the Basic Space Act, and specifically as a condition for management of satellite permits, where it directly references Article IX of the Outer Space Treaty. Further mentions of Japan's responsibility under international law and the general obligation that all space activity is carried out in accordance with international law, with specific mention of the Outer Space Treaty, makes it apparent that Japan has considered its obligations under Articles VI and IX of the Outer Space Treaty, and has established a licensing procedure, defined consequences to non-observation of the legal obligations, and adopted some environmental protection provisions that include also the outer space environment.

6.2 *Republic of Korea*

The Republic of Korea has a developed space market. In 2022, its space budget was 553 million dollars (US). The following year, it increased 19.5 percent to

471 Daiki Ishikawa, Hiroko Yotsumoto and Tetsuji Odan (2023).

472 Daiki Ishikawa, Hiroko Yotsumoto and Tetsuji Odan (2023).

473 Daiki Ishikawa, Hiroko Yotsumoto and Tetsuji Odan (2023).

474 Act on Promotion of Business Activities Related to the Exploration and Development of Space Resources, Law No. 83 of 2021 (Space Resources Act) (23 June 2021) – Supp. Provisions Article 1.

475 See Artemis Accords, Section 10.

674 million dollars.[476] It has future ambitions including landing a vehicle on the Moon and later on Mars. To facilitate this, the government plans to step up public-to-private transfer of space technologies and launch a funding program for up-and-coming space companies.[477]

Korean legislation relevant for space activities consists of several legal documents.[478] The first one adopted was the Aerospace Industry Development Promotion Act[479] of 1987. In 2005, a more space-specific act was adopted, entitled the Space Development Promotion Act.[480] Both documents are primarily addressed to the State[481] and/or establish new bodies.[482] However, the Space Development Promotion Act contains certain provisions that are also relevant to NSAs.[483]

If Korean nationals, natural or legal persons, intend to launch space objects in or outside Korea, they need to obtain a license from the respective authority – the Minister of Science and Technology.[484] In their application, a launch plan including a safety analysis report, a payloads operation plan, and the damage liability coverage must be presented. Though there are no specific references made to environmental protection amongst the conditions for granting a license or amongst reasons for its termination, a reference is made to safety and security,[485] which could encompass environmental concerns under Korea's international obligations. Regarding enforcement, Article 14 regulates liability and Article 15 demands third-party liability insurance, both aimed at

476 Interagency Operations Advisory Group, 'South Korea aims to establish a national space agency modeled after NASA by next year' (12 January 2022) (available at https://www.ioag.org/SitePages/South-Korea-aims-to-establish-a-national-space-agency-modeled-after-NASA-by-next-year.aspx).

477 Interagency Operations Advisory Group, 'South Korea aims to establish a national space agency modeled after NASA by next year' (12 January 2022) (available at https://www.ioag.org/SitePages/South-Korea-aims-to-establish-a-national-space-agency-modeled-after-NASA-by-next-year.aspx).

478 See Youngshin Ahn, *National Space Law and Policy in the Republic of Korea* (Brill Nijhoff, 2024).

479 Aerospace Industry Development Promotion Act, Law No. 8852 (4 December 1987).

480 Space Development Promotion Act, Law No. 7538 (31 May 2005).

481 See, for example, Aerospace Industry Development Promotion Act, Articles 3, 4 and 12; Space Development Promotion Act, Articles 3 and 5.

482 See, e.g., National Space Committee was established by Article 6 of the Space Development Promotion Act. See Doo Hwan Kim, Space Law and Policy in the Republic of Korea (2012) Report to the United Nations Office for Outer Space Affair (available at https://www.unoosa.org/pdf/pres/2010/SLW2010/02-09.pdf).

483 See, e.g. Article 18.

484 Article 11.

485 See, for example, Article 13.

ensuring that the NSAs are (at least partially) liable for the damage caused by their space objects. These two provisions are regulated in further detail in the Space Liability Act.[486]

The Space Development Promotion Act regulates sanctions for certain violations of its provisions.[487] Both a monetary fine as well as imprisonment are possible. The length of imprisonment and the amount of monetary fine are defined based on the type of offence. For example, for performing a launch of a space object without obtaining a license, imprisonment up to five years is possible, as well as a monetary fine of fifty million Won.[488] In certain cases, dual penalization is possible, meaning that the person that is a representative, agent, servant or other employee of a legal entity, as well as the legal entity, can be charged simultaneously.[489]

Lastly, it is important to mention Korean Space Debris Mitigation Recommendations for the Development and Operation of Spacecraft. These recommendations are based on international UNCOPUOS recommendations, and their purpose is to create an environment in which Korean NSAs can *voluntarily* participate in the international community's efforts to protect the space environment. These efforts include the safe utilization of space assets and the sustainable use of outer space, by specifying matters that should be considered by developers and operators of launch vehicles and satellites to minimize the generation of space debris.[490] While this document is significant as an example of State practice, it remains non-binding in nature, and therefore it is tantamount to provisions transposing SDMG into national legislation, included in certain laws, such as Austrian or Slovenian acts on space activities.

The analysis of Korean space legislation shows that the State has managed to put in place several obligations resting upon the government and other State bodies to act in matters of authorization and supervision of NSA space activities, and has also established several obligations for NSAs directly, as well as several sanctions for non-compliance. While there are no specific references to the environment made in the law, the Korean Space Debris Mitigation Recommendations contain several recommendations for protecting the space environment and minimizing harmful effects of space debris. However, these Recommendations do not contain enforcement mechanisms and operate on a voluntary basis.

486 Space Liability Act, Law No. 8852 (21 December 2007).

487 Articles 27, 28 and 29.

488 Article 27.

489 Article 28.

490 Article 1.

6.3 *China*

China is a notable example of a space-active State without a specifically tailored space law. Despite being highly active in space and undergoing several missions, including, but not limited to satellite operations, global navigational services (BeiDou), celestial missions and even an orbital space station, China has only issued an official National Space Policy in the form of White Papers, which are issued approximately every five years.[491] These indicate that China considers space activities critical to, *inter alia*, its ability to conduct domestic operations. While it has relied on an untrammeled use of space to develop its capabilities, it now seems to recognize that to maintain its space operations it must pay due regard to the protection of the space environment and prioritize sustainability of its access to outer space.[492]

In the 1980s, China recognised the strain its vast population was placing on the environment and the necessity to protect that environment to guarantee its survival. This led to the development of Chinese environmental law,[493] which means environmental protection has ever since needed to be planned into all Chinese activities.[494] China was furthermore an original member of the Inter-Agency Space Debris Coordination Committee (IADC)[495] in 1995, signaling its devotion to space sustainability, developing space object and debris monitoring capabilities as early as 2001. The environment-friendly approach is furthermore mirrored in China's White Papers from 2000, 2006, 2011, 2016 and 2021, which spell out Chinese space policy.

Carns notes that the 2000 White Paper set out the initial roadmap, recognizing the importance of ensuring space sustainability and for China to engage with the international community and adopt necessary measures to protect

---

491 The 2000 China Space White Paper; The 2006 China Space White Paper; The 2011 China Space White Paper; The 2016 China Space White Paper; The 2021 China Space White Paper.

492 Marc Carns, *Orbital Debris Prevention and Mitigation Efforts Among Major Space Actors* (Martinus Njihoff Publisher, 2023), pp. 157–167.

493 Environmental Protection Law of the People's Republic of China (adopted on 26th December 1989). Other legal acts preceded it developing environmental protection in China, for more see Carns (2023), p. 69; Jesse Turiel, Iza Ding, John Chung-En Liu, Environmental Governance in China: State, Society, and Market (Brill, 2020); Lu Ruilan, Handbook of Regulations on Environmental Protection in China (RFF Press, 1994, revived 2016 by Routledge).

494 Carns (2023), p. 169 See also Information Office of the State Council of the People's Republic of China, Environmental Protection in China, Permanent Mission of the People's Republic of China to the United Nations Office at Geneva and Other International Organizations in Switzerland (June 1996).

495 For more on the IADC see: IADC, 'Welcome to the Inter-Agency Space Debris Coordination Committee' (available at https://iadc-home.org/what_iadc).

the space environment.[496] The 2006 White Paper then focused increased attention on environmental protection.[497] However, the 2011 White Paper changed in tone due to the 2007 Chinese ASAT test, which produced copious amounts of space debris.[498] The Paper's language changed to seemingly addressing the international audience rather than a domestic one, and speaking of developing and utilizing space resources prudently, while taking effective measures to protect the space environment.[499] While it mentioned many past activities, it did not refer to the 2007 ASAT test or its environmental impact. Nonetheless, it added, for the first time, a section on space debris, outlining China's monitoring and space situational awareness capabilities, and post-mission disposal efforts as well as early collision warnings.[500] The 2016 Paper revealed a vision of desiring to build China into a space power, through innovative and open development. It also acknowledged the space debris threat, highlighting its success in the space surveillance awareness data and early warnings.[501] The current 2021 Paper presented an ambitious space program, focused on extending China's global reach, *inter alia* through advancing its commercial space capabilities and existing legal issues, with space debris featuring prominently throughout for which China acknowledges an obligation for facilitating global consensus and shared responsibility of safeguarding outer space for the benefit of all humanity.[502]

These white papers highlight China's long involvement in advancing space debris management and sustainability. Its other related efforts include the China-Russia Space Cooperation and Sino-US Expert Workshop, advancement of new technologies, mitigation measures, in-orbit servicing, and even interest in 'space debris cleaning', which Carns assumed to refer to active debris removal even though the term is not employed.[503]

Regarding NSAs, China seems to view partial privatization and further development of commercial space activity as one of the critical cornerstones to

496 Carns (2023), pp. 177–178.
497 The 2006 China Space White Paper. See also Carns (2023), p. 178.
498 See Carns (2023), at 177–183. See also the 2011 China Space White Paper.
499 Carns (2023), p. 179. See also the 2011 China Space White Paper.
500 Carns (2023), p. 179. See also the 2016 China Space White Paper.
501 Carns (2023), p. 179. See also the 2016 China Space White Paper.
502 Carns (2023), pp. 177–182. See also the 2021 China Space White Paper.
503 Carns (2023), pp. 181–182. See also the 2000 China Space White Paper; The 2006 China Space White Paper; The 2011 China Space White Paper; The 2016 China Space White Paper; The 2021 China Space White Paper.

guaranteeing Chinese world leadership in space.[504] NSA space activity in China requires authorization from the State. However, the lack of a national space law as well as the complicated and extensive system of governance currently in place for space matters, seems to result in confused channels of State supervision.[505] Of note are the Measures for the Administration of Objects Launched into Outer Space in 2001, establishing some notification obligations for NSAs in accordance with the Registration Convention, as well as Interim Measures on the Administration of Licensing the Project of Launching Civil Space. These are departmental regulations at the lowest level of the Chinese regulatory framework.[506] The Interim Measures clarify that commercial and civil operators need to acquire a license before launch from Chinese territory or by Chinese citizens anywhere, and for this license must meet certain standards, such as not compromising State security or State benefits, that the activity is beneficial to the public and will meet Chinese international norms which bind China, including the Outer Space Treaty provisions, in particular Articles I, II and IX.[507]

The Interim Measures address protection of the environment, requiring reducing the likelihood of creating space debris, and prohibiting activities that would cause irremediable danger to public health, safety or property during all phases of space operations, especially during space operations due to space debris being considered one such danger to future operations and public property.[508] In this, China directly addresses space debris, requiring that certain safety designs must be met to ensure safety. The instruments also require that the entity undertaking the space activity must provide sufficient information regarding the materials that will be used, the safety systems and their reliability, how assessments of possible malfunctions of the launching rocket will be conducted, and measures that will be taken to avoid pollution and debris production.[509]

---

504 Fabio Tronchetti, 'Space Law and China' *Oxford Research Encyclopedia: Planetary Science* (25 February 2019) (available at https://oxfordre.com/planetaryscience/display/10.1093/acrefore/9780190647926.001.0001/acrefore-9780190647926-e-66;jsessionid=228B9CE470EF03340B6A46E91201B7D0?rskey=4IV574andresult=89), p. 3.

505 Carns (2023), pp. 157–167. For an organizational chart of the Chinese Space Program see: Carns (2023), p. 164.

506 For an organizational Chart see Carns (2023), pp. 164, 172.

507 Laws of the People's Republic of China, Interim Measures on the Administration of Permits for Civil Space Launch Projects (21 November 2002).

508 Carns (2023), p. 174; Laws of the People's Republic of China, Interim Measures on the Administration of Permits for Civil Space Launch Projects (Nov. 21 2002), Article 5.

509 Carns (2023), pp. 174–175; Laws of the People's Republic of China, Interim Measures on the Administration of Permits for Civil Space Launch Projects (21 November 2002), Article 6(d).

These early measures adopted in 2001, prior to the adoption of the UNCOPUOS SDMG, were followed by the 2010 Interim Instrument on Space Debris Mitigation and Management Instrument (distinct from the requirements of the five-year plan).[510] The latter were implementation of domestic best practices and standards, adopted by State Administration of Science, Technology, and Industry for National Defense (SASTIND)[511] and were formally adopted in 2015 as the Measures on the Administration of Space Debris Mitigation and Protection. That instrument sought to enact technical standards and recommended practices to reduce environmental pollution during all phases of spacecraft lifecycle, determining supervision and mitigation measures.[512] Carns concludes that the previous instruments did not actually limit debris creation, but simply required explanation of safety procedures. Conversely, the new Measures implemented a regulatory scheme closely resembling the SDMG, including providing orbital insertion and trajectory data for registration purposes, control of debris release during normal operations, passivation measures for residual propellants, post-mission de-orbiting or moving of satellites to graveyard orbits, constant monitoring of risks and describing mitigation measures in order to receive a permit.[513]

In terms of jurisprudence, though it is scarce, China has demonstrated its willingness to take NSAs to a domestic court of law in one case, where it applied Article II of the Outer Space Treaty to prohibit private appropriation of the lunar surface.[514]

As an overarching observation, in spite of lacking a national space law, China has adopted regulations designed to reflect its international obligations, such as those contained within Articles VI and IX of the Outer Space Treaty. It requires NSAs to respect the space environment. However, doubts could be raised with regards to the reality of the debris situation, referencing the 2007 ASAT test and several other alleged ASAT tests. Chinese national defence strategy seems to rely heavily on the development, testing and use of ASAT

---

510 Carns (2023), p. 175.

511 As indicated China has a complex governmental organisation eloaorately addressed and mapped out by Carns (2023), p. 164. SASTIND is among the most important agencies overseeing civil space activity, reporting directly to the Ministry of Industry and Information, and is primarily tasked with drafting guidelines, policies, plans, research and regulations connected to the science, technology and industry (including satellite operations) as well as mainatining China's space object register, see Carns (2023), pp. 165–166.

512 Tronchetti (2019), p. 7; Carns (2023), pp. 175–176.

513 Carns (2023), p. 176. See also Tronchetti (2019), p. 7.

514 *Lunar Embassy to China v. Beijing Administration of Industry and Commerce*, Haidian District People's Court, November 2005.

technology, raising doubts regarding the protection of the space environment if Chinese sovereignty were threatened. Consequently, China recognizes the imperative of protecting the space environment, and transposing these obligations on the private space sector. However, despite a booming growth in the Chinese space sector, the domestic regulatory framework remains complicated and subject to various agencies, including the military sector, with the standardization of the national scheme not among one of its most pressing issues.[515]

6.4 *India*

India is a rising space power with a regional navigational system in operation, celestial missions including a relatively recent non-manned landing on the dark side of the Moon, considerable numbers of other satellites in orbit, and anti-satellite weaponry, the ability of which is successfully tested in 2019 with an ASAT test.

Notably, India is another example of an active space State without a core piece of legislation in place. In 2017, the Indian Government introduced the Space Activities Bill 2017, which is, however, still in the legislative process. In the meanwhile, India only has a space policy in place issued by the Indian Space Research Organization.[516] The policy is applicable to any space activity directed to or undertaken from Indian territory or within the jurisdiction of India including the area to the limits of its exclusive economic zone.[517] Additionally, exemptions may be provided on a case-by-case basis. Content-wise, the policy seeks to provide regulatory certainty for space activities by various stakeholders and to create a thriving space ecosystem. In this, the policy is quite commercially oriented, making numerous references to NSA space activity, and entailing developing a flourishing private sector participation.

Specific mentions relevant to NSA activity in space include the statement that they shall be allowed to undertake end-to-end activities in space sector

---

515 For more see Carns (2023), pp. 157–187; Tronchetti (2019).

516 Indian Space Policy 2023. For further detail see: Kumar Abhijeet, *National Space Legislation for India* (Springer, 2020); Nitin Sarin, Vinamra Longani and Dhawal Jain, 'India' in Joanne Wheeler (ed.), *The Space Law Review* (Law Business Research Ltd, 2020), pp. 64–74.

517 Indian Space Policy 2023, 9. The 2015 Indian Space Act Draft has proposed to extend and clarify this applicability to all space activity carried on from Indian territory or within the jurisdiction of India including the area to the limits of its exclusive economic zone, off-shore platforms, vessels, aircraft including other air-borne vehicles and space objects registered by India as well as to actions of Indian citizens and juridical persons registered or incorporated in India, regardless of their whereabouts (meaning located on Indian territory or abroad), see Government of India, Department of Space, No.E.11020/2/2015-Sec-VI (2015).

through establishment and operation of space objects, ground-based assets and related services, such as communication, remote sensing, navigation, and suchlike to undertake research, innovation and technology development for long-term sustainability of space activities.

Regarding environmental provisions, the Indian policy lists the protection of the environment and lives among its values. The Department of Space shall participate in international efforts by providing critical remote sensing satellite data for disaster management efforts and meeting the requirements of the sustainable development goals formulated by the United Nations in coordination with the Ministry of External Affairs. It is required to establish a framework to ensure safe and sustainable space operations, in compliance with relevant international space debris mitigation guidelines. While the reference to protection of the environment does not specify whether it includes the space environment, it could be read from the overall provisions contained in the policy, especially the dictum that the Space Debris Mitigation Guidelines should be respected, that protection of the space environment is or at least will be warranted in the course of space activities conducted by India and its NSAs. India, for example currently and despite its 2019 ASAT test, maintains that it adheres fully to the UNCOPUOS SDMG, practices de-orbiting of space objects and has advanced Collision Avoidance capabilities (COLA) and Space Objects Proximity Analysis (SOPA) for safeguarding its space assets during ascent, orbital insertion and in-orbit operation.[518]

6.5 *Indonesia*

Indonesia is an active space nation with around 8 satellites in orbit and ambitious plans for a spaceport in 2040.[519] Indonesia implemented its Law of the Republic of Indonesia on Space Activities,[520] Presidential Regulation No. 45 of 2017 on National Plan on Space Activities year 2016 – 2040 and Government Regulation No. 11 of 2018 on Remote Sensing.

Its main Law on Space Activities applies to natural and legal persons on the territory of Indonesia or abroad under its jurisdiction on its behalf or by its

518 Statement of India in UNCOPUOS, Compendium of space debris mitigation standards adopted by States and international organizations, UN Doc. A/AC.105/C.2/2021/CRP.19 (4 June 2021).

519 Neni Ruhaeni and Eka An Aqimuddin and Hadian Afriyadi, 'The Commercialization of Outer Space Under the Outer Space Treaty 1967 and Its Implementation on the Development of Space Industry in Indonesia' (2022). *Proceedings of the 4th Social and Humanities Research Symposium (SoRes 2021).*

520 Indonesia Outer Space Law, Law No. 21 of 2013 on Space Activities.

nationals or legal entities incorporated in Indonesia, thus covering NSA activities.[521] The Law makes several references to the environment, such as defining security as not causing damage to the Earth or space environment,[522] demanding that space activities be implemented with due regard, *inter alia*, to environmental protection and management and the Space environment, as well as provisions of national laws and international treaties that Indonesia became a state party to.[523] It prohibits activities that would violate Article IV of the Outer Space Treaty, and those that may result in environmental pollution and/or damage on Earth or in space and jeopardize activities in space, including the destruction of space objects.[524] It encourages research into, among others, the space environment and space weather,[525] and requires that each space organizer (every entity engaging in space activity)[526] maintains and ensures the preservation of the environment and avoids damage to the Earth and space environment from contamination caused by space activity due to violating quality standards.[527] However, there is no mention of the environment under the Article on establishing the 'master' plan, despite a reference to sustainable and efficient utilization of natural resources and space resources while maintaining the preservation of the environment is referred to under implementation of the space plan.[528]

It is notable that sustainability for present and future generations is included among goals of space activity, next to State independence, defence and competitiveness as well as welfare of its people and protection of the people from negative consequences to ensure safety and security.[529] This indicates that environmental protection must be secured not only for itself, but for the protection of the people as well.[530] Moreover, in the section discussing spaceports, the Indonesian Law requires environmental sustainability and an environmental impact analysis, in accordance with national and international provisions.[531]

---

521 Articles 1, 5.
522 Article 1.
523 Article 7.
524 Article 8.
525 Article 11.
526 see Article 1.
527 Article 87.
528 Article 43.
529 Article 2.
530 As one of the possibilities discussed in the earlier Chapters, See Chapter 4, Section 2.
531 Articles 45, 48.

The Law also reaffirms several international obligations, such as recognizing space as belonging to all mankind,[532] as dictated in Article I of the Outer Space Treaty, mandating national registration of space objects[533] in accordance with Article VIII of the Outer Space Treaty and provisions of the Registration Convention, and liability provisions in line with the Liability Convention. Liability is thus absolute for damage on Earth and to aircraft in flight, and fault-based in outer space, with the possibility of the State seeking recourse against the NSA operator.[534]

Regarding NSAs, the Law references commercial activity specifically and demands compliance to standards for a license,[535] which shall be set out in a government regulation.[536] The most specific provisions concern launching activities. They require that financial requirements and insurance be obtained, that any potential and/or possibility of accidents and/or public health problems or material losses is minimized, as well as ensuring that a space object does not carry nuclear weapons, weapons of mass destruction or other dangerous weapons. They also require guarantees that the launch will not cause possible disruption to national security and will not cause violation of foreign policy and international obligations. They finally require the operator to pay attention to and fulfill provisions on aviation safety.[537] In the event that the launch is carried out abroad (that is, beyond Indonesian territory) the launch license must require an agreement that Indonesia can be released from liability in instances of damage occurring.[538]

Launch safety officers are authorized to enter and inspect space facilities and any space objects and test other equipment located at the facility with the approval of the space activity license holder,[539] and that every space activity license holder, employee, and agent or contractor shall comply with the instructions given by the launch safety officer at the launch facility.[540]

Finally, the Law decrees that immediately after an accident, the launch license concerned shall be suspended until the freeze is lifted by the Minister; it may furthermore be revoked or altered during the freezing period.[541] All

532 Article 3.
533 Articles 71, 72.
534 Article 76–79, 84.
535 See Articles 51, 52, 57.
536 See Articles 37, 42, 55, 56, 69.
537 Article 35.
538 Article 35.
539 Article 55.
540 Article 56.
541 Article 69.

requirements and provisions regarding a freeze, revocation, suspension or alteration of a license will be dealt with by a government regulation.[542] These indicated sanctions are augmented with the possibility of administrative action (such as a warning or the dissolution of a legal entity) for violating the provisions of the Law on Space Activities,[543] and criminal proceedings, in the form of both fines and imprisonment, for example for launches that do not conform to requirements or violate quality standards and criteria of environmental damage, which results in polluted or contaminated environment life.[544]

In sum, the Indonesian Law was adopted after the International Law Association's Model Law, which is discussed below, and provides broad coverage of the key obligations placed on States under international space law. Given that Indonesia is a relatively new entrant to the space exploration context, it is an important step to have the legislation in place. Nonetheless, it remains to be seen how the national regulation will evolve through the indicated Governmental Regulations and how the provisions will be carried out in practice.

7 Middle Eastern States

7.1 *United Arab Emirates*

The United Arab Emirates has a fast-growing space sector and has drastically increased its investments in the space sector in recent years. In 2019, they exceeded Dh22 billion (approx. 6 billion US dollars), with over 50 space-related establishments operating in the country and creating around 1,500 jobs.[545] In 2020, the United Arab Emirates carried out the first Arab unmanned mission to Mars.[546]

542 Article 69.

543 Article 94.

544 Article 95–98.

545 Telecom review, 'An Elevated Future: The UAE Space Sector Is Thriving' (16 January 2023) (available at https://www.telecomreview.com/articles/reports-and-coverage/6699-an-elevated-future-the-uae-space-sector-is-thriving).

546 Agence France-Presse, 'UAE successfully launches Hope probe, Arab world's first mission to Mars' *The Guardian* (20 July 2020) (available at https://www.theguardian.com/science/2020/jul/20/uae-mission-mars-al-amal-hope-space); Emirates News Agency Wam, 'UAE reinforces its journey towards a leading and advanced space sector with qualitative achievements in 2023' (20 November 2023) (available at https://wam.ae/article/apqiq6p-uae-reinforces-its-journey-towards-leading-and).

Its ambitions also include reaching the Moon and deploying a lunar rover.[547]

The core legislation in the United Arab Emirates is its Federal Law Number 12 of 2019.[548] In Article 1 of this Law, it is explained that the Law applies to both physical as well as juridical persons, meaning that this law applies to the activities of NSAs. The objectives of this Law include stimulating investment and encouraging the participation of the private and academic sectors in space activities. Importantly, the objectives include supporting environmentally-oriented (or at least conscious) measures to enhance the sustainability and long-term stability of space activities and related activities. This means that the Law on one hand aims at achieving a significant measure of participation of NSAs with their headquarters in the United Arab Emirates in space activities, but on the other hand includes environmental protection, at least as a means to ensure the sustainability of space activities.

Space activities are defined broadly, including space resources exploration and extraction.[549] This makes the United Arab Emirates one of the very few States that explicitly allow such activities, in line with those members of the Artemis Accords. However, NSAs may only conduct space activities if granted a permit to do so by a specialized Agency.[550] The obligation to obtain a permit applies also in cases when an operator is using space nuclear energy sources.[551] Every operator authorized to use space nuclear energy sources must immediately inform the Agency of any accident or incident encountered, or the risks faced, and any measures undertaken thereby to reduce the same or the effects thereof.

Article 19 of the Federal Law is relevant for the prevention of space pollution of NSAs, as it is dedicated to space debris mitigation. It provides that every operator seeking to own or develop a space object, or carry out or participate in space activities, must take the necessary measures and plans to mitigate space debris and reduce the effects thereof. The operator is liable for damage caused on the surface of the Earth or in aircraft during its flight, by a space object

547 Sally Boyani, 'The Rashid Rover didn't make it to the Moon, but it's a success for science' *Wired.me* (3 May 2023) (available at https://wired.me/gear/rashid-rover-worlds-most-compact-lunar-rover/); Jennifer Bell, 'Dubai's ruler announces new moon mission after UAE's Rashid Rover lunar 'crash'' *English Alarabiya* (27 April 2023) (available at https://english.alarabiya.net/News/gulf/2023/04/27/Dubai-s-ruler-announces-new-moon-mission-after-UAE-s-Rashid-Rover-lunar-crash-).

548 Federal Law No. (12) (19 December 2019) on the Regulation of the Space Sector.

549 Article 4.

550 See Articles 8, 14.

551 Article 17.

participating in the activities authorized for the operator.[552] Environmental damage is not listed as a form of damage recoverable under this provision.

Based on the foregoing, the Emirates' legislation reflects its ambitious space activities. Its Federal Law tackles several fields that are rarely tacked by national laws – for example, the extraction of space resources and the deployment of nuclear energy sources. Despite a strong interest in enhancing the capabilities of its private sector, the Law contains several safeguards aimed at preventing space pollution, such as environmental impact assessment, risk management plan and space debris mitigation.

8 African States

8.1 *South Africa*

South Africa has been active in the field of space activities since the beginning of the space age, and is one of the leading actors of this field on the African continent.[553] According to its Council for Space Affairs, the country has taken meaningful steps towards the aim of sustainable development and the role of space activities in achieving this, as it has since 2002 Johannesburg World Summit on Sustainable Development promoted and coordinated initiatives for sustainable Earth observation, such as the Group on Earth Observations, which then resulted in a globally coordinated Earth observation system – called GEOSS.[554]

The main legal document regulating space activities in South Africa is the Space Affairs Act.[555] It concerns itself with mechanisms to control certain space affairs and the matters related to that issue. Even though the environmental aspect is not explicitly mentioned in it, the Act still contains several important provisions regarding NSAs.

In Article 1, the Act defines 'space activities' to mean 'the activities directly contributing to the launching of spacecraft and the operation of such craft in outer space'. It also defines a distinct category of 'space-related activities', meaning 'all activities supporting, or sharing mutual technologies with, space

552 See Article 20.

553 SACSA, 'Space in South Africa' (available at http://www.sacsa.gov.za/space-in-south-africa/; https://link.springer.com/chapter/10.1007/978-90-481-9008-9_12).

554 SACSA, 'Space in South Africa' (available at http://www.sacsa.gov.za/space-in-south-africa/).

555 Space Affairs Act No. 1157 (2 July 1993), No. 84 – Statutes of the Republic of South Africa – Trade and Industry No. 84 of 1993 (6 September 1993).

activities'. In Article 5, the object of the South African Council for Space Affairs is 'to implement, in the most efficient and economical manner possible, the space policy of the Republic', and to 'take care of the interests, responsibilities and obligations of the Republic regarding its space and space-related activities in compliance with international conventions, treaties and agreements entered into or ratified by the Government of the Republic.' This means that the Council is the relevant national body to regulate space activities in South Africa, including the activities of NSAs.

In order to achieve its purpose, Article 5 lists the tasks of the Council, which include to supervise and implement matters arising from international conventions, treaties and agreements concerning space affairs entered into or ratified by the Government of the Republic. Article 11 regulates licensing, and covers a broad spectrum of NSA activities. According to Article 13, licenses may be amended, suspended and even revoked. The Act does not list environmental concerns as an explicit reason for such a decision, however, it is not excluded that the Council could take this aspect into account. The person holding a license carries certain duties and liabilities, as regulated in Article 14. Violations of the provisions regarding licensing procedures and obligations of the license holders are sanctioned by a monetary fine, imprisonment (for some offenses even for a period up to 10 years) or combination of both.

In addition to the aforementioned Space Affairs Act, South Africa has adopted the Space Affairs Amendment Act.[556] Even though it introduced certain changes to the text of the document from 1992, it does not refer to the environment at any point. Similarly, the Astronomy Geographic Advantage Act,[557] which aims to outline measures to advance astronomy and related scientific endeavours and regulate activities in that field, makes a reference on national environmental laws on several occasions,[558] but only with regard to actions taken on Earth to remove obstacles for astronomical observation.

On these bases, it can be concluded that South Africa has developed a relatively extensive legal framework governing its activities in outer space. Little of it, however, directly concerns space pollution or the preservation of the space environment.

8.2 *Kenya*

Despite its interest in space activities, Kenya has no legislation and instead relies on a space policy. The policy mentions the space environment in the

556 Space Affairs Amendment Act No. 1530 (6 October 1995), No. 64.
557 Astronomy Geographic Advantage Act No. 31157 (17 June 2008), No. 21.
558 See, for example, Articles 29, 33, and 34.

introduction, referencing mapping the environment of outer space. However, aside from that reference the policy seems more concerned with the Earthly environment,[559] and considers monitoring the space environment only as necessary to secure its space-based assets.[560] It furthermore mentions the environment under definitions of Earth observation and space weather,[561] but makes no explicit mention of it under goals, aside from mentioning sustainable capacity building.[562] Kenya, however, does participate in the African Resource and Environmental Management satellite constellation initiative, as well as the African Leadership Conference on Space Science Technology for Sustainable Development. However, whether this policy category could include the protection of the space environment remains unclear. Regarding NSAs, Kenya makes no specific legal provision but does indicate that it will have a space agency with an outreach program and will have a board with relevant advisory committees and representation from key users and stakeholders.

8.3 *Nigeria*

Nigeria has enacted laws establishing national space agencies, which in broad strokes predict a licensing obligation for these entities but do not detail any conditions. Nigeria in its National Space Research and Development Agency Act[563] established its national space agency, detailed its procedures and organs, and determined that the agency shall develop the national space policy ensuring that space activities benefit the social and economic development as well as State security of Nigeria. Section 6 specifies general conditions for licenses, prohibiting any activity that would jeopardize public health, the safety of persons or property, would impair the national security or be inconsistent with the international obligations of the Republic of Nigeria. All licensees must thus provide, as soon as possible, information regarding their space objects and activity (in accordance with Article IV of the Registration Convention and Article XI of the Outer Space Treaty). For any deviation from

559 For example, the potential of space technology to benefit and develop the economic and social position of the country is mentioned throughout the policy document and it also refers to agriculture, resource management and weather. Moreover, in the introduction, technology and innovation are described as having a critical role in improving the quality of life and creating wealth for Kenyan citizens. See Kenya Space Policy 2015 (April 2016) for more.

560 See pp. 6 and 7.

561 See p. 5.

562 Kenya Space Policy 2015 (April 2016), pp. 6 and 7.

563 National Space Research and Development Agency Act, Federal Republic of Nigeria Official Gazette Vol. 97, No.98, (30 August 2010), Government Notice No. 382.

the license (for example deviation from orbital parameters), advance approval from the Council of the Nigerian Space Research and Development Agency must be obtained. As for any unintended deviation, it must immediately inform the Council. The licensees are required to insure themselves against liability incurred in respect of damage or loss suffered by third parties as result of space activity.

Most importantly for the present research, the Nigerian Act specifies that all operations by the license holder are required to be conducted in such a manner as to 'prevent the contamination of outer space or adverse changes in the environment of the earth', as well as to avoid interfering with others' peaceful exploration and use outer space, and to avoid breaching Nigeria's international obligations. In accordance with these provisions, licensees must inform the Council as soon as practicable of the end-of-life operations, the final disposal of space object and payload, and termination of operations. The Act therefore contains some safeguards for NSA space activity, including safeguarding the space environment as a condition for granting a license, and is according to Nigeria's statement to UNCOPUOS in compliance with UNCOPUOS SDMG.[564]

9 Additional States with Regulatory Mechanisms Concerning Space Activities

Several more states enacted decrees establishing space agencies, for example Algeria,[565] Philippines,[566] Colombia,[567] Ecuador,[568] Malaysia (which includes some references to licensing and insurance obligation),[569]

564 Statement of Nigeria in UNCOPUOS, Compendium of space debris mitigation standards adopted by States and international organizations, UN Doc. A/AC.105/C.2/2021/CRP.19 (4 June 2021).

565 Presidential Decree No. 02-49 'Creation, organization and functioning of the Algerian Space Agency (ASAL)' (16 January 2002); Presidential Decree No. 06-225 'Ratifying the Convention for Damage Caused by Space Objects' (24 June 2006); Presidential Decree No. 06-468 'Ratifying the Convention on Registration of Objects Launched into Outer Space' (11 December 2006).

566 Republic Act No. 11363: An Act Establishing the Philippine Space Development and Utilization Policy and Creating the Philippine Space Agency, and for Other Purposes (8 August 2019).

567 Decree 2442 (18 July 2006) on the Creation of the Colombian Commission of Space (CCE).

568 Executive Decree No. 1246 (19 July 2012) on the Creation of the Ecuadorian Space Institute.

569 Communications and Multimedia Act 1998; Strategic Trade Act 2010; Malaysian Space Board Bill 2022; National Space Policy 2030. For more, see: MCMC, Satellite Initiatives

Tunisia,[570] Turkey,[571] Poland,[572] Bolivarian Republic of Venezuela[573] and Belarus.[574]

Chile, for example, specifies that space activities should be used for national defence, to enhance the country's social and economic development, to participate by providing their views in the context of international space organizations, and to unify different sectors in support of the peaceful exploration and use of outer space.[575] The Chilean Space Agency is responsible for developing space policy and advising on space matters, including entering into international cooperation or agreements, promoting space activities, proposing criteria for the allocation of national resources for space development, maintaining and updated information on space activities at national and international level, and proposing relevant improvements or reforms at the institutional and operational level.[576] Chilean authorities are required to identify and propose tools and resources for environmental protection and the control of international drug trafficking, providing assistance in these fields to the National Environment Commission and the National Drug Control Commission.[577]

Another example is Ecuador, which has established the Ecuadorian Space Institute, placed under the authority of Ministry of National Defence. The

---

in Malaysia (available at https://www.mcmc.gov.my/en/sectors/satellite/satellite-initiatives-in-malaysia). See also UNCOPUOS, Schematic Overview of National Regulatory Frameworks for Space Activities, UN Doc. A/AC.105/C.2/2023/CRP.28 (20 March 2023).

570 Decree no. 84-1125 (24 September 1984) (modified by decree no. 931642 (9 August 1993)) on the creation of the National Commission for outer space; Law 88-83 (11 June 1988) forming a National Mapping and Remote Sensing Centre of Tunisia (CNCT).

571 Turkey for example issued a Presidential Decree on the establishment of a national space agency alongside a strategy document: Presidential Decree on the Establishment of Turkish Space Agency (Türkiye Uzay Ajansı Hakkında Cumhurbaşkanlığı Kararnamesi) (13 December 2018); 2022–2030 National Space Programme Strategy Document (24 May 2022).

572 Dz. U. 2014 poz. 1533, USTAWA z dnia 26 września 2014 r. o Polskiej Agencji Kosmicznej. For more information on Polish space activities and its legislative framework see Anna Konert and Frans von der Dunk (eds.), *National Space Law in Poland* (Martinus Nijhoff Publishers, 2023).

573 Decree number 3.389 of December 2004; Decree No. 4.114 of 28 November 2005; Law on the Establishment of the Bolivarian Agency for Space Activities (Official Gazette No. 38.796 of 25 October 2007).

574 Decree 609 of the President of the Republic of Belarus (22 December 2004).

575 Supreme Decree No. 338: Establishment of a Presidential Advisory Committee known as the Chilean Space Agency (17 July 2001).

576 Supreme Decree No. 338: Establishment of a Presidential Advisory Committee known as the Chilean Space Agency (17 July 2001).

577 Supreme Decree No. 338: Establishment of a Presidential Advisory Committee known as the Chilean Space Agency (17 July 2001).

Centre for Integrated Surveys of Natural Resources by Remote Sensing has become part of the Ecuadorian Space Institute, and is required to conduct research, development and operation of space activities for the development of the State, for external and internal state security, use, management and conservation of natural resources.[578] However, the decree itself does not seem to mention the environment of outer space or NSA activity.

In a similar vein, the Polish Act creating the Polish Space Agency (POLSA)[579] does not mention the environment or authorization of NSAs. It lists the tasks of the Space Agency and its general objectives for space activities to profit the economy and defence development of the State. The Act provides that the Polish Space Agency will support the space industry and specifies that Agency members shall include representatives of industry, including from entrepreneurs' satellite technology companies involved in the implementation of European Space Agency projects.[580]

Colombia's Space Agency Act is publicly oriented and only mentions the private sector when it decrees that national policy shall be coordinated to create incentives for private initiative participation in space activities,[581] and where it states that public officials and private citizens may be invited to participate in the deliberations of the technical committee, with the right to speak but without voting rights.[582] Otherwise, the Colombian Act seeks to develop the Colombian space sector, enlisting international cooperation as a means to achieving its goal. For this, an intersectoral body for the coordination and execution of national policy for the development of space activities is proposed, to be composed of various public personnel from almost all ministries and the air force, including one representative from universities with the right to speak but without a vote.

578 The act has been unofficially translated by the authors.

579 Act Number 1533 of 2014 (Dz. U. 2014 poz. 1533, USTAWA z dnia 26 września 2014 r. o Polskiej Agencji Kosmicznej). Poland is also in the process of enacting a law on space activities, however, as of July 2024 the Act remains in the drafting phase, for more see for example Anna Konert and Frans von der Dunk (eds.), *National Space Law in Poland: Past, Present and Future* (Brill, 2023); Mahulena Hofmann and Katarzyna Malinowska, 'Poland Goes to Space. The Draft Polish Act' in: P.J. Blount, Tanja Masson-Zwaan, Rafael Moro-Aguilar and Kai-Uwe Schrogl (eds.), *Proceedings of the International Institute of Space Law 2022* (Eleven International Publishing, 2024), pp. 419–431.

580 Act Number 1533 of 2014 (Dz. U. 2014 poz. 1533, USTAWA z dnia 26 września 2014 r. o Polskiej Agencji Kosmicznej).

581 Article 4(3).

582 Article 8.

The Colombian Space Commission is tasked with responsibility for space activities and the national program. Space technologies constitute an important factor for the economic, social and cultural development of peoples, due to their contribution to numerous fields, such as education, health, peacekeeping and public safety, environmental surveillance, natural resource management, disaster prevention and response, land use monitoring, weather forecasting, climate change studies, land transportation, maritime, river and air navigation, and telecommunications, and due to the fact that the application of space technologies contributes to increasing productivity, efficiency and competitiveness in agriculture, industry, commerce, the service sector and other sectors, including government entities. While not specific, the reference to the environment in this respect seems more oriented toward the Earthly environment. Nonetheless, it might be amenable to interpretation to encompass the space environment.

Some States enacted acts in specific areas, such as for example Tunisia, which passed a law on the formation of the National Mapping and Remote Sensing Centre of Tunisia and a decree on the establishment of the National Commission of Outer Space.[583]

The Philippines adopted its national space legislation in 2019 establishing the Philippine Space Agency (PhilSA) and national space policy.[584] The Philippines' private space industry is still evolving, primarily supporting governmental and research actors.[585] It has numerous acts pertaining to space activity, particularly provisions on streamlining export controls to establish a booming industry,[586] controlling devices and technology that could be used to manufacture weapons of mass destruction,[587] internet,[588] funding

583 Decree No. 84-1125 (24 September 1984) (modified by decree No. 931642 (9 August 1993)) on the creation of the National Commission of the Outer space; Law 88-83 (11 June 1988) forming a National Mapping and Remote Sensing Centre of Tunisia (CNCT).

584 Philippine Space Development and Utilization Policy and Creating the Philippine Space Agency, and for other purposes, Republic Act No. 11363 (2019). For more see Rogel Mari Sese, 'The Philippine Space Program: A Modern Take on Establishing a National Space Program' in Q. Verspieren, M. Berthet, G. Coral, S. Nakasuka, H. Shiroyama (eds), *ASEAN Space Programs* (Springer, 2022), pp. 57–77.

585 JAXA, Space Research and Development in the Philippines' (available at https://iss.jaxa.jp/en/kuoa/news/pdf/06_APRSAF22_Philippines.pdf); Cristina Arayata, 'Yearender: PhilSA 'resolutely' expands domestic space ecosystem' *pna.gov.ph* (26 December 2022) (available at https://www.pna.gov.ph/articles/1191408).

586 Republic Act No. 7844 (1994); Presidential Decree No. 930 (1976); Executive Order No. 1016 (1985).

587 Republic Act No. 10697 (2015); Republic Act No. 9516.

588 Executive Order No. 127 (1998); Republic Act No. 10929 (2020).

programs,[589] and telecommunications, which are an essential interest to the State.[590] Under the latter, the purposely established National Telecommunications Commission is responsible, with wide discretionary powers, for granting licenses and certificates to private actors, including Philippine natural and legal persons. The remaining acts likewise make mention of natural and legal persons, and require private persons to gain licenses. They place general supervisory duties on the Philippines for State security and prosperity. However, none of the acts seem to mention the space environment or debris concerns. Nonetheless, the Philippines' first rocket company is aiming for green and sustainable launches.[591]

Some States such as Argentina,[592] and Spain,[593] have enacted registration legislation establishing national space object registries and procedures to comply with Article VIII of the Outer Space Treaty and the Registration Convention. Argentina, with several satellites in orbit,[594] has a number of national acts establishing the national space agency, space registry, and the Argentine Company of Satellite Solutions. These acts result in space activities in Argentina being 'monitored, managed and administered by the National Commission on Space Activities (CONAE)'.[595] NSAs are *inter alia* tasked with

589 Republic Act No. 10692 (2015), An Act Providing for the Modernization of the Philippine Atmospheric, geophysical and Astronomical Services Administration (PAGASA), providing Funds therefor for other purposes also known as The PAGASA Modernization Act of 2015; Administrative Order No. 76 (2011).

590 Executive Order No. 467 (1998) providing for a national policy on the operation and use of international satellite communications in the country. Other identified Acts pertaining to telecommunication are: Republic Act No. 7925; Implementing Guidelines on International Satellite Communications of the National Telecommunications Commission; Republic Act No. 7925 (Public Telecommunications Policy Act); Act No. 3846. as amended (Radio Law), Executive Order No. 546 (1979); Executive Order No. 467 (1998); Presidential Decree No. 576-A; Republic Act No. 3846 (1963).

591 Deyana Goh, 'The Philippines' first rocket company aims for green launches' *Space Tech Asia* (20 October 2020) (available at https://www.spacetechasia.com/the-philippines-first-rocket-company-aims-for-green-launches/).

592 Argentina has enacted numerous laws pertaining to space activity, as summarized in the See UNCOPUOS, Schematic Overview of National Regulatory Frameworks for Space Activities, UN Doc. A/AC.105/C.2/2023/CRP.28 (20 March 2023) and the UNOOSA, *Online Index of Objects Launched into Outer Space* (20 December 2023).

593 Royal Decree 278/1995 (24 February 1995), establishing in the Kingdom of Spain the Registry foreseen in the Convention adopted by the United Nations General Assembly on 2nd November 1974.

594 See Rome (2022).

595 UNCOPUOS, Schematic Overview of National Regulatory Frameworks for Space Activities, UN Doc. A/AC.105/C.2/2023/CRP.28 (20 March 2023).

the duty to register objects (in accordance with the Registration Convention), including the requirement to submit to the national registry information about the 'anticipated date of disintegration, recovery, or loss of contact with the space object (…) information on precautions taken with regard to non-pollution of outer space, including celestial bodies'[596] and insurance obligations.[597]

It is furthermore noteworthy that several of the States mentioned in this Chapter are forming new international organizations, such as the Latin American and Caribbean Space Agency (ALCE),[598] and the African Space Agency (AfSA),[599] while several of the Middle-Eastern States are part of the Arab Satellite Communications Organization (ARABSAT).[600] How these will affect the evolution of space activities within its member States remains to be seen, but it demonstrates the regionalization of space exploration activities.

Finally, Azerbaijan enacted a Presidential Order establishing the State Program for the development of Earth observation services, which stressed the importance of Earth observation satellites for the protection of the environment.[601] Without stating it explicitly, this is directed toward the Earthly environment. Similar intentions were expressed in the Presidential Order on the creation and development of the space industry in Azerbaijan, with special importance (key priority) placed on communication services with regard to Azerbaijan's oil sector.[602] The two orders are supplemented by the Charter of the national space agency Azercosmos, which in broad terms predicts economic and commercial space activity, but in the end again concentrates on public activity, determining only the goal of establishing a national space

596 UNCOPUOS, Schematic Overview of National Regulatory Frameworks for Space Activities, UN Doc. A/AC.105/C.2/2023/CRP.28 (20 March 2023).

597 UNCOPUOS, Schematic Overview of National Regulatory Frameworks for Space Activities, UN Doc. A/AC.105/C.2/2023/CRP.28 (20 March 2023).

598 For more information see Annette Froehlich and Diego Aloso Amande Soria, *A Regional Space Agency for Latin America* (Springer, 2021).

599 Space TV, 'African Space Agency (AfSA)' (available at https://www.spacetv.net/african-space-agency-afsa/).

600 ARABSAT (available at https://www.arabsat.com/).

601 The program mentions the importance of earth observation services for defence purposes and such activities as disaster management. This furthermore strengthens the belief that the policy is oriented toward the earthly environment. See Order #696 of the President of the Republic of Azerbaijan (15 November 2018) on 'The State Program for the development of the satellite Earth observation services in the Republic of Azerbaijan'.

602 Order #443 of the President of the Republic of Azerbaijan (17 August 2009) on 'The State Program on Creation and Development of Space Industry in the Republic of Azerbaijan'.

industry without specifying any authorization or supervision procedures.[603] The Charter does not seem to address the space environment. However, in its statement to UNCOPUOS, Azerbaijan's stated that the Presidential Order Ref. 3303 (from 10 October 2017) and Ref. 3738 (from 1 March 2018) entrust Azercosmos with carrying out activities to implement the launch, operation and exploitation of satellites missions, applying 'inter alia to space debris (if any) in relation to the satellites that fall under jurisdiction and responsibility of the Republic of Azerbaijan'.[604] Presidential orders 'are applicable to all satellite related activities in the republic of Azerbaijan within and outside the country'.[605]

In addition to these national acts, Azerbaijan has entered into two international agreements with the Russian Federation,[606] and France's Airbus DS.[607] The first has the stated aim of ensuring that the space industry conforming with international standards. This could potentially open the door to licensing and environmental provisions, in accordance with international standards such as space debris mitigation guidelines. However, the agreement is State-oriented, mentioning the needs of the population, such as, for example, TV and internet communications especially in rural mountainous areas, establishment of infrastructure, personnel training, manufacture and operation of first Azeri satellites, and the environment, which restricts its ambit to the terrestrial environment. No specific references to authorization and supervision procedures or licenses with regard to NSA are made.

Regarding the second agreement with France's Airbus DS, the agreement numbers satellites of interest, including Azersky for which it states a lifespan of twelve years, without noting end-of-life procedures following the twelve years. In general, this agreement is largely State-oriented, as it mentions the necessity for developing capabilities and human resources for it, and mentions

603 See The Charter of 'Space Agency of the Republic of Azerbaijan (Azercosmos)', adopted by decision #54 of the Cabinet of the Ministries of the Republic of Azerbaijan (26 February 2022).

604 Statement of Azerbaijan to the UNCOPUOS in the UNCOPUOS, Compendium of space debris mitigation standards adopted by States and international organizations, UN Doc. A/AC.105/C.2/2021/CRP.19 (4 June 2021).

605 Statement of Azerbaijan to the UNCOPUOS in the UNCOPUOS, Compendium of space debris mitigation standards adopted by States and international organizations, UN Doc. A/AC.105/C.2/2021/CRP.19 (4 June 2021).

606 'Economic Cooperation Agreement' between the Republic of Azerbaijan and the Russian Federation, Space Data Receipt Complex UNISCAN-24.

607 Agreement signed between national satellite operator Azercosmos and France's Airbus DS in 2014.

as its objective the assurance of sustainability and environmental protection of Azerbaijani territory, as well as improving the country's touristic and economic strength including export. It does not explicitly address NSA responsibility, authorization or supervision procedures or matters to do with the space environment.

Some of the former Soviet States, such as Kazakhstan and Azerbaijan, exhibit certain common tendencies in national space acts such as State-oriented programs and the building of national space programs on the capabilities and activities developed during the times of the Soviet Union.[608] How these will proceed in the future will be significant. However, the Russian invasion of Ukraine in 2022 calls much of the prospects for international cooperation in space endeavours into question.

Many other States, however, remain without national space legislation even as they consider, possibly even embark on, space activities. Israel, a space-active State, is among these.[609] In 2023, it announced to the UNCOPUOS Legal Subcommittee that it intends to draft and adopt national space legislation, as well as referring to Israel's international obligations under the space law treaties and international standards.[610] It did not specify which standards it was referring to, but alluded to its obligations vis-a-vis the private sector, especially in an era of NewSpace,[611] a term which refers to the rise of private space actors and the ensuing commercialization of the space industry.[612] Given the recent Houthi attempted attack on Israel, it may cause the latter to re-invigorate its space activities, but more for military purposes than those of exploration and peaceful scientific study.

The acts mentioned above (State space policies, acts establishing space agencies or national space object registries) are primarily enacted by space

608 For more see Nataliia, R. Malysheva, *Space Law and Policy in the Post-Soviet States* (Eleven International Publishing, 2018).

609 Israel is evaluated to have around 20 satellites in orbit, see Rome (2022). For more information on Israel's space program see Astronautics Now, 'Early Israel's Space Program' (available at http://www.astronauticsnow.com/israelspace/index.html); Yuval Azulay, 'Star wars: 'Israel is interested in space weapons. Every one of our satellites is a machine of war' (27 September 2023) (available at https://www.calcalistech.com/ctechnews/article/frkow8u03); Seth J. Frantzman, 'Israel launches Ofek 16 satellites to complete intelligence coverage' (6 July 2020) (available at https://www.defensenews.com/space/2020/07/06/israel-launches-ofek-16-satellite-to-complete-intelligence-coverage/).

610 Israel's Statement to the LSC 2023 under General exchange of views (2023).

611 Israel's Statement to the LSC 2023 under General exchange of views (2023).

612 Pierre Henriquet, 'New Space: the changing face of the space industry' Polytechnique Insights (3 November 2022) (available at https://www.polytechnique-insights.com/en/columns/space/new-space-the-changing-face-of-the-space-industry/).

actors still emerging with limited space activity. In general, these address largely broad goals, and revolve primarily around the promotion and establishment of a national space sector. Their focus lies on firstly establishing space capabilities and secondly using these activities to boost their national economy, State security and the wellbeing of their citizens. References to the environment seem primarily aimed at the protection of the State's Earthly environment, for example use of Earth observation technologies to help with agriculture and disaster management. The majority of the emerging space States are less focused on controlling their NSAs, and instead are looking to develop NSAs and public space bodies, and guaranteeing their access to outer space when their national space sectors are able to utilize it.[613] While this may demonstrate itself as calls for the preservation and protection of the space environment, it is primarily aimed at safeguarding their future access to outer space and development of their national space sectors for the benefit of their national economies and defence.[614] The position seems to be that established space actors should take measures to protect the space environment as they have been utilizing it, while emerging space actors should give priority to development of their respective space capabilities.[615] Nonetheless it should be noted that several emerging actors do, for example, follow the space debris mitigation guidelines, such as Kazakhstan.[616]

10 International Law Association Model Law for Domestic Systems

There is some variation in State approaches to regulating NSAs conducting space activities under their jurisdiction, as set out in the preceding analysis. For the purposes of harmonizing the analysis of State approaches, the International Law Association's Model Law on national space legislation provides guidance.[617] This non-binding instrument contains minimal and optimal provisions that should be included in national space acts.[618] The Model Law proposes national legislators adopt in national space acts provisions on

613 See generally Viikari (2008).

614 See Viikari (2008), p. 179.

615 See Viikari (2008), p. 179.

616 For more information and analysis see Martha Mejia-Kaiser, *The Geostationary Ring: Practice and Law* (2020). Leiden: Martinus Nijhoff, pp. 174–322.

617 See Annex: 'Sofia Guidelines for a Model Law on National Space Legislation' to the International Law Association, Resolution No. 6/2012 on Space Law (26–30 August 2012).

618 Hobe (2013), pp. 81–95.

authorization and supervision of NSA space activity, compensation, transfer of activity, environmental protection including space debris mitigation measures and registration of space objects.

The Model Law defines 'space activity' broadly, as including 'the launch, operation, guidance and re-entry of space objects into, in and from outer space and other activities essential for the launch, operation, guidance and re-entry of space objects into, in and from outer space.' The term 'operator' refers to a 'natural or legal person carrying out space activities.' There are various conditions required for granting a license, including an appropriate financial situation, sufficient technical knowledge and reliability that space activity is compatible with public safety standards, that space activity does not run counter to national security interests, that space activity does not run counter to international obligations and foreign policy interests of the State, that the operator has complied with ITU Regulations with regard to frequency allocations and orbital positions, and that the operator complies with insurance requirements. Importantly, the conditions also require that the activity does not cause environmental damage to the Earth and to outer space, and that the space activity is undertaken in such a manner as to mitigate to the greatest possible extent any potential space debris.[619]

In accordance with Article VI of the Outer Space Treaty, the Model Law requires State supervision of NSA conduct,[620] the State's ability to withdraw, suspend or amend its authorization,[621] and that any transfer of space activity or object to a new operator should require prior authorization from the competent authority, checking again the conditions for granting a license.[622]

Concerning liability, the Model Law provides that States reserve for themselves the right to (limited or capped) reimbursement from the operator for compensation it has paid as the launching State to third parties for damage caused by NSA space activity.[623] The Model Law furthermore proposes that all NSA operators should be required to present proof of insurance to cover damage caused to third parties, with specific amounts established by national laws, which may, however, be waived if the operator has sufficient equity capital to cover the amount of damage or if the activity is in the public interest.[624] It provides for sanctions (fines) for violations of national space legislation,

619 Article 4.
620 Article 5.
621 Article 6.
622 Article 9.
623 Article 11.
624 Article 12.

specifically for instances of carrying out space activities or transferring these without authorization.[625]

Regarding dispute resolution, the Model Law proposes the use of general rules of administrative procedural law, with appropriate costs and tariffs for the procedure specified, and any dispute resolution methods, for which the Model Law suggests bringing claims before a national jurisdiction and failing this (including through the exhaustion of national remedies)[626] the Permanent Court of Arbitration (New Rules of the Permanent Court of Arbitration (PCA) for Arbitration of Disputes relating to Outer Space Activities).[627]

In relation to environmental harm, the Model Law requires that 'space activities shall not cause environmental damage to the Earth and outer space or parts thereof, either directly or indirectly'. It adds that 'an environmental impact assessment is required before the beginning of a space activity'.[628] It specifies that space activities should mitigate to the greatest extent possible any potential space debris, any potential for in-orbit break-ups, and should prepare for post-mission disposal and avoid in-orbit collisions in accordance with international space debris mitigation standards,[629] referring to the IADC SDMG, the UNCOPUOS SDMG and the ILA International Instrument on the Protection of the Environment from damage caused by space debris.[630]

The Model Law ascribes States the primary role in regulating NSA conduct. However, this is not the exclusive means of addressing NSA activity, with the Permanent Court of Arbitration also cited as a venue for resolving conflicts.[631] Significantly, the Model Law expressly prohibits environmental harm to outer space or Earth and requires environmental impact assessment reports. This provides hortatory support for the conclusion reached above that space law, in accordance with international environmental law, contains a prohibition of space pollution. Moreover, although there is a strong presumption of ensuring

625 Article 14.

626 UNCOPUOS, Information on the activities of intergovernmental and non-governmental organizations relating to space law, UN Doc. A/AC.105/C.2/2013/CRP.6 (26. March 2013).

627 Permanent Court of Arbitration, Optional Rules for Arbitration of Disputes Relating to Outer Space Activities (6 December 2011). Annex: 'Sofia Guidelines for a Model Law on National Space Legislation' to the International Law Association, Resolution No. 6/2012 on Space Law (26–30 August 2012), Article 13.

628 Article 7.

629 Article 8.

630 UNCOPUOS, Information on the activities of international intergovernmental and non-governmental organizations relating to space law, UN Doc. A/AC.105/C.2/2013/CRP.6 (26. March 2013).

631 See, e.g., Permanent Court of Arbitration, Optional Rules for Arbitration of Disputes Relating to Outer Space Activities (6 December 2011).

accountability via State apparatus, there is an additional basis for using international law (at least private international law) to determine the responsibility of NSA for harm including environmental pollution.

The analysis of the national legislation above shows that various States' regulatory frameworks cover many of the topics contained in the Model Law. In this way, the Model Law provides a guide to the form and contents of a putative space law instrument setting out the common approach of States, which would contribute to the coherence and consistency of national approaches. In this way, the Model Law contributes to harmonizing State practice and new national space legislation, and in promoting adherence to the minimum requirement for implementation of Article VI of the Outer Space Treaty. However, the Model Law does not contain enforcement provisions expressly applicable to NSAs, and so would not provide direct redress for NSA space pollution even if adopted as a binding instrument.

11 Conclusions on Domestic and Regional Practice

The analysis demonstrates the existence of State practice regarding the authorization and supervision of NSA space activities mandated by Article VI of the Outer Space Treaty. However, considerable differences and levels of detail exist across space-faring countries. This is consistent with Larsen's observation concerning space debris mitigation guidelines that '[t]he IADC guidelines are not universally adopted and, where adopted, they are implemented differently by the nation-states.'[632] The near ubiquity of environmental protection (to a lesser or greater degree) under domestic space law supports the conclusion that there is a prohibition of space pollution as a general matter shared by space-faring nations, which in turn reinforces the existence of that prohibition as a matter of international law.[633] It also supports the contention that the prohibition is widely seen as applicable to NSAs. However, the variation in how the prohibition is formulated under domestic law, with some States including criminal sanctions and others treating it purely as a licensing issue, renders it difficult to conclude that the prohibition of space pollution has sufficient consistency to be considered criminalized.[634] Moreover, it lacks the precision to be operationalized as an enforceable protection under non-criminal international

632 Larsen (2018), p. 492.

633 Chapter 2, Section 1.

634 See Chapter 4, Section 2.2 for the Tadić conditions for establishment as a criminal provision under international law.

law processes. In the absence of any definitive decision by international courts or international bodies capable of generating binding normative statements, the existence of an operationalized prohibition of space pollution will remain contentious.

Out of the approximately 80 space-active States, the majority have adopted some type of national regulation regarding space activities. However, not all of these acts are comprehensive space laws incorporating detailed authorization and supervision procedures for NSAs. Some have enacted only legal acts establishing national space agencies or space object registries, or even only national space policies. Nonetheless, several common features could be identified in a majority of the inspected acts.

Almost all analyzed legal acts of States determine their scope of application so as to apply to NSAs. Of those, many differentiate between them, separating mostly two types of NSAs: NSAs, active in the territory of that state (including that State's vessels), as well as NSAs, incorporated in that State (even when they are active outside of the State's territory).

Many of the domestic legal acts thus establish concrete rules governing the procedures in which the NSAs can request a license, permission or similar document allowing them to conduct a particular space activity.[635] In most of these cases the law prescribes the basic information that needs to be provided in the application, in a similar manner to the Model Law. States that have detailed authorization procedures in their national acts furthermore often include insurance obligations, generally tied to damages that the authorizing State may need to pay in case of damage by space objects as the launching State. Typically, States that include these requirements include the possibility for a State to claim back the damages it had paid as the launching state from the NSA which was operating the damaging object. Many States that have detailed authorization procedures, additionally set out detailed supervision procedures. These notification obligations include the requirement to alert the host State about changes in operator, space object ownership transfer, and dangers posed to third parties or the authorizing State. Finally, in most cases sanctions are determined as well, which can include fines and compensation as well as, in some cases, potential criminal charges.

From the perspective of protection against space pollution, many of the acts that contain specific and detailed licensing procedures include references to the space environment, either as self-standing provisions, or more commonly

635 However, Hobe notes that only 20 States have what he terms 'comprehensive' space regulation under their domestic systems.

as part of the licensing procedure. The latter approach is prevalent and useful, especially when environmental impact on outer space is explicitly listed as a condition, as limiting the discretion of the decision-making authority leaves less room for private interests to play a dominant role. In case of discretion, the chances of those interests prevailing over environmental protection increase.

Those legal acts that list environmental protection as a condition to issuing authorization of space activities, rarely concretize the content of this condition. Most of the time they refer to either national environmental laws (see, for example: Australia), or to international legal standards on environmental protection (see Austria, Belgium, Denmark, Finland, Slovenia). Often, they refer to UNCOPUOS Space Debris Mitigation Guidelines or in some cases to documents of the International Standardization Organization. This leaves considerable discretion to States and room for inconsistent approaches, which could in turn lead to forum shopping by NSAs, as discussed herein.[636] Therefore, it remains disputed whether the current practice suffices for the emergence of Space Debris Mitigation Guidelines as customary international law.[637]

Examples of US-based space NSAs being legally sanctioned indicates that domestic provisions which reflect international obligations regarding authorization and supervision, including in some instances those regarding environmental provisions, are being enforced in some States. However, in many States the policy statements, national strategies or acts establishing national space agencies or national space objects registries are too vaguely formulated to be justiciable in the courts.

Among the space-faring States, common practices are: permitting NSAs to engage in space activities, but only pursuant to State-granted licenses; referring to environmental protection, set out in broad terms; referring to the State's international obligations, but without any specificity; and imposing a mix of insurance obligations and potential financial and penal sanctions including fines and incarceration, for violating the national regulatory framework. Whilst there is often no specific prohibition of space pollution *per se* in national legislation, it can be seen that many national acts reflect environmental protection as a key concern, most often in the form of a necessary requirement for a license (for example, the creation of a space debris mitigation plan). In such a way, States have, in many cases, incorporate their obligations under the Outer Space Treaty into domestic law, including Article IX.

636 Chapter 3, Section 2.

637 See, for example, Carns (2023), pp. 339–341.

In terms of jurisprudence on space-related matters, it mainly emanates from the United States and has focused largely on cases of individual companies seeking profits or cutting regulatory corners, with little in relation to responsibility for space pollution *per se* (particularly in the absence of any anthropocentric harms), apart from some cases of harm to the Earth's environment.

Finally, on the issue of space resource extraction, the survey shows that some States have decided to adopt legislation which permits certain entities under their jurisdiction to explore and use space resources. The examples of such legislation (from the United States, Luxembourg, Japan, the United Arab Emirates) are the first of their kind, and provide a precedent for future legislation governing this activity. Concerningly, early examples of such legislation do not make any reference to the environment. Several experts have warned that the extraction of space resources could potentially be harmful and could result in space pollution.[638] Accordingly, legislation enabling these space activities should take account of environmental protection.

638 Melissa de Zwart, Stacey Henderson, Michelle Neumann, 'Space resource activities and the evolution of international space law' (2023) 211 *Acta Astronautica*, pp. 155–162, p. 156; Fengna Xu, 'The approach to sustainable space mining: issues, challenges, and solutions' (2020) *738 IOP Conf. Series: Materials Science and Engineering*, p. 5.

CHAPTER 6

Lex ferenda: Normative Options to Redress Future NSA Space Pollution

Based on the preceding survey, multiple questions emerge regarding the legal basis to proceed against NSAs for space pollution. First, there is the question of whether a prohibition of space pollution exists under international law. As shown above,[1] though there is a robust basis to make this claim, it is not beyond any dispute. The prohibition must be read into Article IX of the Outer Space Treaty's reference to 'harmful contamination'. That reading of Article IX is all the stronger in light of international environmental law and State practice, which widely condemns and often criminalizes space pollution as a violation of the State's obligations (typically referred to in the context of space debris).[2]

Proceeding on the basis that the prohibition of space pollution exists, as set out above, enforcement options are nonetheless limited. Space law itself does not provide for an enforcement mechanism capable of ensuring accountability for polluting the outer space environment. If the pollution amounts to a violation of international criminal law or international humanitarian law, then NSAs can be proceeded against, albeit subject to finding an appropriate forum such as the International Criminal Court or a domestic court applying universal jurisdiction.[3] If the pollution amounts to a violation of international environmental law or international human rights law, then the basis to proceed against NSAs is less clear, particularly as there is no legal forum with clear jurisdiction to apply these bodies of law to NSAs in an enforceable way.[4] Although arbitral proceedings or the lodging of claims in domestic courts are conceivable, these approaches would face considerable hurdles and are untested in relation to space pollution. Moreover, they are not regulatory mechanisms, but instead are party-driven proceedings, which would likely be undertaken to obtain or defend financial benefits rather than to protect the environment. On this basis, a schism emerges between the discernible prohibition of space pollution, potentially applicable to NSAs, and the absence of an enforcement architecture capable of ensuring respect for its observance.

1 Chapter 2.

2 See Chapter 2, Section 2.

3 Chapter 4.

4 Chapter 4.

Bearing in mind those questions and the non-comprehensive nature of space law in these respects, it is apposite to look at how space law may develop in the future. To this end, the analysis explores three potential paths: retrenchment, reinterpretation, and reform. Based on that analysis, it extracts observations which can be reached regarding the nature of international law and its formation itself. This normative assessment of international law as a regulatory tool for NSA space conduct constitutes a novel and detailed assessment of options to develop space law at the systemic level.

1 Retrenchment

One possible response to the threat of NSA space pollution would be retrenchment back to international law's traditional State-centric focus.[5] Under this approach, NSA conduct would be exclusively regulated through the juridical gateway of the State. Any emerging alternatives, such as the direct responsibility of NSAs under international law, would be eschewed.[6] At the conceptual level, this would accord with a strict positivist conception, as it would see States as the exclusive subjects of international law, with NSAs lacking legal personality at the international level and falling to States to control.[7] In this way, it would take space law back to its exclusively State-centric genesis.

---

5 Robert Jennings, Arthur Watts, *Oppenheim's International Law, vol 1, 9th ed.* (Oxford University Press, 2008), p. 16; Colin Warbrick, 'States and Recognition in International Law' (2006) in Malcolm Evans (ed.) *International Law*, 2nd ed. (Oxford University Press, 2006), pp. 205–267; Murray (2016), p. 25.

6 Kramer (2017), p. 135. Whilst the current monograph focuses on international law in its current Westphalian form, in the pre-Westphalian eras, NSA conduct was highly relevant to the development of early aspects of international regulation. Notable examples include the Poor Fellow-Soldiers of Christ and of the Temple of Solomon (Knights Templar), which was active from the 12th Century, and the Dutch East India Company, formed in 1602, both of which engaged in consequential operations across a wide range of territories. Several non-State entities have continued to be recognised as subjects of international law in its modern era, including the Holy See and armed groups recognised as belligerents; Ian Brownlie, *Principles of Public international Law, 7th ed.* (Oxford University Press, 2008), p. 64; James Crawford, *Brownlie's Principles of Public International Law*, 8th ed (Oxford University Press, 201), p. 118; Murray (2016), p. 26. For a detailed development of the increasing scope of subjects of international law see Philip C. Jessup, 'The Subjects of a Modern Law of Nations' (1947) 45 *Michigan Law Review*, p. 4; Gerd Droesse, *Membership in International Organizations* (Springer, 2020) (Chapter on Subjects of International Law and International Legal Personality).

7 Jennings and Watts (2008), p. 16; Clapham (2004), pp. 35–36; Murray (2016), pp. 23–24. See also Fergus Green, 'Fragmentation in Two Dimensions: The International Court of Justice's Flawed Approach to Non-State Actors and International Legal Personality'

Robust in its simplicity, the retrenchment approach finds support in the framing of the key space law instruments. Most significantly, there is the Outer Space Treaty, which affords NSAs only a truncated, uni-directional, and contingent legal status. As a result of Article VI of the Outer Space Treaty, States must supervise and authorize *all* NSA space activities emanating from their territory, under their jurisdiction, or by their nationals.[8] Similarly, as a result of Article VII of the Outer Space Treaty and the Liability Convention, it is States which are imbued with the power to hold NSAs responsible for damage caused by such activities. For their part, NSAs must channel their claims for damages through States, as indicated by the language of Article XI of the Liability Convention (which refers to claims that may be conducted in domestic courts by 'a State, or natural or juridical persons it might represent').[9]

There is some support for the efficacy of the strict positivist reading of the Outer Space Treaty and associated conventions, which was favoured until recent years. For example, UNCOPUOS contends that 'United Nations treaties on outer space had established a *comprehensive legal framework* that encouraged the exploration of outer space and supported increasingly complex activities in outer space by both government and private entities, with benefits for both space-faring and non-space-faring countries.'[10] Moreover, the retrenchment approach would fit with the broader tenet of space law, the roots of which tilt in favour of States being the exclusive legal subjects of international law relevant to space conduct.

However, those restrictive readings of the core legal instruments collide with the growing role of NSAs in space exploration in practice. Retrenching back to an exclusively State-centric position will accentuate the current risks presented by NSAs. As surveyed above, these include States struggling to keep pace with technologically sophisticated NSAs engaged in space activities;[11] States being unwilling to regulate NSA activities emanating from their territories;[12] or unable to do so in parts of States' territories outside the control of the central Government;[13] enterprising corporations, and other individuals or groups, seeking to exploit weaker regulatory regimes, utilizing so-called 'flag

(2008) 9 *Melbourne Journal of International Law*, p. 50; Anthony Clark Arend, *Legal Rules and International Society* (Oxford University Press, 1999), p. 176.

8 Stubbe (2018), p. 82.

9 Chapter 2, Section (2).

10 United Nations Report of the Committee on the Peaceful Uses of Outer Space, 2007, para. 186 (italics added).

11 See Chapter 3, Section 2.

12 See Chapter 3, Section 2.

13 Chapter 3, Section 2 citing Clunan and Trinkunas (2010); Tsagourias (2016); Rabasa (2007).

of convenience countries';[14] the indeterminacy of the attributes of Statehood; and, finally, the extra layers of linkage, and specifically causation and attribution, plus the restrictive effect of the foreign acts of State doctrine. Moreover, as shown in Chapter 5, where States have enacted domestic legislation concerning space activities, it is often vague and unclear as to how environmental obligations would be enforced.[15] Those regulatory approaches can be enhanced by better adherence to best standards, but will not address the problems with ungoverned spaces set out in Chapter 3, Section 2.

Additionally, the retrenchment model would exacerbate a potential loophole in the Outer Space Treaty. This is the framing of Article II prohibiting the Moon and other celestial bodies from being subject to 'national appropriation by claim of sovereignty, by means of use or occupation, or by any other means.' That reference to 'national' appropriation could be exploited by unscrupulous NSAs (potentially backed by States) to argue that they can take possession of resources from those bodies and argue that this is commercial in nature rather than national appropriation. Furthermore, questions persist regarding the legality of space resource extraction, and dangers arise from *de facto* appropriation of space mining sites through permitted use or complete depletion to the point where it impacts the surface of celestial bodies and/or outer space itself.[16] By failing to regulate how NSA ownership would be exercised, the legal framework leaves a significant gap open for exploitation. These risks may lead to pollution and misuse of the outer space environment, as has been shown all too often on Earth.

In the modern era of international law, it has become increasingly evident that the State-centric model of international law has significant limitations in addressing collective problems involving NSAs. In defence of the State-centric model, Thirlway argues that '[i]nternational law, like all law, responds ultimately to the interests and needs of human beings, and the structure of international society is such that it is States that best embody and represent those interests and needs'.[17] However, many States are not democratic representations of the

---

14 Chapter 3, Section 2 citing Larsen (2018), pp. 491–492, 515; Von der Dunk (2012), pp. 76–90.

15 See Chapter 5.

16 An overall depletion of space resources in one area may impact the integrity of outer space/celestial bodies itself, for more on the issue see, Melissa De Zwart et al., 'Space resource activities and the evolution of international space law' (2023) *Acta Astronautica*, 211, p. 156 and Fenga Xu 'The approach to sustainable space mining: issues, challenges, and solutions' (2020) *IOP Conf. Series: Materials Science and Engineering*, p. 5.

17 Thirlway (2017), p. 144. See also Hugh W.A. Thirlway, *International Customary Law and Codification* (Martinus Nijhoff Publishers, 1972) (adopting the view that international

people who live in their borders.[18] Additionally, some States are simply unwilling or unable to address serious problems of communal import. Because of this, the traditional model of State-exclusivity is increasingly problematic and incomplete, particularly in relation to NSAs.[19]

At the normative level, international space law itself has been largely static since 1979, with the exception of certain soft-law instruments.[20] Davis and Lee observe that 'no international treaties have been concluded under the UN framework since the adoption of the Moon Agreement in 1979.'[21] Commentators have observed that 'public international law does not appear to be really fit for purpose [of controlling space debris]'.[22] These shortcomings have been noted by Radi, who observes that 'there is no tailor-made binding instrument or rule which addresses space debris specifically' and 'international space treaties currently in force were concluded decades ago, at a time when space debris was not at the forefront of the policy agenda', meaning that 'they simply do not address a number of issues raised by space debris.'[23] Retrenchment risks continuing this stagnation.

---

law should be understood as what an impartial court would say if seized of the issue in question).

18 Thirlway (2017), p. 145 (arguing that his approach 'does not necessarily require that the State be democratically organized: even a dictator is, in relation to other governments, and on the international level generally, acting for (what he sees as) the good of his country/State'). Similarly, Rawls demonstrates how the law of the peoples, the law governing relations between what he calls liberal societies on one hand and hierarchical societies on the other, consists merely of certain basic rules on which both types of societies can agree. See John Rawls, 'The Law of Peoples' (1993) 20(1) *Critical Inquiry*, pp. 36–68.

19 Chapter 3, Section 2.

20 In the absence of any space law treaties since 1979, the UNGA has taken a 'proactive and pragmatic attitude towards the adoption of UNGA resolutions' issuing the Principles Governing the Use by States of Artificial Earth Satellites for International Direct Television Broadcasting in 1982; Principles Relating to Remote Sensing of the Earth from Outer Space in 1986; Principles Relevant to the Use of Nuclear Power Sources in Outer Space in 1992; Declaration on International Cooperation in the Exploration and Use of Outer Space for the Benefit and in the Interest of All States, Taking into Particular Account the Needs of Developing Countries in 1996; Application of the Concept of the 'Launching State' in 2004; and Recommendations on Enhancing the Practice of States and International Intergovernmental Organizations in Registering Space Objects in 2007 (UN Res. 62/101, 2007).' Zhao (2018), p. 3 citing Michael Bourély, 'The institutional framework of space activities in outer space' (1998) 26 *Journal of Space Law*, p. 1 (these instruments can 'serve as a testing bed for possible future international legislation.').

21 Michael E. Davis, Ricky J. Lee, 'Twenty years later: The Moon agreement and its legal controversies' (1999) *Australian International Law Journal*.

22 Radi (2023), p. 4.

23 Radi (2023), p. 4.

Another limitation of the State-centric model is that States may decline to exercise jurisdiction over acts in global commons. Whereas Thirlway argues that '[e]very individual person, the basic unit, is at any given moment geographically subject to the sovereignty of a State, on its physical territory or (for example) a ship or aircraft of its nationality',[24] the global commons (the high seas and Antarctica) are areas in which no particular State may have territorial jurisdiction.[25] Individuals may try to operate there without flying a national flag (or flying the flag of a national State which is unable or unwilling to enforce international law). In relation to outer space, geo-political and legal constructs on Earth may not be automatically applicable.[26] Because of these factors, outer space presents a unique operating environment that differs from Earth's terrestrial environment in several appreciable respects, and potentially features limitless ungoverned spaces.[27]

At the operational level, if a prohibition against space pollution is to be enforced, it will require a forum capable of entertaining proceedings against a space polluting entity.[28] With regard to the Outer Space Treaty, during the negotiation stage the Soviet bloc rejected the US proposal to confer obligatory jurisdiction to the International Court of Justice for disputes concerning interpretation and application of the treaty.[29] Ultimately, the Soviet Union would not go beyond direct negotiations as a dispute remedy.[30] The Outer Space

24 Thirlway (2017), pp. 145–147. He demonstrates that his views are highly contingent on a terrestrial setting: '[t]he reason why international law is built round States is not because they have selfishly created such a system, or fought off any strivings for equality on the part of other entities: it is because they represent the interests of their human citizens in general terms, in the area where it matters, literally "on the ground"'.

25 See ILC, Articles on Prevention of Transboundary Harm from Hazardous Substances, Article 1 Commentary, paragraph 10 ('[s]ometimes, because of the location of the activity, there is no territorial link between a State and the activity such as, for example, activities taking place in outer space or on the high seas.').

26 For a further discussion see Howard J. Taubenfeld (Ed.), *Space and Society Studies for the Seminar on Problems of Outer Space* (Oceana Publications, 1964).

27 Baker (1987), p. 169 ('[d]ifferent characteristics of outer space and terrestrial environments demand different approaches; although the principles may be identical, the details vary considerably.').

28 The lack of *forum conveniens* for establishing and ensuring State accountability for any space pollution caused by NSAs raises the question of what forum could be used to address NSA conduct directly. In this respect, there are also limitations, but experience from other domains, such as international criminal law, suggest that expanding the legal framework and interpretation to encompass direct application of international norms to non-State actors can be followed by the establishment of institutions capable of applying those norms in specific cases, as detailed herein.

29 Cheng (1997), p. 270.

30 Cheng (1997), p. 270.

Treaty therefore makes no reference to a dispute resolution method or body.[31] The lack of any centralized enforcement body is a major omission from the architecture of international space law. Retrenching back to the State-centric model will only serve to exacerbate this lacuna and accentuate the variability and inconsistency of approaches taken by States to regulating NSA conduct in outer space.

From a conceptual perspective, a more foundational limitation arises from an exclusively State-centric approach to the regulation of NSA conduct in outer space. Namely, if international law only places duties on States with respect to activities in outer space, and does not directly impose any duties on NSAs, then international law cannot serve as a basis for proceedings against NSAs in foreign courts, pursuant to the principle of universal jurisdiction. To date, universal jurisdiction has been used as a basis for cases involving torture, genocide, war crimes and crimes against humanity, to name the most notable examples.[32] These are all prohibitions which are anchored in conventional and customary international law (see the Genocide Convention of 1947, the Geneva Conventions of 1949, the Convention Against Torture of 1984, and the Rome Statute of the International Criminal Court, for example). Importantly, these sources prohibit States and NSAs (and the leaders thereof) alike from engaging in the offending conduct. Contrastingly, if space law is read as only imposing international obligations on States and not directly on NSAs (albeit requiring States to in turn place obligations on NSAs in accordance with Article VI of the Outer Space Treaty),[33] then domestic proceedings based on universal jurisdiction would be restricted to those against States or their representatives (and such proceedings would potentially conflict with the principle of State immunity, as upheld by the International Court of Justice in *Germany v. Italy*).[34] In this manner, there would potentially be no jurisdictional basis to proceed against NSAs, depriving those States and organizations eager to protect the pristine outer space environment of a significant tool in the legal arsenal.

The retrenchment approach has the further drawback of exacerbating existing shortcomings under the international law regulatory apparatus. Lambach and Wesel note that '[t]oo many [space governance] institutions represent

---

31 Space law in general was largely formulated on the basis of conflict avoidance, rather than dispute resolution or enforcement; Goh (2007), p. 20.

32 See, e.g., Máximo Langer, Mackenzie Eason, 'The Quiet Expansion of Universal Jurisdiction' (2019) 30 *European Journal of International Law*, p. 3.

33 See Chapter 3, Section 1.

34 ICJ, *Jurisdictional Immunities of the State* (Germany v. Italy: Greece intervening), Judgment of 3 February 2012 (ICJ Reports 2012, p. 99).

the geopolitical bargains of the 1950s and 1960s, when the majority of them were created.'[35] For example, Article VIII of the Outer Space Treaty is currently hindering attempts to solve the space debris issue. If space debris is flagged to another State, then the State (or States) trying to take measures to clean the space debris may face objections. This issue applies even to unidentifiable small objects, such as particles of an object. Simply because these cannot be identified, and regardless of the perceived value of the object or particle, the situation with regard to jurisdiction does not alter and States may not interfere with these objects without the registering the relevant State's consent. To wit, even an attempt by ESA to reduce space debris (by introducing a satellite servicing satellite that would help prevent active satellites from becoming space debris) was objected to by some States.[36] Normally States are protective of the data that their satellites possess and are protective of the intellectual property in the satellites themselves. They will object to a satellite from another State getting too close as they are afraid of espionage attempts. On this basis, certain States may claim that under Article VIII they have enduring jurisdiction over their satellites and will not allow another satellite near their own.

In terms of the most applicable obligation incumbent on States, Article IX of the Outer Space Treaty does not specify which measures are to be adopted in order to avoid harmful contamination. This constitutes 'a major shortcoming of Article IX of the Outer Space Treaty' when it comes to limiting and redressing space pollution.[37]

Other facets of traditional space law present difficulties when applied to NSA activities. For example, the Registration Convention of 1976 established a system whereby all State Party space launches were entered into the Convention Register.[38] This built on the separate registry of space launches established pursuant to Resolution 1721 of the UN General Assembly from 1961.[39] UNGA Resolution 62/101 from 2007 issued further recommendations on enhancing the practice of States and international organisations in registering space

35 Daniel Lambach, Luca Wesel, 'Tackling The Space Debris Problem: A Global Commons Perspective' in Proc. 8th European Conference on Space Debris, 20 – 23 April 2021, Darmstadt, Germany, published by the ESA Space Debris Office.

36 See Chapters 2 and 5.

37 Stubbe (2018), p. 160 (also arguing that 'the obligation of conduct under Article ix sentence 2 of the Outer Space Treaty indicates the measures to be taken; they must be appropriate for achieving a particular result: the avoidance of harmful contamination.').

38 The Convention Register is operated by UNOOSA, pursuant to Article 3 of the Registration Convention. See also Viikari (2008), pp. 72–74.

39 UNGA Res. 1721(XVI). This Resolution Registry is broader than the Convention Registry, as it applies in theory to all States.

objects, *inter alia* calling on States to ratify and adhere to the Registration Convention and supply information to the United Nations.[40] The information which States must provide to the UN Secretary General includes (i) the identification of the launching State or States; (ii) a designation or registration number to be applied to the space object; (iii) the territory or location from which the launch took place and the date thereof; and iv) the essential orbital information.[41]

Both the UNGA Resolution Registry and the Registration Convention Online Index now contain essentially the same data fields – meaning that the key difference between them is the range of States covered (with the latter only applying to States Parties). However, the actual amount of data provided by States varies widely. Concerningly, the information in most cases remains 'very basic', sometimes consisting of only a couple of words or sentences.[42] Because the specific data on space launches are critical to ensure collective management of the anthropogenic objects placed in space, and to reduce and redress collisions of space objects, it is problematic that States are limiting the information they provide to collective registries.

The Registration Convention entails several limitations even on its own terms. Its terms are in some cases ambiguous; Viikari notes that 'launching State' and 'space object' are unclear, and that this treaty does not clarify whether only unitary space objects must be registered, which does not assist once there are fragments thereof in orbit in space.[43] Additional varied registration practices have emerged with large satellite constellations, with some registering individual satellites and some registering only units of satellites.[44]

The Rescue Agreement is complementary to the Registration Convention, at least in theory. Under the Rescue Agreement, guidance is provided for situations where space objects or astronauts are in distress.[45] State Parties are required to provide assistance in such circumstances where feasible.[46] These

40 United Nations General Assembly, Recommendations on enhancing the practice of States and international intergovernmental organizations in registering space objects, UN Doc. A/RES/62/101 10 January 2008.

41 Registration Convention, Article IV (i). The orbital information that is required under Article IV(1)(d) comprises: a) the nodal period; b) the inclination; c) the apogee; and d) the perigee. See also Viikari (2008), p. 73.

42 'Practice of States and international organizations in registering space objects' 2005, paras. 54–77; Viikari (2008), p. 73.

43 Viikari (2008), p. 76.

44 Kazlouskaya (2021), pp. 571–585.

45 Viikari (2008), p. 81.

46 Rescue Agreement, Articles 2 and 3.

situations could arise from environmental damage – such as the falling apart of a space object resulting in a potential collision for another space object or astronaut. In such circumstances, the assisting State(s) would be obliged to provide assistance, potentially by clearing the space debris. However, the terminology of this instrument is again vague – with 'space object' left open for interpretation.

In relation to incidents which could involve collisions or explosions, the logic of the Rescue Agreement is clear – where threats emerge, the launching authority (clarified in Article 6 as the State responsible for launching, or, where an international organisation is responsible for launching, that organisation) should be notified of the threat and given the chance to remove it. If that State is unable or unwilling to do so, then it has been argued that the obligation to assist in rescuing the space object or astronaut should result in 'a qualified right to de-orbit inactive satellites, comparable to that concerning removal of derelict vessels on the high seas.'[47] But this right is speculative and would often require considerable cooperation and communication among potentially affected and involved States to conduct the removal of the space debris.[48]

In relation to NSAs, further problems compound. Corporate entities engaged in space activities frequently transfer ownership of space objects in orbit, particularly geostationary communication satellites, which may be leased or sold even years after their launching. Yet these transfers of ownership are 'usually not reported to the UN, even though the initial launching state may no longer have any control over the satellite.'[49] That information gap causes an imbalance between the international and domestic regulatory regimes.

In- or on-orbit transfers of ownership are one of the unregulated aspects of space activity.[50] The practice has varied in this respect, ranging from double national registration in the event of BSB-1/Sirius-1, a change of national registrations for AsiaSat1, and no national registration for ANIK.[51] Notification

47 Viikari (2008), pp. 82–83 (The proposal would be to add the following clause '[i]f the state of registration, after notification and consultation, is not going to remove debris which endangers outer space or the Earth within a reasonable time, a nonstate of registration or a non-launching state will have the right to salvage, take away or destroy that object.').

48 Viikari (2008), p. 82.

49 Viikari (2008), p. 77.

50 Armel Kerrest, Legal Aspects of Transfer of Ownership and Transfer of Activities (2017), in *Ownership of Satellites: 4th Luxembourg Workshop on Space and Satellite Communication Law* (Mahulena Hofmann and Andreas Loukakis (eds.)) (Nomos Verlagsgesellschaft, 2017), pp. 75–84; Sancin, Grünfeld, Ramuš Cvetkovič (2021), pp. 25–28.

51 See e.g. Dasgupta (2016), pp. 641–666; Upasana Dasgupta, 'Reconciling State Practice of In-Orbit Satellite Transfer with the Law of Liability and Registration in Outer Space', in

to the United Nations is left to the discretion of relevant States, for example in event of NSS-6 and NSS-7 bought in-orbit by a Dutch company New Skies, the Netherlands notified the United Nations that it considers itself the State of registry for purposes of Article VIII of the Outer Space Treaty, but not the launching State, which in the opinion of the Netherlands rests with the initial launching States.[52] Some States have regulated such transfers and changes in registry in their national space legislation, but practice remains scarce.[53]

If States themselves are not typically providing thorough and detailed information regarding space launches and space object registrations, then the addition of another layer between the entity undertaking the launch and the international community increases the risk of unclear or incorrect information being recorded in the Registry (known as the Index). This in turn raises the spectre of collisions and further space debris. NSAs may act in good faith and provide ample information to their government only to have that information restricted from further sharing due to national political, security, or military interests. Conversely, nefarious NFAs may not provide detailed and full information to governments because of their own competitive interests. Both paradigms increase the risk of insufficient information resulting in collisions between space objects when orbiting the Earth.

A separate problem highlighted by the example of space object registries is that NSAs may in the future seek to use the territories of unregulated or failed States or else areas in the global commons not belonging to any State to conduct launches. If the NSA does not have a nationality in a legal sense, or it evades identification with a specific country, then its activities may not be authorized, registered or notified to the United Nations thus not tied to a State. Although this is a speculative possibility at present, technology is adapting rapidly and the ability to launch small objects, such as profit-seeking satellites, into space will likely augment and democratize in the coming years, particularly as launches become cheaper.

Monograph Series VI: Global Space Governance and the UN 2030 Agenda (Aram Daniel Kerkonian (ed.)) (Centre for Research in Air and Space Law, 2018), pp. 55–72.

52 Note verbale dated 29 July 2003 from the Permanent Mission of the Netherlands to the United Nations (Vienna) addressed to the Secretary-General, UN Doc. A/AC.105/806; Note verbale dated 18 February 2004 from the Permanent Mission of the Netherlands to the United Nations (Vienna) addressed to the Secretary-General, UN Doc. A/AC.105/824; Note verbale dated 29 July 2003 from the Permanent Mission of the Netherlands to the United Nations (Vienna) addressed to the Secretary-General, UN Doc. A/AC.105/806; Note verbale dated 18 February 2004 from the Permanent Mission of the Netherlands to the United Nations (Vienna) addressed to the Secretary-General, UN Doc. A/AC.105/824.

53 See Chapter 5 above.

The issues arising from registration have ramifications for the liability of States and other entities.[54] Identifying the responsible party in case of a collision is largely dependent on either the acknowledgement of the party itself or else the availability of information from which that identification can be conducted. Given that liability is a key means of ensuring deterrence and eventually reducing and eliminating the production of space debris, the inability to determine liability will remove a key plank of international efforts to redress space pollution. Channeling all accountability measures through the prism of the State will result in a heightened risk of gaps in the coverage of international law being exploited by bad faith actors or simply allowing for damage to be caused to the space environment by negligence and neglect without appropriate redress.

On the basis of the foregoing, there are significant limitations which arise from pursuing an approach exclusively focused on States as the regulatory vehicle to ensure the protection of the outer space environment. In this light, it is apposite to look to alternative approaches to conceptualizing, and potentially adapting, international space law to address NSA activity.

2 Re-interpretation

Alternative to the retrenchment approach, is that of re-interpreting space law as it currently exists in a purposive and teleological manner. The re-interpretation approach has precedents in related sub-branches of international law. For example, a similar 'paradigm shift' has occurred in the broader area of international environmental law.[55] Because environmental law balances anthropocentric against ecocentric interests and contains terms broad enough to encompass both in many respects,[56] it is adaptable according to the interpretations given to its provisions.[57]

---

54 Viikari (2008), p. 75.

55 Stubbe (2018), p. 181 (observing that '[a] corresponding paradigm shift in international environmental law, induced by the Rio Conference, shifted the understanding of environmental protection from a sovereignty-centered thinking to the recognition of a common interest in the preservation of an intact environment.').

56 As can be seen for example in Convention on International Trade in Endangered Species of Wild Fauna and Flora, which allows the open trade of animals that are not listed as in its annexes. See also Marina Lostal, 'One-Dimensional Law: A Critique of the Human Right to a Clean, Healthy and Sustainable Environment', *The International Journal of Human Rights* (online edition, 2024).

57 Stubbe (2018), p. 181.

Similarly, the establishment of the *ad hoc* international criminal tribunals (for the former Yugoslavia and Rwanda), saw a dramatic shift in the interpretation and applicability of international humanitarian and criminal law. Whereas in the early 1990s, many entities, including the ICRC, did not consider that violations of international humanitarian law committed in non-international armed conflicts were criminalized as a matter of international law, the ICTY found that in fact such violations did entail criminal responsibility.[58] The shift in legal interpretation arose against the backdrop of the explicit recognition by the ICTY of the prevalence of non-international armed conflicts among the wars in the world in the seminal *Tadić* Jurisdictional Decision of 1995. In that decision, the ICTY Appeals Chamber found that there was liability for individuals in non-international armed conflicts. It declared that a discernible shift had occurred, from a State-sovereignty-oriented approach to a human-being-oriented approach during the twentieth century, in line with the principle of *hominum causa omne jus constitutum est* (all law is created for the benefit of human beings).[59]

In this light, and given the increasing prevalence of NSAs in space activities, the question arises as to whether international space law could be similarly re-interpreted to encompass their conduct and place duties on NSAs to avoid harming the pristine outer space environment. International law recognizes the possibility of evolving interpretations of conventions in light of contemporary circumstances that vary from those prevalent at the time of a treaty's adoption.[60] However, an evolving interpretation must remain faithful to the terms of a convention. It cannot be used as a means of adding new terms to a

58 See Thomas Graditzky, 'Individual criminal responsibility for violations of international humanitarian law committed in non-international armed conflicts' (1998) 322 *International Review of the Red Cross*, pp. 29–56 referring to ICTY, *Prosecutor v. Tadić*, Case No. IT-94-1-AR72, Decision on the Defence Motion for Interlocutory Appeal on Jurisdiction (2 October 1995), para. 137.

59 ICTY, *Prosecutor v. Tadić*, Case No. IT-94-1-AR72, Decision on the Defence Motion for Interlocutory Appeal on Jurisdiction (2 October 1995), para. 97 ('[a] State-sovereignty-oriented approach has been gradually supplanted by a human-being-oriented approach. Gradually the maxim of Roman law *hominum causa omne jus constitutum est* (all law is created for the benefit of human beings) has gained a firm foothold in the international community as well').

60 See ICJ, *Award in the Arbitration regarding the Iron Rhine ('Ijzeren Rijn') Railway (Belgium v. Netherlands)* ICJ Reports 2005, para. 80; ICJ, *In the Case concerning the Gabčikovo-Nagymaros Project (Hungary v. Slovakia)* ICJ Reports 1997, para. 112.

treaty or substituting the existing terms with broader ones, as that would constitute legislating rather than interpreting.[61]

Looking to potential bases for international space law to apply to NSAs, Article IX of the Outer Space Treaty refers to 'harmful interference with activities of other States Parties in the peaceful exploration and use of outer space, including the moon and other celestial bodies' resulting from 'an activity or experiment planned by [a State Party] or its nationals in outer space, including the moon and other celestial bodies'. Whilst this does mention NSAs (as encompassed by the word 'nationals'), it places the responsibility to take action on States Parties. Moreover, the preceding passage of Article IX, which refers to the 'harmful contamination' of outer space, explicitly links the prohibition of causing such harm to States. In addition, Article VI of the same treaty takes a strongly State-centric approach to responsibility, providing that 'States Parties to the Treaty shall bear international responsibility for national activities in outer space'. Given the obligation under the Vienna Convention on the Law of Treaties to interpret provisions 'in accordance with the ordinary meaning to be given to the terms of the treaty in their context and in the light of its object and purpose',[62] it would stretch the ordinary meaning of Article IX, in context to interpret it as directly binding NSAs in order to by-pass State responsibility.

An ardent re-interpretivist may argue that the need to avoid any harmful contamination under Article IX compels a teleological reading whereby any such harm is prohibited under Article IX irrespective of whether it emanates from a State or NSA. However, that would allow the object and purpose of the treaty to extinguish its ordinary meaning in context. It would beg the question of why NSAs are not mentioned in relation to harmful contamination despite being mentioned in the later part of the same provision. Allowing that latitude to the interpretation and application of international law would significantly undermine the basic precepts of international law formation, including the process of drafting and agreeing treaties and the process of customary international law crystallization. If such extreme interpretations of the words of treaties were permitted, it would result in a perceived immediate gain for the object of restraining NSAs in risking harmful contamination to space but risk a more systemic loss in terms the acceptance and legitimacy of the Outer Space Treaty among States, by undermining the coherence of core precepts of international law.

---

61 Gerhard Hafner and Christina Binder, 'The Interpretation of Article 21(3) ICC Statute Opinion Reviewed', *Austrian Review of International and European Law*, 9 (2006), p. 172.

62 Article 31 of the VCLT.

Other provisions of international space law exhibit a State-orientation paralleling that of Article IX of the Outer Space Treaty, and would be similarily difficult to re-interpret.[63] As noted above, Article 4(1) of the Moon Agreement has some broad potential applicability through its reference to 'due regard shall be paid to the interests of present and future generations'. However, Article 7(1) restricts the specific obligations to States, providing that '[i]n exploring and using the Moon, States Parties shall take measures to prevent the disruption of the existing balance of its environment, whether by introducing adverse changes in that environment, by its harmful contamination through the introduction of extra-environmental matter or other-wise.' Furthermore, whereas space treaties to some extent foresee that States are not the only actors in outer space, this is not reflected in explicit obligations placed on NSAs. Article VI of the Outer Space Treaty provides that '[w]hen activities are carried on in outer space, including the moon and other celestial bodies, by an international organization, responsibility for compliance with this Treaty shall be borne both by the international organization and by the States Parties to the Treaty participating in such organization', meaning that it recognizes that international organizations also partake in outer space activities and shall therefore bear appropriate amount of responsibility. Along the same line, Article XIII of the Outer Space Treaty states that '[t]he provisions of this Treaty shall apply to the activities of States Parties to the Treaty in the exploration and use of outer space, including the moon and other celestial bodies, whether such activities are carried on by a single State Party to the Treaty or jointly with other States, including cases where they are carried on within the framework of international intergovernmental organizations.' Even if an analogy with international organizations could be made, in order to include NSAs in the responsibility scheme, the explicit language of the space law instruments counters the attempt to directly attribute NSAs responsibility in this manner.

UNGA Resolution 68/74, which is not binding international law *per se*, but can influence is interpretation and can demonstrate *opinio juris*, refers to the 'need to maintain the sustainable use of outer space, in particular by mitigating space debris, and to ensure the safety of space activities and minimize the potential harm to the environment' and the 'need for a practical regulatory system for the involvement of non-governmental entities to provide further

63 See Zhao (2018), p. 1 ('space activities during the cold-war period were mainly state-oriented ... Consequently, the space rules formulated under the framework of the United Nations mainly regulate the activities conducted by states and aim to realize peaceful uses of outer space.'); Joanne I. Gabrynowicz, 'Space law: Its Cold War origins and challenges in the era of globalization' (2004) 37 *Suffolk University Law Review*, pp. 245–273.

incentives for enacting regulatory frameworks at the national level'. However, it has no specific reference to NSAs having an independent obligation under international law to avoid space pollution, and instead envisages an essentially State-centred framework: 'noting that some States also include national space activities of a governmental character within that framework' and that 'space activities should require authorization by a competent national authority'. This is an insufficient basis to support a purely teleological reading of the existing provisions whereby NSAs would be compelled to avoid space pollution. Instead, it supports a wide reading, whereby States are responsible for NSA space-conduct emanating from their territory as well as space activities by their nationals wheresoever launched from. To this effect, it refers to a State's 'obligations as a launching State and as a State responsible for national activities in outer space under the United Nations treaties on outer space, [and requires that it] should ascertain national jurisdiction over space activities carried out from territory under its jurisdiction and/or control; likewise, it should issue authorizations for and ensure supervision over space activities carried out elsewhere by its citizens and/or legal persons established, registered or seated in territory under its jurisdiction and/or control.'[64]

Customary international law provides a broad and detailed set of environmental protections, which are potentially applicable to activities in outer space.[65] It is arguably imported into the specific Outer Space Treaty regime under Article III, as discussed above, and can certainly assist to interpret the meaning of the terms of the treaty.[66] However, what it brings in flexibility, it sacrifices in legal specificity and applicability. There are few precise principles of international environmental law which could be said to definitively prohibit NSAs from causing space pollution.[67] Although enterprising judges may find a basis to read such prohibitions into customary international law, this could clash with the principle of *lex certa* and legality, particularly when it comes to enforcement through judicial processes.[68] If different courts in different jurisdictions took varying readings of the applicable customary international law, which is a distinct possibility, then the certainty and predictability of the legal position would be compromised. In turn, NSAs seeking to plan and conduct

64 UN General Assembly Resolution A/RES/68/74, adopted on 11 December 2013.

65 Larsen (2018), p. 490; Breccia (2016), p. 8.

66 Larsen (2018), p. 491.

67 Chapter 2, Section 1.

68 Although these principles are usually cited in the criminal context, they can also be alleged in the civil regulatory context, insofar as an entity is held responsible for acts which were not established as clear prohibitions at the time the acts occurred.

activities in space would be left speculating as to the nature and extent of the precise legal parameters for their behaviour, and other entities interested in protecting the outer space environment would be similarly prejudiced in their ability to predict and apply the law.

More broadly, if space law were re-interpreted and NSAs were generally considered subjects of international space law, it would be difficult to operationalize this system under the current framework of international law, particularly as no express prescriptive guidance would be provided in the governing instruments. Questions would arise as to whether NSAs can have independent claims over space objects under international law. Moreover, confusion would arise as to which entity would regulate international clean-up efforts and whether that would result in NSAs being subject to double layers of regulatory oversight. Already the limitations of the Inter-Agency Space Debris Coordination Committee's (IADC)[69] Space Debris Mitigation Guidelines have been noted,[70] particularly their non-mandatory nature, despite the fact they were adopted by UNCOPUOS.[71]

These issues demonstrate that a teleological interpretation seeking to treat NSAs akin to States for the purposes of international space law raises at least as many questions as it answers. Christina Isnardi, who has reviewed the ability of the Permanent Court of Arbitration, the World Trade Organization, the International Telecommunication Union, and domestic courts to address the conduct of NSAs in space in general, ultimately concludes that redressing this regulatory gap cannot be done by interpretation alone and would require a new legal entity.[72] The origins of space law in the State-centric Cold War era resulted in instruments too dependent on State jurisdiction as the primary vehicle for the enforcement of its provisions, which has not been able to keep pace with the rising role of NSAs in the space sector. In this light, the analysis now turns to the options for reform of international space law, particularly in relation to NSAs.

---

69 Whereas UNCOPUOS is an inter-State body, the IADC is not an inter-State organization. The IADC is agile and focuses on technical issues, while COPUOS can get mired in discussions of State security and other core State interests.

70 See Larsen (2018), p. 475.

71 Larsen (2018), p. 476 ('The IADC has no legal authority to monitor, change, or strengthen the international guidelines as debris accumulation increases. Moreover, the IADC lacks legal enforcement authority'), 500 ('The IADC has no prospect of being able to produce mandatory space debris standards because it is not an organization of member countries').

72 Isnardi (2020), p. 532.

3 Reform

Given the limitations of the retrenchment and re-interpretation approaches identified above, a further alternative is to reform space law and seek to bring into effect new legal instruments, applicable to NSAs and able to ensure their accountability for space pollution.[73] This could be done through the adoption of a protocol to the Outer Space Treaty, as set out in the example annexed to this book, or a new convention developing the Outer Space Treaty regime.

Substantively, such an instrument would set out the specific obligations of NSAs in an explicit manner, similar to the way in which Common Article 3 to the Geneva Conventions and Additional Protocol I set out prohibitions applicable to all parties to non-international armed conflicts including NSAs. Those prohibitions have been applied directly to individuals and NSAs, including by international courts imposing criminal sanctions.[74] They provide a precedent for international law instruments to be used to directly regulate NSA conduct and enforce sanctions against them (at least against their leaders and members) as set out above. International aviation law provides an example where international instruments set down primary obligations which are directly enforceable against NSAs through claims in domestic courts, as set out above. Importantly, a new instrument regulating NSA conduct could fill the gap that is arguably left by Article II of the Outer Space Treaty prohibiting 'national' appropriation of celestial bodies, without specifying that this also covers NSAs taking ownership of resources on those bodies. In this way, a new instrument could address the question of space resources and the legality of their extraction and exploitation, all of which are suggested to be imminent by the UNCOPUOS Working group on Legal Aspects of Space Resource Activities and the Artemis Accords.[75] In its absence, the failure to regulate space resource activities and to explicitly prohibit private appropriation of outer space, results in a significant risk that NSAs could engage in *de facto* appropriation and resource

73 Vernile suggests that reform of international space law is required through 'space districts', but does not explain what these would consist of from a legal perspective; Vernile (2018), p. 74.

74 See Chapter 1.

75 The proposed Protocol to the Outer Space Treaty Annexed to this book is focused on NSA space pollution rather than NSA ownership of celestial bodies per se, but could be adjusted to add a provision replicating the prohibition in the Outer Space Treaty of States appropriating outer space including celestial bodies. Alternatively, a separate agreement could clarify this issue.

stripping of whole areas, raising the risk of their pollution.[76] Reform of the space law architecture is pressingly needed to regulate any such activities.

Regarding space pollution, a new bespoke instrument concerning NSA responsibility would contribute to the efficacy of complying with those responsibilities, and the oversight of enforcement mechanisms, such as international courts or domestic courts applying international law. This would assist in achieving regulatory aims, such as protecting the accessibility of space and the pristine nature of the space environment.

Reform could also benefit private actors. Vernile argues that establishing a legal regime which ensures that private entities abide by the obligations of their host States but also protects the rights of the private actors is essential for 'creating certainty for private actors and investors about the lawfulness of their activities and the products of these activities' and that it 'may also promote investment in outer space ventures due to the greater certainty provided by a robust legal regime'.[77]

To this end, a draft protocol to the Outer Space Treaty (or declaration), which has been formulated by the authors, is annexed to this book. This draft instrument is formulated flexibly, so that it could be adopted as a declaration, consistent with the approach to developing space law in recent decades. In this way, it would serve as a stepping stone towards the eventual adoption of the full protocol to the Outer Space Treaty. The draft instrument aims to address the gap concerning NSA accountability for space pollution under international law. It reiterates the foundational preambular principles of the Outer Space Treaty and other international space treaties, including the common interest of all humankind in the progress of the exploration and use of outer space for peaceful purposes, and that outer space, including the moon and other celestial bodies, shall not be subject to national appropriation, but shall instead be free for exploration and use by all States without discrimination of any kind, on a basis of equality and in accordance with international law, and there shall be free access to all areas of celestial bodies.

Substantively, the draft protocol makes explicit two key phenomena which have become increasingly prominent in recent decades, by recognizing, first, the deleterious impact that human actions can have on the outer space environment and, second, that non-State actors are playing an increasingly prevalent role in outer space. In this light, the draft protocol reflects Article IX of the Outer Space Treaty's prohibition against the harmful contamination of outer

76 Chapter 1, Section 3.

77 See Vernile (2018), p. 74 ('[t]he legal uncertainty around private activities deprives private actors of the assurance that they will gain from the capital invested.').

space, and explains that such contamination can occur through space pollution of all forms, including intentional or negligent causation of disproportionate amounts of space debris. It adds that the prohibition applies irrespective of whether the harmful contamination is caused by State actors, NSAs, or a combination of these entities.

To operationalize this prohibition, it sets out a number of steps that space-active entities must take, including reporting obligations regarding harmful contamination of the space environment, registration obligations, and cooperation obligations regarding space pollution remediation and removal efforts. Finally, it requires States Parties to adopt such measures as may be necessary under domestic law to enforce the prohibition in the protocol, and requires that State Parties maintain, designate or establish independent national space protection mechanisms to monitor and prevent harmful space pollution being caused by entities under their jurisdiction.

To effect the protection set out in this new instrument or a similar one, the most impactful reform would be the creation of an international court or entity capable of enforcing its provisions. In broad terms, Isnardi argues that a new legal entity needs to be established with 'regulatory, adjudicative, or arbitral authority necessary to compel private actors to comply with the space law treaties.'[78] There are indications of political will in this respect; States involved in negotiating the regulation of outer space have expressed desire for reform of the regulatory framework under international law, as surmised by UNCOPUOS:

> [delegations considered that] a new, comprehensive convention on space law to further strengthen the international legal regime governing outer space activities was needed to take account of developments in space activities, such as the commercialization of space and the involvement of the private sector, and in order to prevent the militarization of outer space. Those delegations were of the view that a single, comprehensive convention could regulate all aspects of outer space activities.[79]

Various models for NSA responsibility can be gleaned from existing initiatives. By way of precedent closer to Earth, international aviation law provides guidance for the imposition of obligations on NSAs via international treaties. While international aviation law is definitionally not applicable to the outer space

78 Isnardi (2020), p. 523.
79 United Nations Report of the Committee on the Peaceful Uses of Outer Space, para. 187.

domain,[80] it addresses human activity with considerable similarities to space exploration (and with growing overlap in the NewSpace era of space tourism and extraterrestrial habitation). Regarding NSA conduct, the Convention for the Unification of Certain Rules for International Carriage by Air of 1999 (Montreal Convention),[81] like the Warsaw Convention it replaced, is a treaty that sets out a number of detailed obligations that airlines and aircraft operators ('carriers') must abide by when conducting international air transport operations (subject to the relevant State's ratification). Coverage extends to private airlines and partially State-held ones, so long as they are engaged in air carriage as defined under the Convention. It covers the liability of carriers for death and injury to passengers, as well as damage to cargo and delays in arrival.[82] It also provides carriers with rights, including exoneration[83] levels of compensation and limits on liability. Jurisdictionally, it sets out the various domestic courts in which plaintiffs may seek damages.[84] In this way, national law is directly integrated into international law,[85] and international law is directly applied to the conduct of airlines and aircraft operators. This provides a model of international law being directly applicable to the actions of, and the interactions between, NSAs, thereby combining the international and domestic legal levels.[86]

International aviation law also provides guidance on the issue of environmental protection. The International Standards and Recommended Practices (SARPS) set out in Annex 16 to the Chicago Convention on Civil Aviation, lay down a number of obligations incumbent on aeroplane operators and States to protect the environment. Among others, aeroplane operators are required

---

80 See Dempsey and Manoli, p. 9 ('[t]he legal regimes that govern air space and outer space are distinct, and create a distinct conflict: while air space is an area to which State sovereignty can be attributed, outer space falls beyond sovereignty claims').

81 Convention for the Unification of Certain Rules for International Carriage by Air, 28 May1999, UNTS 2004 (entered into force on 4 November 2003), p. 309.

82 Articles 17–19.

83 Article 20 ((in whole or in part) if "the damage was caused or contributed to by the negligence or other wrongful act or omission of the person claiming compensation.").

84 Article 33(1) ("An action for damages must be brought, at the option of the plaintiff, in the territory of one of the States Parties, either before the court of the domicile of the carrier or of its principal place of business, or where it has a place of business through which the contract has been made or before the court at the place of destination").

85 Havel and Gabriel Sanchez, pp. 259–260 (because of 'Warsaw (and subsequently Montreal), therefore, each national law of contract is integrated automatically into the international liability system by each airline's contract of carriage with its customers.').

86 However, these conventions do not establish dispute resolution mechanisms and so may become untenable if multiple States start deviating from their responsibilities thereunder.

to monitor their CO_2 emissions,[87] and submit emissions monitoring plans and emissions reports to the relevant State.[88] The environmentally oriented technical annexes to the Chicago Convention cover Volume I – Aircraft Noise; Volume II – Aircraft Engine Emissions; Volume III – Aeroplane CO2 Emissions; and Volume IV – Carbon Offsetting and Reduction.[89] Although it can be debated whether these technical annexes are strictly binding as a matter of international law,[90] the Convention requires States to provide 'immediate' notice of any relevant deviation between its regulatory framework and those set out in the Annexes, which must then be communicated by the Council to all State Parties, indicating that non-compliance with those standards does have ramifications under international law.[91]

In the outer space domain, guidance can also be taken from the ILA's Model Law, discussed in Chapter 5, which contains specific provisions on environmental protection. It defines an 'operator' as 'a natural or legal person carrying out space activities.'[92] The Model Law on National Space Legislation includes environmental protection and space debris provisions in the authorization procedures for licenses to engage in space activities. During the authorization procedure, the Model Law suggests ascertaining whether the operator has the required technical knowledge, and requiring that '[t]he space activity does not cause environmental damage to the Earth and outer space in accordance with article 7;' as well as that '[t]he space activity is undertaken in such a manner as to mitigate to the greatest possible extent any potential space debris in accordance with article 8;'.[93] Additionally, it requires that the 'space activity does not run counter to international obligations and foreign policy interests of [relevant State(s)]'.[94] Appropriate documentation and evidence must be submitted to substantiate these requirements.[95]

87 ICAO Annex 16, Volume IV, para. 2.2.1.1.

88 ICAO Annex 16, Volume IV, para. 2.2.2.1, 2.3.1.1.

89 ICAO, 'Article 16' (2017) (available at https://applications.icao.int/postalhistory/annex_16_environmental_protection.htm#:~:text=Volume%20I%20of%20the%20reorganized,manuals%20on%20noise%20and%20emissions).

90 The annexes are based on Article 37 of the Chicago Convention, which requires that State Parties secure 'the highest practicable degree of uniformity in regulations, standards, procedures, and organization'. See Tanveer Ahmad, 'Global Civil Aviation Emissions Standards – from Noise to Greener Fuels', Centre for Research in Air and Space Law (McGill, 2016), p. 6.

91 See Article 38 of the Chicago Convention.

92 ILA Model Law for National Space Legislation, Article 4.

93 ILA Model Law, Article 4(1).

94 ILA Model Law, Article 4(1).

95 ILA Model Law, Article 4(2).

Articles 7 and 8 add, respectively, the requirement to undertake environmental impact assessment to prove the activity does not cause those harms, and that debris release is limited 'during normal operations, to minimize the potential for in-orbit break-ups, to prepare for post-mission disposal and to avoid in-orbit collisions in accordance with international space debris mitigation standards.' Explanatory comments from the drafters state that space activities undertaken by private actors should meet the highest environmental standards.[96]

Commentators have argued that space debris could be partly redressed if countries were to form an international agreement waiving their sovereign rights to unidentified space debris.[97] This is because the 'uncertainty of property rights to debris causes third party states to hesitate to remove unregistered and unclaimed space debris.'[98] They posit that by relinquishing possible claims to unidentified space debris, which can be valuable and which Article VIII of the Outer Space Treaty may protect,[99] States would be reassured that their efforts to remove space debris would not violate any such claims. In either event, involving NSAs in space debris mitigation efforts has mutual benefits – for States in terms of observing their obligations to maintain space as an accessible and environmentally sustainable public good, and for NSAs as a promising business opportunity.[100]

A proposed complementary remedy to mitigate space debris is to introduce amendments to the reporting obligations placed on State Parties to the Registration Convention. For example, if the required information were to include power sources, particularly in case of nuclear power sources being utilized, this would assist in reducing the threats to the space environment.[101] Similarly, reporting on the location of the object relative to the surface of the Earth, as well as the space object's mass, and providing information on the

96 United Nations Committee on the Peaceful Uses of Outer Space, Questions on the definition and delimitation of outer space: reply to Pakistan, UN Doc. A/AC.105/C.2/2013/CRP.6 (5 April 2013).

97 Larsen (2018) citing Humaid Alshamsi, Roy Balleste, Michelle L.D. Hanlon, 'As the Grapefruit Turns Sixty, It's Time to Get Serious About Clean Up in Outer Space' (2018) 83 *Journal of Air Law and Commerce*. See also Caitlin Kim, 'The Space Debris Race' *The Regulatory Review* (24 November 2021) (available at https://www.theregreview.org/2021/11/24/kim-space-debris-race/).

98 Larsen (2018), p. 483.

99 Larsen (2018), pp. 485–486.

100 See Vladimir Atanasov and Gianluigi Baldesi, 'An Analysis of Two Space Business Opportunities' in Stella Tkatchova, *Space-Based Technologies and Commercialized Development: Economic Implications and Benefits* (2011) IGI Global, pp. 206–210.

101 Viikari (2008), p. 77.

break-up of any space objects and the change of ownership of space objects, would all assist in reducing the probability of harmful collisions in space.[102]

Separate from the normative limitations of space law in its current form, the critical issue for effective implementation is the existence of an enforcement mechanism. Simply put, there must be a legal body able to address potential violations of international space law, including by NSAs, or else the deficiencies in the State-centric model, as detailed above, will continue to persist.[103] The ILA Draft Convention on the Settlement of Disputes Related to Space Activities[104] foresees a number of options to be selected by the parties to a dispute. These include the International Court of Justice, an arbitral tribunal or panel, and the idea of establishing a special international tribunal for space law, which has been raised previously.[105]

In terms of existing institutions, the International Court of Justice does not have jurisdiction in contentious cases over NSAs. Moreover, it is heavily dependent on voluntary participation by States. According to Article 34, paragraph 1 of the International Court of Justice Statute, only States can be parties before the Court. Moreover, pursuant to Article 36 the International Court of Justice's jurisdiction is possible only when the parties to a dispute refer the case to it, or its jurisdiction is specifically provided for the disputed matter in the UN Charter or relevant treaties, or the Court's jurisdiction is accepted by States parties to a dispute. Prominent authors, for example Lauterpacht, have advocated for compulsory jurisdiction, but such a concept has to date not been accepted in a universal manner.[106] In relation to space law, the International Court of Justice's jurisdiction was touted during negotiations of the Outer Space Treaty. However, as mentioned above, the Soviet Union-led bloc rejected the proposal of the United States to provide the International Court of Justice with compulsory jurisdiction.[107] Consequently, the Outer Space Treaty only refers to consultations between States rather than any specific dispute resolution body.[108]

102 Viikari (2008), pp. 77–78.

103 See Isnardi (2020), p. 591–593.

104 The revised version was adopted in 1998, in Taiwan, see ILA, *Report of the 68th Conference*, 1998, pp. 249–267.

105 Goh (2007), p. 66 (noting that the 'ILA Space Law Committee duly prepared to formulate a Draft Convention on the Settlement of Space Law Disputes' in 1984).

106 See Hersch Lauterpacht, 'The Function of Law in the International Community' (2011), 22 *European Journal of International Law*, p. 4.

107 See Chapter 1, Section 4.

108 Outer Space Treaty, Article IX. See Goh (2007), pp. 75–76.

Another potential forum is a specialized tribunal for resolving disputes arising out of space activities. A related type of dispute settlement mechanism at the domestic level has been established by the United Arab Emirates.[109] It is, however, unlikely, that such a mechanism would be established on a global level, and it is even less likely that this body would be conferred compulsory jurisdiction. This is so not only due to the polarization of the global order that has started since the 2022 Russian invasion of Ukraine, but also for several other reasons, for example the empirically proven fact that States usually prefer to choose a non-specialized forum.[110] Nonetheless, the lack of a short term options should not prevent exploring the conceptual underpinnings and operational considerations necessary to establish an international space law judicial entity.

Some scholars believe that space law evinces a preference for arbitration. As discussed in Chapter 4, ESA also envisioned arbitration as a method of resolving disputes between its members.[111] A potential forum could therefore have been created by the PCA. This attempt is confirmed by the fact that in 2011 the PCA formulated Optional Rules for Arbitration of Disputes Relating to Outer Space Activities.[112] The PCA generally adjudicates cases between States, State entities, international organizations and private parties,[113] and so could potentially encompass NSAs. As noted, its 2011 Optional Rules for Arbitration of Disputes Relating to Outer Space Activities were adopted 'in order to fill the gap left by UN treaties in the field of dispute settlement, where private

109 Agence France-Presse, 'Dubai Creates 'Space Court' for Out-of-This-World Disputes' *Courthouse News Service* (1 February 2021) (available at https://www.courthousenews.com/dubai-creates-space-court-for-out-of-this-world-disputes/).

110 For more reasons on why a specialized space tribunal is not likely to be established anytime soon, see Ramuš Cvetkovič (2021), pp. 36, 37.

111 Art XVII, Convention for the Establishment of a European Space Agency, 1297 UNTS 161, 187.

112 Permanent Court of Arbitration (PCA), Optional Rules for Arbitration of Disputes Relating to Outer Space Activities (Effective 6 December 2011). Many prominent space law scholars participated in the formulation, including Tare Brisibe, Frans von der Dunk, Zhao Haifeng, Stephan Hobe, Joanne Gabrynovicz, Ram Jakhu, Armel Kerrest, Justine Limpitlaw, Francis Lyall, VS. Mani, Rose Montserrat-Filho, Maureen Williams, and until stepping down in 2010 former judge of the International Court of Justice Vladlen Vereshchetin. See Hobe (2019), p. 204.

113 PCA, PCA Arbitration (17 December 2012); see also PCA, Optional Rules for Arbitration Between International Organizations and Private Parties (1996), Article 1; PCA, Optional Rules for Arbitrating Disputes between Two Parties of Which only One is a State (1993), Article 1. For more information, see PCA, 'Dispute Resolution Services' *pca-cpa.org* (available at https://pca-cpa.org/en/services/).

parties do not have locus standi.'[114] These Optional Rules 'reflect the particular characteristics of disputes having an outer space component involving the use of outer space by States, international organizations and private entities.'[115] However, the voluntary nature of such proceedings limits their utility as a basis for enforcement of accountability for wrongful pollution of outer space. On this basis, reform of the legal framework would need to be matched by institutional reform to ensure the new regulations were effective and not merely paper tigers with no utility to redress the growing scourge of space pollution, including when committed by NSAs.

Reforming the parameters and content of international space law to provide for direct NSA accountability for space pollution would match the adjustments that have occurred in international criminal law, international humanitarian law, and are beginning to be seen in international environment.[116] It would reflect the reality of NSAs as active, and in many respects dominant, space actors. NSAs play an active role in the negotiation and formation of international environmental law instruments, particularly in relation to climate change.[117] Sands notes that the categories of NSAs involved in environmental law formation include

> the scientific community because, to a great extent, international environmental law is driven by scientific considerations; the corporate sector is involved because of the significant implications which decisions taken at the global level have even for individual companies; and environmental non-governmental organizations (NGOs) are involved because they advocate for concerns often not pursued by states and see the need for active participation at the international level as the lines dividing local, national and global issues disintegrate.[118]

Each of these groups, and the rationales for their environmental law, are critical for the formation of space law, particularly in relation to space pollution. Space ventures have always been scientifically-founded but are increasingly reliant on corporations working alongside Governmental bodies or even on

---

114 PCA, Optional Rules for Arbitration of Disputes Relating to Outer Space Activities (Effective 6 December 2011). See also Shaw (2008), p. 669.

115 PCA, Optional Rules for Arbitration of Disputes Relating to Outer Space Activities (Effective 6 December 2011), Introduction, p. 4.

116 Sands and Peel (2018), p. 13.

117 Sands and Peel (2018), p. 52.

118 Sands and Peel (2018), p. 52.

their own. In relation to environmental considerations in outer space, NGOs are becoming more heavily involved. Bringing them together under one umbrella of accountability, which they also contribute to shaping, would enhance the acceptance, clarity and predictability of space law and its implementation.

The legal reforms designed to accommodate NSAs would have a democratizing effect and may also assist in relation to the technical aspects of space negotiations,[119] as noted by Viikari:

> Governments may even have an interest in involving these actors in political processes, for they often possess special expertise which governments find advantageous to be channeled into decision-making. Furthermore, their inclusion may serve as a tool to reveal relevant societal views, yet in a manageable way, which can enhance the decision-makers' sensitivity to domestic opposition and support.[120]

In terms of the range of actors which may be relevant to the reform of international law, a significant expansion in the type and character of entities involved in space exploration and utilization has occurred. Traditionally, there were NSAs involved in discussions of the formation of international regulations, for instance via UNCOPUOS, but these have typically been scientific and legally oriented quasi-public bodies such as the International Council for Science (ICSU), International Astronomical Union (IAU), International Astronautical Federation (IAF), the International Institute of Space Law (IISL), and the International Astronautical Academy (IAA).[121]

By involving businesses and other relevant NSAs in the formation of international space law, the key State actors will help to form a cadre of organizations with experience contributing to negotiations and facilitate their ongoing constructive contributions.[122] To determine which entities have the appropriate balance of expertise and constructive commitment, a system of trusted contributors could be established. This would list NSAs with proven track

---

119 See Goran Petrović, 'Non-Governmental Organization (NGO) Participation in Civil Aviation Policy and Decision Making', (2023) 88 *Journal of Air Law and Commerce*, p. 474 (noting that enabling NGO participation in treaty negotiation and treaty making has led to 'further democratization in the field of international law').

120 Viikari (2008), pp. 25–26.

121 Viikari (2008), p. 28.

122 See Viikari (2008), p. 26 ('the fact that states promote (or at least permit) the participation of such groups [NSAs] in the domestic preparation of international accords enhances the possibilities of those groups to be involved in subsequent international deliberations as observers, for instance.').

records of engaging in responsible space exploration as participants in space law treaties' negotiation. Those trusted entities could receive consultative status similar to consultative status in other organizations.[123]

Moving from the formation of international law to NSA's role in its implementation, NSAs could be further included in the regulatory aspects of space activities through consultation and coordination of operations. Under Article IX of the Outer Space Treaty, States are under an obligation to undertake 'appropriate international consultations' before proceeding with planned space activities or experiment which might cause 'potentially harmful interference' with other states parties' space activities. Relatedly, the Moon Agreement sets out, in Article 7(2), that parties have the obligation to inform the UN Secretary-General of the measures being adopted for the prevention of harm to the Moon's environment or back-contamination of the Earth. It continues that, 'to the maximum extent feasible', they should provide prior notification of any placement of radioactive materials on the Moon and the reasons therefor. Given the rising number of NSAs involved in space activities, including with their own satellites in orbit, it would considerably reduce the risks of collisions if those NSAs were directly involved in sharing the information regarding space objects and coordinating responses.

The governance of matter brought from Earth's surface into space is increasingly a concern, particularly as NSAs become more involved in space. Radioactive materials may well be used to power activities on the Moon, as they can potentially provide a reliable energy source at the lunar South Pole, which is an area of considerable interest for human exploration due to the presence of frozen water ice, but has less consistent access to solar energy due to its low sun angle.[124] In the effort to develop nuclear energy sources for use on the moon, private companies have been leading the charge, particularly pursuant to US Department of Defense contracts.[125] Whilst innovative solutions are

123 For example, the United Nations Economic and Social Council (ECOSOC) grants NGO consultative status via its NGO Committee; See United Nations Department of Economic and Social Affairs, 'How to apply for consultative status with ECOSOC?', United Nations (available at https://social.desa.un.org/issues/civil-society/how-to-apply-for-consultative-status-with-ecosoc). See further examples from Birnie–Boyle (2002), p. 67.

124 Jon Kelvey, 'Solar Panel Robots and Mini Nuclear Reactors Could Power NASA's Future Moon Base', Space Ref, 22 June 2023 (https://spaceref.com/newspace-and-tech/solar-panel-robots-and-mini-nuclear-reactors-could-power-nasas-future-moon-base/).

125 Kelvey (2023) ('[s]pace robotics company Astrobotic Technology and electric power behemoth Westinghouse are joining forces to develop nuclear power for NASA and the Department of Defense'.).

being investigated, such as shipping a container-size mini-reactor, the weight of the materials constituting the reactor is currently prohibitive of the delivery of the system and further research and design is ongoing to render the prospect of nuclear energy on the moon possible.[126]

Under Article V of the Outer Space Treaty and Article 5(3) of the Moon Agreement, States must inform the UN Secretary-General of any phenomena in space that could endanger human life or health.[127] This duty is sufficiently broad to entail considerable environmental protection. For example, if a State conducts anti-satellite testing, which was done by China in 2007 as discussed above, it would have the duty to inform the UN Secretary-General of any dangerous debris or other outputs generated thereby. Similarly, Article 7(3) of the Moon Agreement requires States to provide information 'concerning areas of the Moon having special scientific interest' to the UN Secretary-General. Again, this has direct relevance for the protection of the lunar environment. Upon receiving such information, the United Nations may seek to encourage all States (or at least space-faring States) to designate some of those areas as reserved areas ('planetary parks') for scientific studies.[128] However, the Moon Agreement is not widely subscribed to, and so the obligation to take these measures which may protect the environment is of limited real effect.

As the space environment, including the lunar surface, becomes more crowded with anthropocentric objects, it will become increasingly important for information to be shared among space-faring entities regarding the location and nature of their space objects in accordance with Article XI of the Outer Space Treaty and Article 5 of the Moon Agreement. Eventually, it may be necessary for all such activities to be reported in order to avoid any collisions or other destructive interactions between space objects.[129] Whereas there is currently a basis in space law for such an obligation inuring on States, there

126 Kelvey (2023).

127 Viikari (2008), p. 63.

128 John D. Rummel, Margaret S. Race, and Gerda Horneck, 'Ethical Considerations for Planetary Protection in Space Exploration: A Workshop', *Astrobiology*, 2012 (Nov); 12(11), pp. 1017–1023; Leonard David, "Planetary Parks' Could Protect Space Wilderness', *Space.com* (17 January 2013). David notes that the proposed rules in these planetary parks would require: 'No spacecraft or vehicle parts to be left within the park; No landing of unmanned spacecraft within the park; No waste to be left within the park Access only on foot or via surface vehicle along predefined routes, or by landing in a rocket-powered vehicle in predefined landing areas; All suits, vehicles and other machines used in the park to be sterilized on their external surfaces to prevent microbial shedding.'

129 Viikari (2008), p. 61 ('since space objects tend to turn into (or at least produce some) space debris that may gravely interfere in the space activities of all states, such consultations might be necessary before any future launch of a space object.'); Fasan, Ernst, *Space*

is no corresponding basis to place that requirement on NSAs. In looking to amend the architecture of space law to account for the increase in NSA activity, an option is to mirror the consultation and coordination obligation currently limited to States. Mirroring that obligation with a corresponding obligation for NSAs would ensure that all entities sending objects into space consult and cooperate when planning space activities, not just States, and would in turn reduce the likelihood of regulatory and operational knowledge and safety gaps.

It is notable in this respect that States are developing an international space traffic management system termed the rules of the road for space. The United States has included mention of space traffic management in its national space legislation,[130] the European Union is developing an EU approach to space traffic management,[131] and the Institute of Air Law, Space Law and Cyber Law at the University of Cologne in Germany is developing the Cologne Manual on the International Law of Space Traffic Management.[132] As the proposals and the system are still developing, there is an opportunity for NSAs to be included in the substance and formation of the evolving norms.

Although Article IX's etymology and text suggest that it is aimed at avoiding interference with the space activities of other States, it provides a robust basis to reduce space pollution. Space debris, in particular, is often a product of collisions between objects launched into space by different States or NSAs. The risk of such collisions can be reduced through a formalized system ensuring regular exchanges of information. Indeed, a level of consultation and cooperation is a first step towards creating a comprehensive system designed to prevent collisions in space.

Nonetheless, a consultation obligation is not a silver bullet to prevent any future space pollution being accidentally generated. Viikari points out that the duty under Article IX of the Outer Space Treaty has significant limitations, including that

> the obligation of the Outer Space Treaty to enter into consultations does not entitle the potentially affected state to bar the planned activity, nor

Debris – A Functional Approach. Proceedings of the 35th Colloquium on the Law of Outer Space, IISL, 28 August – 5 September, 1992 (AIAA, 1993). p. 285.

130 See e.g. U.S.C. Title 51; Chapter 5 above.

131 For more information on development of this initiative, see Defense Industry and Space, Space Traffic Management *European Commission* (available at: https://defence-industry-space.ec.europa.eu/eu-space-policy/space-traffic-management_en).

132 See Institute for Air Law, Space Law and Cyber Law, Cologne Manual on the International Law of Space Traffic Management *University of Cologne* (available at: https://ilwr.jura.uni-koeln.de/cologne-manual).

> does it specify any procedure or time limits for the consultations (or disputes arising therefrom) or requirements for providing the other state(s) involved with information of any kind. Furthermore, the consultations need not lead to a certain (or any) result, and even if they do, there is no obligation to take into account the result in any way when eventually conducting the space activities concerned.[133]

Experience bears out that the lack of specific binding obligations results in little likelihood that meaningful consultation on the activities that are the most likely to cause space debris will occur.[134] China's 2007 anti-satellite test, which is discussed above,[135] was not preceded by meaningful consultation despite its obligations under Article IX of the Outer Space Treaty.

From these experiences, it can be seen that an obligation to consult and cooperate is a helpful normative goal, but needs to be paired with specific parameters for the consultations. These parameters should include minimum time before the launch or other potentially harmful activity on which the consultations must occur, the range of States and NSAs which should be involved and how the information should be further circulated to interested space actors, and the potential sanctions for failing to adhere to these parameters.

Article XII of the Outer Space Treaty gives States Parties the right to inspect each other's 'stations, installations, equipment and space vehicles on the moon and other celestial bodies'. Viikari suggests that these inspections could be undertaken subject to 'reasonable advance notice of a projected visit [being given], in order that appropriate consultations may be held and that maximum precautions may be taken to assure safety and to avoid interference with normal operations in the facility to be visited'.[136] Again, this could be transposed to NSAs which are actively involved in space, in order to form a comprehensive regulatory web.

A model for the conduct of inspections could be based on the Organization for the Prohibition of Chemical Weapons (OPCW). In the Verification Annex of the Chemical Weapons Convention, provisions are set out governing the

---

133 Viikari (2008), p. 61.

134 Viikari (2008), p. 61 ('anti-satellite tests, which clearly have the potential to create orbital debris that can be harmful for all other spacefaring nations: apparently, international consultations never preceded such experiments'); Bhupendra Jasani, 'Remote Sensing From Space: national and international security. Disarmament Forum' (1999) 1 *The New Security Debate*, pp. 31–40 (available at https://unidir.org/publication/disarmament-forum-the-new-security-debate/).

135 See Chapter 1.

136 Viikari (2008), p. 62.

conduct of inspections. The subject matter has some similarities to space exploration; both involve considerable scientific expertise, technical engineering skills, and can cause harmful effects in States other than the State engaging in the action. Moreover, the two major space powers (the United States and Soviet Union) are key players in the disputes over chemical weapons, and so have experience with operationalizing its provisions. The OPCW has conducted multiple inspection missions and could share operational guidance with a putative space agency established at the international level.

On this basis, it can be seen that reforming space law to provide for NSA accountability for space pollution would align with the trend in international environmental law towards recognizing NSAs as key actors, as well as the developments that have occurred in other areas where NSAs have been attributed rights and responsibilities. Reform, expanding to encompass NSAs in addition to States, is long over-due given the significant shift in the governance structures of the entities underlying international geo-politics.

In relation to the filing of requests for GEO slots (as well as the planning of activities in the LEO and MEO), there have been problems with obtaining filing fees from private entities.[137] Because the ITU, which administers the filings and payments in order to conduct its work of designating slots, does not consider itself to have any legal relationship with companies under international law (as it does not consider them actors under international law), its ability to enforce those obligations rest only with its ability to compel States to pay for debts essentially incurred by satellite operators which over-file in an effort to ensure that they get at least a slot for their payloads to enter.[138] In this lacuna, satellite operators have begun to form their own solutions. Viikari notes that

> given the inability of the international community to provide common rules, satellite operators have begun to act on their own to coordinate their procedures. They have established a Satellite Users Interference Reduction Group (SUIRG), which is comprised of representatives from both private industry and the public sector.[139]

Reportedly, the SUIRG has worked for over a decade seeking to identify and mitigate the growing problem of satellite interference and the economic harm it inflicts on the space exploration and utilization industry.[140] Significantly, the

137 See Thompson (1996), pp. 280–283.

138 See Chapter 3, Section 2.

139 Viikari (2008), p. 93.

140 Viikari (2008), p. 93.

SUIRG cooperates with the satellite industry in seeking to define standards for equipment and to facilitate better training for operators.[141] Those efforts to establish standards and provide effective training would be particularly helpful to limit and mitigate the potential environmental impacts of space exploration and the utilization of space to host satellites for commercial, military and other purposes.

The organic creation of bodies able to communicate and coordinate to address problems at the operational level is an important means to ensure the efficient and effective redress of challenges which arise on the ground. More profoundly, it could provide a model for the adaptation of international law to recognize such groups and attribute them status as actors under international law. This would have the benefit of allowing the ITU and similar regulatory bodies to directly apply international norms to NSAs which constitute an increasingly large share of the entities active in space. It would remove the layer of Statehood which currently stands between the international community and the operators, potentially shielding the latter when conducting space launches and managing space objects providing services to Earth.

Ultimately, the reform avenue would require significant changes to draw NSAs into the direct formation and application of international law. Nonetheless, the approach of reforming the law provides an opportunity to craft well-balanced regulations, directly applicable to NSAs when they conduct acts that are not readily addressed by States. In this way, international law could move towards a more comprehensive web of accountability for space pollution and thereby better the best prospects to protect the space environment.

4 Conclusions regarding Options to Redress the Gap in Space Law Regarding NSAs

From the preceding, it can be seen that several factors augur in favour of the reform approach, rather than the retrenchment or re-interpretation means of proceeding. For example, as discussed above, interpretive issues surround Article IX of the Outer Space Treaty. Most notably, the part of the Article IX referring to 'harmful contamination' only refers explicitly to 'the exploration' of outer space, but not its 'use'.[142] Given that space pollution will likely occur

141 Jason Bates, 'Satellite Operators Target Interference Problem' *Via Satellite* (1 August 2005) (available at: https://www.satellitetoday.com/connectivity/2005/08/01/satellite-operators-target-interference-problem/); Viikari (2008), pp. 93–94.

142 See Chapter 2, Section 1.

when conducting activities other than exploration in the narrow sense (such as launching satellites and sending testing equipment to outer space and celestial bodies) uncertainty surrounds how this provision will be interpreted. This is a significant drawback for the 'retrenchment' approach, which favours traditional and highly literal readings. Moreover, whereas an interpretation of 'exploration' to cover all uses of space is potentially available and could even be applied to NSAs under the 're-interpretation' approach, that would nonetheless render space law dependent on the various interpretations that scholars and judges may adopt in the future.

Contrastingly, the reform approach provides the means to establish a clear and unambiguous normative framework for NSAs to conduct their business relating to space will both enhance the regulation of NSAs while also allowing them to engage in their space activities on the basis of explicit prescriptions. For these reasons, the preceding survey indicates that the 'reform' approach, with new provisions added to the framework of international space law, would best serve the aims of redressing and deterring space pollution and ensuring that avenues for accountability under international law are created for the harmful contamination of outer space. The proposed draft protocol to the Outer Space Treaty (or declaration) annexed to this book stands as a model for developing the architecture of international law to better redress space pollution whether by NSAs or States or a combination of the two.

5 Insights from the Avenues for Redress regarding the Nature of International Law

Confronting a novel threat such as NSA space pollution shines a light on the underlying nature of established international law. The analysis shows that, at the level of legal prescriptions, international law is currently ill-suited to address NSA space pollution. It provides no specific rules directly applicable to NSAs in this respect. Instead, it is heavily reliant on the construct of traditional State responsibility, which suffers from serious limitations in the field of space activities.[143] Other fields of international law, such as international humanitarian law, international criminal law, and international human rights law have some oblique applicability to activities in space, but only in highly truncated circumstances, such as armed conflict, the commission of atrocious crimes, or if the NSA is in control of territory. This leaves a lacuna, which is of increasing

143 See Chapter 3, Section 2.

magnitude as NSA space activity grows, and demonstrates that retrenchment to the existing framework will become even more unfeasible over time. To effectively remedy the legal gap in accountability for NSAs would require either considerable re-interpretation (to the point of exceeding the text of the Outer Space Treaty) or, preferably, reform of existing international law. While regulatory reform is welcome, and a model to achieve that is proposed herein, the analysis also generates insights regarding the formation and construction of international law when confronted with emerging challenges.

At the theoretical level, the retrenchment approach rests on an extremely strict positivist and State-centric understanding of international law. That restrictive conception has the benefit of clarity, systematicity and adherence to established norms and practices. In its purest form, this approach holds that, whereas international law is formed by and strictly applies to States (and international organizations in some respects),[144] sub-State level actors (referred to as NSAs in this paper) are exclusively regulated under domestic law. Such an approach avoids entities being subjected to multiple levels of legal regulation. It also allows for a measure of subsidiarity, whereby States can interpret and apply their international obligations in accordance with their national regulatory frameworks.

However, the State-centric approach has been undermined by developments in multiple areas of international law, including humanitarian,[145] criminal law entailing violations of human rights obligations,[146] and even environmental law. Each of these branches of international law has seen, to a greater or lesser extent, NSAs recognised as being directly subjected to, and subjects of, international law.[147] The distillation of rules applicable to NSAs

---

144 The status of international organizations under international law has been recognised by the International Court of Justice, see ICJ, *Reparations for injuries suffered in the services of the United Nations*, Advisory Opinion of. 11 April 1949 (ICJ Reports 1949, p. 174), p. 179.

145 In the *Tadić Jurisdictional Decision*, the Appeals Chamber of the ICTY observed that internal armed conflicts, or civil wars, have become increasingly prevalent, cruel, and protracted and that NIACs increasingly impact on third states; and recognised that NSAs have responsibilities under IHL; ICTY, *Prosecutor v. Tadić*, Case No. IT-94-1-AR72, Decision on the Defence Motion for Interlocutory Appeal on Jurisdiction (2 October 1995).

146 NSAs have increasingly been ascribed duties, such as human rights obligations, based on instruments directed towards States; see, e.g. ICTY and ICTR cases in which members of NSAs were ascribed with responsibility for violating rights to security, which are usually rights incumbent on States to protect and uphold, through their speech acts: IRMCT, *Prosecutor v. Šešelj*, Case No. IRMCT-16-99-A, Appeal Judgement (11 April 2018) (hereafter '*Šešelj* Appeal Judgment'), para. 163; ICTR, *Prosecutor v. Nahimana et al.*, Appeal Judgement, ICTR-99-52-A, 28 November 2007 (hereafter '*Nahimana et al.* Appeal Judgment'), para. 988.

147 Chapter 1, Section 5.

allowed the actions of groups, such as ISIS, to be judged in foreign courts and their members to be sentenced to imprisonment under international law.[148] Similarly, international aviation law, although not applicable in space, has numerous provisions directly requiring NSAs to engage conduct such as monitoring and reducing CO_2 emissions, which are environmentally-oriented.[149]

These legal developments have caused views to shift regarding the applicability of international law to NSAs. What has made these instances legally meaningful and legitimizing is that trappings of personhood have been ascribed to NSAs on the basis of recognised sources of international law, such as treaties and customary law, as interpreted by Courts established by the UN Security Council or by treaty. The ICTY, for example, went to great lengths to base its decisions on recognised precepts of international law, particularly customary international law.[150] The fact that provisions of those areas of law have been applied to NSAs (at least in the areas of humanitarian and criminal law) and upheld by international courts demonstrates that an exclusively State-bound conception of international law does not reflect the reality of its application in the 21st century. In this respect, Higgins notes (pointing to the increasing frequency of State-to-corporation arbitral agreements) that 'there is no inherent reason why the individual should not be able directly to invoke international law and to be the beneficiary of international law.'[151]

In the field of space law, an overt rejection of the applicability of international space law to NSAs would introduce a schism between branches of international law. An NSA which caused serious space pollution by detonating an explosive device in space, for example, would not have violated international space law. Yet the same NSA could potentially be directly held responsible under international humanitarian and criminal law if the explosion were linked to an armed conflict. That fragmentation portends incoherence in the development of sub-fields of international law.[152] It presumes a level of State-exclusivity as

---

148 See Chapter 1.

149 See Chapter 6, Section 3.

150 See ICTY, *Prosecutor v. Tadić*, Case No. IT-94-1-AR72, Decision on the Defence Motion for Interlocutory Appeal on Jurisdiction (2 October 1995) (assessing classical sources of international law to discern the status of joint criminal enterprise, for example, and finding that crimes can be charged under the Tribunal's Statute for acts committed in non-international armed conflicts). Whilst the accuracy of the Tribunal's reading of specific classical sources is sometimes questioned, the court's legal orientation clearly adhered to the core precepts of international law as a conceptual approach.

151 Higgins (1994), pp. 54–55.

152 See Anne Peters, 'The refinement of international law: From fragmentation to regime interaction and politicization' (2017) 15(3) *International Journal of Constitutional Law*, pp. 690, 692, 702.

subject of international law, which is not borne out by doctrine and practice in the current era.

Moreover, at the operational level, the risks of a solely State-centric approach to the regulation of space activities have been elaborated in Chapter 2. These include accountability gaps, especially where States are unable and unwilling to take measures against NSAs, and where NSAs engage in forum shopping to either maximize profits or opportunities for nefarious conduct.[153] These limitations jeopardize the core aim of regulatory law, which is to prevent negative outcomes for protected values, such as the environment, while allowing people and organizations to engage in productive activity. The retrenchment approach risks exacerbating these shortcomings in the development and operationalization of international space law. By insisting on an exclusively State-centric model, it will accentuate the gaps that are already present in the coverage of international space law.[154]

At the conceptual level, the State-centric approach clashes with several new conceptions of the formation and functioning of international law. For example Higgins conceives international law as 'an authoritative system of decision-making available in a decentralized system to all authorized decision-makers'.[155] According to her approach,[156] the subject-object dichotomy of legal positivists would be replaced by a 'decision-making process' (terming it a 'process' based approach).[157] Andrew Clapham presents a complementary line of reasoning to Higgins, arguing that whereas

153 See Chapter 3, Section 2.

154 See Chapter 6, Section 1.

155 Rosalyn Higgins, 'Policy Considerations and the International Judicial Process' (1968) 17(1) *International and Comparative Law Quarterly*, p. 58–59 ('When … decisions are made by authorized persons or organs, in appropriate forums, within the framework of certain established practices and norms, then what occurs is legal decision-making. In other words, international law is a continuing process of authoritative decisions. This view rejects the notion of law merely as the impartial application of rules. International law is the entire decision-making process, and not just the reference to the trend of past decisions which are termed 'rules'. There inevitably flows from this definition a concern, especially where the trend of past decisions is not overwhelmingly clear, with policy alternatives for the future.').

156 Somewhat paradoxically, Rosalyn Higgins (1994) also writes that '[c]onsent and sovereignty are constraining factors against which the prescribing, invoking, and applying of international law norms must operate.' (p.1).

157 Higgins (1994), p. 50.

> international law is mostly generated by accepted processes between nation states … public international law can apply in the networks and sectors that focus on duties for non-state actors.[158]

Those new 'process-based' conceptions conflict with the 'rules-based' approach, such as the traditional orientation of international space law. The converse approach (retrenching back to State exclusivity as decision-makers) will deny the role of NSAs as subjects of international law. This would be incongruous with NSA's increasingly central role in contemporary space activity. The incongruity further highlights the gap emerging between the strict traditionalist conception of State exclusivity under international law and the operational practice of applying branches of international law to pressing global problems.

Whereas some commentators do not accept that NSAs (apart from international organizations) can possess international legal personality,[159] even among those who would attribute NSAs with a measure of international legal personality there is variation. Some give NSAs a more central role in the formation of international law, as discussed above.[160] Others, such as Ronen, acknowledge that NSAs are capable of carrying out actions that would be, if conducted by States, considered violations of human rights, but maintain that, despite this, human rights law does not extend beyond traditional State-centric ambit.[161] Another view is the 'functional approach', which avoids conceptualizing the basis on which NSAs can be described as subjects,[162] and instead focuses on the utility of international law addressing NSAs in a specific circumstance. Thus, Ruth Wedgewood has argued that

> [t]he test for the 'privatization' of the international legal order must be a functional one. In the case of non-governmental organizations, their role has been seen as beneficial and creative, subject to suitable cautions. In the case of non-state political entities, the international community has treated them from necessity where the nation state did not have full control of its own domain, but it remains to be seen whether these political

158 Clapham (2016), pp. 28–29.

159 See, e.g. Robert Jennings and Arthur Watts (Eds.), *Oppenheim's International Law (9th Edition): Volume 1 Peace* (Oxford University Press, 2008), p. 120.

160 Chapter 6, Section 4 and Section 5.

161 Yaël Ronen, 'Human Rights Obligations of Territorial Non-State Actors' (2013) 46 *Cornell International Law Journal*, p. 47.

162 Clapham (2006), pp. 60–61.

imperatives may require a more formal status outside the state orientation of the Westphalian system.[163]

However, such a pragmatic approach is inherently context-bound and unable to generate insights that can assist in determining the legal personality and competencies of NSAs in circumstances other than the immediate case being observed. Nor can the 'functional' approach provide insight as to the axiomatic principles of international law, and to what extent those undergirding principles have shifted in recent decades with the increased NSA activity at the global level.

Going beyond the rules-based, process-based, and functional conceptions, the assessment provides a basis to argue that a flexible approach, prioritizing the interpretive principle of *effet utile* but anchored to the axiomatic foundations of international law, emerges as the best explanatory vehicle and conceptual basis for the development of international space law. This could be termed 'progressive positivism', as it seeks to interpret the applicable international law based on its express terms in light of the purpose it seeks to achieve in the dynamic context of changing technology, whilst still adhering to its core precepts as a legal discipline (namely international law comprising conventions and customary sources, as well as the general principles of law, as reflected in Article 38(1) of the Statute of the International Court of Justice).[164] NSA

163 Ruth Wedgewood, 'Legal Personality and the Role of Non-Governmental Organizations and Non-State Political Entities in the United Nations System' (1999) in R. Hofmann (ed.) *Non-State Actors as New Subjects of International Law: International Law – From the Traditional State Order Towards the Law of the Global Community* (Duncker and Humblot, 1999), p. 36.

164 This approach incorporates the view of Hart and Sacks view that '[u]nderlying every rule and standard ... is at the least a policy and in most cases a principle. This principle or policy is always available to guide judgment in resolving uncertainties about the arrangement's meaning.' Henry Hart and Albert Sacks, *The Legal Process: Basic Problems in the Making and Application of Law* (Tentative edition, 1958), pp. 166–167. However, whereas the approach of Hart and Sacks concerned adjudication, the current discussion concerns law reform to address the novel challenge of NSA space activities. Moreover, the present discussion adheres tangibly to the parameters of law formation, requiring interpretive tools and influences to be based on authoritative and recognised sources of international law. The approach of Hart and Sacks emphasizes the discernible substratum of values underlying legal provisions, against which existing and developing law may be assessed (see Vincent Wellman, 'Dworkin and the Legal Process Tradition: The Legacy of Hart & Sacks' (1987) 29 Arizona Law Review, pp. 418–423). That approach is particularly apposite for international law formation given the relatively broadbrush formulation of many treaties, the largely uncodified nature of customary international law, and the paucity of jurisprudence at the international level. Principles and policies underlying international law, which are relevant to discerning the capacity of space law to adapt to this challenge

conduct has been recognised by several commentators as contributing to the formation of customary international law, and arguably to general principles, as well as on occasion being referred to in treaties, as set out herein.[165] Under progressive positivism, NSA contributions to the development of international law are anchored to foundational principles and processes of law formation, such as treaty drafting and adoption and customary international law identification based on *opinio juris* and State practice. By adhering to those core systemic elements, this approach imbues new actors with legitimacy and status as contributors to the law, while affording them recognition based on the pre-existing legal framework of international law formation. The conclusions are thereby reached with legal authority, respecting the coherence of international law as a system. This adheres to the observation of the International Court of Justice, according to which:

> Law exists, it is said, to serve a social need; but precisely for that reason it can do so only through and within the limits of its own discipline. Otherwise, it is not a legal service that would be rendered.[166]

The question of legal personality is fundamental in this regard. By relying on established legal concepts to determine such personality, the approach of progressive positivism reinforces the validity of the core precepts of international law, while allowing its application to an expanding array of actors, which are increasingly involved in the formation of international law.[167] In Brolman's terms:

> inside the system "legal personality" is the attire which enables an entity to function in a legal order; more importantly, this attire is awarded by

include the recognition of the protection of the environment (and avoidance of its contamination) as a critical goal of international law (as can be seen from the proliferation of treaties, customary international law and other legal developments designed to protect the environment in the post-Cold War World). They also include the need to ensure effective accountability, which was foreshadowed at Nuremberg (with the Judges' observation that crimes are committed by humans and not abstract entities) but emerged more fully with international criminal law institutions from 1990s onwards.

165 Chapter 1, Section 5.

166 ICJ, South West Africa Case, para. 49.

167 See, e.g. Ayelet Berman, 'Between Participation and Capture in International Rule-Making: the WHO Framework of Engagement with Non-State Actors', (2021) 31(1), *European Journal of International Law*.

> that same legal order, which determines which entities participate in its sphere and which do not.[168]

To maintain both the effectiveness and conceptual coherence of international law, particularly in the field of space law, it is proposed that the progressive positivist approach should prioritize the *effet utile* interpretation technique.[169] This follows fundamental international law parameters such as Article 31(1) of the Vienna Convention on the Law of Treaties, which seeks to interpret provisions, and the treaty as a whole, to give them meaningful effect in light of the object and purpose of the treaty and to avoid either rendering the provisions superfluous or depriving them of significance in governing the parties' relationship.[49] In order to determine the object and purpose of a treaty in space law, soft law instruments by space-active States can provide considerable insight, particularly in relation to the interpretation of a treaty's aims when applied to new phenomenon, such as space debris (or pollution), which was not directly referred to in the treaty itself. Here, it is relevant that several soft law declarations provide that NSAs must abide by the environmental protections contained therein, as detailed extensively above.[170]

The context of NSA involvement in space pollution raises the need for clarity regarding the status, rights and obligations of NSAs under international space law.[171] Commentators have argued that space pollution such as debris could be redressed if countries were to form an international agreement waiving their sovereign rights to unidentified space debris.[172] Underlying this argument is the recognition that States' rights count under international law and cannot be simply overborne by efforts to achieve policy goals no matter how laudable, if those efforts are not reflected in legal developments of the applicable doctrine.

---

168 Catherine Brolman, *The Institutional Veil in Public International Law: International Organizations and the Law of Treaties* (Hart, 2007), p. 68.

169 In support of the *effet utile* (or 'effectiveness') principle, see Inter-American Court of Human Rights: *Case of the "Mapiripán Massacre" v. Colombia*, Judgment of September 15, 2000 (Merits, Reparations, and Costs), para. 105; ICC: *The Prosecutor v. Omar Hassan Ahmad Al Bashir*, Appeals Chamber, ICC-02/05-01/09-397-Anx2, 06 May 2019, para. 69, Joint Dissenting Opinion of Judge Luz Del Carmen Ibáñez Carranzaa and Judge Solomy Balungi Bossa; ICC: *Situation in Uganda*, Decision on the Prosecutor's Application that the Pre-Trial Chamber disregard as irrelevant the Submission filed by the Registry on 5 December 2005, Pre-Trial Chamber II, ICC-02/04-01/05-147, 09 March 2006, para. 25.

170 See, e.g. the European Code of Conduct for Space Debris Mitigation, discussed in Chapter 5.

171 Fogo (2017), p. 214.

172 Larsen (2018) citing Alshamsi, Balleste, Hanlon (2018).

Aside from the obvious operational limitation to such an approach (its utility would be significantly curtailed if even one space-faring State did not sign on to the agreement, as the unclaimed space debris could theoretically belong to that State), the proposal highlights the destabilizing impact of scholars simply declaring that NSAs are subjects of international space law without establishing the basis to claim that NSAs are recognised as subjects under established sources of international law. To a degree, this approach is premised on being compatible with a State-centric understanding of international law.[173] On the presumption that the Outer Space Treaty only applies to States, and that accordingly all claims over space objects ultimately vest in States as a matter of international law,[174] the proposal is at least conceptually coherent. However, it is operationally unsound, as it clashes with the reality on the ground (or above the sky), where NSAs are increasingly predominant in launching and operating space objects.

Conversely, if an alternative approach were taken, along the lines of Higgins' open and fluid process-based formulation,[175] and NSAs were considered subjects of international space law without anchoring that recognition on existing principles of international law, it would engage in a self-contradictory project of ascribing them status in a system whilst at the same time undermining the coherence of that system. At present, the framework of space law does not explicitly ascribe NSAs legal status to be directly proceeded against, and does not set out other means to enforce the protections of the space environment. Simply declaring space law to do so will not overcome the overwhelming tenor of the terms of the key space instruments, which are State-centric.

The survey above indicates that bluntly considering NSAs to be participants under international space law, without founding that view in the established framework of international law, has little explanatory or practical utility. It would potentially create as many questions and limitations as the

173 Larsen (2018), pp. 485–486. Larsen's state-centric outlook is reinforced by the subsequent analysis of 'Removal of Debris by Its Launching State' and 'Removal of Debris by Third Party States', which are not matched by a review of removal of debris by NSAs. Larsen does review the possibility of regulation of space activities by a non-governmental entity; Larsen (2018), pp. 508–511. However, he does not address the legal foundation and status of such a body under international law. Moreover, he concludes that a non-governmental body 'would not be able to establish mandatory regulations or enforce regulations without the enforcement of government agencies, because they cannot enforce regulations on other private operators'.

174 This premise is contestable, as Article II of the Outer Space Treaty leaves the position ambiguous in relation to NSAs appropriating space resources.

175 Albeit, Higgins does make reference to the importance of State consent and sovereignty.

retrenchment approach would in the other direction. Conversely, relying on enforceable rules of international law in accordance with its own precepts ensures its ongoing integrity as a system of law.[176]

Nonetheless, directly applying space law to NSAs while adhering to the foundational precepts of international law is not a straight forward matter and cannot simply be achieved by re-interpreting existing space law instruments. When prohibitions of international law are applied directly to NSAs, a host of other provisions of international law must necessarily also accompany the application of those provisions. These provisions should be enforceable in a realistic sense or else they risk undoing even the normative force that they may bear. Such ancillary (but important) rules and principles include human rights, to the extent specific individuals are involved. Thus, when international criminal law provisions were applied directly to individuals at the ICTY, ICTR, and ICC, for example, those individuals also became the direct bearers of human rights under international law such as the presumption of innocence and the right to silence.[177] In this light, the question is not just whether NSAs can be held accountable, but also whether the imputation of other status and rights under international law will necessarily follow, and whether that shift coheres with the structures and functioning of international law.

As present, although NSAs are significantly impacted by international space law, as detailed at length in Chapter 5's survey of domestic frameworks,[178] their involvement in the formation and interpretation of international law is truncated, uni-directional, and contingent.[179] It is truncated, as NSAs are only invited to provide views for consideration rather than practice for incorporation into the formation of international law. It is uni-directional, as NSAs are subjected to rules created by States rather than involved in the creation of rules controlling State conduct. It is also contingent, because the involvement of NSAs in the processes of distilling applicable guidelines for space conduct

---

176 'Enforceable' in this respect does not exclusively refer to sanctions, though of course that is a particularly robust way of demonstrating the existence and effectiveness of international law. Instead, enforceability is used to refer to the enshrining of principles into legal rules which could potentially be relied on before Courts competent to apply international law. But see Clapham (2006), pp. 28–29 (stating that he would 'reject the prevalent assumptions that: first, the bearers of international obligations are limited to presumed, so-called, 'subjects' of international law; and second, that public international law is inoperative outside established enforcement regimes such as international tribunals.')

177 See, e.g. Rome Statute of the International Criminal Court, Article 67.

178 See Chapter 5.

179 See Chapter 1, Section 5.

remains at the behest of their host States. This limited legal role contrasts with their growing actual activity in space.

Legal personality is not a strictly binary phenomenon, and competencies will vary even among entities recognised as subjects of international law.[180] However, basing the recognition of NSA's status under international law on its existing foundations will strengthen the legitimacy and effectiveness of activities conducted with that status.

As Anthony Clark Arend has articulated, there are challenges in expanding international law to encompass a wider array of subjects:

> If, however, the state were to lose its monopoly in a neomedieval system, the most basic general principle about the nature of international law – the notion that states create international law through their consent – would now have to be expanded. If this were to be the case, the international law-creating process would be fundamentally changed … [T]he process of creating customary international law could become much more complex. There could, in fact, be multiple levels of customary international law.[181]

Higgins opposes the subject-object dichotomous view of international law, for being based on 'conservative belief that what presently is, necessarily always has to remain so'.[182] She posits that 'the further one moves away from positivism and rules, the less important becomes the distinction between *lex lata* and *lex ferenda* – the law as it is and the law as it might be.'[183] However, the statement inherently acknowledges the cost of loosening the underlying approach to international law. Instead of the firm clarity and reliability of *lex lata*, actors under international law would be exposed to a much broader field of concepts which may or may not constitute *lex ferenda*, without any established criteria to delineate that category from simply the desires or preferred policy position of any actor in any specific situation.

---

180 ICJ, *Reparations for injuries suffered in the services of the United Nations*, Advisory Opinion of. 11 April 1949, p. 178 ("the subjects of law in any legal system are not necessarily identical in their nature or in the extent of their rights.'); Murray (2016), p. 29 ('the consequences of international legal personality are not uniform and an entity's ability to act on the international plane is determined on the basis of factors specific to that entity; i.e. on the basis of an entity's subject-specific competence.').

181 Arend (1999), pp. 176–177.

182 Rosalyn Higgins (1994), p. 49.

183 Rosalyn Higgins (1994), p. 10.

In this light, international space law can undergo a normative development towards a more constitutionalized system characterized by obligations *erga omnes*,[184] which would match those undertaken by other fields including humanitarian, criminal, and increasingly human rights and environmental law.[185] However, there must be a coherent conceptual basis invoked when doing so, as has been done for those other fields and as proposed herein, or the legitimacy and forces of the *erga omnes* obligations themselves may be undermined.

184 Viikari (2008), p. 183. See further, by analogy, Stubbe (2018), p. 11.
185 See Chapter 4.

CHAPTER 7

Overall Conclusions: An Emerging Threat that Tests the Underpinnings of International Law

> [S]pace can be explored and mastered without feeding the fires of war, without repeating the mistakes that man has made in extending his writ around this globe of ours.[1]

Humankind has made major advances, including accessing outer space, and also missteps, such as harming the environment, in the arc of its existence on Earth to date. In recent years a growing awareness of the fragility of the planet to anthropogenic harm has emerged. Spurred on by this environmental cognizance, international treaties concerning the protection of the terrestrial and maritime domains have been concluded. However, such protections have not been concertedly examined in the context of outer space, particularly in relation to NSAs. The imperative to do so is all the more pressing with these NSAs engaging in potentially harmful space activities at an ever-greater rate. In this light, the present analysis approaches the problem of space pollution from an ecocentric perspective, placing potential legal protections of the environment under the microscope.

The analysis in this book demonstrates that international law contains an emergent prohibition of space pollution.[2] Article IX of the Outer Space Treaty provides a robust basis for this prohibition, based on its reference to avoiding 'harmful contamination' of the outer space environment.[3] International environmental law, which is incorporated as an interpretive aide by reference in Article III of the Outer Space Treaty, supports reading Article IX as banning space pollution. Specifically, this aligns with the no-harm principle, which

1 President John F. Kennedy, 'We choose to go to the Moon', address at Rice University (12 September 1962) (available at https://www.rice.edu/jfk-speech#:~:text=Well%2C%20space%20is%20there%2C%20and,which%20man%20has%20ever%20embarked).

2 See Chapter 2, Section 2.

3 See Stubbe (2018); Viikari (2008); Dennerley (2018).

augurs in favour of interpreting Article IX's reference to harmful contamination to prohibit space pollution.[4] That reading is further reinforced by the State practice examined in Chapter 5, which demonstrates how States convert their international obligations into domestic licensing regimes. In several instances, States impose criminal sanctions, including incarceration, for failing to adhere to environmental protection in space launches and operations.[5] This State practice is significant for the present inquiry, as it shows that many States consider NSAs must avoid polluting the space environment, particularly, though not exclusively, in the form of space debris.

However, the enforceability of this prohibition constitutes a legal blind spot. Specifically, the terms of Article IX's reference to 'harmful contamination' lacks precision. It does not set out a procedure for determining harmful contamination and it fails to specify any concrete consequence in cases of non-compliance.[6] It is difficult to envisage how the prohibition could be operationalized to ensure accountability. Moreover, no enforcement mechanism is identified under the Outer Space Treaty, and there is no international environmental court to address such cases. In circumstances where the pollution amounts to a violation of international criminal law, there are options such as the International Criminal Court and domestic courts operating under universal jurisdiction. But these only cover very specific circumstances, and will exclude a significant proportion of space pollution which can arise from events such as anti-satellite tests and other collisions. Moreover, only a minority of space-faring States have established national mechanisms to ensure the enforcement of their obligations at the domestic level, emphasizing the need for international responses.[7]

The accountability gap is particularly aggravated when it comes to NSAs. States could theoretically be taken to the International Court of Justice if their space activities violated a treaty under which the Court was provided jurisdiction, and also could be brought before human rights courts if the conduct amounted to violations of rights such as to a clean, healthy, and sustainable environment. However, those institutions do not entertain cases against NSAs. In the absence of an international court for the environment (including outer space), there are few options to proceed against NSAs. Arbitration is party-driven and non-regulatory in nature. Domestic courts of the home State of the NSA (or launching State) provide a promising option. But, for the reasons set

4 See Larsen (2018), pp. 4901–491.
5 See Chapter 5, Section 11.
6 Hobe (2019), p. 89.
7 See Chapter 5.

out above (including inability or unwillingness on the part of the State and/ or forum shopping by the NSA),[8] these courts may decide not to undertake proceedings against offending NSAs. On this basis, the putative prohibition of space pollution stands as a bridge to nowhere. It is an important provision, which provides the key basis for a prohibition of space pollution under international law. But it does not lead to repercussions. In this light, it is a tool without teeth, normatively setting down an important environmental protection, but operationally insufficiently precise for any enforcement action through legal venues.

Several causes have contributed to this lacuna. Primarily, there are historical factors such as the State-dominated era in which leading space law treaties were formed. Outer space presents the environmental context *par excellence* for a purist Statist legal regime. With activities in space limited to States for the early decades of space exploration, there were simply no other entities engaging in conduct that could even potentially influence the development of international space law. The language and orientation of the major space conventions of early years reflects this State-exclusivity.[9] The Outer Space Treaty only provides for the possibility of NSA conduct in outer space under the 'control' of one or more States. Similarly, the Liability Convention (in its preamble) refers to 'the precautionary measures to be taken by States and international intergovernmental organizations involved in the launching of space objects, damage may on occasion be caused by such objects' without referencing NSAs. Given the temporal and environmental context in which space law was formed, the lack of attention to NSAs, though limiting, is unsurprising.

In the modern world, the disconnect between this State-oriented terminology and the increasing role of NSAs in space is incongruous. To date, there has been little appetite to amend the terms of the core space treaties. That inertia derives partly from States' comfort with the current conventional framework (and its adaptability to a variety of intents, including certain States being content to let private companies do what States perhaps cannot). However, that homeostasis is becoming untenable in light of the growing interest in the commercial exploitation of outer space, including through resource extraction, and the legislative moves in certain countries to allow private entities to engage in that behaviour irrespective of whether it may clash with established interpretations of the prohibition on national appropriation.[10] More States have signed up to the Artemis Accords, which appear to endorse resource extraction and

8 See Chapter 3, Section 2.

9 Chapter 1, Section 4.

10 See Chapter 1, Section 3.

utilization in outer space, than are party to the Moon Agreement, which contains the apex of environmental protection in Article 7.[11] Consequently, the danger of States and NSAs exploiting the lack of an explicit prohibition on private appropriation in the Outer Space Treaty is growing.[12]

The limitations in the current space law framework, which have been identified in this book, render it all the more important to look at other avenues to ensure accountability for such harm to the outer space environment. In this respect, the following conclusions can be drawn in relation to harmful NSA conduct in outer space.

Normatively, there is the traditional orientation of international law towards State acts and State responsibility. Even in other domains where NSA conduct has a long history, such as under international humanitarian law, the framework of international law has only been applied to NSAs in fits and starts, and with particular intensity by institutions such as the ICTY.[13] Likewise, the application of international human rights law to NSAs remains an area of heated debate,[14] notwithstanding the volume of human rights abuses conducted by such actors and the proliferation of international human rights law treaties.[15] That context suggests that adjusting space law to regulate the conduct of NSAs will be similarly uneven and unpredictable.

Then there is the medium in issue. Space itself lies outside of the jurisdiction of any State, as noted by the Outer Space Treaty, the Liability Convention, and the Moon Agreement (establishing the States should not take ownership of celestial objects). Because the extent of State territorial jurisdiction (and

11 Saudi Arabia, for example, was first critical of the Artemis Accords and had ratified the Moon Agreement. Since then however, it has signed the Artemis Accords and withdrawn from the Moon Agreement, effective as of January 2024.

12 It should be mentioned that the Nemitz case presented an apt example on why States should be encouraged to continue prohibiting private appropriation of outer space as in that instance a private USA citizen sued NASA for payment of parking fees on the Moon incurred by NASA spacecraft on Nemitz alleged property. As such States would be placing themselves in a disadvantageous position compared to NSAs.

13 For example, the terms of Additional Protocol I, applicable to international armed conflicts, continue to be more extensive and comprehensive than those of Additional Protocol II, which applies to non-international armed conflicts, and several war crimes in the Rome Statute only apply in State-to-State conflicts, such as the Article 8(2)(b)(iv) offences of launching attacks risking excessive harm (specifically '[i]ntentionally launching an attack in the knowledge that such attack will cause incidental loss of life or injury to civilians or damage to civilian objects or widespread, long-term and severe damage to the natural environment which would be clearly excessive in relation to the concrete and direct overall military advantage anticipated').

14 Bourdonnaye (2020), pp. 592–593.

15 See Chapter 4, Section 2.4.

therefore potential accountability) is limited in relation to space, the establishment of an international legal regime governing NSA conduct is particularly important. As analyzed above, currently the most direct and likely means of addressing space pollution by NSAs is through the traditional approach of State responsibility.[16] This approach funnels all redress and remedial action through the State. Efforts to protect the outer space environment have been grafted onto this legal framework. For example, the UNCOPUOS SDMG are directed to States (and international organisations) and do not explicitly address NSAs.[17] In this way, all avenues for redress are directed through the State apparatus, which renders enforcement efforts vulnerable to falling into gaps in States' willingness and ability to regulate space conduct.

However, the study has shown that exclusively relying on State responsibility has limitations in relation to NSA space pollution. As noted in Chapter 3, Section 2 above, shortcomings of the State-exclusivity enforcement model include: States struggling to match the technological sophistication to monitor NSA activities in outer space; States being unwilling or unable to regulate NSA space activities due to financial pressures from well-resourced NSAs or due to a lack of control over certain parts of their territory, such as during armed conflict; nefarious NSAs exploiting weak regulatory regimes through forum shopping to maximize profits at the expense of environmental protections; some governments and territorial entities having unclear status under international law, such as in Afghanistan and Kosovo; NSA activities emanating from areas outside any State's control, such as the high seas or the poles; and, finally, addressing establishing causation and/or attribution, which are complex and dynamic notions.[18] Moreover, the variation in how States are implementing their international obligations, as examined in detail in Chapter 5, suggests that discrepancies are already evident in transferring their international obligations to domestic settings.

Bearing in mind those limitations, the study has postulated that NSAs can play a role in the development and application of international space law. In accordance with other branches of international law, NSAs can have both passive and active international legal personality in important respects. However, the recognition of NSA active international legal personality must accord with the broader framework of international law. At present, the basis for holding NSAs *directly* responsible under space law is speculative.[19] Article IX, which is

16 See Chapter 3.
17 Chapter 1, Section 3.
18 Chapter 3, Section 2.
19 See Chapter 4, Section 1.

the core provision of the Outer Space Treaty concerning a potential prohibition of space pollution, refers to '*States Parties to the Treaty*' having the obligations to avoid the harmful contamination of outer space including the Moon and other celestial bodies. It is difficult to interpret this as imposing direct obligations on NSAs.[20] The context of the Outer Space Treaty reinforces that it is premised on a model of State enforcement for NSA conduct. For example, Article VI holds that NSA conduct in space requires 'authorization and continuing supervision by the appropriate State Party', and Article VII makes State Parties liable for damage to other State Parties or their natural or juridical persons on the surface of the Earth, to aircraft in flight, or in outer space.

Legal flexibility is introduced by Article III, which imports broader international law concepts and principles into the Outer Space Treaty framework, including customary international environmental law. On this basis, international environmental law notions, such as the 'no-harm' principle, could be incorporated into interpretations of the Outer Space Treaty, particularly Article IX's reference to harmful contamination. Moreover, in line with State obligations to undertake environmental impact assessments before conducting or authorizing potentially environmentally harmful activities such as space launches, this requirement is provided for in the legislation of several space-active States. That imposes a legal obligation, at least normatively, on NSAs from those countries or operating under the jurisdiction.[21]

However, these principles lack specificity for their implementation *per se* and the enforcement of more detailed regulations at the domestic level reflecting these obligations is inconsistent between States. Consequently, the basis to argue that NSAs are directly bound by international environmental law remains thin and lacks precision. Additionally, even to the extent that NSAs are referred to in some areas of environmental law, such as under the Aarhus Convention, there is no specific environmental court in which they could be proceeded against at the international level, undermining its direct applicability to this growing category of space actors.

As an alternative means of protecting the environment, this study has examined how other areas of international law could be used to collaterally address space pollution by NSAs. International criminal law has provided an example of direct application of international law to NSAs, including individual natural persons.[22] Equally, human rights practice (particularly that of United Nations

20 See Chapter 4, Section 2.1.

21 See Chapter 5.

22 Chapter 4, Section 2.2.

entities) is increasingly recognizing the responsibility of NSAs.[23] Under international human rights law, the recently recognised right to a healthy, clean, and sustainable environment, is the most directly relevant, not only due to its content, but the fact that it represents a basis and a prerequisite for exercising several other human rights.[24] The possibility of finding violations of criminal and human rights law, and potentially criminal sanctions, against individuals and NSA groups has been an important facet of establishing international accountability for atrocities and is increasingly touted as a means of protecting the Earth's environment. Specific provisions under international criminal law, which could be engaged by space pollution caused intentionally, would include war crimes such as those of launching attacks against civilian objects, launching attacks knowing that excessive harm to the natural environment would ensue, and the destruction of an enemy's (adversary's) property.[25] The corresponding provisions of international humanitarian law would be violated in such circumstances, particularly where attacks in space on communications and other infrastructure systems significantly impact civilian life on Earth. There are emerging ways in which the obligation to respect that right has been imposed on NSAs, including businesses. However, there remains a lack of fora in which NSAs can be directly proceeded against, even for these prospective violations.

If a basis for liability of NSAs for space pollution can be established under substantive law, then compensation for space pollution by an NSA could theoretically be sought in the domestic courts of the launching State or via diplomatic channels. However, the Liability Convention does not explicitly provide for liability for damages to the outer space environment. Furthermore, the dangers facing the claimant in front of domestic courts include the insolvency of the NSA in question (particularly if it is a corporation) as well as the ability to enforce the judgment and the restraints of national space acts. It is likely that any claim for space pollution in front of domestic courts would face other obstacles, such as causation, attribution, and potentially the act of State doctrine, if the corporation were tied to the State of the domestic courts.

On the other hand, this book proposes a possibility to be able to pursue NSAs in front of international tribunals as a complement to domestic proceedings. There has been a proliferation of international courts in recent decades. However, the international framework lacks clear rules on how the causation of space pollution, for example through the unnecessary and reckless creation

23 See Chapter 3, Section 2.
24 Chapter 2, Section 1.3.
25 Chapter 4, Section 2.2.

of space debris, can provide a basis for legal proceedings. Examples include Article IX of the Outer Space Treaty, the no-harm principle, and others, as explored in Chapters 2 to 4. Nonetheless, each of the examples examined appears too vague to give rise to an enforceable prohibition directly applicable to NSA space pollution.

As the risk to the space environment from NSA conduct rises, a widening gap can be discerned between the stated aims of the Outer Space Treaty (to preserve the exploration and use of outer space as the province of all humankind, which is jeopardized by space pollution both due to the restricting of access to outer space and the non-preservation of the outer space environment itself) and the possibility of holding NSA misfeasors accountable for serious harm to the outer space environment. This will be especially important in the evolving commercial age where technology has enabled easier and cheaper launches and smaller satellites and subsequently allowed a larger array of actors to participate in space activity.

Among the three avenues for redress, the retrenchment (State-centric) avenue provides a conservative response to the growing problem of NSA space pollution. Whereas space law could continue to assert itself as the appropriate deterrent, it is inherently dependent on each individual State's ability to supervise and control its NSAs. This in turn creates a danger of the risks set out above which limit States' ability to regulate NSA conduct, including when conducted from areas outside their control or jurisdiction.[26] Engaging in more of the same approach without adjustment is unlikely to resolve the growing problem.

The second approach of re-interpretation bears some promise, but will struggle to take hold given the vagueness of the provisions of space law which could potentially apply to NSAs. No specific principles of international environmental law definitively prohibit NSAs from causing space pollution. Even with creative readings under the 'reinterpretation' approach, there is simply insufficient procedural specificity to enforce Article IX in the context of binding legal proceedings. Creative interpretations which deviate from the terms of established law would challenge the legitimacy of the fora in which they are made and may undermine the certainty and predictability of the international law they apply more generally. NSAs planning space activities in space would have to speculate as to the nature and extent of legal obligations falling on them.

As for the third 'reform' approach whereby new provisions would be added to the framework of international space law, this has the benefit of clarity,

26 See Chapter 3, Section 2.

effectiveness, and specificity. An expanded legal framework, with provisions directly applicable to NSAs could achieve significant progress on this front. The UNCOPUOS SDMG could be used as a model, as they cover the life-cycle of a space objects launch, activity, and decommission. In addition to ensuring that the specific duties and rights were also directed to NSAs, it would be necessary to ensure that such an instrument covered all foreseeable harmful activities. This would help avoid legal vacuums in the coverage of State-led regulation, which can be exploited by bad faith private actors looking to maximize profits. Importantly, any such instrument should contain an enforcement branch or link to an enforcement institution, capable of applying international law directly to NSAs.[27] In this way, it would best redress and deter NSA space pollution in both theory and practice. On this basis, it is argued that a new rule, protocol, or treaty is required, or else State practice must develop to the point that it convincingly demonstrates the existence of such a rule as a matter of State practice.[28] For this purpose, the draft protocol to the Outer Space Treaty annexed to this book, provides a model for consideration to be considered for further development and adoption in order to ensure NSA (and State) accountability for space pollution under international law.

Whereas considerable political capital would be required to achieve sufficient consensus to bring about changes to the conventional provisions of space law, the growing communal risks of cutting off access to outer space will provide strong motivation for States and other entities to reach accords in this respect. Moreover, even if conventional amendment or new treaty creation is not achieved, soft law instruments could help to shape the contours of space law – particularly in relation to the application of international environmental law to NSAs, which would infuse space law via Article III of the Outer Space Treaty.

At the conceptual level, the study reveals several insights. In the modern era of international law, it has become increasingly evident that the State-centric model of international law has significant practical limitations.[29] Many States suppress minorities and even majorities within their territorial bounds.[30]

27 See Chapter 4, Section 3.

28 See Chapter 6.

29 It has to be noted, however, that international regulation of NSA activities also raises concerns. See, for example, Chapter 6, Section 2.

30 Thirlway (2017), p. 145 argues that his approach 'does not necessarily require that the State be democratically organized: even a dictator is, in relation to other governments, and on the international level generally, acting for (what he sees as) the good of his country/State'. Similarly, Rawls demonstrates how the law of the peoples, the law governing relations between what he calls liberal societies on one hand and hierarchical societies on the

Moreover, some States are simply unwilling or unable to address serious problems of communal import.[31] Because of this, the traditional model of State-exclusivity has retreated, and NSAs are being increasingly recognised as objects of international law, as well as potentially contributing to its formation. There are some initial signs that space law may be following in this same direction. For example, the UNCOPUOS Guidelines for the Long-term Sustainability of Outer Space Activities refer to their basis consisting of a substantial body of knowledge provided by 'States, international intergovernmental organizations and relevant national and international non-governmental entities'.[32] Nonetheless, that recognition remains the exception rather than the rule at the present stage of space law development.

Until recent decades States had a near monopoly over space activity.[33] All space exploration occurred well after the Westphalian State system became established. In the initial years of space activity, the prospect of NSAs accessing space *en masse* was not widely recognised. Whilst NSAs have been sending communications satellites to space since IntelSat I in 1965, it is only very recently that NSAs have begun sending crewed missions to outer space.[34] In comparison with the exploration of the high seas, for example, the historical shift between State and private activity is reversed. The high seas were first explored well before States were established, but more recently States have sought to place all activities at sea under a State flag. Conversely, there was no private exploration of space prior to State-led missions. That historical

---

other, consists merely of certain basic rules on which both types of societies can agree. See Rawls (1993), 43–54.

31 Chapter 3, Section 2.

32 Committee on the Peaceful Uses of Outer Space Guidelines for the Long-term Sustainability of Outer Space Activities, para. 11.

33 Martin N. Ross, Leonard David, 'Space Pollution: The new private launch industry can learn a lot from aviation about sustainability' (2021) 324(2) *Scientific American*, pp. 56–59 (noting that less than fifty years ago the only satellites allowed in space were government owned/operated but now most rockets and satellites are launched by public-private partnerships and that the shift to private space access will increase rapidly in the near future).

34 History of Information, 'INTELSAT 1, the First Commercial Communication Satellite, is Placed in Geosynchronous Orbit' *historyinformation.com* (available at https://historyofinformation.com/detail.php?entryid=3595); Monica Grady, 'Private companies are launching a new space race – here's what to expect' *The Conversation* (3 October 2017) (available at https://theconversation.com/private-companies-are-launching-a-new-space-race-heres-what-to-expect-80697); Scott Dutfield, Vicky Stein, 'Inspiration 4, The first all-civilian spaceflight on SpaceX Dragon' *Space* (5 January 2022) (available at https://www.space.com/inspiration4-spacex.html); Denise Chow, 'SpaceX makes history with first all-civilian spaceflight' *NBC News* (16 September 2021) (available at https://www.nbcnews.com/science/space/spacex-makes-history-first-civilian-spaceflight-rcna2027).

context has shaped the development and topography of international space law. However, it should not be permitted to freeze space law in an increasingly unsuitable mold, which is insufficiently adaptable to address the emerging challenges presented by large numbers of NSA space objects accessing and maneuvering in space.

In light of the limits of a retrenchment to the State-centric approach as well as the consequent risks of engaging in re-interpreting the provisions of space law without importing additional guarantees, and in light of the ambiguity in major key provisions of the dated instruments of space law, it is essential to identify additional and alternative means of holding NSAs to account for serious destruction of communally important phenomenon such as the space environment. Reform, whether through a new protocol to the Outer Space Treaty, as annexed to this book, or a new free-standing treaty (or alternatively as a declaration), promises the more coherent means of achieving a lasting regime governing NSA conduct in space. Such an instrument would have to place the prohibition of space pollution at its core, and provide for clear guidance to NSAs looking to operate in space, as well as for States and international and domestic courts looking to apply their terms.

Whatever approach is ultimately taken, the preceding analysis shows that it is critical to look beyond the traditional State-focused route to accountability for space activities. It is imperative that the international community also develop alternative mechanisms and legal regimes under which NSAs could be held responsible for misconduct in outer space, in order to preserve humankind's access to space and the outer space environment itself.

Annex: Proposed New Protocol to the Outer Space Treaty of 1967 Addressing NSA Responsibility for Space Pollution

Non-State Actor Accountability for Space Pollution

1 Proposed Optional Protocol to the Outer Space Treaty to Address Space Pollution by State and Non-State Actors

1.1 *Rationale*

As set out in the monograph, harm to the space environment is an increasingly recognised threat to the continued accessibility of outer space. Equally, the role of non-State actors has emerged as a key feature of modern space activity. The Outer Space Treaty will benefit from clarification to address these phenomena which have become far more prevalent and potent since its adoption in 1967.

1.2 *Provisions*

The States Parties to this Protocol,

Reiterating the aims set out in preamble of the Outer Space Treaty of 1967, and, in *particular,*

Reaffirming the common interest of all humankind in the progress of the exploration and use of outer space for peaceful purposes, and

Recalling that outer space, including the moon and other celestial bodies, shall not be subject to national appropriation,[1] but shall instead be free for exploration and use by all States without discrimination of any kind, on a basis of equality and in accordance with international law, and there shall be free access to all areas of celestial bodies;

Noting the deleterious impact that human actions can have on the outer space environment,

Further noting that non-State actors are playing an increasingly prevalent role in outer space,

1 As a separate note, on the issue of appropriation, this Protocol or a similar instrument could clarify that NSAs may not appropriate outer space, including the Moon and other celestial bodies.

 | DOI:10.1163/9789004724624_009

Convinced that an Optional Protocol to the Treaty on Principles Governing the Activities of States in the Exploration and Use of Outer Space, including the Moon and Other Celestial Bodies of 1967, will further the purposes and principles of the Charter of the United Nations,

Have agreed on the following:

1. The harmful contamination of outer space through space pollution of all forms, including intentional or negligent causation of disproportionate amounts of space debris, is prohibited. This prohibition applies irrespective of whether the harmful contamination is caused by State actors, non-State actors, or a combination of these entities. All entities sending objects into outer space or maintaining, operating, controlling, or otherwise responsible for objects in outer space must adhere to this prohibition and the requirements in Article 2.
2. For the avoidance of harmful contamination, all entities conducting outer space activities shall take the following steps, in accordance with guidelines issued by the United Nations and other international and regional organisations:
   a. Limit pollution, including debris, released during normal operations;
   b. Minimize the potential for break-ups of spacecraft and launch vehicles, as well as space objects, during operational phases and ensure that disposal and passivation measures are planned in conjunction with any space activities; when intentional break-ups are necessary, they should be conducted at sufficiently low altitudes to limit the orbital lifetime of resulting fragments;
   c. Limit the probability of accidental collisions in orbit;
   d. Strictly avoid intentional destruction of space objects and other harmful activities that generate space pollution;
   e. Minimize potential for post-mission break-ups resulting from stored energy, including by ensuring that all on-board sources of stored energy should be depleted or made safe when they are no longer required for mission operations or post-mission disposal;
   f. Limit the long-term presence of spacecraft and launch vehicle orbital stages in the low-Earth orbit (LEO) region after the end of their mission;
   g. Limit the long-term interference of spacecraft and launch vehicle orbital stages with the geosynchronous Earth orbit (GEO) region after the end of their mission;
   h. Designate and use appropriate space traffic management measures and best practices for the avoidance of collisions, including

use of space situational awareness data prior to, during and after the operation of space objects.

3. Any entity conducting outer space activities which receives information or discovers that harmful contamination of the outer space environment has occurred or that there is a likelihood that such contamination will imminently occur shall notify the launching authority (insofar as known to the entity) and, in any event, the Secretary-General of the United Nations.
4. Any entity conducting outer space activities shall cooperate in studies and efforts to remediate and remove harmful contamination in outer space, including space debris.
5. Any entity conducting outer space activities shall ensure that its space objects are registered with the United Nations, including through the provision of prompt and updated information to the national authorities in the launching State or other appropriate State.
6. Each State Party shall adopt such measures as may be necessary under domestic law to prohibit the conduct set forth in Article 1 of this Protocol, including through criminal offences and sanctions for serious and intentional violations of Article 1 and through civil sanctions for other violations of Article 1. All criminal and civil offences and sanctions should extend both to natural and, *mutatis mutandis*, legal persons, and should be applied in accordance with internationally recognised human rights protections. In assessing violations of Article 1 of this Protocol, enforcement entities shall take into account compliance with the measures set out in Article 2 of this Protocol.
7. Each State Party shall maintain, designate or establish, at the latest one year after the entry into force of the present Protocol or of its ratification or accession, one or several independent national space protection mechanism(s) (NSPM) to monitor and prevent harmful space pollution being caused by entities under its jurisdiction. The States Parties undertake to make available the necessary resources for the functioning of the NSPMs.

Bibliography

Monographs, Articles, and Other Written Works Attributable to Authors

Abbott KW, Snidal D, 'Strengthening International Regulation Through Transnational New Governance' (2009) 42(2) Vanderbilt Journal of Transnational Law 501–578.

Abhijeet K, National Space Legislation for India (2020) Heidelberg: Springer.

Ad Hoc Expert Group IAA (McKnight D et al.) 'Orbital Debris – Status and Possibilities for Control' (1993) 9(3) Space Policy.

Adams R, 'The New York Times Co. v. National Aeronautics & Space Administration' (available at: https://rickadams.org/chall/legal.html).

Afonso AJ, 'Brazil relaunches its space industry by opening the Alcantara base to the US' Universidad de Navarra (available at: https://www.unav.edu/web/global-affairs/detalle/-/blogs/brazil-relaunches-its-space-industry-by-opening-the-alcantara-base-to-the-us).

Aganaba-Jeanty T, 'Space Sustainability and the Freedom of Outer Space' (2018) 14(1) Astropolitics: The International Journal of Space Politics & Policy.

Aglietti GS, 'Current Challenges and Opportunities for Space Technologies' (2020) 1 Frontiers in Space Technologies.

Ahn, Y, National Space Law and Policy in the Republic of Korea (2024) Leiden: Brill Nijhoff.

Akiyama H, 'Japan's space agency to be freed to invest in private businesses' NikkeiAsia (13 June 2023) (available at: https://asia.nikkei.com/Business/Aerospace-Defense-Industries/Japan-s-space-agency-to-be-freed-to-invest-in-private-businessessss).

Aliberti M, Lisitsyna K, Russia's Posture in Space (2019) Vienna: Springer.

Alsahlawi AM, Chebbi K, Ammer MA, 'The Impact of Environmental Sustainability Disclosure on Stock Return of Saudi Listed Firms: The Moderating Role of Financial Constraints' (2021) 9(4) International Journal of Financial Studies.

Alshamsi H, Balleste R, Hanlon MLD, 'As the Grapefruit Turns Sixty, It's Time to Get Serious About Clean Up in Outer Space' (2018) 83 Journal of Air Law and Commerce.

Anderson JL, 'Piracy and World History: An Economic Perspective on Maritime Predation' (1995) 6(2) Journal of World History.

Aoki S, 'In Search of the Current Legal Status of the Registration of Space Objects' (2010) in: 61st International Astronautical Congress, Prague, Czech Republic.

Arangio-Ruiz G, 'State Responsibility Revisited: The Factual Nature of the Attribution of Conduct to the State' (2017) 6 Rivista di diritto internazionale.

Arato J, 'Corporations as Lawmakers', (2015) 56(2) Harvard International Law Review.

Arayata C, 'Yearender: PhilSA 'resolutely' expands domestic space ecosystem' pna.gov.ph (26 December 2022) (available at: https://www.pna.gov.ph/articles/1191408).

Arend AC, Legal Rules and International Society (1999) New York: Oxford University Press.

Arzo TF, 'Starlink satellites increased nearly 50% in space in 2021' techgenyz (8 March 2022) (available at https://www.techgenyz.com/2022/03/08/starlink-satellites-increased-nearly-space/).

Atanasov V & Baldesi G, 'An Analysis of Two Space Business Opportunities' in: Space-Based Technologies and Commercialized Development: Economic Implications and Benefits (Stella Tkatchova (ed.)) (IGI Global, 2011).

Atapattu S, 'International environmental law and soft law: a new direction or a contradiction?' (2012) in: Non-state actors, soft law and protective regimes: from the margins (C. Bailliet (ed.)) (Cambridge University Press).

Austin J, Lectures on Jurisprudence or the Philosophy of Positive Law (5th Edition) (1885) London: John Murray.

Azubuike L, 'International Law Regime Against Piracy' (2009) 15 Annual Survey of International & Comparative Law.

Azulay Y, 'Star wars: 'Israel is interested in space weapons. Every one of our satellites is a machine of war' Ctech (27 September 2023) (available at: https://www.calcalistech.com/ctechnews/article/frkow8u03).

Bailey M, 'Frequent and Reliable Launch for Small Satellites: Rocket Lab's Electron Launch Vehicle and Photon Spacecraft' (2020) in: Handbook of Small Satellites (J.N. Pelton, S. Madry (eds.)) (Cham: Springer).

Baker HA, 'Protection of the Outer Space Environment: History and Analysis of Article IX of the Outer Space Treaty' (1987) 12 Annals of Air & Space Law.

Baker HA, 'The ESA and USS reports on Space Debris' (1990) 6 Space Policy.

Baker HA, Space Debris: Legal and Policy Implications (1989) Leiden: Nijhoff.

Baker M, 'NASA Astronaut Anne McClain Accused by Spouse of Crime in Space' The New York Times (23 August 2019) (available at: https://www.nytimes.com/2019/08/23/us/astronaut-space-investigation.html).

Baker M, 'Space Crime Allegation Leads to Charges Against Astronaut's Ex-Wife' The New York Times (6 April 2020) (available at: https://www.nytimes.com/2020/04/06/us/space-crime-allegation-indictment.html).

Ballard O, '15 Star companies of the UK space sector' (2 July 2019) (available at: https://www.businessleader.co.uk/15-stars-of-the-uk-space-sector/).

Barash M, 'Astra Space Fends Off Investor Lawsuit Over Rocket Launch Claims' Bloomberg Law News (3 August 2023) (available at: https://news.bloomberglaw.com/securities-law/astra-space-fends-off-investor-lawsuit-over-rocket-launch-claims).

Barber H, 'How Israel shot down a ballistic missile in space for the first time' Telegraph (5 November 2023) (available at: https://www.telegraph.co.uk/world-news/2023/11/04/how-israel-shot-down-ballistic-missile-in-space-houthis/).

Barral V, 'Sustainable Development in International Law: Nature and Operation of an Evolutive Legal Norm' (2012) 23(2) European Journal of International Law.

Basu A, Kurlekar A, 'Highway to the Danger Zone: United States Legislative Framework Regulating the Commercial Space Sector' (2016) 14(1) Astropolitics.

Bates J, 'Satellite Operators Target Interference Problem.' Via Satellite (August 2005) (available at: http://www.suirg.org/press/ViaSat_08–05.pdf).

Beard J. and Stephens D (eds.), The Woomera Manual on the International Law of Military Space Operations (2024) (Oxford University Press).

Bell Jennifer, 'Dubai's ruler announces new moon mission after UAE's Rashid Rover lunar 'crash" English Alarabiya (27 April 2023) (available at: https://english.alarabiya.net/News/gulf/2023/04/27/Dubai-s-ruler-announces-new-moon-mission-after-UAE-s-Rashid-Rover-lunar-crash-).

Benkö M, Schrogl KU, Digrell D, Jolley E, Space Law: Current Problems and Perspectives for Future Regulation (2005) The Hague: Eleven International Publishing.

Berger B, 'SpaceX Sues Boeing and Lockheed Martin' Space.com (21 October 2005) (available at: https://www.space.com/1701-spacex-sues-boeing-lockheed-martin.html).

Berger E, 'Russia threatens criminal charges against a NASA astronaut' arstechnica (30 November 2021) (available at: https://arstechnica.com/science/2021/11/russia-threatens-criminal-charges-against-a-nasa-astronaut/).

Berman A, 'Between Participation and Capture in International Rule-Making: the WHO Framework of Engagement with Non-State Actors' (2021) 31(1) European Journal of International Law.

Besson S, 'Due Diligence and Extraterritorial Human Rights Obligations – Mind the Gap!' (2020) 9(1) ESIL Reflections.

Biachini A, 'Environmental Harm Resulting from the Use of Nuclear Power Sources in Outer Space: Some Remarks on State Responsibility and Liability' (1991) in: International Responsibility for Environmental Harm (F. Francioni (ed.)) (London: Graham and Trotman).

Bini A, 'The Moon Agreement: Its effectiveness in the 21st century' (2008) 14 European Space Policy Institute Perspectives.

Birnie PW, Boyle AE, International Law and the Environment (2nd ed.) (2002) Oxford: Oxford University Press.

Bittencourt Neto O, 'Preserving the outer space environment: The 'precautionary principle' approach to space debris' (2013) Proceedings of the International Institute of Space Law.

Bittlinger H, 'Private Space Activities: Questions of International Responsibility' (1987) in: Proceedings of the 30th Colloquium on the Law of Outer Space, (Washington, D.C.: American Institute of Aeronautics and Astronautics).

Blount P.J. and Hofmann M. (eds.), Space Law in a Networked World (2023) (Koninklijke Brill).

Blount PJ, 'Renovating Space: The Future of International Space Law' (2011) 40(1) Denver Journal of International Law & Policy.

Blount PJ, 'Targeting in Outer Space: Legal Aspects of Operational Military Actions in Space' Harvard Law School: National Security Journal (25 November 2012) (available at: https://harvardnsj.org/2012/11/25/targeting-in-outer-space-legal-aspects-of-operational-military-actions-in-space/).

Böckstiegel KH, 'Term Appropriate State in International Space Law, The Definitional Issues in Space Law' (1994) 37(77) Proc Law Outer Space.

Böckstiegel KH, Benkö M, Hobe S, Space Law: Basic Legal Documents (2005) The Hague: Eleven Publishing.

Bothe M, 'Protection of the Environment in Relation to Armed Conflicts' (2021) in: The Handbook of International Humanitarian Law (4th ed.) (D. Fleck (ed.)) (Oxford: Oxford University Press).

Bourély M, 'The institutional framework of space activities in outer space' (1998) 26 Journal of Space Law.

Boyani S, 'The Rashid Rover didn't make it to the Moon, but it's a success for science' Wired.me (3 May 2023) (available at: https://wired.me/gear/rashid-rover-worlds-most-compact-lunar-rover/).

Boyle A, Redgewell C, Birnie, Boyle, and Redgewell's International Law and the Environment (4th ed.) (2021) Oxford: Oxford University Press.

Breccia P, 'Article III of Outer Space Treaty and Its Relevance in the International Space Legal Framework' (2016) 67th International Astronautical Congress (IAC).

Brekke P, "Norwegian Space Activities – Arctic Access to Space" (2015) 2(2) Journal of Space Safety Engineering 91.

Brolman C, The Institutional Veil in Public International Law: International Organizations and the Law of Treaties (2007) Oxford: Hart.

Brown A, 'New space race holds promise, but possible environmental risks, too', Washington Post (31 July 2022) (available at: https://www.washingtonpost.com/science/2022/07/31/spaceports-environmental-harm/).

Brunner C, Soucek A (eds.), Outer Space in Society (2011) Heidelberg: Springer.

Brunswick S, 'How Canada is Shaping the World's Future in Space' SpaceNews (23 January 2023) (available at: https://spacenews.com/op-ed-how-canada-is-shaping-the-worlds-future-in-space/).

Bryan SM, 'CEO Interview: Richard Branson on Space Travel', Seattle Times (23 November 2010) (available at: https://www.seattletimes.com/business/ceo-interview-richard-branson-on-space-travel/).

Burgueño Salas E, 'Space industry worldwide – statistics & facts' Statista (20 November 2022) (available at https://www.statista.com/topics/5049/space-exploration/).

Butash T, 'Low-Earth orbit megaconstellations reach record capacity' (available at: https://aerospaceamerica.aiaa.org/year-in-review/low-earth-orbit-megaconstellations-reach-record-capacity/).

Butt Y, 'Avoiding Collisions in Outer Space' N.Y. Times (19 March 2018) (available at: https://www.nytimes.com/2018/03/19/opinion/space-race-regulation.html).

Byers M & Boley A, Who Owns Outer Space? (2023) Cambridge: Cambridge University Press.

Byers M, Wright E, Boley A, Byers C, 'Unnecessary Risks Created by Uncontrolled Rocket Reentries' (2022) 6 Nature Astronomy.

Cabello A, Michels Freitas LH, and Melo M, 'Brazilian Space Sector: Historical Analysis of the Public Budget' (2022) 62 Space Policy.

Cabello AF, de Melo MC, Ferreira GV, Michels Freitas LH, Moreira Couto de Lima F, 'The Incipient Brazilian Private Space Sector: A Brief Description' (2022) 11(3) New Space.

Cabello AF, de Melo MC, Viana Ferreira G, Michels Freitas LH, Moreira Couto de Lima F, 'The Incipient Brazilian Private Space Sector: A Brief Description' (2022) 11(3) New Space.

Cassese A, Gaeta P, International Criminal Law (2nd ed.) (2008) Oxford: Oxford University Press.

Castillo Y, 'The Appeal to Human Rights in Arbitration and International Investment Agreements' (2012) XII Anuario Mexicano Derecho Internacional.

Čeferin G, Mednarodnopravna ureditev rudarjenja na neesnih telesih (Master Thesis) (2018) Ljubljana: University of Ljubljana.

Chang K, 'Moon Landing by Israel's Beresheet Spacecraft Ends in Crash' New York Times (11 April 2019) (available at: https://www.nytimes.com/2019/04/11/science/israel-moon-landing-beresheet.html).

Charlesworth H, 'Customary International Law and the Nicaragua Case', (1984–87) 11 Australian Year Book of International Law.

Charnovitz S, 'Two Centuries of Participation: NGOs and International Governance' (1997) 18 Michigan Journal of International Law.

Chartier B, 'Chamber for Environmental Matters: International Court of Justice (ICJ)' Max Planck Encyclopedias of International Law (2018) (available at: https://opil.ouplaw.com/display/10.1093/law-mpeipro/e3339.013.3339/law-mpeipro-e3339).

Cheng B, 'Article VI of the 1967 Space Treaty Revisited: 'International Responsibility', 'National Activities' and 'The Appropriate State'' (1998) 26(1) Journal of Space Law.

Cheng B, Studies in International Space Law (1997) Oxford: Oxford University Press.

Cheng K, 'Elon Musk Says SpaceX Could Land on Mars in 3 to 4 Years' New York Times (5 October 2023) (available at: https://www.nytimes.com/2023/10/05/science/elon-musk-spacex-starship-mars.html).

Chow D, 'SpaceX makes history with first all-civilian spaceflight' NBC News (16 September 2021) (available at: https://www.nbcnews.com/science/space/spacex-makes-history-first-civilian-spaceflight-rcna2027).

Chow D, 'To cheaply go: How falling launch costs fueled a thriving economy in orbit', NBC News (8 April 2022) (available at: https://www.nbcnews.com/science/space/space-launch-costs-growing-business-industry-rcna23488).

Chung G, 'Jurisdiction and Control Aspects of Space Debris Removal' (2019), in: Space Security and Legal Aspects of Active Debris Removal (A. Froehlich (ed.)) (Heidelberg: Springer).

Chung G, 'The Emergence of Environmental Protection Clauses in Outer Space Treaty: A Lesson from the Rio Principles' (2018) in: A Fresh View on the Outer Space Treaty (A. Froehlich (ed.)) (Cham: Springer).

Cinelli C, Pogorzelska K, 'The Current International Legal Setting for the Protection of the Outer Space Environment: The Precautionary Principle Avant La Lettre' (2013) 22(2) RECIEL.

Cirkovic E, 'International Law beyond the Earth system: Orbital debris and interplanetary pollution' (2022) 13(2) Journal of Human Rights and the Environment.

Cirkovic E, 'The Next Generation of International Law: Space, Ice, and the Cosmolegal Proposal' (2021) 22 German Law Journal.

Clapham A, 'Human Rights Obligations of Non-State Actors in Conflict Situations' (2006) 88 International Review of the Red Cross.

Clapham A, 'Non-State Actors' (2022) in: International Human Rights Law (4th ed.) (Moeckli D, Shah S, Sivakumaran S, Harris D (eds.)) (Oxford University Press).

Clapham A, 'The Complexity of International Criminal Law: Looking Beyond Individual Responsibility to the Responsibility of Organizations, Corporations and States' (2004) in: From Sovereign Impunity to International Accountability: The Search for Justice in a World of States (Thakur R, Malcontent P (eds.)) (Tokyo: United Nations University Press).

Clerc P, Space Law in the European Context: National Architecture, Legislation and Policy in France (2018) The Hague: Eleven International Publishing.

Clunan AL, Trinkunas HA, Ungoverned Spaces: Alternatives to State Authority in an Era of Softened Sovereignty (2010) Redwood City: Stanford University Press.

Colvin TJ, Karcz J, Wusk G, 'Cost and Benefit Analysis of Orbital Debris Remediation' NASA Office of Technology, Policy, and Strategy Report (10 March 2023) (Available at: https://www.nasa.gov/wp-content/uploads/2023/03/otps_-_cost_and_benefit_analysis_of_orbital_debris_remediation_-_final.pdf).

Cottam J, 'How to Prevent a War in Space' The Cove (8 November 2022) (Available at: https://cove.army.gov.au/article/how-prevent-war-space-part-2).

Cowig, K. 'United Nations General Assembly Adopts Draft Resolutions Regarding Space Weapons' SpaceRef. (9. December 2022) (Available at: https://spaceref.com/newspace-and-tech/united-nations-general-assembly-adopts-draft-resolution-regarding-space-weapons/).

Crawford J, 'The System of International Responsibility' (2010) in: The Law of International Responsibility (Crawford J, Pellet A, Olleson S & Parlett K (eds.)) (New York: Oxford University Press).

Crawford J, Brownlie's Principles of Public international Law (7th ed.) (2008) Oxford: Oxford University Press.

Crawford J, Brownlie's Principles of Public International Law (8th ed) (2012) Oxford: Oxford University Press.

Crawford J, Brownlie's Principles of Public International Law (9th ed.) (2019) Oxford: Oxford University Press.

Crist R, 'Starlink Explained: What to Know About Elon Musk's Satellite Internet Service' CNET (15 April 2023) (available at: https://www.cnet.com/home/internet/starlink-satellite-internet-explained/https://www.faa.gov/newsroom/faa-requires-spacex-take-over-75-actions-mitigate-environmental-impact-planned).

Cryer R, et al. An Introduction to International Criminal Law and Procedure (2nd ed.) (2010) Cambridge University Press.

Cusato E, 'From Ecocide to Voluntary Remediation Projects: Legal Responses to Environmental Warfare in Vietnam and the Spectre of Colonialism' (2018) 19 Melbourne Journal of International Law.

D'Alessandra F, Gillett M, 'The War Crime of Starvation in Non-International Armed Conflicts' (2019) 17 Journal of International Criminal Justice.

Dale L, Macor Heath N, 'Space Law Update: One Person's Space Junk is Another's Treasure – Who is Legally Responsible for Damage Caused by Space Debris?' HWL Ebsworth Lawyers (6 February 2023) (available at: https://hwlebsworth.com.au/space-law-update-one-persons-space-junk-is-anothers-treasure-who-is-legally-responsible-for-damage-caused-by-space-debris/).

Daly J, 'LTTE: Technologically Innovative Rebels,' (2007) ISN, Centre for Security Studies (CSS), ETH Zurich, Switzerland.

Dasgupta U, 'On-Orbit Transfer of Satellites Between States: Legal Issues – with Special Emphasis on Liability and Registration' (2016) in: 59th International Institute for Space Law Colloquium on the Law of Outer Space (T. Masson-Zwaan et al. (eds.)) (The Hague: Eleven International Publishing).

Dasgupta U, 'Reconciling State Practice of In-Orbit Satellite Transfer with the Law of Liability and Registration in Outer Space' (2018) in: Monograph Series VI: Global Space Governance and the UN 2030 Agenda (A.D. Kerkonian (ed.)) (Montreal: Centre for Research in Air and Space Law).

Davalos J, 'International standards in regulating space travel: Clarifying ambiguities in the commercial era of outer space' (2016) 30(4) Emory International Law Review.

David L, "Planetary Parks' Could Protect Space Wilderness' Space.com (17 January 2013) (available at: https://www.space.com/19302-planetary-parks-space-wilderness-protection.html).

Davis ME, Lee RJ, 'Twenty years later: The Moon agreement and its legal controversies' (1999) 6 Australian International Law Journal 9–32.

Dawson L, War in Space: The Science and Technology Behind Our Next Theater of Conflict (2018) Cham: Springer.

de La Bourdonnaye T, 'Greener insurgencies? Engaging non-State armed groups for the protection of the natural environment during non-international armed conflicts' (2020) 102 International Review of the Red Cross.

De Lucia V, 'Splashing Down the International Space Station in the Pacific Ocean: Safe Disposal or Trashing the Ocean Commons' EJIL:Talk! (23 February 2022) (available at: https://www.ejiltalk.org/splashing-down-the-international-space-station-in-the-pacific-ocean-safe-disposal-or-trashing-the-ocean-commons/).

De Man P, 'The Commercial Exploitation of Outer Space and Celestial Bodies – A Functional Solution to the Natural Resource Challenge,' (2011) in: New Perspectives on Space Law (Sundahl MJ, Gopalakrishnan V (eds.)) (International Institute of Space Law).

De Man P, Munters W, 'Reciprocal Limits to the Freedom to Use Outer Space by All States: Common but Differentiated Responsibilities?' (2018) 43(1) Air and Space Law.

De Schutter O, Eide A, Khalfan A, Orellana M, Salomon M, Seiderman I, 'Commentary to the Maastricht principles on extraterritorial obligations of states in the area of economic, social and cultural rights' (2012) 34(4) Human Rights Quarterly.

de Selding PB, 'Intelsat Vows to Stop Piracy by Sri Lanka Separatist Group' Space News (18 April 2007) (available at https://spacenews.com/intelsat-vows-stop-piracy-sri-lanka-separatist-group/).

de Selding PB, 'Sea Launch Ordered to Pay HNS $52 Million', Space News (23 April 2009) (available at: https://spacenews.com/sea-launch-ordered-pay-hns-52-million/).

de Zwart M, 'GOOGLE in Space? How will space governance accommodate non-State actors?' (2016) RUMLAE Research Paper.

de Zwart M, Henderson S, Neef R, 'The Principle of 'Harmful Contamination' Applied to Human Missions to Mars' (2021) 45(2) Journal of Space Law.

de Zwart M, Henderson S, Neumann M, 'Space resource activities and the evolution of international space law' (2023) 211 Acta Astronautica.

Debuf E, Captured in War: Lawful Internment in Armed Conflict (2013) Paris/Oxford: Hart Publishing.

Delgado López L, 'What Are the Implications of Peru Joining the Artemis Accords?', (6 June 2024) Center for Strategic and International Studies (available at: https://www.csis.org/analysis/what-are-implications-peru-joining-artemis-accords).

Dembling PG, Arons DM, 'The Evolution of the Outer Space Treaty' (1967) 33 Journal of Air Law and Commerce.

Dempsey PS, 'National laws governing commercial space activities: Legislation, regulation, & enforcement.' (2016) 36 Northwestern Journal of International Law & Business.

Dempsey PS, Manoli M, 'Suborbital Flights and the Delimitation of Air Space Vis-À-Vis Outer Space: Functionalism, Spatialism and State Sovereignty' (2017) International Association for the Advancement of Space Safety.

Dennerley JA, 'State Liability for Space Object Collisions: The Proper Interpretation of 'Fault' for the Purposes of International Space Law' (2018) 29(1) European Journal of International Law.

Di Giovanni A, 'A Pebble in the Shoe: Assessing the Uses of Do No Harm in International Assistance' (2014) 47(2) Law and Politics in Africa, Asia and Latin America.

Diederiks-Verschoor I, Kopal V, An Introduction to Space Law (3rd Revised Version) (2008) The Netherlands: Wolters Kluwer International.

Diederiks-Verschoor IHP, 'Environmental Protection in Outer Space' (1987) 30 German Yearbook of International Law.

Dinstein Y, The Conduct of Hostilities Under the Law of International Armed Conflict (2004) Cambridge University Press.

Do TT, 'Canada's space agency to take back seat to private sector' CBC News (7 February 2014) (available at: https://www.cbc.ca/news/politics/canada-s-space-agency-to-take-back-seat-to-private-sector-1.2527149).

Doo HK, *Space Law and Policy in the Republic of Korea* (2012) Report to the United Nations Office for Outer Space Affair (available at: https://www.unoosa.org/pdf/pres/2010/SLW2010/02-09.pdf).

Droesse G, Membership in International Organizations (2020) Heidelberg: Springer.

Dunn M, 'SpaceX successfully uses recycled parts to launch third crew into orbit' PBS (23 April 2021) (available at: https://www.pbs.org/newshour/science/spacex-successfully-uses-recycled-parts-to-launch-third-crew-into-orbit).

Dutfield S, Stein V, 'Inspiration 4: The first all-civilian spaceflight on SpaceX Dragon' Space.com (5 January 2022) (available at: https://www.space.com/inspiration4-spacex.html).

Earl MA, 'The CASTOR Satellite Survey, 2007 January 1 to 2009 December 31' (2010) 104(4) Journal of the Royal Astronomical Society of Canada.

Erdbrink T, Anderson C, 'In Sweden's Far North, a Space Complex Takes Shape', New York Times (23 May 2021) (available at: https://www.nytimes.com/2021/05/23/world/europe/sweden-space-arctic-satellites.html).

Fasan E, Space Debris – A Functional Approach. Proceedings of the 35th Colloquium on the Law of Outer Space, IISL, 28 August – 5 September, 1992 (Washington, DC). AIAA. 1993.

Fernholz T, 'An unauthorized satellite launch in India threatens US regulatory reform in space' (13 March 2018) Quartz (available at: https://qz.com/1226962/an-unauthorized-satellite-launch-in-india-threatens-us-regulatory-reform-in-space).

Ferreira-Snyman A, 'Outer Space Exploration and the Sustainability of the Space Environment – An Uneasy Relationship' (2023) 26 Potchefstroom Electronic Law Journal/Potchefstroomse Elektroniese Regsblad.

Ferreira-Snyman A, 'The environmental responsibility of states for space debris and the implications for developing countries in Africa' (2013) 46(1) The Comparative and International Law Journal of Southern Africa.

Fichera A, 'Posts misinterpret space travel carbon emissions finding' AP NEWS (14 December 2021) (available at https://apnews.com/article/fact-checking-55839 8031858).

Fogo H, 'A Legal Mirage: State Responsibility for Non-State Actor Interference with Space Systems' (2017) 55 Canadian Yearbook of International Law/Annuaire Canadien De Droit International.

Fortin K, The Accountability of Armed Groups under Human Rights Law (2017) Oxford University Press.

Foust J, 'An opening door for hosted payloads' SpaceNews (30 October 2012) (available at: http://spacenews.com/an-opening-door-for-hosted-payloads/).

Foust J, 'FAA again delays completion of Starship environmental review' Space News (26 March 2022) (available at: https://spacenews.com/faa-again-delays-complet ion-of-starship-environmental-review/).

Foust J, 'FAA proposes fining SpaceX for missing launch data' Space News (17 February 2023) (available at: https://spacenews.com/faa-proposes-fining-spacex-for-miss ing-launch-data/).

Foust J, 'FCC approves Starlink license modification' Space News (3. November 2023) (available at: https://spacenews.com/fcc-approves-starlink-license-modification/).

Foust J, 'Lawsuit claims Amazon's board erred in awarding Kuiper launch contracts to Blue Origin and others' Space News (31 August 2023) (available at: https://spacen ews.com/lawsuit-claims-amazons-board-erred-in-awarding-kuiper-launch-contra cts-to-blue-origin-and-others/).

Foust J, 'More countries encouraged to commit to halt destructive ASAT tests' SpaceNews (15 June 2023) (available at: https://spacenews.com/more-countr ies-encouraged-to-commit-to-halt-destructive-asat-tests/).

Foust J, 'Senate passes orbital debris bill' Space News (1 November 2023) (available at: https://spacenews.com/senate-passes-orbital-debris-bill/).

Fox S, '6 Private Companies That Could Launch Humans Into Space' Space.com (4 June 2010) (available at https://www.space.com/8541-6-private-companies-launch-hum ans-space.html).

Foye H and Hernández GR, 'UN First Committee Calls for ASAT Test Ban' Arms Control Association (December 2022) (available at: https://www.armscontrol.org/act/2022 -12/news/un-first-committee-calls-asat-test-ban#:~:text=(See%20ACT%2C%20N ovember%202022.,United%20Kingdom%20have%20followed%20suit).

Frantzen B, 'Umweltbelastungen durch Weltraumaktivitäten' (1991) in: Handbuch des Weltraumrechts (Böckstiegel KH) Cologne: Carl Heymanns Verlag.

Frantzman SJ, 'Israel launches Ofek 16 satellites to complete intelligence coverage' *DefenseNews* (6 July 2020) (available at: https://www.defensenews.com/space/2020/07/06/israel-launches-ofek-16-satellite-to-complete-intelligence-coverage/).

Freeland S, 'Impact of space tourism on the International Law of Outer Space' (2005) in: Proceedings of the 48th Colloquium on the Law of Outer Space (IISL) Fukuoka: the American Institute of Aeronautics and Astronautics Inc.

Freeland S, 'Overview of Current International Space Law in the Context of Planetary Defense' (2021) in: Legal Aspects of Planetary Defense (Marboe I (ed.)) Leiden: Martinus Nijhoff.

Freeland S, Ireland-Piper D, 'Space Law, Human Rights and Corporate Accountability' (2022) 26(1) UCLA Journal of International Law and Foreign Affairs.

Freeland S, Jakhu R, 'Article II' (2009) in: The Cologne Commentary on Space Law: Vol. I (Hobe S, Schmidt-Tedd B, Schrogl K, Meishan Goh G (eds.)) Cologne: Carl Heymanns.

Friedberg J, 'Bracing for the Impending Rocket Revolution: How to Regulate International Environmental Harm Caused by Commercial Space Flight' (2013) 24(1) Colorado Natural Resources, Energy & Environmental Law Review.

Froehlich A, Amande Soria DA, A Regional Space Agency for Latin America (2021) Heidelberg: Springer.

Froehlich A, Seffinga V, National Space Legislation: A Comparative and Evaluative Analysis (2018) Cham: Springer.

Froehlich A, Space Resource Utilization A View from an Emerging Space Faring Nation (2018) Vienna: ESPI/Springer.

Froehlich A, Space Security And Legal Aspects of Active Debris Removal (2019) Cham: Springer.

Froehlich A, Taiatu CM, Space in Support of Human Rights (2022) Vienna: ESPI/Spirnger.

Gabriel RA, Koven BS, 'Malicious Non-state Actors and Contested Space Operations' Report to DHS S&T Office of University Programs and DoD Strategic Multilayer Assessment Branch (February 2018) (available at: https://nsiteam.com/social/wp-content/uploads/2018/07/START_Malicious-Non-state-Actors-and-Contested-Space-Operations-Final.pdf).

Gabrynowicz JI, 'Space law: Its cold war origins and challenges in the era of globalization' (2004) 37 Suffolk University Law Review.

Gangale T, 'The Non Kármán Line: An Urban Legend of the Space Age' (2017) 41 Journal of Space Law.

Garner M, 'Transnational Alignment of Non-Governmental Organizations for Global Environmental Action' (1991) 24 Vanderbilt Journal of Transnational Law.

Garrick M, 'Equatorial Launch Australia hit with lawsuit, including allegations of bullying against director Michael Jones' ABC (13 October 2022) (available at: https://www.abc.net.au/news/2022-10-13/michael-jones-equatorial-launch-australia-ceo-bullying-lawsuit/101526340).

Gaskill B, 'SpaceX vs Boeing and Lockheed: Case Closed' Nasa Spaceflight (20 May 2006) (available at: https://www.nasaspaceflight.com/2006/05/spacex-vs-boeing-and-lockheed-case-closed/).

Genta G, 'Private space exploration: A new way for starting a spacefaring society?' (2014) 104 Acta Astronautica.

Gerhard M, 'Article VI' (2009) in: The Cologne Commentary on Space Law: Vol. I (Hobe S, Schmidt-Tedd B, Schrogl K, Meishan Goh G (eds.)) (Cologne: Carl Heymanns).

Gillespie A, Protected Areas and International Environmental Law (2007) Leiden: Martinus Nijhoff.

Gillett M, 'A Tale of Two Definitions: Fortifying Four Key Elements of the Proposed Crime of Ecocide' Opinio Juris (20 June 2023) (available at: https://opiniojuris.org/2023/06/20/a-tale-of-two-definitions-fortifying-four-key-elements-of-the-proposed-crime-of-ecocide-part-i/).

Gillett M, 'Eco-Struggles: Using International Criminal Law to Protect the Environment During and After Non-International Armed Conflict' (2017) in: Environmental Protection and Transitions from Conflict to Peace: Clarifying Norms, Principles and Practices (C. Stahn, J. Iverson, J.S. Easterday (eds.)) (Oxford: Oxford University Press).

Gillett M, Prosecuting Environmental Harm before the International Criminal Court (2022) Cambridge: Cambridge University Press.

Goehring JS, 'Can We Address Orbital Debris with the International Law We Already Have? An Examination of Treaty Interpretation and the Due Regard Principle' (2020) 85(2) Journal of Air Law and Commerce.

Goh, G, Dispute Settlement in International Space Law: A Multi-Door Courthouse for Outer Space (2007) Martinus Nijhoff Publishers.

Goka T, 'The Space Environment: Natural and Induced' (2009) in: Safety Design for Space Systems (G.E. Musgrave, A. (Skip) M. Larsen, T. Sgobba (eds.)) (Oxford: Butterworth-Heinemann).

Goldman NC, 'Space Law' (2002): in: Space Politics and Policy: an evolutionary perspective (E. Sadeh (ed.)) (Kluwer Academic Publishers: Dordrecht, Boston, London).

Gorove S, 'Pollution and Outer Space: A Legal Analysis and Appraisal' (1972) 5 NYU Journal of International Law and Politics.

Gorove S, 'The Concept of "Common Heritage of Mankind": A Political, Moral or Legal Innovation?' (1972) 9 San Diego Law Review.

Gorove S, Gorove MA, Cases on Space Law (1996) Journal of Space Law, University of Mississippi.

Graditzky T, 'Individual criminal responsibility for violations of international humanitarian law committed in non-international armed conflicts' (1998) 322 International Review of the Red Cross.

Grady M, 'Private companies are launching a new space race – here's what to expect' The Conversation (3 October 2017) (available at: https://theconversation.com/private-companies-are-launching-a-new-space-race-heres-what-to-expect-80697).

Green F, "Fragmentation in Two Dimensions': The International Court of Justice's Flawed Approach to Non-State Actors and International Legal Personality' (2008) 9 Melbourne Journal of International Law.

Grego L, 'A History of Anti-Satellite Programs, Union of Concerned Scientists' (January 2012) (available at: https://www.ucsusa.org/sites/default/files/2019-09/a-history-of-ASAT-programs_lo-res.pdf).

Grünfeld K, Influence of the Russian Federation on International Law in the 21st Century (Master Thesis) (2020) (Ljubljana: University of Ljubljana, Faculty of Law) (23 September 2020) (available at: https://repozitorij.uni-lj.si/IzpisGradiva.php?id=120616).

Grush L, 'Company that launched satellites without permission gets new license to launch more probes' The Verge (4 October 2017) (available at: https://www.theverge.com/2018/10/4/17928452/swarm-technologies-spacebees-satellites-spacex-falcon-9-fcc-license).

Grush L, 'Israel's attempted Moon landing fails moments before touchdown' The Verge (11 April 2019) (available at: https://www.theverge.com/2019/4/11/18306294/spaceil-beresheet-lunar-lander-failure-crash-engine-shut-down).

Grush L, 'The first alleged crime committed in space raises questions about jurisdiction in orbit' The Verge (27 August 2019) (available at: https://www.theverge.com/2019/8/27/20833761/nasa-iss-international-space-station-alleged-crime-anne-mcclain-jurisdicition-framework).

Gupta B, Agasti T, 'The Curious Case of Article IX and Outer Space Environment' (2022) 2(2) Journal of Environmental Impact and Management Policy.

Gutzman J, 'State Responsibility for Non-State Actors in Times of War: Article VI of the Outer Space Treaty and the Law of Neutrality' (2017) Institute of Air and Space Law, McGill University.

Hacket GT, Space Debris and the Corpus Iuris Spatialis (1994) Editions Frontières.

Hafner G and Binder C, 'The Interpretation of Article 21(3) ICC Statute Opinion Reviewed', *Austrian Review of International and European Law*, 9 (2006).

Harding T, 'Why space debris is a threat to the world' The National News (16 July 2021) (available at: https://www.thenationalnews.com/world/2021/07/16/why-space-debris-is-a-threat-to-the-world/).

Haroun F, Ajibade S, Oladimeji P, Igbozurike JK, 'Toward the Sustainability of Outer Space: Addressing the Issue of Space Debris' (2021) 9(1) New Space.

Hart H, Sacks A, The Legal Process: Basic Problems in the Making and Application of Law (1958) Tentative edition.

Hasin G, 'Confronting Space Debris Through the Regime Evolution Approach' (2021) 97 International Law Studies.

Havel B, Sanchez G, The Principles and Practice of International Aviation Law (2014) Cambridge University Press.

Heffes E, Kotlik MD, Ventura MJ, International Humanitarian Law and Non-State Actors: Debates, Law and Practice (2020) Heidelberg: Springer.

Heilweil R, 'The space debris problem is getting dangerous' Vox (16 November 2021) (available at: https://www.vox.com/recode/2021/11/16/22785425/international-space-station-russia-missle-test-debris).

Heintschel von Heinegg W, Donner M, 'New Developments in the Protection of the Natural Environment in Naval Armed Conflicts' (1994) 37 German Yearbook of International Law.

Helmore E, 'Chinese Rocket's Chaotic Fall to Earth Highlights Problem of Space Junk' The Guardian (8 May 2021) (available at: https://www.theguardian.com/science/2021/may/08/chinese-rocket-space-junk-long-march-5gb).

Henckaerts JM, Doswald-Beck L, Customary International Humanitarian Law, Vol. 1: Rules (2005) Cambridge: Cambridge University Press.

Henderson S, 'To the Moon and Beyond: Australia's Space Activities and Obligations Under International Law' Australian Institute of International Affairs (3 April 2023) (available at: https://www.internationalaffairs.org.au/australianoutlook/to-the-moon-and-beyond-australias-space-activities-and-obligations-under-international-law/).

Henriquet P, 'New Space: the changing face of the space industry' Polytechnique Insights (3 November 2022) (available at: https://www.polytechnique-insights.com/en/columns/space/new-space-the-changing-face-of-the-space-industry/).

Henry C, 'SpaceX submits paperwork for 30,000 more Starlink satellites' Space News (15 October 2019) (available at: https://spacenews.com/spacex-submits-paperwork-for-30000-more-starlink-satellites/).

Higgins P, Short D, South N, 'Protecting the planet: a proposal for a law of ecocide' (2013) 59(3) Crime Law Soc Change.

Higgins R, 'Policy Considerations and the International Judicial Process' (1968) 17(1) International and Comparative Law Quarterly.

Higgins R, Problems and Process: International Law and How We Use It (1994) Oxford: Clarendon Press.

Hobe S, 'Artikel 189 AEUV' (2015) in: Europäisches Unionsrecht, Vertrag über die Europäische Union – Vetrag über die Arbeitsweise der Grundrechte der Europäischen Union, Band 4, (H von der Groeben, J Schwarze, A Hatje (eds.) (7th ed)) (Nomos Baden-aden: Verlag).

Hobe S, 'International Space Law in its First Half Century' (2006) in: Proceedings of the 49' Colloquium on the Law of Outer Space (Corinne M. Contant Jorgenson (ed.)) (Washington D.C.: American Institute of Aeronautics and Astronautics).

Hobe S, 'The ILA Model Law for National Space Legislation' (2013) 62 Zeitschrift für Luft- und Weltraumrecht.

Hobe S, 'The Impact of New Developments on International Space Law (New Actors, Commercialisation, Privatisation, Increase in the Number of Space-Faring Nations)' (2010) 15(3-4) Uniform Law Review.

Hobe S, 'The Legal Framework for a Lunar Base Lex Data and Lex Ferenda' (1997) in: Outlook on Space Law over the Next 30 Years (G. Lafferranderie, D. Crowther (eds.)) (The Hague: Kluwer Law International).

Hobe S, Pellander E, 'Space Law: A 'Self-Contained Regime?' (2012) in: In Heaven as on Earth? The Interaction of Public International Law on the Legal Regulation of Outer Space (S. Hobe, S. Freeland (eds.)) (Bonn: Institute of Air and Space Law of the University of Cologne).

Hobe S, Space Law: a Handbook (2019) Baden-Baden: Nomos/Hart.

Hobe S. et al. Cologne Commentary on Space Law: Volume I (2009) Cologne: Carl Heymanns.

Hofmann M and Malinowska K, 'Poland Goes to Space. The Draft Polish Act' (2024) in: Proceedings of the International Institute of Space Law 2022 (P.J. Blount, T. Masson-Zwaan, R. Moro-Aguilar and K. Schrogl (eds.)) (Eleven International Publishing).

Hollis DB, 'Private Actors in Public International Law: Amicus Curiae and the Case for the Retention of State Sovereignty' (2002) 25 Boston College International and Comparative Law Review.

Holmes M, 'Activities in Kazakhstan' Via Satellite (24 September 2021) (available at: https://www.satellitetoday.com/business/2021/09/24/eurasian-space-ventures-looks-to-boost-space-activities-in-kazakhstan/).

Housen-Couriel D, 'Disruption of Satellite Transmissions Ad Bellum and In Bello: Launching a New Paradigm of Convergence' (2012) 45(3) Israel Law Review.

Howell E, 'Canada assigns astronauts to launch on Boeing's Starliner, back up Artemis 2 moon mission' Space.com (22 November 2023) (available at: https://www.space.com/canadian-space-agency-astronaut-assignments-spaceflight).

Hsu D, Siggelkow N, 'Why Big Business Is Making a Giant Leap into Space' Knowledge at Wharton (4 June 2019) (available at: https://knowledge.wharton.upenn.edu/article/commercial-space-economy/).

Hui Y, 'Joint development of mineral resources: An Asian solution' (1994) in: Asian Yearbook of International Law (S. Lee, H.E. Lee (eds.)) (Leiden: Martinus Nijhoff).

Hulme K, 'Using International Environmental Law to Enhance Biodiversity and Nature Conservation During Armed Conflict' (2022) 20 Journal of International Criminal Justice.

Hurst L, 'Japan's ispace is set to become the first private company to land on the Moon' Euronews (25 April 2023) (available at: https://www.euronews.com/next/2023/04/25/japans-ispace-is-set-to-become-the-first-private-company-to-land-on-the-moon).

Iavicoli V, 'The legal regime of outer space in light of the Law of the Sea' (2015) in: Ocean Sustainability in the 21st Century (S. Aricò (ed.)) (Cambridge: Cambridge University Press).

Ireland-Piper D & Freeland S, 'Human Rights and Space: Reflections on the Implications of Human Activity in Outer Space on Human Rights Law' (2021) 9 Groningen Journal of International Law 1.

Ireland-Piper D, 'Space Laws: Criminal Jurisdiction in Outer Space' ILA Reporter (17 October 2019) (available at: https://ilareporter.org.au/2019/10/space-laws-criminal-jurisdiction-in-outer-space-danielle-ireland-piper/).

Ishikawa D, Yotsumoto H, Odan T, 'In review: space law, regulation and policy in Japan' Lexology (5 January 2023) (available at: https://www.lexology.com/library/detail.aspx?g=f0a661ce-b787-4bb5-95ab-d07fd4159fe6).

Isnardi C, 'Problems with Enforcing International Space Law on Private Actors' (2020) 58 Columbia Journal of Transnational Law.

Jacobs B, 'Debris Mitigation Certification and the Commercial Space Industry: A New Weapon in the Fight against Space Pollution' (2011) 20(1) Media Law & Policy.

Jakhu RS, Freeland S, McGill Manual on International Law Applicable to Military Uses of Outer Space: Volume 1 – Rules, Montreal, Quebec, Canada: McGill University.

Jakhu RS, Jasani B, McDowell JC, 'Critical issues related to registration of space objects and transparency of space activities' (2018) 143 Acta Astronautica.

Jakhu RS, National Regulation of Space Activities (2010). Heidelberg: Springer.

Jakhu RS, Pelton JN, Global Space Governance: An International Study (2017) Heidelberg: Springer.

Jakhu RS, Pelton JN, Small satellites and their regulation (2014) New York, NY: Springer.

Jasani B, 'Remote Sensing From Space: National and International Security' (1999) in: The New Security Debate (K Hoffman (ed.)) UNIDIR Disarmament Forum (available at https://unidir.org/publication/disarmament-forum-the-new-security-debate/).

Jennings R, Watts A, Oppenheim's International Law: Volume 1 Peace (9th ed.) (2008) Oxford: Oxford University Press.

Jensen E, 'The International Law of Environmental Warfare: Active and Passive Damage During Armed Conflict' (2005) 38 Vanderbilt Journal of Transnational Law.

Jerbi S, 'The International Code of Conduct for Private Security Service Providers' (2013) Geneva Academy of International Humanitarian Law and Human Rights.

Jessup PC, 'The Subjects of a Modern Law of Nations' (1947) 45(4) Michigan Law Review.

Jewett R, 'OneWeb Adjusts Target Constellation Size Down to 7,000 Satellites' Via Satellite (14 January 2021) (available at https://www.satellitetoday.com/broadband/2021/01/14/oneweb-adjusts-target-constellation-size-down-to-7000-satellites).

Joffre T, 'Russia stops space cooperation with US: 'Let them fly on brooms'' The Jerusalem Post (3 March 2022) (available at https://www.jpost.com/breaking-news/article-699203).

Johnson CD, Porras D, Hearsey CM, O'Sullivan S, 'The curious case of the transgressing tardigrades (part 1)' The Space Review (26 August 2019) (available at https://thespacereview.com/article/3783/1).

Johnson LM, 'The Consequences of Somali Piracy on International Trade' (2014) 8 Global Tides.

Jones A, 'Norway opens Andøya spaceport' Space News (3 November 2023) (available at: https://spacenews.com/norway-opens-andoya-spaceport/).

Jones A, 'UK Space Agency signs deal with Axiom Space for human spaceflight mission' Space.com (27 October 2023) (available at: https://www.space.com/uk-space-agency-axiom-human-spaceflight-mission).

Jones T, Macken T, 'Australia' (2019) in: The Space Law Review (J. Wheeler (ed.)), London: Law Business Research Ltd.

Kaineg S, 'The Growing Problem of Space Debris' (2020) 26(2) Hastings Environmental Law Journal.

Kazlouskaya M, 'Large Satellite Constellations: Legal Challenges in Addressing Space Sustainability and Astronomical Observations' (2021) 70(4) Zeitschrift für Luft- und Weltraumrecht.

Kelsen H, General Theory of Law and State (1949) Cambridge Massachusetts: Harvard University Press.

Kelvey J, 'Solar Panel Robots and Mini Nuclear Reactors Could Power NASA's Future Moon Base' Space Ref (22 June 2023) (available at: https://spaceref.com/newspace-and-tech/solar-panel-robots-and-mini-nuclear-reactors-could-power-nasas-future-moon-base/).

Kerrest A, 'International Organizations as Active Subjects of International Law of Outer Space' (1999) Proceedings of Third ECSL Colloquium on International Organizations and Space Law, Perugia, 6–7 May 1999.

Kerrest A, 'Legal Aspects of Transfer of Ownership and Transfer of Activities' (2017) in: Ownership of Satellites: 4th Luxembourg Workshop on Space and Satellite Communication Law (M. Hofmann and A. Loukakis (eds.)) (Baden-Baden: Nomos Verlagsgesellschaft).

Kerrest A, 'Remarks on the Notion of Launching State' (1999) International Institute of Space Law.

Kerrest A, 'The concept of the 'launching State' in commercial launch ventures (2017) in: Commercial Uses of Space and Space Tourism (J. Wouters, P. De Man, R. Hansen (eds.)) (Cheltenham: Edward Elgar).

Kerrest A, Schmidt L, 'Article VII' (2009) in: The Cologne Commentary on Space Law: Vol. I (S. Hobe, B. Schmidt-Tedd, K.-U. Schrogl, G.M. Goh (eds.)) (Cologne: Carl Heymanns).

Kessler DJ, Cour-Palais BG, 'Collision Frequency of Artificial Satellites: The Creation of a Debris Belt' (1978) 38 JGR Space Physics.

Kim C, 'The Space Debris Race' The Regulatory Review (24 November 2021) (available at: https://www.theregreview.org/2021/11/24/kim-space-debris-race/).

Kimball D.G., 'U.S. Commits to ASAT Ban' Arms Control Association (May 2022) (available at: https://www.armscontrol.org/act/2022-05/news/us-commits-asat-ban).

Klabbers J, 'The Concept of Legal Personality' (2005) 11 Ius Gentium.

Klotz I, 'Lawsuit seeks to stop Boeing, SpaceX work on NASA space taxi' Reuters (16 October 2014) (available at: https://www.reuters.com/article/idUSKCN0I52O8/).

Klotz I, 'Virgin Galactic's SpaceShipTwo Makes 1st Test Flight of Revamped Re-Entry System' Space.com (2 May 2017) (available at: https://www.space.com/36679-virgin-galactic-spaceshiptwo-unity-feather-system-test-flight.html).

Kolmar C, 'The 15 Largest Satellite Companies In The World' ZIPPIA (26 July 2022) (available at https://www.zippia.com/advice/largest-satellite-companies/).

Kolodny L, 'FAA orders Musk's SpaceX to take 63 corrective actions on Starship, keeps rocket grounded' CNBC (3 November 2023) (available at: https://www.cnbc.com/2023/09/08/faa-starship-grounded-corrective-action.html).

Konert A, von der Dunk FG (eds.), National Space Law in Poland (2023) Martinus Nijhoff Publishers.

Koplow DA, 'ASAT-isfaction: Customary International Law and the Regulation of Anti-Satellite Weapons' (2009) 30 Michigan Journal of International Law.

Koren M, 'Launching Rogue Satellites Into Space Was a 'Mistake'' The Atlantic (7 September 2018) (available at: https://www.theatlantic.com/technology/archive/2018/09/spacebees-swarm-unauthorized-satellite-launch/569395/).

Kramer WR, 'In dreams begin responsibilities – environmental impact assessment and outer space development' (2017) 19(3) Environmental Practice.

Kravchenko S, Chowdhury TMR, Bhuiyan JH, 'Principles of International Environmental Law' (2013) in: Routledge Handbook of International Environmental Law (S. Alam, J.H. Bhuiyan, T.M.R. Chowdhury, E.J. Techera (eds.)) (London: Routledge).

Kütting G, Environment, Society and International Relations: towards more effective international environmental agreements (2000) New York: Routledge.

Lachs M, The Law of Outer Space (2010) Leiden: Martinus-Nijhoff Publishers.

Lafferanderei G, 'Jurisdiction and Control of Space Objects and the Case of an International Intergovernmental Organization (ESA)' (2005) 54 Zeitschrift für Luft- und Weltraumrecht.

Lal B, 'Reshaping Space Policies to Meet Global Trends' (2016) 32(4) Issues in Science and Technology.

Lamb RD, 'Ungoverned Areas and Threats from Safe Havens: Final Report of the Ungoverned Areas Project' (2008) Office of the Deputy Assistant Secretary of Defense for Policy Planning (available at: https://dgi.umd.edu/sites/default/files/2019-07/ugash_report_final.pdf).

Lambach D, Wesel L, 'Tackling The Space Debris Problem: A Global Commons Perspective' (2021) Proc. 8th European Conference on Space Debris (virtual), 20 – 23 April 2021, Darmstadt, Germany, published by the ESA Space Debris Office.

Langer M, Eason M, 'The Quiet Expansion of Universal Jurisdiction' (2019) 30(3) European Journal of International Law.

Lanovoy V, 'The Use of Force by Non-State Actors and the Limits of Attribution of Conduct' (2017) 28(2) European Journal of International Law.

Larsen PB, 'Application of the Precautionary Principle to the Moon' (2006) 71(2) Journal of Air Law and Commerce.

Larsen PB, 'International regulation of global navigation satellite systems' (2017) 80(2) Journal of Air Law and Commerce.

Larsen PB, 'Solving the Space Debris Crisis' (2018) 83 Journal of Air Law and Commerce.

Larsson ML, 'Legal Definitions of the Environment and of Environmental Damage' (1999) Scandinavian Studies in Law.

Lauer RS, 'When States Test Their Anti-Satellite Weapons' (2022) 20(1) Astropolitics.

Lauterpacht H, The Function of Law in the International Community (2011) Oxford: Oxford University Press.

Lay SH, Tauenfeld HJ, The Law Relating to Activities of Man in Space (1970) Chicago: University of Chicago.

Layachi O, 'International Liability for Pollution Damage in Outer Space Environment' (2020) 16 WSEAS Transactions On Environment And Development.

Lazare B, 'The French Space Operations Act: Technical Regulations (2013) 92 Acta Astronautica 2.

Lee R, Law and Regulation of Commercial Mining in Outer Space (2012) Heidelberg: Springer.

Limperis PT, 'Orbital Debris and the Spacefaring Nations: International Law Methods for Prevention and Reduction of Debris, and Liability for Damage Caused by Debris' (1998) 15 Arizona Journal of International and Comparative Law.

Listner, MJ, 'Iridium 33 and Cosmos 2251, Three Years Later' Space Safety Magazine (10 February 2012) (available at: https://www.spacesafetymagazine.com/space-debris/kessler-syndrome/iridium-33-cosmos-2251-years-later-learned-then/).

Liu L, Jia P, Huang Y, Han J, Liechtfouse E, 'Space industrialization' (2023) 21(1) Environmental Chemistry Letters.

Livingston S, 'Commercial Remote Sensing Satellites and the Regulation of Violence in Areas of Limited Statehood' (2015) 5 CGCS Occasional Paper Series on ICTs, Statebuilding, and Peacebuilding in Africa.

Livingstone D, Lewis P, 'Space, the Final Frontier for Cybersecurity?' (2016) Research paper, Chatham House The Royal Institute of International Affairs, International Security Department, London (available at: https://www.chathamhouse.org/sites/default/files/publications/research/2016-09-22-space-final-frontier-cybersecurity-livingstone-lewis.pdf).

López C, 'The 'Ruggie process': From legal obligations to corporate social responsibility?', in Surya Deva, David Bilchitz (eds), *Human Rights Obligations of Business: Beyond the Corporate Responsibility to Respect?*, (Cambridge University Press, 2013).

Lostal M, 'One-Dimensional Law: A Critique of the Human Right to a Clean, Healthy and Sustainable Environment', *The International Journal of Human Rights* (online edition, 2024).

Lubell N, Extraterritorial Use of Force Against Non-State Actors (2010) Oxford University Press.

Lyall F, Larsen PB, Space Law: A Treatise (2009) Surrey: Ashgate.

Macchi C, 'Business, Human Rights And International Space Law: Filling The Gaps Of Corporate Accountability In The 'New Space', in Claudia Cinelli (ed.), *Regulation of Outer Space International Space Law and the State* (Routledge, advance edition (full book forthcoming 2025)).

Mack E, Ryan J, 'SpaceX sends Israel's historic moon mission on its way' CNET (21 February 2019) (available at: https://www.cnet.com/science/spacex-space-x-beresheet-moon-mission-israel/).

Maishman E, 'Space Debris Australia: Piece of SpaceX capsule crashes to Earth in field' BBC News (3 August 2022) (available at: https://www.bbc.com/news/world-australia-62414438).

Malanczuk P, 'Review of the Regulatory Regime Governing the Space Environment' (1996) 45(1) Zeitschrift für Luft und Weltraumrecht.

Malik T, 'Virgin Galactic's SpaceShipTwo Unity 22 launch with Richard Branson' Space.com (11 July 2021) (available at: https://www.space.com/virgin-galactic-richard-branson-unity-22-launch-explained).

Malysheva Nataliia R, Space Law and Policy in the Post-Soviet States (2018) The Hague: Eleven International Publishing.

Mandow R, 'NASA and Australia Continue Strategic Partnership with Artemis' Space Australia (21 March 2023) (available at: https://spaceaustralia.com/news/nasa-and-australia-continue-strategic-partnership-artemis).

Mann A, 'Rocket Lab poised to provide dedicated launcher for CubeSat science' Science (6 December 2017) (available at: https://www.science.org/content/article/rocket-lab-poised-provide-dedicated-launcher-cubesat-science).

Marboe I, 'National space law' in: Handbook of Space Law (von der Dunk FG & Tronchetti F (eds.)) (2015) (Cheltenham/Northampton: EE Publishing).

Marboe I, Soft Law in Outer Space: The Function of Non-Binding Norms in International Space Law (2012) Vienna: Böhlau.

Marchisio S, 'Article IX' (2009) in: The Cologne Commentary on Space Law: Vol. I (S. Hobe, B. Schmidt-Tedd, K.-U. Schrogl, G.M. Goh (eds.)) (Cologne: Carl Heymanns).

Marchisio S, 'Il Trattato sullo spazio: passato, presente e future' (2018) 1 Rivista di diritto internazionale.

Marchisio S, 'The ITU Regulatory System: a Self-Contained Regime or a Part of International Law?' (2014) in: Governing the Geostationary Orbit Orbital Slots and Spectrum Use in an Era of Interference (G. Penent (ed.)) (IFRI).

Maslow SA, 'Non-Financial Reporting and the Model Contract Clauses, Version 2.0' Business Law Today (26 May 2021) (available at: https://businesslawtoday.org/2021/05/non-financial-reporting-and-the-model-contract-clauses-version-2-0/).

Masson-Zwaan T, 'Registration of Small Satellites and the Case of the Netherlands' (2016) in: Small Satellites – Regulatory Challenges and Chances (I. Marboe (ed.)) (Brill).

Matte NM, 'Environmental Implications and Responsibilities in the Use of Outer Space' (1989) 14 Annals of Air and Space Law.

May A, Dobrijevic D, 'The Kármán Line: Where does space begin?' Space.com (14 November 2022) (available at: https://www.space.com/karman-line-where-does-space-begin).

Mayence JF, 'Granting Access to Outer Space: Rights and Responsibilities for States and their Citizens, An Alternative Approach to Article VI of the Outer Space Treaty, Notably Trough the Belgian Space Legislation' (2011) in: National Space Legislation in Europe (FG. von der Dunk (ed.)) Martinus Nijhoff.

McCall SM, 'Challenges to the United States in Space' (2020) Congressional Research Service Report IF10337.

McCallion K, Sharma R, 'Environmental Justice without Borders: The Need for an International Court of the Environment to Protect Fundamental Environmental Rights' (2000) 32 George Washington Journal of International Law and Economics.

McFadden C, Ballantine D, 'Dual-Use Technologies and National security' (1997) in: International Friction and Cooperation in High-Technology Development and Trade: Papers and Proceedings (National Research Council) (Washington, DC: The National Academies Press).

McGirr D, Bovaird M, Jones T, 'In review: space law, regulation and policy in Australia' Lexology (5 January 2023) (available at: https://www.lexology.com/library/detail.aspx?g=29a0fde0-b441-4d49-858d-f7b5759fd050).

McGoogan C, 'What is SpaceX and is it the future of space exploration?' Telegraph (26 July 2017) (available at: https://www.telegraph.co.uk/technology/0/spacex-future-space-exploration/).

McLachlan C, *The Principle of Systemic Integration in International Law* (online edn, Oxford Academic) (2024).

McLachlan C, 'The Principle of Systemic Integration and Article 31(3)(C) of the Vienna Convention', *International and Comparative Law Quarterly*, 54 (2005).

Mégret F, 'The Problem of an International Criminal Law of the Environment' (2011) 36 Columbia Journal of Environmental Law.

Mejia-Kaiser Martha, The Geostationary Ring: Practice and Law (2020) Leiden: Martinus Nijhoff.

Melo M, Vasconcellos P, 'High hopes for Brazil's space ambitions' (2020) 25 Room: Space Journal of Asgardia 3 (available at: https://room.eu.com/article/high-hopes-for-brazils-space-ambitions).

Meron T, 'Extraterritoriality of Human Rights Treaties' (1995) 89(1) The American Journal of International Law.

Milde M, International Air law and ICAO (Essential Air and Space Law Series) (2008) (The Hague: Eleven International Publishing).

Miller GD, 'Space Pirates, Geosynchronous Guerrillas, and Non-terrestrial Terrorists: Nonstate Threats in Space' (2019) 33(3) Air & Space Power Journal.

Mineiro MC, 'FY-1C and USA-193 ASAT Intercepts: An Assessment of Legal Obligations under Article IX of the Outer Space Treaty' (2008) 34 Journal of Space Law.

Moir L, The Law of Internal Armed Conflict (2002) Cambridge University Press.

Morabito GS, 'How Did Maritime Piracy Affect Trade in Southeast Asia?' (2018) 18 Journal of East Asian Studies.

Morozova E, Laurenava A, 'International Liability for Commercial Space Activities and Related Issues of Debris' (published online 2021) Planetary Science.

Moskowitz C, 'Private Spaceship Could Start Carrying Tourists Within a Year', SPACE.com (30 November 2010) (available at: https://www.space.com/9621-private-spaceship-start-carrying-tourists-year.html).

Mrema EM, Bruch C, Diamond J, Protecting the Environment during Armed Conflict: An Inventory and Analysis of International Law (2009) Nairobi: United Nations Environment Programme.

Murphy SD, 'Does the World Need a New International Environmental Court?' (2000) 32(3) George Washington Journal of International Law and Economics.

Murray D, Human Rights Obligations of Non-State Armed Groups (2016) Oxford: Hart Publishing Limited.

Mustow SE, 'Environmental impact assessment (EIA) screening and scoping of extra-terrestrial exploration and development projects' (2018) 36(6) Impact Assessment and Project Appraisal.

Nader R, Kelso TS, 'The Pegasus Incident: The Loss of the First Ecuadorian Satellite and its Recovery' (2014) Conference Paper at the International Astronautical Congress.

Nienass N, 'Europe leads on environmental concerns on earth, it must do the same in space' Euractiv (3 July 2023) (available at: https://www.euractiv.com/section/global-europe/opinion/europe-leads-on-environmental-concerns-on-earth-it-must-do-the-same-in-space/).

Nishimura L, Adaptation and Anticipatory Action: Integrating Human Rights Duties into the Climate Change Regime (2022) Brill.

Nixon J, Michaels J, Modern English for Aeronautics and Space Technology (2021) Munich: Carl Hanser Verlag.

Noortmann M, NGOs in international law (2019) in: Routledge Handbook of NGOs and International Relations (T Davied (ed.)) Oxon/New York: Routledge.

O'Callaghan J, 'Hardy water bears survive bullet impacts-up to a point' Science (18 May 2021) (available at https://www.science.org/content/article/hardy-water-bears-survive-bullet-impacts-point).

O'Shea M, 'The Wild, Wild West of Space Law' The Walrus (4 April 2023) (available at: https://thewalrus.ca/space-the-wild-wild-west-of-space-law/).

Öberg M, 'The Legal Effects of Resolutions of the UN Security Council and General Assembly in the Jurisprudence of the ICJ', (2005) 16(5) European Journal of International Law.

Oberhaus D, 'A Crashed Israeli Lunar Lander Spilled Tardigrades on the Moon' Wired (5 August 2019) (available at https://www.wired.com/story/a-crashed-israeli-lunar-lander-spilled-tardigrades-on-the-moon/).

Oduntan G, Sovereignty and Jurisdiction in the Airspace and Outer Space: Legal Criteria for Spatial Delimitation (2011) Oxon/New York: Routledge.

Ormsbee MH, 'Fair Enough?: Procedural Fairness When the ICAO Council Excercises Its Judicial Function' (2023) 48 Air and Space Law 4/5.

Osofsky H, 'The creation of the international law of climate change: complexities of sub-state actors' (2012) in: Non-state actors, soft law and protective regimes: from the margins (C. Bailliet) (Cambridge: Cambridge University Press).

Paladini S, Castellucci I, 'Sovereign states, private actors, and (national) space laws. A rapidly evolving landscape' (2022), in: The Institutions of Extraterrestrial Liberty (C.S. Cockell (ed.)) (Oxford: Oxford Academic online).

Palkowitz N, Regulating a Revolution (2019) The Netherlands: Wolters International Law BV.

Parlett K, Ewad S, 'Protection of the Environment in Investment Arbitration – A Double-Edged Sword', Kluwer Arbitration Blog (22 August 2017) (available at: https://arbitrationblog.kluwerarbitration.com/2017/08/22/protection-environment-investment-arbitration-double-edged-sword/).

Pavesi G, 'Legal Consequences of Environmental Pollution in Outer Space' (2018) in: A Fresh View on the Outer Space Treaty (A. Froehlich (ed.)) (Cham: Springer).

Peculjic AN, Tugnoli M, Promoting Productive Cooperation Between Lawyers and Engineers (2019) Hershey: IGI Global.

Pelton JF, Space 2.0 (2019) Springer International Publishing.

Pelton JN, Space Debris and Other Threats from Outer Space (2013) New York: Springer.

Pereira R, Environmental Criminal Liability and Enforcement in European and International Law (2015) Leiden: Koninklijke Brill.

Perek L, 'Maintaining the Space Environment' (2001) in: Luft- und Weltraumrecht im 21. Jahrhundert (Böckstiegel KH, Benkö M, Kröll W (eds.)) Cologne: Carl Heymanns Verlag.

Peters A, 'The refinement of international law: From fragmentation to regime interaction and politicization' (2017) 15(3) International Journal of Constitutional Law.

Petrova M, 'The first crop of space mining companies didn't work out, but a new generation is trying again' CNBC (9 October 2022) (available at: https://www.cnbc.com/2022/10/09/space-mining-business-still-highly-speculative.html).

Petrović G, 'Non-Governmental Organization (NGO) Participation in Civil Aviation Policy and Decision Making', (2023) 88 Journal of Air Law and Commerce.

Pietkiewicz M, 'Protection of the space environment against space debris pollution' (2019) 45 Studia Prawnoustrojowe.

Pincus W, 'Boeing Fined $10 Million For Data Transfer To Ukraine, Russia', Washington Post (3 October 1998) (available at: https://www.washingtonpost.com/archive/politics/1998/10/03/boeing-fined-10-million-for-data-transfer-to-ukraine-russia/307b7709-655a-4572-84f9-0202ce5e5352/).

Pinto-Bazurco JF, 'Deep Dive: The Precautionary Principle' International Institute for Sustainable Development (23 October 2020) (available at: https://www.iisd.org/articles/deep-dive/precautionary-principle).

Pocar F, 'An Introduction to the PCA's Optional Rules for Arbitration of Disputes Relating to Outer Space Activities' (2012) 38 Journal of Space Law.

Pop V, 'The men who sold the Moon: science fiction or legal nonsense?' (2001) 17(3) Space Policy.

Portmann R, Legal Personality in International Law (2010) Cambridge: Cambridge University Press.

Portree DSF, Loftus JP, 'Orbital Debris: A Chronology' (1999) NASA/TP-1999-208856.

Pozza MA, Dennerley JA, Risk Management in Outer Space Activities: An Australian and New Zealand Perspective (2022). Heidelberg: Springer.

Proulx VJ, 'A Postmortem for International Criminal Law? Terrorism, Law and Politics, and the Reaffirmation of State Sovereignty' (2020) 11(1) Harvard National Security Journal.

Pultarova T, 'The 10 Hottest Companies in Satellite 2018' ViaSatellite (January 2019) (available at http://interactive.satellitetoday.com/via/january-2019/the-10-hottest-companies-in-satellite-2018/).

Rabasa A, Boraz S, Chalk P, Craigin K, Karasik TW, Ungoverned Territories: Understanding and Reducing Terrorism Risks (2007) (Rand).

Radi Y, 'Clearing up the Space Junk: On the Flaws and Potential of International Space Law to Tackle the Space Debris Problem' (2023) 12(2) ESIL Reflections.

Ramuš Cvetkovič I, Space law as lex specialis to international law (Master Thesis) (2021) Ljubljana: University of Ljubljana, Faculty of Law (available at: https://repozitorij.uni-lj.si/Dvokument.php?id=147587&lang=slv).

Randall I, 'SpaceX loses control of three of its Starlink internet satellites just WEEKS after launch amid fears the surge in space junk could one day trap humanity on Earth' Mail Online (1 July 2019) (available at https://www.dailymail.co.uk/sciencetech/article-7200885/SpaceX-loses-control-three-Starlink-internet-satellites-just-WEEKS-launch.html).

Rawls J, 'The Law of Peoples' (1993) 20(1) Critical Inquiry.

Raymond N, 'Boeing sues Sea Launch partners for $350 million' Reuters (4 February 2013) (available at: https://www.reuters.com/article/us-boeing-sealaunch-idUSBRE9130RU20130204).

Reinert AP, 'Updating the Liability Regime in Outer Space: Why Spacefaring Companies Should Be Internationally Liable For Their Space Objects' (2020) 62 William & Mary Law Rev.

Remuss NL, 'The Need to Counter Space Terrorism: A European Perspective' (2009) European Space Policy Institute.

Reyhani R, 'Protection of the Environment During Armed Conflict' (2006) 14 Missouri Environmental Law & Policy Review.

Ria U, 'Top 4 Canadian Space Companies & their Contribution' Space Impulse (4 July 2023) (available at: https://spaceimpulse.com/2023/07/04/canadian-space-companies/).

Ribbelink O, 'Article III' (2009) in: The Cologne Commentary on Space Law: Vol. I (S. Hobe, B. Schmidt-Tedd, K.-U. Schrogl, G.M. Goh (eds.)) (Cologne: Carl Heymanns).

Rigby M, Carter B, 'A chunk of Chinese satellite almost hit the International Space Station. They dodged it – but the space junk problem is getting worse' The Conversation (12 November 2021) (available at: https://theconversation.com/a-chunk-of-chinese-satellite-almost-hit-the-international-space-station-they-dodged-it-but-the-space-junk-problem-is-getting-worse-171735).

Rinner A, 'Small Satellites – Smart Laws – Small Satellite Projects in the Face of National Space Legislation – Austria' (2013) in: Proceedings of the International Institute of Space Law (PJ Blount (ed.)) The Hague: Eleven International Publishing.

Roberts A, 'Clash of Paradigms: Actors and Analogies Shaping the Investment Treaty System' (2013) 107(1) American Journal of International Law.

Robinson D, 'Ecocide – Puzzles and Possibilities' (2022) 20(2) Journal of International Criminal Justice.

Rome P, 'Every Satellite Orbiting Earth and Who Owns Them' DEWESoft (18 January 2022) (available at: https://dewesoft.com/blog/every-satellite-orbiting-earth-and-who-owns-them).

Ronen Y, 'Human Rights Obligations of Territorial Non-State Actors' (2013) 46 Cornell International Law Journal.

Ross M, Vedda JA, 'The policy and science of rocket emissions' (2018) Center for Space Policy and Strategy.

Ross MN, David L, 'Space Pollution: The new private launch industry can learn a lot from aviation about sustainability' (2021) 324(2) Scientific American.

Routh A, 'Near-Earth Space Government is all About the Money' The Space Review (11 November 2019) (available at: https://www.thespacereview.com/article/3830/1).

Ruhaeni N, Aqimuddin EA, Afriyadi H, 'The Commercialization of Outer Space Under the Outer Space Treaty 1967 and Its Implementation on the Development of Space Industry in Indonesia' (2022) in: Proceedings of the 4th Social and Humanities Research Symposium (SoRes 2021) (Ahamadi D *et al.* (eds.)) (Advances in Social Science, Education and Humanities Research).

Ruilan L, Handbook of Regulations on Environmental Protection in China (1994) (RFF Press, 1994, revived 2016 by Routledge).

Rummel JD, Race MS, Horneck G, 'Ethical Considerations for Planetary Protection in Space Exploration: A Workshop' (2012) 12(11) Astrobiology.

Ryngaert C, 'Non-State Actors: Carving out a Space in a State-Centred International Legal System' (2016) 63 Netherlands International Law Review.

Sancin V, Grünfeld K, Ramuš Cvetkovič I, 'Contemporary Challenges of International Law-Making for Outer Space' (2021) 76(138) Pravnik.

Sands P, 'International Law, the Practitioner and Non-State Actors' (2000) in: The International Lawyer as Practitioner (C. Wickremasinghe (ed.)) (British Institute of International and Comparative Law).

Sands P, Principles of International Environmental Law (2nd Edition) (2012) Cambridge: Cambridge University Press.

Sands P, Peel J, Principles of International Environmental Law (4th ed.) (2018) Cambridge: Cambridge University Press.

Sapir A, Schraepen T, Tagliapietra S, 'Green Public Procurement: A Neglected Tool in the European Green Deal Toolbox' (2022) 57(3) Intereconomics: review of European Economic Policy (available at: https://www.intereconomics.eu/contents/year/2022/number/3/article/green-public-procurement-a-neglected-tool-in-the-european-green-deal-toolbox.html).

Sarin N, Longani V, Jain D, 'India' (2020) in: The Space Law Review (ed. J. Wheeler (ed.)) (London: Law Business Research Ltd).

Scharf MP, Sterio M, Williams PR, The Syrian Conflict's Impact on International Law (2020) Cambridge: Cambridge University Press.

Schellekens J, 'The Legality of Antisatellite ASAT Weapons' (Master Thesis) (2008) University of Leiden (available at: https://www.researchgate.net/publication/344493662_The_Legality_of_Antisatellite_ASAT_Weapons).

Schlom D, 'When Terrorists Threatened Apollo' (2001) Nov/Dec Ad Astra.

Schmalenbach K, 'International Organizations or Institutions, General Aspects (Status: July 2014)' in: The Max Planck Encyclopaedia of Public International Law: Online Edition (R. Wolfrum (ed.)) (Oxford: Oxford University Press).

Schmidt V, Brüning-Pfeiffer A, 'Environmental Aspects in Public Procurement in Europe: Conference Report' (2021) Berlin: German Environmental Agency (available at: https://www.umweltbundesamt.de/sites/default/files/medien/5750/publikationen/2021-04-22_dokumentationen_02-2021_public_procurement_0.pdf).

Schmidt-Tedd B, Mick S, 'Article VIII' (2009) in: The Cologne Commentary on Space Law: Vol. I (S. Hobe, B. Schmidt-Tedd, K.-U. Schrogl, G.M. Goh (eds.)) (Cologne: Carl Heymanns).

Schmidt-Tedd B, Soucek A, 'Registration of Space Objects' in: Oxford Research Encyclopedia of Planetary Science (P. Read et al. (eds.)) (Oxford: Oxford University Press).

Schmitt M, Tinkler K, 'War in Space: How International Humanitarian Law Might Apply' (2020) Just Security (available at: https://www.justsecurity.org/68906/war-in-space-how-international-humanitarian-law-might-apply/).

Schmitt MN, 'International Law and Military Operations in Space', Max Planck Yearbook of United Nations Law, (2006).

Schmitt MN, Tallinn Manual on the International Law Applicable to Cyber Warfare (2013) Cambridge: Cambridge University Press.

Schreurs F, 'Revisiting the Possibility of Corporate Criminal Responsibility in International Criminal Law: Amending Article 25 of the Rome Statute to Include Legal Entities Within the Jurisdiction of the ICC' (2020) Research paper DCL 7066, University of Ottawa.

Schröder M, 'Precautionary Approach/Principle' (2014) in: Max Planck Encyclopedia of Public International Law (R. Wolfrum (ed.)) online edition.

Schultz I, "Jeff Bezos' Space Joyride Emitted a Lifetime's Worth of Carbon Pollution' GIZMODO (10 December 2021) (available at: https://gizmodo.com/jeff-bezos-space-joyride-emitted-a-lifetime-s-worth-of-1848196182).

Seibert J, 'Top 4 Canadian Space Companies & their Contribution' Space Impulse (4 July 2023) (available at: https://spaceimpulse.com/2023/07/04/canadian-space-companies/).

Selivon M, 'Cooperation Between Judiciary and International Commercial Arbitration' (2011) 2 Law of Ukraine: Legal Journal.

Sese RM, 'The Philippine Space Program: A Modern Take on Establishing a National Space Program' (2022) in: ASEAN Space Programs (Q Verspieren, M Berthet, G Coral, S Nakasuka, H Shiroyama (eds.)) (Springer).

Shammas VL, Holen TB, 'One giant leap for capitalist kind: private enterprise in outer space' (2019) 5 Palgrave Communications.

Shaw M, International Law (6th ed.) (2008) Cambridge: Cambridge University Press.

Sheetz M, 'Bezos' Blue Origin loses NASA lawsuit over SpaceX $2.9 billion lunar lander contract' CNBC (4 November 2021) (available at: https://www.cnbc.com/2021/11/04/bezos-blue-origin-loses-lawsuit-against-nasa-over-spacex-lunar-lander.html).

Sinchak J, 'The Extraterritorial Application of Human Rights Treaties: Al-Skeini et al. v. United Kingdom (2011)' (2013) 3 Pace International Law Review.

Sivakumaran S, The Law of Non-International Armed Conflict (2012) Oxford University Press.

Slivka J, 'Managing Environmental Liabilities through Contracts' IRMI (1 January 2003) (available at: https://www.irmi.com/articles/expert-commentary/managing-environmental-liabilities-through-contracts).

Smith LJ, 'EU Competition Law and Issues of National Authorization of Private Space Activities' (2011) in: National Space Legislation in Europe (FG von der Dunk (ed.)) (Leiden: Martinus Nijhoff).

Smith LJ, Baumann I, Wintermuth SG, Routledge Handbook of Commercial Space Law (2023) Taylor and Francis.

Smith LJ, Kerrest A, 'The 1972 Convention on International Liability for Damage Caused by Space Objects' (2013) in: The Cologne Commentary on Space Law: Vol. II (S. Hobe, B. Schmidt-Tedd, K.-U. Schrogl (eds.), P. Stubbe (assist. ed.)) Cologne: Carl Heymanns.

Smith M, 'Anti-Satellite Weapons: History, Types and Purpose' Space.com (10 August 2022) (available at https://www.space.com/anti-satellite-weapons-asats).

Smith M., 'United States' (2019) in: The Space Law Review (J. Wheeler (ed.)) (London: Law Business Research Ltd.).

Sommariva A, 'The Evolution of Space Economy: The Role of the Private Sector and the Challenges for Europe' ISPI (7 December 2020) (available at: https://www.ispionline.it/en/pubblicazione/evolution-space-economy-role-private-sector-and-challenges-europe-28604).

Soucek A, Brünner C, Outer Space in Society, Politics and Law (2012) Vienna: Springer.

Soucek A, Space Law Essentials: Volume 1: Textbook (2020) Vienna: NWV.

Sreejith SG, 'Whither International Law, Thither Space Law: A Discipline in Transition' (2008) 38 California Western International Law Journal.

Steer C, Stephens D, 'International Humanitarian Law and Its Application in Outer Space' (2020), in: War and Peace in Outer Space: Law, Policy, and Ethics (C. Steer, and M. Hersch (eds.)) (New York: Oxford Academic Press).

Stepanova E, Terrorism in Asymmetrical Conflict Ideological and Structural Aspects – SIPRI Research Report No. 23 (2008) Oxford: Oxford University Press.

Stubbe P, 'Legal Consequences of the Pollution of Outer Space with Space Debris' (2020) in: Oxford Research Encyclopedia of Planetary Science (P. Read et al. (eds.)) (Oxford: Oxford University Press).

Stubbe P, State Accountability for Space Debris: a Legal Study of Responsibility for Polluting the Space Environment and Liability for Damage Caused by Space Debris (2018) Leiden/Boston: Brill/Martinus Nijhoff Publishers.

Sucharitkul S, 'State Responsibility and International Liability Under International Law' (1996) 18 Loyola of Los Angeles International and Comparative Law Journal.

Sundahl M, 'Legal Status of Spacecraft' (2017) in: Routledge Handbook of Space Law (R. Jakhu, P.S. Dempsey (eds.)) (London/New York: Routledge).

Susskind LE, Environmental Diplomacy: negotiating more effective global agreements (1994) New York/Oxford: Oxford University Press.

Szondy D, 'First private moon mission lifts off aboard SpaceX Falcon 9 rocket' NewAtlas (22 February 2019) (available at: https://newatlas.com/beresheet-lunar-mission-launch/58587/).

Tallis J, 'Remediating Space Debris: Legal and Technical Barriers' (2015) 9 Strategic Studies Quarterly.

Tan A, Zhang TX, Dokhanian M, 'Analysis of the Iridium 33 and Cosmos 2251 Collision using Velocity Perturbations of the Fragments' (2013) 3(1) Advances in Aerospace Science and Applications.

Tan D, 'Towards a New Regime for the Protection of Outer Space as the 'Province of All Mankind' (2000) 25 The Yale Journal of International Law.

Tangermann V, 'FCC Fines Startup for Launching Satellites Without Permission' Futurism (21. December 2018) (available at: https://futurism.com/fcc-fine-settlement-swarm-technologies-unauthorized).

Tanveer A, Global Civil Aviation Emissions Standards – from Noise to Greener Fuels (2016) Centre for Research in Air and Space Law, McGill.

Tapio J, 'The Finnish Space Act: En Route to Promoting Sustainable Private Activities in Outer Space' (2018) 43(4–5) Air and Space Law.

Tapio J, Soucek A, The European Space Agency's Contribution to National Space Law (2022) Heidelberg: Springer.

Thirlway H, 'The Role of Non-State Actors: A Response to Professor Ryngaert' (2017) 64 International Law Review.

Thirlway HWA, International Customary Law and Codification (1972) Leiden: Martinus Nijhoff Publishers.

Thompson J, 'Space for Rent: The International Telecommunications Union, Space Law, and Orbit/Spectrum Leasing', (1996) 62 Journal of Air Law and Commerce.

Tiberghien G, Mukhamedjanova R, and Xiw PF, 'Authenticity and spectrality of space heritage: Baikonur Cosmodrome, Kazakhstan' (14 July 2023) 25(5) An International Journal of Tourism Space, Place and Environment.

Tignino M, Bréthaut C, 'The role of international case law in implementing the obligation not to cause significant harm' (2020) 20 International Environmental Agreements: Politics, Law, and Economics.

Tillman NT, 'Virgin Galactic launches researchers to suborbital space on 5th commercial flight' Space.com (2 November 2023) (available at: https://www.space.com/virgin-galactic-05-mission-success-stern-gerardi).

Timtchenko I, 'Firefly looks to bolster aerospace ties with US, investing in Ukraine for the long-haul' Kyiv Post (20 August 2018) (available at: https://www.kyivpost.com/post/8390).

Tingkang A, 'These Aren't the Asteroids You Are Looking For: Classifying Asteroids in Space as Chattels, Not Land' (2012) 35 Seattle University Law Review.

Titi C, Public Actors in International Investment Law (2021), Springer Nature (Open Access).

Tkatchova S, Space-Based Technologies and Commercialized Development: Economic Implications and Benefits (2011) Hershey/New York: Engineering Science Reference (IGI Global).

Tremayne-Smith R, 'Environmental Protection and Space Debris Issues in the Context of Authorization,' (2011) in: National Space Legislation in Europe (FG von der Dunk (ed.)) (Leiden: Martinus Nijhoff Publishers).

Tronchetti F, (2013) 'The Legal Framework Regulating International Outer Space Activities' in: Fundamentals of Space Law and Policy (F Tronchetti) (SpringerBriefs in Space Development).

Tronchetti F, 'Space Law and China' Oxford Research Encyclopedia: Planetary Science (25 february 2019) (available at: https://oxfordre.com/planetaryscience/display/10.1093/acrefore/9780190647926.001.0001/acrefore-9780190647926-e-66;jsessionid=228B9CE470EF03340B6A46E91201B7D0?rskey=4IV574&result=89).

Tronchetti F, The Exploitation of Natural Resources of the Moon and Other Celestial Bodies (2009) Leiden: Koninklijke Brill.

Tsagourias N, 'Non-State Actors, Ungoverned Spaces and International Responsibility for Cyber Acts' (2016) 21(3) Journal of Conflict and Security Law.

Turiel J, Ding I, Chung-En Liu J, Environmental Governance in China: State, Society, and Market (2020) (Brill).

Turns D, 'Implementation and Compliance' (2007) in: Perspectives on the ICRC Study on Customary International Humanitarian Law (E. Wilmshurst and S. Breau (eds.)) (Cambridge: Cambridge University Press).

Uchitomi M, Sustainable Development in Outer Space: Applicability of the Concept of Sustainable Development to Space Debris Problems (2000) (American Institute of Aeronautics and Astronautics, Inc).

Undseth M, Jolly C, Olivari M, 'The Economics of Space Debris in Perspective' (2021) 8th European Conference on Space Debris, 20 April 2021 – 23 April 2021, Darmstadt, Germany, published by ESA Space Debris Office.

Vereshchetin VS, 'International Space Law and Domestic Law: Problems of Interrelations' (1981) 9 Journal of Space Law.

Vernile A, The Rise of Private Actors in the Space Sector (2018) Cham: Springer.

Verschuuren J, Principle of Environment Law (2003) Nomos Verlagsges.

Viets M, 'Piracy in an Ocean of Stars: Proposing a Term to Identify the Practice of Unauthorized Control of Nations' Space Objects' (2018) 54(2) Stanford Journal of International Law.

Viikari L, 'Environmental aspects of space activities (2015) in: Handbook of Space Law (von der Dunk FG & Tronchetti F (eds.)) (Cheltenham/Northampton: EE Publishing).

Viikari L, The Environmental Element in Space Law (2008) Leiden/Boston: Martinus Nijhoff Publishers.

Villasanta A, 'SpaceX to Build 1 Million Earth Stations to Track 12,000 Satellites, FCC License Details,' International Business Times (10 February 2019) (available at: https://www.ibtimes.com/spacex-build-1-million-earth-stations-track-12000-satellites-fcc-license-details-2761987).

Vitt E, Die Marskolonie (Doctoral Thesis) (1989) Cologne: University of Cologne.

Vitzthum WG, Volkerrecht (5th ed.) (2010) Berlin: De Gruyter Recht.

von der Dunk FG & Nikolaisen A, 'VIKINGS FIRST IN NATIONAL SPACE LAW: OTHER EUROPEANS TO FOLLOW – The Continuing Story Of National Implementation Of International Responsibility And Liability' (2001) Space, Cyber, and Telecommunications Law Program Faculty Publications.

von der Dunk FG (ed.), National Space Legislation in Europe (2011a) Leiden: Martinus Nijhoff.

von der Dunk FG, 'Armed Conflicts in Outer Space: Which Law Applies?' (2021) 97 International Law Studies.

von der Dunk FG, 'Effective Exercise of "In-Space Jurisdiction": The US Approach and the Problems it is Facing' (2015–2016) 40 Journal of Space Law.

von der Dunk FG, 'From Space Tourists to Unruly Passengers? The US Struggle with 'On-Orbit' Jurisdiction' (2015b) in: Proceedings of the International Institute of Space Law 2014 (Institute of International Space Law).

von der Dunk FG, 'International space law' (2015a) in: Handbook of Space Law (von der Dunk F & Tronchetti F (eds.)) (Cheltenham/Northampton: Edward Elgar).

von der Dunk FG, 'Liability versus Responsibility in Space Law: Misconception or Misconstruction?' (1992) 21 Space, Cyber, and Telecommunications Law Program Faculty Publications.

von der Dunk FG, 'Property Rights Over the Moon or On the Moon? The Legality of Space Resource Exploitation on Celestial Bodies' (2023) 6 Journal of Law & Innovation.

von der Dunk FG, 'The Origins of Authorization: Article VI of the Outer Space Treaty and International Space Law' (2011b) 69 Space, Cyber, and Telecommunications Law Program Faculty Publications.

von der Dunk FG, 'Towards ´Flags of Convenience´in Space?' (2012) 3 Space and Telecommunications Law Program Faculty Publications Paper 76.

von der Dunk FG, Advanced Introduction to Space Law (2020) (Edward Elgar).

Waelde T, Kolo A, 'Environmental Regulation, Investment Protection and 'Regulatory Taking' in International Law' (2001) 50(4) The International and Comparative Law Quarterly.

Wallach O, 'The World's Tech Giants, Compared to the Size of Economics' Visual Capitalist (7 July 2021) (available at: https://www.visualcapitalist.com/the-tech-giants-worth-compared-economies-countries/).

Warbrick C, 'States and Recognition in International Law' (2006) in: International Law (2nd ed.) (M. Evans (ed.)) (Oxford: Oxford University Press).

Wasser A, Jobes D, 'Space Settlements, Property Rights, and International Law: Could a Lunar Settlement Claim the Lunar Real Estate It Needs to Survive' (2008) 73(1) Journal of Air Law and Commerce.

Wedgewood R, 'Legal Personality and the Role of Non-Governmental Organizations and Non-State Political Entities in the United Nations System' (1999) in: Non-State Actors as New Subjects of International Law: International Law – From the Traditional State Order Towards the Law of the Global Community (R. Hofmann (ed.)) (Berlin: Duncker & Humblot).

Weinzierl M, Sarang M, 'The Commercial Space Age Is Here' Harvard Business Review (12 February 2021) (available at: https://hbr.org/2021/02/the-commercial-space-age-is-here).

Weisberger M, 'There Are Thousands of Tardigrades on the Moon. Now What?' LIVE SCIENCE (15 August 2019) (available at: https://www.livescience.com/moon-tardigrades-future.html).

Weiss EB, 'Climate Change, Intergenerational Equity, and International Law' (2008) 615 Vermont Journal of Environmental Law.

Wellman V, 'Dworkin and the Legal Process Tradition: The Legacy of Hart & Sacks' (1987) 29 *Arizona Law Review*.

Werneck MF, Hoorn GZ, and Almeida Braga AC, 'Brazil' (2020) in: The Space Law Review (J Wheeler (ed.)) (Business Law Research Ltd).

Wheeler J, 'Space Debris: Legal Framework, Issues Arising and New ISO Guidelines in 2010/2011' (2013) in: Yearbook on Space Policy 2010/2011: The Forward Look (P Hulsroj, S Pagkratis, B Baranes (eds.)) (Heidelberg: Springer).

Wheeler J, The Space Law Review (4th ed.) (2023) London: Lexology.

Whitt KK, 'Who owns all the satellites?' EarthSky (8 February 2022) (available at: https://earthsky.org/space/who-owns-satellites-company-country/).

Williams M, 'Eye-Opening Numbers on Space Debris' Universe Today (21 March 2017) (available at: https://phys.org/news/2017-03-eye-opening-space-debris.html).

Williamson M, 'Protecting the Space Environment' (2000) 9(4) Earth Space Review.

Williamson M, 'Space Ethics and Protection of the Space Environment' (2003) 19(1) Space Policy.

Wilmshurst E, 'The Chatham House Principles on International Law on the Use of Force in Self-Defence' (2006) 55 International & Comparative Law Quarterly.

Wins E, Weltraumhaftung im Völkerrecht (2000) Berlin: Duncker & Humblot.

Woodard C, 'High-seas launch worries islanders' The Christian Science Monitor (22 September 1999) (available at: https://www.csmonitor.com/1999/0922/p5s1.html).

Wrench JG, 'Non-Appropriation, No Problem: The Outer Space Treaty Is Ready for Asteroid Mining' (2019) 51 Case Western Reserve Journal of International Law.

Xu F, 'The approach to sustainable space mining: issues, challenges, and solutions' (2020) 738 IOP Conf. Series: Materials Science and Engineering.

Young S, 'The Number of Active Satellites in Space Skyrockets ... Literally' The Equation (27 July 2021) (available at: https://blog.ucsusa.org/syoung/number).

Zannoni D, 'The Liability Regime for Private Activities in Outer Space: Is There a Normative Gap?' (2021) 59(1) Archiv des Völkerrechts.

Zegveld L, Accountability of Armed Opposition Groups in International Law (2002) Cambridge: Cambridge University Press.

Zhou W, 'War, law and outer space: pathways to reduce the human cost of military space operations', *Humanitarian Law and Policy* (15 August 2023)

Zhao Y, 'Space Commercialization and the Development of Space Law' (2018) Oxford Research Encyclopedia of Planetary Science.

Ziemblicki B & Oralova Y, 'Private Entities in Outer Space Activities: Liability Regime Reconsidered' (2021) 56(2) Space Policy.

Zimmerman A, Geiß R, 'Article 8 – para. 2 (e)' in: The Rome Statute of the International Criminal Court: A Commentary (2.3 substantive crimes) (O. Triffterer and K. Ambos (eds.)) (Baden-Baden: C.H. Beck/Hart Publishing/Nomos, 2016).

Zubaşcu F, 'Ukraine war disrupting East-West cooperation in space' ScienceBusiness (8 March 2022) (available at: https://sciencebusiness.net/news/ukraine-war-disrupting-east-west-cooperation-space).

Websites

ACIL Allen, 'Australian Space Industry Capability' (October 2017) (available at: https://acilallen.com.au/uploads/projects/673/ACILAllen_AustralianSpaceIndustryCapability_2017.pdf).

Aerospace Review, 'Volume 2: Reaching Higher: Canada's Interests and Future in Space' *Aerospace Review* (November 2012) (available at: https://publications.gc.ca/site/eng/432242/publication.html).

Agence France-Presse, 'UAE successfully launches Hope probe, Arab world's first mission to Mars' *The Guardian* (20 July 2020) (available at: https://www.theguardian.com/science/2020/jul/20/uae-mission-mars-al-amal-hope-space).

Agence France-Presse. 'Dubai Creates 'Space Court' for Out-of-This-World Disputes' *Courthouse News Service* (1 February 2021) (available at: https://www.courthousenews.com/dubai-creates-space-court-for-out-of-this-world-disputes/).

Airbus, 'Constellations' *Airbus* (available at: https://www.airbus.com/en/space/telecom/constellations).

Airbus, 'Space technology made in Germany' *Airbus* (5. November 2023) (available at: https://www.airbus.com/en/products-services/space/space-technology-made-in-germany).

ARABSAT (available at: https://www.arabsat.com/).

Arianespace, 'Who does what?' *Arianespace* (5. November 2023) (available at: https://www.arianespace.com/spaceport-facility/who-does-what/).

Associated Press, 'Bomb Shatters Office of Europe Space Unit,' *New York Times* (3 August 1984) (available at: https://www.nytimes.com/1984/08/03/world/bomb-shatters-officeof-europe-space-unit.html).

Astronautics Now, 'Early Israel's Space Program' *Astronautics Now* (available at: 7).

Australian Trade and Investment Commission, 'Space' *Australian Government* (5 November 2023) (available at: https://www.globalaustralia.gov.au/industries/space).

Austria in Space, 'Austrian Space Industry and Research' *Austria in Space* (5. November 2023) (available at: https://austria-in-space.at/en/austria-in-space/austrian-space-industry-and-research.php).

Austria in Space, 'Space Activities' *Austria in Space* (5. November 2023) (available at: https://austria-in-space.at/en/european-space-activities/).

Base Camp, 'The Basics of LEO Satellite Systems' *Base Camp* (23 February 2022) (available at: https://www.basecampconnect.com/leo-satellite-systems/).

BBC, 'Ecuador Pegasus satellite fears over space debris crash' *BBC News* (24 May 2013) (available at: https://www.bbc.com/news/world-latin-america-22635671).

BBC, 'SpaceX loses 40 satellites to geomagnetic storm a day after launch' *BBC News* (9 February 2022) (available at https://www.bbc.com/news/world-60317806).

Belfer Center for Science and International Affairs, Harvard Kennedy School, 'Starlink and the Russia-Ukraine War: A Case of Commercial Technology and Public Purpose?' *BelferCenter* (9 March 2023) (available at: https://www.belfercenter.org/publication/starlink-and-russia-ukraine-war-case-commercial-technology-and-public-purpose).

BELSPO, 'The Belgian Space Industry' *Belspo.be* (5. November 2023) (available at: https://www.belspo.be/belspo/space/beindu_en.stm).

Bloomberg News, 'China, US are racing to make billions from mining the moon's minerals' *Mining.com* (17 May 2022) (available at: https://www.mining.com/web/china-us-are-racing-to-make-billions-from-mining-the-moons-minerals/).

Blue Origin, 'Blue Origin safely launches four commercial astronauts to space and back' *Blue Origin* (available at: https://www.blueorigin.com/news/first-human-flight-updates).

China National Space Administration (CNSA), 'Probe makes historic landing on Mars' *China National Space Administration* (17 May 2021) (available at: https://www.cnsa.gov.cn/english/n6465652/n6465653/c6812005/content.html).

CNES, 'French Space Industry Capabilities Catalogue' *cnes.fr* (available at:https://cnes.fr/en/entreprises/catalogue-industrie-spatiale).

CNET, 'Satellite Hack Raises Security Questions' *CNET* (2 January 2002) (available at: https://www.cnet.com/tech/mobile/satellite-hack-raises-security-questions/).

Copenhagen Suborbitals, 'About us' *Copenhagen Suborbitals* (available at: https://copenhagensuborbitals.com/about-us/).

Court of Justice of the European Union, 'Press Release No. 156/22' (20 September 2022) (available at: https://curia.europa.eu/jcms/upload/docs/application/pdf/2022-09/cp220156en.pdf).

Cyberlaw, 'Viasat KA-SAT attack' *cyberlaw.ccdcoe.org* (29 May 2022) (available at: https://cyberlaw.ccdcoe.org/wiki/Viasat_KA-SAT_attack_(2022)).

Defense Industry and Space, 'Space Traffic Management' *European Commission* (available at: https://defence-industry-space.ec.europa.eu/eu-space-policy/space-traffic-management_en).

Defense Industry and Space, 'Targeted consultation on EU space law' *European Commission* (13 September 2023) (available at: https://defence-industry-space.ec.europa.eu/public-consultations/targeted-consultation-eu-space-law_en).

Deloitte, 'Space Galaxy' *Deloitte* (available at: https://www2.deloitte.com/lu/en/pages/technology/articles/luxembourg-space-initiatives.html).

DLR, 'DLR ceases bilateral cooperation with Russia' *dlr.de* (3 March 2022) (available at: https://www.dlr.de/content/en/articles/news/2022/01/20220303_dlr-ceases-bilateral-cooperation-with-russia.htm).

Dragonfly Aerospace, 'Applications of a LEO Satellite' *Dragonfly Aerospace* (19 Aperil 2022) (available at: https://dragonflyaerospace.com/what-are-some-applications-of-a-leo-satellite/).

Emirates News Agency Wam, 'UAE reinforces its journey towards a leading and advanced space sector with qualitative achievements in 2023' *wam.ae* (20 November 2023) (available at: https://wam.ae/article/apqiq6p-uae-reinforces-its-journey-towards-leading-and).

ESA, '50 years of space activity for Norway' *ESA* (17 August 2012) (available at: https://www.esa.int/About_Us/ESA_history/50_years_of_space_for_Norway).

ESA, 'ariane' *ESA* (available at: https://www.esa.int/Enabling_Support/Space_Transportation/Ariane).

ESA, 'Clean Space – Latest' *ESA* (available at: https://www.esa.int/Space_Safety/Clean_Space).

ESA, 'Clean Space' *ESA* (available at: https://www.esa.int/Space_Safety/Clean_Space/Clean_Space2).

ESA, 'Eco Design' *ESA* (available at: https://www.esa.int/Space_Safety/Clean_Space/ecodesign).

ESA, 'ESA's Annual Space Environment Report' (22 April 2022) (available at https://www.sdo.esoc.esa.int/environment_report/Space_Environment_Report_latest.pdf).

ESA, 'ESA Facts' *ESA* (available at: https://www.esa.int/About_Us/Corporate_news/ESA_facts).

ESA, 'ESA Green Agenda' *ESA* (available at: https://www.esa.int/About_Us/Responsibility_Sustainability/ESA_Green_Agenda).

ESA, 'ESA's Space Environment Report 2023' *ESA* (2. November 2023) (available at: https://www.esa.int/Space_Safety/ESA_s_Space_Environment_Report_2023).

ESA, 'European space sector commits: Earth is ours, we must cherish it' *ESA* (21 November 2022) (available at: https://www.esa.int/Space_Safety/European_space_sector_commits_Earth_is_ours_we_must_cherish_it).

ESA, 'For Planet Earth and Beyond', European Space Agency (26 February 2024) (available at: https://connectivity.esa.int/news/satellite-services-and-applications-vital-cornerstone-modern-society).

ESA, 'Highlights of ESA rules and regulations' *ESA* (available at: https://www.esa.int/About_Us/Law_at_ESA/Highlights_of_ESA_rules_and_regulations).

ESA, 'International Space Station Legal Framework' *ESA* (available at: https://www.esa.int/Science_Exploration/Human_and_Robotic_Exploration/International_Space_Station/International_Space_Station_legal_framework).

ESA, 'Managing mega-constellations' *ESA* (available at: https://www.esa.int/Enabling_Support/Preparing_for_the_Future/Discovery_and_Preparation/Managing_mega-constellations).

ESA, 'Member States & Cooperating States' *ESA* (available at: https://www.esa.int/About_Us/Corporate_news/Member_States_Cooperating_States).

ESA, 'Space Debris by the Numbers' *ESA* (22 December 2022) (available at https://www.esa.int/Safety_Security/Space_Debris/Space_debris_by_the_numbers).

ESA, 'Space debris: assessing the risk' *ESA* (16 March 2005) (available at https://www.esa.int/About_Us/ESOC/Space_debris_assessing_the_risk).

ESA, 'Space law cases' *ESA* (17 March 2022) (available at: https://www.esa.int/About_Us/ECSL_-_European_Centre_for_Space_Law/Space_law_cases).

ESA, 'Space Law Cases' *ESA* (available at: https://www.esa.int/About_Us/ECSL_-_European_Centre_for_Space_Law/Space_law_cases).

ESA, 'The origins of Ariane' *ESA* (18 December 2009) (available at: https://www.esa.int/About_Us/ESA_history/The_origins_of_Ariane).

EU SST, 'EU SST is the key operational capability for the EU approach to Space Traffic Management' (available at: https://www.eusst.eu/newsroom/eu-sst-key-operational-capability-eu-approach-stm/).

Eurasian Bank, 'A Private Space Company from Kazakhstan Together with SpaceChain is Preparing to Launch a Satellite on Elon Musk's SpaceX Falcon 9 Rocket' *eubank.kz* (available at: https://astanatimes.com/2021/07/kazakh-company-launches-cryptocurrency-and-quran-satellite-projects-on-board-of-spacex-falcon-9-rocket/).

EUR-Lex, 'Environment and climate change' *eur-lex* (available at: https://eur-lex.europa.eu/summary/chapter/20.html).

European Commission, 'Corporate sustainability reporting' *European Commission* (available at: https://ec.europa.eu/info/business-economy-euro/company-reporting-and-auditing/company-reporting/corporate-sustainability-reporting_en).

European Commission, 'The European Green Deal' *European Commission* (available at: https://commission.europa.eu/strategy-and-policy/priorities-2019-2024/european-green-deal_en).

European Commission, 'The future of the European Space Sector' *European Investment Bank* (2019) (available at: https://www.eib.org/attachments/thematic/future_of_european_space_sector_en.pdf).

European Environmental Bureau, 'Environmental Law and Justice' EEB (available at: https://eeb.org/work-areas/environmental-law-and-justice/EU-environmental-law/).

European Parliament, 'Environment policy: general principles and basic framework' *European Parliament* (available at: https://www.europarl.europa.eu/factsheets/en/sheet/71/environment-policy-general-principles-and-basic-framework).

EUSPA, 'How EU Space Supports Europe's environmental policies' *EUSPA* (1 June 2023) (available at: https://www.euspa.europa.eu/newsroom/news/how-eu-space-supports-europe-environmental-policies).

EUSPA, 'The EU Space Programme' *EUSPA* (2 February 2024) (available at: https://www.euspa.europa.eu/european-space/eu-space-programme).

EUSTM, 'European space traffic management for the 21st century' *EU STM* (available at: https://eustm.eu/).

FAA, 'FAA Proposes 175.000 Fine Against SpaceX for Not Submitting Required Pre-Launch Data' *FAA* (17 February 2023) (available at: https://www.faa.gov/newsroom/faa-proposes-175000-fine-against-spacex-not-submitting-required-pre-launch-data).

FAA, 'Environmental Review' *FAA* (21 December 2020) (available at: https://www.faa.gov/space/stakeholder_engagement/spacex_starship/environmental_review).

FAA, 'FAA Closes SpaceX Starship Mishap Investigation' *FAA* (8 September 2023) (available at: https://www.faa.gov/newsroom/faa-closes-spacex-starship-mishap-investigation).

FAA, 'FAA Proposes $175,000 Fine Against SpaceX for Not Submitting Required Pre-Launch Data' *FAA* (17 February 2023) (available at: https://www.faa.gov/newsroom/faa-proposes-175000-fine-against-spacex-not-submitting-required-pre-launch-data).

FAA, 'Licensing and Permitting Process' *FAA* (12 November 2020) (available at: https://www.faa.gov/space/stakeholder_engagement/spacex_starship/license_review_process).

FAA, 'SpaceX Starship Super Heavy Project at the Boca Chica Launch Site' *FAA* (17 November 2023) (available at: https://www.faa.gov/space/stakeholder_engagement/spacex_starship).

FCC, 'Application for Fixed Satellite Service by Kuiper Systems LLC' *FCC Report* (30 July 2020) (available at: https://fcc.report/IBFS/SAT-LOA-20190704-00057).

FCC, 'FCC Authorizes SpaceX to Provide Broadband Satellite Services' *FCC* (29 March 2018) (available at: https://www.fcc.gov/document/fcc-authorizes-spacex-provide-broadband-satellite-services).

FCC, 'FCC Reaches $900,000 Settlement for Unauthorized Satellite Launch' *FCC* (20 December 2018) (available at: https://www.fcc.gov/document/fcc-reaches-900000-settlement-unauthorized-satellite-launch).

Federal Ministry for Transport, Innovation and Technology, 'Austrian Space Applications Programme' *FFG* (available at: www.ffg.at/content/austrian-space-applications-programme).

FFG, 'Austria in Space' *ffg.at* (available at: https://www.ffg.at/en/space/austria-in-space).

Foust J, 'FCC approves Starlink license modification' *Space News* (27 April 2021) (available at: https://spacenews.com/fcc-approves-starlink-license-modification/).

Glaser M, Schiller B, Jeschke S, Radbruch M, 'Global Outer Space Guide: Germany' *Norton Rose Fulbright* (February 2024) (available at: https://www.nortonrosefulbright.com/de-de/knowledge/publications/582a6d62/global-outer-space-guide-germany).

Global Terrorism Database, 'National Consortium for the Study of Terrorism and Responses to Terrorism' *Global Terrorism Database* (2018) (available at: https://www.start.umd.edu/gtd).

GlobalSecurity.org, 'Denmark in Space' *GlobalSecurity.org* (available at: https://www.globalsecurity.org/space/world/denmark/index.html).

Göbel J., 'Strong start-ups' *deutschland.de* (25 May 2022) (available at: https://www.deutschland.de/en/topic/business/germany-aerospace-start-ups-innovative-technology-in-space).

Government of Canada, '2020 State of the Canadian Space Sector Report – Facts and Figures 2019' *asc-csa* (available at: https://www.asc-csa.gc.ca/pdf/eng/publications/2020-state-canadian-space-sector-facts-figures-2019-v2.pdf).

Government of Canada, 'Canada's Views on Reducing Space Threats through norms, rules and principles of Responsible Behaviour' (2021) (available at: https://documents.unoda.org/wp-content/uploads/2022/05/EN-Canada-working-Paper-on-Norms-75-36.pdf).

Government of Canada, 'Canadian space industry' *ised-isde.canada* (available at: https://ised-isde.canada.ca/site/canadian-space-industry/en).

Government of Canada, 'Government of Canada supports commercial space launches in Canada' *canada.ca* (20 January 2023) (available at: https://www.canada.ca/en/transport-canada/news/2023/01/government-of-canada-supports-commercial-space-launches-in-canada.html).

Government of Canada, 'Government of Canada supports commercial space launches in Canada' *canada.ca* (20 January 2023) (available at: https://www.canada.ca/en/transport-canada/news/2023/01/government-of-canada-supports-commercial-space-launches-in-canada.html).

Government of Canada, 'Programs' *ised-isde.canada* (available at: https://ised-isde.canada.ca/site/canadian-space-industry/en/programs).

Government of Canada, 'Stakeholder directories' *ised-isde.canada* (available at: https://ised-isde.canada.ca/site/canadian-space-industry/en/stakeholder-directories).

Government of the Netherlands, 'Space research generates new technologies' *Government of the Netherlands* (available at: https://www.government.nl/topics/space/space-research-generates-new-technologies#:~:text=The%20Dutch%20space%20sector%20is,services%20based%20on%20satellite%20data).

History of Information, 'INTELSAT 1, the First Commercial Communication Satellite, is Placed in Geosynchronous Orbit' *historyinformation.com* (available at: https://historyofinformation.com/detail.php?entryid=3595).

IADC, 'Welcome to the Inter-Agency Space Debris Coordination Committee' *IADC* (available at: https://iadc-home.org/what_iadc).

ICAO, 'Article 16' *Icao.int* (2017) (available at https://applications.icao.int/postalhistory/annex_16_environmental_protection.htm#:~:text=Volume%20I%20of%20the%20reorganized,manuals%20on%20noise%20and%20emissions).

ICEYE, 'ICEYE Signs Contract to Provide Government of Ukraine with Access to Its SAR Satellite Constellation' *ICEYE* (18 August 2022), (available at: https://www.iceye.com/press/press-releases/iceye-signs-contract-to-provide-government-of-ukraine-with-access-to-its-sar-satellite-constellation).

ICRC, Convention (III) relative to the Treatment of Prisoners of War. Geneva, 12 August 1949, Commentary 2020 (available at: https://ihl-databases.icrc.org/en/ihl-treaties/gciii-1949/toc/commentary/2020?activeTab=undefined).

Intelsat General Corporation, 'Hosted Payloads' *Interlsat General* (available at: https://www.intelsat.com/space/products/hosted-payloads/).

Interagency Operations Advisory Group, 'South Korea aims to establish a national space agency modeled after NASA by next year' *IOAG* (12 January 2022) (available at: https://www.ioag.org/SitePages/South-Korea-aims-to-establish-a-national-space-agency-modeled-after-NASA-by-next-year.aspx).

Independent Expert Panel, 'Definition of Ecocide' *Stop Ecocide* (June 2021) (available at: https://www.stopecocide.earth/legal-definition).

International Trade Administration, 'Brazil Space Sector' *International Trade Administration* (15 March 2021) (available at: https://www.trade.gov/market-intelligence/brazil-space-sector).

International Trade Administration, 'Japan Space Industry Commercialization' *International Trade Administration* (26 August 2021) (available at: https://www.trade.gov/market-intelligence/japan-space-industry-commercialization).

International Trade Administration, 'South Korea Space Industry' *International Trade Administration* (26 September 2023) (available at: https://www.trade.gov/market-intelligence/south-korea-space-industry).

Isar Aerospace, 'Isar Aerospace participates in inauguration of new Spaceport Esrange in Sweden' *Isar Aerospace* (13 January 2023) (available at: https://www.isaraerospace.com/press/isar-aerospace-participates-in-inauguration-of-new-spaceport-esrange-in-sweden).

Japan Brandvoice, 'These Japanese Startups Are Powering Space Development' *Forbes* (18 March 2021) (available at: https://www.forbes.com/sites/japan/2021/03/18/these-japanese-startups-are-powering-space-development/).

JAXA, 'Japan's Space Industry' *JAXA* (available at: https://aerospacebiz.jaxa.jp/en/partner/).

Jessica, 'Towards a Clean Space: ESA's Zero Debris Approach' *ESA* (16 June 2023) (available at: https://blogs.esa.int/cleanspace/2023/06/16/a-clear-path-to-a-sustainable-space-esas-zero-debris-approach/).

Johnson N, 'The Collision of Iridium 33 and Cosmos 2251: The Shape of Things to Come, Conference paper 20100002023 at 60th International Astronautical Congress' *NASA* (16 October 2009) (available at: https://ntrs.nasa.gov/citations/20100002023).

Jones A, 'China, Russia enter MoU on international lunar research station' *Space News* (9 March 2021) (available at: https://spacenews.com/china-russia-enter-mou-on-international-lunar-research-station/).

Kinstellar, 'Ukraine allows private sector involvement in space activities' *Kinstellar* (November 2019) (available at: https://www.kinstellar.com/news-and-insights/detail/971/ukraine-allows-private-sector-involvement-in-space-activities).

Klotz I, 'Lawsuit seeks to stop Boeing, SpaceX work on NASA space taxi' *Reuters* (16 October 2014) (available at: https://www.reuters.com/article/idUSKCN0I52O8/).

Klotz I, 'Virgin Galactic's Space Ship Two makes 1st test flight of revamped re-entry system' *Space.com* (2 May 2017) (https://www.space.com/36679-virgin-galactic-spaceshiptwo-unity-feather-system-test-flight.html).

Launch UK, 'A guide to UK spaceports' *GOV.UK* (available at: https://assets.publishing.service.gov.uk/government/uploads/system/uploads/attachment_data/file/1151003/Spaceport_brochure_17.4.23.pdf).

Law Insider, 'Environmental Disclosure Sample Clauses' *Law Insider* (available at: https://www.lawinsider.com/clause/environmental-disclosure).

Luxembourg Space Agency, 'Space Campus: The Future Centre of Gravity of the Luxembourg Space Ecosystem' *LSN* (3 August 2022) (available at: https://space-agency.public.lu/en/news-media/news/2022/spacecampus.html).

Malaysian Communications and Multimedia Commission, 'Satellite Initiatives in Malaysia' *MCMC* (available at: https://www.mcmc.gov.my/en/sectors/satellite/satellite-initiatives-in-malaysia).

Metallurgprom, 'Firefly Aerospace ordered at the Pivdenmash missile parts to $ 15 million' *Metallurgprom* (31 October 2019) (available at: https://metallurgprom.org/en/news/ukraine/1657-firefly-aerospace-zakazala-na-juzhmashe-detali-raket-na-15-millionov-dollarov.html).

Ministry of Higher Education and Science, 'Space and Denmark' *ufm.dk* (22 August 2023) (available at: https://ufm.dk/en/research-and-innovation/space-and-denmark).

Ministry of the Economy, Tourism and Sport, 'Catalogue of Slovenian Space Industry' *GOV.SI* (2023) (available at: https://www.gov.si/assets/ministrstva/MGTS/Dokumenti/ESA/Slovenia-space-catalogue-2023-SPREAD.pdf).

Mordor Intelligence, 'Space Mining Market Size & Share Analysis – Growth Trends & Forecasts (2023 – 2028)' *Mordor Intelligence* (available at: https://www.mordorintelligence.com/industry-reports/space-mining-market-industry).

NASA Science Editorial Team, 'Space Debris and Human Spacecraft' *NASA* (21 July 2022) (available at https://www.nasa.gov/mission_pages/station/news/orbital_debris.html).

NASA, 'Artemis Accords' (available at: https://www.nasa.gov/artemis-accords/).

NASA, '15 Ways the International Space Station is Benefiting Earth' *NASA* (30 October 2015) (available at: https://www.nasa.gov/missions/station/15-ways-the-international-space-station-benefits-humanity-back-on-earth/).

NASA, 'Basics of Space Flight: Section 3: Operations, Chapter 14: Launch' *NASA* (available at: https://solarsystem.nasa.gov/basics/chapter14-1/#:~:text=If%20a%20spacecraft%20is%20launched,hour%20relative%20to%20Earth's%20center).

NASA, 'NASA's Perseverance Rover Begins its First Science Campaign on Mars' *NASA* (9 June 2021) (available at: https://www.nasa.gov/solar-system/nasas-perseverance-rover-begins-its-first-science-campaign-on-mars/).

Nasir S, 'UK and South Korea join US-led efforts to ban anti-satellite testing' *The National News* (6 October 2022) (available at: https://www.thenationalnews.com/world/uk-news/2022/10/06/uk-and-south-korea-join-us-led-efforts-to-ban-anti-satellite-testing/).

Office of Public Affairs, 'Lafarge Pleads Guilty to Conspiring to Provide Material Support to Foreign Terrorist Organizations' *US Department of Justice* (18 October 2022) (https://www.justice.gov/opa/pr/lafarge-pleads-guilty-conspiring-provide-material-support-foreign-terrorist-organizations).

OHB, 'First launches in the North Sea planned for 2024' *ohb.de* (18 October 2023) (available at: https://www.ohb.de/en/news/first-launches-in-the-north-sea-planned-for-2024-gosa-starts-its-first-demo-mission).

OHCHR, 'Frequently Asked Questions about the Guiding Principles on Business and Human Rights' *ohchr.org* (1 October 2014) (available at: https://www.ohchr.org/sites/default/files/Documents/Publications/FAQ_PrinciplesBussinessHR.pdf).

Orbex, 'Launch Site' *orbex.space* (available at: https://orbex.space/launch-services/launch-site).

Orbital Today, 'The Lunar 'Gold Rush' Is On: How Could Mining Moon Minerals Change Life On Earth?' *Orbital Today* (9 October 2023) (available at: https://orbitaltoday.com/2023/10/09/the-lunar-gold-rush-is-on-how-could-mining-moon-minerals-change-life-on-earth/).

Orbital Today, 'The Magnificent Seven' *Orbital Today* (5. August 2021) (available at:https://orbitaltoday.com/2021/08/05/the-magnificent-seven-the-main-uk-rocket-launch-sites-their-benefits/).

Permanent Court of Arbitration, 'Dispute Resolution Services' *pca-cpa.org* (available at: https://pca-cpa.org/en/services/).

Permanent Court of Arbitration, 'PCA Arbitration Rules' *pca-cpa.org* (available at: https://pca-cpa.org/en/services/arbitration-services/pca-arbitration-rules-2012/).

Portugal Space, 'Space Catalogue: Industry' *Portugal Space* (available at: https://www.newspaceportugal.org/en).

Republic of Slovenia, 'First Slovenian satellites launched into orbit' *GOV.SI* (3 September 2020) (available at: https://www.gov.si/en/news/2020-09-03-first-slovenian-satellites-launched-into-orbit/).

SatNews, 'Nine Canadian Space Companies Create The Space Canada Association' *satnews.com* (20 March 2022) (available at: https://news.satnews.com/2022/03/20/nine-canadian-space-companies-create-the-space-canada-organization/).

Sese RM, 'Space Research and Development in the Philippines' *JAXA* (available at: https://iss.jaxa.jp/en/kuoa/news/pdf/06_APRSAF22_Philippines.pdf).

Sheetz M, 'FCC approves SpaceX change to its Starlink network, a win despite objections from Amazon and others' *CNBC* (27 April 2021) (available at: https://www.cnbc.com/2021/04/27/fcc-approves-spacex-starlink-modification-despite-objections.html).

Silk Way, 'Startups in aerospace industry to be developed in Kazakhstan' *Silky Way Channel* (25. August 2022) (available at: https://jibekjoly.tv/en/startups-in-aerospace-industry-to-be-developed-in-kazakhstan).

Skyrora, 'Trends in the UK Space Industry' *skyrora.com* (available at: https://www.skyrora.com/trends-in-the-uk-space-industry/).

Space TV, 'African Space Agency' *AfSA* (available at: https://www.spacetv.net/african-space-agency-afsa/).

Spacewatch Global, 'Kazakhstan to start its own satellite design and manufacturing industrial base' *SpaceWatch* (available at: https://spacewatch.global/2020/02/kazakhstan-to-start-its-own-satellite-design-and-manufacturing-industrial-base/).

'Space Security 2004'. Spacesecurity.org, (June 2005) (available at:https://www.belfercenter.org/sites/default/files/pantheon_files/files/publication/ssi2004.pdf).

STA, 'Third Slovenian satellite launched in space' *STA* (13 July 2022) (available at: https://english.sta.si/3060191/third-slovenian-satellite-launched-in-space).

Starlink (available at: https://www.starlink.com/).

Statista Research Department, 'Number of satellites in orbit by major country as of January 1, 2022' *Statista* (8 December 2023) (available at https://www.statista.com/statistics/264472/number-of-satellites-in-orbit-by-operating-country/).

Stop Ecocide Foundations, 'Definition of Ecocide proposed by Independent Expert Panel for the Legal Definition of Ecocide' (June 2021) (available at: https://static1.squarespace.com/static/5ca2608ab914493c64ef1f6d/t/60d1e6e604fae2201d03407f/1624368879048/SE+Foundation+Commentary+and+core+text+rev+6.pdf).

T&F, 'The proliferation of corporate war-crimes cases' (3 November 2023) (available at: https://www.tandfonline.com/doi/full/10.1080/13567888.2023.2279864?src=).

Telecom Review, 'An Elevated Future: The UAE Space Sector Is Thriving' *Telecom Review* (16 January 2023) (available at: https://www.telecomreview.com/articles/reports-and-coverage/6699-an-elevated-future-the-uae-space-sector-is-thriving).

The Economist, 'Ukrainian Cities Are Suffering Internet Blackouts.' *The Economist Newspaper*, (26 February 2022) (available at: https://www.economist.com/graphic-detail/2022/02/26/ukrainian-cities-ar).

The Independent Expert Panel for the Legal Definition of Ecocide, 'Commentary and Core Text' *Stop Ecocide* (June 2021) (available at https://www.stopecocide.earth/legal-definition).

The South African Council for Space Affairs, 'Space in South Africa' *SACSA* (available at: http://www.sacsa.gov.za/space-in-south-africa/;https://link.springer.com/chapter/10.1007/978-90-481-9008-9_12).

The White House, 'FACT SHEET: Vice President Harris Advances National Security Norms in Space' *The White House* (18 April 2022) (available at: https://www.whitehouse.gov/briefing-room/statements-releases/2022/04/18/fact-sheet-vice-president-harris-advances-national-security-norms-in-space/).

Tracxn, 'NewSpace Startups in France' *tracxn.com* (17 June 2023) (available at: https://tracxn.com/d/explore/newspace-startups-in-france/__cRjAOQ4LjYjRQRTbpe8ZNxuwovS2FRTMkXyNx4zC4Aw/companies).

United Arab Emirates Space Agency, 'About UAE Space Agency' *space.gov.ae* (available at: https://space.gov.ae/Page/20120/20230/About-UAE-Space-Agency).

United Nations Department of Economic and Social Affairs, 'How to apply for consultative status with ECOSOC?' *United Nations* (available at https://social.desa.un.org/issues/civil-society/how-to-apply-for-consultative-status-with-ecosoc).

UNOOSA, 'United Nations Online Index of Objects Launched into Outer Space' *UNOOSA* (available at: https://www.unoosa.org/oosa/osoindex/index.jspx?lf_id).

UNOOSA, 'Committee on the Peaceful Uses of Outer Space and its Subcommittees' *UNOOSA* (available at: https://www.unoosa.org/oosa/en/ourwork/copuos/comm-subcomms.html#:~:text=The%20Committee%20on%20the%20Peaceful,membership%20has%20continued%20to%20expand).

UNOOSA, 'Status of International Agreements relating to Activities in Outer Space' *UNOOSA* (available at: https://www.unoosa.org/oosa/en/ourwork/spacelaw/treaties/status/index.html).

UNOOSA, 'Working Group on Legal Aspects of Space Resource Activities' *UNOOSA* (available at: https://www.unoosa.org/oosa/en/ourwork/copuos/lsc/space-resources/index.html).

UNOOSA, 'Working Group on the Definition and Delimitation of Outer Space of the Legal Subcommittee' *UNOOSA* (available at: https://www.unoosa.org/oosa/en/ourwork/copuos/lsc/ddos/index.html).

UNOOSA, 'Notifications to the UN' UNOOSA (available at https://www.unoosa.org/oosa/sk/spaceobjectregister/submissions/states-organisations.html).

UNOOSA, 'United Nations Register of Objects Launched into Outer Space' UNOOSA (availa-ble at https://www.unoosa.org/oosa/sk/spaceobjectregister/index.html).

Urban R, 'The 20 Most Important UK Space Companies' *Space Impulse* (24 April 2023) (available at: https://spaceimpulse.com/2023/04/24/the-20-most-important-uk-space-companies/).

US Department of Defense *Quadrennial Defense Review* (2014) (available at: https://www.acq.osd.mil/ncbdp/docs/2014_Quadrennial_Defense_Review.pdf).

Virgin Galactic, 'Virgin Galactic successfully completes first fully crewed spaceflight' *Virgin Galactic* (available at: https://www.virgingalactic.com/news/virgin-galactic-successfully-completes-first-fully-crewed-spaceflight).

Venditti B, Smith M, 'SPACE Which Companies Own the Most Satellites?' *Visual Capitalist* (available at: https://www.visualcapitalist.com/who-owns-the-most-satellites/).

WECOOP, 'EU Environment Policy' *WECOOP* (available at: https://wecoop.eu/regional-knowledge-centre/eu-policies-regulations/).

White House, 'National Space Council' *White House* (available at: https://www.whitehouse.gov/spacecouncil/).

World Commission on Environment and Development: Our Common Future (1987), Oxford: Oxford University Press.

Wormbs N, Källstrand G, 'A Short History of Swedish Space Activities' *ESA* (December 2007) (available at: https://www.esa.int/esapub/hsr/HSR_39.pdf).

Treaties, Other Instruments and Documents

Treaties

Agreement between the Government of the Russian Federation and the Cabinet of Ministers of Ukraine on Technology Safeguards Associated with Cooperation in the Field of the Exploration and Use of Outer Space for Peaceful Purposes and in the Development and Operation of Space Rocket and Rocket Equipment, Signed in Moscow on 11th of June 2009.

Agreement Between the United States of America and Other Governments Concerning Cooperation on the Civil International Space Station, 29 January 1998 (entered into force on 27 March 2001).

Agreement Governing the Activities of States on the Moon and Other Celestial Bodies, 5 December 1979, 1363 UNTS 3 (entered into force on 11 July 1984).

Agreement on the Rescue of Astronauts, the Return of Astronauts and the Return of Objects Launched into Outer Space, 19 December 1967, 672 UNTS 119 (entered into force on 3 December 1968).

Basel Convention on the Control of Transboundary Movements of Hazardous Wastes and Their Disposal, 22 March 1989, 1673 UNTS 125 (entered into force 5 May 1992).

Bilateral and Multilateral Agreements Governing Space Activities: Disintegration of Cosmos 954 Over Canadian Territory in 1978, Protocol Between The Government of Canada and The Government of the Union Of Soviet Socialist Republics, 2 April 1981 (entered into force on the date of signature).

Buenos Aires International Instrument on Damage caused by Space Debris, August 1994, reprinted in 23 Journal of Space Law 113 (1995).

Consolidated Version of the Treaty on the Functioning of the European Union, OJ C 326, 26 October 2012.

Constitution and Convention of the International Telecommunication Union, 22 December 1992, 1825/1826 UNTS (entered into force on 1 July 1994).

Convention for Protection of Cultural Property in the Event of Armed Conflict 1954, 249 UNTS 240 (entered into force on 7 August 1956).

Convention for the Prevention of Marine Pollution from Land-Based Sources, 4 June 1974, 1546 UNTS 119 (entered into force on 6 May 1978).

Convention for the Unification of Certain Rules for International Carriage by Air (Montreal Convention), 28 May 1999, 2242 UNTS 309 (entered into force on 4 November 2003).

Convention IV Respecting the Laws and Customs of War on Land and Its Annex: Regulation Concerning the Laws and Customs of War on Land (Hague Regulations), 1899 and 1907, 187 CTS 227 (entered into force on 26 January 1910).

Convention on Biological Diversity, 5 June 1992, 1760 UNTS 79 (entered into force on 29 December 1993).

Convention on International Interests in Mobile Equipment, 16 November 2001, 2307 UNTS 285.

Convention on International Liability for Damage Caused by Space Objects, 29 March 1972, 961 UNTS 187 (entered into force on 1 September 1972).

Convention on International Trade in Endangered Species of Wild Fauna and Flora, 3 March 1973, 993 UNTS 243 (entered into force on 1 July 1975).

Convention on the Prevention and Punishment of the Crime of Genocide, 9 December 1948, 78 UNTS 277 (entered into force on 12 January 1951).

Convention on the Prohibition of Military and Other Hostile Use of Environmental Modification Techniques (ENMOD), 10 December 1976, 1108 UNTS 151 (entered into force on 5 October 1978).

Declaration of the United Nations Conference on the Human Environment (Stockholm Declaration), 15 December 1972.

Energy Charter Treaty (opened for signature 17 December 1994, entered into force 16 April 1998) (ECT).

ESA Convention and Council Rules of Procedure (SP-1337/EN, November 2019).

GATT 1994: General Agreement on Tariffs and Trade 1994, 15 April 1994, Marrakesh Agreement Establishing the World Trade Organization, Annex 1A, 1867 U.N.T.S. 187, 33 I.L.M. 1153 (1994).

ILC Draft articles on Prevention of Transboundary Harm from Hazardous Activities with Commentaries (DAPTHAA), Yearbook of the International Law Commission, Volume II, Part II (2001).

ILC Draft Code of Crimes Against the Peace and Security of Mankind, Yearbook of the International Law Commission (1991).

International Convention for the Prevention of Pollution from Ships, 2 November 1973, 1340 UNTS 61 (entered into force on 2 October 1983).

International Convention for the Suppression of the Financing of Terrorism, 9 December 1999, 2178 UNTS 197 (entered into force on 10 April 2002).

Kyoto Protocol to the United Nations Framework Convention on Climate Change, 11 December 1997, 2303 UNTS 148 (entered into force on 16 February 2005).

Montreal Protocol on Substances that Deplete the Ozone Layer 1522 UNTS 3 (entered into force on 20 January 1989).

Optional Protocol to the Convention against Torture and Other Cruel, Inhuman or Degrading Treatment or Punishment (OPCAT), 18 December 2002, 2375 UNTS 237 (entered into force 22 June 2006).

Outer Space Treaty (Treaty on Principles Governing the Activities of States in the Exploration and Use of Outer Space, Including the Moon and Other Celestial Bodies), 27 January 1967, 610 UNTS 205 (entered into force on 10 October 1967).

Protocol I to the Geneva Convention, 8 June 1977, 1125 UNTS 3 (entered into force on 7 December 1978).

Protocol II Additional to the Geneva Conventions of 12 August 1949 and Relating to the Protection of Victims of Non-International Armed Conflicts, 8 June 1977, 1125 UNTS 609 (entered into force on 7 December 1978).

Protocol to the Convention on International Interests in Mobile Equipment on Matters Specific to Space Assets, 9 March 2012.

Responsibility of States for Internationally Wrongful Acts (ARSIWA), Yearbook of the International Law Commission (2001).

Rome Statute of the International Criminal Court, 17 July 1998, 2187 UNTS 38544 (entered into force on 1 July 2002).

Statute of the International Court of Justice, 26 June 1945, 33 UNTS 993 (entered into force on 24 October 1945).

The Convention on International Civil Aviation, 7 December 1944, 15 UNTS 295 (entered into force on 4 April 1947).

Treaty Banning Nuclear Weapon Tests in the Atmosphere, 5 August 1963, 480 UNTS 43 (entered into force on 10 October 1963).

Treaty on Principles Governing the Activities of States in the Exploration and Use of Outer Space, including the Moon and Other Celestial Bodies, 27 January 1967, 610 UNTS 205 (entered into force on 10 October 1967).

United Nations Agreement Governing the Activities of States on the Moon and Other Celestial Bodies, 5 December 1979, 1363 UNTS 3 (entered into force on 11 July 1984).

United Nations Convention on the Law of the Sea (UNCLOS), 10 December 1982, 1833/1834/1835 UNTS 3 (entered into force on 16 November 1994).

United Nations Framework Convention on Climate Change, 9 May 1992, 1771 UNTS 107 (entered into force on 21 March 1994).

Vienna Convention for the Protection of the Ozone Layer, 22 March 1985, 1513 UNTS 323 (entered into force on 22 September 1988).

Vienna Convention on the Law of Treaties, 23 May 1969, 1155 UNTS 331 (entered into force 27 January 1980).

Documents Prepared by or for the Uncopuos and/or UNOOSA

Committee on the Peaceful Uses of Outer Space, *Compendium on Space Debris Mitigation Standards Adopted by States and International Organizations,* UN Doc. A/AC.105/2023/CRP.12 (15 May 2023).

Committee on the Peaceful Uses of Outer Space, Definition and delimitation of outer space, UN Doc. A/AC.105/C.2/2022/CRP.24 (6 April 2022).

Committee on the Peaceful Uses of Outer Space, *Guidelines for the Long-term Sustainability of Outer Space Activities*, UN Doc. A/AC.105/2018/CRP.20 (28 June 2018).

Committee on the Peaceful Uses of Outer Space, Information on the activities of international intergovernmental and on-governmental organizations relating to space law, UN Doc. A/AC.105/C.2/2013/CRP.6 (8-19 April 2013).

Committee on the Peaceful Uses of Outer Space, *Report of the Committee on the Peaceful Uses of Outer Space: Sixty-fifth session*, UN Doc. A/77/20 (1-10 June 2022).

Committee on the *Peaceful Uses of Outer Space, Report of the Committee on the Peaceful Uses of Outer Space*, UN Doc. A/62/20 (2007).

Committee on the Peaceful Uses of Outer Space, *Report of the Legal Sub-Committee on the Work of its Fourth Session (20 September–1 October 1965) to the Committee on the peaceful uses of outer space*, UN Doc. A/AC.105/29 (1 October 1965).

Committee on the Peaceful Uses of Outer Space, *Report of the Scientific and Technical Subcommittee on its 42nd session, held in Vienna from 21 February to 4 March 2005*, UN Doc. A/AC.105/848 (21 February–4 March 2005).

Committee on the Peaceful Uses of Outer Space, *Schematic Overview of National Regulatory Frameworks for Space Activities*, UN Doc. A/AC.105/C.2/2023/CRP.28 (20 March 2023).

Committee on the Peaceful Uses of Outer Space, *Space Debris Mitigation Guidelines of the Committee on the Peaceful Uses of Outer Space*, UN Doc. ST/SPACE/49 (2010).

Committee on the Peaceful Uses of Outer Space, *Technical Report on Space Debris*, UN Doc. A/AC.105/720 (1999).

Inter-Agency Space Debris Coordination Committee (IADC), *Inter-Agency Space Debris Coordination Committee (IADC) Space Debris Mitigation Guidelines, 2002; revised 2007; revision 2 2020*, IADC-02-01 (2020).

Office for Outer Space Affairs, *Press Release: New Partnership between UN Office for Outer Space Affairs, UN Development Programme and Brazilian Space Agency*, UN Doc. UNIS/OS/575 (15 December 2022) (available at: https://www.unoosa.org/oosa/en/informationfor/media/2022-unis-os-575.html).

Office for Outer Space Affairs, *United Nations Treaties and Principles on Outer Space and related General Assembly Resolutions*, United Nations publication, October 2009.

Schematic Overview of National Regulatory Frameworks for Space Activities, UNCOPUOS, UN Doc. A/AC.105/C.2/2024/CRP.10 (15 April 2024).

Statement of Australia to the UNCOPUOS in: Committee on the Peaceful Uses of Outer Space, *Compendium of space debris mitigation standards adopted by States and international organizations*, UN Doc. A/AC.105/C.2/2021/CRP.19 (4 June 2021).

Statement of Austria to the UNCOPUOS in: Committee on the Peaceful Uses of Outer Space, *Compendium of space debris mitigation standards adopted by States and international organizations*, UN Doc. A/AC.105/C.2/2021/CRP.19 (4 June 2021).

Statement of Azerbaijan to the UNCOPUOS in: Committee on the Peaceful Uses of Outer Space, *Compendium of space debris mitigation standards adopted by States and international organizations*, UN Doc. A/AC.105/C.2/2021/CRP.19 (4 June 2021).

Statement of Belgium to the UNCOPUOS in: Committee on the Peaceful Uses of Outer Space, *Compendium of space debris mitigation standards adopted by States and international organizations*, UN Doc. A/AC.105/C.2/2021/CRP.19 (4 June 2021).

Statement of Canada to the UNCOPUOS in: Committee on the Peaceful Uses of Outer Space, *Compendium of space debris mitigation standards adopted by States and international organizations*, UN Doc. A/AC.105/C.2/2021/CRP.19 (4 June 2021).

Statement of Denmark to the UNCOPUOS in: Committee on the Peaceful Uses of Outer Space, *Compendium of space debris mitigation standards adopted by States and international organizations*, UN Doc. A/AC.105/C.2/2021/CRP.19 (4 June 2021).

Statement of ESA to UNCOPUOS in: Committee on the Peaceful Uses of Outer Space, *Compendium of space debris mitigation standards adopted by States and international organizations*, UN Doc. A/AC.105/C.2/2021/CRP.19 (4 June 2021).

Statement of Finland to the UNCOPUOS in: Committee on the Peaceful Uses of Outer Space, *Compendium of space debris mitigation standards adopted by States and international organizations*, UN Doc. A/AC.105/C.2/2021/CRP.19 (4 June 2021).

Statement of France to the UNCOPUOS in: Committee on the Peaceful Uses of Outer Space, *Compendium of space debris mitigation standards adopted by States and international organizations*, UN Doc. A/AC.105/C.2/2021/CRP.19 (4 June 2021).

Statement of Germany to the UNCOPUOS in: Committee on the Peaceful Uses of Outer Space, *Compendium of space debris mitigation standards adopted by States and international organizations*, UN Doc. A/AC.105/C.2/2021/CRP.19 (4 June 2021).

Statement of Greece to the UNCOPUOS in: Committee on the Peaceful Uses of Outer Space, *Compendium of space debris mitigation standards adopted by States and international organizations*, UN Doc. A/AC.105/C.2/2021/CRP.19 (4 June 2021).

Statement of India to the UNCOPUOS in: Committee on the Peaceful Uses of Outer Space, *Compendium of space debris mitigation standards adopted by States and international organizations*, UN Doc. A/AC.105/C.2/2021/CRP.19 (4 June 2021).

Statement of Italy to the UNCOPUOS in: Committee on the Peaceful Uses of Outer Space, *Compendium of space debris mitigation standards adopted by States and international organizations*, UN Doc. A/AC.105/C.2/2013/CRP.6 (26 March 2013).

Statement of Japan to the UNCOPUOS in: Committee on the Peaceful Uses of Outer Space, *Compendium of space debris mitigation standards adopted by States and international organizations*, UN Doc. A/AC.105/C.2/2021/CRP.19 (4 June 2021).

Statement of Peru to the UNCOPUOS in the UNCOPUOS, Compendium of space debris mitigation standards adopted by States and international organizations, UN Doc. A/AC.105/C.2/2021/CRP.19 (4 June 2021).

Statement of the Netherlands to the UNCOPUOS in: Committee on the Peaceful Uses of Outer Space, *Compendium of space debris mitigation standards adopted by States and international organizations*, UN Doc. A/AC.105/C.2/2021/CRP.19 (4 June 2021).

Statement of the Russian Federation to the UNCOPUOS in: Committee on the Peaceful Uses of Outer Space, *Compendium of space debris mitigation standards adopted by States and international organizations*, UN Doc. A/AC.105/C.2/2021/CRP.19 (4 June 2021).

Statement of the United Kingdom of Great Britain and Northern Ireland to the UNCOPUOS in: Committee on the Peaceful Uses of Outer Space, *Compendium of space debris mitigation standards adopted by States and international organizations*, UN Doc. A/AC.105/C.2/2021/CRP.19 (4 June 2021).

Statement of the USA to the UNCOPUOS in: Committee on the Peaceful Uses of Outer Space, *Compendium of space debris mitigation standards adopted by States and international organizations*, UN Doc. A/AC.105/C.2/2021/CRP.19 (4 June 2021).

Statement of Ukraine to the UNCOPUOS (regarding Article 9 of the Law of Ukraine) (15 November 1996) in: Committee on the Peaceful Uses of Outer Space, *Compendium of space debris mitigation standards adopted by States and international organizations*, UN Doc. A/AC.105/C.2/2021/CRP.19 (4 June 2021).

Statement of Ukraine to the UNCOPUOS in: Committee on the Peaceful Uses of Outer Space, *Compendium of space debris mitigation standards adopted by States and international organizations*, UN Doc. A/AC.105/C.2/2021/CRP.19 (4 June 2021).

UNOOSA, International Space Law: United Nations Instruments (United Nations, 2017).

UN General Assembly Documents

United Nations General Assembly, *Declaration on International Cooperation in the Exploration and Use of Outer Space for the Benefit and in the Interest of All States, Taking into Particular Account the Needs of Developing Countries*, UN Doc. 51/122 (13. December 1996).

United Nations General Assembly, *Fiftieth anniversary of the first United Nations Conference on the Exploration and Peaceful Uses of Outer Space: space as a driver of sustainable development*, UN Doc. A/RES/73/6 (26 October 2018).

United Nations General Assembly, *International co-operation in the peaceful uses of outer space*, UN Doc. A/RES/1721 (XVI) (20 December 1961).

United Nations General Assembly, *International cooperation in the peaceful uses of outer space*, UN Doc. A/RES/73/91 (7 December 2018).

United Nations General Assembly, *International cooperation in the peaceful uses of outer space*, UN Doc. A/RES/77/121 (15 December 2022).

United Nations General Assembly, *Permanent sovereignty over natural resources,* UN Doc. A/RES/1803 (XVII) (14 December 1962).

United Nations General Assembly, *Principle relating to remote sensing of the Earth from Outer Space*, UN Doc. A/RES/41/65 (3 December 1986).

United Nations General Assembly, *Principles Relevant to the Use of Nuclear Power Sources in Outer Space*, UN Doc. A/RES/47/68 (14 December 1992).

United Nations General Assembly, *Question of the Peaceful Use of Outer Space,* UN Doc. A/RES?1348 (XIII) (13 December 1958).

United Nations General Assembly, *Recommendations on national legislation relevant to the peaceful exploration and use of outer space,* UN Doc. A/RES/68/74 (11 December 2013).

United Nations General Assembly, *Report of the Committee on the Peaceful Uses of Outer Space*, UN Doc. A/RES/61/20 (2007).

United Nations General Assembly, Report of the International Law Commission on the work of its fifty-third session, 23 April–1 June and 2 July–10 August 2001, Official Records of the General Assembly, Fifty-sixth session, Supplement No.10, UN Doc. A/56/10 (2001) (23 April–1 June and 2 July–1 August 2001).

United Nations General Assembly, *Space and global health*, UN Doc. A/RES/77/120 (15 December 2022).

United Nations General Assembly, *The human right to a clean, healthy and sustainable environment*, UN Doc. A/RES/76/300 (28 July 2022).

United Nations General Assembly, *World Charter for Nature*, UN Doc. A/RES/37/7 (28 October 1982).

Other International Instruments and Documents

Agreement signed between national satellite operator Azercosmos and France's Airbus DS in 2014.

Council of Europe, *Model Act on the Protection of the Environment 1994*, Dela/Model Act (94)1 (1994).

Economic Cooperation Agreement between the Republic of Azerbaijan and the Russian Federation, Space Data Receipt Complex UNISCAN-24.

ESA Contract 14471/00/D/HK: Update of the ESA Space Debris Mitigation Handbook, Ref: QINETIQ/KI/SPACE/CR021539.

ESA Director General's Office (2014), *Space Debris Mitigation Policy for Agency* Projects, ESA/ADMIN/IPOL(2014)2.

ESA Space Debris Mitigation Policy for Agency Projects, EUR SPACE AGENCY, ESA/ADMIN/IPOL (2014)2 (28 March 2014).

ESA, ESA Space Debris Mitigation Requirements, Reference: ESSB-ST-U-007 Issue 1 (30 October 2023).

ESA, ESA's Annual Space Environment Report, ESA Space Debris Office Report (22 April 2022).

ESA, Zero Debris Charter (2022).

ESPI, ESPI Report 82 – Space Environment Capacity (April 2022).

ESPI, Executive brief No. 11 updated: Delimitation of Outer Space (1 March 2017).

European Code of Conduct for Space Debris Mitigation (Issue 1.0) (28 June 2004).

European Space Agency (ESA), (resolution for a European Policy on the Protection of the Space Environment from Debris), ESA Res. E/SA/C/(2000)93.

European Space Policy Institute (ESPI), 'ESPI Perspectives 51: Space Activities Ukraine Looking for New Developments' (August 2011).

European Space Policy Institute (ESPI), 'Executive Brief No. 57' (5 May 2022).

Hague Institute for the Internationalisation of Law, 'General Rules and Principles of International Criminal Procedure and Recommendations of the International Expert Framework' (October 2011) (available at: https://www.legal-tools.org/doc/ee4de3/pdf/).

ICRC (2020), *Guidelines on the Protection of the Natural Environment in Armed Conflict,* Geneva 2020.

ICRC (2021), *The Potential Human Cost of the Use of Weapons in Outer Space and the Protection Afforded by International Humanitarian Law: Position paper submitted by the International Committee of the Red Cross to the Secretary-General of the United Nations on the issues outlined in General Assembly Resolution 75/36* (available at:https://www.icrc.org/en/document/potential-human-cost-outer-space-weaponization-ihl-protection).

ICRC (2022), *Constraints under International Law on Military Operations in Outer Space during Armed Conflicts* (Working paper submitted by the International Committee of the Red Cross to the open-ended working group on reducing space threats through norms, rules and principles of responsible behaviours, as convened under United Nations General Assembly Resolution 76/231, and to the Secretary-General of the United Nations in reply to General Assembly Resolution 76/230 on "Further practical measures for the prevention of an arms race in outer space").

ICRC, Convention (III) relative to the Treatment of Prisoners of War. Geneva, 12 August 1949, Commentary 2020 (available at: https://ihl-databases.icrc.org/en/ihl-treaties/gciii-1949/toc/commentary/2020?activeTab=undefined).

International Law Association, *Resolution No. 6/2012 on Space Law (26-30 August 2012), including Annex: Sofia Guidelines for a Model Law on National Space Legislation*, 6/2012 (30 August 2012).

International Law Commission, *Identification of customary international law*, UN Doc. A/CN.4/691 (9 February 2016).

International Law Commission, *Identification of customary international law*, UN Doc. A/CN.4/L.872 (30 May 2016).

International Law Commission, *Report of the ILC to the fifty-eight session of the General Assembly*, UN Doc. A/61/10 (2006).

International Panel on Climate Change, *Sixth Assessment Report of the Intergovernmental Panel on Climate Change*, IPCC AR6 WGI (2021).

International Standardisation Organisation, *ISO Space Debris Mitigation Requirements*, ISO 24113 (last updated: 24113:2023) (2023).

International Telecommunications Union (ITU), *Recommendation on Environmental Protection of the Geostationary Satellite Orbit*, ITU–R S.1003-2 (December 2010) (available at: [link](https://www.unoosa.org/documents/pdf/spacelaw/sd/R-REC-S1003-2-201012-IPDF-E.pdf)).

Letter from United Nations Special Procedures to Saudi Arabia and to companies operating on behalf of Saudi Arabia in relation to the NEOM project, April 2023.

Note verbale dated 18 February 2004 from the Permanent Mission of the Netherlands to the United Nations (Vienna) addressed to the Secretary-General, UN Doc. A/AC.105/824.

Note verbale dated 18 February 2004 from the Permanent Mission of the Netherlands to the United Nations (Vienna) addressed to the Secretary-General, UN Doc. A/AC.105/824.

Note verbale dated 29 July 2003 from the Permanent Mission of the Netherlands to the United Nations (Vienna) addressed to the Secretary-General, UN Doc. A/AC.105/806.

Note verbale dated 29 July 2003 from the Permanent Mission of the Netherlands to the United Nations (Vienna) addressed to the Secretary-General, UN Doc. A/AC.105/806.

Note verbale dated 3 December 2021 from the Permanent Mission of China to the United Nations (Vienna) addressed to the Secretary-General, UN Doc. A/AC.105/1262 (Dec. 10, 2021).

OECD, Recommendation of the Council on Guiding Principles concerning International Economic Aspects of Environmental Policies, 2020.

OHCHR, *Guiding Principles on Business and Human Rights: Implementing the United Nations 'Protect, Respect and Remedy' Framework*, 2011.

Permanent Court of Arbitration (PCA), Optional Rules for Arbitration of Disputes Relating to Outer Space Activities (Effective 6 December 2011).

Permanent Court of Arbitration, Optional Rules for Arbitration Between International Organizations and Private Parties (1996).

Permanent Court of Arbitration, Optional Rules for Arbitration of Disputes Relating to Outer Space Activities (6 December 2011).

Proposal of the Union of Socialist Soviet Republics: Declaration of the Basic Principles governing the Activities of States pertaining to the Exploration and Use of Outer Space, UN Doc. A/AC.105/C.2/L.1 (1962).

Report of the Committee on the Peaceful Uses of Outer Space, UN Doc. A/62/20, General Assembly Official Records Sixty-Second Session Supplement No. 20 (2007).

Report of the Working Group on international liability for injurious consequences arising out of acts not prohibited by international law, A/CN.4/L.284 and Corr.1, New York, 1978.

Report of United Nations sixty-second session of the Committee on the Peaceful Uses of Outer Space, A/62/20.

Seventh report of the Special Rapporteur Barboza on international liability for injurious consequences arising out of acts not prohibited by international law, UN Doc. A/CN.4/437 and Corr.1, New York, 1991.

Space Sustainability Adoption Notice of ISO 24113: Space Systems Space Debris Mitigation Requirements, Eur. Cooperation for Space Standardisation, ECSS-U-AS-10C (10 February 2012).

SpaceX Commercial Crew Transportation Capability Contract (CCtCap) NNK14MA74C, signed between NASA and SpaceX (available at: https://www.nasa.gov/sites/default/files/files/CCtCap_SpaceX_508.pdf).

SpaceX, Mars and Beyond, SpaceX (available at: https://www.spacex.com/humanspaceflight/mars/).

SpaceX, The Gateway to Mars, SpaceX (available at: https://www.spacex.com/vehicles/starship/assets/media/Starbase%20Overview.pdf).

The Artemis Accords (2020), available at https://www.nasa.gov/specials/artemis-accords/img/Artemis-Accords-signed-13Oct2020.pdf.

UNIDROIT Principles of International Commercial Law (International Institute for the Unification of Private Law, 1994).

United Nations Human Rights Committee, *Views adopted by the Committee under article 5 (4) of the Optional Protocol, concerning communication No. 2751/2016*, (Communication No. 2751/2016, Views of 25 July 2019), UN Doc. CCPR/C/126/D/2751/2016 (20 September 2019).

United Nations Human Rights Council, *Situation of human rights in Yemen, including violations and abuses since September 2014*, UN Doc. A/HRC/42/CRP.1 (3 September 2019).

United Nations Mission in the Republic of South Sudan (UNMISS), Conflict in South Sudan: A Human Rights Report (8 May 2014).

United Nations Secretary-General, *Report of the Secretary-General's Panel of Experts on Accountability in Sri Lanka* (31 March 2011).

United Nations Security Council, *Resolution 2235*, UN Doc. S/RES/2235 (7 August 2015).

United Nations Security Council, *Third Report of the Organization for the Prohibition of Chemical Weapons – United Nations Joint Investigative Mechanism*, UN Doc. S/2016/738/Rev.1 (24 August 2016).

National and Regional Instruments

Algeria

Presidential Decree No. 02-49 'Creation, organization and functioning of the Algerian Space Agency (ASAL)' of 16 January 2002.

Presidential Decree No. 06-225 'Ratifying the Convention for Damage Caused by Space Objects' of 24 June 2006.

Presidential Decree No. 06-468 'Ratifying the Convention on Registration of Objects Launched into Outer Space' of 11 December 2006.

Argentina

Decree PEN No. 125/1995: Creates the 'National Registry of Objects Launched into Outer Space' under the Authority of the National Commission of Space Activities (CONAE).

DNU Decree No. 267/2015: 'Creates the National Communications Entity (ENACOM)', authority on communications that grants the radiofrequency licenses'.

Law No 23.335: Approves the 'Convention on International Liability for Damage Caused by Space Objects' by the United Nations (UN) signed by the Argentine Republic.

Law No. 17.989: Approve the 'Treaty on Principles Governing the Activities of States in the Exploration and Use of Outer Space, including the Moon and Other Celestial Bodies' and the 'Agreement on the Rescue of Astronauts, the Return of Astronauts and the Return of Objects Launched into Outer Space' by the Organization of the United Nations (UN) signed by the Republic of Argentina.

Law No. 24.158 Approves the 'Convention on Registration of Objects Launched into Outer Space' by the United Nations (UN) signed by the Republic of Argentina.

Law No. 26.092: 'Creates the Argentine Company of Satellite Solutions Sociedad Anonima AR-SAT. Social Statute. Grant said company the authorization to use the orbital position 81° West Longitude and its associated frequency bands. Law No. 26.306: 'Regime of the Registry of Cultural Heritage on Meteorites and other celestial bodies that are on or enter in the future the Argentine territory, its airspace and jurisdictional waters'.

Law No. 27.078: 'Argentina Digital. Information Technology and communications'.

Law No. 27.208 'Declares the development of the satellite industry as a state policy and a national priority regarding geostationary telecommunications satellites, and approved the Argentine Geostationary Satellite Plan 2015-2035 to be executed by the company AR-SAT'.

National Decree No. 995/91, Creation of the National Commission on Space Activities (28 May 1991).

PEN Decree No. 1330/99 Modifies PEN Decree No. 2076/94 and Establishes the National Space Plan 1997-2008, as well as that the actions provided for in it have the character of Strategic Plan of the National Commission for Space Activities.

PEN Decree No. 2076/94: First National Space Plan that declares space activity as an area of scientific-technological activity and as a national priority, and CONAE's strategical plan.

PEN Decree No. 532/05 Declares the development of space activity as a State policy and a national priority. It establishes that this plan and the actions planned for said period have the character of Strategic Plan of the National Commission for Space Activities.

Armenia

Basic Law No. HO-152-N on Space-related Activities of the Republic of Armenia (Original Source: RAPT 2020.04.01/30(1585) Art. 356), Yerevan: RA National Assembly (Date of Signature by RA President 26.03.2020, Date of entry into force 11.04.2020).

Australia

Space Launches and Returns Act 2018 (No. 74, 2023) (as amended and in force on 18 October 2023)Maximum Probable Loss Methodology.

Space (Launches and Returns) (General) Rules 2019 made under section 110 of the Space (Launches and Returns) Act 2018.Space (Launches and Returns) (High Power Rocket) Rules 2019.

Space Activities Act 1998 (No. 123, 1998) (as amended, taking into account amendments up to Act No. 8 of 2010).

Austria

Austrian Explanatory Memorandum, Zu § 4 Zu Abs. 1 Zu Z 5.

Federal Law on the Authorization of Space Activities and the Establishment of a National Registry (Outer Space Act), BGBl. I No. 132/2011 of 27 December 2011.

Regulation of the Federal Minister for Transport, Innovation and Technology in Implementation of the Federal Law on the Authorization of Space Activities and the Establishment of a National Space Registry (Outer Space Regulation; Bundesgesetzblatt II Nr. 36/2015 of 26 February 2015) issued on the basis of § 12 of Outer Space Act (Bundesgesetzblatt. I No. 132/2011).

Azerbaijan

The Charter of 'Space Agency of the Republic of Azerbaijan (Azercosmos)', adopted by decision #54 of the Cabinet of the Ministries of the Republic of Azerbaijan (26 February 2022).

Order #443 of the President of the Republic of Azerbaijan (17 August 2009) on 'The State Program on Creation and Development of Space Industry in the Republic of Azerbaijan'.

Order #696 of the President of the Republic of Azerbaijan (15 November 2018) on 'The State Program for the development of the satellite Earth observation services in the Republic of Azerbaijan'.

Belarus

Decree 609 of the President of the Republic of Belarus (22 December 2004).

Belgium

Law of 17 September 2005 on the Activities of Launching, Flight Operation or Guidance of Space Objects (*consolidated text as revised by the Law of 1 December 2013 (B.O.J. of 15 January 2014)*).

Royal Decree implementing certain provisions of the Law of 17 September 2005 on the activities of launching, flight operations and guidance of space objects form the legal basis for the regulation of space activities.

Canada

Canadian Space Agency Act (S.C. 1990, c. 13) (10 May 1990).

Client Procedures Circular (CPC) 2-6-02 – Procedure for the Submission of Applications for Spectrum Licenses for Space Stations issued by the Innovation, Science and Economic Development Department of Canada.

Government of Canada, 'Canada's Views on Reducing Space Threats through norms, rules and principles of Responsible Behaviour' (2021), available at: https://documents.unoda.org/wp-content/uploads/2022/05/EN-Canada-working-Paper-on-Norms-75-36.pdf.

Remote Sensing Space Systems Act (S.C. 2005, c. 45) (amended 5 April 2007).

Chile

Supreme Decree No. 338: Establishment of a Presidential Advisory Committee known as the Chilean Space Agency (17 July 2001).

China

Environmental Protection Law of the People's Republic of China (adopted on 26th December 1989).

Information Office of the State Council of the People's Republic of China, Environmental Protection in China, Permanent Mission of the People's Republic of China to the United Nations Office at Geneva and Other International Organizations in Switzerland (June 1996).

Laws of the People's Republic of China, Interim Measures on the Administration of Permits for Civil Space Launch Projects (21 November 2002), available at: http://www.asianlii.org/cn/legis/cen/laws/imotaopfcslp771/, Art. 6(d).

The 2000 China Space White Paper.

The 2006 China Space White Paper.

The 2011 China Space White Paper.

The 2016 China Space White Paper.

The 2021 China Space White Paper.

Colombia

Decree 2442 (18 July 2006) on the Creation of the Colombian Commission of Space (CCE).

Costa Rica

Law No. 9770 (29 October 2019) on the Creation of the Registry of Spatial Objects.

Law No. 9960 (8 February 2021) on the creation of the Costa Rican Space Agency.

Denmark

Executive Order on requirements in connection with approval of activities in outer space, etc., No. 552 of 31 May 2016.

Outer Space Act (Act no. 409 of 11 May 2016).

Ecuador

Executive Decree No. 1246 (19 July 2012) on the Creation of the Ecuadorian Space Institute.

EU

Commission implementing decision (EU) 2022/1245 of 15 July 2022.

Regulation (EU) 2021/695.

Regulation (EU) 2021/696.

Regulation (EU) 2023/588.

Regulation (EU) No 1321/2004.

Regulation (EU) No. 912/2010.

Finland

Act on Space Activities (63/2018).

Criminal Code (39/1889).
Decree of the Ministry of Economic Affairs and Employment on Space Activities (74/2018).
Publication of the Ministry of employment and the economy, Finland's space strategy for years 2013 to 2020.
Tort Liability Act (412/1974).

France

Decree No. 2008-518 of June 3, 2008, March 31, 2011.
Decree No. 2009-643 of June 9, 2009.
Decree No. 2009-1657 of December 24, 2009.
Decree No. 62-153 of February 10, 1962.
French Finance Act 2024 (La loi de finances (LOLF)) 2024.
French Space Operations Act No. 2008-518 (2008) (Law No. 2008-518 of June 3, 2008 relating to space operations (1)).

Germany

Raumfahrtaufgabenübertragungsgesetz, 22 August 1998, BGBl. I, 2510.
Telekommunikationsgesetz, 23 June 2021, BGBl. I, 1858, as amended 10 September 2021, BGBl. I, 414.
2590 Bundesgesetzblatt Jahrgang 2007 Teil I Nr. 58, ausgegeben zu Bonn am 28. November 2007 – Gesetz zum Schutz vor Gefährdung der Sicherheit der Bundesrepublik Deutschland durch das Verbreiten von hochwertigen Erdfernerkundungsdaten (Satellitendatensicherheitsgesetz – SatDSiG).

Greece

Law 4508/2017 (22 December 2017), on 'Authorization of space activities, Registration in the National Register of Space Objects- Establishment of a Greek Space Organization and other provisions' (amended by Law 4712/2020/146/A'/29-07-2020) (29. July 2020).

India

Government of India, Department of Space, No.E.11020/2/2015-Sec-VI (2015).
Indian Space Act Draft 2015.
Indian Space Policy 2023.

Indonesia

Governmental Regulation No. 11 (2018) on remote Sensing.
Indonesia Outer Space Law, Law No. 21 of 2013 on Space Activities.
Law No. 21 (2013) on Space Activities.

Presidential Regulation NO. 45 (2017) on National Plan on Space Activities year 2016-2040.

Israel

Israel's Statement to the LSC 2023 under General exchange of views (2023) (available at: https://www.unoosa.org/documents/pdf/copuos/lsc/2023/Statements/22_AM/3_Israel_22Mar_AM.pdf).

Italy

Law Decree No. 128, 4 June 2003, Reorganization of the Italian Space Agency (A.S.I.).

Law of the 12 July 2005, n. 153 Accession of the Italian Republic to the Convention on the registration of objects launched into outer space, made in New York on 14 January 1975 and its execution. (GU General Series n.177 of 01-08-2005).

Law No. 7, 11 January 2018 on Measures for the coordination of space and aerospace policy and provisions concerning the organization and operation of the Italian Space Agency (18G00025) (Official Gazette, General Series, No. 34, 10 February 2018).

Japan

Act No. 76 of 2016, the Act on the launch of artificial satellites, and the management of artificial satellites.

Act on Promotion of Business Activities Related to the Exploration and Development of Space Resources, Law No. 83 of 2021 (Space Resources Act) (23 June 2021) – Supp. Provisions Article 1.

Basic Space Law, Law No. 43 of 2008 (27 August 2008).

National Research and Development Agency Japan Aerospace Exploration Agency Act No. 161 (13 December 2002).

Kazakhstan

Law of the Republic of Kazakhstan on Space Activities, No. 528-IV (6 January 2012).

Kenya

Kenya Space Policy 2015 (April 2016).

Luxembourg

Law of 27 July 1991 on Electronic Media.

Law of 20 July 2017 on the exploration and use of space resources.

Law of 15 December 2020 relating to space activities.

Malaysia

Communications and Multimedia Act 1998.

Malaysian Space Board Bill 2022.
National Space Policy 2030.
Strategic Trade Act 2010.

New Zealand

Outer Space and High-altitude Activities Act 2017.
Outer Space and High-altitude Activities (Licenses and Permits) Regulations 2017.

Nigeria

National Space Research and Development Agency Act, Federal Republic of Nigeria Official Gazette Vol. 97, No.98, (30 August 2010), Government Notice No. 382.

Norway

Act on launching objects from Norwegian territory etc. into outer space, 13 June. No. 38. 1969.

Peru

Decree-Law No. 20643 (11 June 1974) on establishing the Comision Nacional de Investigacion y Desarrollo Aeroespacial – CONIDA.
Law No. 28799 'Declaring the establishment and operation of a National Centre for Satellite Imagery Operations' (Ley 28799, Que declara de interés nacional la creación, implementación y desarrollo de un Centro Nacional de Operaciones de Imágenes Satelitales).
Supreme Decree No. 008-2016-DE establishing the National Register of Objects Launched into Outer Space (Decreto Supremo N° 008-2016/DE que crea el Registro Nacional de Objetos Lanzados al Espacio Ultraterrestre).

Philippines

Act No. 3846. as amended (Radio Law).
Administrative Order No. 76 (2011).
Executive Order No. 1016 (1985).
Executive Order No. 127 (1998).
Executive Order No. 467 (1998) providing for a national policy on the operation and use of international satellite communications in the country.
Executive Order No. 467 (1998).
Executive Order No. 546 (1979).
Implementing Guidelines on International Satellite Communications of the National Telecommunications Commission.
Philippine Space Development and Utilization Policy and Creating the Philippine Space Agency, and for other purposes, republic Act No. 11363 (2019).

Presidential Decree No. 576-A.

Presidential Decree No. 930 (1976).

Republic Act No. 10692 (2015), An Act Providing for the Modernization of teh Philippine Atmospheric, geophysical and Astronomical Services Administration (PAGASA), providing Funds therefor for other purposes also known as The PAGASA Modernization Act of 2015.

Republic Act No. 10697 (2015).

Republic Act No. 10929 (2020).

Republic Act No. 3846 (1963).

Republic Act No. 7844 (1994).

Republic Act No. 7925 (Public Telecommunications Policy Act).

Republic Act No. 7925.

Republic Act No. 9516.

Poland

Dz. U. 2014 poz. 1533, USTAWA z dnia 26 września 2014 r. o Polskiej Agencji Kosmicznej.

Portugal

Decree-Law no. 16/2019, of 22 January, Legal regime of access to and exercise of space activities.

Regulation no. 697/2019, of 5 September, regulation on access to and exercise of space activities.

Republic of Korea

Aerospace Industry Development Promotion Act, Law No. 8852 (4 December 1987).

Space Development Promotion Act, Law No. 7538 (31 May 2005).

Space Liability Act, Law No. 8852 (21 December 2007).

Russian Federation

Act No. Pr-906, 'Fundamentals of the Russian Federation's State Policy in the Field of Space Activities for the Period up to 2030 and beyond' (19 April 2013).

Federal Law of the Russian Federation No. 162-FZ 'On Standardisation in the Russian Federation' (29 June 2015).Federal Law of the Russian Federation No. 215-FZ, 'On the State Corporation for Space Activities ROSCOSMOS' (13th July 2015).

Federal Law of the Russian Federation No. 216-FZ, 'On Amendments to Certain Legislative Acts of the Russian Federation Following the Adoption of the Federal Law on the State Space Corporation 'Roscosmos' of 13 July 2015' (8 July 2015) as amended by Federal Law No. 578-FZ (29 December 2022).

Outer Space Treaty R 52925-2018 (1 January 2019) on 'Space Technology Items. General Requirements for Space Vehicles for Near-Earth Space Debris Mitigation' (developed by the Federal State Unitary Enterprise Central Research Institute for Machine Building, approved by Order of the Federal Agency for Technical Regulation and Metrology on September 21, 2018 N 632-st), substitute GOuter Space Treaty R 52925-2008.

Slovenia

Decree on the Implementation of the Space Activities Act, Official Gazette of the Republic of Slovenia 122/22.

Space Activities Act, Official Gazette of the Republic of Slovenia, 43/22.

South Africa

Astronomy Geographic Advantage Act No. 31157 (17 June 2008), No. 21.

Space Affairs Act No. 1157 (2 July 1993), No. 84 – Statutes of the Republic of South Africa – Trade and Industry No. 84 of 1993 (6 September 1993).

Space Affairs Amendment Act No. 1530 (6 October 1995), No. 64.

South Korea

Space Liability Act, Law No. 8852 (21 December 2007).

Spain

Royal Decree 278/1995 (24 February 1995), establishing in the Kingdom of Spain the Registry foreseen in the Convention adopted by the United Nations General Assembly on 2nd November 1974.

Sweden

Act on Space Activities (1982:963).

Decree on Space Activities (1982:1069).

The Netherlands

Decree of 19 January 2015 expanding the scope of the Space Activities Act to include the control of unguided satellites (Unguided Satellites Decree).

Rules Concerning Space Activities and the Establishment of a Registry of Space Objects (Space Activities Act), in force since 1 January 2008.

Tunisia

Decree n°84-1125 (24 September 1984) (modified by decree n°931642 (9 August 1993)) on the creation of the National Commission of the Outer space.

Law 88-83 (11 June 1988) forming a National Mapping and Remote Sensing Centre of Tunisia (CNCT).

Turkey

2022-2030 National Space Programme Strategy Document (24 May 2022).

Presidential Decree on the Establishment of Turkish Space Agency (Türkiye Uzay Ajansı Hakkında Cumhurbaşkanlığı Kararnamesi) (13 December 2018).

Ukraine

Industrial Standard URKT-11.03 on 'Limitation of the Near-Earth Orbital debris Making at Operation of Space Technical Equipment' (19 July 2006).

Law of Ukraine (15 November 1996): Ordinance of the Supreme Soviet of Ukraine on Space Activity.

United Arab Emirates

Federal Law No. (12) (19 December 2019) on the Regulation of the Space Sector.

United Kingdom

UK Outer Space Act of 1968 (c. 38).

UK Space Industry Act of 2018 (c. 5).

UK Government, 'Press Release from 3. October 2022' (3 October 2022) (available at: https://www.gov.uk/government/news/responsible-space-behaviours-the-uk-commits-not-to-destructively-test-direct-ascent-anti-satellite-missiles).

United States of America

51 United States Code (USC).

Alien Tort Statute (codified in 1948 as 28 U.S.C. para. 1350).

FCC, FCC Grants SpaceX's Satellite Broadband Modification Application, Document FCC-21-48 (36 FCC Rcd) 7995 (11) (27 April 2021).

FCC, *Intelsat-22 Grant of Application for Satellite Space Systems Authorization with Attachment to Grant (IBFS) File No. SAT-LOA-20110929-00193* (2012).

FCC, Statement of Commissioner Michael O'Really, FCC 18-184.CC.

FCC, FCC Takes First Space Debris Enforcement Action, DOC-397412A1 (2 October 2023).

NOAA, 'Regulatory Affairs', (available at www.nesdis.noaa.gov/commercial-space/regulatory-affairs); 51 U.S.C. Sections 60101; CFR 15 Part 960.

Orbital Sustainability Act of 2023 – S.447 – 118th Congress (2023-2024).

U.S. Government, *Orbital Debris Mitigation Standard Practices* (November 2019 Update).

U.S., *Spurring Private Aerospace Competitiveness and Entrepreneurship Act* of 2015, Pub L No 114-90, 129 Stat 704 (2015) ('*US Commercial Space Launch Competitiveness Act*').

Cases

International Court of Justice

ICJ, *Application of the Convention on the Prevention and Punishment of the Crime of Genocide* (Bosnia and Herzegovina v. Serbia and Montenegro), Judgment of 11 July 1996 (ICJ Reports 1996, p. 595).

ICJ, *Barcelona Traction, Light and Power Company, Limited* (Belgium v. Spain), Judgment of 5 February 1970 (ICJ Reports 1970, p. 3).

ICJ, *Gabčikovo-Nagymaros Project* (Hungary v. Slovakia), Judgment of 25 September 1997 (ICJ Reports 1997, p. 7).

ICJ, *Military and Paramilitary Activities in and against Nicaragua* (Nicaragua v. United States of America), Judgment of 27 December 1986 (ICJ Reports 1986, p. 14).

ICJ, *Certain Activities Carried Out by Nicaragua in the Border Area (Costa Rica v. Nicaragua) and Construction of a Road in Costa Rica along the San Juan River (Nicaragua v. Costa Rica)*, Judgment of 16 December 2015 (ICJ Reports 2015, p. 665).

ICJ, *Corfu Channel Case* (U.K. v. Albania), Judgment of 15 December 1949 (ICJ Reports 1949, p. 244).

ICJ, *Legal Consequences of the Construction of a Wall in the Occupied Palestinian Territory*, Advisory Opinion of 9 July 2004 (ICJ Reports, p. 136).

ICJ, *Legal Consequences for States of the Continued Presence of South Africa in Namibia (South West Africa) notwithstanding Security Council Resolution 276*, Advisory Opinion of 21 June 1971 (ICJ Reports 1971, p. 16).

ICJ, *Legality of the Threat or Use of Nuclear Weapons*, Advisory Opinion of 8 July 1996 (ICJ Reports 1996, p. 226).

ICJ, *Reparation for Injuries Suffered in the Service of the United Nations*, Advisory Opinion of 11 April 1949 (ICJ Reports 1949, p. 174).

ICJ, *South West Africa Cases* (Ethiopia v. South Africa; Liberia v. South Africa), Preliminary Objections Judgment of 21 December 1962 (ICJ Reports 1962, p. 319).

ICJ, *South West Africa Cases* (Ethiopia v. South Africa; Liberia v. South Africa), Joint Dissenting Opinion of Sir Percy Spender and Sir Gerald Fitzmaurice to the Preliminary Objections Judgment of 21 December 1962, (ICJ Reports 1962, p. 465–563).

ICJ, *Pulp Mills on the River Uruguay* (Argentina v. Uruguay), Judgment of 20 April 2010 (ICJ Reports 2010, p. 14).

ICJ, *Reparations for injuries suffered in the services of the United Nations*, Advisory Opinion of. 11 April 1949 (ICJ Reports 1949, p. 174).

ICJ, *Jurisdictional Immunities of the State* (Germany v. Italy: Greece intervening), Judgment of 3 February 2012 (ICJ Reports 2012, p. 99).

PCIJ, *Factory at Chorzow Case* (Germany v. Poland), Series A – No. 9, Judgment (26 July 1927).

ICJ, *Interpretation of the Agreement of 25 March 1951 between the WHO and Egypt*, Advisory Opinion of 20 December 1980 (ICJ Reports 1980, p. 73).

ICJ, *Arrest Warrant of 11 April 2000* (Democratic Republic of the Congo v. Belgium), Jurisdiction of the Court and Admissibility Judgment of 14 February 2002 (ICJ Reports 2002, p. 3).

ICJ, *Corfu Channel Case* (U.K. v. Albania), Judgment of 9 April 1949, merits (ICJ Reports 1949, p.4).

International Criminal Tribunals

ICC, *The Prosecutor v. Omar Hassan Ahmad Al Bashir*, Appeals Chamber, ICC-02/05-01/09-397-Anx2, (06 May 2019), Joint Dissenting Opinion of Judge Luz Del Carmen Ibáñez Carranzaa and Judge Solomy Balungi Bossa.

ICC, *Situation in Uganda*, Decision on the Prosecutor's Application that the Pre-Trial Chamber disregard as irrelevant the Submission filed by the Registry on 5 December 2005, Pre-Trial Chamber II, ICC-02/04-01/05-147, (09 March 2006).

ICTR, *Jean-Bosco Barayagwiza vs. Prosecutor*, Case No. ICTR-97-19-AR72, Decision of the Appeals Chamber (3 November 1999).

ICTR, *Prosecutor v. Nahimana et al.*, Case No. ICTR-99-52-A, Appeal Judgement, (28 November 2007).

ICTY, *Prosecutor v. Mrkšić (Mile) and Šljivančanin (Veselin)*, Case No. IT-95-13/1-A, Appeal Judgement (5 May 2009).

ICTY, *Prosecutor vs. Stanislav Galić*, Case No. IT-98-29/A, Appeals Chamber Judgment (30 November 2006).

IRMCT, *Prosecutor v. Šešelj*, Case No. IRMCT-16-99-A, Appeal Judgement (11 April 2018).

Nuremberg Judgement 1, 'Trial of the Major War Criminals Before the International Military Tribunal', Nuremberg 14 November 1945 – 1 October 1946, at 186 (1947); reprinted in 172 Am. J. Int'l L. (1947) 186.

Special Tribunal for Lebanon, *Akhbar Beirut S.A.L. and Ibrahim Mohamed Ali Al Amin*, Case No. STL-14-06/I/CJ, Contempt Judge (Public Redacted Version of the Judgment) (15 July 2016).

ICTY, *Prosecutor v. Lahi Brahimaj*, Case No. IT-04-84-T, Public Judgment with Confidential Annex (29 November 2012).

ICTY, *Prosecutor v. Ratko Mladić*, Case. No. IT-09-92-T, Judgment (22 November 2017).

ICTY, *Prosecutor v. Tadić*, Case No. IT-94-1-AR72, Decision on the Defence Motion for Interlocutory Appeal on Jurisdiction (2 October 1995).

ICC, *Prosecutor v. Ahmad Al Faqi Al Mahdi*, Case. No. ICC-01/12-01/15, Judgment and Sentence, Trial Chamber VIII (27 September 2016).

ICTY, *Prosecutor v. Radovan Karadžić*, Case No. IT-95-5/18-T, Judgment (24 March 2016).

ICC, *Prosecutor v. Katanga*, Case No. ICC-01/04-01/06 A5, Judgment on the appeal of Mr Thomas Lubanga Dyilo against his conviction (1 December 2014).

ICC, *Prosecutor v. Thomas Lubanga Dyilo*, Case No. ICC-01/04-01/06-2842, Judgment pursuant to Article 74 of the Statute (14 March 2012).

ICC, *Prosecutor v. Thomas Lubanga Dyilo*, Case No. ICC-01/04-01/06 A5, Judgment on the appeal of Mr Thomas Lubanga Dyilo against his conviction (1 December 2014).

ICC, *Prosecutor v. Katanga*, Case No. ICC-01/04-01/07, Decision pursuant to Article 74 of the Statute (7 March 2014).

Other Cases

(Canada) *Nevsun Resources Ltd v Araya*, SCC 5 (2020).

(China) *Lunar Embassy to China v. Beijing Administration of Industry and Commerce*, Haidian District People's Court (November 2005).

CJEC, *Guiseppe Sacchi*, Court of Justice of the European Communities, C-155/73, Preliminary Ruling (30 April 1974).

CJEC, *Guiseppe Sacchi*, Court of Justice of the European Communities, C-52/79, Judgement (18 March 1980).

CJEC, *Procureur du Roi v. Marc LV.C. Debauve and Others*, Court of Justice of the European Communities, C-62/79, Judgement (18 March 1980).

CJEC, *S.A. Compagnie Gènérale pour la Diffusion de la Télévision, Coditel, and Others*, Court of Justice of the European Communities, C-352/85, Judgement (26 April 1988).

CJEC, *Bond van Adverteerders and Others v. The Netherlands State*, Court of Justice of the European Communities, C-222/94, Judgement (10 September 1996).

CJEC, *Commission of the European Communities v. United Kingdom of Great Britain and Northern Ireland*, Court of Justice of the European Communities, C-11-11/95, Judgement (10 September 1996).

CJEC, *Commission of the European Communities v. Kingdom of Belgium*, Court of Justice of the European Communities, Judgement (12 December 1996).

ECJ, *Bundesrepublik Deutschland v SpaceNet AG (C-793/19) and Telekom Deutschland GmbH (C-794/19)*, European Court of Justice, Judgement of the Grand Chamber in Joined Cases C-793/19, SpaceNet and C-794/19 (20 September 2022).

ECJ, *Commissioner of An Garda Síochána and Others, (C-140/20)*, European Court of Justice, Judgement of 5 April 2022, (see also Press Release No 58/22), and of 6 October 2020, La Quadrature du Net and Others, C-511/18, C-512/18 and C-520/18 (see also Press Release No 123/20).

ECJ, *Konsumentombudsmannen (KO) v De Agostini (Svenska) Förlag AB (C-34/95) og TV-Shop i Sverige AB (C-35/95 og C-36/95)*, European Court of Justice, Judgement in Joined Cases C-34/95 and C-36-95,(July 9 1997).

ECJ, *Reti Televisive Italiane SpA* (*RTI*) (*C-320/94*), *Radio Torre* (*C-338/94*), *Rete A Srl* (*C-329/94*), *Vallau Italiana Promomarket Srl* (*C-337/94*), *Radio Italia Solo Musica Srl and Others* (*C-338/94*), *and GETE Srl* (*339/94*) *v. Ministerio delle Poste e Telecommunicazioni*, European Court of Justice, Judgement in Joined Cases C-320/94, C-328/94, C-329/94, C-337/94, C-338/94 and C-339/94 (12 December 1996).

ECtHR, *Giacomelli v. Italy*, Application no. 59909/00, Judgment (2 November 2006).

ECtHR, *Verein KlimaSeniorinnen Schweiz v. Switzerland*, Application no. 53600/20, Application lodged (26 November 2020).

ECtHR, *Öneryıldız v. Turkey*, Application no. 48939/99, ECHR Grand Chamber Judgment (30 November 2004).

Human Rights Committee, *Portillo Cáceres et al. v. Paraguay*, Communication No. 2751/2016, UN Doc. CCPR/C/126/D/2751/2016 (25 July 2019).

IACtHR, *Case of the Indigenous Communities of the Lhaka Honhat (Our Land) Association v. Argentina*, Inter-American Court of Human Rights, Judgment of 6 February 2020 (Merits, Reparations and Costs).

IACtHR, *Case of the "Mapiripán Massacre" v. Colombia*, Judgment of September 15, 2000 (Merits, Reparations, and Costs).

IACtHR, *Comunidades Indígenas Miembros de la Asociación Lhaka Honhat (Nuestra Tierra) v. Argentina* ('Lhaka Honhat') Judgement (6 February 2020).

IACtHR, *State Obligations in Relation to the Environment in the Context of the Protection and Guarantee of the Rights to Life and to Personal Integrity*, Case No. OC-23/17, Advisory Opinion (15 November 2017).

ICSID, *Burlington Resources Inc v Republic of Ecuador*, Case No. ARB/08/5, Decision on Ecuador's Counterclaims (7 February 2016).

ICSID, *Urbaser v. The Argentine Republic*, Case No. ARB/07/26, Award (8 December 2016).

ICSID, *Mondev Internationall Ltd. v. United States*, Case No. ARB(AF)/99/2, Award (11 October 2022).

ICSID, *Total S.A. v. Argentine Republic*, Case No. ARB/04/1, Decision on Liability (27 December 2010).

ITLOS, *Responsibilities and Obligations of States Sponsoring Persons and Entities with Respect to Activities in the Area*, ITLOS Reports 2011, p. 10, Advisory Opinion (1 February 2011).

Lake Lanoux Arbitration, France v. Spain, 12 R.I.A.A. 281, 24 I.L.R. 101, Award (16 November 1957).

Settlement of Claim between Canada and the Union of Soviet Socialist Republics for Damage Caused by 'Cosmos 954' (2 April 1981).

STL, *Interlocutory Decision on the Applicable Law: Terrorism, Conspiracy, Homicide, Perpetration, Cumulative Charging*, Case No. STL-11-01/I, Appeals Chamber Interlocutory Decision (16 February 2011).

Trail Smelter Arbitration (*USA v. Canada*), Decision of 16 April 1938, published in: 33 *American Journal of International Law* 1, 1938.

Trail Smelter Arbitration (*USA v. Canada*), Decision of 11 March 1941, Published in: 35 *American Journal of International Law* 4, 1941.

PCA, *Iron Rhine Arbitration, Belgium v Netherlands*, Case No. ICGJ 373, Arbitral Award (24 May 2005).

SpaceNet and Telekom Deutschland, available at: https://curia.europa.eu/jcms/upload/docs/application/pdf/2022-09/cp220156en.pdf.

(UK) *R v Reeves Taylor*, UKSC 51 (2019).

(UK) *R v TRA*, EWCA Crim 2843 (2018).

(USA) *Berg v. Reaction Motors Division*, 37 NJ 396, 181 A.2d 487 (1962).

(USA) *Blue Origin v. United States & Space Exploration Technologies Corp*, No. 21-1695C, Federal Court of Public Opinion (4 November 2021).

(USA) *Centre for Biological Diversity et. al. vs Federal Aviation Administration and Billy Nolen*, US District Court for the District of Columbia, Case No. 1:23-cv-01204, (1 May 2023).

(USA) Eastern Airlines, Inc. v. Floyd, 499 U.S. 530 (1991).

(USA) *Florida Coalition for Peace and Justice v. George Herbert Walker Bush*, Civil Action No. 89-2682-OG, D.D.C., (10 October 1989).

(USA) *Florida Coalition for Peace and Justice v. George Herbert Walker Bush*, Civil Action No. 89-2682-OG, D.D.C., (5 October 1990).

(USA) *Kadic v Karadzic*, 70 F 3d 232, 243–4 (1995).

(USA) *Martin Marietta v. INTELSAT*, 763 F. Supp. 1327 (1991).

(USA) *Martin Marietta v. INTELSAT*, 991 F.2d 94 (1992).

(USA) *Michie v Great Lakes Steel Division* 495 F 2d 213 (1974).

(USA) *Nemitz v N.A.S.A*, 126 Fed Appx. 343, 9th Cir. Nev. (10 February 2004).

(USA) *Nemitz v US*, 2004 WL 316704, D. Nevada, 2004 (26 April 2004).

(USA) *Pigott v. Boeing Co.*, 240 So. 2d 63 (1970).

(USA) *Smith v. Lockheed Propulsion Co.*, 246 Cal. App. 2d 774, 56 Cal. Rptr. 128 (1967).

(USA) *The Boeing Company v. KB Yuzhnoye, et al.*, U.S. District Court, Central District of California, 13-00730 (13 May 2016).

Index

Printed in the United States
by Baker & Taylor Publisher Services